Integrating Technology in Problem-Solving Educational Practices

Jingru Zhang
Universiti Sains Malaysia, Malaysia

Wan Ahmad Jaafar Wan Yahaya
Universiti Sains Malaysia, Malaysia

Mageswaran Sanmugam
Centre for Instructional Technology and Multimedia, Universiti Sains Malaysia, Malaysia

Darren Lim
Universiti Sains Malaysia, Malaysia

IGI Global
Publishing Tomorrow's Research Today

Vice President of Editorial	Melissa Wagner
Managing Editor of Acquisitions	Mikaela Felty
Managing Editor of Book Development	Jocelynn Hessler
Production Manager	Mike Brehm
Cover Design	Phillip Shickler

Published in the United States of America by
IGI Global Scientific Publishing
701 East Chocolate Avenue
Hershey, PA, 17033, USA
Tel: 717-533-8845
Fax: 717-533-8661
E-mail: cust@igi-global.com
Website: https://www.igi-global.com

Library of Congress Cataloging-in-Publication Data

Names: Zhang, Jingru, 1995- editor. | Yahaya, Wan Ahmad Jaafar Wan, 1968- editor. | Sanmugam, Mageswaran, 1982- editor. | Lim, Darren, 1997- editor.
Title: Integrating technology in problem-solving educational practices / Jingru Zhang, Wan Ahmad Jaafar Wan Yahaya, Mageswaran Sanmugam, Darren Lim.
Description: Hershey, PA : IGI Global Scientific Publishing, [2025] | Includes bibliographical references and index. | Summary: "The book explores how emerging technologies are changing the problem-solving landscape and how educational technology can improve problem-solving skills in the digital age, which offers insights into how educators and students can leverage these tools to enhance learning outcomes"-- Provided by publisher.
Identifiers: LCCN 2024052883 (print) | LCCN 2024052884 (ebook) | ISBN 9798369367452 (hardcover) | ISBN 9798369367469 (paperback) | ISBN 9798369367476 (ebook)
Subjects: LCSH: Educational technology. | Problem solving. | Education--Effect of technological innovations on.
Classification: LCC LB1028.3 .I56539 2025 (print) | LCC LB1028.3 (ebook) | DDC 371.33--dc23/eng/20241203
LC record available at https://lccn.loc.gov/2024052883
LC ebook record available at https://lccn.loc.gov/2024052884

British Cataloguing in Publication Data
A Cataloguing in Publication record for this book is available from the British Library.

Table of Contents

Detailed Table of Contents

To respond to the requirements of the national strategy for cultivating innovative talents, stimulate the enthusiasm of digital media art professional students in learning professional skills, and tap the creative potential of students, this paper introduces the concept of project-based teaching method, the status quo of the application of project-based teaching method in digital media art majors, and analyzes the characteristics of this project-based teaching method, and at the same time build up a theoretical framework of project-based teaching for professional courses in digital media art and design. It also proposes the principles and strategies for introducing the project-based teaching method into the classroom of digital media art majors to improve the teaching quality of higher vocational digital media art major courses and the practical ability of students.

Students in vocational colleges in China play a crucial role in supporting the digital transformation of education. In this study, a vocational institute in Jiangsu province was selected for investigation, involving 79 students. The findings revealed that traditional classrooms still face limitations in enhancing students' digital literacy and skills. To address this issue and better equip students with the digital literacy and learning skills required by society, a serious game model was developed for the architecture professional course "Architecture CAD Drawing." This model presents core course content through case pictures and promotes interactive engagement. A user study involving 42 vocational architecture students was then conducted to compare the effectiveness of serious games with traditional video classes. The results demonstrate that Serious Games significantly enhance student interest in utilizing digital technology for learning, improve their efficiency in acquiring professional skills, and deepen their comprehension of digital literacy.

Since the beginning of the 21st century, the number of studies on serious games has been surging, and more and more serious games are being used for educational purposes to facilitate students' learning and increase their motivation. This study systematically reviewed seven empirical studies on the application of serious games in higher arts education from 2019 to 2024, aiming to reveal the current state of recent research in the field, incorporating trends in the use of technology and the results of the impact on learners. The results show that most articles indicate that serious games are effective in higher arts education. Currently, researchers pay relatively little attention to this area, but this area has good research potential. In addition, integrating serious games with technologies such as augmented reality, virtual reality and mixed reality in higher arts education is a promising avenue for future research and development.

This research paper examines the impact of gamification on academic achievement in undergraduate students. The study used a quasi-experimental design, comparing pre- and post-test scores. Results showed a significant improvement in post-test scores for the gamified group compared to the control group. The study also found that pre-test scores and engagement metrics significantly influenced the outcomes. The study suggests that the effectiveness of gamification depends on factors like design, intervention duration, and alignment with educational objectives. It recommends further longitudinal studies and exploring gamification's applicability across diverse educational settings.

This study analyses how game-based learning motivates Malaysian ESL students. The mixed-method research employed questionnaires and semi-structured interviews with students and teachers. Students were in favour of the game-based lessons, suggesting that game-based learning might solve motivational issues. However, several obstacles prevented teachers from delivering a game-based lesson. The study stresses the need of motivation in ESL classes since disengaged students may hinder learning. To promote learning, teachers must inspire and meet student needs. The findings suggest that game-based learning may motivate and engage students, but educators must be flexible to overcome its challenges. This research helps educators, policymakers, and administrators improve ESL education and student motivation.

Gamification is known as the use of game-like elements within a non-game context. The use of gamification in a classroom setting, also known as gamified learning aims to improve the learning process by constructing a low-risk and well-structured learning environment for students. The use of gamification in the educational context has proven to be able to increase motivation, engagement, retention of knowledge and performance. In this paper, the authors inquired into previous relevant research and wish to contribute to the field by proposing the DAMP model which dealt with the depth (shallow, deep and total), annex (plugged or unplugged, online or offline), motion (static and dynamic), and placement (intra and extra) of gamification with the consideration of 8Ts namely task, target, technology, time, technique, tariff, tensity and terrain. The proposed model hopes to serve as a guideline and provide new insights for future educators and instructional designers when constructing a gamified learning classroom.

This study aims to explore the potential of gamified teaching strategies in enhancing classroom effectiveness. In response to the prevalent issues of low student engagement and lack of motivation in current teaching practices, we propose a series of instructional designs grounded in gamification principles. These designs use the BOPPPS teaching model as the core and incorporate SWOT analysis to thoroughly assess the potential benefits, challenges, opportunities, and risks associated with integrating game elements into the teaching process. We anticipate that carefully crafted gamification strategies will significantly improve student interaction and participation in the classroom, spark their interest in learning, and facilitate a deeper understanding of the subject matter.

As technology advances at breakneck speed, reliance on software grows exponentially. This growth has given rise to multiple issues encountered during software development, including increased occurrences of software bugs. The conventional methods previously used by developers, such as manual code checking or testing, may involve greater chances of human error and extended timelines, resulting in more significant expense budgets towards revenue leakage due to late deliveries or failed outcomes. This chapter per the authors aim to explore how artificial intelligence (AI) solutions can identify potential vulnerabilities more accurately than before. By utilizing machine learning algorithms, deep learning, and natural language processing, AI-based bug detection not only enhances precision and efficiency but also saves costs on the development process, ultimately giving better software quality and reduced monetary costs. This chapter per the authors present some applications of AI techniques in bugs detection to select bugs accurately and suggest possible optimizations for the buggy codes.

Artificial Intelligence (AI) is taking us by storm, and Human Resources functions are no exception. Future of work for nearly 40% of the companies are in the algorithms of Artificial Intelligence (AI). AI is the most powerful acronym that pulls every human resource professional into challenge. Almost 33% of the employees' jobs, roles, tasks are to be augmented by AI in the near future is the prediction by Deloitte. This paper analyses the Skill development challenges for the developing countries like India to handle AI related training by conducting meta Analysis and presents suggestive measures to counter these challenges. The aim of the paper is to comprehend the issues surrounding vocational education and training by putting the Learner first. It suggests measures for implementation of planned activities with the augmentation of training initiatives to reskill, right skill and align those skills for the emerging jobs.

Visual arts and design education is an important area in higher education, and artificial intelligence (AI), which can provide personalised learning experiences, plays a pivotal role in facilitating the learning process and student creativity within it. This chapter provides an insight into the current use of AI technologies in the teaching of visual arts and design, highlighting their impact on student engagement. Through the integration of current research findings as well as detailed case studies, it reveals how AI can be effective in fostering creativity and meeting specific pedagogical needs in the field of visual arts and design. In addition, the article explores the role of AI in visual arts and design education and highlights the ethical issues encountered when integrating technology into educational frameworks. Finally, the chapter looks at future research trends and calls for further studies to improve the quality of teaching and learning in visual arts and design education and to prepare students for a technology-led future.

This abstract examines the many facets of artificial intelligence, outlining its reach, development, and effects, with an emphasis on how it can be used in education. The study explores the evolutionary history of artificial intelligence, which has been fueled by exponential gains in computer power, data availability. The research looks at how AI is changing teaching, learning, and administrative procedures in educational institutions. The abstract explores the ways in which artificial intelligence is transforming education, outlining the nature, uses, implications, difficulties, and importance of AI. It explores how artificial intelligence technologies which include learning, reasoning and self-correction are revolutionizing traditional teaching methods and administrative procedures. It also facilitates automatic grading, data-driven decision-making, and lifelong learning. AI has significant ramifications that highlight its critical role in transforming educational paradigms internationally, helping both students and educators, despite its limitations.

Virtual reality has a lot of potential, and researchers are becoming increasingly interested in using it in the classroom. However, there is little systematic work on how researchers can apply VR to higher education for the purpose of improving student engagement. Therefore, we propose to use systematic mapping to investigate how VR can be used to improve engagement in higher education. The review synthesizes the results of various studies conducted over the past five years, highlights the effectiveness of VR in creating immersive and interactive learning environments, and provides a literature review of related studies. The results of the study show that students who use VR technology are more engaged and motivated to learn. The demand for virtual reality technology is surging as a means to enhance student engagement in educational settings. Consequently, the future development of effective tools that promote student involvement is imperative. Nevertheless, it is crucial to meticulously consider design, accessibility, and pedagogical strategies to optimize its efficacy.

This systematic review analyzes research up to 2024 on the effects of creative metacognition on creative performance. Following PRISMA guidelines, the study screened and examined 30 high-quality journal articles, focusing on creative metacognition, divergent thinking, metacognitive monitoring skills, their application in educational settings, and the effectiveness of various assessment methods and tools. Key findings highlight a significant increase in research interest in creative metacognition, which positively affects creative performance. Most studies currently use subjective or indirect objective measurement methods. The crucial role of metacognitive monitoring skills is emphasized, supporting the hypothesis that creative metacognition can enhance creative performance. This review identifies gaps in applying creative metacognition theory in educational practice. It suggests future research directions, emphasizing the need for in-depth exploration to promote the development of students' creative abilities.

This article explores the impact of using anthropomorphic graphics in multimedia learning materials on learners' attention allocation and learning outcomes. Anthropomorphic graphics refer to images that possess human-like characteristics, meaning they are described and conceived based on human traits(Salles et al., 2020). In the context of multimedia education, the integration of anthropomorphic graphics has been widely discussed as a means to enhance learners' attention and overall learning outcomes. This paper reviews multiple studies, summarizing the role of anthropomorphic graphics in attracting and maintaining students' attention, and whether this can improve learning outcomes. The authors hold that while the effect of anthropomorphic graphics on final learning outcomes is unclear, they positively influence student attention, deepen understanding, and facilitate knowledge transfer. Despite the uncertain impact on outcomes, their potential to enhance learning effectiveness should not be overlooked.

In recent years, the integration of social media into educational settings has emerged as a significant trend, revolutionizing traditional teaching and learning practices. Social media integration into learning environments is becoming more and more common, providing innovative ways to improve teaching and learning. This book chapter presents a detailed analysis of the role, benefits, challenges, and strategies associated with social media integration in teaching and learning. It aims to discuss the effective utilization of social media platforms, such as Facebook, Twitter, Instagram, YouTube, and other applications, to promote student and teacher engagement, collaboration, and knowledge sharing. The chapter explores various theoretical frameworks such as connectivism and constructivism, which support the integration of social media in fostering active learning environments. However, there are challenges as well, like maintaining academic integrity, protecting data privacy, and managing distractions.

Society is currently going through major changes in the educational field due to technological changes. The impact of EdTech on teaching methods, learner commitment, and effectiveness is explored in this paper. Adaptive learning systems differentiate students, utilizing technology like VR and AR for immersive learning, encouraging participation, understanding, and empowering students with control over their learning. We emphasize the need to employ technology judiciously and cautiously to find the right balance between implementing modern technology and using traditional instructional techniques. The future of EdTech also looking bright with such developments as AI adding a more personalized element and metaverse allowing everyone to go to school online. The effective implementation of EdTech allows for the development of a promising future for everyone since education should be open and engaging for all students and transform education into a lifelong process.

With its interactive and captivating learning experiences, touchscreen technology has become a particularly promising new direction for music learning in recent years. This paper reports the preliminary study which investigates the impact of a touchscreen-technology-based multi-user collaborative musical instrument application in middle school students' music learning. Four secondary school students were chosen as participants and participated in interviews and non-participant observation. The evaluation revealed that this application fulfilled the usability aspect; it was confirmed to be easy to use and contributes to fostering collaborative skills and increasing student engagement in music learning. As there is no existing mobile music instrument application for multi-users to support middle school students in music learning, this study would be considered a groundbreaking attempt. The insights provide valuable implications for educators and developers aiming to integrate touchscreen technology into music curricula, promoting more interactive and collaborative learning environments

Today, in the digital world, the security of systems is crucial because, with continuous information exchange and huge quantities of data being processed, the protection of operation processes and data assets becomes paramount. Threat modeling is an important part of cybersecurity management methodology that looks for any possible threats or weaknesses that can break the system or endanger the environment. This paper is an attempt to analyze all the models of threat modeling by taking STRIDE, PASTA, DREAD, TREK, VAST and Attack Trees as references. An integrated model is suggested that combines the benefits of existing approaches, which includes the adoption of a comprehensive frame to deal with cyber threats. This methodology emphasizes iterative refinement and rigorous testing to ensure the effectiveness of threat mitigation strategies. By incorporating user-friendly web portals and the integration of new technologies, this framework enhances usability and addresses emerging threats.

Preface

Technology has become an integral part of our daily lives, reshaping every aspect of how we live, work, and learn. As we advance into an increasingly digital age, the role of technology in education continues to expand, providing new tools and methods for enhancing problem-solving skills among students. This book, *Integrating Technology in Problem-Solving Educational Practices*, explores the transformative power of emerging technologies in the classroom and how they can foster critical thinking, creativity, and problem-solving abilities in learners.

The chapters in this book delve into the various ways educators can harness technology to create dynamic, interactive learning environments. These environments not only engage students but also equip them with the skills needed to navigate and solve real-world problems. By incorporating experiential learning, collaborative projects, and cutting-edge technological tools, educators can help students develop crucial problem-solving skills that are essential in today's interconnected and complex world.

Drawing on a blend of theoretical frameworks and practical applications, this book offers educators, researchers, and instructional designers the strategies and resources necessary to seamlessly integrate technology into their teaching practices. It emphasizes the importance of adapting educational methods to meet the needs of modern learners, preparing them for the challenges they will face in their personal and professional lives.

Our target audience includes educators looking to enhance their teaching with technology, instructional designers seeking to develop innovative learning experiences, and researchers aiming to understand the evolving intersection between technology and education. Students studying education, technology, or related fields will also find valuable insights in this book, helping them to understand how technology can be effectively used to improve learning outcomes.

By exploring these diverse perspectives, this book aims to provide educators and learners alike with the tools they need to thrive in the ever-changing educational landscape. Through the integration of technology, we can build a brighter, more innovative future for students, equipping them with the problem-solving skills needed for success in an increasingly complex world.

Jingru Zhang
Universiti Sains Malaysia, Malaysia

Wan Ahmad Jaafar Wan Yahaya
Universiti Sains Malaysia, Malaysia

Mageswaran Sanmugam
Centre for Instructional Technology and Multimedia, Universiti Sains Malaysia, Malaysia

Darren Lim
Universiti Sains Malaysia, Malaysia

Acknowledgment

The journey of creating Integrating Technology in Problem-Solving Educational Practices has been a collaborative effort that would not have been possible without the valuable contributions of many individuals.

First and foremost, the editor would like to extend sincere appreciation to the chapter authors, whose dedication and insightful research have brought depth and innovation to this book. Your work has truly shaped this volume into a resource that will impact both educators and students in understanding the role of technology in enhancing problem-solving skills.

Secondly, a special note of thanks goes to the team at IGI Global for their professionalism and support throughout the publication process. Your expertise and guidance were crucial in ensuring the success of this project.

Lastly, the editor would be deeply grateful to the reviewers who generously gave their time and expertise to provide critical feedback on the chapters. Their thoughtful evaluations and rigorous suggestions have greatly enhanced the quality of this book. The following individuals should be acknowledged:

Da Yan, Du Shaoxu, Fenglin Song, Hanjun Su, Hanben Yao, Irfan Kösesoy, Jiawei Wang, Jinya Liu, Li Ji, Lin Chuxuan, Musabah, Purushothman, Rajat Pandit, Xin Li, Yue Shi, Yuting Dai, and Yuhe Lu.

Chapter 1
Exploration of Project Teaching Method for Higher Vocational Digital Media Arts Majors

Xiao Gu
Nanjing City Vocational College, China

ABSTRACT

To respond to the requirements of the national strategy for cultivating innovative talents, stimulate the enthusiasm of digital media art professional students in learning professional skills, and tap the creative potential of students, this paper introduces the concept of project-based teaching method, the status quo of the application of project-based teaching method in digital media art majors, and analyzes the characteristics of this project-based teaching method, and at the same time build up a theoretical framework of project-based teaching for professional courses in digital media art and design. It also proposes the principles and strategies for introducing the project-based teaching method into the classroom of digital media art majors to improve the teaching quality of higher vocational digital media art major courses and the practical ability of students.

1. INTRODUCTION

The rapid advancement of digital technology, the diversified development of the media industry, and the increasing emphasis in higher education on integrating emerging technologies with creativity have collectively contributed to the emergence and growth of digital media art as a significant discipline within higher education

DOI: 10.4018/979-8-3693-6745-2.ch001

(Du, 2015). This field has developed swiftly, largely due to the combined influences of technology, industry, creativity, and education, making substantial contributions to the cultivation of professionals in modern digital media (Wang & Zhang, 2022).

Given that this article discusses the project-based teaching method for digital media art in higher vocational education in China, some of the references are sourced from the China National Knowledge Infrastructure (CNKI) database. Digital media art, as an interdisciplinary field encompassing digital media design, animation production, visual effects, game development, and related areas, requires the cultivation of new, well-rounded talents who are creative, technologically proficient, and market-oriented. At present, China's colleges and universities have taken the teaching of digital media art as the focus of teaching, and every year there are about 160,000 graduates of digital media art majors who are engaged in the fields of network media, game and television, film and digital, animation and industrial design, etc. It can be seen that the teaching of digital media art majors has a good prospect of market development. Compared with foreign countries, China's digital media art education development is late, but the development speed is fast. The current social market demand for digital media art talent and standards have changed, resulting in the past traditional education model not being able to adapt to the development of higher requirements for the profession, the urgent need to change the mode of education to cultivate talents, change the traditional teaching methods and other means to cultivate qualified composite digital media art talent. Digital media art as a new professional synthesis is very strong, it almost covers all branches of art and design, such as photography and video, visual communication, television production, animation production, etc., which is higher than other professional requirements. In addition, the development and growth of the digital media industry can not only rely on learning from others but more importantly, we must give full play to our strengths and develop our characteristics. As the basic pillar of the development of the digital media industry, higher education should be adapted to the times, and the requirements of the development of enterprises to create the required technology, style, and form, but these are not possible under the guidance of the current teaching ideology, therefore, the teaching ideology must be reformed, not only to change the original not adapt to the industry's requirements of the idea, but also to go beyond the current reality, put forward new professional teaching ideas, teaching methods, and so on.Therefore, in teaching digital media art design, particularly in higher vocational colleges, the introduction of project-based teaching is essential. This approach not only emphasizes the theoretical knowledge imparted during the teaching process but also focuses on the practical application of that knowledge and the skills acquired by students through hands-on projects (Jia, 2020).

Incorporating project-based teaching into classroom instruction, where students actively participate in real-world projects, provides them with a platform to develop practical skills (Wang, 2023). Furthermore, through these projects, students can enhance their proficiency in digital media design, animation production, visual effects, and other related skills, thereby improving their practical abilities and professional competence. Additionally, project participation fosters teamwork, stimulates creativity, and encourages innovative thinking by presenting open-ended challenges (Han, 2024). As students from higher vocational institutions engage in these projects, they accumulate valuable practical experience, laying a solid foundation for their future employment.

1. The background of the problems faced by the teaching of digital media art is not adequately expressed;

A:Page 1-Page 2("At present,... ...but also to go beyond the current reality, put forward new professional teaching ideas, teaching methods, and so on.")

2. OVERVIEW OF PROJECT TEACHING METHOD

2.1 Definition of Project Teaching Method

The origins of the project teaching method can be traced back to 18th-century European work-study education and 19th-century cooperative education in the United States (Jiao et al., 2024). In the early 20th century, American educator John Dewey introduced the educational concept of "learning by doing," which laid the theoretical foundation for the development of the project teaching method (Cui, 2021). In September 1918, William Heard Kilpatrick, an American scholar, published an article entitled "The Project Method" in Columbia University's Teachers College Journal, and the "project method" was formally introduced. William Heard Kilpatrick extended John Dewey's idea of "learning by doing" by elaborating and defining project-based teaching for the first time: "teaching and learning that occurs in a specific social context and that requires the whole person of the learner". Project teaching was first elaborated and defined as "a planned action that takes place in a particular social context and requires the full commitment of the learner" (Kilpatrick, W.H.,1918) . He believes that the project method advocates students' interest as the starting point, learning knowledge in practical activities, emphasizes the status of learners in learning, abandons traditional textbooks and classroom teaching in the form of "subjects", enables students to formulate plans and take responsibility for their actions independently, and embodies the behavioral and democratic model of social practice. In addition, Rudolf Pfeifer and Fu Xiaofang believe that project teaching is a kind of teaching activity in which students put forward ideas and problems, agree on a project with the teacher, set up a learning group, determine the content and learning mode according to the objectives, and carry out the program and then carry out evaluation(Rudolf Pfeifer,&Fu, 2007). Professor Xu Guoqing defines the project teaching method as a teaching method and proposes that the core of project teaching is "task-centered teaching, linking knowledge and work tasks with practical problems, and stimulating students' motivation to learn through completing complete work by-products. The American educator John Dewey put forward the theory of pragmatism in education, believing that "education is life" and advocating "learning by doing", suggesting that teaching and learning should be designed with practice as the core and that real-life problems should be integrated into teaching and learning. The empiricist curriculum system he created theoretically laid the foundation for the project-based curriculum (Liu,2010) . William Heard Kilpatrick, an American progressivist educator, researched project teaching on this basis and improved the theoretical framework of project teaching in his book Project Teaching Method. He divided project teaching into four parts: first, determining the purpose, in which students put forward learning objectives or problems based on their interests and needs; then, formulating a plan, in which students are responsible for formulating an action plan based on the purpose, with the teacher acting as a mentor; then, implementing the plan, in which students use the available materials and take practical actions to complete the plan, with the teacher guiding them at the right time; and lastly, evaluating the learning outcomes, in which students use the assessment methods and assessment criteria formulated by the teacher to assess the learning outcomes. Finally, the students are responsible for assessing the learning outcomes according to the assessment methods and criteria set by the teacher, and the teacher is responsible for checking and correcting the students' mistakes. In his book Principles of Educational Methods, he discusses the project teaching method again and divides the project teaching design into four ways: producer's design, consumer's design, problem design, and practice design(Feng,2005). William Heard Kilpatrick's research on the project teaching method has led to the widespread application of the project teaching method in general education teaching in the United States and its gradual adoption by other countries. In the book Multiple Intelligences and Problem-based Learning, Robin Fogarty of the United States proposes that project teaching is an innovation in curriculum design, arguing that the curriculum framework can be embodied by five kinds of projects, namely, relevant types of projects, structural projects, template projects, open-ended projects, and thematic projects and that the teacher is responsible for helping the students to construct " collection-processing-application" in the project activities. Teachers are responsible for helping students construct a three-level intellectual model of "collection-processing-application" during project activities. Robin Fogarty, based on the integration of project-based teaching and the theory of multiple intelligences, focuses on the process of project-based teaching and how it works.

By the 1960s, this method was widely adopted and popularized in German vocational education, eventually spreading to other countries and regions as an effective approach for developing students' key competencies, particularly in vocational education settings (Huang, 2022). In 1969, Germany enacted the Vocational Education Act, and the "dual system" of vocational education took shape. The so-called "dual system" refers to the "dual" education and teaching of theoretical knowledge learning and technical training on the one hand, and the "dual" main body of vocational schools and related enterprises on the other (Gao,2017)"The "dual system" requires students to receive both curriculum learning in schools and certain training in enterprises, and emphasizes the cultivation of students' vocational skills . In the 1980s, "action-oriented teaching method" was first proposed in Germany, and its theoretical basis is constructivist learning theory. "Action-oriented teaching method" means that teachers and students discuss together to determine the action product, teachers guide the teaching organization process according to this action product, and students achieve the unity of mental and physical work through active learning. Teaching methods such as the "project teaching method", "role-playing method" and "case teaching method" are all derivatives of the "action-oriented method". The "action-oriented approach" is a derivative of the "project approach", "role-playing approach" and "case study approach". Due to the rapid development of the economy and the shortage of skilled personnel in society, the German federal government has paid more attention to the development of vocational education. in July 2003, the German Federal Institute for Vocational Education (Bundesanstalt für Bildung und Bildung (BFIB)) formulated the action-oriented project teaching method, which embodies the concept of dual system vocational education in Germany, i.e., "taking the student as the main body and the vocational competence as the goal of development. The whole learning process is broken down into several specific events, and the teaching ideas and corresponding project teaching programs are designed according to the logic of action. Students work in small groups to complete the project tasks, while ensuring that they are involved in every step of the process. In this way, knowledge and skills are transferred to the students, and their methodological, learning, and collaborative skills are developed .In Germany, project-based teaching can be realized from one lesson to one course. Teachers at Siemens Vocational and Technical College organize the teaching contents into project forms, assign project tasks, and students form groups to discuss, design, and produce the projects, and then the teachers evaluate the completion of the projects comprehensively at the end . The Hamburg Technical and Vocational School also uses the project approach to integrate learning and employment to ensure that the students graduate as skilled workers and can work directly in the workplace. According to Smith, Managing Director of METOP at the University of Hamburg, "The project approach makes the students the subject of the classroom, with the teacher playing the role of guide and advisor, providing space for independent thinking and maximizing the potential of the students" (F.W. Krohn.,2005). In summary, both in theory and practice, the research and application of project teaching methods have been relatively mature in foreign countries. On the one hand, foreign scholars have conducted in-depth research on the development concept and implementation strategy of project teaching methods and formed a certain project teaching system. On the other hand, foreign countries have conducted a lot of practical exploration of project teaching methods, and have used the theory of project teaching methods to guide the implementation of teaching at various stages of education. Especially, the successful practical experience of applying project teaching methods in vocational education is worth learning from our country.

Regarding the early development of the project teaching method in China, most mathematicians believe that the project teaching method sprouted in China at the end of the 20th century. 1995, Ms. Anneliese Pollack of Germany introduced two translations of "Examples of Project Design Teaching in the General Knowledge Classes in the German Hometowns" at the Sino-German Symposium on General Knowledge of Nature, which were successively published in the journal Science Lessons and explained the value of the project teaching method and its application in the teaching of basic education in Germany. In 1998, Hong Changli explored the application of the project teaching method in business administration training in his article "A preliminary study of the training effect of project teaching method", proposing that the application of project teaching in training can stimulate students' interest in learning, improve teachers' teaching work, and enhance the level and efficiency of enterprises, and it was the first paper explaining the application of project learning in adult education. In addition, in 1999, China Training introduced the effect of applying the project teaching method in enterprise training under the title of "Project Teaching Method" - a useful attempt. 2000, Yang Yan published the article "Teaching Methods of Vocational Education in Foreign Countries", introducing project teaching into the field of vocational education in China for the first time. In 2000, Yang Yan published the article "Teaching Methods of Foreign Vocational Education", which introduced project teaching into the field of vocational education for the first time. Since then, the research on project teaching has been gradually expanded to various educational fields in China(Chen&S,2021).The project teaching method is defined as a teaching approach that is project-driven, teacher-guided, and student-led, where students engage in preliminary research, program design, project implementation, and project proposal development for a relatively independent project, thereby promoting the acquisition of knowledge and skill enhancement (Liang et al., 2024).

2. Project-based teaching method originated in Europe and the United States. In the chapter of definition and international application, extensive English literature should be introduced for more detailed description, and the literature should be as accurate as possible.

A:(In September 1918, William Heard Kilpatrick, ...Robin Fogarty, based on the integration of project-based teaching and the theory of multiple intelligences, focuses on the process of project-based teaching and how it works.(In 1969, Germany enacted the Vocational Education Act, ...Since then, the research on project teaching has been gradually expanded to various educational fields in China(Chen&S,2021).)

2.2 Project Teaching Method Characteristics

The most significant feature of the project teaching method is its emphasis on student initiative, teacher-student interaction, and the practical nature of projects throughout the teaching process (Zhang, 2024). It integrates students' "learning, thinking, and acting," reflecting the organic combination of "teaching, learning, and doing." Through real-world projects, students develop independent problem-solving abilities, as they are encouraged to autonomously resolve project-related challenges. This approach stimulates students' initiative in learning and embodies the "student-centered" philosophy of the project teaching method (Liu, 2020).

Moreover, the method follows a sequence where teachers assign project tasks, students work on problem-solving, teachers provide guidance, and students complete the project (Wang, 2021). This process highlights the interaction between teachers and students, with a strong focus on practical operations. By combining theoretical knowledge with practical skills, students enhance their ability to solve real-world problems. Additionally, the project teaching method fosters the application of learned knowledge, enabling students to develop comprehensive qualities, cultivate critical thinking, and improve their problem-solving skills. Simultaneously, teachers achieve innovation and breakthroughs in their teaching methods. The project teaching method also features synthesis, teamwork, openness, and strong connections to enterprise attributes (Xing, 2023).

2.3 Comparison Between Project Teaching Method and Traditional Teaching Method

The project teaching method differs significantly from traditional teaching methods in terms of teaching philosophy, approach, learning outcomes, and teaching environment. Rooted in the principle of "work demand-oriented, vocational skills as the core, project tasks as a carrier," the project teaching method disrupts the conventional design of course chapters. Instead, it structures the curriculum around various stages of project work, allowing students to acquire professional skills through hands-on project practice (Fan, 2023).

At the conceptual level, traditional teaching methods emphasize the transmission of theoretical knowledge and the results of summative assessments, with teachers acting as the "dominant" figures while students passively receive knowledge. In contrast, the project teaching method prioritizes student initiative, encouraging active participation in practical activities where students learn and master new knowledge by solving real-world problems (Xu, 2022). This approach fosters the development of students' active learning and practical abilities.

In terms of teaching methods, traditional instruction primarily involves "classroom lectures," whereas the project teaching method begins with a project and uses real-world tasks as the framework. This approach guides students to practice, explore, research, and solve problems within the classroom, cultivating both practical skills and innovative thinking (Wang et al., 2024).

Regarding learning outcomes, traditional teaching methods focus more on theoretical instruction and test preparation, whereas the project teaching method allows for a deeper integration of theory and practice, enabling students to understand and apply knowledge more effectively. Additionally, the learning environment in project-based teaching differs from the single classroom setting typical of traditional teaching. The project approach emphasizes practical experience and collaboration, leading to the coexistence of various teaching environments.

Moreover, there are differences in teaching objectives, processes, and the roles of teachers and students (Yang, 2021). The project teaching method aims to cultivate students' practical, problem-solving, teamwork, and innovation abilities, emphasizing the enhancement of comprehensive skills. In contrast, traditional teaching focuses on transmitting knowledge to ensure that students systematically master the disciplinary knowledge. In terms of role transformation, in the project teaching method, students act as executors and decision-makers of the project, while teachers serve as guides and advisors. In traditional teaching, teachers are the primary transmitters of knowledge and authority figures, and students are the recipients of this knowledge (see Figure 1).

Figure 1. Comparison between traditional teaching method and project teaching method

Picture 1-Traditional Teaching method VS Project-based Learning (PBL)

	Traditional Teaching method	PBL
Teaching Philosophy	Focusing on knowledge transfer and test scores, teacher-led teaching, and students' passive acceptance of knowledge	Focus on student engagement and practice, with students taking an active role in the program
Teaching method	Classroom lectures, notes, assignments, and exams are the main focus	Organize hands-on practice, research and exploration, and problem-solving for students using projects as a vehicle
Learning effect	Emphasis on theoretical mastery and test-taking ability, lack of practical ability, and innovative thinking	Deeper understanding and application of knowledge
Educational Environment	classrooms	Emphasis on practice and collaboration, with multiple environments coexisting

Given these differences, the project teaching method offers considerable advantages for digital media art majors, whose educational goals include cultivating multidisciplinary professionals with advanced digital media technology skills. By emphasizing the integration of theory and practice and focusing on the development of highly skilled professionals with strong artistic literacy, the project teaching method clearly demonstrates its superiority in application.

3. THE SITUATION OF PROJECT TEACHING METHOD IN DIGITAL MEDIA ART MAJORS

Internationally, the development of digital media art majors began relatively early, and the application of project teaching methods has matured over time (Qi, 2023). As early as the 1980s, some universities in Europe and the United States introduced project teaching methods in digital media art programs to cultivate students' innovative and practical abilities. With the widespread adoption of computer technology and the Internet, the use of project teaching methods in these programs has expanded and deepened (Wang, 2021). However, challenges remain in implementing this method, including difficulties in selecting appropriate projects. If the projects are too simple, they may fail to engage students; if too complex, students may struggle to complete them, negatively affecting the learning outcome. Therefore, project selection should follow the "jump and reach the peach" principle, meaning it should be challenging yet attainable for students at various levels (Li, 2023).

Another significant issue is the role of teachers in project-based learning (Chen, 2022). This method requires teachers to have a broad range of skills, and some may lack the project experience or guidance abilities necessary to effectively mentor students through the project. Additionally, insufficient teaching resources pose a challenge to successfully implementing the project teaching method (Kong, 2016).

In China, the digital media art major emerged in the early 21st century (Xian & Liu, 2023), and has rapidly developed due to advancements in digital technology and growing market demand (Lu, 2019). The application of project teaching methods in digital media art education is gaining attention, with many institutions beginning to incorporate it into their curricula (Yang, 2020). While this shift represents a reform in teaching methodology, improving teaching quality and stimulating students' enthusiasm for learning, it is primarily observed in key universities. In contrast, many vocational colleges, particularly those with less comprehensive capabilities, face significant challenges. These include a superficial understanding of the project teaching method among teachers and students, leading to a lack of depth in its implementation, and the persistence of formalism during its execution (Qu et al., 2023). Furthermore, issues with project management and evaluation systems result in uncontrolled project progress, low-quality outcomes, and subjective assessments, which undermine the effectiveness of the teaching process.

The essential element of "school-enterprise cooperation" in the project teaching method is also problematic. The depth and breadth of collaboration between schools and enterprises are often insufficient. Even when institutions establish partnerships with enterprises, they may struggle to implement the project teaching method effectively. Some colleges miss opportunities for meaningful cooperation due to their limited resources, leading to "blank cooperation" where students lack access to real projects and practical experiences (Zhang, 2022).

As a field with significant growth potential, digital media art equips students with extensive knowledge and skills while fostering creativity and practical abilities. The booming digital media industry, driven by rapid advancements in Internet and information technology, highlights the growing demand for professionals in this sector. According to the China Digital Economy Development Report 2022, the digital economy reached 45.5 trillion yuan in 2021, accounting for 39.8% of GDP (Liu, 2023). This trend underscores the accelerating digital transformation and the increasing demand for digital media art and design professionals (Zhang, 2022).

The revision of the 2021 National Catalogue of Higher Vocational Education Professions, which introduced digital media art as a new field, reflects the recognition of its importance by academic experts (Zhang et al., 2020). However, despite this recognition, the large-scale development of digital media art education in China is relatively recent, and there is a significant talent gap due to the limited number of higher vocational institutions offering this specialization (Zhu, 2024). While short-term training programs have emerged to address the employment crisis, they may hinder the healthy development of this emerging field, as the market urgently needs highly skilled professionals.

The goal of digital media art education is to cultivate well-rounded professionals with strong ideals, ethics, and innovative thinking, capable of mastering the specialized knowledge and technical skills required for digital content services, multimedia, interactive design, and related fields. Graduates are expected to become high-quality, versatile talents within 3-5 years of graduation, capable of roles such as web design, interface design, 3D design, video post-processing, and branding design for new media (Jian & Shen, 2021). The broad application of digital media arts, including dynamic web design, interactive multimedia, digital animation, and game design, demonstrates its pervasive influence in modern society, impacting education, media, publishing, communication, entertainment, and more (Li et al., 2024).

Despite the rapid development of the digital media art profession, the growth within higher vocational education remains slow, with several challenges such as curriculum design, faculty expertise, practical teaching, student motivation, and alignment with industry needs (Sun, 2021). Faculty members often lack practical industry experience and a deep understanding of current trends, limiting their ability to effectively teach the latest developments. Additionally, practical teaching suffers due to the limited number of internship opportunities and insufficient depth in school-enterprise cooperation, making it difficult for students to engage in meaningful project-based learning.

A review of the literature reveals commonalities and differences in the application of project teaching methods in digital media art programs domestically and abroad (Sun, 2021). Both contexts recognize the method's alignment with the practical needs of the digital media art profession, enhancing students' practical and innovative abilities. However, foreign institutions have a longer history of applying these methods, resulting in richer experience and more in-depth research. In contrast, domestic applications face unique challenges, such as educational system constraints and uneven resource distribution, requiring targeted research and exploration.

In conclusion, as digital media art programs in higher vocational institutions continue to develop, it is essential to consider the unique characteristics of these institutions, regional features, educational resources, and student profiles. Collaborative efforts among schools, teachers, students, and enterprises are necessary to address these challenges and improve professional training and talent development. By continuously enhancing the quality of digital media art education, this field can play a more significant role in higher vocational education and contribute to the cultivation of outstanding digital media art professionals.Based on the problems existing in the digital media art specialty of China's higher vocational education, such as the lack of professional teachers' understanding of enterprise projects, and failure to carry out the project practice promptly; secondly, the students are not able to contact the project practice in the first time, and they cannot put what they have learned into practice; thirdly, how to combine the project pedagogy with the vocational tournaments of colleges and universities, to achieve the goal of "promoting teaching and learning by competition". Thirdly, how to combine the project teaching method with university vocational events to achieve the purpose of "promoting teaching and learning through competition" will be discussed in the following article.

4. THE THEORETICAL FRAMEWORK OF DIGITAL MEDIA ART DESIGN PROFESSIONAL CURRICULUM PROJECT TEACHING

The digital media art curriculum integrates art creation with digital technology, embodying interdisciplinary, practice-oriented characteristics that encourage innovation, experimentation, and project-driven learning (Yan, 2024). Therefore, the course aims to develop an effective teaching process and a replicable project-based teaching program tailored to the learning characteristics of students in higher vocational institutions and the unique attributes of the digital media art curriculum, thus achieving systematic learning objectives.

A Digital media art, as a critical component of vocational education, is characterized by its interdisciplinary nature and strong emphasis on technology and practice. As technological advancements continue, the field of digital media art maintains close ties with industry, necessitating continuous change and innovation (Wang & Zhang, 2022). Given these attributes, the project-based teaching method, with its strong "practical" focus, can be effectively applied to numerous areas within digital media art education. This includes, but is not limited to, multimedia design and production. For example, students can engage in multimedia projects from concept to execution, mastering the processes and skills essential for digital media art production, such as "Graphic Design," "3D Animation Production," "Video Post-Editing," and "Interactive Content Design."

As interaction design rapidly evolves, project-based teaching enables students to gain a deeper understanding of interaction design principles and user experience. Through hands-on project practice, students can enhance their interface design and user experience capabilities. Moreover, project-based teaching allows students to explore the application of emerging technologies, such as virtual reality (VR) and augmented reality (AR), in digital media art. Projects might include the design and implementation of virtual exhibitions, interactive experiences, and the presentation of digital artworks.

Thus, the project-based teaching method has a broad range of applications within digital media art education. It not only equips students with professional knowledge and skills but also fosters teamwork, problem-solving, and innovation abilities, which are crucial for the future development and practice of digital media art. A teaching framework for digital media art courses can be structured around the logical sequence of “project process + teaching content.” This framework involves forming a project team, selecting project themes, defining project modules, finalizing course chapters, drafting lesson plans, implementing project-based teaching, evaluating project outcomes, and refining the teaching content (Jian, 2024). The sequence is visualized in Figure 2.

Figure 2. The construction of project teaching method

STEP 1	PROJECT THEME SCREENED
STEP 2	PROJECT MODULE DETERMINED
STEP 3	COURSE CHAPTER FINALIZED
STEP 4	LESSON PLAN WRITTEN
STEP 5	PROJECT TEACHING IMPLEMENTED
STEP 6	PROJECT RESULTS ACCEPTED
STEP 7	PROJECT TEACHING CONTENT ADJUSTED

For the formation of project teams, collaboration between schools and enterprises is essential. This can be achieved through a “dual mentor system” involving both on-campus and off-campus mentors or a “dual training base system” combining institutional and corporate resources (Deng, 2023). These collaborations allow the integration of real-world enterprise projects into the curriculum, ensuring that students learn “real knowledge,” apply “real skills,” and handle “real projects.” Throughout the project teaching process, a progressive, spiral approach should be maintained, enabling students to incrementally improve their professional skills. For instance, in the "Film and Television Packaging" course, students may work with an enterprise as the client (Party A) while they, as the service providers (Party B), apply their professional skills to deliver satisfactory results. Alternatively, students may participate in project practices as the core of project-based learning, with project outcomes evaluated in skills competitions and project assessments. Teachers, acting as guides, promoters, and supervisors, should encourage students to independently pursue project practices under the guidance of dual mentors from both academia and industry (Xiong et al., 2021).

Drawing from enterprise management processes, simulating corporate workflows, and creating project-based core classrooms can enhance the standardization and practicality of the art design curriculum. This approach not only standardizes the curriculum but also increases its relevance to real-world social and practical contexts (Tan, 2023).

5. THE PROJECT TEACHING METHOD IN DIGITAL ART MEDIA APPLICATION PRINCIPLES

5.1 The Principle of Practicality

The principle of practicality is a fundamental characteristic of the project teaching method. As noted by Guo (2023), "through a real project environment, students can gain practical operating experience." Therefore, the focus of project-based teaching is for instructors to select projects that closely resemble real-world work scenarios. Instead of merely conveying theoretical knowledge in a didactic manner, instructors integrate real projects that students may encounter in their future careers into classroom activities. This approach shifts teaching towards a project-oriented method that mirrors actual work environments. By engaging with these real-world projects, professional teachers can connect with ongoing projects within enterprises and institutions, offering students authentic practice opportunities(Qiu,2014). These practical experiences significantly enhance the skills of digital media art and design students, laying a solid foundation for their future careers.

5.2 The Principle of Rationality

When applying the project teaching method to digital media art courses, professional teachers must adhere to the principle of scientific rationality in selecting projects for students (Guo, 2023). Research on the current status of project-based learning in digital media art programs, both domestically and internationally, reveals that some projects are either too challenging or too simplistic, failing to align with the student's actual skill levels. Furthermore, the lack of innovation and challenge in these projects can hinder student engagement and limit their potential (Wang, 2020).

In the context of domestic higher vocational institutions, where students may have varying levels of ability, it is crucial for professional teachers to consider factors such as contemporary relevance, student characteristics, and regional attributes when selecting projects. Projects should be chosen to ensure consistency between curriculum objectives and project goals. Teachers must design projects that are moderately challenging, aligned with students' knowledge and abilities, and foster partnerships with enterprises to introduce real, innovative project cases. Regular updates to project content are also necessary.

For example, in the "Layout Design" course offered in the second semester at our university, students generally have basic proficiency in software such as Adobe Photoshop and Adobe Illustrator but lack experience with dynamic design software. Therefore, when designing a project for this course, it is advisable to avoid dynamic production tasks. Instead, professional teachers could guide students to complete graphic design projects similar to those undertaken by partnering enterprises. In short, under the principle of rationality, project selection should follow the "jumping, picking a peach" approach, choosing projects that are challenging yet attainable. This ensures that students remain motivated and engaged, preventing a loss of interest in their studies.

5.3 The Principle of Process

The process principle involves breaking down a project into multiple stages, each with clearly defined goals and tasks. For example, these stages may include pre-project research, mid-term project design, and post-project presentation (Guo, 2023). Each stage must have distinct phases, with specific responsibilities assigned to each team member. Additionally, an effective monitoring mechanism should be established to regularly check and provide feedback on project progress (Zhou, 2020). Professional teachers and external tutors play a critical role in providing students with ongoing assessments and feedback during the project, helping them understand their progress and make necessary adjustments and improvements (Long, 2022). Furthermore, students should be encouraged to report on project progress promptly throughout the implementation or teaching process. This includes key decisions, problem-solving processes, and any difficulties encountered. The entire teaching process should engage students proactively in solving project-related challenges, creating a closed loop from project implementation to project outcome reporting.

5.4 The Principle of Evaluative

The project teaching method emphasizes student agency, and when evaluating student performance, teachers should adhere to the principle of diversified evaluation. Professional instructors need to reform traditional evaluation systems by incorporating a variety of assessment methods, including evaluations of project outcomes, process evaluations, team assessments, and individual evaluations (Ye, 2010). Among these, process evaluation has become the most critical assessment method in digital media art courses (Wu, 2023). Additionally, a combination of multiple evaluation approaches should be employed, including assessments by enterprise tutors, on-campus tutors, self-assessments, and peer evaluations (Ma, 2023). Implementing the evaluative principle ensures that students receive timely feedback on the projects they are responsible for, thereby enhancing their initiative, and sense of responsibility, and cultivating their professional spirit.

3. The chapter on the principles of the application of project teaching method in digital art media should be supported by relevant literature cases;

A:Added

6. THE PROJECT TEACHING METHOD IN DIGITAL ART MEDIA APPLICATION STRATEGY

The project teaching method is a pedagogical approach that emphasizes student participation and practicality (Du, 2021). As professional teachers, we are the designers of digital media art professional courses, the builders of course structure, and the lecturers of course content, therefore, when introducing the project-based teaching method into the digital media art professional classroom, the teachers should also start from themselves to improve the professional teachers' ability of project design, instructing ability, and teaching and management ability, etc. In addition, teachers need to consider specifically "what project to introduce, how to do the project, how to promote the project, why to evaluate the project, and finally improve the students' professional ability". In addition, teachers need to consider specific strategies such as "what project to introduce, how to do the project, how to promote the project, why to evaluate the project, and ultimately enhance the students' vocational ability", to form a "project to promote teaching, teaching to do the project". "Feedback" mode, through challenging and innovative projects, guides students to learn and master various skills in practice.

6.1 Teachers of Digital Media Art Programs "Introduce" Projects

When integrating projects into digital media art courses, teachers should ensure that the projects align with the contemporary attributes of the field. Given that digital media art is a rapidly evolving discipline, the design concepts, software, and requirements must be current. Teachers should incorporate the latest and most representative projects into the curriculum to enhance students' practical abilities (Chen & Yang, 2023). This requirement places high demands on teachers' personal design skills and project experience. However, many educators in higher education may be limited by traditional teaching methods, leading to a lack of awareness of current design trends.

To address this, teachers should engage in enterprise practice to stay informed about evolving design trends. By immersing themselves in the industry, teachers can identify and integrate relevant projects into their courses. For instance, in the "Information Visualization Design" course, a core component of the digital media art program, students already possess foundational skills in software and layout design. This course focuses on information organization and visualization. Teachers can leverage enterprise practices to study real-world projects, guiding students through the stages of information visualization design, including pre-project research, mid-term design, and final presentation.

By introducing enterprise projects into the classroom through this practical approach, teachers enable students to engage with cutting-edge design projects, align their work with industry standards, and better understand their own design capabilities through comparison with professionals.

6.2 Group Participation in "Doing" Projects

Introducing the project teaching method into the classroom teaching of digital media art majors, the most important thing is that students can participate in the various processes of the project. As a professional teacher, after the introduction of the enterprise's high-quality projects into the curriculum, students can be guided to the group in the form of small groups and assigned roles so that they can more quickly participate in the project, similar to the division of the enterprise's departments, the grouping of students and role allocation in the project teaching method plays a crucial role (Wei, 2024). Take the "Film and Television Coloring" course as an example, once the teacher releases the task, students can form groups formulate the division of roles according to their needs, and begin to research the current project, including the color grading styles of similar films and tonal tendencies, etc., which can be combined with the analysis of the existing project. Compared with individual independent completion, group work can promote mutual motivation, cooperation, and common progress, while role allocation enables each student to play different roles in the team and utilize their respective strengths to achieve the best team results. At the same time, role assignment also helps to develop students' leadership, communication skills, and team awareness, helping them to better adapt to the teamwork environment in their future work and life.

Overall, the moderate application of the project teaching method in the teaching of digital media art majors and the organization of student grouping and role allocation through the project can not only promote cooperation among students but also lay a good foundation for vocational students to master a skill based on the future development of the students to get ready.

6.3 Combination of Project and Competition "to Promote" the Project

The integration of project-based teaching in digital media art education effectively stimulates students' learning enthusiasm and hones their vocational skills. Vocational skills competitions serve as a direct method to assess the outcomes of project-based learning (Zhou & Huang, 2023). The "learning through competition" model is widely utilized in vocational education, as it boosts student engagement, improves professional skills, and enhances the quality of the teaching team. Furthermore, it fosters stronger partnerships between educational institutions and industry.

Based on the above professional background, the digital media art major combines different teacher-student competitions according to the characteristics of each teaching project and mobilizes the project practice enthusiasm of teachers and students by participating in teachers' teaching competitions and students' skill competitions, which plays a good role in promoting the overall project teaching construction and development of the digital media art professional curriculum. Taking the annual college students' advertising art competition as an example, most of the selected topics in the competition are based on the real topics of enterprises, which guide students to express their design creativity. However, in the process of participating in the competition in recent years, we found that most of the students in this major stayed in the finalist award and excellence award, compared with other dual colleges and universities or higher undergraduate colleges and universities, there is still a big gap, and these gaps mainly exist in our students' lack of creativity and insufficient depth of thinking. Based on the above problems, teachers of digital media art majors, in the teaching process, increase the part of the teaching content of the preliminary research, guide students to understand and think deeply about the project, introduce the demand for research, problem analysis, design thinking, etc. in the preliminary analysis, and actively guide the students to carry out multi-creative expression, the teacher will be a combination of the requirements of the competition and the content of the curriculum, leading students to carry out the presentation and expression of the project. Teachers combine the requirements of the competition with the course content and lead students to present and express their projects. Under the teaching method of combining "project and competition", the scoring standard is refined to improve students' enthusiasm for the competition, and students' enthusiasm for participating in the competition is significantly increased, and the awards won are higher than before.

6.4 Multi-System "Assessment" Program

Traditional teaching methods often rely on homework or exams to provide feedback on student learning. However, the introduction of project-based teaching methods in digital media courses necessitates a diversified evaluation system to effectively assess project outcomes (Wang & An, 2019). This system should incorporate various evaluation modes, including process evaluation, multi-perspective assessment, continuous feedback, and iterative improvement.

In this context, professional teachers assume the roles of mentors and guides, helping students navigate both theoretical and practical aspects of digital media art. They offer necessary support and encourage problem-solving and creativity. Additionally, a multi-entity evaluation approach is employed, involving both on-campus and external mentors. External mentors, typically industry professionals, evaluate student projects using industry standards and provide timely guidance. This dual-mentor system—combining on-campus and off-campus support—ensures that students receive relevant resources and technical assistance to successfully complete their projects.

Moreover, a structured reporting and assessment mechanism should be integrated into the teaching process. Students are expected to regularly update teachers on their project progress, including accomplishments, encountered challenges, and needed support. Professional teachers, in turn, provide feedback and guidance based on these reports, addressing any issues promptly. Adjustments to the project plan and work arrangements may be made as needed, optimizing the project implementation process and ensuring timely and high-quality completion.

The multi-dimensional evaluation process can be summarized in the following steps: (a) Teachers transition into mentoring roles, (b) Implement dual-mentor guidance, (c) Establish regular reporting and evaluation mechanisms, and (d) Adjust program arrangements as necessary (Chen, 2024). By employing these methods, professional teachers can effectively oversee and guide students throughout the project implementation process, ensuring its successful progress. This approach allows students to fully engage their creativity and initiative, thereby achieving the learning objectives of digital media art courses.

6.5 Continuous Improvement of the Project

In the process of implementing the project teaching method, it is inevitable to encounter some difficult-to-solve problems, so the professional teacher team, the student team, and the off-campus enterprise team must work together to continuously improve the problems encountered, to better complete the project. In the process of continuous improvement, teachers and students reflect together, analyze, and discuss the strengths and weaknesses, such students in the project have accumulated a wealth of experience and skills, that need to be summarized and shared promptly, you can organize an experience exchange meeting or write a project report to share the success of the project and lessons learned, and to promote learning and growth among each other. Secondly, for the application of the project teaching method in the overall design of digital media art majors, we can reflect on more detailed points, for example, from the project design and planning, grouping and task allocation, as well as the implementation of the entire project process for review, in the reflection to constantly refine their teaching ability, but also to better apply our project teaching method in digital media art majors in the course practice. At the same time, we also aim to better apply our project teaching method to the practice of digital media art courses.

7. CONCLUSION

With the ongoing advancement of digital media arts programs, the implementation of project-based teaching methods is anticipated to undergo further development and refinement. As an innovative pedagogical approach, project-based learning infuses new vitality and opportunities into education. Despite facing challenges during its implementation, continuous exploration and enhancement of this method will increasingly contribute to cultivating high-quality talent aligned with contemporary needs. Educators should embrace this method actively, integrating it with practical applications to foster educational reform and progress.

For students in higher vocational colleges and universities, the practical nature of project-based learning is particularly beneficial, as it encourages the application of acquired knowledge and skills in real-world contexts. This approach effectively integrates technology, art, and design, thereby nurturing students' comprehensive abilities and innovative thinking. It enables them to leverage various technical tools for creation and practice within the digital media field.

As student needs continue to diversify, future project-based teaching methods are likely to focus more on personalized learning and tailored courses. Projects and tasks will be designed to align with students' interests and capabilities. Consequently, the future of project-based teaching in digital media arts is expected to be increasingly diversified, personalized, and forward-looking, aimed at enhancing students' overall competence, creativity, and social responsibility to meet the evolving demands of education and industry in the digital era.

REFERENCES

Chen, J., & Yang, W. H. (2023). Research on the project teaching method of landscape design courses in higher vocational colleges. *Modern Gardening, 24*, 197–200. https://doi.org/DOI: 10.14051

Chen, X. Y. (2024). The reform and exploration of project teaching methods in the course of graphic design software: Taking the direction of visual communication as an example. *Shoes, 13*, 15–17.

Cui, L. B. (2021). The research of mixed work order classroom teaching practice based on CDIO. *Master's Dissertation, Shandong Normal University*. https://doi.org/DOI: 10.27767

Deng, G. (2023). The vocational college double division team innovates the mechanism and path of "Post Course Competition Certificate." *University, 35*, 7–10.

Du, L. N. (2021). Higher vocational pre-school art education to carry out project-based teaching. *China Educational Technology & Equipment, 13*, 48–49.

Du, X. M. (2015). Research on project-driven practical teaching reform of digital media design major. *China Packaging, 11*, 65–68.

Fan, Q. Q. (2023). Research on the "deep learning" strategy of higher vocational art students' informationization based on project-based teaching. *Dazhongwenyi, 10*, 127–129. https://doi.org/DOI: 10.20112/j.cnki.issn1007-5828.2023.10.044

Guo, J. Q. (2023). Research on the construction of project teaching methods in art design teaching. *Grand Spectacle, 5*, 153–155.

Han, R. (2024). The application research of project teaching methods in electronic and electrical engineering teaching of higher vocational education. *Theoretical and Practice of Innovation and Entrepreneurship, 8*, 161–163.

Huang, S. D. (2022). The application of project teaching methods in the construction of top-quality online open courses in electrical and electronic technology. *China Educational Technology & Equipment, 20*, 54–57.

Jia, R. (2020). Research on the status quo and problems of digital media talent training in higher vocational colleges. *Journalists Cradle, 10*, 51–52.

Jian, B., & Sun, X. J. (2024). The reform and practice of the teaching mode of digital media art in colleges and universities. *Journal of Taiyuan Urban Vocational College, 5*, 86–90. https://doi.org/DOI: 10.16227/j.cnki.tycs.2024.0279

Jiao, Z. X., Yuan, G. H., & Wu, C. Z. (2024). Practice of project teaching methods in the course of electrical machinery and electrical control. *Electronic Technology & Software Engineering, 1*, 88–89.

Jin, T. (2024). Master of practical research on project-based teaching methods in digital audio-visual editing and synthesis. *Dissertation*. https://link.cnki.net/doi/10.27280/d.cnki.gsdsu.2024.001504

Kilpatrick, W. H. (1918). The Project Method. *Teachers College Record*, •••, 318–330.

Krohn, F. W. (2005). *Foundations of Pedagogy*. Educational Science Press.

Li, X. Y. (2023). *An empirical study on the application of project-based teaching methods in technical environmental monitoring courses in secondary vocational education* (Master's thesis, Shandong Normal University). https://doi.org/DOI:10.27280/d.cnki.gsdsu.2023.001113

Liang, W. L.. (2024). Research on the application of project-based teaching methods in Tea Art Association courses from the perspective of curriculum ideology and politics. *Guangdong Tea Industry*, 01, 65–69.

Liu, J. Y. (2020). Reform and practice of the project-driven mode of cultivating innovative and enterprising talents through school-enterprise cooperation. *Education Teaching Forum, 12*, 8–9.

Liu, L. (2024). On the development of digital media art education in the context of art science and technology integration. *University*, 11, 134–137.

Liu, Y. (2001). A Brief Overview of Higher Teacher Education Reform in the United States. *Educational Researcher*, 10, 74–77.

Long, W. L. (2022). *Based on the idea of project management: PBL teaching method in secondary vocational "Dynamic web design" course of practical research* (Master's thesis, Jiangxi Science and Technology Normal University). DOI: 10.27751/d.cnki.gjxkj.2022.000050

Lu, J. (2019). Research on the status quo and problems of digital media art professional training in higher vocational colleges. *Home Drama*, 01, 172–174.

Qu, S. L., Yang, J. J., & Xie, Z. H. (2023). The application of project teaching methods in the teaching of environmental art design in colleges and universities. *Journal of Shanxi University of Finance and Economics*, S1, 181–183.

Song, T. W. (2019). This paper discusses the innovation of digital media art teaching mode. *Da Guan*, 12, 113–114.

Sun, Y. J. (2021). *Research on immersive scene design of digital media art* (Doctoral dissertation, Chinese National Academy of Arts). DOI: 10.27653/d.cnki.gzysy.2021.000013

Tan, Z. P. (2023). Discussion on the reform and optimization strategy of art design teaching methods in higher vocational colleges. *Journal of Harbin Vocational Technical College*, 02, 37–39. DOI: 10.16145/j.cnki.cn23-1531/z.2023.02.012

Wang, D., & Zhang, Q. M. (2022). Research on the reform and innovation of digital media art education in colleges and universities. *Grand View (Forum)*, 02, 147–149.

Wang, L. (2023). The application of project-based approach to English teaching in secondary vocational schools. *Examination Questions and Research*, 32, 106–108.

Wang, T. (2020). Research on project teaching methods for digital media art specialties. *SP, 11*, 281.

Wang, T. (2021). Research on the teaching of professional English courses in higher vocational colleges based on a project-based approach. *Journal of Chongqing Vocational College of Electronic Engineering*, 02, 98–101. DOI: 10.13887/j.cnki.jccee.2021(2).23

Wang, Y., & An, H. (2019). The application research of project teaching methods in the course of information technology teaching theory. *Knowledge Library*, 21, 174–178.

Wei, T. X. (2024). Exploring the application of project teaching methods in mathematics teaching in secondary vocational schools. *Guangdong Vocational Technical Education and Research*, 01, 10–13. DOI: 10.19494/j.cnki.issn1674-859x.2024.01.034

Wu, C. F. (2023). *The project teaching method in secondary vocational "Interior design": The optimization practice research* (Master's thesis, Guangxi Normal University). https://doi.org/DOI: 10.27036/d.cnki.ggxsu.2023.001052

Xian, Y., & Liu, N. (2023). Research on the core curriculum construction standard of digital media art majors for vocational undergraduates. *Western Radio & Television*, 04, 85–88.

Xing, W. L. (2023). Research on teaching innovation in electrical and electronic specialties in secondary vocational schools. *New Wisdom*, 36, 7–9.

Xiong, H. F., Ning, C., & Huang, H. (2021). Project-based teaching: Reform and practice of the packaging design course in higher vocational education under the integration of industry and education. *Theoretical Research and Practice of Innovation and Entrepreneurship, 05*, 22–23+26.

Xu, M. (2022). *Applied research of project teaching methods in the course of "Foundation of Fashion Design" in secondary vocational schools* (Master's thesis, Nanning Normal University). DOI: 10.27037/d.cnki.ggxsc.2022.000278

Xue, D. S., & Li, C. H. (2019). An analysis of the economic dynamics of personnel training in digital media art. *Times of Fortune*, 12, 168.

Yang, M. Y. (2021). *The application research of project teaching methods in junior Chinese reading teaching*. Liaoning Normal University., DOI: 10.27212/d.cnki.glnsu.2021.001379

Yang, Y. J. (2020). The application and research of project teaching methods in the teaching of graphic design. *Journal of Science and Education (Mid-Magazine), 32*, 146–147. DOI: 10.16400/j.cnki.kjdkz.2020.11.068

Ye, S. Y. (2010). The application and exploration of project teaching methods in the course of art design specialty. *Vocational and Technical Education in China, 14*, 70–71+82.

Zhang, C. (2024). The application of project teaching methods in graphic design teaching. *PACK*, 04, 226–228. DOI: 10.19446/j.cnki.1005-9423.2024.04.073

Zhang, C. Y. (2022). Reflection and innovation research on digital media art design teaching. *Guangdong Vocational Technical Education and Research*, 05, 137–140. DOI: 10.19494/j.cnki.issn1674-859x.2022.05.036

Zhang, H. M., Zhang, C. Y., & Liu, Q. (2020). Research on the international professional talents training of digital media majors from the perspective of creativity. *Modern Computers*, 07, 95–99.

Zhang, Y. Y. (2022). Market-oriented exploration of higher vocational art design teaching reform: Digital media art design as an example. *DAGUAN*, 10, 124–126.

Zhou, A. Q. (2020). Research on the application of project teaching methods in design courses: Taking the design of animation scenes as an example. *Grand Spectacle*, 06, 138–139.

Zhou, W. T., & He, H. Y. (2023). Research and practice on the teaching reform of landscape architecture design courses in the context of rural revitalization: Taking the preliminary course of landscape architecture design as an example. *Anhui Agricultural Science Bulletin*, 19, 129–133. DOI: 10.16377/j.cnki.issn1007-7731.2023.19.031

Zhu, X. L. (2024). Research on the talent training path of the digital culture industry in our country. *Chinese Personnel Science*, 02, 45–52.

Chapter 2
Serious Games:
A Study on Digital Literacy and Skill Improvement of Architecture Students in China Vocational Institute

Yuting Dai
Jiangsu Vocational Institute of Architectural Technology, China

Jingru Zhang
https://orcid.org/0009-0002-6537-2334
Universiti Sains Malaysia, Malaysia

ABSTRACT

Students in vocational colleges in China play a crucial role in supporting the digital transformation of education. In this study, a vocational institute in Jiangsu province was selected for investigation, involving 79 students. The findings revealed that traditional classrooms still face limitations in enhancing students' digital literacy and skills. To address this issue and better equip students with the digital literacy and learning skills required by society, a serious game model was developed for the architecture professional course "Architecture CAD Drawing." This model presents core course content through case pictures and promotes interactive engagement. A user study involving 42 vocational architecture students was then conducted to compare the effectiveness of serious games with traditional video classes. The results demonstrate that Serious Games significantly enhance student interest in utilizing digital technology for learning, improve their efficiency in acquiring professional skills, and deepen their comprehension of digital literacy.

DOI: 10.4018/979-8-3693-6745-2.ch002

1 INTRODUCTION

The digital transformation of higher vocational education is the key to the high quality development of higher vocational education(Wang et al.,2023). In 2007, The International Society for Technology in Education (ISTE) identified "digital citizenship literacy" as one of the six standards of National educational technology standards for students.The Digital Education Action Plan (2021-2027) is a EU policy initiative aiming to support the adaptation of the education and training systems of Member States to the digital age. This plan is inspired by the common vision of high-quality, inclusive and accessible digital education(Outeda, 2024). China's vocational education has also entered an era of rapid digital development. Students in China's vocational colleges are not only crucial supporters of the digital transformation of education but also the core force behind the digital advancement of modern vocational education. Therefore, students need to be trained in digital literacy skills for the world of work(Jatmoko et al.,2023).

In 2020, China's Ministry of Education and nine other departments issued the Action Plan for Improving the Quality of Vocational Education (2020-2023). This plan clearly proposed: "The implementation of vocational education information 2.0 construction action should vigorously improve the level of vocational education information construction, and comprehensively improve the digital literacy of vocational college students, including the use of network information technology and high-quality online resources for independent learning ability." Since 2022, China's Ministry of Education has frequently referenced digital literacy in its conferences and policies. For example, at the National Education Work Conference in January 2022, the implementation of education digitization action was proposed as a crucial reform measure for China's education sector. In 2024, the Chinese government issued Key Points of Work to Upgrade Digital Literacy and Skills for all by 2024(2024), which explicitly stated the need to cultivate high-level composite digital talents. This initiative aims to comprehensively improve the digital literacy and skills of both teachers and students.

Europe and the United States have conducted in-depth research on cultivating teachers' digital literacy for some time, developing relatively mature models and practical experiences. The United Kingdom, the United States and other countries have attached great importance to the cultivation of digital literacy.(Polizzi,2020; Alexander et al.,2017). For example, the United Kingdom proposed a strategy for cultivating digital literacy in the British Digital Strategy. Different policies, initiatives and strategies are currently being proposed in Germany, addressing educational technology innovations in Higher Education(Bond et al.,2018). In 2020, the EU issued the Digital Education Action Plan 2021-2027, which proposed two key measures: (1) requiring countries to build and improve digital infrastructure, create high-performance digital education ecosystems, and develop digital literacy learning platforms; and (2) cultivating students' digital skills and literacy while enhancing digital skills and transformation capabilities. Compared to these countries, research on students' digital literacy and skills in China began relatively late and has developed rapidly over a short period. However, China has a strong foundation in information literacy. Scholar Chen puts forward the basic path to promote the comprehensive governance system of "intelligent +" digital literacy education, and puts forward specific suggestions on lifelong education of digital literacy for all people, cultivation of comprehensive digital talents with legal ethics and data analysis, as well as promoting the aggregation of industry-university-research resources(Chen,2022). Scholar Wu discussed the concept digital literacy features the subjective initiatives to actively improve one's and others' skills, competence, awareness and thinking mode for adapting to, qualifying for and creating a new digital age and society(Wu, 2023).

Serious Games(SG) usually refer to a hybrid approach, often mediated by technology(Malegiannaki, 2017). The terms edutainment (Okan, 2011), playful learning (Resnick, 2004), gamification (De Sousa Borges, Durelli, Reis,&Isotani, 2014), game-based learning (Whitton, 2011). Scholars believe that serious games may be more effective in promoting learning than games that focus primarily on entertainment(Laamarti et al., 2014). This trend is supported by educational theories such as experiential learning, active learning, and situated learning (Ortiz, Bowers, & Cannon-Bowers, 2015). Some scholars have adopted serious games as a learning method for students to acquire knowledge, such as using serious games to increase motivation for learning about cultural heritage (Ye et al., 2021).

The educational goals for students majoring in architecture at vocational colleges in China are consistent with the teaching objectives of serious games. However, there has been limited exploration into leveraging serious games to improve professional competencies and digital proficiency among these students. Most research on the design of serious games for cultural heritage education focuses on immersive digital technology applications or narrative game flow design to create a scene re-enactment experience or a vivid storytelling process for participants (Malegiannaki & Daradoumis, 2017; Ibrahim & Ali, 2018). While this gaming format may be suitable for museum settings or architectural ruins (Ye et al., 2021), its efficacy is diminished when applied to fostering building-related skill acquisition and enhancing digital literacy, as emphasized in this study.

Consequently, this study has chosen vocational college students as the survey sample. It has integrated the contemporary context and relevant literature to elucidate the present status of digital education development, the concept of digital literacy and skills for vocational college students. A comprehensive survey was conducted to assess the current level of digital literacy and skills among these students. Additionally, this study undertook systematic applied research aimed at enhancing digital literacy and skills through interactive serious games within traditional architecture classes.

This paper aims to address the following research questions:

> RQ1: What is the current status of digital literacy among vocational architecture students? What are their learning needs and expectations regarding professional skills?
> RQ2: How can interactive serious game applications be designed to cultivate vocational students' interest in digital technology, improve their learning efficiency, and enhance their digital literacy during the learning process?

To answer these questions, we selected the China Jiangsu Vocational and Technical College of Architecture, a public full-time institution in Jiangsu Province, recognized as a national model higher vocational college and a national quality higher vocational college. As a higher vocational college specializing in architecture, the school offers a rich architecture curriculum, making it an ideal choice to explore the use of serious games to improve the digital learning literacy of architecture majors in vocational colleges. First, we conducted a questionnaire survey of 79 students to understand their current digital literacy, professional skills learning needs, and expectations. Based on these findings, we designed a serious game program aimed at transforming traditional professional skill operation knowledge into multimedia form and integrating virtual multimedia content with practical skill training. We then conducted a study involving 42 students majoring in architectural animation technology, who were asked to experience teaching in a traditional classroom and learning from serious games, and then complete a 5-point Likert scale questionnaire. The results indicated that, compared to traditional classroom teaching, serious games significantly improved students' learning efficiency and digital literacy.

We make the following contributions to this work:

(1) Analyze the characteristics of vocational college students' current digital literacy.
(2) Use serious games for interactive teaching, combining multimedia presentation of knowledge points with practical exercises.
(3) Through the adoption of serious games to enable vocational students to acquire professional skills, enhance their own digital literacy. Therefore, to expand the significance of experience design and methodology of serious game teaching.

2 LITERATURE REVIEW

To enhance vocational architecture students' skill learning and digital literacy through digital learning, we conducted literature research and analysis in the following fields: serious games, digital literacy, and vocational students' digital literacy training.

2.1. Serious Games

The concept of serious games was first coined by Abt, who described them as follows: "We are concerned with serious games in the sense that these games have an explicit and carefully thought-out educational purpose and are not intended to be played primarily for amusement" (Abt, 1987). Serious games are considered one of the most effective means of learning as they influence the mood of the learner (Shabir Ahmad et al., 2022). his is because they can capture and hold the attention of players through entertaining mechanics such as animations, narrative, and interactivity (Dyck et al., 2003; Ritterfeld & Weber, 2006), while also enabling them to learn and improve in the game by specifying learning principles (Gee, 2006, 2009).Education has been one of the main focuses of action for serious games, based on the principle that learning while having fun is possible and efficient(Pérez et al., 2023). For example, teachers have used games like Civilization and The Sims in conjunction with traditional classroom activities to effectively teach students about history and societal development (McCall, 2016). This means that serious games can be a useful tool for teaching and learning(Rosenthal, 2022). Serious games are more likely to be successful when they balance the serious and the playful nature of the game by embedding the educational goal into the gameplay itself, building the content on a strong foundation of domain expertise, utilizing appropriate interaction technologies, and offering intuitive game mechanics that naturally support the game's serious intent without adverse effects (Caserman et al., 2020).

Virtual reality (VR) games, augmented reality (AR) games, and artificial intelligence (AI) have also been incorporated into serious game design, and many researchers have explored and developed them. For example, Holly et al. conducted a user study for over six years to find the challenges and expectations of VR platforms in science education(Holly et al.,2021). It is widely believed that simulation-based AR games in science, especially in physical education, can improve learners' motivation and learning effectiveness (Ullah et al.,2022). Graeske et al. show that implementing VR-based teaching tools increases the possibility of co-creation, co-design, and customized learning, thereby increasing student motivation. It improves students' problem-solving skills in high school (Graeske et al.). Dyulicheva et al. explored the use of AI and immersive technology in serious educational games. In particular, it focuses on using AI to customize and personalize the player experience. It also works on AI-based serious games for teachers and students who don't need programming skills(Dyulicheva et al.,2021). This is different from traditional classroom education. Serious games emphasize students' individual practical learning, while traditional classrooms focus on abstract learning(Checa & Bustillo, 2020). Unlike traditional teaching environments, where the teacher controls the learning (e.g., teacher-centered), Serious Games present a learner-centered approach to education. In Serious Games, the trainee feels in control of an interactive learning process, thereby facilitating active and critical learning (Stapleton, 2004). Therefore, we begin by understanding the needs and expectations of architecture students regarding digital literacy and professional skills. Student feedback was used to explore ways to design serious games for architecture courses.

2.2. Digital Literacy

The concept of digital literacy was first proposed by Israeli scholar Professor Alkalai in 1994. He believed that digital literacy should contain five aspects: visual literacy, re-creation literacy, branching literacy, information literacy, and social-emotional literacy. However, there are differences in the way digital literacy is conceptualized (Eshet-Alkalai, 2004). For instance, the European Commission defines digital competence as one of eight key competencies for lifelong learning including "the confident and critical use of information society technology (IST) for work, leisure and communication" (European Commission, 2006). Tuamsuk et al. refer to both US and EU policy documents as well as research when using the following definition of digital literacy: "Digital literacy is composed of technical skill, cognitive skill and emotional-social skills"(Tuamsuk et al., 2017).

With the rapid development of digital information technology in the 21st century, various views and understandings of the definition of digital literacy have emerged. Cazco et al. defines digital competence as: " Values, beliefs, knowledge, capacity and attitudes to use technology in an adequate way, including computer as well as different programmes and Internet, which allow for the possibility of research, access, organisation and the use of information to produce knowledge"(Cazco et al., 2016). In 2018, United Nations Education Scientific and Cultural Organization(UNESCO) defined digital literacy as "the ability to access, manage, understand, integrate, communicate, evaluate and create information securely and rationally, using digital devices and network technologies for employment, access to decent work and entrepreneurship." It mainly includes computer literacy, information and communication technology literacy, information literacy and media literacy(Law et al., 2018). Most frameworks on skills development, although only TPACK(Reyes et al.,2017), UNESCO frameworks(2011) and, to a lesser extent, ISTE(2017) standards explicitly link these frameworks to related changes in pedagogy and curriculum.

These skills typically focus on the technical and operational aspects of ICT and information skills, particularly how to use devices and software to access, process, and evaluate information for a range of curricular and instructional purposes, along with the associated types of thinking (e.g., analysis, evaluation, criticism). The frameworks vary greatly in structure, with ISTE standards, UNESCO competencies, and the ICTE-MM Maturity Model adopting a generic "checklist" format, while others are more conceptual, providing a broader range of ideas for custom development.

Currently, digital literacy has become a key component of professional development for educators (Nguyen & Habók, 2024). The challenge lies in integrating technology into the academic curriculum (Blauet al., 2020). Various tools have been developed and tested by scholars to assess teachers' digital literacy in real-world educational contexts (e.g., Quaicoe & Pata, 2020). For instance, Potyrała and Tomczyk (2021) explore teachers' knowledge and skills in addressing cybersecurity issues, such as assessing the reliability of electronic information, cyberbullying, and other issues related to the educational application of technology. Hasan et al. reviewed 43 articles from databases including WoS/Clarivate Analytics, Proquest Central, Emerald Management Journals, Jstor Business College Collections, and Scopus/ Elsevier. The initial results indicate an upward trend in academic papers focused on digital literacy (Tinmaz et al., 2022).

At the same time, Chinese scholars have also conducted in-depth analyses of digital literacy. The following articles are from China National Knowledge Network (CNKI), the largest literature retrieval website in China. Chinese scholars believe that digital literacy is an integrated, dynamic, and open concept, formed through the evolution of media literacy, computer literacy, information literacy, and network literacy (Wang et al., 2013). Sun believes that digital literacy is what people need to survive, work, study and develop in the digital social environment, including a comprehensive ability to understand, use, evaluate and create digital technology in economic and social development(Sun et al., 2020). Some scholars have further refined the concept of digital literacy, suggesting that it includes the ability to use digital technologies in work, study, and life, as well as the associated emotions, attitudes, qualities, and values. This includes aspects such as "digital access," "digital communication," "digital creation," "digital consumption," "digital security," "digital ethics," "digital norms," and "digital health" (Zhou, 2023). These studies highlight the importance of improving digital literacy among higher vocational college students, as it is a necessary skill for their future success in a digital society.

2.3. Vocational College Students Digital Literacy Training

On January 27, 2023, France issued the "Strategy for the Digitalisation of Education 2023–2027," which stated that digitalisation is transforming every sphere of society, and digital technologies are playing an increasingly important role in people's work and lives (Voronkova et al., 2023). As most students will pursue digital careers in the future, schools need to educate students with the appropriate literacy and skills. The strategy proposes a series of initiatives to strengthen students' digital skills and promote student success through digital tools (Bilohur, Vlada, & Andriukaitiene, Regina, 2020). This study posits that digital literacy is an extension and expansion of information literacy, a dynamic and evolving concept. It encompasses traditional elements of information awareness, information ability, and information ethics, while also emphasizing the application of digital technology in a digital environment. From the students' perspective, digital literacy involves proficiency in using emerging digital technologies and various digital tools, from which professional skills and educational values are derived. Lazonder et al. conducted a three-year study measuring the development of children's digital literacy skills by testing 151 students three times a year to monitor their progress in collecting, creating, transforming, and securely using digital information (Lazonder et al., 2020). Amin et al. explored the contribution of communication and digital literacy to critical thinking in biology. Their findings suggest that educators need to incorporate communication skills and digital literacy components into their teaching to improve students' critical thinking skills (Amin et al., 2023). Quraishi et al. investigated the integration of digital literacy into higher education curricula. A sample of 150 university students and lecturers provided insights into digital literacy, technology use, and educational experiences. The findings highlight the importance of incorporating digital literacy into higher education curricula and emphasize that upgrading digital literacy skills for students and educators requires ongoing support and training (Quraishi et al., 2024).

At present, Chinese scholars Zhang integrated and refined the influencing factors of college students' digital literacy education from five dimensions, and analyzed the key factors affecting digital literacy education(Zhang, 2021). Gu & Ding reviews Chinese academic papers from the past 20 years to investigate the digital literacy of normal students of pedagogical faculties(Gu & Ding,2022). Huang et al. review the current research and existing frameworks of digital literacy both domestically and internationally. They conduct a comparative analysis and propose an index reference framework. Additionally, they preliminarily construct an evaluation index for the digital literacy of higher vocational students(Huang et al., 2023). Previous research has primarily focused on identifying problems in digital literacy and solving students' ability issues, often overlooking how digital technology in teaching can enhance students' digital literacy. This study attempts to visualize professional skill points using serious games in a classroom-based environment to improve students' skill learning ability and digital literacy.

3 PURPOSE

The purpose of this study is to stimulate students' interest in learning professional skills and enhance their digital literacy through the use of serious games. Therefore, this study selected a fundamental course for architecture majors—Architectural CAD Drawing. This study explores an effective design method that transforms the traditional classroom explanation mode into an interactive jigsaw game. Serious games (SG) can not only better demonstrate the structural relationships of various parts of CAD architectural drawings and the operation of quick commands, but also provide an interactive discussion platform that stimulates learners' motivation for exploration and active learning (Ye et al., 2021). Additionally, Serious games can improve students' digital literacy. Based on this concept, the study developed a computer game called "Explore Architectural Drawings." Using a complete CAD drawing from a course case study, this research assesses the advantages of using serious games to promote digital literacy by comparing them with traditional classroom teaching. The main purposes of this study are as follows: 1. Analyze the characteristics of vocational college students' current digital literacy. 2. Develop a AutoCAD digital jigsaw puzzle game to help students understand the structural composition of each part of the architectural drawing and the key points of software drawing, including quick commands and drawing steps. 3. Examine the differences between classroom learning and the completion of serious games in acquiring professional skills and knowledge; 4. Assess the impact of students playing serious games on digital literacy.

4 METHOD

In this study, in order to better understand the target audience, we designed a pre-test to survey the profile of vocational architecture students, mainly including their current digital literacy, their needs and expectations for professional skills, their satisfaction with existing curriculum skill carriers, and their awareness of serious games. This is followed by a serious game experiment. The game group completes the game process for learning. The classroom group completes the learning through the course. Both groups learnt the same content i.e. architectural pattern drawing techniques and steps through the learning method that they could not. Finally, the performance of the participants in both groups in terms of knowledge acquisition and knowledge transfer was assessed using the pattern test and the change in motivation of the participants in the game group was assessed using the Digital Literacy Scale.

4.1. Pre-Investigation

4.1.1. On-Site Investigation Among the Visitors

To better understand the target audience, we surveyed the profile of vocational college architecture students, including their current status of digital literacy, their needs and expectations for professional skills, their satisfaction with existing curriculum skill carriers, and their awareness of serious games. In this study, 79 vocational college students were randomly recruited and participated in semi-structured interviews on campus, each lasting about 20 to 30 minutes.

4.1.2. Demographics

Demographics Of the 79 respondents, 47 are female and 32 are male. There are 21 freshmen, 56 sophomores, 1 junior and 1 graduate students. Regarding their geographic origins, 45 students are from townships, 12 from county-level cities, 18 from prefecture-level cities, and 4 from provincial capitals or municipalities.

4.1.3. Findings

4.1.3.1. Analysis of Current Situation of Students' Digital Literacy

To understand the current state of digital literacy among architecture students in vocational colleges, we first asked them about their understanding of the digital development goals of their professional courses and the connotations of personal digital literacy. The students were then presented with an explanation of the content of the professional training program and digital literacy (quoting the European Union interpretation).The results show that most respondents (N=58) do not have a clear understanding of professional digital training goals and the connotation of digital literacy. For example, V23 said that" *Teachers put more emphasis on the acquisition of skills and knowledge when giving professional lessons, and did not specifically emphasize the professional numerical training goa*ls". V30 indicates" *I have received specific training related to digital literacy"* . V47 mentioned" *I do not have a particular understanding of the numerical training objectives. However, some respondents believe that practical professional courses, compared to theoretical ones, are helpful in improving personal digital literacy"*. V6 said"*The practical course teacher lets us use relevant digital devices for practice, and my personal digital literacy has improved."* V65 stated" *I heard the teacher talk about* *this concept, and because I am curious about it, I personally conducted in-depth discussions with the teacher."* This curiosity for new ideas and training goals prompts some students to explore more about digital training goals and the connotation of digital literacy. Additionally, respondents mentioned that although they have read the digital training objectives of some professional courses, their understanding of the connotation is not clear enough to apply to their learning. As V2 and V71 said" *The teacher has talked about it before class, but my understanding is not clear during the course learning process."*

4.1.3.2. Students' Needs and Expectations for Learning Professional Skills

Secondly, the research also asked the students about their needs and expectations for professional skills learning, and showed the students the professional skills cultivation goals of 3-5 courses at random. The results show that about half of the students think that the setting of the skill development objectives of the existing professional courses is very reasonable (N=53). "*It is the professional skills I want to learn in this course* (V5)" . "*The goal is very clear and consistent with the teacher's teaching content*(V21)" . However, 1/3 of the students (N=18) indicated that these goals were not fully achieved in their learning process, which raised more learning needs and expectations. For example, V19 shows that "*the teacher's explanation in class may only meet most of the goals, and a small part of them need to be achieved by other teaching resource*". V68 believes that "*professional skill learning hopes to increase the interaction of skill learning, so that the classroom will be more interesting*".

4.1.3.3. Students' Satisfaction with the Existing Professional Curriculum Skills Learning Vector

We asked respondents about their attention to professional books for their courses and the skills taught in the classroom, as well as whether they have used digital media or digital applications (such as online courses or MOOCs) to acquire skills and knowledge. Most of them (N=43) are not satisfied with the current methods of skills learning in professional courses (such as textbooks, online courses, and classroom lectures), which they feel do not effectively improve personal digital literacy. They reported that "*the individual skill steps in the textbook do not provide a better understanding of why certain skills are used in a particular way, and the content related to digital literacy is also dry*(V23)". "*The explanation in online classes is better; it can be more vivid with a teacher's explanation, and it has improved my personal digital literacy to some extent. However, we encounter different problems from those addressed by teachers during practice, and online courses do not allow for real-time communication with teachers to answer questions* (V76)."

Additionally, some students believe that the most satisfactory medium for learning professional skills is classroom teaching. In this setting, teachers can explain the reasons behind certain skills and answer students' questions in real-time. The inclusion of practical computer operations greatly helps in improving personal digital literacy. However, one-third of the students (N=21) also pointed out that classroom learning is insufficient; classroom time is limited, and they cannot continue interactive learning to improve personal digital literacy after class. As V19 stated, "*The skills used in the internship company during the holidays were explained by the teacher before, but I forgot some of the skills without practicing for a month, and many digital goals were forgotten.*" V42 noted that "*pure online courses can be helpful for after-school learning, but they lack interaction. Many problems cannot be solved in a timely manner, making it difficult to improve personal digital literacy.*"

4.1.3.4. Students' Awareness of Serious Games

In this study, the respondents were asked about their knowledge of serious games, their learning experiences using serious games, and their attitudes towards the application of serious games to the learning of professional skills in vocational architecture. According to the study, about 35% of respondents don't know much about serious games. "*It is also the first time I have heard of this concept, and I hope to get an answer(V12)*", "*I do not understand what his learning process is like*(V21)". However, some students (N=30) have experienced the learning of serious games, such as serious games in thinking logic courses, interactive experiences in entrepreneurship courses. Respondents indicated that "*serious games are fun and allow me to concentrate on learning knowledge* (V32)", and "*games and interactions can give me more real-time feedback and allow me to keep track of my learning status*(V8)" . However, some respondents also mentioned their doubts about using serious games to learn professional skills, which is the top concern of students. As V48 saids "*Serious games sound interesting, but can they be combined with practical skills to learn, will they improve learning efficiency?*" V53 indicates that "*Can serious games be used independently in class or after class?*" but some interviewees also mentioned that they do not want serious games to require interaction with strangers, and hope that they can be used alone, easy to operate, and more targeted to improve the learning effect of professional skills.

4.1.3.5. Discussion

Through semi-structured interviews with vocational college students, we found that their digital literacy learning objectives are currently unclear, their expectations for professional skills learning are high, and they are dissatisfied with the existing professional skills learning carriers. Additionally, the use of serious games to improve learning efficiency has not been deeply explored. This gap is mainly due to the lack of effective skill learning carriers that can bridge the gap between professional skill learning, digital literacy goals, and interactive learning. While online classes and lectures can aid in improving students' skills and digital literacy, they are not sufficient in the current vocational teaching framework.

Students expressed interest in developing professional skills and interacting through serious games. Firstly, they are curious about the potential of serious games to enhance skill learning and digital literacy, although they have not yet tried them. Secondly, they desire serious games that are independent and easy to operate. Thirdly, they need opportunities to engage with serious games in various environments to improve their practical skills and digital literacy effectively.

4.2. Serious Game Test

In this study, participants were divided into two groups: one group learned the lesson in a traditional classroom, while the other group used a serious game. Both groups covered the same content, specifically key commands in AutoCAD software and the architectural drawing process, but through different learning mediums. The researchers developed learning materials based on expert advice to ensure effective teaching of professional skills. To evaluate the outcomes, a pattern test was used to assess knowledge acquisition, and a digital literacy scale was employed to measure changes in digital literacy among students in the game group.

4.2.1. Introduction to AutoCAD Puzzle Projects

The core drawings used in this study are two floor plans, see Figure 1.

Figure 1. AutoCAD core drawing drawings.

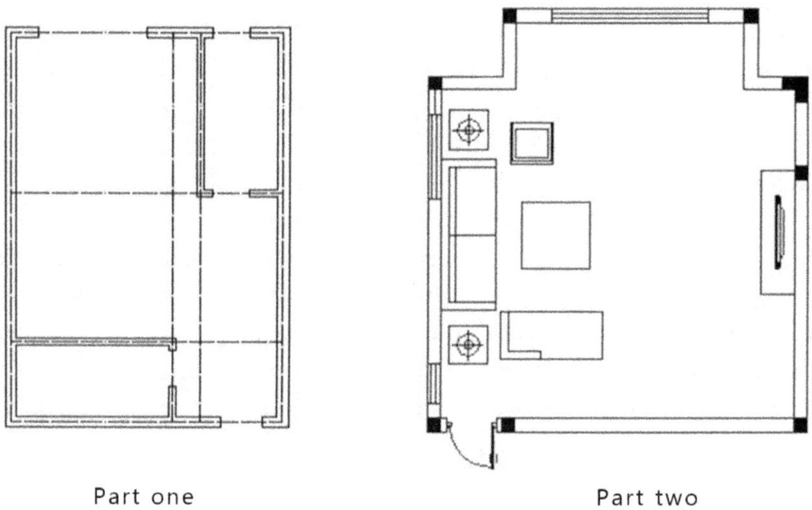

4.2.2. Serious Game Design

A digital jigsaw puzzle called "Exploring cad Architectural Drawings" was used in this study. This game, designed by the author, follows the rules of a traditional jigsaw puzzle. Players are asked to assemble scrambled AutoCAD patterns, with complete architectural drawingsavailable for reference throughout the process. Due to the large number of AutoCAD patterns, players need to carefully compare and explore the ways the patterns fit together. After determining the relationships between the graph patterns, the corresponding patterns can be placed on the building base map to complete the puzzle.

The first pattern is a wall layout of a room, which has less content. The second pattern is the layout of a single room, which is more complex and increases the difficulty. During the game, players are not only asked to identify the shape and structure of the patterns but also guided to discover various drawing methods hidden within the patterns, thereby increasing their knowledge of professional skills. Scaffolding is provided in the game to guide players in exploring the drawing methods, helping them to better complete the game and learn from it. These prompts can be accessed at any time. To facilitate students' learning, the game interface and process are designed to be simple and efficient, including the puzzle page and scaffolding two interfaces. Players assemble patterns on the puzzle page. The top of the interface is the complete reference map, the right side of the interface is the target patterns selection area, and the left side of the interface is the puzzle position. When exploring architectural drawings, players can select a target patterns from the right side and place it in the correct jigsaw position on the left. If placed correctly, text and video explanations of the drawing commands for the target patterns are displayed. If incorrect, an error message appears, allowing the player to try again. If the player is unable to identify the correct position, they can access the scaffolding interface for additional information about the target patterns.

The game is divided into two exploration levels, which take a total of 20min, and the running process is shown in Figure 2. Before exploring, players are required to watch the video explaining the operation of the building mold. Then enter level one after the exploration of a single room plan drawing. Once completed, the player can begin to assemble the floor plan of the overall building of Level 2. Players are encouraged to explore the composition of the patterns on their own, but scaffolding prompts help them overcome obstacles when they fail. Players who are not good at positional reasoning or are not sensitive to modeling features must put a lot of effort into carefully examining the composition and placement of patterns, but this is necessary for the skill learning process. The diversity of patterns compositions and the instructions for drawing skills provide greater autonomy and openness throughout the process.

The final game content was integrated into Microsoft PowerPoint, with interactive prompts implemented through hyperlinks and keystroke responses. PowerPoint's ease of use makes it suitable for quickly arranging and updating course content to facilitate more efficient teaching activities, and it can even create virtual interactions with vivid effects (Price, 2008; Siko & Barbour, 2012; Ye et al., 2021). The hyperlink function in Microsoft PowerPoint supports response modes and content switching, and also allows for secondary development and further control using Visual Basic (Ye et al., 2021). By utilizing PowerPoint, we were able to display relevant information, instructions, and hints in alignment with the game's design intent. Ultimately, the serious game was run on the PC platform.

Figure 2. Serious game running process.

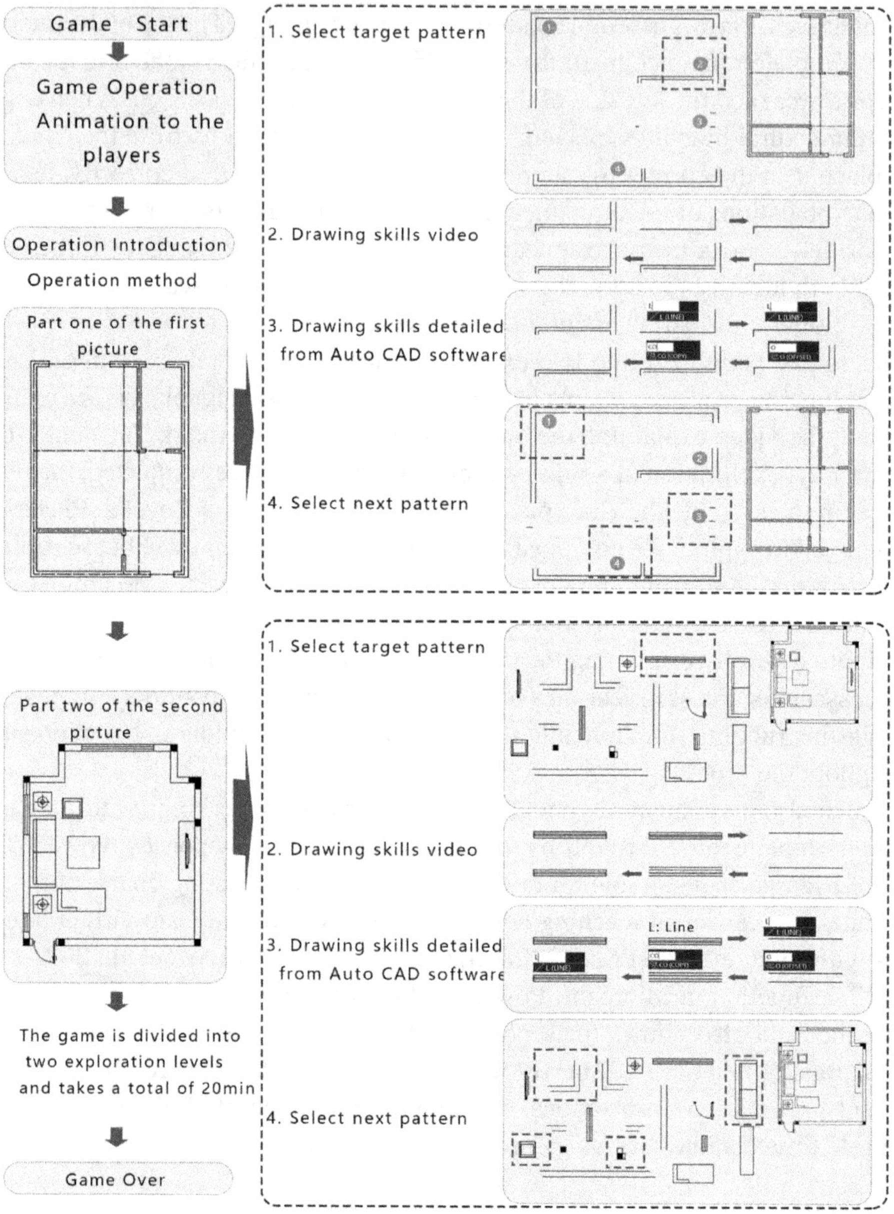

4.2.3. Classroom Learning

The traditional classroom group was set up as the control group. In this classroom,a combination of teacher-led instruction and video teaching methods was used. Compared with the "game experimental group" which employed serious games as the teaching method, the total teaching time was the same for both groups, set at 20 minutes. The teaching content is combined with textbook theory explanations with practical course case demonstrations. First, the textbook PowerPoint and video content were used to comprehensively and thoroughly explain AutoCAD software drawing commands and the drawing steps for architectural projects. AutoCAD software was then utilized to demonstrate the actual operation of the case, showing and explaining the drawing commands, the combination of drawing patterns, and the drawing steps in sequence. To ensure the effectiveness of the class, the explanation included timed pauses and repeated explanations to help learners fully understand the content, so that learners can understand the learning content.

4.2.4. Skill Learning Test

To examine the validity of using serious games based on the interactive model of digital puzzles for learn professional skills in architecture, this study designed a series of tests to assess student performance. The pattern test evaluates participants' learning performance from two aspects: knowledge acquisition and knowledge application. The post-test includes a skill application test and a skill extension test, assess skills acquisition and digital literacy improvement after completing the games or the classroom learning. To ensure the validity of the test content, we invited four experienced architectural experts, who had participated in content review during the game development process, to evaluate the feasibility of our test content. The specific test contents are shown in Table 1, including a basic skill knowledge test, a skill application test and a skill extension test.

Table 1. Student drawing work.

Testing Content			
1	Basic Test (10min)	Question 1	
		Question 2	
		Question 3	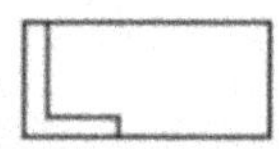
		Question 4	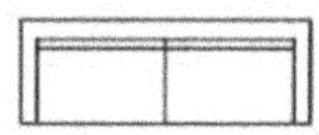
2	Skill Application Test (30min)	Question 1	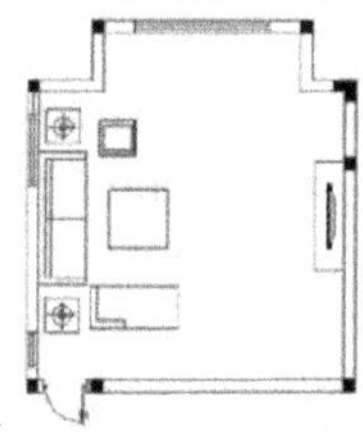
3	Extended Testing and Digital Literacy Testing (30min)	Question 1	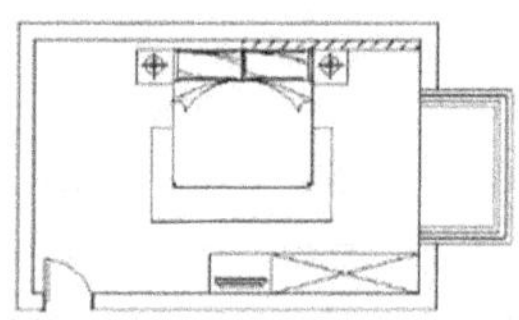

The basic test contains four questions designed to determine whether participants have achieved a minimum level of skill learning. The first test assesses the participants' familiarity with the drawing skills commands for the patterns. Questions 1 and 2 use patterns from the wall layout of a single room in level 1. Questions 3 and 4 use patterns from the floor plan of the entire room in Level 2. Participants input drawing commands in the answer area by referring to the given patterns picture. There were no key tips in the test, and the overall time was 10 minutes. The second skill application test. Participants are required to refer to the complete architectural plan drawing in level two. They used 30 minutes to complete the drawing exercises in AutoCAD software, after which they take screenshots and upload them to their personal homework library for teachers to review. These two tests reflect the learning outcomes of participants using the serious game design and traditional classroom teaching. However, these results may not be sufficient for evaluating the practical application of the skills or the improvement in the participants' digital literacy.

Architectural cases in games and classroom learning are classic examples and cannot encompass all knowledge areas. This requires participants to transfer the skills they have learned. Therefore, the third test—the Extension Test and the Digital Literacy Test—primarily assesses the ability of the participants to apply and expand their knowledge and the level of digital literacy improvement. The Extension Test involves architectural drawing content from unfamiliar building patterns that participants have not seen before but are similar to the structures and drawing commands used in games and classes. This means that both groups of participants must transfer their previously learned skills to the new building patterns. The new building patterns used in the extension test is detailed in Table 1, which is a complete room layout plan, including furniture and wall patterns. Participants are given 30 minutes to complete drawing exercises in AutoCAD software according to the pattern of drawing patterns. They take screenshots and upload them to their personal homework library for teachers to review. A screenshot of the extended and digital literacy test assignment is shown in Figure 3.

Figure 3. Extended Testing and Digital Literacy Testing.

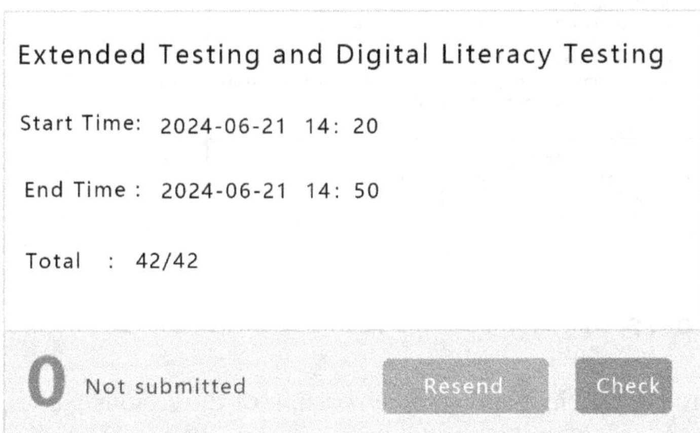

4.2.5. Digital Literacy Test of Subjects

The Digital Literacy scale was adapted with reference to Tang(Tang,2021). A 5-point Likert scale was employed to investigate changes in digital literacy among the two groups before and after the experiment. Students were asked to choose the option that best reflected their actual situation, ranging from "very non-conforming" to "very conforming." Each response was assigned a score from 1 to 5. The contents of the digital literacy scale are detailed in Table 2.

Table 2. Digital literacy scale.

Digital literacy scale					
Digital literacy	**Score**				
	1	**2**	**3**	**4**	**5**
1.I understand the development process, basic status and future trend of digital technology related to this major.	Very non-conforming	Inconformity	Normal	Conformity	Very conforming
2.I am familiar with the technical tools, software platforms and digital resources commonly used in my study.	Very non-conforming	Inconformity	Normal	Conformity	Very conforming
3.I can choose and use digital devices, tools or software platforms appropriately for my learning needs.	Very non-conforming	Inconformity	Normal	Conformity	Very conforming
4.I can use digital technology in my field to solve professional problems and create professional works.	Very non-conforming	Inconformity	Normal	Conformity	Very conforming
5.I was able to use digital technology to observe and experience work scenes and simulation skills training in virtual environments.	Very non-conforming	Inconformity	Normal	Conformity	Very conforming
6.I can actively pay attention to the frontier of integration of my major and digitalization, actively expand my knowledge, and keep learning status.	Very non-conforming	Inconformity	Normal	Conformity	Very conforming
7.I recognize the value of digital technology in my study and life, and I am willing to actively use digital resources and devices in my study and life.	Very non-conforming	Inconformity	Normal	Conformity	Very conforming

4.2.6. Process

To ensure the efficient and stable operation of the serious games, we used HP graphical workstations to display the game interface. The control group's classroom learning was also conducted using the same equipment. During the experiment, the participants used individual equipment to perform the tasks without external interference. Before the experiment began, the experimenter introduced the test content and competition rules to the participants. Once the participants read and understood the rules, the test commenced. The test was divided into three stages: the first stage involved 20 minutes of game or classroom learning; the second stage was the skill learning test, lasting 70 minutes; and the third stage was the digital literacy test, which took 10 minutes and had no specific time limit. A total of 42 freshmen majoring in architectural animation technology at a vocational college participated in this study. Written consent was obtained from all participants before the experiment began. The participants consisted of 23 males and 19 females, with an average age of 19. They were randomly divided into the game group and the classroom learning group by drawing lots, with 21 participants in each group.

Before the experiment, the participants were briefly interviewed to ensure that they had no prior knowledge of AutoCAD software and architectural drawing; thus, everything learned in the experiment was new. Finally, the collected data were analyzed, including the skill learning test time, extended test practice scores, and digital literacy scale test results.

5 RESULTS AND DISCUSSION

5.1. Building Patterns Drawing Test Analysis

The results of the building patterns drawing test analysis were used to compare the skill learning performance of participants in the game group and the classroom learning group. These results effectively reflect the students' learning performance. The accuracy rate of the drawings determined the test score, with higher accuracy rates resulting in higher scores. Efficiency was measured by the time taken to complete the practice, with shorter times indicating faster response speeds. Figure 4 illustrates the accuracy and efficiency with which the two groups of students completed all three tests. The results indicate that, compared to the classroom learning group, the game group demonstrated significant advantages in both the skill learning test and the extension test. The game group achieved higher accuracy and faster completion times, indicating superior skill learning performance and more effective knowledge transfer.

Figure 4. Test results.

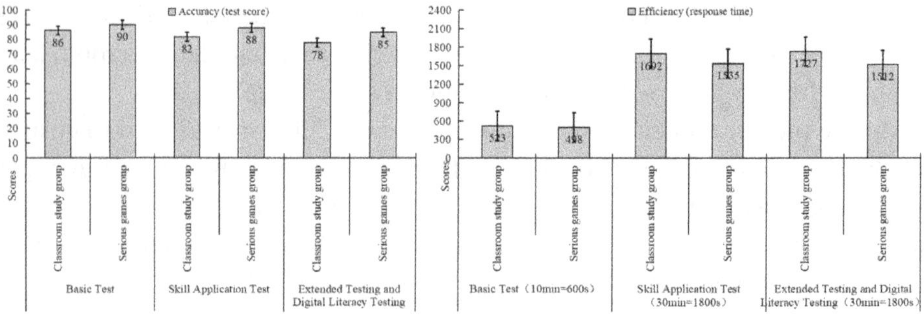

In the test of basic skills and knowledge, there was no significant difference between the two groups, with the game group scoring 86 points and the classroom learning group scoring 90 points. This indicates that both groups were able to achieve the basic skills learning objectives. However, in the skill application test, the game group demonstrated generally higher accuracy and efficiency, scoring 88 points compared to the classroom learning group's 82 points. This suggests that while classroom learning's repeated explanations offer certain advantages, game-based learning may be more effective overall. In the skill development test, the game group again showed clear advantages in both accuracy and efficiency, scoring 85 points compared to the classroom learning group's 78 points. This further confirms significant differences in performance between the two teaching methods. Proficiency in graphics-based visual tasks is primarily influenced by long-term memory (Blalock, 2015), and the results suggest that game-based learning enhances the retention of learned content (Malegiannaki & Daradoumis, 2017). With appropriate challenges and scaffolding, participants tend to focus more on the learning process, especially when correcting mistakes. This approach is more engaging and memorable compared to traditional methods, which can become monotonous (Ye et al., 2021).

5.2. Changes in Digital Literacy Before and After the Test

The 42 participants in the experiment completed the digital literacy scale both before and after the implementation. All results were valid and included in the analysis. To assess the reliability of the questionnaires, we used Cronbach's Alpha coefficient method. The Cronbach's Alpha reliability coefficient ranges from 0 to

1, with higher values indicating greater reliability. Typically, a coefficient value greater than 0.8 is considered very good, between 0.6 and 0.8 is good, and below 0.6 suggests insufficient reliability (Cronbach, 1951). The Kaiser-Meyer-Olkin (KMO) value was used to measure the validity of the questionnaire, with KMO values ranging from 0 to 1. A KMO value greater than 0.8 indicates good validity (Tabachnick, 2013).

Table 3-A presents the digital literacy performance of the subjects before the experiment, showing a reliability of 0.911 and a validity of 0.879. Table 3-B presents the digital literacy performance after the experiment, with a reliability of 0.882 and a validity of 0.815. These results indicate that the reliability and validity of both the pre-test and post-test questionnaires for digital literacy are excellent.

Table 3. Questionnaire reliability and Validity analysis.

A	Cronbach's Alpha	Kaiser-Meyer-Olkin
Pre-test questionnaire	0.911	0.879
B	Cronbach's Alpha	Kaiser-Meyer-Olkin
Post-test questionnaire	0.882	0.815

To evaluate the impact of learning through serious games versus traditional classroom methods on students' digital literacy, we analyzed the results as follows: Figure 5 illustrates the digital literacy performance of participants before the experiment, showing that there was no significant difference between the two groups, with no clear pattern emerging. Figure 6 presents a comparison of digital literacy performance from the pre-test to the post-test for both the classroom group and the game group.Compared with the classroom learning group, most of the students in the game group showed an improved level of digital literacy after the experiment.

Figure 5. Pre-test questionnaire data.

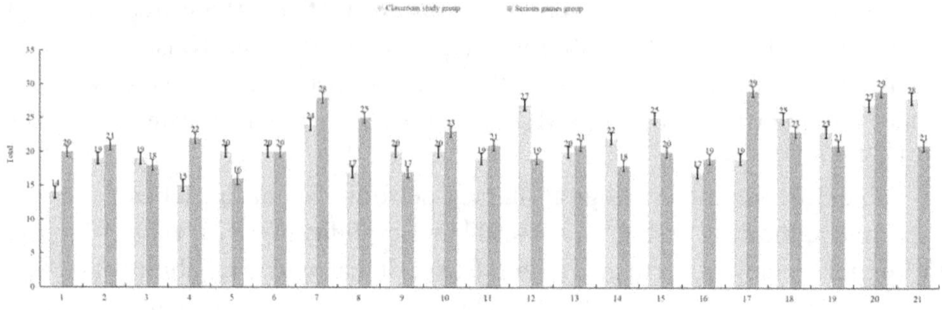

Figure 6. Comparison of three sets of data.

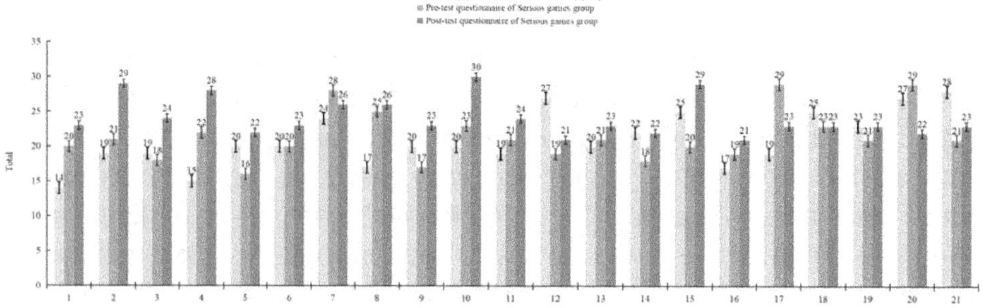

6 CONCLUSIONS

This study surveyed Chinese vocational college students to assess their current levels of digital literacy, their needs and expectations for professional skills learning, their satisfaction with existing professional curriculum skills, and their perceptions of serious games. The research involved designing a serious game model for an architecture course, specifically "Architecture CAD Drawing," which combines multimedia presentations of teaching content with practical exercises. A user study was conducted on 42 vocational architecture students to comparethe effectiveness of serious games versus traditional classroom teaching. The experimental results indicate that serious games offer significant advantages in vocational skill acquisition and are more effective in achieving digital literacy training goals. The game group demonstrated superior performance in skill learning, skill extension, learning efficiency, and overall performance.

Furthermore, the pre-test and post-test results for the game group confirmed that serious games not only enhance students' interest in learning but also provide a more comprehensive understanding of AutoCAD software skills and architectural graphic creation. This study contributes to the exploration of effective learning methods and expands instructional design approaches aimed at improving students' digital literacy.

However, this study has several limitations that need to be acknowledged. Firstly, the teaching cases used in the experiment were relatively homogeneous, with a limited scope of overall instructional content. Future research should aim to develop more comprehensive professional curricula that integrate a broader range of instructional materials. This would allow for a more thorough assessment of the impact of serious games on students' skill acquisition and digital literacy. Secondly, the duration of the experimental study was relatively short, which constrains the ability to evaluate the long-term impact of the acquired skills and the sustainability of improvements in digital literacy. To gain a deeper understanding of these effects, it is imperative to conduct longitudinal studies that span a more extended period. Third, the lack of diversity in the participants' professional backgrounds affects the universality of the research results. In the future, it will be necessary to include participants from a broader range of professional backgrounds to enhance the validity and scientific rigor of the findings. This approach will provide more comprehensive and practical strategies for designing serious games.

REFERENCES

Abt, C. C. (1987). Serious games. University press of America.

Ahmad, S., Umirzakova, S., Jamil, F., & Whangbo, T. K. (2022). Internet-of-things-enabled serious games: A comprehensive survey. *Future Generation Computer Systems*, 136, 67–83. DOI: 10.1016/j.future.2022.05.026

Alexander, B., Becker, S. A., Cummins, M., & Giesinger, C. H. (2017). *Digital literacy in higher education, Part II: An NMC Horizon project strategic brief.* The New Media Consortium.

Amin, A. M., Adiansyah, R., & Hujjatusnaini, N. (2023). The contribution of communication and digital literacy skills to critical thinking. [Indonesian Journal of Science Education]. *Jurnal Pendidikan Sains Indonesia*, 11(3), 697–712. DOI: 10.24815/jpsi.v11i3.30838

Bilohur, Vlada, & Andriukaitiene, Regina (2020). Sports culture as a means of improving the integrity of sports personality: philosophicalcultural and anthropological analysis. Humanities studies. N° 6 (83). P. 136–152.

Blalock, L. D. (2015). Stimulus familiarity improves consolidation of visual working memory representations. *Attention, Perception & Psychophysics*, 77(4), 1143–1158. DOI: 10.3758/s13414-014-0823-z PMID: 25720758

Blau, I., Shamir-Inbal, T., & Avdiel, O. (2020). How does the pedagogical design of a technology-enhanced collaborative academic course promote digital literacies, self-regulation, and perceived learning of students? *The Internet and Higher Education*, 45, 100722. DOI: 10.1016/j.iheduc.2019.100722

Blau, I., Shamir-Inbal, T., & Avdiel, O. (2020). How does the pedagogical design of a technology-enhanced collaborative academic course promote digital literacies, self-regulation, and perceived learning of students? *The Internet and Higher Education*, 45, 100722. DOI: 10.1016/j.iheduc.2019.100722

Bond, M., Marín, V. I., Dolch, C., Bedenlier, S., & Zawacki-Richter, O. (2018). Digital transformation in German higher education: Student and teacher perceptions and usage of digital media. *International Journal of Educational Technology in Higher Education*, 15(1), 1–20. DOI: 10.1186/s41239-018-0130-1

Caserman, P., Hoffmann, K., Müller, P., Schaub, M., Straßburg, K., Wiemeyer, J., Bruder, R., & Göbel, S. (2020). Quality criteria for serious games: Serious part, game part, and balance. *JMIR Serious Games*, 8(3), e19037. DOI: 10.2196/19037 PMID: 32706669

Cazco, G. H. O., González, M. C., Abad, F. M., Altamirano, J. E. D., & Mazón, M. E. S. (2016). Determining factors in acceptance of ICT by the university faculty in their teaching practice. In: *Proceedings of the Fourth International Conference on Technological Ecosystems* DOI: 10.1145/3012430.3012509

Checa, D., & Bustillo, A. (2020). A review of immersive virtual reality serious games to enhance learning and training. *Multimedia Tools and Applications*, 79(9), 5501–5527. DOI: 10.1007/s11042-019-08348-9

Chen, Y. (2022, July). Research on comprehensive management of digital literacy education in the era of big data. In *Proceedings of the 6th International Conference on Education and Multimedia Technology* (pp. 421-427). DOI: 10.1145/3551708.3551766

Cronbach, L. J. (1951). Coefficient alpha and the internal structure of tests. psychometrika, 16(3), 297-334.

Cyberspace Administration of the CPC Central Committee. Ministry of Education, Ministry of Industry and Information Technology, Human Resources and Social Security(2024).*Key points of work to upgrade digital literacy and skills for all by 2024*.https://bit.ly/3Y7cP0e

De Sousa Borges, S., Durelli, V. H. S., Reis, H. M., & Isotani, S. (2014). A systematic mapping on gamification applied to education. Proceedings of the 29th Annual ACM Symposium on Applied Computing - SAC '14, (Icmc), 216e222. DOI: 10.1145/2554850.2554956

Dyck, J., Pinelle, D., Brown, B., & Gutwin, C. (2003). *Learning from games: HCI design innovations in entertainment software*. Graphics Interface.

Dyulicheva, Y. Y., & Glazieva, A. O. (2021). Game based learning with artificial intelligence and immersive technologies: An overview. CS&SE@ SW, 146-159.

Eshet, Y. (2004). Digital literacy: A conceptual framework for survival skills in the digital era. *Journal of Educational Multimedia and Hypermedia*, 13(1), 93–106.

European Commision. (2006). Recommendation on key competences for lifelong learning. Council of 18 December 2006 on key competences for lifelong learning, 2006/962/EC, L. 394/15. Retrieved December 7, 2017, from http://eur-lex.europa .eu/legal-content/ en/TXT/?uri=CELEX:32006H0962&qid= 1496720114366.

EUROPEAN UNION (EU).Digital Education Action Plan (2021 -2027) [EB/OL]. [2023- 02-13].https: / / education.ec.europa.eu /node /1518

Gee, J. P. (2006). Are video games good for learning? *Nordic Journal of Digital Literacy*, 1(3), 172–183. DOI: 10.18261/ISSN1891-943X-2006-03-02

Gee, J. P. (2009). Deep learning properties of good digital games: How far can they go? In Ritterfeld, U., Cody, M., & Vorderer, P. (Eds.), *Serious games: Mechanisms and effects* (pp. 67–82). Routledge.

Graeske, C., & Sjöberg, S. A. (2021). VR-Technology in Teaching: Opportunities and Challenges. *International Education Studies*, 14(8), 76–83. DOI: 10.5539/ies.v14n8p76

Gu, J., & Ding, R. (2022). Digital Literacy of Chinese Normal Students: A Literature Review. Digital Literacy for Teachers, 191-210.

Holly, M., Pirker, J., Resch, S., Brettschuh, S., & Gütl, C. (2021). Designing VR experiences–expectations for teaching and learning in VR. *Journal of Educational Technology & Society*, 24(2), 107–119.

Huang, S., Xu, J., Sang, Q., & Shao, Z. (2023, September). Research on the digital literacy model construction and practice of higher vocational students in the digital era. In *Proceedings of the 15th International Conference on Education Technology and Computers* (pp. 370-377). DOI: 10.1145/3629296.3629356

Ibrahim, N., & Ali, N. M. (2018). A conceptual framework for designing virtual heritage environment for cultural learning. [JOCCH]. *Journal on Computing and Cultural Heritage*, 11(2), 1–27. DOI: 10.1145/3117801

International Society for Technology in Education. (2007). *National educational technology standards for students. ISTE*. Interntl Soc Tech Educ.

International Society for Technology in Education. (2017). *ISTE standards for educators*. International Society for Technology in Education.

Jatmoko, D., Suyitno, S., Rasul, M. S., Nurtanto, M., Kholifah, N., Masek, A., & Nur, H. R. (2023). The Factors Influencing Digital Literacy Practice in Vocational Education: A Structural Equation Modeling Approach. *European Journal of Educational Research*, 12(2), 1109–1121. DOI: 10.12973/eu-jer.12.2.1109

Laamarti, F., Eid, M., & El Saddik, A. (2014). An overview of serious games. *International Journal of Computer Games Technology*, 2014, 358152. DOI: 10.1155/2014/358152

Law, N. W. Y., Woo, D. J., De la Torre, J., & Wong, K. W. G. (2018). A global framework of reference on digital literacy skills for indicator 4.4. 2.

Lazonder, A. W., Walraven, A., Gijlers, H., & Janssen, N. (2020). Longitudinal assessment of digital literacy in children: Findings from a large Dutch single-school study. *Computers & Education*, 143, 103681. DOI: 10.1016/j.compedu.2019.103681

Malegiannaki, I., & Daradoumis, T. (2017). Analyzing the educational design, use and effect of spatial games for cultural heritage: A literature review. Computers &amp. *Education*, 108, 1–10.

McCall, J. (2016). Teaching history with digital historical games. *Simulation & Gaming*, 47(4), 517–542. DOI: 10.1177/1046878116646693

Ministry of Education, National Development and Reform Commission, Ministry of Industry and Information Technology, et al. (2020). *Action Plan for Improving the Quality and Excellence of Vocational Education (2020-2023).*The Chinese Ministry of Education, National Development and Reform Commission, Ministry of Industry and Information Technology, et al. https://bit.ly/3WaFHSJ

Nguyen, L. A. T., & Habók, A. (2024). Tools for assessing teacher digital literacy: A review. *Journal of Computers in Education*, 11(1), 305–346. DOI: 10.1007/s40692-022-00257-5

Okan, Z. (2011). Edutainment and learning. In Seel, N. M. (Ed.), *Encyclopedia of the Sciences of learning (pp. 1080e1082)*. Springer.

Ortiz, S. A., Bowers, C., & Cannon-Bowers, J. (2015). Video game self-efficacy and its effect on training performance. International Journal of Serious Games, 2(3), 63e75.

Outeda, C. C. (2024). European Education Area and Digital Education Action Plan (2021–2027): One More Step Towards the Europeanisation of Education Policy. In *E-Governance in the European Union: Strategies, Tools, and Implementation* (pp. 187–206). Springer Nature Switzerland. DOI: 10.1007/978-3-031-56045-3_13

Pérez, J., Castro, M., & López, G. (2023). Serious games and ai: Challenges and opportunities for computational social science. *IEEE Access : Practical Innovations, Open Solutions*, 11, 62051–62061. DOI: 10.1109/ACCESS.2023.3286695

Polizzi, G. (2020). Digital literacy and the national curriculum for England: Learning from how the experts engage with and evaluate online content. *Computers & Education*, 152, 103859. DOI: 10.1016/j.compedu.2020.103859

Potyrała, K., & Tomczyk, Ł. (2021). Teachers in the lifelong learning process: Examples of digital literacy. *Journal of Education for Teaching*, 47(2), 255–273. DOI: 10.1080/02607476.2021.1876499

Price, C. B. (2008). Unreal PowerPointTM: Immersing PowerPoint presentations in a virtual computer game engine world. *Computers in Human Behavior*, 24(6), 2486–2495. DOI: 10.1016/j.chb.2008.03.009

Quaicoe, J. S., & Pata, K. (2020). Teachers' digital literacy and digital activity as digital divide components among basic schools in Ghana. *Education and Information Technologies*, 25(5), 4077–4095. DOI: 10.1007/s10639-020-10158-8

Quraishi, T.Helena ULUSIAsma MUHIDMusawer HAKIMIMohammad Reshad OLUSI. (2024). Empowering students through digital literacy: A case study of successful integration in a higher education curriculum. *Journal of Digital Learning and Distance Education*, 2(9), 667–681. DOI: 10.56778/jdlde.v2i8.208

Resnick, M. (2004). Edutainment? No thanks. I prefer playful learning. Associazione civita report on edutainment.

Reyes, V. C.Jr, Reading, C., Doyle, H., & Gregory, S. (2017). Integrating ICT into teacher education programs from a TPACK perspective: Exploring perceptions of university lecturers. *Computers & Education*, 115, 1–19. DOI: 10.1016/j.compedu.2017.07.009

Ritterfeld, U., & Weber, R. (2006). Video games for entertainment and education. In Vorderer, P., & Bryant, J. (Eds.), *Playing video games: Motives, responses, and consequences* (pp. 399–413). Lawrence Erlbaum Associates.

Rosenthal, S., & Ratan, R. A. (2022). Balancing learning and enjoyment in serious games: Kerbal Space Program and the communication mediation model. *Computers & Education*, 182, 104480. DOI: 10.1016/j.compedu.2022.104480

Siko, J. P., & Barbour, M. K. (2012). Homemade PowerPoint Games: Game Design Pedagogy Aligned to the TPACK Framework. *Computers in the Schools*, 29(4), 339–354. DOI: 10.1080/07380569.2012.734430

Stapleton, A. J. (2004, December). Serious games: Serious opportunities. In *Australian Game Developers" Conference*. Academic Summit.

Sun, X., Yue, L., & Li, S. (2020). Digital Literacy in the Era of Globalization: Connotation and evaluation. *World Education Information*, (08), 13–17.

Tabachnick, B. G., Fidell, L. S., & Ullman, J. B. (2013). Using multivariate statistics (Vol. 6, pp. 497-516). Boston, MA: pearson.

Ting, T. (2021). Master's Degree in the Construction and Application of Digital Literacy Evaluation Model for Higher Vocational Students (Dissertation, Guangdong Technical Normal University). Master of https://link.cnki.net/doi/10.27729/d.cnki.ggdjs.2021.000067doi:10.27729/d.cnki.ggdjs.2021.000067

Tinmaz, H., Lee, Y. T., Fanea-Ivanovici, M., & Baber, H. (2022). A systematic review on digital literacy. *Smart Learning Environments*, 9(1), 21. DOI: 10.1186/s40561-022-00204-y

Tuamsuk, K., & Subramaniam, M. (2017). The current state and influential factors in the development of digital literacy in Thailand's higher education. *Information and Learning Science*, 118(5/6), 235251. DOI: 10.1108/ILS-11-2016-0076

Ullah, M., Amin, S. U., Munsif, M., Yamin, M. M., Safaev, U., Khan, H., Khan, S., & Ullah, H. (2022). Serious games in science education: A systematic literature. *Virtual Reality & Intelligent Hardware*, 4(3), 189–209. DOI: 10.1016/j.vrih.2022.02.001

United Nations Educational, Scientific and Cultural Organisation (UNESCO). (2011). *ICT competency standards for teachers (version 2)*. UNESCO.

Voronkova, V., Vasyl'chuk, G., Nikitenko, V., Kaganov, Y., & Metelenko, N. (2023). Transformation of digital education in the era of the fourth industrial revolution and globalization.

Wang, X., Li, A., Li, T., Zhao, X., Liu, S., Gai, J., & Zhang, R. (2023). Research on Strategies and Methods of Improving Teachers' Digital Literacy in Classroom Teaching in Higher Vocational Colleges. In SHS Web of Conferences (Vol. 179, p. 02016). EDP Sciences.

Wang Y M, Yang X L, Hu W & Wang J. (2013). From Digital Literacy to digital competence: conceptual evolution, constitutive elements and integration model. Remote education magazine (03), 24-29.

Whitton, N. (2011). Games-based learning. In Seel, N. M. (Ed.), *Encyclopedia of the Sciences of learning (pp. 1337e1340)*. Springer.

Wu, D. (2023). Exploring digital literacy in the era of digital civilization: A framework for college students in China. Information Services & Use, (Preprint), 1-23.

Ye, L., Wang, R., & Zhao, J. (2021). Enhancing learning performance and motivation of cultural heritage using serious games. *Journal of Educational Computing Research*, 59(2), 287–317. DOI: 10.1177/0735633120963828

Zhang, K. (2021). Determining the influencing factors affecting the digital competencies of colleges students in blended teaching. *Contemporary Educational Research Journal*, 11(4), 210–224. DOI: 10.18844/cerj.v11i4.5974

Zhou, R. (2023). Digital Literacy of vocational college Students: Connotation change, theoretical logic, Framework Construction and Practical Direction. *Vocational and Technical Education in China*, (21), 5–13.

APPENDIX

Table 4.

Reviewer 1: Minor revisions				
No.	**Comments**	**Amendments**	**Pg No. (before)**	**Pg No. (after)**
1	Update and Expand Content: Incorporate recent studies on technological advancements in serious games (e.g., VR, AR, AI).	Modified and updated (see Literature review. 2.1. Serious Games)	3-4	3-4
2	Updated digital literacy frameworks, and recent pedagogical theories. Include references to policy documents and research findings post-2022 to ensure the chapter is current and relevant.	Modified and updated (see Literature review. 2.2. Digital literacy)	4-5	4-5
3	Offer practical strategies for integrating serious games into curricula, discuss the long-term impact of digital literacy.	Modified and updated (see Literature review. 2.3. Vocational college students digital literacy training)	5-6	5-6
Reviewer 2: Minor revisions				
No.	**Comments**	**Amendments**	**Pg No. (before)**	**Pg No. (after)**
1	Delve deeper into the challenges of implementing serious games.	Modified and updated (see Literature review. 2.1. Serious Games)	3-4	3-4
2	Add more case studies from different disciplines or vocational education contexts.	Modified and updated (see Literature review. 2.3. Vocational college students digital literacy training)	5-6	5-6

Chapter 3
A Systematic Literature Review of Serious Games in Higher Arts Education

Yue Shi
https://orcid.org/0009-0002-7501-4717
Universiti Sains Malaysia, Malaysia

Yun Yi Tan
Universiti Sains Malaysia, Malaysia

Hanben Yao
Universiti Sains Malaysia, Malaysia

ABSTRACT

Since the beginning of the 21st century, the number of studies on serious games has been surging, and more and more serious games are being used for educational purposes to facilitate students' learning and increase their motivation. This study systematically reviewed seven empirical studies on the application of serious games in higher arts education from 2019 to 2024, aiming to reveal the current state of recent research in the field, incorporating trends in the use of technology and the results of the impact on learners. The results show that most articles indicate that serious games are effective in higher arts education. Currently, researchers pay relatively little attention to this area, but this area has good research potential. In addition, integrating serious games with technologies such as augmented reality, virtual reality and mixed reality in higher arts education is a promising avenue for future research and development.

DOI: 10.4018/979-8-3693-6745-2.ch003

1. INTRODUCTION

Nowadays, serious games (SGs) find effective applications across various fields such as healthcare, education, military and defense, and ecology, serving diverse objectives including teaching and learning, training, raising awareness, and altering attitudes and behaviors; their intended audience spans across all age groups (Daoudi et al., 2021). These apps are used at all educational levels, including a wide range of disciplines and subjects in primary, secondary, and tertiary education, such as computer architecture, math, science, computational thinking and programming concepts, and language learning (Daoudi, 2022; Hainey et al., 2016).

All areas of the world have witnessed an unprecedented acceleration in the use of innovative technological tools. Specifically within the educational sector, emerging technologies—including social and collaborative learning tools, intelligent and adaptive tutoring systems, as well as augmented and mixed reality applications—have been extensively integrated into conventional educational methodologies by examining the dynamics between digital innovations and learning processes (Hantoobi et al., 2021; Klašnja-Milićević et al., 2017).. In recent years, there has been an increased interest in researching the impact of SGs on learning outcomes in higher education, as it integrates gaming and learning functions (Girard et al., 2013). SGs are activities designed to entertain the user, who learns in that environment and is educated and trained in well-defined domains and tasks (Wouters et al., 2009). The main goal of this tool is learning, with the fun aspect of the activity taking a back seat, and it aims to achieve the acquisition of competencies and skills that lead to the holistic development of the student (Sandí Delgado & Bazán, 2021; Taipe et al., 2017). In the field of education, educational software is now revolutionized thanks to the incorporation of specific designs based on SGs (Fraga-Varela et al., 2021).

Indeed, numerous studies have demonstrated that integrating SGs as supplementary educational resources into the learning process can significantly enhance students' learning experiences, including knowledge acquisition and content comprehension, as well as their overall satisfaction, which encompasses motivation and engagement (De Freitas, 2018; Fokides, 2018). Furthermore, SGs are regarded as a viable alternative to conventional teaching methods, offering significant benefits by enhancing students' academic performance and also fostering higher-level skills such as problem-solving and collaboration (Gómez & Suárez, 2021; Vlachopoulos & Makri, 2017).

Zhonggen (2019) published a study that conducted a meta-analysis of the effectiveness of SGs in education to understand trends in the use of SG in education. Gómez & Suárez (2021), through a scoping review of the existing literature within the period from January 2002 to September 2020, aimed to collect, synthesize, and map SGs in higher education design and impact. Khaldi et al. (2023) systematically reviewed the literature on the gamification of e-learning in higher education between 2010 and 2021. Gamification of e-learning encompasses SG, exploring the different game elements and theories of gamification used in the empirical research, establishing the different ways in which these game elements are combined, and reviewing the literature to present the higher education state-of-the-art approaches to the gamification of e-learning systems. More recently, Brandl & Schrader (2024) conducted a systematic review of how the Education 4.0 shift has impacted the way SG is designed and used in higher education contexts.

The findings stated that over the past decade, the number of research publications with applications of SG in education has steadily increased over time, and SG has begun to receive more attention from scholars (Zhonggen, 2019). Brandl & Schrader (2024) found that SG in the context of higher education demonstrated positive results in their respective studies, mainly in terms of increases in motivation, learning outcomes, and transfer of new knowledge or soft skills. Insights from assessments employing a variety of questions should inform the future design of SGs, particularly regarding the integration of multimedia and consideration of students' emotional states. However, the lack of consistency in the evidence regarding the pedagogical, instructional, and technological principles involved in SG design and their impacts poses a challenge for educational practitioners, game developers, and researchers (Gómez & Suárez, 2021). Khaldi et al. (2023) have also stated that the majority of applied gamification research is not theoretically based, and that when designing gamified learning systems without using a gamification framework.

Zhonggen's (2019) review covered the arts and humanities, science, engineering, and medicine. Based on the results of his study, it is evident that researchers have shown more interest in the application of SG in the fields of science, medicine, and mathematics (Connolly et al., 2012). However, the number of studies related to SGs in the field of arts education is still very limited.

Art education is important for the promotion of human beings, life, society, and the world (Fürst & Nylander, 2023; Sharma, 2022). Ye et al. (2024) stated that the value of SGs is recognized and attempts can be made to use digital means such as SGs for art education. On the other hand, with the development of time and technological advancement, the integration of virtual and real has generated more new teaching models, such as exploring the immersive experience of music education based on artificial intelligence and rich interactive content worthy of expanding the teaching methodology (Qiusi, 2022). However, how to better utilize these technological tools to enhance student interactivity and immersion and aid teaching and learning in the arts is a concern for educators (Ye et al., 2024). At the same time, the lack of systematic identification of impacts on student learning and achievement poses a challenge for educational practitioners, game developers, and researchers seeking to identify, develop, or adapt best practices in SG design (Gómez & Suárez, 2021).

Current research, however, does not provide a common or proven result, especially about the potential of SGs for learning in higher art education(HAE). Bonfield et al. (2020) suggest that there are currently new tests in terms of new technologies as well as pedagogical innovations in the context of higher education. For these reasons, there is a need to systematically review and analyze the state-of-the-art in incorporating the use of technology in SGs, as well as the academic achievements and trends in SG in the field of art applications. Therefore, this study will examine the status of the use of SGs in HAE.

2. METHODS

The methodological approach employed in this review is referred to as a 'Systematic Literature Review' (SLR). The primary objective of an SLR is to identify, summarize, explain, and categorize the essential components of existing research within a specific topic or field (Liberati et al., 2009). Additionally, an SLR serves to pinpoint and analyze potential research gaps that could be further explored. This study adhered to a structured process comprising (1) defining the research question, (2) conducting the study by establishing search terms, (3) reviewing the articles based on inclusion and exclusion criteria, and (4) presenting and synthesizing the key features and principal findings of the included studies. The process was conducted in accordance with the reporting guidelines outlined in the Protocol for Systematic Reviews and Meta-Analyses (PRISMA) to enhance methodological rigor (Liberati et al., 2009).

2.1 Research Questions

This SLR aims to capture the most up-to-date information on the use of SG in HAE settings over the past 5 years, to investigate research trends in the use of SG in HAE, and to provide a roadmap for possible future research. The timeframe of the literature selected for review in this study is 2019-2024, due to the meta-analysis already made by Zhonggen (2019) for SGs used in education and the limited number of empirical studies on SGs in HAE before 2019. Therefore, in this study, empirical studies before 2019 were not included in the review. For this reason, this study is guided by the following research questions:

(1) What is the current state of research regarding the use of SG in the field of HAE?
(2) What are the trends regarding the use of SG in conjunction with technology in HAE?

(3) What is the impact on learners of using SG in the field of HAE?
(4) What is the state of the art regarding the application of theories or models for SGs in HAE?

2.2 Databases Searched

The electronic databases consulted for this literature review encompassed IEEE Xplore, SpringerLink, Web of Science, Scopus, and Taylor & Francis. In the electronic search phase, the study employed the following keyword search terms based on Boolean operations: "serious game" OR "serious educational game" AND "art" OR "design" OR "painting" AND "education" OR "learning" OR "teaching". The chosen search terms were applied to the titles, keywords, and abstracts of each article, and a thorough review of each selected study was conducted to ensure relevance.

2.3 Inclusion and Exclusion Criteria

The literature search process was carried out on July 30, 2024, with the objective of identifying pertinent articles that addressed the research question by evaluating the titles and abstracts of each article. To achieve this, specific inclusion and exclusion criteria were established (Table 1), and each paper was meticulously reviewed to assess its eligibility for inclusion in the analysis.

Table 1. Inclusion and Exclusion criteria

Inclusion criteria	Exclusion criteria
Papers from international peer-reviewed journals Papers published between 2019 and 2024	The article is not written in English
The article offers an analysis of empirical evidence concerning the application of SG to HAE	Articles for which the full text is not accessible online
The article focuses on the use of SG within the context of HAE	The article discusses another educational field (medical, engineering, social science, etc.)

2.4 Selection and Synthesis of the Publications

Figure 1 shows a flowchart of this literature review illustrating the process used, including identification, screening, eligibility assessment, and final selection of articles. The initial search yielded a total of 1001 results, leaving 603 articles after removing duplicate entries. Two reviewers (S and Y) unanimously identified seven articles for inclusion in this study after an initial screening and a second round of screening based on predetermined criteria.

Figure 1. Flowchart for the PRISMA-based selection process

Inclusion criteria	Exclusion criteria
Papers from international peer-reviewed journals Papers published between 2019 and 2024	The article is not written in English
The article offers an analysis of empirical evidence concerning the application of SG to HAE	Articles for which the full text is not accessible online
The article focuses on the use of SG within the context of HAE	The article discusses another educational field (medical, engineering, social science, etc.)

3. RESULTS

This section presents the answers to the four research questions posed in this study. Firstly, we focused on the current state of development of SG in HAE. Then, trends in the use of SG in combination with technology in HAE are identified. Next, we investigated what impact SG in combination with other technologies has had on learners in HAE. Finally, we reveal what theories have been applied to guide SG design and development in HAE.

3.1 Current Status of Research on the Use of SG in HAE

As can be seen in Figure 2, a total of seven publications that met the final inclusion criteria were screened for this study, covering the period from 2019 to 2024. Specifically, no relevant literature applicable to this study area was identified between 2019 and 2020. In contrast, the number of publications between 2021 and 2024 showed a gradual increase in the number of papers published, especially in 2024, where the number of publications was significantly higher than in the previous years.

Figure 2. Number of publications issued between 2019 and 2024

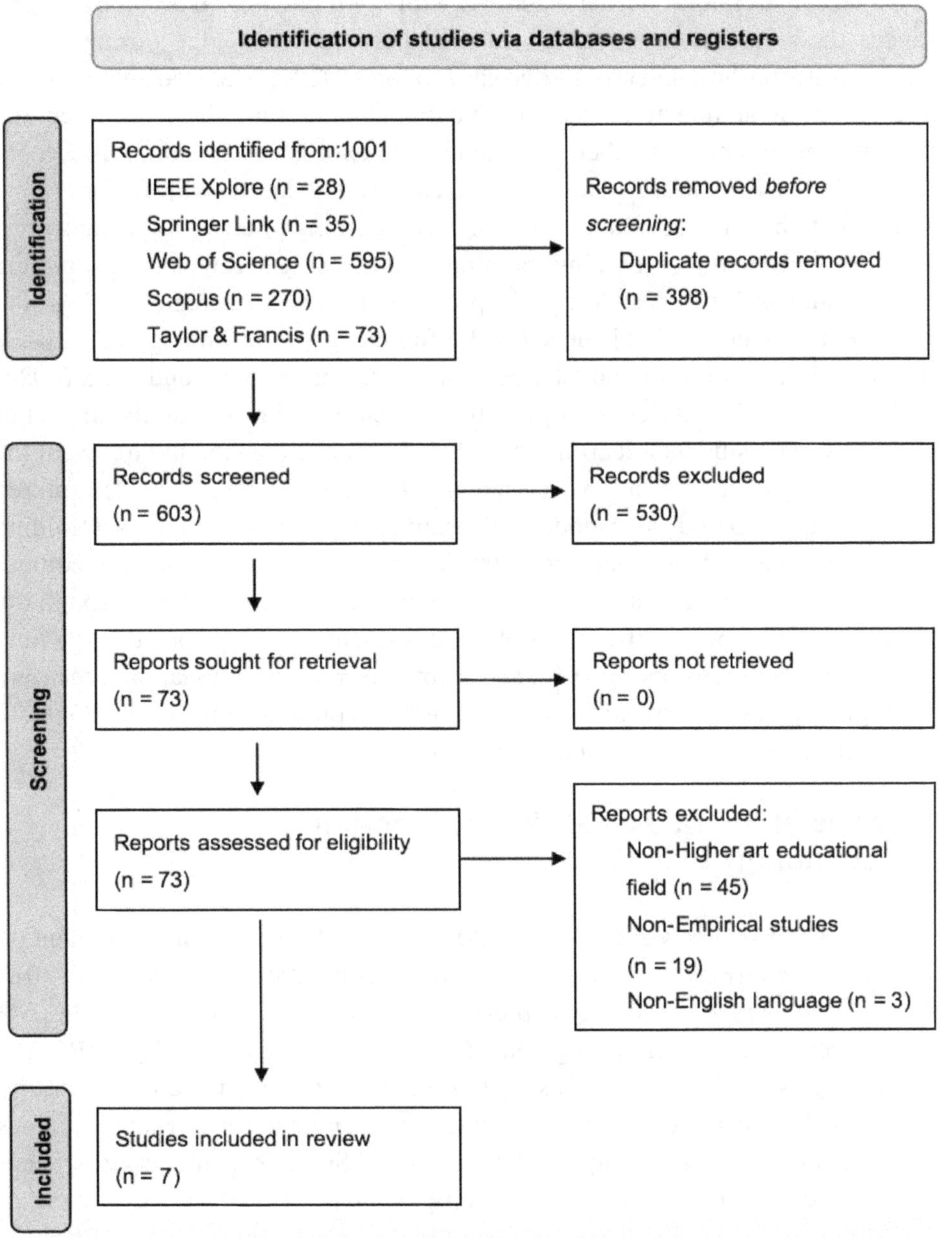

The specific research content and research objectives of these seven articles are as follows:

Zhang et al. (2021) proposed a SG for cultural heritage education based on the experiential learning cycle model, which provides a single-player experiential environment in a cultural heritage context with 3D modeling on a computer, and enhances the active construction of cultural heritage knowledge through game narratives, interactions, and knowledge cards. Goli (2022) developed an interactive digital game for architectural design educational tools that allows architectural design students to challenge their knowledge and experience. In addition, Cecotti (2023) designed a SG based on fully immersive VR with hidden objects for art history, aiming to better engage users in immersive learning of art history. Hang et al. (2023) developed a SG for learning traditional crafts using MR technology, aiming to improve students' attitudes through the promotion of digital teaching and learning environments. Ye et al. (2024) developed a SG using AR technology to enhance students' learning of traditional Chinese mural painting culture, and Kara (2024) used the computer-based SG "Europe in the Museum" to investigate the impact of SGs on university students' learning of cultural heritage content and to reveal the factors affecting their learning experience in SGs. Finally, Li et al. (2024) explored an adventure game-based game model for learning cultural heritage using scaffolding theory to enhance students' learning of traditional Chinese mural painting culture.

Overall, the researchers aimed to enhance learners' learning of art through the application of SG. The specific topics of these seven articles distributed in the field of art were cultural heritage (n = 3), art history (n = 1), traditional patterns (n = 1), intangible cultural heritage (n = 1), and architectural design (n = 1). Overall, cultural heritage-related research dominated this field.

3.2 Trends in the Use of SG in Conjunction with Technology in HAE

Table 2 shows that between 2021 and 2022, SG in HAE is mainly dependent on computer technology devices for its application and operation. However, from 2023 to 2024, researchers are gradually exploring and adopting ways of combining SG with new technologies such as augmented reality (AR), mixed reality (MR), and virtual reality (VR). Cecotti (2023) suggests that there is a need to embed learning activities into SGs in immersive environments to communicate the learning outcomes to learners. Hang et al. (2023) argued that MR-based SGs allow students to observe the structure of mortise and tenon from multiple perspectives during operation. In addition, the combination of AR and SG is also more useful for long-term memory and understanding of complex traditional art forms (Ye et al., 2024).

Overall, computer technology platforms continue to be the primary vehicle for SG applications in the field. This shift reflects the continuous advancement and diversification trends in educational technologies, although the application of these new technologies in HAE is still in its initial stages; however, with the current maturing of AR, MR, and VR technologies, researchers are beginning to explore ways to integrate these technologies with SG to create more creative and interactive ways of learning.

Table 2. Technology platforms used by SGs in HAE

Number	Author(s), year of publication	Technology platforms used in conjunction with SG
1	(Zhang et al., 2021)	Computer
2	(Goli et al., 2022)	Computer
3	(Cecotti, 2023)	Immersive Virtual Reality
4	(Hang et al., 2023)	Mixed Reality
5	(Ye et al., 2024)	Augmented Reality
6	(Kara, 2024)	Computer
7	(Li et al., 2024)	Computer

3.3 Impact of Using SG in HAE on Learners

The third research question of this study aimed to determine what impact the implementation of SG in HAE had on learners, which consisted of undergraduates, postgraduates, and adult participants. Table 3 shows the study population, independent variables, and dependent variables in the research content of the seven articles.

The findings of the first article indicated that SG-based learning of cultural heritage was effective in improving learners' learning outcomes and motivation and had a positive impact on learners' learning experience. The second article indicated that SG-based learning of architectural design not only engages architectural students in learning but also helps them to achieve better results from the learning activities compared to face-to-face teaching methods. The third study found that an immersive environment in virtual reality is not sufficient for learning art history, but it can provide additional value and enhance learning. The fourth article suggested that MR-SG-based learning of Mortise and Tenon has advantages in terms of knowledge retention and can motivate and contextualize students' interest in learning. The fifth article stated that both regular SG and AR SG had good teaching and learning effects, and AR SG significantly reduced students' cognitive load. The results of the sixth study showed that SG-based experience of cultural heritage positively affected students' learning experience, with significantly higher scores on the knowledge posttest and delayed posttest than those taught using traditional methods. The last article indicated that SG-based learning of traditional Chinese mural culture had better learning outcomes and knowledge retention, higher intrinsic motivation, related load, and engagement than traditional video learning.

As can be seen from some of the studies in the above articles, most of the studies in this field have positively affected learners' knowledge retention, learning achievement, motivation, engagement, and learning experience. Meanwhile, the application of SG in HAE has significantly reduced students' cognitive load.

Table 3. Variables and research object used in research on the use of SG in HAE

Number	Author(s), year of publication	Research object	Dependent variable(s)	Independent variable
1	(Zhang et al., 2021)	Postgraduates	Learning effect, learning experience and learning motivation	SG-based learning of cultural heritage
2	(Goli et al., 2022)	College students	The game's effectiveness, satisfaction, usability, and usefulness	SG-based learning of architectural design
3	(Cecotti, 2023)	Adult participants	Workload, availability, traffic, VR disease symptoms, and game engagement	IVR SG-based learning of art history
4	(Hang et al., 2023)	College students	Knowledge retention, learning motivation and situational interest	MR SG-based learning of mortise and tenon
5	(Ye et al., 2024)	College students	Learning motivation, cognitive load, short-term and long-term memory	AR SG-based learning of traditional pattern
6	(Kara, 2024)	College students	Knowledge retention and learning experience	SG-based experience of cultural heritage
7	(Li et al., 2024)	College students	Knowledge retention, learning performance, cognitive load, learning motivation and engagement	SG-based learning of traditional Chinese murals culture

3.4 Application of Theories or Models on SGs in HAE

Table 4 lists the theories and models used in the seven studies in the field. The studies by Goli et al. (2022), Hang et al. (2023), and Kara (2024) do not explicitly suggest the use of any particular theory, model, or framework.

In contrast, Zhang et al.'s (2021) study used the experiential learning cycle model as a learning methodology; however, the authors found the theory to be controversial when applied to the context of cultural heritage education, and therefore, the study incorporated flow theory. Cecotti's (2023) study is based on the Learning Mechanics-Game Mechanics (LM-GM) framework, which allows the viewer to explore and analyze the details of the painting through visual search. Ye et al.'s (2024) study was guided by pattern theory to explore the different effects of common SGs and AR SGs to find the best innovative teaching model. Li et al. (2024) used scaffolding theory to understand cultural heritage based on adventure games.

Table 4 Theories or models for the use of SGs in HAE

Number	Author(s), year of publication	Theories and models
1	(Zhang et al., 2021)	Flow Theory and the Experiential Learning Cycle Model
2	(Goli et al., 2022)	Not mentioned
3	(Cecotti, 2023)	Learning Mechanics-Game Mechanics
4	(Hang et al., 2023)	Not mentioned
5	(Ye et al., 2024)	Pattern Theory
6	(Kara, 2024)	Not mentioned
7	(Li et al., 2024)	Scaffolding Theory

Krath et al. (2021) concluded from a systematic review and analysis of theories in gamification, SGs, and game-based learning research that flow theory is the theory that focuses on effect and motivation; the experiential learning cycle model is a core component of experiential learning theory; and social learning theory and scaffolding theory are the theoretical foundations of the theory that focuses on learning. The Learning Mechanics-Game Mechanics (LM-GM) framework is a theoretical framework that combines Learning Mechanics (LM) with Game Mechanics (GM) and aims to optimize learning through gamified interactive elements (Arnab et al., 2015). In the arts, schema theory has been applied to explain the content and semantics of traditional schemas and for storing information (Ye et al., 2024).

4. DISCUSSION

The main objective of this study is to systematically review the use of SG in HAE from 2019 to 2024. Three main research questions aim to reveal the current state of recent research, trends in incorporating technology use, and results of impact on learners.

Among the most recent current research, Lee et al. (2024) explored the current status of integrating SG into education to improve the quality of learning, including trends in the use of technologies such as AR, VR, and MR in conjunction with SG. They stated that SG developed under VR and AR-based technologies is particularly suitable for skills and knowledge-based education and can engage students' interest in learning. In addition, the application of VR and AR in education allows learners to develop skills and gain knowledge within a secure and controlled virtual environment, It offers experiences and resources that may not be accessible in a conventional classroom setting (Radianti et al., 2020).

In the results of this study, it was shown that the majority of computer-based use of SGs in HAE has gradually shifted from 2023; for example, Cecotti (2024) designed an art history hidden object SG based on full IVR. Ye et al. (2024) developed an SG for teaching traditional patterns using AR technology. In addition, Hang et al. (2023) developed an SG for learning traditional crafts using MR technology. Over the past decade, the affordability and user-friendliness of VR- and AR-enabled (collectively referred to as IVR) hardware and software have continued to improve, leading to their increasing use in education (Ng et al., 2020).

Currently, recent developments in visualization and interaction in IVR technologies are becoming increasingly attractive to academics (Radianti et al., 2020). This is because they help to present difficult and abstract concepts, especially intangible content (Liu et al., 2022). However, it is important to note that immersion in SG when combined with VR does not guarantee that learners achieve effective learning when interacting with the content (Cecotti, 2023). Meanwhile, the findings of Ye et al. (2024) indicated that AR SGs are not much different from regular SGs in terms of motivation to learn, although AR is more suitable for understanding complex knowledge. Therefore, in the design of HAE, although AR and VR combined with SG can enhance the learning experience, their effectiveness still needs to be evaluated based on specific learning objectives and content. In addition, researchers should focus on the introduction of effective educational strategies and activity mechanisms when SG is applied in IVR environments to ensure that learners can achieve their learning goals and absorb knowledge effectively.

Only seven articles in this study found the application of SG in HAE. Overall, there are still a limited number of studies on the application of SG in HAE and a relatively low level of researchers' attention to this area. Five of these seven articles focused on investigating the effects of SG on learners, with most of the dependent variables being knowledge retention, academic performance, motivation, engagement, and learning experience. The remaining two articles mainly investigated the usability, effectiveness, satisfaction, and usefulness of the developed SG. However, it is important to note that there are also some SGs that, due to their nature, add to the psychological and mental workload of the students, thus reducing learning outcomes (Cowley et al., 2013). Therefore, researchers may note that when designing SGs, their nature, content, and gameplay tasks should also take into account students' thoughts.

In addition, regarding the application of theories and models of SGs in HAE, only four out of seven articles described or mentioned their use, while the remaining three did not. For example, Zhang et al. (2021) stated in their study that the experiential learning cycle model can be a convenient way to acquire tacit knowledge and improve learning efficiency by acquiring knowledge that is difficult to express in words through experiential learning. However, experiential learning theory has also been criticized by various researchers (Morris, 2019). Researchers have raised questions about the lack of theoretical underpinnings, lack of clarity, or conceptual weaknesses (Fromm et al., 2021). In this context, Zhang et al. (2021) integrated flow theory and the experiential learning cycle model in their study to propose a new framework for serious educational game design. However, the impact of gamification and SGs on the flow experience has not been established (Krath et al., 2021).

The learning mechanics-game mechanics (LM-GM) framework used in the article by Cecotti (2023) aims to optimize learning outcomes through the interactive elements of gamification, making the learning process more engaging and interactive. The current version of the LM-GM, if it is required to present effective SGs for education and training, will also require proper user evaluation to be able to meet educational objectives and provide appropriate user feedback (De Gloria et al., 2012). However, inserting this new dimension into the model is a major challenge for future research (Arnab et al., 2015).

The scaffolding theory mentioned by Li et al. (2024) refers to teachers or more experienced learners who support students during the learning process. As the learner's ability increases, these supports are gradually reduced until the learner can complete the task on his/her own. Some researchers have contended that designers of game-based learning systems need to carefully consider the interplay between scaffolding and pedagogical goals, as this relationship can influence the outcomes of the final experiments (Li et al., 2024).

Finally, Ye et al. (2024) stated that in the field of art, in addition to the use of schema theory to analyze artworks, researchers are gradually emulating educational activities in other disciplines, but at present, schema theory is less used in art education, which needs to be confirmed through progressive research.

For researchers and educators in HAE, the application of SG is both an opportunity and a challenge. In conclusion, the combination of SGs and emerging technologies has become a mainstream trend in this research field, although there are inevitably technical problems that are currently being addressed. For example, the cost of current VR devices is still high, and the popularization of SGs that incorporate new technologies is a challenge; VR devices offer unparalleled immersion and efficient learning environments, but 3D vertigo is still a problem that cannot be ignored, and the causes of this symptom are related to the individual's physical factors, the device's factors, and the quality of the content. (Marougkas et al., 2023). On the other hand, there is a lack of basic learning theories about the application development and design elements of VR in combination with gamification, SGs, or game-based learning (Radianti et al., 2020).

5. CONCLUSION

The results of this study show a shallow trend towards the use of SG in HAE between 2019 and 2024. However, the number of publications has started to gradually increase since 2024. This suggests that researchers are starting to recognize the potential of this field. As mentioned earlier, most of the papers in this field show that SG is effective in HAE. Researchers and educators can use SG as an adjunct tool to support teaching and learning materials in HAE.

Integrating SG with technologies such as AR, VR, and MR in HAE is indeed a promising avenue for future research and development, which can help university students better understand and enhance their interaction with artworks. Scholars have also tried to find more innovative approaches to SG applications and collect data related to learning outcomes. As Hwang et al. (2023) indicated, researchers advocate for game-based learning approaches, which can be the best catalyst for students to experience art education.

However, the field is also faced with the same problems, as almost all SGs developed in existing empirical studies are stand-alone, which means that users need to invest a certain amount of learning costs for each SG. In the future, it may be possible to substitute the concept of iterative design for SGs, where experience is gained by creating and evaluating several designs and iteratively optimizing them until the final game meets the desired criteria, resulting in a higher quality of SGs and more experience in SG design.

Overall, there is a need to consider more empirical evidence on the theoretical and practical aspects of the application of SG under HAE, as well as guidance on the successful incorporation of SG into AR, VR, and MR environments. Given the limited number of researchers currently focusing on this topic, this area holds significant research potential. In this review, we have provided a possible trajectory for the development and implementation of these technologies in HAE. In the future, it may be possible to consider students taking SG assessments as they learn higher arts content and explore how they can better participate in the classroom (Cecotti, 2023).

We need to acknowledge some of the limitations of this review study. Seven articles of review were published in conference proceedings and journals. This indicates that certain resources were not included in this review, such as book reviews and dissertations. Therefore, not all of the results from the resources that were available were included in our review. Future study endeavours should consider this constraint and broaden their reviews by incorporating articles published with a broader range of references. In addition, we focused only on investigating the current state of research, incorporating trends in the use of technology, and the resulting aspects of impact on learners. Other aspects (e.g., research methodology and design) are also important but beyond the scope of the research examined in this review. Future research could consider exploring other aspects of the use of SG under HAE.

REFERENCES

Arnab, S., Lim, T., Carvalho, M. B., Bellotti, F., De Freitas, S., Louchart, S., Suttie, N., Berta, R., & De Gloria, A. (2015). Mapping learning and game mechanics for serious games analysis. *British Journal of Educational Technology*, 46(2), 391–411. DOI: 10.1111/bjet.12113

Bonfield, C. A., Salter, M., Longmuir, A., Benson, M., & Adachi, C. (2020). Transformation or evolution?: Education 4.0, teaching and learning in the digital age. *Higher Education Pedagogies*, 5(1), 223–246. DOI: 10.1080/23752696.2020.1816847

Brandl, L. C., & Schrader, A. (2024). Serious Games in Higher Education in the Transforming Process to Education 4.0—Systematized Review. *Education Sciences*, 14(3), 281. DOI: 10.3390/educsci14030281

Cecotti, H. (2023, June). A Serious Game Based on Hidden Objects for Art History in Fully Immersive Virtual Reality. In International Conference on Immersive Learning (pp. 223-238). Cham: Springer Nature Switzerland.

Connolly, T. M., Boyle, E. A., MacArthur, E., Hainey, T., & Boyle, J. M. (2012). A systematic literature review of empirical evidence on computer games and serious games. *Computers & Education*, 59(2), 661–686. DOI: 10.1016/j.compedu.2012.03.004

Cowley, B., Ravaja, N., & Heikura, T. (2013). Cardiovascular physiology predicts learning effects in a serious game activity. *Computers & Education*, 60(1), 299–309. DOI: 10.1016/j.compedu.2012.07.014

Daoudi, I. (2022). Learning analytics for enhancing the usability of serious games in formal education: A systematic literature review and research agenda. *Education and Information Technologies*, 27(8), 11237–11266. DOI: 10.1007/s10639-022-11087-4 PMID: 35528757

Daoudi, I., Chebil, R., Tranvouez, E., Chaari, W. L., & Espinasse, B. (2021). Improving learners' assessment and evaluation in crisis management serious games: An emotion-based educational data mining approach. *Entertainment Computing*, 38, 100428. DOI: 10.1016/j.entcom.2021.100428

De Freitas, S. (2018). Are games effective learning tools? A review of educational games. *Journal of Educational Technology & Society*, 21(2), 74–84.

De Gloria, A., Bellotti, F., & Berta, R. (2012). Building a comprehensive R&D community on serious games. *Procedia Computer Science*, 15, 1–3. DOI: 10.1016/j.procs.2012.10.051

Fokides, E. (2018). Digital educational games and mathematics. Results of a case study in primary school settings. *Education and Information Technologies*, 23(2), 851–867. DOI: 10.1007/s10639-017-9639-5

Fraga-Varela, F., Vila-Couñago, E., & Martínez-Piñeiro, E. (2021). The impact of serious games in mathematics fluency: A study in Primary Education. *Comunicar*, 29(69), 125–135. DOI: 10.3916/C69-2021-10

Fromm, J., Radianti, J., Wehking, C., Stieglitz, S., Majchrzak, T. A., & vom Brocke, J. (2021). More than experience?-On the unique opportunities of virtual reality to afford a holistic experiential learning cycle. *The Internet and Higher Education*, 50, 100804. DOI: 10.1016/j.iheduc.2021.100804

Fürst, H., & Nylander, E. (2023). *The value of art education: Cultural engagements at the Swedish folk high schools*. Springer Nature. DOI: 10.1007/978-3-031-14061-7

Girard, C., Ecalle, J., & Magnan, A. (2013). Serious games as new educational tools: How effective are they? A meta-analysis of recent studies. *Journal of Computer Assisted Learning*, 29(3), 207–219. DOI: 10.1111/j.1365-2729.2012.00489.x

Goli, A., Teymournia, F., Naemabadi, M., & Garmaroodi, A. A. (2022). Architectural design game: A serious game approach to promote teaching and learning using multimodal interfaces. *Education and Information Technologies*, 27(8), 11467–11498. DOI: 10.1007/s10639-022-11062-z PMID: 35578701

Gómez, R. L., & Suárez, A. M. (2021). Gaming to succeed in college: Protocol for a scoping review of quantitative studies on the design and use of serious games for enhancing teaching and learning in higher education. *International Journal of Educational Research Open*, 2, 100021. DOI: 10.1016/j.ijedro.2020.100021

Hainey, T., Connolly, T. M., Boyle, E. A., Wilson, A., & Razak, A. (2016). A systematic literature review of games-based learning empirical evidence in primary education. *Computers & Education*, 102, 202–223. DOI: 10.1016/j.compedu.2016.09.001

. Hang, Y., Wang, H., Sang, Z., Huang, R., & Ye, L. (2023). The impact of mixed reality serious games on mortise and tenon learning in college students. Computers & Education: X Reality, 3, 100042.

. Hantoobi, S., Wahdan, A., Al-Emran, M., & Shaalan, K. (2021). A review of learning analytics studies. Recent advances in technology acceptance models and theories, 119-134.

Hwang, G. J., Chiu, M. C., Hsia, L. H., & Chu, H. C. (2023). Promoting art appreciation performances and behaviors in effective and joyful contexts: A two-tier test-based digital gaming approach. *Computers & Education*, 194, 104706. DOI: 10.1016/j.compedu.2022.104706

Kara, N. (2024). A mixed-methods study of cultural heritage learning through playing a serious game. *International Journal of Human-Computer Interaction*, 40(6), 1397–1408. DOI: 10.1080/10447318.2022.2125627

Khaldi, A., Bouzidi, R., & Nader, F. (2023). Gamification of e-learning in higher education: A systematic literature review. *Smart Learning Environments*, 10(1), 10. DOI: 10.1186/s40561-023-00227-z

Klašnja-Milićević, A., Ivanović, M., & Budimac, Z. (2017). Data science in education: Big data and learning analytics. *Computer Applications in Engineering Education*, 25(6), 1066–1078. DOI: 10.1002/cae.21844

Krath, J., Schürmann, L., & Von Korflesch, H. F. (2021). Revealing the theoretical basis of gamification: A systematic review and analysis of theory in research on gamification, serious games and game-based learning. *Computers in Human Behavior*, 125, 106963. DOI: 10.1016/j.chb.2021.106963

Lee, L. K., Wei, X., Chui, K. T., Cheung, S. K., Wang, F. L., Fung, Y. C., Lu, A., Hui, Y. K., Hao, T., U, L. H., & Wu, N. I. (2024). A Systematic Review of the Design of Serious Games for Innovative Learning: Augmented Reality, Virtual Reality, or Mixed Reality? *Electronics (Basel)*, 13(5), 890. DOI: 10.3390/electronics13050890

Li, Q., Wang, P., Liu, Z., Zhang, H., Song, Y., & Zhang, Y. (2024). Using scaffolding theory in serious games to enhance traditional Chinese murals culture learning. *Computer Animation and Virtual Worlds*, 35(1), e2213. DOI: 10.1002/cav.2213

Liberati, A., Altman, D. G., Tetzlaff, J., Mulrow, C., Gøtzsche, P. C., Ioannidis, J. P., & Moher, D. (2009). The PRISMA statement for reporting systematic reviews and meta-analyses of studies that evaluate health care interventions: Explanation and elaboration. *Annals of Internal Medicine*, 151(4), W-65. DOI: 10.7326/0003-4819-151-4-200908180-00136 PMID: 19622512

Liu, R., Wang, L., Koszalka, T. A., & Wan, K. (2022). Effects of immersive virtual reality classrooms on students' academic achievement, motivation and cognitive load in science lessons. *Journal of Computer Assisted Learning*, 38(5), 1422–1433. DOI: 10.1111/jcal.12688

Marougkas, A., Troussas, C., Krouska, A., & Sgouropoulou, C. (2023). Virtual reality in education: A review of learning theories, approaches and methodologies for the last decade. *Electronics (Basel)*, 12(13), 2832. DOI: 10.3390/electronics12132832

Morris, T. H. (2020). Experiential learning–a systematic review and revision of Kolb's model. *Interactive Learning Environments*, 28(8), 1064–1077. DOI: 10.1080/10494820.2019.1570279

Ng, S. C., Lee, L. K., Lui, A. K. F., Wong, K. F., Chan, W. Y., & Tam, H. H. (2020). Using immersive reality in training nursing students. *International Journal of Innovation and Learning*, 27(3), 324–343. DOI: 10.1504/IJIL.2020.106815

Qiusi, M. (2022). Research on the improvement method of music education level under the background of AI technology. *Mobile Information Systems*, 2022(1), 7616619. DOI: 10.1155/2022/7616619

Radianti, J., Majchrzak, T. A., Fromm, J., & Wohlgenannt, I. (2020). A systematic review of immersive virtual reality applications for higher education: Design elements, lessons learned, and research agenda. *Computers & Education*, 147, 103778. DOI: 10.1016/j.compedu.2019.103778

Sandí Delgado, J. C., & Bazán, P. A. (2021). Diseño de juegos serios: Análisis de metodologías. *E-Ciencias de la Información*, 11(2), 80–106. DOI: 10.15517/eci.v11i2.45505

Sharma, B. P. (2022). Digital Tools in Art Education: From Expanding Creative Horizons and Facilitating Collaboration to Increasing Access and Resources for a Diverse Student Population. *Applied Research in Artificial Intelligence and Cloud Computing*, 5(1), 55–65.

Taipe, M. S. A., Pesántez, D. Á., Rivera, L., & Vizueta, D. O. (2017). Juegos serios en el proceso de aprendizaje. *UTCiencia*, 4(2), 111–122.

Vlachopoulos, D., & Makri, A. (2017). The effect of games and simulations on higher education: A systematic literature review. *International Journal of Educational Technology in Higher Education*, 14(1), 1–33. DOI: 10.1186/s41239-017-0062-1

Wouters, P., Van Nimwegen, C., Van Oostendorp, H., & Van Der Spek, E. D. (2013). A meta-analysis of the cognitive and motivational effects of serious games. *Journal of Educational Psychology*, 105(2), 249–265. DOI: 10.1037/a0031311

Ye, L., Li, J., Yang, S., & Hang, Y. (2024). The effect of augmented reality-based serious game on traditional pattern learning. *Interactive Learning Environments*, •••, 1–29. DOI: 10.1080/10494820.2024.2327042

Zhang, Y., Li, W., Luo, Y., Nie, X., Tan, G., Qin, Y., & Sin, Y. K. (2021, November). Serious game design of cultural heritage education based on the experiential learning cycle model. In 2021 2nd International Conference on Information Science and Education (ICISE-IE) (pp. 1193-1200). IEEE. DOI: 10.1109/ICISE-IE53922.2021.00269

Zhonggen, Y. (2019). A meta-analysis of use of serious games in education over a decade. *International Journal of Computer Games Technology*, 2019(1), 4797032. DOI: 10.1155/2019/4797032

Chapter 4
Effects of Gamification on Student Achievement in Learning:
A Comparative Analysis of Pre- and Post-Test Outcomes for Secondary Students in Johor, Malaysia

Mageswaran Sanmugam
https://orcid.org/0000-0003-3313-4462
Universiti Sains Malaysia, Malaysia

ABSTRACT

This research paper examines the impact of gamification on academic achievement in undergraduate students. The study used a quasi-experimental design, comparing pre- and post-test scores. Results showed a significant improvement in post-test scores for the gamified group compared to the control group. The study also found that pre-test scores and engagement metrics significantly influenced the outcomes. The study suggests that the effectiveness of gamification depends on factors like design, intervention duration, and alignment with educational objectives. It recommends further longitudinal studies and exploring gamification's applicability across diverse educational settings.

DOI: 10.4018/979-8-3693-6745-2.ch004

INTRODUCTION

Gamification, integrating game-like elements into non-game contexts, has gained significant attention in education as a potential strategy to enhance student engagement and learning outcomes. However, the empirical evidence on the effectiveness of gamification in improving academic performance remains mixed. While some studies have reported positive effects of gamification on student learning, others have found inconclusive or even negative results. (Khaldi et al., 2023)(Bai et al., 2020)(Yıldırım & Şen, 2019). The intriguing aspect of gamification in educational contexts is its promise to transform traditional learning environments into engaging and interactive spaces. This potential has been acknowledged and explored through various studies aiming to understand how integrating game elements—such as points, badges, and leaderboards—into educational settings can foster a more dynamic learning experience.(An, 2020) The premise of employing game mechanics is to leverage the intrinsic motivation and engagement that games naturally elicit, applying these to academic settings to boost students' interest and participation in their learning journey. (Kucher, 2021)(Laine & Lindberg, 2020)(Václavíková, 2020)Despite this promising outlook, the impact of gamification on actual learning outcomes has been met with mixed results, presenting an intriguing paradox. While some scholars highlight the positive implications of gamification, noting improved student engagement and performance, others cast a shadow of doubt, pointing out instances where gamification does not yield significant enhancements or might even detract from learning outcomes. (Amo et al., 2018)(Bai et al., 2020)This divergence in findings underscores the complexity of effectively integrating gamification in education. It suggests that not all gamified approaches are created equal or universally effective across different educational settings and student demographics. The effectiveness of gamification, therefore, seems to hinge on several critical factors, including the design of the gamification elements themselves. For instance, merely adding points or leaderboards to an educational activity without considering how these elements align with the learning objectives and content might not improve student achievement. (Furdu et al., 2017)(Landers, 2014) Additionally, the duration of the intervention and the extent to which students engage with the gamified elements play crucial roles in determining the impact of gamification. Short-term interventions may not capture the full extent of gamification's potential benefits, while longer-term implementations could provide more insights into how these strategies foster sustained engagement and learning. Aligning game mechanics with educational objectives is paramount to ensure that the gamification strategy does not become a distraction but a potent tool for enhancing the learning experience. (Botra et al., 2014)(Urh et al., 2015) Furthermore, acknowledging the variability in how different students respond to gamified learning is crucial. Individual differences in learning preferences, motivation, and engagement with game elements can significantly affect the outcomes of gamification interventions. As such, future research should continue to dissect these nuances, exploring how gamification strategies can be tailored to maximize their effectiveness across diverse learning environments and student populations. This will advance our understanding of gamification's role in education and refine its implementation, ensuring that it serves as a meaningful complement to traditional teaching methods rather than a superficial addition.

To gain a deeper understanding of the impact of gamification on student achievement, this research paper adopts a comparative approach, analyzing the effects of gamification on pre-and post-test scores(Hanus & Fox, 2015)(Ibáñez et al., 2014). The study is guided by the following research question: What are the effects of gamification on students' academic achievement, as measured by pre-and post-test performance?

The existing literature review suggests that gamification in educational settings can promote behavioural, cognitive, and emotional engagement among students (Bai et al., 2020)(Jiang, 2016). Nevertheless, the impact on actual learning outcomes could be clearer, with some studies reporting positive effects while others find no significant improvements(Khaldi et al., 2023)(Dichev & Dicheva, 2017). This study aims to contribute to the ongoing debate by providing a rigorous analysis of the effects of gamification on academic achievement in a specific educational context. A meta-analysis by Lamprinou and Paraskeva found an overall medium effect size favouring gamification over traditional learning approaches regarding academic performance(Lamprinou & Fotini, 2015). Similarly, a longitudinal study by Koivisto and Hamari observed that gamification's motivational and psychological benefits may diminish over time, highlighting the importance of understanding the long-term implications(Koivisto & Hamari, 2019). Besides that, Simoes et al. emphasize the need to carefully design and implement gamification strategies to ensure their effectiveness in enhancing student learning. This is because the mere inclusion of game elements does not guarantee improved learning outcomes, and the specific design and execution of the gamification approach can significantly influence its impact (Simões et al., 2013).

Taken together, the existing research suggests that gamification can be a promising approach to enhance student engagement and potentially improve learning outcomes, but various factors, such as the specific design of the gamification elements, the duration of the intervention, and the alignment with the learning objectives may influence its effectiveness. Also, the effects of gamification may vary across different educational contexts and subject areas(Khaleel et al., 2015). The present study aims to contribute to this ongoing debate by conducting a comprehensive investigation of the effects of gamification on student achievement, as measured by pre-and post-test comparisons. By examining the differences in student performance before and after the implementation of gamification, this study seeks to provide a more nuanced understanding of the impact of gamification on learning.

LITERATURE REVIEW

A meta-analysis of independent interventions found a significant medium-sized effect of gamification on student academic performance compared to non-gamified learning conditions. (Bai et al., 2020) Specifically, the study reported a Hedges' g effect size of 0.504, indicating a moderate advantage of gamified learning over traditional approaches. Similarly, a longitudinal study examining the effects of gamification on intrinsic motivation and learning outcomes in a classroom setting found that gamification elements such as points, badges, and leaderboards positively impacted student motivation and engagement over time. Another study by Simoes et al. suggests that the effectiveness of gamification in education may depend on the specific design and implementation of the gamification elements and their alignment with the learning objectives(Simões et al., 2013). Also, the review by Hamari, Koivisto, and Sarsa highlights the need to consider the long-term effects of gamification, as the motivational benefits may diminish over time (Hamari et al., 2014). Meanwhile, Sanmugam et al. emphasize the importance of carefully integrating gamification into the learning process to avoid potential negative impacts on student learning(Sanmugam et al., 2016)(Sanmugam et al., 2014). The existing research suggests that while gamification can enhance student engagement and motivation, its impact on learning outcomes is more complex and context-dependent.

However, not all studies have reported the positive effects of gamification on learning. A review by Aldemir et al. identified a mix of findings, with some studies showing improved learning outcomes and others finding no significant differences between gamified and non-gamified conditions. (Alsawaier, 2018) The authors suggested that the effectiveness of gamification might be influenced by factors such as the specific game elements used, the integration of gamification with the learning content, and the overall design of the gamified learning environment.

There are also concerns about the potential negative effects of gamification, such as the risk of over-emphasis on extrinsic rewards, which could undermine intrinsic motivation and lead to a decline in long-term engagement. Koivisto and Hamari's longitudinal study found that gamification's motivational and psychological benefits may wear off over time, highlighting the need for a deeper understanding of the long-term effects of gamification on learning(Koivisto & Hamari, 2019). Besides that, gamification has also been criticized for potentially being “exploitative” and undermining the intrinsic value of learning. Another study by Lee and Hammer argued that gamification should be designed carefully to avoid such pitfalls and to effectively support learning goals. (Lee & Hammer, 2011)This is due to mixed findings and the lack of a clear consensus on the effectiveness of gamification in education. Also, according to Zichermann and Cunningham (2011), gamification can become "exploitationware" rather than a tool for engagement and learning when gamification is not well designed. In summary, while growing evidence suggests that gamification can enhance student engagement and motivation, the impact on learning outcomes is more complex and context-dependent.

Overall, the available evidence suggests that gamification can positively impact student achievement. However, the effectiveness may depend on factors such as the specific game elements used, the duration of the intervention, and the learning context. Educators should carefully consider the design and implementation of gamification strategies to maximize their potential benefits for student learning. To address these mixed findings and concerns, the present study aims to provide a comprehensive analysis of the effects of gamification on student achievement, focusing on comparing pre- and post-test results.

METHODOLOGY

The study will employ a quasi-experimental research design, with an experimental group exposed to gamification-based instruction and a control group receiving traditional instruction. The participants will be drawn from a pool of high school students enrolled in normal schools in southern Malaysia, in the state of Johor. The students are also selected from those who learn computer science in their school. The study will measure student achievement using pre- and post-tests designed to assess the student's understanding of the key concepts and learning objectives covered in the instruction.

The study will consist of the following steps:

1. Pre-test: All participants will complete a pre-test to assess their baseline knowledge and understanding of the subject matter.
2. Intervention: The experimental group will receive a gamified instructional intervention, which may include elements such as points, badges, leaderboards, and challenges. The control group will receive the same content and instruction but without the gamification elements.
3. Post-test: The experimental and control groups will complete a post-test to measure their learning outcomes after the intervention.

4. Data Analysis: The pre-test and post-test scores will be compared between the experimental and control groups to assess the effects of gamification on student achievement.
5. Statistical Analysis: Appropriate statistical tests, such as t-tests, will determine the statistical significance of the observed differences in student performance between the two groups.

The sample is chosen via a purposive method, as they are enrolled in a relevant course. As well as based on the availability during times of COVID. The study will be conducted over six weeks, with the gamified instruction taking place during the four weeks in the middle of the study.

Ethical Considerations

The study was conducted according to the ethical guidelines of Universiti Sains Malaysia. All participants were informed about the study's purpose and procedures, and their consent was obtained before the data collection. The participants' privacy and confidentiality were protected, and all data was anonymized to ensure their identities were not revealed. The Institutional Review Board (IRB) of Universiti Sains Malaysia approved the study before the data collection commenced.

Results

The pre-test and post-test scores of the experimental and control groups will be analyzed and presented as tables and figures. The key findings from the data analysis are as follows:

Figure 1. Pre and Post-Test Scores Comparison between the Control and Intervention Group

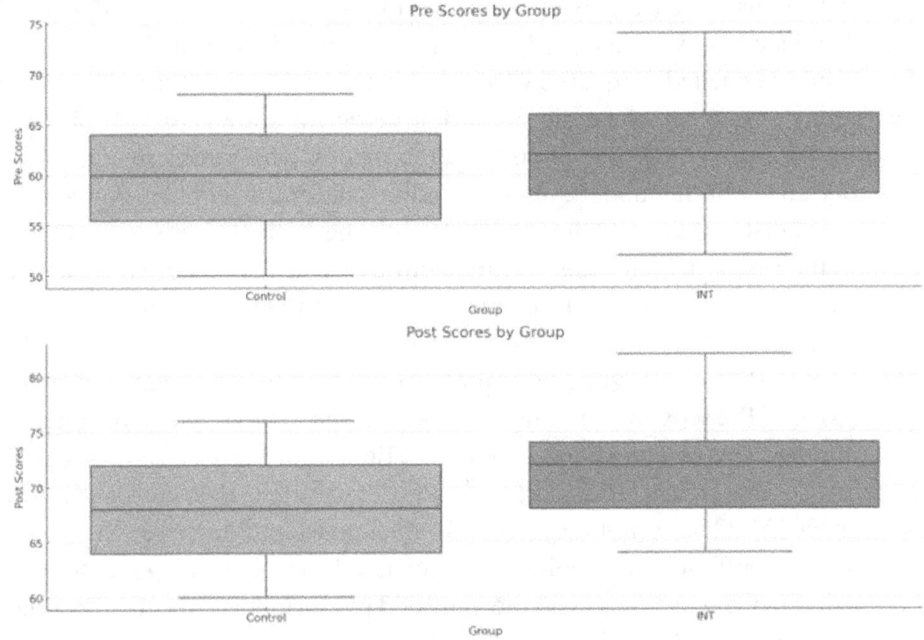

The statistical analysis of score improvements between Pre and Post scores reveals the following:

The experimental group (gamified learning) showed a significantly greater improvement in their post-test scores than the control group (traditional instruction).

- **t-statistic**: -12.87
- **p-value**: 8.64×10−188.64 \times 10^{-18}8.64×10−18
- **Mean Improvement**: 9.13
- **Standard Deviation of Improvement**: 5.17

The negative t-statistic indicates that the control group had a significantly higher score increase than the experimental group. The extremely low p-value suggests that the difference in score improvements between the two groups is statistically significant at the $p < 0.001$ level. The extremely low p-value indicates that the improvement from Pre to Post scores is statistically significant. The mean improvement of 9.13 suggests a substantial increase in scores post-intervention. Overall, this suggests that gamification-based instructional practices were more effective in improving student achievement compared to traditional instruction.

Meanwhile, based on the R-squared value of 0.857, the model explains 85.7% of the variance in the score improvements. The pre-scores and login frequency can explain approximately 85.7% of the variance in the post-scores. This indicates a strong relationship between the predictors and the dependent variable.

Based on the adjusted R-squared with the value of 0.852, the adjusted R-squared accounts for the number of predictors in the model. It shows that 85.2% of the variance in the Post scores is explained by the model, which confirms the strong explanatory power of the model even when adjusting for the number of predictors. Also, the F-statistic shows a value of 192.0 with the Prob (F-statistic): 3.87e-23. Therefore, the F-statistic tests the overall significance of the model. The very low p-value (close to 0) indicates that the model is statistically significant.

Based on the Coefficients, the Constant (Intercept) has a value of 2.5789. This is the expected Post score when both pre-scores and Login Frequency are zero. However, since a Pre score of zero might not be realistic in this context, the intercept is more of a baseline reference point. The coefficient for the Pre score is 0.8722, indicating that for every one-unit increase in the Pre score, the Post score is expected to increase by 0.8722 units, holding other variables constant. Moreover, the analysis reveals that the coefficient for Login Frequency is 1.1732, suggesting that for every additional login or engagement with the gamified platform, the expected Post score is predicted to increase by 1.1732 units, holding other variables constant. For each one-unit increase in Pre scores, the Post score is expected to increase by approximately 0.876 units, holding the Login Frequency constant. The very low p-value indicates that this relationship is highly statistically significant.

Additional statistics were obtained from the Omnibus Test, which showed the tests for the normality of the residuals. A p-value > 0.05 (0.267) suggests that the residuals are normally distributed. A Durbin-Watson statistic of 1.993, close to 2, indicates that the residuals are independent and not autocorrelated. Durbin-Watson Statistic showed a value of 1.890, which suggests that the tests for the presence of autocorrelation in the residuals. Values close to 2 suggest no autocorrelation. Also, the Jarque-Bera (JB) Test is another test for normality. A non-significant p-value (0.299) indicates normal distribution of residuals. The statistical analysis suggests that the gamification-based instructional approach was more effective in improving student achievement than traditional instruction. The regression model shows that Pre scores and Login Frequency are significant predictors of Post scores, explaining a substantial portion of the variance in the outcomes. The model appears robust and statistically significant, indicating that improvements in Pre scores and increased Login Frequency are associated with higher Post scores.

It can be seen from the analysis that there has been an increase in both control and experimental group academic performance throughout the study. This indicates that gamification can enhance student achievement relative to traditional instruction, although the long-term effects may vary. The findings of this study echo the mixed results reported in the literature. While some studies have found positive effects of gamification on learning outcomes, others have reported no significant differences or even a decline in effectiveness over time. It is important to note that the specific design and implementation of the gamification elements may have played a crucial role in determining the effectiveness of the intervention. Factors such as the alignment of the game-based activities with the learning objectives, the level of student engagement, and the long-term sustainability of the gamification approach can influence student achievement.

Limitations

While the findings suggest that the gamification-based instructional approach was more effective in improving student achievement than traditional instruction, the study has a few limitations. First, it was conducted in a specific educational context and may not be generalizable to other settings. Second, it focused on overall achievement outcomes and did not explore the effects of gamification on specific learning processes or engagement metrics.

DISCUSSION

Based on the findings, several potential factors could have contributed to the observed effects. First, the gamification elements implemented in this study, such as points, badges, and leaderboards, may have enhanced student motivation and engagement, improving learning outcomes in computer science. This aligns with previous research suggesting that gamification can positively impact intrinsic motivation and learning outcomes.

However, the results also suggest that the effects of gamification may diminish over time as the novelty of the game-like elements wears off. This highlights the importance of designing gamification strategies that maintain student interest and engagement throughout the learning process.

Furthermore, the specific context and characteristics of the student population may have contributed to the effectiveness of the gamification intervention. For instance, the study participants' prior familiarity with game-based learning, their personal preferences, and the alignment of the gamification elements with their learning styles could have influenced the outcomes.

FUTURE RECOMMENDATIONS

Based on the findings of this study, several recommendations can be made for future research and practice:

1. Conduct longitudinal studies to examine the long-term effects of gamification on student achievement and engagement.
2. Explore the design of gamification elements and their alignment with specific learning objectives and student characteristics.
3. Investigate the combined effects of gamification and other instructional strategies, such as problem-based learning or collaborative learning, to optimize the impact on student achievement.
4. Develop a deeper understanding of the factors that influence the effectiveness of gamification, such as the duration of the intervention, the level of integration with the curriculum, and the specific game elements used.
5. Explore the potential of adaptive gamification, where the game-based elements are tailored to individual student needs and preferences.
6. Expand the research to different educational contexts, such as K-12 classrooms, professional development programs, and online learning environments, to assess the broader applicability of gamification.
7. Incorporate qualitative methods, such as interviews and observations, to better understand the student experience and the underlying mechanisms through which gamification influences learning.
8. Collaborate with cross-disciplinary teams, including educational researchers, game designers, and learning technologists, to develop and evaluate effective gamification strategies for education.
9. Make the study and dataset available for other researchers to build upon, enabling replication and meta-analyses to strengthen the evidence base on the effects of gamification in education.
10. Engage in knowledge dissemination and professional development activities to help educators understand gamification's potential benefits and limitations and provide guidance on its appropriate implementation.
11. Potential limitations should be acknowledged, such as the study's specific context, sample size, and the potential for self-selection bias in the participant pool.

CONCLUSIONS

This study investigated the effects of gamification on student achievement in learning computer science. The findings suggest that gamification can lead to improved learning outcomes, with the experimental group demonstrating higher post-test scores than the control group. However, the long-term sustainability of these effects remains a concern, highlighting the need for further research and refinements in the design and implementation of gamification strategies.

The study contributes to the growing body of literature on the effectiveness of gamification in education, providing insights into this approach's potential benefits and limitations. Future research should focus on exploring the nuances of gamification, its alignment with specific learning objectives, and its long-term impact on student engagement and achievement.

ACKNOWLEDGEMENTS

We acknowledge the Universiti Sains Malaysia Short Term Grant, 304/PME-DIA/6315350 for supporting this research

REFERENCES

Alsawaier, R S. (2018, January 2). The effect of gamification on motivation and engagement. Emerald Publishing Limited, 35(1), 56-79. https://doi.org/DOI: 10.1108/IJILT-02-2017-0009

Amo, L., Liao, R., Rao, H R., & Walker, G. (2018, June 18). Effects of Leaderboards in Games on Consumer Engagement. https://doi.org/DOI: 10.1145/3209626.3209708

An, Y. (2020, February 21). Designing Effective Gamified Learning Experiences. *Designing Effective Gamified Learning Experiences.*, 3(2), 62–62. DOI: 10.46328/ijte.v3i2.27

Bai, S., Hew, K F., & Huang, B. (2020, June 1). Does gamification improve student learning outcomes? Evidence from a meta-analysis and synthesis of qualitative data in educational contexts. Elsevier BV, 30, 100322-100322. https://doi.org/.DOI: 10.1016/j.edurev.2020.100322

Botra, A., Rerselman, M., & Ford, M. (2014, May 1). Gamification beyond badges. https://doi.org/DOI: 10.1109/ISTAFRICA.2014.6880651

Dichev, C., & Dicheva, D. (2017, February 20). Gamifying education: what is known, what is believed and what remains uncertain: a critical review. *International Journal of Educational Technology in Higher Education*, 14(1), 9. Advance online publication. DOI: 10.1186/s41239-017-0042-5

Furdu, I., Tomozei, C., & Köse, U. (2017, January 1). Pros and cons gamification and gaming in classroom. Cornell University. https://doi.org/DOI: 10.48550/arXiv.1708

Gabe, J. (2020). Does educational gamification improve students' motivation? *Proceedings of the Second International Conference on Technological Ecosystems for Enhancing Multiculturality*, 701-707.

Hamari, J., Koivisto, J., & Sarsa, H. (2014, January 6). Does Gamification Work? A Literature Review of Empirical Studies on Gamification. https://www.semanticscholar.org/paper/Does-Gamification-Work-A-Literature-Review-of-on-Hamari-Koivisto/0768149ce1170691bcde8b4539153a282f0cc74c

Hanus, M., & Fox, J. (2015, January 1). Assessing the effects of gamification in the classroom: A longitudinal study on intrinsic motivation, social comparison, satisfaction, effort, and academic performance. Elsevier BV, 80, 152-161. DOI: 10.1016/j.compedu.2014.08.019

Ibáñez, M. B., Serio, Á. D., & Kloos, C. D. (2014, July 1). Gamification for Engaging Computer Science Students in Learning Activities: A Case Study. *IEEE Transactions on Learning Technologies*, 7(3), 291–301. DOI: 10.1109/TLT.2014.2329293

Jiang, S. (2016, January 1). A Review of the Effectiveness of Gamification in Education. RELX Group (Netherlands). DOI: 10.2139/ssrn.3163896

Khaldi, A., Bouzidi, R., & Nader, F. (2023, January 31). Gamification of e-learning in higher education: A systematic literature review. *Springer Nature*, 10(1), 10. Advance online publication. DOI: 10.1186/s40561-023-00227-z

Khaleel, F L., Ashaari, N S., Wook, T S M T., & Ismail, A. (2015, April 1). User-enjoyable learning environment based on Gamification elements. DOI: 10.1109/I4CT.2015.7219570

. Koivisto, J., & Hamari, J. (2019, April 1). The rise of motivational information systems: A review of gamification research. Elsevier BV, 45, 191-210. https://doi.org/DOI: 10.1016/j.ijinfomgt.2018.10.013

Kucher, T. (2021, March 17). Principles and Best Practices of Designing Digital Game-Based Learning Environments. *Principles and Best Practices of Designing Digital Game-Based Learning Environments.*, 5(2), 213–223. DOI: 10.46328/ijtes.190

Laine, T. H., & Lindberg, R. S. N. (2020, October 1). Designing Engaging Games for Education: A Systematic Literature Review on Game Motivators and Design Principles. *IEEE Transactions on Learning Technologies*, 13(4), 804–821. DOI: 10.1109/TLT.2020.3018503

Lamprinou, D., & Fotini, P. (2015, November 1). Gamification design framework based on SDT for student motivation. DOI: 10.1109/IMCTL.2015.7359631

Landers, R. N. (2014, December 1). Developing a Theory of Gamified Learning. *Simulation & Gaming*, 45(6), 752–768. DOI: 10.1177/1046878114563660

Lee, J. J., & Hammer, J. (2011, January 1). Gamification in Education: What, How, Why Bother? Rapid Intellect Group, 15(2). https://www.uwstout.edu/soe/profdev/resources/upload/Lee-Hammer-AEQ-2011.pdf

Nah, F. F. H., Zeng, Q., Telaprolu, V. R. A., Ayyappa, S., & Eschenbrenner, B. (2014). Gamification of education: a review of literature. *Proceedings of the 1st international conference on HCI in business*, 401-409. DOI: 10.1007/978-3-319-07293-7_39

Sanmugam, M., Abdullah, Z., & Zaid, N M. (2014, December 1). Gamification: Cognitive impact and creating a meaningful experience in learning. DOI: 10.1109/ICEED.2014.7194700

Sanmugam, M., Zaid, N M., Abdullah, Z., Aris, B., Mohamed, H., & Meijden, H V D. (2016, December 1). The impacts of infusing game elements and gamification in learning. DOI: 10.1109/ICEED.2016.7856058

Simões, J., Redondo, R P D., & Vilas, A F. (2013, March 1). A social gamification framework for a K-6 learning platform. Elsevier BV, 29(2), 345-353. https://doi.org/DOI: 10.1016/j.chb.2012.06.007

. Urh, M., Vukovič, G., Jereb, E., & Pintar, R. (2015, July 1). The Model for Introduction of Gamification into E-learning in Higher Education. Elsevier BV, 197, 388-397. https://doi.org/DOI: 10.1016/j.sbspro.2015.07.154

. Václavíková, Z. (2020, April 1). Game: Experience as an Educational Tool. IntechOpen. DOI: 10.5772/intechopen.88853

Yıldırım, İ., & Şen, S. (2019, July 3). The effects of gamification on students' academic achievement: a meta-analysis study. Taylor & Francis, 29(8), 1301-1318. https://doi.org/DOI: 10.1080/10494820.2019.1636089

Zichermann, G., & Cunningham, C. (2011). *Gamification by Design*. "O'Reilly Media, Inc." http://books.google.ie/books?id=Hw9X1miVMMwC&printsec=frontcover&dq=gabe+zichermann&hl=&cd=1&source=gbs_api

Chapter 5
Using Games in the Classroom to Boost Motivation Among ESL Students

Puteri Zarina Megat Khalid
Sultan Idris Education University, Malaysia

Haddi Junaidi Kussin
Sultan Idris Education University, Malaysia

Nurihan Nasir
https://orcid.org/0000-0002-5429-736X
Sultan Idris Education University, Malaysia

Hannatul Akila Esahak
Sultan Idris Education University, Malaysia

ABSTRACT

This study analyses how game-based learning motivates Malaysian ESL students. The mixed-method research employed questionnaires and semi-structured interviews with students and teachers. Students were in favour of the game-based lessons, suggesting that game-based learning might solve motivational issues. However, several obstacles prevented teachers from delivering a game-based lesson. The study stresses the need of motivation in ESL classes since disengaged students may hinder learning. To promote learning, teachers must inspire and meet student needs. The findings suggest that game-based learning may motivate and engage students, but educators must be flexible to overcome its challenges. This research helps educators,

DOI: 10.4018/979-8-3693-6745-2.ch005

policymakers, and administrators improve ESL education and student motivation.

INTRODUCTION

The rapid development of technology has revolutionised English Language instructions in the twenty-first century, particularly in the context of English as a second language (ESL) acquisition (Ahmed et al., 2022) as well as for professional development (Akhter, 2022). According to Galloway and Rose (2021), the fact that English is one of the language disciplines taught in schools all over the world is evidence of the relevance of the language in society. In the same vein, English is the medium of instruction in schools, educational institutions, and workplaces in Malaysia and other countries where English is not the native language of the people (Anak Yunus & Hua, 2021; Aziz & Kashinathan, 2021;). English is considered the language of knowledge and is vital for accessing global information, enhancing skills, and facilitating communication among people from diverse linguistic backgrounds (Ali, 2022). Its importance is evident as it is a core subject in schools worldwide. It is also gazetted as the medium of instruction in many non-native English-speaking countries, including Malaysia. However, teaching English in such countries is challenging when students lack motivation in their academic pursuit. Studies have shown that students' reluctance to learn English can hinder the teaching process, manifesting as lack of participation (Ahmad, 2021).Digital games, brought about by the emergence of technology, have evolved from mere entertainment tools to becoming effective learning methods, known as digital game-based learning (Adnan et al., 2020; Mukaromah et al., 2019). This game-based approach to learning has significantly impacted ESL instructions. Research has shown that integrating technology, specifically digital games, into English language teaching is becoming increasingly important for second and foreign language acquisition (Munisa & Mohinur, 2024; Yaacob et al., 2022; Yaacob & Yunus, 2019).

Motivation is crucial in influencing students' behaviour, attitudes and language performance. This research explores using game-based learning to boost motivation in ESL classrooms. Motivation is a crucial factor in influencing behaviour, attitudes, and language performance (Hussain et al., 2020). The challenges of teaching English in a non-native country are well-documented, particularly when students lack motivation to learn the language (Yuzulia, 2021). Game-based learning enhances conceptual understanding, motivation, and provides an engaging learning experience. This research aims to investigate the use of game-based learning as a strategy to boost students' motivation in ESL classrooms. Game-based learning has been shown to not only improve conceptual comprehension but also enhance motivation to study and provide a fun and engaging learning experience (Byusa et al., 2022).

There are two primary types of motivation: intrinsic motivation, which drives students to learn English for personal growth, and extrinsic motivation, which drives students to learn English for pragmatic objectives (Ajmal et al., 2021). Additionally, motivation can be categorized into four dimensions: competence, autonomy, interest, and relatedness (Hussain et al., 2020). Game-based learning is a learning method that employs attractive educational game concepts, often with electronic devices (Liu & Gazizova, 2020). Teachers can utilize available educational gaming apps to implement game-based learning in their classrooms (Liu & Gazizova, 2020).

The issue of students who lack motivation in the learning processes has emerged as a topic of attention, as shown by prior studies (Altun & Abdullah Khdir, 2022; Ramzan et al., 2023; Khan et al., 2023). Investigating strategies to boost students' motivation is crucial as motivation drives positive behaviours and constructive learning performances. However, generating motivation is challenging due to individual differences among students. Ideally, students should feel motivated to learn English as it relates to real-life practice. Yet, not all students are inclined to learn English despite understanding its importance. The findings from this research are significant in investigating a potential teaching practice to boost students' motivation. Working on students' motivation is important in any teaching pedagogy because motivation influences students' positive behaviours for constructive learning performances (Ajmal et al., 2021). Nevertheless, generating students' motivation is difficult considering students' individual differences. Ideally, students should feel motivated to learn English because topics for English lessons are closely related to students' real-life practice. However, not all students want to learn English despite knowing its importance (Uddiniyah & Silfia, 2020). Thus, the purpose of this study is to assess the dimensions of motivation that game-based learning can produce. This paper will provide further study in line with two research questions on how game-based learning affects students' motivation in ESL classrooms and what are the challenges of applying game-based learning in ESL classrooms faced by teachers.

RELATED LITERATURE REVIEW

Theoretical Background

Numerous researchers in the area of education undertake investigations with the application of theoretical knowledge in order to assemble conclusive findings that may lead to the development of improved teaching and learning experiences for individuals of all generations (Schunk, 2002). In English as a Second Language (ESL) classes, the issue that has been discovered is students who are not motivated, which may be shown via the students' poor behaviour. As a result, it is very important for this research to investigate the idea of game-based learning approach in enhancing students' motivation to learn the target language.

The Use of Game-Based Learning and its Impact on Learners' Motivation

Game-based learning is an educational approach that uses elements of games to disseminate information and nurture skills in an engaging and hands-on learning environment (Kolb and Kolb, 2005; Jaccard et al., 2022). The motivating impact of game-based learning has been analysed in several fields, including computer science, education, and psychology. Studies have shown that game-based learning approach have the potential to both enhance and diminish students' motivation.

In order to create settings that promote learning, it is important for students to be interested, motivated, and engaged (Järvelä and Renninger, 2014) in an active learning environment (Silvola et al., 2021). Dabbous et al. (2022) found that game-based learning settings may promote meaningful learning and motivation, provided that learners' cognitive processing of the instructional information is ascertained. Digital game-based learning solutions have the capability to create learning environments that promote reflection, hands-on experience, and curiosity (Bygstad et al., 2022). As a result, they are well-suited for project-based classroom assignments. According to Jääskä and Aaltonen (2022), educators suggest that game-based learning approaches have the potential to create a lasting learning experience for students by influencing emotions.

Game elements such as the organisation of the game, the level of engagement it offers, and its attractiveness may encourage students and help them achieve their targeted learning goals (Breien and Wasson, 2021; Jääskä et al., 2021; Naul and Liu, 2020). Prior studies have found that game-based learning helps enhance students' activation, motivation and behaviour (Barbosa & de Ávila Rodrigues, 2020), as well as their feelings of interest and immersion (Hamari et al., 2016), and their overall engagement (Hartt et al., 2020). It is also suggested that students' motivation is promoted when positive emotional states, such as joy and enthusiasm, are induced (Barbosa & de Ávila Rodrigues, 2020).

Despite the numerous benefits of game-based learning as students' motivation booster, there are potential setbacks of this approach such as eliciting negative feelings and dissatisfaction among learners. Perceived difficulties can appear as time-consuming and demanding within a game or problems related to the game's environment (Boghian et al., 2019). Some of the problems are related to technical instability (Jääskä and Aaltonen, 2022) as well as the complexity of the games themselves (Lomas et al., 2017). Additionally, students may experience discomfort with the presence of competition and the comparison of performance in game-based learning scenarios (Velaora et al., 2022). Unfavourable experiences often reduce motivation, but an appropriate level of challenge in the form of positive stress may enhance motivate and improve learning outcomes (Yu et al., 2021). Game-based learning approaches are feasible to enhance students' desire to study. However, it is crucial to be cautious of possible drawbacks and ensure they are avoided.

The Correlation Between Students' Motivation and Learning

Motivational theories aim to understand the factors that drive people to engage in activities (Thomas & Gupta, 2022). Catacutan et al. (2022) aim to elucidate the factors that contribute to people's motivation and involvement, as well as their thereof and disconnection. The motivation to learn, driven by individual factors such as the need for challenge, curiosity, control and fantasy, as well as interpersonal factors such as collaboration, competitiveness, and recognition, has been extensively examined (Mohamadbahuldin, 2022).

The self-determination theory of motivation, proposed by Ryan and Deci (2000), views human beings as pro-active individuals who are driven by goals and are naturally inclined towards learning. Fulfilling psychological demands for competence, autonomy, and relatedness improves self-regulation and well-being, all of which are important in the field of education (Guay, 2022). Motivation may be analysed by valuing the intrinsic and extrinsic elements. Intrinsic motivation refers to personal aspirations and interests meanwhile extrinsic motivation concerns one's goal attainment while engaging in certain tasks (Ryan and Deci, 2000). Within the education realm, it is crucial to address both elements to help improve students' motivation (Leitão Et al., 2022). According to Martin-Hernandez et al. (2021), game-based learning approaches have the potential to enhance intrinsic motivation by providing engaging and innovative learning experiences. The entire gaming process, scoring and competitiveness of instructional games may build students' extrinsic motivation.

Student motivation has a positive effect on their learning results, which is impacted by new experiences, challenges, and task variety (Elshareif & Mohamed, 2021). Positive emotions and pleasurable experiences boost cognitive activity, amplify motivation, and aid in the learning of competence. Bewilderment may also influence motivation, promoting the development of critical thinking abilities and facilitating profound learning. Student motivation is thus an essential determinant in the learning process (Pnevmatikos et al., 2023).

Past Studies on Game-Based Learning and Students' Motivation

Game-Based Learning and Students' Motivation

The integration of game-based learning and technology in education has been gaining traction in recent years, with numerous studies highlighting its potential to enhance student attraction, motivation, and desire to continue learning. Liu and Gazizova's (2020) study, which focused on improving the quality of learning and memorizing in 9-10 year old students, found that game-based learning can be a valuable teaching practice in today's rapidly evolving educational landscape. The study revealed that 70.93% of students expressed interest in game-based lessons, and 51.16% were enthusiastic about the next game-based lesson. Furthermore, students expressed a greater interest in studying if they could work using educational game applications.

Similarly, Roohani and Heidari Vincheh's (2023) study explored the use of mobile-assisted language learning (MALL) and gaming applications and social media as instructional methods for English phrasal verbs. The results showed statistically significant improvements in learning English phrasal verbs in all three groups, with the game-based method being found to be the most effective. This highlights the potential of integrating gaming applications into the English teaching curriculum for pedagogical purposes.

Another study by Almusharraf (2023) focused on the integration of Kahoot!, a game-based student response system, into English literature courses in EFL online classrooms. The study involved 276 undergraduate learners and found that Kahoot! positively influenced students' learning experiences, boosting enthusiasm, encouraging inquisitiveness, and contributing to identifying knowledge gaps. The study concluded that students have positive attitudes towards a game-based approach in English learning, suggesting that educational competitions in the classroom can reduce interferences and enhance teaching quality beyond traditional classrooms.

Numerous technologies have been created in order to meet the needs of constructing a course as a game. Games are becoming more frequent in learning settings, and in order to meet these requirements, a range of technologies have been. Game-based learning has become more popular in a variety of different contexts, including professional training and social media, in addition to the educational sector. Students will experience increased engagement, motivation, and productivity when they use game-based learning platforms since these platforms use gaming components as a teaching strategy. While game-based learning is more than simply the creation of games for students to play on the surface, it also involves the establishment of learning activities that progressively teach topics and lead users to reach objectives.

Ismaizam et al. (2022) analysed the tools that were used and the disciplines that were carried out by twenty-one researchers on the game-based learning method. With regard to the development of the game-based learning approach, their data indicate that the majority of research have achieved exceptional outcomes. Generally speaking, game-based learning in education finds the ideal balance between the subject matter and gaming, as well as the students' ability to remember and apply the information they have gained in the classroom to real-world situations.

According to the findings of the studies by Muhridza et al., (2018) and Partovi (2019), game-based learning has a good impact on the acquisition and adaption of complicated abilities. It is possible that learning environments that are based on games have the ability to facilitate learning that is applicable outside the context of instructional settings. Making the most of the students' participation in the classroom is thus essential. According to Zakaria et al. (2021), game-based learning also gave students the opportunity to study in a collaborative manner with their classmates, which resulted in increased student engagement in the classroom. Active participation in the conversation was place both before and after the class.

Students are said to experience increased engagement, motivation, and productivity when they use game-based learning platforms since these platforms use gaming components as a teaching strategy. While game-based learning is more than simply the creation of games for students to play on the surface, it also involves the establishment of learning activities that progressively teach topics and lead users to reach objectives. The two aspects of a review by Ismaizam et al. (2022) are the tools that were used and the disciplines that were carried out by twenty-one researchers on the game-based learning method. With regard to the development of the game-based learning approach, their findings indicate that the majority of research have achieved exceptional outcomes. Generally speaking, game-based learning in education finds the ideal balance between the subject matter and gaming, as well as the students' ability to remember and apply the information they have gained in the classroom to real-world situations.

The studies presented above suggest that game-based learning can be a valuable teaching practice in today's rapidly evolving educational landscape. By combining game concepts with technology and updated elements, students can become more competitive, critical thinkers, and interested in learning. Moreover, the use of mobile-assisted language learning (MALL) and gaming applications can be an effective way to improve language learning outcomes. Furthermore, the integration of game-based systems like Kahoot! into English language courses can enhance student engagement and learning experiences. Overall, these studies highlight the potential of game-based learning to enhance student motivation, engagement, and learning outcomes in various educational settings.

Game-Based Learning and Teacher's Challenges

Game-based learning is a promising approach that has the potential to enhance language learning, but it also presents challenges and limitations, particularly to the teachers. The cost of developing or purchasing educational games and simulations may be prohibitive for some schools and teachers, limiting access to valuable resources (Adipat et al., 2021). Furthermore, technological advancements can hinder the implementation of game-based learning, leading to a digital divide and affecting students from different backgrounds.

An investigation into the experiences of educators who had used game-based learning methodologies in the context of project management in higher education was carried out by Jääskä and Aaltonen (2022) as part of their study. Through the use of semi-structured interviews as their technique of data collection, they identified the advantages and obstacles for students of using game-based learning techniques in project management education. The study also aimed to discover the benefits and challenges for teachers of implementing game-based learning methods in project management education. Twenty-two educators who had prior experience managing projects in higher education. Australia, Austria, Canada, China, Denmark, Finland, Iceland, Norway, Sweden, the United Kingdom, and the United States of America were among the nations that produced the sample data. In light of the findings of their research, Jääskä and Aaltonen arrived at the conclusion that the implementation of game-based learning necessitates more effort on the part of teachers in order to prepare the relevant lessons. In the ESL context, teachers are commonly saddled with challenges in the rapidly growing digital world, where students are "native speakers" of the numerous digital gadgets and tools. This has led to increased pressure for teachers to promote a higher level of technology use in the ESL teaching and learning processes (Ghazy et al., 2021).

Adipat et al. (2021) found that a game-based strategy requires a significant amount of information about how to carry it out in the appropriate manner. Because of this, it is necessary for a teacher to have a strong drive in order to adapt game-based learning for activities that take place in a classroom environment. As a consequence of the process of modernization, technology has developed into a suitable instrument that may be used to execute game-based learning. For the purpose of putting this into perspective, the implementation of game-based learning requires not only the inventiveness of teachers but also their positive attitudes toward learning and the use of technology. As a consequence of this, it is essential for educators to have the knowledge and skills required to make use of technology, which is a challenge for them (Varas et al., 2023). In addition, Liu and Gazizova (2020) asserted that in order for teachers to be able to adopt game-based learning, they are required to attend specialised courses that may provide them with the skills necessary to implement game-based learning methods. According to Adipat et al. (2021), one of the challenges that teachers need to surmount in order to effectively implement game-based learning is the policy of administration. In point of fact, there are certain schools that choose not to let teachers utilise games in the lessons.

Game-based learning approaches are deemed to be beneficial by these individuals because they believe in the efficacy of other teaching methods to educate students. Concerns have been raised by the administration over the fact that children are more involved in having fun than they are in studying. There is a potential that studying will result in learning development that is not as effective as it is purported to be. According to Jääskä and Aaltonen (2020), it is not the duty of a teacher to be put at fault if they are not authorized to include game-based learning into a lesson. This is the case despite the fact that there are a number of benefits that game-based learning may bring in a classroom context. Once again, Adipat et al. (2021) articulated that game-based learning is helpful for the goal of ensuring that students participate in the teaching and learning processes. This should be done in order to obtain the desired learning outcomes. Therefore, in refuting Jääskä and Aaltonen's (2020) belief earlier, the onus is on the teachers to make additional efforts for game-based learning to be fun for students. One possible strategy to make the learning fun is by injecting elements of competitiveness where students will be motivated to pursue the lesson due to the excitement of potential winnings (Nusi et al., 2024).

Tirasin (2023) found that although the majority of educators approve of the benefits of game-based teaching materials, they often have problems with the implementation of games in their lessons. Carillo (2019) highlights the significant impact that teacher training and professional development may have in overcoming the deficiency in understanding the appropriate implementation processes. It was discovered that teachers who had training in game-based learning had a higher likelihood of successfully incorporating games into their instructional practices. Thus, it is imperative for ESL teachers to have frequent access to seminars, online courses, or coaching sessions that provide help on the design and implementation of game-based activities. teachers can collaborate with colleagues and peer educators who have experience in implementing game-based learning. Time constraints is another form of obstacle for teachers to implement game-based learning in their lessons (Low et al., 2023). One strategy to overcome this time-related challenge among teachers is by collaborating with colleagues who have had similar experiences. This is because teachers can learn from their experiences and gain insights into effective strategies from one another (Lindland, 2021).

Additionally, game-based instruction requires more facilities than traditional methods, which can be a drawback (Adipat et al., 2021). Another challenge associated with the implementation of technological-based games for learning is poor access to the digital resources. Such limitations cause great difficulties for teachers to incorporate digital games into their classroom setting (Yang et al., 2018). In order to facilitate the adoption of game-based learning in the classroom, it is recommended that the Ministry of Education, together with the Ministry of Information and Communications Technology, improve the internet access in all the schools.

Implementing game-based learning in project management education is a complex process that requires educators to overcome various challenges, including investing time and effort to develop game concepts and gather materials, possessing knowledge and skills to use technology effectively, and navigating school administration policies that may not allow games in the classroom. Despite the numerous challenges, there are possible measures that can be adopted to ensure a smooth implementation of game-based learning in an ESL classroom as discussed above. Educators must consider incorporating games into their language lessons to enhance student engagement and motivation (Wang and Tahir, 2020). As Abdullaev (2021) suggests, a positive attitude towards teaching strategies like games can influence students' acceptance of the lesson, leading to a more favourable learning environment and a more appreciative attitude among students.

METHODOLOGY OF THE STUDY

Research Design

This study adopted a mixed-methods research design. According to Clark et al. (2020), action research is a study where a teacher-researcher identifies a problem in a classroom and collects relevant data to facilitate better teaching practice. The combination of quantitative and qualitative research design can promote a comprehensive understanding of the research from various perspectives (Noyes et al., 2019). According to Montoya and Lugo-Ocando (2020), a mixed method design is any research methodology that combines qualitative and quantitative methods in order to reveal the truth. A definition of mixed method research was provided by Plano-Clark and Ivankova (2016), who said that it is "the intentional integration of quantitative and qualitative research approaches to better address a research problem" (p. 57). Increasing the validity of the study that was carried out is accomplished by combining the two different designs. As an additional benefit, it provides a comprehensive understanding of the phenomenon that was investigated (Creswell & Clark, 2018).

Sampling

There were two groups of respondents in this study. The first group comprised thirty participants aged 16 years old who were upper secondary students at a public school in Malaysia. The second group comprised two English Language teachers. Both of the selected teachers who were qualified academicians had more than ten years of teaching experience. One was an upper secondary teacher while another was from a lower secondary school. Both groups of respondents were chosen based on a convenience sampling method as they resided at the school where one of our research team members had her teaching practicum.

Research Instruments

To answer the first research question, a survey questionnaire was distributed to the students via Google Form for data collection purposes. The respondents were chosen based on a convenience sampling method since the researcher had the access to them. Five parameters were provided for each question in the survey questionnaire which were "Strongly Agree", "Agree", "Moderately Agree", "Disagree" and "Strongly Disagree". The survey questionnaire was adapted from Liu and Gazizova (2020) who studied the concept of game-based learning in education. Data from the two English teachers who were chosen from the same public school were collected via interview sessions. The semi-structured interviews were conducted using a set of predetermined questions which was adapted from Samarasinghe et al., (2023).

Ethical Considerations

Prior to collecting data, a consent form was distributed to all the respondents, both students and teachers, to inform them that their anonymity and confidentiality were guaranteed. They were also allowed to voluntarily withdraw from the study without any implications on them.

Data Collection Procedures

Administration of Survey Questionnaire

The survey was carried out by use of an online platform known as Google Forms. In the event that they had a device that was linked to the Internet, students were able to respond to the survey questions from any location. In the beginning, one of us who was also a practising teacher collected volunteers in a WhatsApp group before sending out instructions to complete the survey. Before students gave their responses to the survey, they were given the opportunity to ask any questions they had about the methods for data collecting that they did not fully comprehend about. After students had clicked on the link to the survey, they were required to successfully log in to their respective email accounts. Following the completion of the registration process, students were prompted to fill out their demographic information, which included their age and gender, before moving on to the survey questions. Ten minutes were allotted for each student so that they may respond to all of the questions without pressure or coercion.

Interview Sessions

All of the interviews were conducted in person during school hours. Different interviews were performed by the researcher, who was also a practicum teacher, taking into account the availability of the respondents. Interview questions were sent to respondents one hour before the beginning of the sessions in order to provide them with sufficient time to prepare their responses. It was possible for respondents to arrange a collection of detailed replies if they did so. A wide-angle video recorder was placed in the rear corner of their office area for each and every interview. This recorder was used to capture the environment in which the interview was taking place. In order to ensure that the whole session was captured on camera, the video recorder was activated. The duration of the first interview session was around eleven minutes, while the duration of the second interview session was approximately six minutes. Interview questions were given to respondents an hour before starting the sessions. For every interview, a video recorder was placed in the back corner of their office room with a wide-angle view to capture the setting. Videos for interview sessions were transcribed to highlight information from teachers' perspectives. Responses that were given by both teachers were analysed to organize findings and initiate discussions.

FINDINGS OF THE STUDY

As stated by Borah (2021), a teacher who is able to effectively conduct an entertaining class has the ability to stimulate pupils' drive to study. The findings of the research shown in Table 1 below indicate that the majority of students consider game-based learning to be an engaging form of instruction. It is important to note that students would have attended English as a Second Language classes if they had been aware that game-based learning were being used.

Table 1. Students' responses to the questionnaire survey

Components	Insights of Students' Behavior (Percentage %)				
	Strongly Agree	**Agree**	**Moderately Agree**	**Disagree**	**Strongly Disagree**
Q1. I am interested in learning the English language if my teacher uses game concepts in a lesson.	76.67	20.00	0.00	3.33	0.00
Q2. I am interested in learning the English language in the next class if I know my teacher will use game concepts in the lesson.	76.67	16.67	0.00	3.33	3.33
Q3. I am punctual to English classrooms because I am interested in game-based learning.	63.33	23.33	6.67	3.33	3.33
Q4. I am interested in completing all tasks given in the English classroom if I know my teacher will give me a reward after class.	46.67	43.33	3.33	6.67	0.00
Q5. I am committed to group work during English class to gain rewards from my teacher.	56.67	16.67	16.67	6.67	3.33

It is clear that game-based learning addresses one of the motivating aspects of learning, which is the interest that is involved in the process. The findings of this research are corroborated by a prior study conducted by Ersoz (2020), which was mentioned in Yudha and Mandasari (2021). This study found that lessons that include game learning would produce students' desire (motivation) to do well in learning since game ideas are entertaining and intriguing. Through the incorporation of educational game elements into English courses, students are intuitively motivated to acquire English language skills without feeling any pressure (ibid). All questions from the questionnaire survey were designed to observe students' behaviors in ESL classrooms. Indeed, Ajmal et al., (2021) mentioned that motivation can influence people's behavior toward learning. Students with high motivation will behave positively in a classroom. Q1, Q2, and Q3 from Table 1 show that students are interested in attending English classes that apply game-based learning. Q4 and Q5 show that the majority of students would behave positively in ESL classrooms such as finishing tasks on time and committed to group work when they are competing to achieve something. The sense of competency, autonomy, interest, and relatedness are indeed the dimensions of students' motivation (Borah, 2021).

Table 2 below presents the transcriptions of the interview sessions mainly on the challenges that teachers faced when applying game-based learning in a classroom. The challenges are mainly regarding teachers' efforts to encourage students to use the English language in game-based lessons. In understanding any game rules, teachers need to give more attention to students with low English proficiency.

Table 2. Teachers' responses on the semi-structured interview questions

Question	Response
Q1.Have you encountered any challenges or concerns when applying game-based learning in ESL classes?	"*...sometimes, not all games can be interesting or engaging to students. Plus, language can also be a hindrance to those with low proficient skills.*" - Teacher 1
	"*Challenges, yes. To motivate them using the English language during the game is difficult especially when they are having discussions...*" - Teacher 2
Q2. What recommendations do you have for other ESL teachers interested in applying game-based learning?	"*...always experiment. Find out the best educational games that are mostly appealing to students.*" - Teacher 1
	"*...keep on going from group to group and encourage them to use the language. Make sure that they are following the rules given...*" - Teacher 2

Both educators recruited as respondents in this interview concurred that game-based learning yields advantages in terms of student motivation. However, if a teacher neglects to supervise their language use, students have a tendency to resort to their native tongue, such as engaging in discussions with friends in the Malay language. Therefore, language acts as an obstacle that hinders the progress of students' English language development during game-based learning activities, particularly for those who have low proficiency levels. Purba and Katemba (2022) conducted a research in which a teacher described a classroom scenario including the usage of game-based learning. In this scenario, students were more focused on participating in the game activities rather than adhering to the prescribed norms for using the English language. Therefore, including a second language (L2) into a first language (L1) classroom without careful teacher preparation to accommodate the level of difficulty may hinder students from attaining the desired learning outcomes.

Another aspect to investigate is the difficulties encountered by instructors in implementing game-based learning in ESL classrooms, particularly in terms of classroom management. During the interview sessions, both instructors emphasised the need of carefully implementing game-based learning by selecting appropriate games and establishing clear rules. However, a teacher who wishes to include game-based learning into a lesson must take a more rigorous approach to classroom management. This involves designing engaging and appropriate courses, providing clear explanations of complicated game rules, and closely monitoring each student to ensure they follow all provided directions. Game-based learning is not only labor-intensive, but it also requires the instructor to diligently oversee every component of the learning process (Smith, 2022). In addition, Camilleri (2023) said that while implementing game-based learning in a classroom, it is important for the management to prioritise the distribution of time, facilities, and resources.

Irkinovich (2022) asserts that game ideas are compelling in English courses due to their ability to foster a sense of connectedness among students. For instance, activities and games like role play captivate students due to their utilisation of real-life scenarios that students can easily connect with (ibid.). According to Borah (2021), relatedness is a component of motivation. Furthermore, engaging in gaming activities might contribute to the attainment of higher educational credentials, since game ideas often include diverse cultural viewpoints (Borowiecki & Bakshi, 2017, as referenced in Pellas et al., 2019). Therefore, game-based learning may enhance students' existing understanding of cultural issues. In addition, students are well-acquainted with the utilisation of digital gadgets in the present era of modernization. Mobile phones, tablets, and PCs are often used in game-based learning as technological gadgets. Students may engage in gaming activities via the usage of electronic gadgets due to their familiarity with technological advancements. Therefore, students' motivation is elevated when a teacher incorporates known gaming aspects and tools into the classroom.

IMPLICATIONS OF STUDY

According to the quantitative findings, game-based learning is a teaching method that has the potential to generate student motivation in a classroom. Liu and Gazizova (2020) mentioned that educational games include teachers assigning catchy names for group work, adapting movies or gaming concepts, playing familiar roles as well as creating a competitive environment that aligns with the dimension of motivations. From this knowledge, a teacher-researcher may consider adapting game-based concepts in English lessons to create motivational classroom settings especially when they have the ability to use technology. Nowadays, technology has become the tool for teachers to execute game-based approaches besides being creative (ibid.).

Based on the qualitative findings, there are challenges in applying game-based learning in ESL classrooms. The challenges of language difficulties require teachers to put extra effort into choosing educational games that are friendly to all levels of students' proficiency. Indeed, a game-based approach requires a lot of teachers' willingness to execute it effectively (Adipat et al., 2021). In addition, Liu and Gazizova (2020) stated that a teacher needs to attend special courses that can equip them with the ability to execute game-based learning. A teacher should always facilitate better teaching practice despite many difficulties. Indeed, students have the utmost right to receive a quality level of education in schools. According to Abdullaev (2021), if a teacher has a positive attitude towards executing a lesson, students' positive behavior can be easily shaped in a classroom.

CONCLUSION

In conclusion, the research findings provide an in-depth understanding of the use of game-based learning in ESL classrooms. By associating educational game concepts with English lessons, students are unconsciously driven to learn English without pressure. In fact, applying game-based learning can lessen students' fear of learning English through fun and interactive lesson settings. The insights from this research are obtained from a small sampling. Thus, the result of the study might only be representative of those groups of students and therefore could not be extended to another classroom. The recommendation for further study is to expand the data size to strengthen data validity. Additionally, the acquired sample data was accessed through an online platform where the researcher could not verbally explain the aim of the overall research. It is also recommended for future studies to conduct research in a physical setting to closely monitor the procedure of data collection.

REFERENCES

Abdullaev, Z. K. (2021). Second Language Learning. *Mental Enlightenment Scientific-Methodological Journal*, 2021(06), 1–11.

Adipat, S., Laksana, K., Busayanon, K., Asawasowan, A., & Adipat, B. (2021). Engaging Students in the Learning Process with Game-Based Learning: The Fundamental Concepts. *International Journal of Technology in Education*, 4(3), 542–552. DOI: 10.46328/ijte.169

Adnan, N. H., Norman, H., & Nordin, N. M. (2020). Instructor-generated hand-drawn 2D animations for ESL vocabulary learning in secondary education. *The Asian ESP Journal, 16*(1.2), 67-81. https://www.elejournals.com/asian-esp-journal/aesp-february-2020-16-1-2/

Ahmad, C. V. (2021). Causes of students' reluctance to participate in classroom discussions. ASEAN Journal of Science and Engineering Education, 1(1), 47-62. https://ejournal.upi.edu/index.php/AJSEE/

Ahmed, A. A. A., Ampry, E. S., Komariah, A., Hassan, I., Thahir, I., Hussein Ali, M., Fawzi Faisal, A., & Zafarani, P. (2022). Investigating the effect of using game-based learning on EFL learners' motivation and anxiety. *Education Research International*, 2022, 1–9. DOI: 10.1155/2022/6503139

Akther, F. (2022). English for personal and career development and its importance for better employment opportunities. *Journal of Languages. Linguistics and Literary Studies*, 2(3), 95–100.

Ali, H. H. H. (2022). The importance of the four English language skills: Reading, writing, speaking, and listening in teaching Iraqi learners. *Humanitarian and Natural Sciences Journal*, 3(2), 155–165. DOI: 10.53796/hnsj3210

Anak Yunus, C. C., & Hua, T. K. (2021). Exploring a gamified learning tool in the ESL classroom: The case of Quizizz. *Journal of Education and e-learning Research*, 8(1), 103–108. DOI: 10.20448/journal.509.2021.81.103.108

Aziz, A. A., & Kashinathan, S. (2021). ESL learners' challenges in speaking English in Malaysian classroom. *Development*, 10(2), 983–991. DOI: 10.6007/IJARPED/v10-i2/10355

Barbosa, M. W., de Avila, ´., & Rodrigues, C. (2020). Project portfolio management teaching: Contributions of a gamified approach. *International Journal of Management Education*, 18(2), 100388. DOI: 10.1016/j.ijme.2020.100388

Boghian, I., Cojocariu, V.-M., Popescu, C. V., & Mat , L. (2019). Game-based learning. Using board games in adult education. *J. Educat. Sci. Psychol.*, 9, 51–57.

Breien, F. S., & Wasson, B. (2021). Narrative categorization in digital game-based learning: Engagement, motivation & learning. *British Journal of Educational Technology*, 52(1), 91–111. DOI: 10.1111/bjet.13004

Byusa, E., Kampire, E., & Mwesigye, A. R. (2022). Game-based learning approach on students' motivation and understanding of chemistry concepts: A systematic review of literature. *Heliyon*, 8(5), 1–10. DOI: 10.1016/j.heliyon.2022.e09541 PMID: 35663764

Camilleri, V. (2023, October). *Designing GBL for Higher Education: Pitfalls & Recommendations*, In European Conference on Games Based Learning, *17*(1), 869-875. https://papers.academic-conferences.org/index.php/ecgbl/article/view/1900

Carrillo, E. (2019). *Digital game-based learning: An analysis of teacher preparation* (Doctoral dissertation, University of West Georgia). https://www.proquest.com/docview/2234237055?pq-origsite=gscholar&fromopenview=true&sourcetype=Dissertations%20&%20Theses

Catacutan, A. B., Malbas, M. H., Valiente, M. P. M., Moneva, J. C., & Mauring, L. (2022). Social disconnectedness and anxiety. *Asian Education, 2022*, 3-3. https://www.lynnp.org

Clark, J. S., Porath, S., Thiele, J., & Jobe, M. (2020).. . *Action Research.*

Creswell, J. W., & Plano Clark, V. L. (2018). *Designing and Conducting Mixed Methods Research* (3rd ed.). Sage Publications.

Dabbous, M., Kawtharani, A., Fahs, I., Hallal, Z., Shouman, D., Akel, M., Rahal, M., & Sakr, F. (2022). The role of game-based learning in experiential education: Tool validation, motivation assessment, and outcomes evaluation among a sample of pharmacy students. *Education Sciences*, 12(7), 434. DOI: 10.3390/educsci12070434

Elshareif, E., & Mohamed, E. (2021). The effects of e-learning on students' motivation to learn in higher education. *Online Learning : the Official Journal of the Online Learning Consortium*, 25(3), 128–143. DOI: 10.24059/olj.v25i3.2336

Framework of Educational Innovation. *Comunicar: Media Education Research Journal, 28*(65), 9-20. DOI: 10.3916/C65-2020-01

Galloway, N., & Rose, H. (2021). English medium instruction and the English language practitioner. *ELT Journal*, 75(1), 33–41. DOI: 10.1093/elt/ccaa063

Ghazy, A., & Wajdi, M. Ikhsanudin, & Sada, C. (2021). The use of game-based learning in English class. *Journal of Applied Studies in Language, 5*(1), 67—78. https://ojs.pnb.ac.id/index.php/JASL

Guay, F. (2022). Applying self-determination theory to education: Regulations types, psychological needs, and autonomy supporting behaviors. *Canadian Journal of School Psychology, 37*(1), 75-92. s://DOI: 10.1177/08295735211055355

Hamari, J., Shernoff, D. J., Rowe, E., Coller, B., Asbell-Clarke, J., & Edwards, T. (2016). Challenging games help students learn: An empirical study on engagement, flow and immersion in game-based learning. *Computers in Human Behavior*, 54, 170–179. DOI: 10.1016/j.chb.2015.07.045

Hartt, M., Hosseini, H., & Mostafapour, M. (2020). Game on: Exploring the effectiveness of game-based learning. *Planning Practice and Research*, 35(5), 589–604. DOI: 10.1080/02697459.2020.1778859

Hussain, M. S., Salam, A., & Farid, A. (2020). Students' motivation in English language learning (ELL): An exploratory study of motivation-al factors for EFL and ESL adult learners. *International Journal of Applied Linguistics and English Literature*, 9(4), 15–28. DOI: 10.7575/aiac.ijalel.v.9n.4p.15

Irkinovich, N. R. (2022). The importance of role-playing game in teaching English in a non-linguistic university. *International Journal of Pedagogics*, 2(09), 29–32. https://theusajournals.com/index.php/ijp/article/view/376

Ismaizam, N. M., Rahman, S. F. A., Ahmad, S. N. S. M., Nazri, N. I. I. M., Idris, N. A. A., & Ali, N.

Ismaizam, N. M., Rahman, S. F. A., Ahmad, S. N. S. M., Nazri, N. I. I. M., Idris, N. A. A., Ali, N. A., & Aldaba, A. M. A. (2022). An integration of game-based learning in a classroom: An overview (2016-2021). *International Journal of Academic Research in Progressive Education and Development*, 11(1).

Jääskä, E., & Aaltonen, K. (2022). Teachers' experiences of using game-based learning methods in project management higher education. *Project Leadership and Society, 3*, 100041. https://www.sciencedirect.com/science/article/pii/S2666721522000011

Jääskä, E., Aaltonen, K., & Kujala, J. (2021). Game-based learning in project sustainability management education. *Sustainability (Basel)*, 13(15), 8204. DOI: 10.3390/su13158204

Jaccard, D., Bonnier, K.E., & Hellstrom, M. (2022). How might serious games trigger a

Järvelä, S., & Renninger, K. A. (2014). Designing for learning: interest, motivation, and engagement. In Sawyer, R. K. (Ed.), *The Cambridge Handbook of the Learning Sciences, Cambridge Handbooks in Psychology* (pp. 668–685). Cambridge University Press., DOI: 10.1017/CBO9781139519526.040

Kolb, A. Y., & Kolb, D. A. (2005). Learning styles and learning spaces: Enhancing experiential learning in higher education. *Academy of Management Learning & Education*, 4(2), 193–212. DOI: 10.5465/amle.2005.17268566

Leitão, R., Maguire, M., Turner, S., & Guimarães, L. (2022). A systematic evaluation of game elements effects on students' motivation. *Education and Information Technologies*, 27(1), 1–23. DOI: 10.1007/s10639-021-10651-8

Lester, D., Skulmoski, G. J., Fisher, D. P., Mehrotra, V., Lim, I., Lang, A., & Keogh, J. W. (2023). Drivers and barriers to the utilisation of gamification and game-based learning in universities: A systematic review of educators' perspectives. *British Journal of Educational Technology*, 54(6), 1748–1770. DOI: 10.1111/bjet.13311

Lindland, K. (2021). *Gaming as a Tool in English Language Teaching What is Game-based Learning, and how do teachers experience digital games as an educational tool?* (Master's thesis, University of South-Eastern Norway).

Liu, Z. Y., Shaikh, Z., & Gazizova, F. (2020). Using the concept of game-based learning in education. [iJET]. *International Journal of Emerging Technologies in Learning*, 15(14), 53–64. DOI: 10.3991/ijet.v15i14.14675

Lomas, J. D., Koedinger, K., Patel, N., Shodhan, S., Poonwala, N., & Forlizzi, J. L. (2017). Is difficulty overrated? The effects of choice, novelty and suspense on intrinsic motivation in educational games. In: *Proceedings of the 2017 CHI Conference on Human Factors in Computing Systems,* CHI '17. Association for Computing Machinery, New York, NY, USA, pp. 1028–1039. DOI: 10.1145/3025453.3025638

Low, J. Y., Balakrishnan, B., & Yaacob, M. I. H. (2023). Game-Based Learning: Current Practices and Perceptions of Secondary School Physics Teachers in Malaysia. *The international journal of science, mathematics and technology learning, 31*(1), 1-21. DOI: 10.18848/2327-7971/CGP/v31i01/1-21

Mohamadbahuldin, U. Q. (2022). Challenge of Way of Teaching. *Journal of Arts, Literature, Humanities, and Social Sciences*, 80, 144–165. DOI: 10.33193/JALHSS.80.2022.687

Muhridza, N. H., Rosli, N. A., Sirri, A., & Abdul Samad, A. (2018). Using Game-based Technology, kahoot! for Classroom Engagement. *LSP International Journal*, 5(2). Advance online publication. DOI: 10.11113/lspi.v5n2.77

Mukaromah, D., Mutoharoh, A., Pramudwiatmoko, A., Tsutoh, S., Gutmann, G., Konagaya, A., & Cahyono, T. D. (2019). Digital quiz as media to review material for English education students. *Script Journal: Journal of Linguistic and English Teaching*, 4(2), 88–100. DOI: 10.24903/sj.v4i2.319

Munisa, I., & Mohinur, S. (2024). Teaching English To Elementary School Students Through Different Games. *Western European Journal of Linguistics and Education*, 2(5), 4–8. https://westerneuropeanstudies.com/index.php/2

Naul, E., & Liu, M. (2020). Why story matters: a review of narrative in serious games.

Naul, E., & Liu, M. (2020, June). Why Story Matters: A Review of Narrative in Serious Games. *Journal of Educational Computing Research*, 58(3), 687–707. DOI: 10.1177/0735633119859904

Noyes, J., Booth, A., Moore, G., Flemming, K., Tunçalp, Ö., & Shakibazadeh, E. (2019). Synthesising quantitative and qualitative evidence to inform guidelines on complex interventions: clarifying the purposes, designs and outlining some methods. *BMJ global health, 4*(Suppl 1).

Nusi, A., Dewirahmadanirwati, D., Novia, N., & Ardi, H. (2024). Factors and Challenges in Using Gamification In Teaching ESP. *Jurnal Ilmiah Pendidikan Scholastic, 8*(1), 15-25. https://e-journal.sastra-unes.com/index.php/JIPS

Partovi, T., & Razavi, M. R. (2019). The effect of game-based learning on academic achievement motivation of elementary school students. *Learning and Motivation*, 68, 101592. DOI: 10.1016/j.lmot.2019.101592

Pellas, N., Fotaris, P., Kazanidis, I., & Wells, D. (2019). Augmenting the learning experience in primary and secondary school education: A systematic review of recent trends in augmented reality game-based learning. *Virtual Reality (Waltham Cross)*, 23(4), 329–346. https://surl.li/qxcdw. DOI: 10.1007/s10055-018-0347-2

Plano-Clark, V., & Ivankova, N. (2016). What is mixed methods research?: considering how mixed methods research is defined. In Plano-Clark, V., & Ivankova, N. (Eds.), *Mixed methods research: A guide to the field* (pp. 55–78). Sage., DOI: 10.4135/9781483398341.n6

Pnevmatikos, D., Christodoulou, P., Georgiadou, T., & Lithoxoidou, A. (2023). Undergraduate students' conceptualization of critical thinking and their ideas for critical thinking acquisition. *Education Sciences*, 13(4), 416. DOI: 10.3390/educsci13040416

Purba, F. A., & Katemba, C. V. (2022). English Teachers Perception of Using Game-Based Learning (GBL) to Enhance Students' Vocabulary. *8ISC Proceedings: Arts and Education*, 35-46.

Ramírez-Montoya, M.S., & Lugo-Ocando, J. (2020). Systematic Review of Mixed Methods in the

Ryan, R. M., & Deci, E. L. (2000). Self-determination Theory and the Facilitation of Intrinsic Motivation, Social Development, and Well-Being. *The American Psychologist*, 55(1), 68–78. DOI: 10.1037/0003-066X.55.1.68 PMID: 11392867

Samarasinghe, R., Hettiarachchi, T., & Adihetti, I. (2023). Examining Teacher Perspectives on the Use of Gamification Within Classrooms to Enhance Student Engagement. *Journal of Physical Education and Sport*, 121(2), 482–491. DOI: 10.7752/jpes.2023.02060

Silvola, A., Näykki, P., Kaveri, A., & Muukkonen, H. (2021). Expectations for supporting student engagement with learning analytics: An academic path perspective. *Computers & Education*, 168, 104192. DOI: 10.1016/j.compedu.2021.104192

Smith, C. (2022). *Understanding Middle School Teachers' Use of Instructional Practices for Online Reading Comprehension* (Doctoral dissertation, Walden University).

Thomas, A., & Gupta, V. (2022). The role of motivation theories in knowledge sharing: An integrative theoretical reviews and future research agenda. *Kybernetes*, 51(1), 116–140. DOI: 10.1108/K-07-2020-0465

Tıraşın, K. D. (2023). *Games Teachers Play: An investigation of upper secondary EFL teachers' practices, beliefs, and attitudes regarding digital game-based language learning in Norway* (Master's thesis, University of Stavanger, Norway).

transformation in project management education? Lessons learned from 10 Years of

Uddiniyah, N. D., & Silfia, E. (2020). An analysis of students' motivation in learning English at SMAN 8 Kota Jambi academic year 2018/2019. JELT. *Journal of English Language Teaching*, 3(2), 139–149.

Varas, D., Santana, M., Nussbaum, M., Claro, S., & Imbarack, P. (2023). Teachers' strategies and challenges in teaching 21st century skills: Little common understanding. *Thinking Skills and Creativity*, 48, 101289. DOI: 10.1016/j.tsc.2023.101289

Velaora, C., Dimos, I., Tsagiopoulou, S., & Kakarountas, A. (2022). A game-based learning approach in digital design course to enhance students' competency. *Information (Basel)*, 13(4), 177. DOI: 10.3390/info13040177

Wang, A. I., & Tahir, R. (2020). The effect of using Kahoot! For learning – a literature review. *Computers & Education*, 149, 103818. DOI: 10.1016/j.compedu.2020.103818

Wooldridge, J. (2022). Teaching Pragmatic Suprasegmentals in the Adult ESL Classroom. *School of Education and Leadership Student Capstone Projects,* 776. https://digitalcommons.hamline.edu/hse_cp/776

Yaccob, N. S., Rahman, S. F. A., Mohamad, S. N. A., Rahim, A. A. A., Rashid, K. K. A., Aldaba, A. M. A., Yunus, M. M., & Hashim, H. (2022). Gamifying ESL Classrooms through Gamified Teaching and Learning. *Arab World English Journal (AWEJ). Special Issue on CALL*, 8, 177–191. DOI: 10.24093/awej/call8.12

Yaccob, N. S., & Yunus, M. M. (2019). Language Games in Teaching and Learning English Grammar: A Literature Review. *Arab World English Journal*, 10(1), 209–217. DOI: 10.24093/awej/vol10no1.18

Yang, J.-C., Lin, M., & Chen, S. (2018). Effects of anxiety levels on learning performance and gaming performance in digital game-based learning. *Journal of Computer Assisted Learning*, 34(3), 324–334. DOI: 10.1111/jcal.12245

Yang, J. C., Quadir, B., & Chen, N. S. (2016). Effects of the badge mechanism on self-efficacy and learning performance in a game-based English learning environment. *Journal of Educational Computing Research*, 54(3), 371–394. DOI: 10.1177/0735633115620433

Yu, Z., Gao, M., & Wang, L. (2021). The effect of educational games on learning outcomes, student motivation, engagement and satisfaction. *Journal of Educational Computing Research*, 59(3), 522–546. DOI: 10.1177/0735633120969214

Yudha, H. T., & Mandasari, B. (2021). The analysis of game usage for senior high school students to improve their vocabulary mastery. *Journal of English Language Teaching and Learning*, 2(2), 74–79. http://jim.teknokrat.ac.id/index.php/english-language-teaching/article/view/1329. DOI: 10.33365/jeltl.v2i2.1329

Yuzulia, I. (2021). A study on students' motivation towards learning English language. *Eltin Journal: Journal of English Language Teaching in Indonesia*, 9(1), 10–17.

Zakaria, N. Y. K., Yunus, M., Hashim, H., Nordin, M. N., Norman, H., & Adnan, N. H. (2021b). Pre-Service Teachers' Views on the Implementation of Game-Based Learning for Academic Writing Skills. *Sains Insani*, 6(1), 11–16. DOI: 10.33102/sainsinsani.vol6no1.226

Chapter 6
Forming the Depth–Annex–Motion–Placement (DAMP) Conceptual Model for Gamified Learning

Darren Lim Yie
https://orcid.org/0000-0002-3708-4784
University of Science Malaysia, Malaysia

Mageswaran Sanmugam
https://orcid.org/0000-0003-3313-4462
Universiti Sains Malysia, Malaysia

Wan Ahmad Jaafar Wan Yahaya
https://orcid.org/0000-0002-8605-0062
Universiti Sains Malaysia, Malaysia

Syahrini Shawalludin
https://orcid.org/0000-0001-9087-3566
Universiti Sains Malaysia, Malaysia

Jingru Zhang
https://orcid.org/0009-0002-6537-2334
Universiti Sains Malaysia, Malaysia

ABSTRACT

Gamification is known as the use of game-like elements within a non-game context.

DOI: 10.4018/979-8-3693-6745-2.ch006

The use of gamification in a classroom setting, also known as gamified learning aims to improve the learning process by constructing a low-risk and well-structured learning environment for students. The use of gamification in the educational context has proven to be able to increase motivation, engagement, retention of knowledge and performance. In this paper, the authors inquired into previous relevant research and wish to contribute to the field by proposing the DAMP model which dealt with the depth (shallow, deep and total), annex (plugged or unplugged, online or offline), motion (static and dynamic), and placement (intra and extra) of gamification with the consideration of 8Ts namely task, target, technology, time, technique, tariff, tensity and terrain. The proposed model hopes to serve as a guideline and provide new insights for future educators and instructional designers when constructing a gamified learning classroom.

INTRODUCTION

Gamification is the use of game elements which is a collection of tools to create a sense of a game in a non-game context (Deterding et al., 2011). In modern days, the development of the gamification concept can be discerned by the research in video game-based learning and the "serious games" movement (Khaitova, 2021). It is one of the most well-known contemporary technologies which is based on an abundance of educational theories that help to provide a stimulation-based educational system (Al-Hafdi & Alhalafawy, 2024). In essence, games have a very strong ability to motivate individuals. They do this by using a variety of strategies, frequently for no payoff, but only for the enjoyment of playing and the chance to win (Dicheva et al., 2015). Whether we play them for entertainment, relaxation, or to satisfy our competitive spirit, games are an integral part of our daily life. Nowadays, there is a growing trend of applying game principles outside of the traditional playing environment (Cavus et al., 2023). As mentioned, the enjoyment of players is essential for the success of any gamification effort (Cunico et al., 2022). Along with the integration of gamification, mundane and dull tasks can be transformed into fun and enjoyable activities.

In the context of the educational field, the success of students' learning is generally dependent on the extent of how motivated and how involved they are in the learning process which presumably originates from the need for greater independence, time management, self-regulation and intrinsic motivation (Dicheva & Dichev, 2016). Gameful learning which offers new opportunities to develop skills and advance knowledge is seemingly to be ideal and has drawn more interest from the education sector, as well as from academia and industry (Putz et al., 2020). Within the past two decades, research on gamified learning has stretched to different learning environments (e.g. e-learning, m-leaning etc.) that seek to understand the effect on learners of all ages from early childhood education to professional education (Zeybek & Saygı, 2024). Its use can even be integrated into cutting-edge technology like Virtual Reality, which its application may contribute to the realisation of the digital transformation of education, satisfy contemporary needs in education, enhance the instructional process, and embellish learning outcomes (Lampropoulos & Kinshuk, 2024). Anyhow, gamified learning must fulfil several criteria which include i) to utilize components of game design and game thinking, ii) providing various options, iii) allowing low-risky engagement, iv) constructing a well-structured (regardless of formal or informal) learning environment (Osheim, 2013).

Anyhow, despite the ethical concerns discussed by O'Sullivan et al., (2021) which include manipulation towards users, exploiting users through game elements, causing users to be addicted, causing users to be overly competitive, cheating, or acting in an undesired manner, and also user's privacy etc. Previous research has found that gamified learning has been applied successfully to achieve goals in information acquisition, skill development, affective and perceptual goals, behavioral change, cognitive and physiological results, communicative prowess, inventiveness, and adaptability (Rita, Wong Mee Mee; Lim, Seong Pek; Wong, Yee Von; Khatipah Abd, Ghani; Tengku Shahrom Tengku, Shahdan; Md Rosli, Ismail; Yugeshineey, 2021). Furthermore, educational gamification enhances learning by fostering interest and curiosity by employing emotional neuroscience and neuroplasticity (the brain's capacity for change) (Serice, 2023). Also, studies have found that gamification could allow learners to focus for a longer period of time, spark creativity, and prompt them to adjust to challenging conditions which eventually leads to the obtainment of problem-solving skills (Aibar-Almazán et al., 2024).

As much as gamification benefits the educational sector, at times it might cause indifference, demotivation and loss of performance and more (O'Sullivan et al., 2021). This is due to the fact that gamified depth, annex, motion, and placement are not contemplated, and as a matter of fact, its discussion are still rare. Although researchers believe that certain approaches to gamification are more powerful than others, the authors of this study believe that the inclusivity of various contexts of learning should be taken into consideration. Thus, in this chapter, the authors further discuss the conditions prior to the gamification of one's teaching and learning environment and propose the DAMP model which hopes to provide insight for fellow instructional designers and educators.

LITERATURE REVIEW

Gamified Depth

Gamified depth is mainly appertained to the level of transforming the teaching and learning (T&L) core processes. Shallow gamification is the addition of a layer over the basic procedures without altering their fundamental nature. On the other hand, deep gamification is the introduction of game features that alter the primary procedures of the activity (Gurjanow et al., 2019). Deep gamification aims to develop gamified educational systems that, when compared to conventional educational software and conventionally gamified systems (shallow gamification), provide larger learning benefits and are favoured by more users (Boyce & A, 2014). In the recent study by Gil-Aciron, (2024), the author discusses several interchangeable terms to describe the depth of gamification, in which shallow gamification can be replaced with structural or extrinsic gamification; while deep gamification could also be known as content gamification or intrinsic gamification. The continuum between the combination of both shallow and deep gamification is referred to as total gamification.

However, the depth of gamification is interchangeable. By incorporating learning objectives with game objectives, a no-lose condition with success levels, competitive aspects, and social user-generated material, shallow gamification can be expanded to deep gamification (Mozelius, 2021). Hicks et al., (2011) discuss the principles of deep gamification listed by Boyce namely: i) the specific alignment of learning objective to the fundamental play mechanic, ii) the compromise of the system's convenience when in conflict with the learning objectives, iii) reward systems must be closely tied to academic goals, iv) limiting innovation that allow sub-optimal behavior while promoting ideal behavior, and lastly, v) both structured and unstructured elements must exist in the system.

To have a better grasp of the concept, the distinction between the different depths of gamification is summarized in Table. 1 below.

Table 1. Gamified Depth Characteristics

Items	Shallow Gamification	Total Gamification	Deep Gamification
Engagement (Söbke, 2019)	Short-lasting	Long-lasting	Long-lasting
Motivation types (Mozelius, 2021)	Extrinsic	Extrinsic and Intrinsic	Intrinsic
Motivation impact (Mozelius, 2021)	Small	Large	Large

continued on following page

Table 1. Continued

Items	Shallow Gamification	Total Gamification	Deep Gamification
Gamification approaches (Fuchs, 2015), (W. Huang et al., 2023)	Gamify learning structure	Gamify both technological and human resources	Gamify learning content
Changing of T&L Essence (Gurjanow et al., 2019)	Thin layer	Combination of both	Core-process
Difficulty to implement (P. A. Santos, 2015)	Easy	Very difficult	Difficult
Game elements implemented (Gurjanow et al., 2019)	Points, Badges, Leaderboard	Combination of both	More meaningful mechanisms
Skill requirements (P. A. Santos, 2015)	Programming and visual design skills	Combination of both	Game design skills

Gamified Annex

The gamified annex in this study refers to the connection of the network and the involvement of technology when gamifying an activity, event or content. Although recent gamification platforms such as *Kahoot!, Class Dojo, Classcraft* etc. are commonly used by educators in an online setting due to the applications' feature to connect with others. It is important to note that gamification can be cultivated not only in an online setting but in offline conditions as well. In order to maintain the originality of acquiring the elements through this offline gamification method, a gamified offline element that is converted into an online element needs to both preserve its value and be prompted to be given online features (Sanmugam, 2021). On the other hand, plugged gamification is defined as activities created in virtual settings or with some technological assistance using the game's techniques, components, and strategies. On the contrary, unplugged gamification can be referred to as the use of the game's mechanics, elements, and strategies in activities created in non-technological situations (González, 2022). Similar terms such as digital gamification (gamifying the online learning management system environment), analogue gamification (gamification that tends to be classified as "low tech" with not much digital technology involved) and hybrid gamification (combination of both digital and analogue gamification) were defined by Marczewski, (2020) as well.

The summary of the gamified annex is listed in Table. 2 below.

Table 2. Gamified Annex Characteristics

Gamified Annex	Connection to Network	Adoption of Technology
Online Gamification	Yes	Yes
Offline Gamification	No	Yes or No
Plugged Gamification	Yes or No	Yes
Unplugged Gamification	No	No

To decide on a suitable framework to be used in an unplugged gamified learning condition, Oliveira et al., (2020) came up with a study that compared the effectiveness between both the 6D framework and the GAMIFY-SN framework within two separate classrooms. The former was one of the early constructed frameworks done by Hunter, (2012), consisting of six consecutive stages. The steps are i) **D**efine business objectives, ii) **D**elineate target behaviour, iii) **D**escribe the players, iv) **D**evise activity loops, v) **D**on't forget the fun and vi) **D**eploy appropriate tools. The latter framework was introduced by Toda, do Carmo, et al., (2019), comprising four steps which include i) defining the content, ii) defining the game elements, iii) deployment and iv) evaluation. The end results showed that while the 6D framework offers better flexibility and adaptability to instructors, the GAMIFY-SN framework would perform better in an educational setting. Apart from that, Nascimento, (2023) also proposed several designs for unplugged gamification namely social design, ecological design, fictional design, personal design and performance-based design with the hope of adhering to distinct player profiles even under circumstances that lack technology use, the individualization of gamification shall be further discussed in the following section below.

Gamified Motion

Gamified motion within the context of this study can be referred to as the adaptivity of the system towards real-time user/player types and needs. In a gamified world, the one-size-fits-all approach in gamified learning is also known as the traditional gamification which applies homogeneous gamification components to all students. However, users' player traits experience changes as time passes and is deemed to be unstable (A. C. G. Santos et al., 2021). Thus, the over-emphasis on the predominant player types while ignoring other player types that exist as well as the instability of player types might affect the effectiveness and learning outcome.

Hallifax et al., (2019) pointed out that the application of a particular motivation strategy and the selection of player typology will significantly influence the motivation of users. Two adaptive gamification was later proposed namely static adaptation and dynamic adaptation. While static adaptation mainly separates users into groups that contains distinct game elements based on their profiles, dynamic adaptations closely observes users' profiles and behaviour in the activity that was given (Hallifax et al., 2020). However, Oliveira, Hamari, Shi, et al., (2022) suggested that dynamic modelling, also known as the concurrent investigation of several attributes, and comprehending the implications of variables other than users' profiles is needed. Correspondingly, Rodrigues et al., (2022) introduced an automated recommendation system. Apart from the user profile (consisting of demographic, personality and behavioural profile), it should also include items (game elements), transactions (the interrelationship between the user and items, or preference) and context (geographic location and learning activities). Several recommendation systems were mentioned by Vasconcelos et al., (2022) including i) personalized, ii) collaborative, iii) content-based, iv) knowledge-based and v) evidence-based. Future gamification designs may allow for the customization of the gaming experience based on user preferences, motivation, level of engagement, and mood (Schöbel et al., 2021). The process of creating and constructing media-based or mediated learning environments to be utilized as learning tools based on formal models and System Dynamic (SD) expertise is known as "System Dynamic gamification"(Cunico et al., 2022). Kim & Lee, (2015) proposed a dynamic model, hypothesizing that by adjusting the four key variables (Challenge, Control, Curiosity and Fantasy), in which the efficacy of instruction can be altered.

Anyhow, one of the significant problems with this is that fellow researchers still could not come to a consensus on the various definitions used. As shown in Table 3 below, several authors tend to use the terms "tailored", "personalized" or "adaptation" and several more in different ways, which would cause disorientation for future research:

Table 3. Distinct Definitions of Individualized Gamification

Author(s)	Personalized gamification/ Personalization	Tailored gamification	Adaptive gamification/ Adaptation	Recommended/ Customized gamification
(García-Barrios et al., 2005)	Personalization is the subset of adaptation, which adapts towards a specific individual.	-	-	-
(Sundar & Marathe, 2010)	Personalization is a system-driven process, in which the users passively receive.	-	-	Customisation is a very user-driven approach as the user has an active role in choosing what information is displayed.
(Ricci et al., 2015)				Recommendation either personalized or non-personalized involves predicting the utility of an item that has been recently suggested or updated.
Hallifax et al., (2019)	-	-	Adaptive gamification is known as the analysis of how game aspects might be modified for students in educational settings to enhance learning.	-
(Hong et al., 2024; Klock et al., 2020)	Personalization gamification system customises the content based on user preferences.	Tailored is used as a general umbrella term to explain the process of individualization.	Adaptive gamification primarily uses the continually changing student data in user profiles to determine the demands of the users and modify the gamified systems accordingly	Recommendations provide individualized suggestions that based on one's previous favoured game elements along with others that have similar interest.

continued on following page

Table 3. Continued

Author(s)	Personalized gamification/ Personalization	Tailored gamification	Adaptive gamification/ Adaptation	Recommended/ Customized gamification
(Altaie & Jawawi, 2021)	-	-	Adaptive gamification is a method that aims to maximize individual expectations by giving priority to their requirements and preferences while also taking into account player types and the motivation they possess as they interact with the gamified system	-
Author(s)	**Personalized gamification/ Personalization**	**Tailored gamification**	**Adaptive gamification/ Adaptation**	**Recommended/ Customized gamification**
(Rodrigues, Palomino, et al., 2021)	Personalization gamification is related to developers or the system itself choosing game components based on user data.			Customized gamification (also referred to as bottom-up gamification) involves the selection of game elements (normally from a predefined list) by taking into account the individual's preferences and traits as well as the situation in which gamification will be employed.
(Oliveira, Hamari, Joaquim, et al., 2022)	Personalized gamification refers to the dynamic adaptation of the specific user during usage time	Tailored gamification is adapted at design time typically based on one or a few selected qualities (stereotypes).	-	-

To avoid any confusion, the author of the current study uses the term "individualized gamification" as an umbrella term to include a gamification approach that contains any kind of "custom-made attempt", while at the same time also distinguishing each of the entities via the gamification process and the components which involved in it. Figure 1 below shows the schematic representation of the individualized gamification types based on the definitions gathered. For clarity, the term "dynamic" or "static" in this context does not refer to the interaction between user and gamification mechanics but rather relates it to the adaptation of users' constant or continuous change of variables (e.g. player profiles, learning styles, learning context etc.). Table 4 below shows the key features of distinct gamified motion and its types.

Figure 1. Schematic Representation of Gamified Motion Types

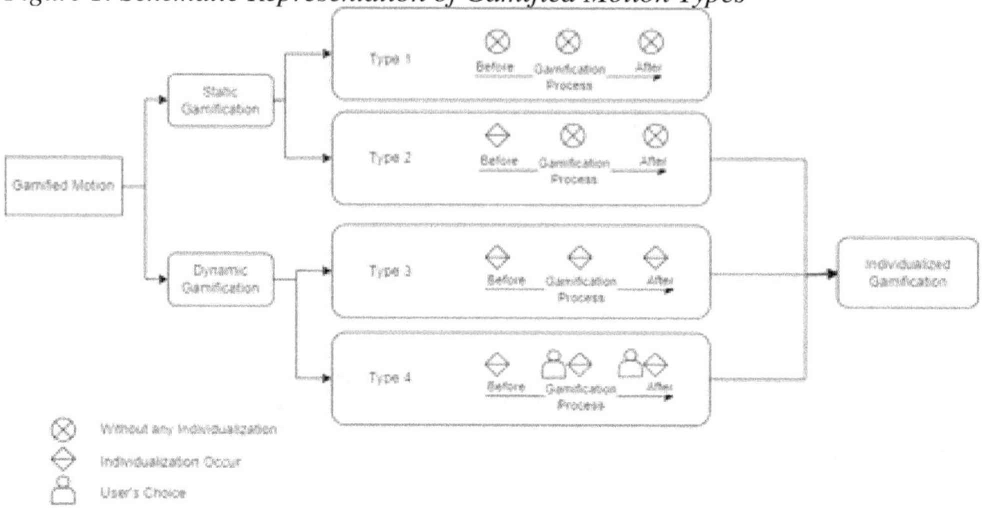

Table 4. Gamified Motion Types Characteristics

Gamified Motion	**Types**	**Player Preferences / Types**	**Game Elements Design**
Static	Type 1	Not considering	Apply the same game elements to all users
	Type 2	Considering prior to the system design	Design the game elements based on selected stereotypes
Dynamic	Type 3	Taking into account throughout the period users are using the system	Constantly changing the game elements that adhere to learners' needs in real-time
	Type 4	Similar to Type 3	Suggestions were given to users but also allowed the freedom of choice on whether to proceed with the same or a different experience.

Gamified Placement

Gamified placement is closely related to the relation between game elements with either the game's plot or its mechanics. "In-Game gamification" or "Intra-game gamification" refers to gamification procedures that take place within the game itself but are connected to game worlds in some way. Conversely, when specific game features that are closely tied to gameplay are discernible outside of the game world, this is referred to as "around game gamification." Or "extra-game gamification" (Ansori, 2015). The author suggested that Intra- game gamification could be used to attain higher learning objectives or to encourage gamers to attempt new things, while Extra-game gamification can be applied to the areas of assessment and learning.

METHOD

According to Colquhoun et al., (2014), there are five stages to propose a methodological model. The authors thus relate the following stages to the context of this study, namely:

Stage 1: Identification of research questions
Research Question 1: How do gamified annex, motion, depth and placement associate with one another?
Research Question 2: How do gamified annex, motion, depth and placement affect learners in the educational setting?
Research Question 3: What should be considered when designing a gamified classroom?
Stage 2: Identification of relevant studies

The authors search for studies that consist of the terms "online gamification", "offline gamification", "plugged gamification", "unplugged gamification" "dynamic gamification", "adaptive gamification", "traditional gamification", "tailored gamification", "personalized gamification", "deep gamification", "shallow gamification", "total gamification", "In-game gamification", "Around-game gamification", "Intra-game gamification", and "Extra-game gamification".

Stage 3: Selection of studies

After that, the authors viewed all the articles found and excluded studies that are irrelevant. The research articles selected should be aligned with the definition of gamified annex, gamified motion and gamified depth in this study.

Stage 4: Depiction of data

The effect of gamified annex, motion and depth is examined and recorded while looking into different types of learning environments as well.

Stage 5: Compilation and description of data

After the analyzation of the selected research articles, the findings are discussed, constructed into a conceptual model and presented in a graphical format.

FINDINGS AND DISCUSSIONS

W. H.-Y. Huang & Soman, (2013) proposed a 5-step procedure guideline for educators when intending to integrate gamification in the educational context, which are i) determine the target audience and context, ii) define goals of learning, iii) construct the experience, iv) analyze resources and v) apply game elements. In coherence with that, the authors proposed the Depth-Annex-Motion-Placement (DAMP) model as portrayed in Figure 1. The association between gamified annex, motion, depth and placement are represented in each outline of a circle. When gamifying a classroom or content, should be referred from the outer layer to the inner layer of the model.

To answer research question 2 posed above, the learning outcomes of each gamified layer are discussed below.

Gamified depth: P. A. Santos, (2015) implemented deep gamification within a higher education setting, and the students came to an uncontested preference towards the new way of learning. Students give feedback on learning more and have more interest in such an approach. Additionally, the passing rate of students increased by 8% compared to previous years (from 22% to 30%). A recent study by (Lim et al., 2023) suggested that shallow gamification tends to lead to an increase in the achievement level of students but deep gamification is capable of retaining and sustaining the intrinsic motivation of learners. Aligning with the findings of (Gurjanow et al., 2019), shallow gamification has a small impact in terms of motivation but is able to impact performance metrics successfully.

Gamified Annex: Results by Ho et al., (2023) show that although both plugged and unplugged gamification methods affect students positively in terms of motivation and engagement, students are more engaged when using the plugged gamification platform. Anyhow, unplugged gamification displayed higher levels of motivation, immersion, and purpose while having lower levels of achievability and intrigue than plugged gamification.

However, when delving into the connectivity of gamification, the analyses review done by Sanmugam et al., (2015) suggested that the implementation of online and offline gamification has mixed results. A study done by Pelegro, (2022) claimed that online gamification affects learners' academic performance significantly. Similarly, positive effects on students' engagement and enjoyment were stronger towards students who experienced online gamification, but they too felt less excited and expressed stronger negative feelings as well compared to offline gamification (Mac Namara & Murphy, 2017). Nevertheless, although Madariaga et al., (2023) stated that online and offline gamified robotics are equitably engaging, the offline counterparts are regarded to be more attractive, approachable and better in terms of game mechanics for students.

Gamified motion: The study's findings showed that people who interacted with the adapted gamified application outperformed participants who interacted with non-adapted gamified, non-gamified, and counter-adapted gamified applications (Lopez & Tucker, 2021). Likewise, the results done by Hassan et al., (2021) also showed that adaptive gamification (Type 3) showed an increase in learners' motivation, interaction and a decline in drop-out rates. The findings supported the statement of Passalacqua et al., (2021), (Type 3) gamification with a focus on the individual user can result in better user performance. Most studies found in regards to dynamic gamification uses the type 3 gamification, further studies on type 4 gamification should be emphasized as well to fully understand the potential of individualized gamification.

Gamified Placement: Unfortunately, no empirical studies or experimentation were found in regard to the effect or learning outcome of intra and extra-game gamification. The gap in the literature is identified and further research in this area is required.

Lastly, to address research question 3, the authors outlined the layer of the circle which consists of the learning conditions and context to be considered when designing a gamified system, which includes task, target, technology, time, technique, tariff, tensity and terrain (8Ts). Each of the featured items will be further discussed below.

Task

As suggested by Bennani et al., (2022), the goals of gamification in education, which provide the learner with greater enjoyment, motivation, and dedication to learning, must guide the adaptive gamification process in an online learning environment. The use of gamification should not dictate or overwhelm the learning experience, but rather act as a support tool to complete the task given.

Target

It was perceived that demographic factors such as age (Sillaots et al., 2020), gender and personality (Denden et al., 2021) as well as player typology (Loria & Marconi, 2018), (Schimanke et al., 2019), acceptance of gamification of the target audience could affect their perception towards gamified learning and the effectiveness of it. The gamification design should be specified whether it is for primary, secondary, tertiary, adult or even learners with special needs education to maximize the learning outcomes.

Terrain

"Terrain" could also be understood as geographical location, or countries/ nations. Policies of countries such as the ban on video games in China (Singleton, 2022), or the ban on students bringing phones to school in the Malaysian context (Ridzaimi, 2022) might affect the difficulty and convenience of implementing gamification within the classroom.

Technology

Gamification of educational activities has numerous challenges, including a lack of Internet service and technological infrastructure (Saleem et al., 2021). Students in rural areas that are unable to receive or have an unstable Internet connection should be considered. The work by D. Lim et al., (2022) discusses the consequences of the failure of technological infrastructure for learners and educators, instead of motivating or engaging learners, an exquisite gamification experience might have done the opposite.

Time

The time consumption of designing, constructing, implementing, and the duration of applying gamified learning within a classroom should be taken into consideration. The intervention duration of gamification has a moderating effect towards learners' intrinsic motivation (Rodrigues, Toda, et al., 2021).

Tariff

An et al., (2021), mentioned that funds are one of the major challenges when it comes to gamifying a Massive Online Open Course (MOOC), tariff (monetary) or the cost of obtaining resources, researching, designing, and purchasing adequate technological tools for the gamification of learning needs before choosing a suitable approach.

Technique

The term "technique" here also resembles the knowledge and skills needed for the creation of a gamification system. Instructional designers not only need to be equipped with game design and visual design skills but in order to construct an adaptive gamification system, programming skills are also required to harness the potential use of Artificial Intelligence (AI) (Bennani et al., 2022).

Tensity

The game elements to be implemented in education such as the ones proposed by Toda, Klock, et al., (2019) and Murillo-Zamorano et al., (2023) hold different purposes. A careful selection of game elements should be made to create a balanced learning environment that has both tense and relaxing moments. This is to prevent learners from feeling discouraged, stressed, or disengaged with the gamified content.

Figure 2. Depth-Annex-Motion-Placement (DAMP) Conceptual Model

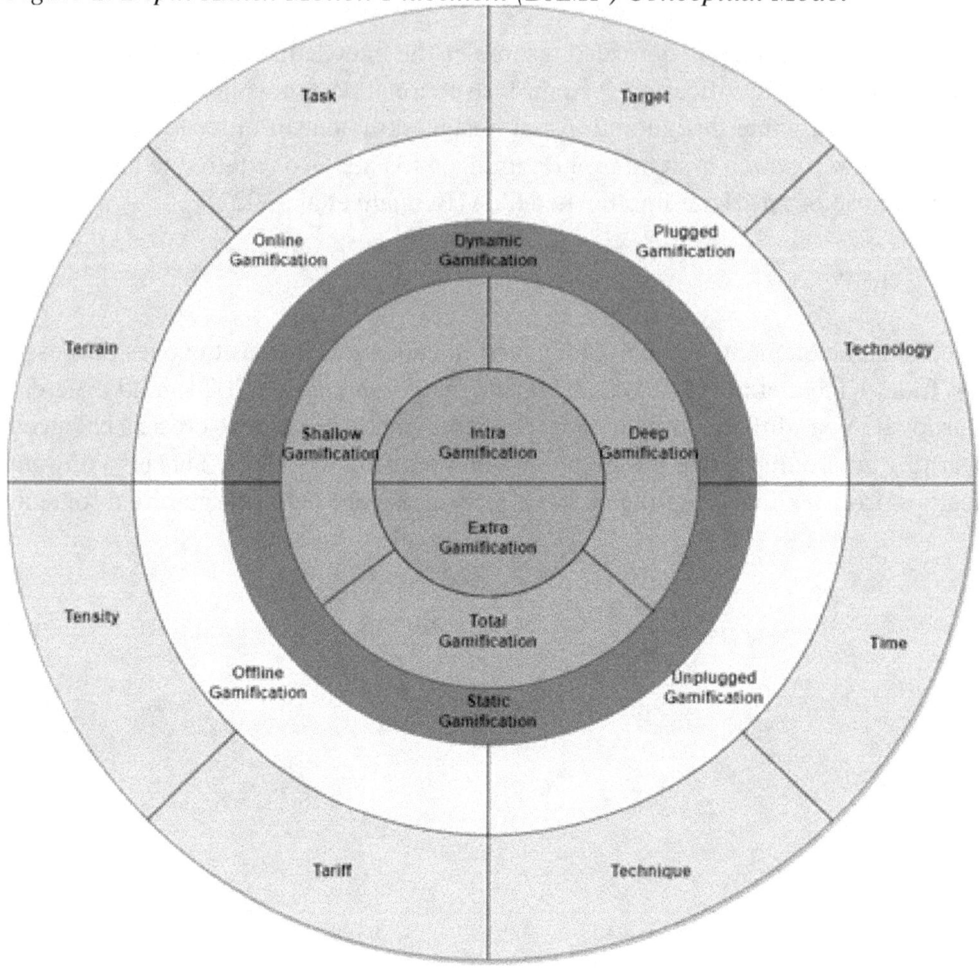

CONCLUSION

In conclusion, the authors proposed the DAMP model which dealt with the depth, annex, motion, and placement of gamification. Although it is believed that certain gamification approaches are more effective than others. However, the gamification of the education setting should be considered and be designed and constructed according to one's learning context, availability of technology, resources (8Ts) and more. The suggested model is believed to provide a more holistic view of the design and development of gamified learning, the authors recommend that the DAMP model be implemented by scrutinizing the factors from the outer layer and slowly progressing to the core of it. Besides that, the authors also identified the gap in literature that exists in relation to gamified placement. Similarly, in the gamified motion segment, more research on Type 4 gamification is also required. The authors wish to point out and emphasize on the need to come into unity of the various definitions especially in the gamification motion types to prevent any consternation or hindrance to future works. Lastly, further research is also needed to test the applicability of the DAMP model in distinct learning environments.

REFERENCES

Aibar-Almazán, A., Castellote-Caballero, Y., Carcelén-Fraile, M. del C., Rivas-Campo, Y., & González-Martín, A. M. (2024). Gamification in the classroom: Kahoot! As a tool for university teaching innovation. *Frontiers in Psychology*, 15(March), 1–8. DOI: 10.3389/fpsyg.2024.1370084 PMID: 38646120

Al-Hafdi, F. S., & Alhalafawy, W. S. (2024). Ten Years of Gamification-Based Learning: A Bibliometric Analysis and Systematic Review. [IJIM]. *International Journal of Interactive Mobile Technologies*, 18(07), 188–212. DOI: 10.3991/ijim.v18i07.45335

Altaie, M. A., & Jawawi, D. N. A. (2021). Adaptive Gamification to Promote Computational Thinking. *Journal of E-Learning and Knowledge Society*, 17(3), 89–100.

An, Y., Zhu, M., Bonk, C. J., & Lin, L. (2021). Exploring instructors' perspectives, practices, and perceived support needs and barriers related to the gamification of MOOCs. *Journal of Computing in Higher Education*, 33(1), 64–84. DOI: 10.1007/s12528-020-09256-w

Bennani, S., Maalel, A., & Ben Ghezala, H. (2022). Adaptive gamification in E-learning: A literature review and future challenges. *Computer Applications in Engineering Education*, 30(2), 628–642. DOI: 10.1002/cae.22477

Boyce, A. K. (2014). *Deep gamification: Combining game-based and play-based methods*. North Carolina State University.

Cavus, N., Ibrahim, I., Ogbonna Okonkwo, M., Bode Ayansina, N., & Modupeola, T. (2023). The Effects of Gamification in Education: A Systematic Literature Review. *BRAIN.Broad Research in Artificial Intelligence and Neuroscience*, 14(2), 211–241. DOI: 10.18662/brain/14.2/452

Colquhoun, H. L., Levac, D., O'Brien, K. K., Straus, S., Tricco, A. C., Perrier, L., Kastner, M., & Moher, D. (2014). Scoping reviews: Time for clarity in definition, methods, and reporting. *Journal of Clinical Epidemiology*, 67(12), 1291–1294. DOI: 10.1016/j.jclinepi.2014.03.013 PMID: 25034198

Cunico, G., Aivazidou, E., & Mollona, E. (2022). System dynamics gamification: A proposal for shared principles. *Systems Research and Behavioral Science*, 39(4), 723–733. DOI: 10.1002/sres.2805

Denden, M., Tlili, A., Essalmi, F., Jemni, M., Chen, N. S., & Burgos, D. (2021). Effects of gender and personality differences on students' perception of game design elements in educational gamification. *International Journal of Human-Computer Studies*, 154(May), 102674. DOI: 10.1016/j.ijhcs.2021.102674

Deterding, S., Dixon, D., Khaled, R., & Nacke, L. (2011). From game design elements to gamefulness: Defining "gamification." *Proceedings of the 15th International Academic MindTrek Conference: Envisioning Future Media Environments, MindTrek 2011,* March 2014, 9–15. DOI: 10.1145/2181037.2181040

Dicheva, D., & Dichev, C. (2016). An Active Learning Model Employing Flipped Learning and Gamification Strategies. *13th International Conference on Intelligent Tutoring Systems (ITS 2016), July*, 7.

Dicheva, D., Dichev, C., Agre, G., & Angelova, G. (2015). Gamification in education: A systematic mapping study. *Journal of Educational Technology & Society*, 18(3), 75–88.

Fuchs, M. (2015). *Total Gamification.*

García-Barrios, V. M., Mödritscher, F., & Gütl, C. (2005). Personalisation versus Adaptation? A User-centred Model Approach and its Application. *International Conference on Knowledge Management (I-Know), Iicm*, 120–127.

Gil-Aciron, L. A. (2024). The gamer psychology: A psychological perspective on game design and gamification. *Interactive Learning Environments*, 32(1), 183–207. DOI: 10.1080/10494820.2022.2082489

González, C. S. G. (2022). *Unplugged Gamification : towards a definition. September.*

Gurjanow, I., Oliveira, M., Zender, J., Santos, P. A., & Ludwig, M. (2019). Shallow and deep gamification in mathematics trails. *Lecture Notes in Computer Science (Including Subseries Lecture Notes in Artificial Intelligence and Lecture Notes in Bioinformatics), 11385 LNCS*(3), 364–374. DOI: 10.1007/978-3-030-11548-7_34

Hallifax, S., Jean, U., & Lyon, M. (2020). *Adaptive gamification of digital learning environments.*

Hallifax, S., Serna, A., Marty, J. C., Lavoué, G., & Lavoué, E. (2019). Factors to consider for tailored gamification. *CHI PLAY 2019 - Proceedings of the Annual Symposium on Computer-Human Interaction in Play*, 559–572. DOI: 10.1145/3311350.3347167

Hassan, M. A., Habiba, U., Majeed, F., & Shoaib, M. (2021). Adaptive gamification in e-learning based on students' learning styles. *Interactive Learning Environments*, 29(4), 545–565. DOI: 10.1080/10494820.2019.1588745

Hicks, A., Zhi, R., Dong, Y., & Barnes, T. (2011). *Applying "Deep Gamification"*. Principles to Improve Quality of User-Designed Levels.

Ho, P. H., Fleitas, Y. B., & González-gonzález, C. S. (2023). Unplugged Versus Plugged Gamification - A Comparative Study in Higher Education on Engagement, Motivation and Teachers '. *Perception*, 1(1).

Hong, Y., Saab, N., & Admiraal, W. (2024). Approaches and game elements used to tailor digital gamification for learning: A systematic literature review. *Computers & Education*, 212(January), 105000. DOI: 10.1016/j.compedu.2024.105000

Huang, W., Li, X., & Shang, J. (2023). Gamified Project-Based Learning: A Systematic Review of the Research Landscape. *Sustainability (Basel)*, 15(2), 940. Advance online publication. DOI: 10.3390/su15020940

Huang, W. H.-Y., & Soman, D. (2013). A Practitioner's Guide To Gamification Of Education. *Early Child Development and Care*, 189(3), 392–404. DOI: 10.1080/03004430.2017.1324434

Hunter, K. W. dan. (2012). *How Game Thinking Can Revolutionize Your Business.* Wharton Digital Press.

Khaitova, N. F. (2021). History of Gamification and Its Role in the Educational Process. *International Journal of Multicultural and Multireligious Understanding*, 8(5), 212. DOI: 10.18415/ijmmu.v8i5.2640

Kim, J. T., & Lee, W. H. (2015). Dynamical model for gamification of learning (DMGL). *Multimedia Tools and Applications*, 74(19), 8483–8493. DOI: 10.1007/s11042-013-1612-8

Klock, A. C. T., Gasparini, I., Pimenta, M. S., & Hamari, J. (2020). Tailored gamification: A review of literature. *International Journal of Human Computer Studies, 144*(September 2019). DOI: 10.1016/j.ijhcs.2020.102495

Lampropoulos, G., & Kinshuk. (2024). Virtual reality and gamification in education: A systematic review. *Educational Technology Research and Development*, •••, 1–95.

Lim, D., Sanmugam, M., & Jaafar, W. A. (2023). *The Effect of Gamified Depth on Malaysian Higher Education Students ' Intrinsic Motivation Level and Achievement Level*. 1–14.

Lopez, C. E., & Tucker, C. S. (2021). Adaptive Gamification and Its Impact on Performance. *Lecture Notes in Computer Science (Including Subseries Lecture Notes in Artificial Intelligence and Lecture Notes in Bioinformatics), 12789 LNCS*, 327–341. DOI: 10.1007/978-3-030-77277-2_25

Loria, E., & Marconi, A. (2018). Player types and player behaviors: Analyzing Correlations in an On-the-field Gamified System. *CHI PLAY 2018 - Proceedings of the 2018 Annual Symposium on Computer-Human Interaction in Play Companion Extended Abstracts, October*, 531–538. DOI: 10.1145/3270316.3271526

Mac Namara, D., & Murphy, L. (2017). Online versus offline perspectives on gamified learning. *CEUR Workshop Proceedings*, 1857, 47–52.

Madariaga, L., Allendes, C., Nussbaum, M., Barrios, G., & Acevedo, N. (2023). Offline and online user experience of gamified robotics for introducing computational thinking: Comparing engagement, game mechanics and coding motivation. *Computers and Education, 193*(July 2022), 1–24. DOI: 10.1016/j.compedu.2022.104664

Marczewski, A. (2020). *Analogue vs Digital Gamification*. Gamified UK. https://www.gamified.uk/2020/01/17/analogue-vs-digital-gamification-2/

Mee, R. W. M., Pek, L. S., Von, W. Y., Ghani, K. A., Shahdan, T. S. T., Ismail, M. R., & Rao, Y. S. (2021). A Conceptual Model of Analogue Gamification to Enhance Learners' Motivation and Attitude. *International Journal of Language Education*, 5(2), 40–50.

Mozelius, P. (2021). Deep and Shallow Gamification in Higher Education, What Is the Difference? *INTED2021 Proceedings, 1*(March 2021), 3150–3156. DOI: 10.21125/inted.2021.0663

Murillo-Zamorano, L. R., López-Sánchez, J. Á., López-Rey, M. J., & Bueno-Muñoz, C. (2023). Gamification in higher education: The ECOn+ star battles. *Computers and Education, 194*(March 2022). DOI: 10.1016/j.compedu.2022.104699

Nascimento, I. M. do. (2023). *UnplugGamify : a didactic material to support user-centered unplugged gamification.*

O'Sullivan, D., Stavrakakis, I., Gordon, D., Curley, A., Tierney, B., Murphy, E., Collins, M., & Becevel, A. (2021). "You Can't Lose a Game If You Don't Play the Game": Exploring the Ethics of Gamification in Education. *International Journal for Infonomics*, 14(1), 2035–2045. DOI: 10.20533/iji.1742.4712.2021.0211

Oliveira, W., Hamari, J., Joaquim, S., Toda, A. M., Palomino, P. T., Vassileva, J., & Isotani, S. (2022). The effects of personalized gamification on students' flow experience, motivation, and enjoyment. In *Smart Learning Environments* (Vol. 9, Issue 1). DOI: 10.1186/s40561-022-00194-x

Oliveira, W., Hamari, J., Shi, L., Toda, A. M., Rodrigues, L., Palomino, P. T., & Isotani, S. (2022). Tailored gamification in education : A literature review and future agenda. In *Education and Information Technologies* (Issue 0123456789). Springer US. DOI: 10.1007/s10639-022-11122-4

Oliveira, W. M., Toda, A. T., Palomino, P., Rodrigues, L., & Isotani, S. (2020). Which one is the best? A quasi-experimental study comparing frameworks for unplugged gamification. *Renote*, 18(1). Advance online publication. DOI: 10.22456/1679-1916.105971

Osheim, D. E. (2013). "THIS COULD BE A GAME!": DEFINING GAMIFICATION FOR THE CLASSROOM. *Journal of Chemical Information and Modeling*, 53(9), 1689–1699.

Passalacqua, M., Sénécal, S., Frédette, M., Nacke, L. E., Pellerin, R., & Léger, P.-M. (2021). Should Gamification be Personalized? A Self- deterministic Approach. *AIS Transactions on Human-Computer Interaction*, 13(3), 265–286. DOI: 10.17705/1thci.00150

Pelegro, R. (2022). Gamification in Online Education. SSRN *Electronic Journal, January*. DOI: 10.2139/ssrn.4054977

Pfeiffer, A., Bezzina, S., König, N., & Kriglstein, S. (2020). Beyond classical gamification: in-and around-game gamification for education.

Putz, L. M., Hofbauer, F., & Treiblmaier, H. (2020). Can gamification help to improve education? Findings from a longitudinal study. *Computers in Human Behavior*, 110(April), 106392. DOI: 10.1016/j.chb.2020.106392

Ricci, F., Shapira, B., & Rokach, L. (2015). Recommender systems handbook, Second edition. In *Recommender Systems Handbook, Second Edition*. DOI: 10.1007/978-1-4899-7637-6

Ridzaimi, S. (2022). *Education Minister: Schools to continue banning smartphones to curb gaming addiction among students*. TechNave. https://technave.com/gadget/Education-Minister-Schools-to-continue-banning-smartphones-to-curb-gaming-addiction-among-students-29174.html

Rodrigues, L., Palomino, P. T., Toda, A. M., Klock, A. C. T., Oliveira, W., Avila-Santos, A. P., Gasparini, I., & Isotani, S. (2021). Personalization Improves Gamification: Evidence from a Mixed-methods Study. *Proceedings of the ACM on Human-Computer Interaction, 5*(CHIPLAY). DOI: 10.1145/3474714

Rodrigues, L., Toda, A. M., Oliveira, W., Palomino, P. T., Avila-Santos, A. P., & Isotani, S. (2021). Gamification Works, but How and to Whom?: An Experimental Study in the Context of Programming Lessons. *SIGCSE 2021 - Proceedings of the 52nd ACM Technical Symposium on Computer Science Education, March*, 184–190. DOI: 10.1145/3408877.3432419

Rodrigues, L., Toda, A. M., Oliveira dos Santos, W., Palomino, P. T., Vassileva, J., & Isotani, S. (2022). Automating Gamification Personalization to the User and Beyond. *IEEE Transactions on Learning Technologies*, 15(2), 1–1. DOI: 10.1109/TLT.2022.3162409

Saleem, A. N., Noori, N. M., & Ozdamli, F. (2021). Gamification Applications in E-learning: A Literature Review. *Technology. Knowledge and Learning*, 0123456789. Advance online publication. DOI: 10.1007/s10758-020-09487-x

Sanmugam, M. (2021). Sustainability and Aptness of Game Elements in A Gamified Learning Environment. *2021 9th International Conference on Information and Communication Technology, ICoICT 2021*, 500–505. DOI: 10.1109/ICoICT52021.2021.9527499

Sanmugam, M., Mohamed, H., Zaid, N. M., Abdullah, Z., Aris, B., & Suhadi, S. M. (2015). Implementation of Gamification as an educative tool via online and offline methods; an analyses review. *1st International Conference On Educational Studies (ICES-2015), July*.

Santos, A. C. G., Oliveira, W., Hamari, J., & Isotani, S. (2021). Do people's user types change over time? An exploratory study. *CEUR Workshop Proceedings*, 2883, 90–99.

Santos, P. A. (2015). Deep Gamification of a University Course. *Conference Proceedings SciTecIN'15 Sciences and Technologies of Interaction 12-13 November 2015 Coimbra, Portugal*, 1–5.

Schimanke, F., Mertens, R., & Huck, B. S. (2019). Player types in mobile learning games – Playing patterns and motivation. *Proceedings - 2018 IEEE International Symposium on Multimedia, ISM 2018, June 2019*, 247–252. DOI: 10.1109/ISM.2018.00035

Schöbel, S., Schmidt-Kraepelin, M., Janson, A., & Sunyaev, A. (2021). Adaptive and Personalized Gamification Designs: Call for Action and Future Research. *AIS Transactions on Human-Computer Interaction*, 13(4), 479–494. DOI: 10.17705/1thci.00158

Serice, L. (2023). Prisms of Neuroscience. *Frameworks for Thinking About Educational Gamification.*, (March), 1–30.

Sillaots, M., Jesmin, T., Fiadotau, M., & Khulbe, M. (2020). Gamifying classroom presentations: Evaluating the effects on engagement across demographic factors. *Proceedings of the 14th International Conference on Game Based Learning, ECGBL 2020, September*, 537–546. https://doi.org/DOI: 10.34190/GBL.20.105

Singleton, T. (2022). *China claims youth gaming addiction resolved.* BBC News. https://www.bbc.com/news/technology-63730316

Söbke, H. (2019). A case study of deep gamification in higher engineering education. *Lecture Notes in Computer Science (Including Subseries Lecture Notes in Artificial Intelligence and Lecture Notes in Bioinformatics), 11385 LNCS*(December 2018), 375–386. DOI: 10.1007/978-3-030-11548-7_35

Sundar, S. S., & Marathe, S. S. (2010). Personalization versus customization: The importance of agency, privacy, and power usage. *Human Communication Research*, 36(3), 298–322. DOI: 10.1111/j.1468-2958.2010.01377.x

Toda, A. M., do Carmo, R. M. C., da Silva, A. P., Bittencourt, I. I., & Isotani, S. (2019). An approach for planning and deploying gamification concepts with social networks within educational contexts. *International Journal of Information Management*, 46(May), 294–303. DOI: 10.1016/j.ijinfomgt.2018.10.001

Toda, A. M., Klock, A. C. T., Oliveira, W., Palomino, P. T., Rodrigues, L., Shi, L., Bittencourt, I., Gasparini, I., Isotani, S., & Cristea, A. I. (2019). Analysing gamification elements in educational environments using an existing Gamification taxonomy. In *Smart Learning Environments* (Vol. 6, Issue 1). DOI: 10.1186/s40561-019-0106-1

Vasconcelos, G., Oliveira, W., Santos, A. C. G., & Hamari, J. (2022). ReGammend: A method for personalized recommendation of gamification designs. *CEUR Workshop Proceedings*, 3147(June), 85–94.

Yie, D. L., Sanmugam, M. A., Yahaya, W. A. J. W., & Abdullah, N. B. (2022, May). The dilemma of online gamified learning in Malaysian educational context: A qualitative study on Malaysian university students' perspective. In 2022 IEEE 12th Symposium on Computer Applications & Industrial Electronics (ISCAIE) (pp. 61-65). IEEE.

Zeybek, N., & Saygı, E. (2024). Gamification in Education: Why, Where, When, and How?—A Systematic Review. *Games and Culture*, 19(2), 237–264. DOI: 10.1177/15554120231158625

Chapter 7
Exploring Gamification Strategies to Enhance Classroom Effectiveness

Xuehua Xu
https://orcid.org/0009-0000-0410-7030
Shanghai University of Engineering Science, China

Yueyang Zhao
https://orcid.org/0009-0004-3309-4004
Shanghai University of Engineering Science, China

ABSTRACT

This study aims to explore the potential of gamified teaching strategies in enhancing classroom effectiveness. In response to the prevalent issues of low student engagement and lack of motivation in current teaching practices, we propose a series of instructional designs grounded in gamification principles. These designs use the BOPPPS teaching model as the core and incorporate SWOT analysis to thoroughly assess the potential benefits, challenges, opportunities, and risks associated with integrating game elements into the teaching process. We anticipate that carefully crafted gamification strategies will significantly improve student interaction and participation in the classroom, spark their interest in learning, and facilitate a deeper understanding of the subject matter.

DOI: 10.4018/979-8-3693-6745-2.ch007

1. INTRODUCTION

At present, a significant challenge in the field of education is how to effectively enhance students' classroom participation and learning interest(David & Weinstein, 2024). In our thorough review of existing literature, we have frequently encountered keywords such as classroom silence, classroom effectiveness, classroom interaction, and teaching models (Ho et al., 2023). These terms highlight the long-standing focus of educational researchers on how to improve student engagement and knowledge absorption efficiency through educational reform. However, with the continuous development of modern technology, traditional teaching methods often struggle to ignite students' enthusiasm for learning, leading to suboptimal teaching outcomes (Saha et al., 2024). To address this issue, our study delves deeply into the realm of gamified teaching and verifies its effectiveness through extensive literature review (Pardim et al., 2023). Nonetheless, when integrating gamification into the classroom, it is crucial to ensure that it does not disrupt the normal teaching pace and order. Hence, this research attempts an innovative integration within the framework of the BOPPPS teaching model (Guo, 2024; Xu, 2023; Yan et al., 2023). Specifically, we combine the interactive and participatory elements of gamification with the "Engagement" phase of the BOPPPS model, aiming to enhance students' classroom interaction, participation, and knowledge absorption. To verify the effectiveness of this integrated approach in real teaching scenarios, our study employs a preliminary SWOT analysis to assess its strengths, weaknesses, and potential risks and challenges.

1.1 The Application of Gamification

1.1.1 Gamification

Gamification is a strategy that involves applying game design elements and mechanics in non-game environments to motivate participants through engaging interactions, enhancing their problem-solving abilities, and increasing their participation and contribution to activities or services(Gil-Aciron, 2024). In the fields of business and marketing, gamification is particularly used in consumer-facing websites and mobile applications to enhance user experience and encourage interaction. This approach integrates game elements such as point systems, level rewards, progress bars, and virtual achievements to activate user participation and increase the appeal of products.

interdisciplinary nature, diversity, and scenario-based approach. These games significantly contribute to various domains such as knowledge acquisition, creativity stimulation, educational expansion, management simulation, skill training, behavior modification, and fostering positive qualities (Christopoulos & Mystakidis, 2023).

Unlike traditional games that focus on entertainment, Serious Games place a stronger emphasis on functionality. Gamification is a design methodology that involves integrating game elements and mechanics into non-game contexts to enhance user experience and motivate behavior. On the other hand, Serious Games are designed with the explicit purpose of solving real-world problems. While they are games at their core, their primary focus lies in their educational or practical application value.

1.1.2 Domains of Gamification Application

Gamification strategies have been widely applied across various fields, including business, health, environmental protection, politics, and education (Abujaber et al., 2023; Farrokhnia et al., 2024; Zaman, 2023).

Case Study 1: Take Alipay's "Ant Forest" as an example, which is a tree-planting game where players accumulate energy by using Alipay for transactions, and this energy can be used to grow virtual trees within 24 hours. Additionally, players can steal energy from their friends. Once a certain amount of energy is collected, players can apply to plant real trees in designated areas in the physical world. This allows users to contribute to public welfare and give back to society while enjoying the entertainment of consumption (HU et al., 2021,from China and in CNKI).

Case Study 2: "Pokémon GO," also known as Pokémon GO, is an augmented reality smartphone game based on location services. This game revolutionizes traditional gameplay by encouraging players to leave their homes and explore the real world to catch Pokémon. While playing the game, players engage in significant physical activity, allowing them to lose weight and achieve better health through entertainment. Consequently, the success of this game has inspired many health and fitness-themed applications that incorporate gamification elements[1].

In the field of education, the use of games or game elements varies according to their level and method, which can be understood as a variety of different terms and concepts, such as educational games, game-based learning, gamification, educational gamification, and functional games (serial games), etc. These concepts each have their own characteristics and aim to enhance the effectiveness and attractiveness of education through the use of games (Heldal et al., 2021).

Since 2000, the field of education has gradually explored gamified teaching, reaching a peak of research interest in 2012. During this period, scholars extensively studied the acceptance of gamified teaching among students of different age groups, the cognitive outcomes of knowledge acquisition, and the application of technologies such as AR and VR in gamified teaching. They also investigated the effectiveness of gamified teaching in specialized fields. Most of these research findings come from scholars in education, psychology, and game design, who focus on different aspects of the topic due to their professional backgrounds, enriching the theoretical foundation and practical experience of gamified teaching. As an educator in the field of gaming, I will continue to delve into the application of gamified teaching in the classroom, seeking more effective teaching methods to advance the field of education. Taenam Kim's (2016) research case successfully integrated classical literature with gamification, targeting middle school students as participants. The results indicated that the application of gamification strategies in learning the Korean language significantly impacted self-efficacy (Heldal et al., 2021).In their study, Stott and Neustaedter reviewed a vast array of literature on gamified teaching, finding that the application of gamification in education has largely yielded effective results. However, some scholars have pointed out that it is precisely the reduction of superficial characteristics of game design that hinders the successful gamification of classrooms. If implemented properly, "gamification can help enrich educational experiences by enabling students to identify and respond." However, reducing the complexity of a carefully designed game to superficial elements (such as badges and experience points) is insufficient to engage students. Besides failing to involve them, restricting the implementation of game dynamics to superficial features could actually damage existing interest and participation; this is not to say that game elements should be avoided, but rather to emphasize the importance of allowing them to surface as part of a deeper implementation that includes the fundamentals of good game design(Stott & Neustaedter, 2013).

1.2 Curriculum Design

Curriculum design is a purposeful, planned, and structured process of developing curriculum plans, standards, and materials (Kumar & Rewari, 2022). The BOPPPS teaching model, originating from teacher training in Canada, is a student-centered approach that is goal-oriented. The "BOPPPS" model is based on constructivist theory and communicative methods, known for its effective instructional design. It emphasizes a closed-loop teaching process model that ensures student participation and feedback.

1.2.1 Bridge-In

The introduction phase is crucial for sparking students' curiosity and enthusiasm for learning. By employing techniques such as storytelling, video presentations, and connections to current trending topics, this phase effectively captures students' attention. However, the introduction strategy must be carefully tailored to the subject matter to ensure it lays a solid foundation for deeper learning and comprehension.

1.2.2 Objective

Learning objectives form the core of each lesson, clearly defining the primary focus of knowledge transfer and acquisition. These objectives typically cover three major areas: knowledge mastery, skill development, and personal growth. In traditional teaching, these objectives are often presented visually through blackboards or PowerPoint slides. When setting learning objectives, it is crucial to consider them from the students' perspective, clearly outlining the key knowledge points they need to master while ensuring that these goals are achievable and understandable.

1.2.3 Pre-Assessment

Pre-assessment refers to the initial evaluation phase designed to determine students' proficiency levels and explore their interest and existing knowledge on a particular subject. This process is essential for adjusting the depth and pace of teaching to ensure precise alignment with the course objectives. To achieve this, teachers can employ various assessment methods, such as brief questionnaires, quizzes, or group discussions, to gather relevant information and optimize the teaching plan accordingly.

1.2.4 Participatory Learning

Participatory learning is the core concept of the BOPPPS teaching model, aimed at fostering active student engagement. This teaching method emphasizes student agency by incorporating a variety of interactive learning activities after the clear communication of concepts, key points, and challenges. These activities may include individual presentations, group discussions, role-playing, hands-on exercises, seminars, and case studies. Not only do these activities stimulate students' enthusiasm for learning, but they also encourage active involvement in the learning process, leading to a deeper understanding of the content. Moreover, participatory learning enhances students' communication, collaboration, and critical thinking skills, which are essential components of their overall development.

1.2.5 Post-Assessment

Unlike traditional teaching methods, the BOPPPS model emphasizes the immediacy of assessment, which should be conducted either after the lesson or during the teaching process. Timely assessments allow for the observation of students' knowledge acquisition levels, enabling them to understand their own progress. Assessments can take various forms, such as quizzes, problem-solving exercises, or practical demonstrations, to evaluate the effectiveness of teaching.

1.2.6 Summary

In contrast to traditional teaching models, the BOPPPS approach emphasizes that summaries should be student-driven, allowing them to synthesize the knowledge they have acquired. As a closed-loop feedback course design model that emphasizes interaction and reflection, it is one of the most effective design methods for teachers in organizing and planning their lessons.

Through comprehensive theoretical analysis, this study reveals two core features of the BOPPPS teaching model. First, it emphasizes comprehensive participatory learning, rather than passive listening. Second, it advocates for timely feedback from students to adjust subsequent teaching activities, aiming to achieve educational goals more effectively. This study examines how game mechanics in gamification can be integrated into the participatory learning phase of the BOPPPS teaching model to enhance student engagement and learning outcomes. By incorporating game elements such as reward systems, competitive mechanisms, role-playing, and challenge tasks, the gamified teaching strategy not only promotes active student participation in the classroom but also significantly improves their understanding of key concepts and challenges. Additionally, by increasing the fun of learning, this teaching design stimulates students' interest and motivation, effectively contributing to their overall development.

Figure 1. BOPPPS Teaching Model + Gamification

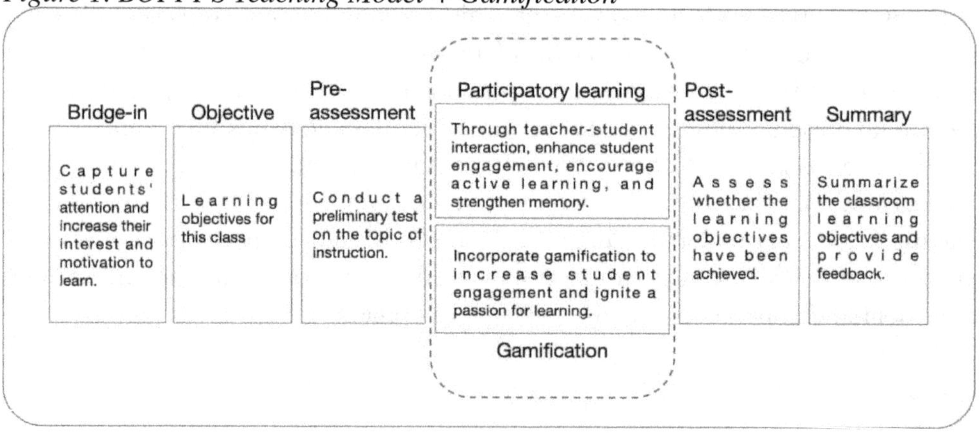

2 RESEARCH METHODOLOGY

Through in-depth analysis of relevant theoretical knowledge points and the study of multiple specific cases, we observed the feasibility of integrating gamification into classroom instruction. This integration not only may transform the traditional teaching paradigm but also offers an innovative approach to foster deeper understanding and mastery of knowledge among students. Next, to comprehensively evaluate the practical effectiveness of integrating game-based learning with the BOPPPS model, we will conduct a SWOT analysis. This will help us identify its strengths, weaknesses, opportunities, and potential risks, thereby providing valuable references and recommendations for educational reform.

2.1 SWOT Analysis

The SWOT-CLPV Theory is a model that has been slightly modified based on the SWOT model. This analytical method is capable of objectively and accurately assessing the current situation of a company (Zhang & Dong, 2024). By utilizing this approach, it is possible to identify factors that are beneficial and worth promoting, as well as those that are detrimental and should be avoided. It helps in discovering existing problems, finding solutions, and clarifying future development directions. The interaction among the four factors—Strengths (S), Weaknesses (W), Opportunities (O), and Threats (T)—significantly impacts the survival and development of a company. Under the interplay of these four major factors, changes occur and four different market environments and strategic situations arise: an advantageous situation with "Leverage" (L); a market situation that affects the company's ability to leverage its strengths, known as "Control" (C); a competitive situation that reduces the intensity of the company's strengths, termed "Vulnerability" (V); and a problematic competitive situation caused by both external threats and internal weaknesses, labeled "Problem" (P).

During the literature search, over 16,000 articles were found using the keyword "SWOT analysis of educational methods." Researcher Li Meifang analyzed whether the "Internet +" online education model could completely replace offline education during the pandemic through the SWOT analysis method. Researcher Tao Shuang conducted a study on the implementation status and optimization strategies of case teaching in high school geography from the perspective of SWOT analysis, employing literature research, questionnaire surveys, and interviews (Yao., 2022,from China and in CNKI). Additionally, the application of SWOT analysis is also widespread in related research fields such as "micro-lessons," "disciplines," and "classroom effectiveness."

First, we establish internal capabilities as the BOPPPS model of instructional design. This model is student-centered and goal-oriented, emphasizing the importance of student participation and feedback to form a closed loop instructional process model that emphasizes comprehensive student engagement in learning. The core feature of this model lies in its ability to promote students' active engagement in learning, spark their interest and motivation, thereby effectively enhancing classroom interactivity and learning outcomes.

Secondly, external factors are set as game-based strategies. Gamification (Gamification) is a strategy that applies gaming elements and mechanisms to non-gaming environments. It aims to stimulate participant motivation through relatively engaging interactions, improve their problem-solving abilities, and increase their participation and contribution to activities or services. This method activates user participation and increases classroom appeal through incorporating elements such as point systems, level rewards, progress bars, and virtual achievements.

2.1.1 Strengths (S)

(1) Student engagement: The BOPPPS model can effectively enhance student participation in class. Through the systematic five stages from introduction to summary, each phase is designed very clearly and orderly, ensuring that students actively participate at every learning stage. This also enhances their understanding and application of knowledge.
(2) Interactivity: The model emphasizes collaboration and communication among students, promoting mutual learning and cooperation through diverse interactive activities such as group discussions and role-playing. This not only improves their social skills but also deepens their understanding of complex concepts.
(3) Timely feedback on student knowledge mastery: The BOPPPS model provides immediate assessment of student learning outcomes through pre-tests and post-tests, allowing teachers to quickly adjust teaching strategies based on these feedbacks. This real-time feedback mechanism helps identify issues promptly and ensures the achievement of learning objectives.

2.1.2 Weaknesses (W)

(1) Varied student acceptance: Despite the significant advantages of the BOPPPS model, not all students can adapt to this highly interactive and participatory teaching mode. Some students may feel uncomfortable or unaccustomed to traditional teaching methods, which could affect their learning outcomes.

(2) Time-consuming for teacher lesson planning: The implementation of the BOPPPS model requires additional class hours and preparation work. Teachers need to design detailed lesson plans and conduct multiple revisions and rehearsals before class, undoubtedly increasing their workload.

(3) Reasonability of methods during participation in learning: Some interactive learning methods may not be suitable for all subjects and teaching content, necessitating flexible adjustment of teaching strategies by teachers based on specific subject characteristics to ensure methodological reasonability and effectiveness.

2.1.3 Opportunities (O)

(1) Enhanced fun: The introduction of gamification elements such as reward systems and competitive mechanisms can significantly increase the fun and attractiveness of learning. This not only stimulates students' interest in learning but also enhances their engagement and enthusiasm for the content.

(2) Increased involvement: Combining game-based elements with the BOPPPS model can further enhance student participation in class. By setting challenging tasks and virtual achievements, students are motivated to actively engage in learning.

(3) Improved interactivity: Through diverse interactive activities like teamwork and role-playing, the interaction and collaboration among students can be significantly enhanced, promoting a deeper understanding of complex concepts and improving their application skills.

(4) Observation of knowledge mastery through gaming participation; Game-based teaching allows real-time feedback on student understanding, helping teachers adjust teaching strategies promptly to ensure the achievement of educational objectives.

2.1.4 Risks (T)

(1) Time-consuming game design: Although gamification elements can enhance the fun and interactivity of learning, their design and implementation also require considerable time and effort. If teachers cannot efficiently utilize this time, it may lead to overall teaching progress delays. Therefore, schools should provide necessary support and resources to assist teachers in better implementing game-based teaching.

(2) Varied student acceptance: As mentioned above, not all students can adapt to gamified teaching. Some students might be uninterested or confused by it, affecting their learning outcomes. Teachers need to provide personalized guidance and support based on individual student situations.
(3) Logical consistency of game content design: Game-based design needs to be scientifically and reasonably integrated into the teaching content to avoid overly entertaining while neglecting core educational values. Teachers must carefully craft game content to ensure it attracts students' interest while effectively delivering knowledge.
(4) Logical consistency between subject content and game mechanisms: When integrating subject content with game mechanisms, it is crucial to ensure logical consistency and rationality. If the game mechanisms are disjointed from the subject content, it may fail to achieve the intended educational effect. Therefore, teachers need to conduct thorough testing and validation to ensure the effectiveness and applicability of the games.

Table 1. Gamification Capabilities

External Factors-Gamification Internal Capabilities - Teaching Design BOPPPS Model	S	W
	1. Student engagement in learning 2. Student interactivity 3. Timely feedback on students' mastery of knowledge	1. Variations in student receptivity 2. Time-consuming for teachers in curriculum design 3. Reasonability of methods during the learning process
O	SO	WO
1. Enhance the fun factor 2. Increase participation 3. Improve interactivity 4. Observe students' mastery of knowledge through game participation;	(1) Provide teacher training and resource support; (2) Use advanced technology to improve teaching processes; (3) Design universally applicable game-based learning schemes; (4) Ensure that educational content takes precedence over entertainment elements; (5) Continuously evaluate and monitor the effectiveness of game-based teaching; (6) Enhance technical support and infrastructure development.	(1) Regularly conduct teacher training to enhance their technological application skills; (2) Establish a comprehensive technical support system to improve teaching efficiency; (3) Flexibly adjust teaching methods to meet the diverse learning needs of students; (4) Offer diverse learning resources to enrich the content of instruction; (5) Ensure a variety of teaching activities to accommodate different learning styles of students; (6) Continuously improve teaching methods to enhance the quality of education.

continued on following page

Table 1. Continued

T	ST	WT
1. Time consumption in game design 2. Variations in student receptivity 3. Reasonability of game content design 4. Reasonability of knowledge points and game mechanisms;	(1) Establish clear priorities to ensure the integrity and systematic nature of learning content; (2) Regularly assess and monitor to promptly identify and address potential issues; (3) Strengthen technical support to enhance the reliability and efficiency of educational equipment; (4) Perfect infrastructure to improve the comfort and convenience of the teaching environment; (5) Gradually implement and pilot new teaching methods to mitigate risks associated with uncertainty; (6) Offer alternative solutions to cope with emergencies and ensure the continuity of instruction.	(1) Implement new teaching methods in stages to avoid the shock of large-scale changes at once; (2) Offer multiple optional teaching methods to meet the diverse learning preferences and needs of students; (3) Focus on long-term development to ensure the stability and sustainability of teaching methods; (4) Regularly collect feedback and analyze data to understand the implementation effects of new methods; (5) Continuously optimize and adjust teaching methods to enhance the quality and effectiveness of education; (6) Provide psychological support and counseling services to help students adapt to new teaching methods.

4 RESULTS AND ANALYSIS

In this paper, through the SWOT analysis of game-based teaching, we have gained a deep understanding of its inherent strengths, external opportunities, inherent weaknesses, and potential risks. Based on this analysis, we propose a series of strategies aimed at optimizing the application of game-based teaching and advancing educational reform.

By leveraging the strengths of game-based teaching and seizing external opportunities (SO strategy), to maximize the benefits of the BOPPPS model and capitalize on the opportunities of gamification, it is recommended to integrate modern technology with the BOPPPS model. This approach promotes interdisciplinary game-based learning methods, supports current educational reforms, and designs teaching activities that align with modern learning habits. These measures can enhance student engagement and learning outcomes while promoting efficient use of educational resources.

In response to the weaknesses of game-based teaching, we also identify several opportunities (WO strategy). To overcome the disadvantages of the BOPPPS model and seize these opportunities, it is suggested to provide teacher training and resource support, utilize technology to improve teaching processes, and design universally applicable game-based learning schemes. These initiatives can ensure that all students benefit regardless of their interest in game-based learning.

To leverage the strengths of the BOPPPS model while mitigating risks (ST strategy), it is recommended to ensure that learning content remains prioritized. Continuous evaluation and monitoring of the effectiveness of game-based teaching should be conducted, along with enhancing technical support and infrastructure. These measures can ensure the smooth progression of teaching activities and reduce potential risk factors.

Finally, in response to the disadvantages and potential risks of game-based teaching (WT strategy), to overcome the limitations of the BOPPPS model and address potential risk factors, we suggest gradually implementing and piloting new teaching methods and providing alternative solutions to accommodate different student learning needs and focus on their long-term development.

In summary, despite the numerous challenges faced by game-based teaching, through proper planning and execution of relevant strategies, it is expected to become a powerful tool for educational innovation and improving student learning efficiency. The future path requires joint efforts by teachers, scholars, and educational decision-makers to realize the full potential of game-based teaching and ensure it brings positive impacts to all students.

REFERENCES

Abujaber, A. A., Abd-Alrazaq, A., Al-Qudimat, A. R., & Nashwan, A. J. (2023). A strengths, weaknesses, opportunities, and threats (SWOT) analysis of ChatGPT integration in nursing education: A narrative review. *Cureus*, 15(11). Advance online publication. DOI: 10.7759/cureus.48643 PMID: 38090452

Christopoulos, A., & Mystakidis, S. (2023). Gamification in education. *Encyclopedia*, 3(4), 1223–1243. DOI: 10.3390/encyclopedia3040089

David, L., & Weinstein, N. (2024). Using technology to make learning fun: Technology use is best made fun and challenging to optimize intrinsic motivation and engagement. *European Journal of Psychology of Education*, 39(2), 1441–1463. DOI: 10.1007/s10212-023-00734-0

Farrokhnia, M., Banihashem, S. K., Noroozi, O., & Wals, A. (2024). A SWOT analysis of ChatGPT: Implications for educational practice and research. *Innovations in Education and Teaching International*, 61(3), 460–474. DOI: 10.1080/14703297.2023.2195846

Gil-Aciron, L. A. (2024). The gamer psychology: A psychological perspective on game design and gamification. *Interactive Learning Environments*, 32(1), 183–207. DOI: 10.1080/10494820.2022.2082489

Guo, Y. (2024). *An investigation into the practice of blended teaching in English courses based on the BOPPPS model*. Applied Mathematics and Nonlinear Sciences. DOI: 10.2478/amns.2023.1.00336

Heldal, I., Helgesen, C., Ali, Q., Patel, D., Geitung, A. B., & Pettersen, H. (2021). Supporting school aged children to train their vision by using serious games. *Computers*, 10(4), 53. DOI: 10.3390/computers10040053

Ho, D. G., Sa'adi, M., He, D., & Hoon, C.-Y. (2023). Silence over the wire: Student verbal participation and the virtual classroom in the digital era. *Asia Pacific Education Review*, 24(4), 599–615. DOI: 10.1007/s12564-023-09834-4

Kumar, V., & Rewari, M. (2022). A responsible approach to higher education curriculum design. *International Journal of Educational Reform*, 31(4), 422–441. DOI: 10.1177/10567879221110509

Pardim, V. I., Contreras Pinochet, L. H., Viana, A. B. N., & Souza, C. A. (2023). Where is the student who was here? Gamification as a strategy to engage students. *The International Journal of Information and Learning Technology*, 40(2), 177–192. DOI: 10.1108/IJILT-05-2022-0122

Saha, M., Islam, S., Akhi, A. A., & Saha, G. (2024). Factors affecting success and failure in higher education mathematics: Students' and teachers' perspectives. *Heliyon*, 10(7), e29173. DOI: 10.1016/j.heliyon.2024.e29173 PMID: 38601642

Stott, A., & Neustaedter, C. (2013). Analysis of gamification in education. *Surrey, BC, Canada, 8*(1), 36.

Xiaoling, H., Lingxia, Z., & Dan, L. (2021). Effectiveness of game-based teaching: A systematic review and meta-analysis. *Open Educ. Res*, 27(02), 69–79.

Xu, J. (2023). Optimizing English Education in the Information Era: A Multimodal Approach Based on BOPPPS Teaching Model. *Journal of Combinatorial Mathematics and Combinatorial Computing*, 118, 33–48. DOI: 10.61091/jcmcc118-03

Yan, L., Lu, Z., & Yu, Y. (2023). Exploration and Practice of BOPPPS Model in Enhancing Effective Teaching--Taking Business Communication as an Example. SHS Web of Conferences, Zaman, M. (2023). ChatGPT for healthcare sector: SWOT analysis. *International journal of research in industrial engineering, 12*(3), 221-233.

Yao, S. (2022) A Study on Case Teaching of High School Geography Courses from the Perspective of. SWOT Analysis (Doctoral dissertation, Henan University).

Zhang, L., & Dong, F. (2024). Development Strategies of Chinese Geriatric Hospitals Based on the SWOT-CLPV Model. *Social Medicine and Health Management*, 5(1), 106–118.

Chapter 8
Applications of Artificial Intelligence for Enhanced Bug Detection in Software Development

Yahya Najib Hamood Al-Shameri
Kocaeli University, Turkey

ABSTRACT

As technology advances at breakneck speed, reliance on software grows exponentially. This growth has given rise to multiple issues encountered during software development, including increased occurrences of software bugs. The conventional methods previously used by developers, such as manual code checking or testing, may involve greater chances of human error and extended timelines, resulting in more significant expense budgets towards revenue leakage due to late deliveries or failed outcomes. This chapter per the authors aim to explore how artificial intelligence (AI) solutions can identify potential vulnerabilities more accurately than before. By utilizing machine learning algorithms, deep learning, and natural language processing, AI-based bug detection not only enhances precision and efficiency but also saves costs on the development process, ultimately giving better software quality and reduced monetary costs. This chapter per the authors present some applications of AI techniques in bugs detection to select bugs accurately and suggest possible optimizations for the buggy codes.

DOI: 10.4018/979-8-3693-6745-2.ch008

1. INTRODUCTION

In the contemporary environment of software development, the complexity and scale of projects have increased, rendering traditional bug detection methods, such as manual code reviews and conventional testing, increasingly inadequate. The limitations of these methods become particularly evident in large-scale software systems, where the volume of code surpasses manual review efforts, leading to overlooked bugs and higher costs associated with late-stage bug fixes. Errors during software development are inevitable, and it is crucial to detect and fix them quickly to ensure reliable software. Traditional methods like code reviews and testing can be time-consuming and not entirely reliable. This has sparked significant interest in leveraging advanced techniques to enhance bug detection processes. Modern techniques, especially those involving artificial intelligence, offer promising solutions to the challenges of bug detection. By analyzing large amounts of code and identifying patterns that could indicate potential errors, these techniques can significantly reduce the time and effort required for manual inspections. Automated tools can detect and classify bugs, improving both the efficiency and accuracy of the process. (Siswantoro & Yuhana, 2023; Tang et al., 2024)

Modern techniques, particularly those involving deep learning and natural language processing, hold great promise for improving the efficiency and reliability of bug detection. For instance, supervised learning models can analyze extensive codebases to identify patterns indicative of potential bugs that might escape human reviewers (Elshamy et al., 2023; Wang, 2023). These models can classify bugs based on historical data, allowing for the proactive identification of error-prone modules before they are subjected to testing (Bala et al., 2023). Additionally, approaches such as Generative Adversarial Networks (GANs) have been explored to enhance bug prediction capabilities, demonstrating advanced accuracy and speed in identifying software bugs (Kumar & Venkatesan, 2020; Song et al., 2024). This shift towards automated and intelligent bug detection not only reduces the time and effort required for manual inspections but also enhances the overall quality of software products. The integration of artificial intelligence (AI) techniques into bug detection processes provides a more nuanced understanding of software quality. AI can effectively address the complexities of modern software systems by detecting subtle and intricate bugs that traditional methods might overlook (Siswantoro & Yuhana, 2023; Tang et al., 2024). For example, hybrid models that combine various machine learning algorithms have been developed to optimize bug prediction, achieving higher accuracy and efficiency in identifying errors (Bala et al., 2023; Zheng et al., 2021). Moreover, the use of data mining techniques has facilitated the classification and prioritization of bugs, enabling developers to focus their efforts on the most critical issues (Prakash et al., 2015; Wang, 2023). This capability is particularly valuable in large-scale projects, where the cost of manual bug detection is prohibitively high.

The implementation of advanced techniques in bug detection represents a transformative shift in software development practices. By harnessing the power of artificial intelligence, developers can significantly enhance the accuracy, efficiency, and reliability of bug detection processes. As technology continues to evolve, the role of these advanced methodologies is expected to expand, offering even more effective solutions for identifying and addressing software defects, ultimately leading to higher-quality software products. (Kumar & Venkatesan, 2020; Siswantoro & Yuhana, 2023; Tang et al., 2024)

In this study, several code snippets containing bugs were tested using various AI tools that have been developed in recent years for the purpose of bug detection. The aim was to evaluate the effectiveness of these tools in identifying and addressing potential issues within the code. AI tools such as Microsoft Copilot, CodePal, ChatGPT and Gemini were used as part of the study. These tools were provided with code snippets containing bugs and their ability to identify and detect these bugs was analyzed and compared.

2. AI TECHNIQUES IN BUG DETECTION

Artificial Intelligence (AI) techniques have significantly transformed the landscape of bug detection in software development. These techniques leverage machine learning, natural language processing, and other AI methodologies to automate and enhance the processes of identifying, diagnosing, and prioritizing bugs. This section will detail various AI techniques utilized in bug detection, highlighting their methodologies, applications, and benefits.

2.1 Machine Learning (ML)

Various machine learning techniques, including decision trees, support vector machines and neural networks, can be utilized for bug detection in software. These algorithms have the ability to predict and categorize defects by being trained on previous data such as bug reports and code repositories. This training enables them to recognize patterns and connections that help with identifying bugs in newly written code. (Menzies & Marcus, 2008)

Neural networks, inspired by the human brain, consist of interconnected layers of nodes (neurons) that process input data. These networks can learn complex patterns and relationships within the data through a process called training. By adjusting the weights of the connections between neurons, neural networks can improve their accuracy in predicting and categorizing defects. This makes them particularly effective for handling large and complex datasets, such as those found in software development.

Ensemble methods, which combine multiple models to improve prediction accuracy, can also be employed for bug detection. Techniques like random forests and gradient boosting are examples of ensemble methods that can enhance the performance of individual models by aggregating their predictions.

2.2 Natural Language Processing (NLP)

One way to detect bugs is by using natural language processing (NLP) methods to examine written data, like comments and documentation. NLP can spot disparities between code and documentation as well as recognize unclear or unfinished requirements that might result in bugs by taking out significant facts from these materials. (Arnaoudova et al., 2016)

Moreover, NLP can be used to analyze bug reports and user feedback. By processing the natural language used in these reports, NLP can identify common patterns and recurring issues, helping developers to prioritize and address the most critical bugs. This can also provide insights into the root causes of bugs, enabling more effective and targeted fixes.

2.3 Deep Learning

Advanced machine learning methods, such as RNNs and CNNs, have demonstrated potential in identifying errors in code by analyzing it either as a sequence of tokens or an image. Such methods can intelligently comprehend intricate patterns and connections within the code, making them capable of detecting bugs that may be challenging to pinpoint using conventional means. (Pradel & Sen, 2018)

RNNs are particularly effective for sequential data, such as code, because they can maintain context across long sequences. This allows them to understand the flow and dependencies within the code, making it easier to identify logical errors and inconsistencies. By processing the code token by token, RNNs can detect anomalies that might indicate the presence of bugs. (Sadkoğlu et al., 2023)

On the other hand, CNNs, which are typically used for image processing, can be applied to code by representing it as a visual structure. For example, the code can be transformed into a graph or matrix, where CNNs can then analyze spatial relationships and patterns. This approach is useful for identifying structural issues and complex bugs that are difficult to detect through traditional text-based analysis.

3. BENEFITS OF AI-DRIVEN BUG DETECTION

Artificial intelligence-based bug identification systems provide several benefits compared to conventional techniques, such as: (Ray et al., 2014)

- **Improved Learning Efficiency**: AI tools can process and analyze large codebases far more quickly than traditional methods, allowing developers to receive feedback faster and focus their efforts on higher-order problem-solving tasks. This reduces frustration and enhances motivation by minimizing time spent on repetitive debugging tasks.
- **Increased accuracy:** By learning from historical data, AI-driven systems can identify patterns and relationships that may be difficult for humans to detect, leading to more accurate bug detection.
- **Reduced development costs:** By automating the bug detection process, AI-driven systems can help reduce the costs associated with manual code reviews and testing.
- **Enhanced Collaboration and Communication**: AI-driven tools such as ChatGPT and Copilot can act as collaborative partners in coding environments. These tools not only help with debugging but also explain code logic, provide suggestions, and facilitate better understanding of coding best practices. By fostering a collaborative coding experience, these AI systems can also enhance teamwork and communication skills.

4. AI TOOLS IN BUG DETECTION

4.1 CodePal AI Tool

CodePal is a powerful AI-driven tool that helps developers find and fix bugs in their code more efficiently. By using advanced machine learning, CodePal not only identifies potential issues but also provides real-time feedback, helping to catch and correct errors early in the development process. (Codepal.ai, 2022)

4.1.1 Key Features

- **Smart Code Analysis:** CodePal scans your code with sophisticated AI models to spot bugs that might be missed in manual reviews.
- **Real-Time Feedback:** Get instant alerts and suggestions as you code, reducing debugging time later.

- **Pattern Recognition:** Trained on vast code datasets, CodePal recognizes common bugs and warns you before they become problems.
- **Automated Testing:** It generates test cases automatically, covering a wide range of scenarios, including edge cases.
- **Seamless Integration:** CodePal works smoothly with popular development environments and version control systems.

4.1.2 Benefits

- **Higher Accuracy:** Fewer false positives and missed issues thanks to AI-driven bug detection.
- **Increased Efficiency:** Real-time feedback and automated testing streamline the development process.
- **Better Code Quality:** Continuous learning and integration ensure consistently reliable and maintainable code.

4.1.3 Challenges

- **Learning Curve:** Developers might need time to fully adapt to and utilize the tool.
- **Resource Intensity:** Running advanced AI models can be resource-heavy, which might be a concern for smaller teams.

In summary, CodePal is a significant advancement in AI-powered bug detection, offering developers a tool that improves code quality and makes the development process more efficient.

4.2 ChatGPT AI Tool

ChatGPT, developed by OpenAI, is a versatile conversational AI model with applications in software development, particularly in bug detection and resolution. Utilizing natural language processing (NLP) and machine learning, ChatGPT aids developers in identifying and fixing bugs more efficiently. (Ge & Wu, 2023; Google, 2023; Surameery & Shakor, 2023)

4.2.1 Key Features

- **Interactive Debugging:** ChatGPT can engage developers in interactive debugging sessions, understanding natural language queries to help diagnose code issues and suggest fixes. This makes debugging more intuitive and less time-consuming.

- **Code Explanation and Documentation:** The tool can explain complex code segments and provide detailed documentation, which is especially useful for understanding legacy code or onboarding new team members. This ensures quicker identification and resolution of potential bugs.
- **Automated Code Reviews:** ChatGPT can conduct automated code reviews, analyzing code for bugs and suggesting improvements, helping maintain high code quality and reducing the risk of overlooked issues.
- **Learning from Developer Interactions:** ChatGPT learns from its interactions with developers, continuously improving its understanding of coding practices and common issues. This adaptive learning enhances its ability to detect and fix bugs.
- **Integration with Development Tools:** ChatGPT integrates with various development tools and platforms, offering real-time assistance as developers write and review code, making bug detection a seamless part of the workflow.

4.2.2 Benefits

- **Enhanced Collaboration:** ChatGPT improves communication and collaboration among development teams by providing clear explanations and helpful suggestions.
- **Increased Efficiency:** By automating routine tasks like code reviews and documentation, ChatGPT allows developers to focus on more complex and creative aspects of software development.
- **Improved Code Quality:** Continuous learning and real-time feedback help maintain high code quality, reducing bugs and enhancing overall software reliability.

4.2.3 Challenges

- **Contextual Limitations:** ChatGPT's suggestions are based on the context it has been trained in, which may not always perfectly match specific project requirements.
- **Dependency on AI:** Over-reliance on AI for debugging and code reviews could lead to a reduced understanding of the code among developers.

In summary, ChatGPT is a powerful tool that enhances the bug detection process in software development. By leveraging its conversational AI capabilities and continuous learning, it helps developers produce cleaner, more reliable code, ultimately leading to better software products.

4.3 Microsoft Copilot

Microsoft Copilot, an AI-powered tool integrated into development environments like Visual Studio Code, enhances software development by improving productivity and code quality. Powered by OpenAI's Codex, it suggests code snippets and provides real-time feedback, reducing the likelihood of bugs during coding. Copilot's vast training on open-source repositories enables it to detect common mistakes and deviations from best practices, helping to prevent bugs early. (Wermelinger, 2023)

4.3.1 Key Features

- **Code Autocompletion**: Copilot reduces manual errors by offering contextual code suggestions based on existing code.
- **Learning from Code Repositories**: It detects potential issues based on patterns from historical data, improving code reliability.
- **Real-time Bug Prevention**: It identifies inefficient loops, unused variables, and unhandled exceptions, minimizing future bugs.
- **IDE Integration**: Seamless integration allows developers to detect potential bugs during coding, reducing later debugging.
- **Code Reviews**: Copilot assists in reviewing code by flagging potential issues and suggesting improvements.
- **AI-Generated Unit Tests**: Copilot aids in writing unit tests, ensuring the code is robust and well-tested.

4.3.2 Benefits

Microsoft Copilot offers several benefits when it comes to improving bug detection and overall software quality:

- **Reduced Human Error**: By automating repetitive tasks and offering context-specific suggestions, Copilot minimizes the chance of human error, which is a common cause of bugs.
- **Early Detection of Potential Bugs**: Copilot's intelligent code suggestions help catch mistakes early, preventing bugs from making their way into production code.

- **Increased Productivity**: Developers spend less time debugging and more time building features, as Copilot helps catch many common errors during the code-writing phase itself.
- **Code Consistency and Best Practices**: Copilot encourages the use of standardized code practices, which leads to more maintainable and consistent codebases, reducing the likelihood of bugs due to varying coding styles

4.3.3 Challenges

- **Code Accuracy**: Generated code might miss edge cases.
- **Dependence on Training Data**: Specialized code not covered by its training data may introduce limitations.
- Copilot's role is to assist and enhance, not replace, comprehensive testing strategies like unit testing, integration testing, or manual code reviews.

In summary, Microsoft Copilot is a powerful tool for reducing bugs early in software development but should be complemented with thorough testing practices.

4.4 Gemini AI Tools

Gemini is an AI-powered tool designed to improve the software development process by offering advanced bug detection capabilities. Using machine learning algorithms, Gemini helps developers find and fix bugs more efficiently, leading to better code quality and reliability (Akter et al., 2023; Pichai, 2023).

4.4.1 Key Features

- **Deep Learning Integration:** Gemini uses deep learning models to analyze code patterns and detect anomalies that could indicate bugs. This allows it to identify complex issues that traditional static analysis tools might overlook.
- **Automated Code Review:** Gemini performs automated code reviews, scanning the codebase to highlight potential errors and suggest improvements. This helps catch bugs early, reducing the time spent on manual reviews.
- **Contextual Understanding:** The tool is trained to understand the context of the code, enabling it to detect bugs that are specific to the overall structure and logic of the project.
- **Continuous Learning:** Gemini learns from new code and bug reports over time, improving its detection capabilities. This ensures that it remains up to date with the latest coding practices and vulnerabilities.

- **Integration with Development Environments:** Gemini integrates seamlessly with popular development environments and version control systems, providing real-time feedback as developers write code. This integration supports a smooth workflow and makes bug detection a natural part of the development process.

4.4.2 Benefits

- **Enhanced Accuracy:** With deep learning and contextual understanding, Gemini offers highly accurate bug detection, minimizing false positives and overlooked issues.
- **Increased Efficiency:** Automated reviews and real-time feedback speed up development, allowing developers to focus on more complex tasks and reducing the time spent debugging.
- **Improved Code Quality:** Continuous learning and tight integration with development environments ensure consistently high code quality, leading to more reliable and maintainable software.

4.4.3 Challenges

- **Complexity of Integration:** Integrating a tool like Gemini into existing workflows can be complex and might require additional training for developers.
- **Resource Intensive:** Deep learning models require significant computational resources, which could be a concern for smaller teams or projects with limited budgets.

In summary, Gemini is a significant advancement in AI-powered bug detection, providing developers with a powerful tool to improve code quality and streamline the development process. Its deep learning and continuous learning capabilities help ensure that software is robust, reliable, and free from critical bugs.

5. AI-POWERED BUG DETECTION CONCEPT

5.1 Understanding the Concept

AI-powered bug detection leverages machine learning algorithms to automatically identify potential errors or defects in software code. These algorithms are trained on vast datasets of code, bugs, and bug patterns. Once trained, they can analyze new code and compare it against known bug patterns, flagging potential issues (Ayewah et al., 2021; Liang et al., 2014; Heaps, Slavin, & Wang, 2018).

5.2 Key Techniques and Approaches

5.2.1 Static Analysis

- **Syntax and Semantic Analysis:** AI tools can examine code for syntax errors, type mismatches, and semantic inconsistencies.
- **Code Style and Best Practices:** They can assess adherence to coding standards, reducing the risk of human error.
- **Vulnerability Scanning:** AI can identify common security vulnerabilities like SQL injection, cross-site scripting, and buffer overflows.

5.2.2 Dynamic Analysis

- **Runtime Error Detection:** AI can monitor code execution for exceptions, crashes, and unexpected behavior.
- **Performance Profiling:** It can identify bottlenecks and performance issues.
- **Fuzz Testing:** AI can generate random inputs to stress-test code and uncover hidden bugs.

5.2.3 Machine Learning Algorithms

- **Supervised Learning:** Algorithms are trained on labeled data (code with known bugs) to learn patterns and predict new ones.
- **Unsupervised Learning:** Algorithms can identify anomalies or outliers in code that might indicate bugs.
- **Reinforcement Learning:** AI can learn through trial and error, experimenting with different code modifications to find optimal solutions.

5.2.4 Natural Language Processing (NLP)

- **Code Comment Analysis:** AI can analyze comments to understand the intended behavior of code and identify inconsistencies.
- **Issue Tracking Integration:** AI can analyze bug reports and code changes to identify recurring patterns and root causes.

5.3 The Role of AI in Modern Development

- **Early Detection:** AI can identify potential bugs early in the development process, saving time and resources.
- **Improved Code Quality:** By catching errors before they become more complex, AI can help ensure higher-quality software.
- **Reduced Manual Effort:** AI can automate many routine testing tasks, freeing up developers to focus on more complex problems.
- **Enhanced Security:** AI can help identify security vulnerabilities that might be missed by traditional testing methods.
- **Continuous Improvement:** AI can learn from its mistakes and improve its accuracy over time.

5.4 Concept Example: Microsoft's BugLab Project

5.4.1 Introduction

BugLab is a deep learning model developed by Microsoft Research that aims to automate the process of detecting and repairing software bugs. This innovative approach leverages the power of machine learning to address the time-consuming and often frustrating task of manual bug hunting.

BugLab is trained using a unique "hide and seek" game, inspired by generative adversarial networks (GANs). In this game, two competing models are trained together: (See Figure 1)

- **Bug Selector:** This model introduces bugs into code snippets, mimicking the behavior of human developers.
- **Bug Detector:** This model tries to identify and fix the bugs introduced by the selector.

Figure 1. The BugLab Deep Learning System

By playing this game repeatedly, both models learn to improve their skills. The bug selector becomes better at creating more challenging bugs, while the bug detector becomes more adept at finding and fixing them (Allamanis et al., 2021).

5.4.2 Example

BugLab can also understand ambiguous natural language hints that developers leave in code comments, variable names, and other parts of the code. This ability enables it to identify and repair bugs that are not immediately apparent from the code's structure alone. An illustration of this is the code excerpt shown in figure 2, which corrects a bug in a GitHub open-source project. (See Figure 2)

Figure 2. Bug detection by AI is Microsoft's BugLab project

```
  def make_id(name):
      """
      Create a random id combined with the creditor name.
      @return string consisting of name (truncated at 22 chars), -,
      12 char rand hex string.
      """
      r = get_rand_string(12)
-     if len(name) <= 22:
+     if len(name) > 22:
          name = name[:22]
      return name + "-" + r
```

In this case, the software developer's intention is evident from both the code's high-level structure and the natural language comment. Despite this, a bug managed to slip through, resulting in the use of an incorrect comparison operator. Microsoft's BugLab deep learning model was capable of detecting this bug accurately and notifying the developer. (Allamanis, & Brockschmidt, 2021)

5.4.3 Key Features of BugLab

- **Self-supervised learning:** BugLab is trained without the need for labeled data, making it more adaptable to different codebases.
- **Graph-based representation:** BugLab represents code as a graph, capturing its rich structure and relationships between different entities.
- **Neural network architectures:** BugLab uses graph neural networks (GNNs) and relational transformers to reason over the code's structure and identify potential bugs.

5.4.4 Results and Limitations

While BugLab has shown promising results in detecting and repairing common types of bugs, it is still under development. Further advancements are needed to improve its accuracy and reliability.

5.4.5 Conclusion

BugLab represents a significant step forward in the field of AI-powered bug detection and repair. Its ability to learn from code and leverage natural language cues offers the potential to significantly reduce the time and effort required for software development. As AI technology continues to evolve, we can expect to see even more innovative approaches to automating the bug detection process. (Allamanis et al., 2021Allamanis, & Brockschmidt, 2021)

6. BUG DETECTION APPLICATIONS BY DIFFERENT AI TOOLS

In this section, we compare and analyze the feedback provided by various AI tools CodePal, Gemini, Copilot, and ChatGPT- on the same piece of code. Each tool offers unique insights and suggestions for improving the code, reflecting their individual approaches to bug detection and code enhancement.

6.1 Applied Code and Instruction

6.1.1 Calculate the Average of a List of Numbers Code

The code under analysis is a Python script written by the author, which calculates the average of a list of numbers. It contains several errors and bugs that prevent it from functioning correctly. (See Figure 3)

Figure 3. The script of Calculation the average Code

```
def calculate_average(numbers):
    total = 0
    for number in numbers:
        total += number
        return total / len(numbers)

numbers = [1, 2, 3, 'four', 5]
average = calculate_average(numbers)
print('The Average:'average)
```

Running this code will result in multiple errors, which will be analyzed by the different AI tools.

6.1.2 Instruction

The instruction provided to the AI tools to have bug detection report is:
"This code was written to calculate the average of a list of numbers. Act as a bug detector and give a bug detection report."

6.2 The Bug Detection Feedback by the Different AI Tools

6.2.1 CodePal Bug Detector

CodePal focuses heavily on code analysis without needing additional instructions. It provides feedback in multiple categories, including syntax errors, runtime errors, code optimization, and performance bottlenecks. Here is the generated bug detection report for **calculate_average** code. (Codepal.ai, 2022)

Syntax Errors

Issue: Incorrect Syntax in Print Statement

- **Context: print('The Average:'average)**
- **Description:** The syntax for the print statement is incorrect. The string and variable are not properly concatenated.
- **Suggested Fix:** Change to **print('The Average:', average)** or use an f-string: **print(f'**The Average**: {average}').**

Issue: Improper Indentation of Return Statement

- **Context: return total / len(numbers)** is indented within the loop.
- **Description:** The **return** statement is incorrectly placed inside the loop, causing the function to return after the first iteration.
- **Suggested Fix:** Move the return statement outside of the **for** loop.

Runtime Errors

Issue: TypeError due to Non-Numeric Value

- **Context:** The list (**numbers**) contains a string **'four'**.
- **Description:** When trying to calculate the average, adding a string to an integer will raise a **TypeError**.
- **Suggested Fix:** Ensure all elements in **numbers** are numeric. You can filter the list to include only numbers before performing calculations.

Memory Leaks

Issue: No Memory Leak Detected

- **Context:** The function does not create any persistent data structures that would lead to memory leaks.
- **Description:** The function operates on a local variable and does not retain references that could lead to memory issues.
- **Conclusion:** No memory leaks are present in this code.

Code Optimization Tips

Issue: Inefficient Handling of Non-Numeric Values

- **Description:** The current implementation does not handle non-numeric values, which can lead to runtime errors. This could be optimized by filtering the input list.
- **Suggested Fix:** Use a list comprehension to filter out non-numeric values before calculating the average: numbers = [num **for** num **in** numbers **if** isinstance(num, (**int**, **float**))]

Issue: Division by Zero

- **Description:** If the list contains no valid numbers after filtering, **len(numbers)** will be zero, leading to a ZeroDivisionError.
- **Suggested Fix:** Add a check to ensure that the list is not empty before performing the division.

Deprecated Functions

Issue: No Deprecated Functions Detected

- **Context:** The code does not utilize any deprecated functions.
- **Conclusion:** All functions used in this code are current and do not have any known deprecations. However, always check the latest Python documentation for updates.

Performance Bottlenecks

Issue: Inefficient Average Calculation

- **Context:** The **return** statement is placed inside the loop.
- **Description:** This causes the function to return after the first iteration, leading to incorrect average calculation.
- **Suggested Fix:** Move the **return** statement outside the loop to ensure all numbers are processed before calculating the average.

Variable Naming Consistency

Issue: Inconsistent Naming

- **Context:** The variable list (**numbers**) is clear, but the function name could be more descriptive.
- **Description:** While **calculate_average** is descriptive, consider renaming it to **calculate_average_of_numbers** for clarity.
- **Suggested Fix:** Ensure all variable names are consistently descriptive and follow a clear naming convention.

Comments Review

Issue: Lack of Comments

- **Context:** The function lacks comments explaining its purpose and parameters.
- **Description:** Comments are essential for understanding the code's intent and usage.
- **Suggested Fix:** Add a docstring to the function to describe its purpose, parameters, and return value.

Potential Refactoring Spots

Issue: Handling Non-Numeric Values

- **Description:** The function does not handle non-numeric values in the list, which can lead to a TypeError during addition.
- **Suggested Fix:** Implement a check to filter out non-numeric values before calculating the average, e.g.: **numbers** = [num **for** num **in** numbers **if** isinstance(num, (**int**, **float**))]

API Misuse

Issue: Incorrect Print Statement Syntax

- **Context: print('The Average:'average)**
- Description: The syntax for the print statement is incorrect; it lacks a comma or proper formatting.
- Suggested Fix: Correct the print statement to: print('The Average:', average)

Code Smells

Issue: Potential Division by Zero

- **Description:** If the input list is empty, **len(numbers)** will be zero, leading to a ZeroDivisionError.
- **Suggested Fix:** Add a check to return **None** or raise an exception if the list is empty before performing the division.

Compatibility Issues

Issue: Type Handling

- **Context:** The function does not handle mixed types in the input list.
- **Description:** The presence of a string (**'four'**) in the list will cause a **TypeError** during the addition operation.
- **Suggested Fix:** Implement type checking to ensure only numeric values are included in the average calculation.

Code Style Violations

Issue: Indentation Error

- **Context:** The return statement is incorrectly indented within the loop.
- **Description:** This violates Python's indentation rules and leads to logical errors.

- **Suggested Fix:** Correct the indentation of the return statement to align with the function's logic. (See Figure 4)

*Figure 4. Suggested Code for Fixing the***return***Statement by CodPal.*

```
def calculate_average(numbers):

    total = 0

    for number in numbers:
        total += number

    return total / len(numbers)
```

Issue: Lack of Whitespace

- **Description:** The code lacks proper whitespace for readability.
- **Suggested Fix:** Add spaces around operators and after commas to improve readability, e.g., **print('The Average:', average)** instead of **print('The Average:'average).**

Here's the corrected code (See Figure 5)

Figure 5. Enhanced Code by CodPal

```
def calculate_average(numbers):

    numbers = [num for num in numbers if isinstance(num, (int, float))]
    if len(numbers) == 0:                          #to avoid a ZeroDivisionError
        return print('No valid numbers found.')

    total = 0
    for number in numbers:
        total += number
    return total / len(numbers)

numbers = [1, 2, 3, 'four', 5]
average = calculate_average(numbers)
print('The Average:', average)
```

Overall, CodePal highlighted a variety of issues including syntax errors, runtime exceptions, potential logical errors, and code optimization opportunities, offering detailed suggestions to fix and enhance the script.

6.2.2 Gemini AI Tool

Gemini provides bug detection through both code-only analysis and with user instructions. It detects logical issues in the code while suggesting optimizations. Here is how the Gemini AI tool responded when code was inserted with the instruction. (GoogleGemini, 2023)

Code Analysis and Feedback:

Issue: The code contains a bug that will result in a **TypeError**.

Explanation: The **TypeError** occurs because the list (**numbers**) contains a string (**'four'**) which cannot be added to integers. Python's addition operator (+) is not defined for different data types, and attempting to add an integer to a string will raise an exception.

Suggestions:

- **Type Checking:** Before performing calculations, check the data type of each element in the numbers list. If a non-numeric element is found, raise an exception or convert it to a numeric type (if possible).
- **Error Handling:** Implement error handling to catch exceptions that may occur during the calculation process, such as TypeError or ZeroDivisionError (if the list is empty).

- **Input Validation:** Consider adding input validation to ensure that the numbers list is not empty and contains only numeric elements.
- **Clarity and Readability:** Improve code readability by using more descriptive variable names and adding comments to explain the purpose of different sections of the code.

Enhanced Code (See Figure 6)

Figure 6. Enhanced Code by Gemini

```
def calculate_average(numbers):
    """Calculates the average of a list of numbers.

    Args:
        numbers: A list of numbers.

    Returns:
        The average of the numbers in the list.

    Raises:
        TypeError: If the list contains non-numeric elements.
        ValueError: If the list is empty.
    """

    if not numbers:
        raise ValueError("List cannot be empty.")

    total = 0
    for number in numbers:
        if not isinstance(number, (int, float)):
            raise TypeError("List contains non-numeric elements.")
        total += number

    return total / len(numbers)

numbers = [1, 2, 3, 5]  # Removed 'four' as it is not a number
average = calculate_average(numbers)
print("The Average:", average)
```

Key improvements in the enhanced code:

- **Type checking:** Ensures that all elements in the **numbers** list are numeric.
- **Error handling:** Raises appropriate exceptions for empty lists and non-numeric elements.
- **Input validation:** Checks if the list is empty before performing calculations.

- **Clarity and readability:** Uses more descriptive variable names and comments to explain the code's purpose.

This enhanced code should now calculate the average of a list of numbers correctly and provide informative error messages if necessary.

6.2.3 Copilot AI Tool

Copilot performs a deep analysis of the code and also responds well to instruction-based bug detection. It integrates code suggestions directly into the workflow.Here is how the Copilot AI tool responded when code was inserted with the instruction. Firstly, Copilot breaks down the code and identify the issues: (Microsoft, 2022)

Issues in the Code:

- **Indentation Error:** The **return** statement is inside the **for** loop, which means it will return the result after the first iteration.
- **Type Error:** The list **numbers** contains a string **'four'**, which will cause an error when trying to add it to the total.
- **Syntax Error:** The **print** statement is missing a comma between the string and the variable **average**.

Suggestions to Enhance the Code:

- **Fix Indentation:** Ensure the **return** statement is outside the **for** loop.
- **Type Checking:** Add a check to ensure all elements in the list are numbers.
- **Correct Print Statement:** Fix the syntax error in the **print** statement.

Enhanced Code:

Here's the improved version of the code: (See Figure 7)

Figure 7. Enhanced Code by Copilot

```
def calculate_average(numbers):
    total = 0
    count = 0
    for number in numbers:
        if isinstance(number, (int, float)):  # Check if the element is a number
            total += number
            count += 1
        else:
            print(f"Warning: '{number}' is not a number and will be ignored.")
    if count == 0:
        return 0  # Avoid division by zero
    return total / count

numbers = [1, 2, 3, 'four', 5]
average = calculate_average(numbers)
print('The Average:', average)
```

Explanation of Enhancements:

- **Indentation:** The **(return)** statement is now correctly placed outside the **(for)** loop.
- **Type Checking:** The (**isinstance**) function checks if each element is an integer or float, and only those are added to the total.
- **Handling Non-Numeric Values:** Non-numeric values are ignored, and a warning is printed.
- **Division by Zero:** Added a check to return 0 if there are no numeric values to avoid division by zero.
- **Correct Print Statement:** The **(print)** statement now correctly separates the string and the variable with a comma.

With these enhancements, the code can now accurately compute the average of numeric values in the list and gracefully handle any non-numeric entries.

6.2.4 ChatGPT AI Tool

ChatGPT provides both general insights and instruction-specific analysis, offering detailed suggestions for fixing errors, optimization, and code structure improvement. Upon analyzing the Python code for calculating the average of a list of numbers, ChatGPT highlighted the following issues and provided solutions:

Bug Detection Report: (OpenAI, 2021)

Incorrect Indentation of the return Statement

- **Issue**: The **return** statement is incorrectly indented inside the (**for**) loop.
- **Explanation**: Since the return statement is inside the loop, the function will return after processing the first number in the list, rather than after processing all numbers.
- **Fix**: Detent the **return** statement to align with the (**for**) loop, so that the return occurs after the loop has finished processing all elements. (See Figure 8)

*Figure 8. Suggested Code for Fixing the***return***Statement by ChatGPT-4*

```
def calculate_average(numbers):

    total = 0

    for number in numbers:
        total += number

    return total / len(numbers)

```

Handling Non-Numeric Values

- **Issue**: The list (**numbers**) contains a non-numeric value (**'four'**), which will cause a TypeError when trying to add it to the total.
- **Explanation**: The function assumes that all elements in the list are numbers, but 'four' is a string, leading to an error when attempting to add it to the running total.
- **Fix**: Add a check to ensure that all elements in the list are numeric before attempting to sum them. You could either skip non-numeric values, raise an error, or convert them if possible. (See Figure 9)

Figure 9. Suggested Code for Handling Non-Numeric Values by ChatGPT-4

```python
def calculate_average(numbers):

    total = 0
    count = 0

    for number in numbers:
        if isinstance(number, (int, float)):  # Check if the number is int or float
            total += number
            count += 1
        else:
            print(f"Warning: Non-numeric value '{number}' ignored.")

    if count == 0:
        return 0  # Avoid division by zero
    return total / count
```

Syntax Error in print Statement

- **Issue**: There is a syntax error in the print statement where the string and the variable average are not correctly concatenated.
- **Explanation**: The print statement is missing a comma or a plus sign to properly concatenate the string with the variable.
- **Fix**: Add a comma or use an f-string to properly format the output. (See Figure 10)

Figure 10. Suggested Code for Fixing the ***print*** *Statement by ChatGPT-4*

```python
# Correct way to print
print('The Average:', average)

# or Using f-string for formatting
print(f'The Average: {average}')
```

Potential Zero Division Error

- **Issue**: If the list (**numbers**) only contains non-numeric values, the function will attempt to divide by zero, causing a **ZeroDivisionError**.
- **Explanation**: If no numeric values are found, the count variable will be zero, leading to a division by zero when calculating the average.
- **Fix**: Add a check to return a default value or raise an appropriate error if the list contains no numeric values. (See Figure 11)

Figure 11. Suggested Code for Potential Zero Division Error by ChatGPT-4

```
def calculate_average(numbers):
    total = 0
    count = 0
    for number in numbers:
        if isinstance(number, (int, float)):
            total += number
            count += 1
        else:
            print(f"Warning: Non-numeric value '{number}' ignored.")
    if count == 0:
        return 0  # Return 0 or raise an error if no valid numbers are found
    return total / count
```

Final Corrected Code (See Figure 12)

Figure 12. Final Corrected Code by ChatGPT-4

```python
def calculate_average(numbers):
    total = 0
    count = 0
    for number in numbers:
        if isinstance(number, (int, float)):
            total += number
            count += 1
        else:
            print(f"Warning: Non-numeric value '{number}' ignored.")
    if count == 0:
        return 0
    return total / count

numbers = [1, 2, 3, 'four', 5]
average = calculate_average(numbers)
print('The Average:', average)
```

The corrected code now properly handles non-numeric values, avoids early returns within the loop, prevents division by zero, and correctly formats the output. Now, the code can handles errors gracefully, computes the average correctly, and is more readable and robust.

6.2.5 Overall Feedbacks'Summary

By comparing the feedback from **CodePal**, **Gemini**, **Copilot**, and **ChatGPT**, it is evident that all four AI tools are effective in identifying major syntax, runtime, and logic errors, but they differ significantly in their approach to optimization and enhancement suggestions.

- **CodePal** provides thorough bug reports without requiring additional instructions, focusing on common issues like incorrect syntax, improper indentation, and type errors. It also offers practical advice on code optimization, such as handling non-numeric values and preventing division by zero. CodePal stands out for its detailed performance insights, emphasizing efficient code handling and improvements.
- **Gemini** combines code analysis with instruction-based feedback, excelling in logical bug detection. It emphasizes type checking, error handling, and input validation, while also suggesting improvements in code readability, naming conventions, and adding comments for clarity. Gemini's strength lies in its focus on making the code robust, readable, and more maintainable.

- **Copilot** integrates smoothly into the development workflow, providing real-time code suggestions based on user input. It focuses on resolving key issues like indentation errors and type mismatches, while also ensuring proper error handling and print statement corrections. Copilot's ease of use and in-context suggestions make it a powerful tool for improving code quality while coding.
- **ChatGPT** provides a holistic analysis, offering both general and instruction-based feedback. It not only identifies technical issues like syntax and type errors but also suggests structural improvements. ChatGPT excels in delivering detailed explanations and solutions for potential problems like division by zero, while also recommending improvements for code formatting and readability.

Overall, while all tools are proficient at detecting bugs, they vary in their approach:

- **CodePal** is more focused on comprehensive, detailed bug reports.
- **Gemini** and **ChatGPT** offer tailored, instruction-based feedback, focusing on readability and robustness.
- **Copilot** seamlessly integrates into the coding process, offering real-time code suggestions and fixing common issues efficiently.

These tools together represent a wide range of capabilities, from real-time assistance to deep analytical insights, allowing developers to address bugs while enhancing code performance and clarity. (Akter et al., 2023; Ray et al., 2014; Surameery & Shakor, 2023; Wermelinger, 2023)

7. COMPARISON BETWEEN DIFFERENT AI TOOLS

Here is a comparison table highlighting the key features, benefits, and challenges of Copilot, Gemini, ChatGPT-4, and CodePal: (See Table 1)

Table 1. Comparison Table of the Different Tools

Feature/Aspect	CodePal	Copilot	ChatGPT-4	Gemini
Primary Function	Intelligent code analysis and bug detection	Code completion and suggestions	Conversational debugging and code assistance	Code completion and suggestions
Real-Time Feedback	Yes	Yes	Yes	Yes
Contextual Understanding	High	High	Very High	High
Automated Code Reviews	Yes	Yes	Yes	Yes
Learning from Interactions	Yes	Yes	Yes	Yes
Integration with Tools	Seamless integration with IDEs	Seamless integration with IDEs	Seamless integration with IDEs	Seamless integration with IDEs
Automated Testing	Yes	Limited	Yes	Yes
Code Explanation	Yes	Limited	Yes	Yes
Adaptive Learning	Yes	Yes	Yes	Yes
Enhanced Collaboration	High	Moderate	Very High	High
Efficiency Improvement	High	High	Very High	High
Code Quality Improvement	High	High	Very High	High
Challenges	Learning curve, Resource requirements	Dependency on AI, Security concerns	Dependency on AI, Contextual limitations	Complexity of integration, Resource intensive

This table provides a clear comparison of the strengths and challenges of each tool:

- **CodePal** is excellent for thorough bug detection and provides detailed analysis but may have a steep learning curve and higher resource requirements.
- **Copilot** offers real-time suggestions and code completion, but its dependency on AI raises potential security concerns.
- **ChatGPT-4** stands out for its deep contextual understanding, detailed explanations, and high efficiency, though it can face limitations with complex contextual queries.
- **Gemini** offers a balance between code completion and contextual suggestions but may require significant resources for optimal integration.

This comparison illustrates the diverse capabilities of these AI tools in enhancing bug detection and code quality improvement. (Akter et al., 2023; Ray et al., 2014; Surameery & Shakor, 2023; Wermelinger, 2023).

8. CHALLENGES OF AI-DRIVEN BUG DETECTION

Although AI-powered bug detection has the potential to offer significant advantages, there are still many challenges such as:

- **Data Quality:** Poor quality training data adversely affects system performance resulting in ineffective identification of bugs
- **Interpretability:** Interpretability poses another significant challenge increasing confusion among developers in addressing identified bugs accurately
- **Integration with existing tools:** complexities in integrating AI algorithms into existing development tools demand considerable time and resources further exacerbating these challenges.
- **False Positives:** AI tools may sometimes flag non-issues, leading to unnecessary investigations.
- **False Negatives:** AI may miss some bugs, especially if they are novel or outside the scope of its training data.
- **Complexity of Code:** AI may struggle to understand complex code or code with unconventional patterns.

Effective solutions demand prioritized research efforts focused on developing new techniques while concurrently solving current shortcomings as a means towards enhancing accuracy and efficiency. (Surameery & Shakor, 2023; Liu et al., 2017)

9. CONCLUSION

This chapter delved into the transformative potential of artificial intelligence (AI) in revolutionizing bug detection practices within software development. Traditional methods, such as manual code reviews and conventional testing, have fallen short in addressing the increasing complexity and scale of modern software projects. AI-powered techniques, including deep learning and natural language processing, offer a more efficient and accurate approach to identifying and classifying bugs.

This can assist developers in resolving bugs more efficiently, resulting in top-quality software and decreased development expenses.

By analyzing vast amounts of code and recognizing patterns indicative of potential errors, AI tools can significantly reduce the time and effort required for manual inspections. This not only enhances the overall quality of software products but also enables developers to focus on more critical tasks. The ability of AI to detect subtle and intricate bugs that might escape human detection is particularly valuable in ensuring the reliability and robustness of software systems. (Elshamy et al., 2023; Wang, 2023)

The chapter also highlighted the effectiveness of various AI tools, such as Microsoft Copilot, CodePal, ChatGPT, and Gemini, in identifying and addressing bugs within code snippets. These tools demonstrated their ability to analyze code and detect potential issues, showcasing the practical application of AI in enhancing bug detection processes.

As AI technology continues to advance, its role in bug detection is expected to expand further. The integration of AI-powered tools into software development workflows can lead to more efficient, reliable, and higher-quality software products. By leveraging the power of AI, developers can proactively address potential issues, reducing the risk of costly errors and improving overall software quality.

REFERENCES

Akter, S. N., Wu, Z., Muhamed, A., Ou, T., Bäuerle, A., Cabrera, Á. A., Dholakia, K., Xiong, C., & Neubig, G. (2023). An in-depth look at Gemini's language abilities. *ArXiv*. https://doi.org//arXiv.2312.11444DOI: 10.48550

Allamanis, M., & Brockschmidt, M. (2021, December 8). Finding and fixing bugs with deep learning. *Microsoft Research*. https://www.microsoft.com/research/blog/finding-and-fixing-bugs-with-deep-learning/

Allamanis, M., Jackson-Flux, H., & Brockschmidt, M. (2021). Self-supervised bug detection and repair. *Advances in Neural Information Processing Systems*, 34, 27865–27876.

Arnaoudova, V., Di Penta, M., & Antoniol, G. (2016). Linguistic antipatterns: What they are and how developers perceive them. *Empirical Software Engineering*, 21(1), 104–158. DOI: 10.1007/s10664-014-9350-8

Ayewah, N., Pugh, W., Hovemeyer, D., Morgenthaler, J. D., & Penix, J. (2008). Using static analysis to find bugs. *IEEE Software*, 25(5), 22–29. DOI: 10.1109/MS.2008.130

Bala, Y. Z., Samat, P. A., Sharif, K. Y., & Manshor, N. (2023). Improving cross-project software defect prediction method through transformation and feature selection approach. *IEEE Access : Practical Innovations, Open Solutions*, 11, 2318–2326. DOI: 10.1109/ACCESS.2022.3231456

Codepal.ai. (2022). *Bug Detector*. https://codepal.ai/bug-detector

Elshamy, N., AbouElenen, A., & Elmougy, S. (2023). Automatic detection of software defects based on machine learning. *International Journal of Advanced Computer Science and Applications*, 14(3). Advance online publication. DOI: 10.14569/IJACSA.2023.0140340

Ge, H., & Wu, Y. (2023). An Empirical Study of Adoption of ChatGPT for Bug Fixing among Professional Developers. *Innovation & Technology Advances*, 1(1), 21–29. DOI: 10.61187/ita.v1i1.19

Google. (2023). *Google Gemini*. https://gemini.google.com/app

Heaps, J., Slavin, R., & Wang, X. (2018). Toward A Code Pattern Based Vulnerability Measurement Model. *InProceedings of the 23rd ACM on Symposium on Access Control Models and Technologies (SACMAT '18)* (pp. 209–211). Association for Computing Machinery. DOI: 10.1145/3205977.3208948

Kumar, P., & Venkatesan, R. (2020). Improving software defect prediction using generative adversarial networks. *International Journal of Science and Engineering Applications*, 9(9), 117–120. DOI: 10.7753/IJSEA0909.1001

Liang, G., Wang, J., Li, S., & Chang, R. (2014). PatBugs: A pattern-based bug detector for cross-platform mobile applications. In *2014 IEEE International Conference on Mobile Services* (pp. 84-91). https://doi.org/DOI: 10.1109/MobServ.2014.21

Liu, W., Wang, Z., Liu, X., Zeng, N., Liu, Y., & Alsaadi, F. E. (2017). A survey of deep neural network architectures and their applications. *Neurocomputing*, 234, 11–26. DOI: 10.1016/j.neucom.2016.12.038

Menzies, T., & Marcus, A. (2008). Automated severity assessment of software defect reports. *2008 IEEE International Conference on Software Maintenance*, 346–355. DOI: 10.1109/ICSM.2008.4658083

Microsoft. (2022). *Copilot*. https://copilot.microsoft.com/

Open, A. I. (2021). *ChatGPT*. https://chatgpt.com/

Pichai, S. (2023). *Google Gemini AI: A new era of intelligence*.

Pradel, M., & Sen, K. (2018). Deepbugs: A learning approach to name-based bug detection. *Proceedings of the ACM on Programming Languages, 2*(OOPSLA), 1–25. DOI: 10.1145/3276517

Prakash, B. V. A., Ashoka, D. V, & Aradya, V. N. M. (2015). Application of data mining techniques for defect detection and classification. *Advances in Intelligent Systems and Computing*, 387–395. DOI: 10.1007/978-3-319-11933-5_42

Ray, B., Posnett, D., Filkov, V., & Devanbu, P. (2014). A large scale study of programming languages and code quality in github. *Proceedings of the 22nd ACM SIGSOFT International Symposium on Foundations of Software Engineering*, 155–165. DOI: 10.1145/2635868.2635922

Sadkoğlu, E., Gök, M., & Mjwl, M. M., & Kösesoy, \.Irfan. (2023). The Evolution and Impact of Large Language Model Chatbots in Social Media: A Comprehensive Review of Past, Present, and Future Applications. *Veri Bilimi*, 6(2), 67–76.

Siswantoro, M. Z. F. N., & Yuhana, U. L. (2023). Software defect prediction based on optimized machine learning models: A comparative study. *Teknika*, 12(2), 166–172. DOI: 10.34148/teknika.v12i2.634

Song, W., Gan, L., & Bao, T. (2024). Software defect prediction via generative adversarial networks and pre-trained model. *International Journal of Advanced Computer Science and Applications*, 15(3). Advance online publication. DOI: 10.14569/IJACSA.2024.01503119

Surameery, N. M. S., & Shakor, M. Y. (2023). Use Chat GPT to Solve Programming Bugs. [IJITC]. *International Journal of Information Technology & Computer Engineering*, 3(01), 17–22. DOI: 10.55529/ijitc.31.17.22

Tang, K., Zhang, Y., & Xia, S. (2024). Software defect prediction and automatic repair based on machine learning. *Highlights in Science. Engineering and Technology*, 98, 439–443. DOI: 10.54097/cwfckw19

Wang, F. (2023). Software defect fault intelligent location and identification method based on data mining. *Journal of Applied Data Sciences*, 4(2), 84–92. DOI: 10.47738/jads.v4i2.92

Wermelinger, M. (2023). Using GitHub Copilot to solve simple programming problems. *SIGCSE 2023: Proceedings of the 54th ACM Technical Symposium on Computer Science Education,* V.1, 172–178. https://doi.org/DOI: 10.1145/3545945.3569830

Chapter 9
Skill Development Challenges in the Era of Artificial Intelligence (AI)

C. Karthikeyan
https://orcid.org/0000-0002-2018-8245
SJB Institute of Technology, India

Sonia Singh
https://orcid.org/0000-0003-3168-8656
Jain University (Deemed), India

ABSTRACT

Artificial Intelligence (AI) is taking us by storm, and Human Resources functions are no exception. Future of work for nearly 40% of the companies are in the algorithms of Artificial Intelligence (AI). Al is the most powerful acronym that pulls every human resource professional into challenge. Almost 33% of the employees' jobs, roles, tasks are to be augmented by AI in the near future is the prediction by Deloitte. This paper analyses the Skill development challenges for the developing countries like India to handle AI related training by conducting meta Analysis and presents suggestive measures to counter these challenges. The aim of the paper is to comprehend the issues surrounding vocational education and training by putting the Learner first. It suggests measures for implementation of planned activities with the augmentation of training initiatives to reskill, right skill and align those skills for the emerging jobs.

DOI: 10.4018/979-8-3693-6745-2.ch009

INTRODUCTION

AI is impacting our daily life. It is transforming all work areas and the HR managers and office supervisors are no exception. AI has come a long way in transforming HR and the workforce. Examples include reducing the Human bias, increasing the efficiency for candidate assessments prior and post interview for jobs, improving the compliance system, increasing the adoption of metrics and improving the workplace learning are some of the benefits of the organizations that are working particularly on the digital platforms today. Any industry in India, like healthcare, advertising, transportation, finance, legal, education and in as many kinds of workplaces including our place of work to the maximum possible extent, reduction of redundant tasks are possible. The rapid advancement of artificial intelligence (AI) is reshaping the landscape of skill development across various sectors, introducing both opportunities and challenges. As organizations increasingly integrate AI technologies into their operations, the demand for new skill sets is becoming critical. This transformation necessitates a comprehensive understanding of the evolving skill requirements and the implications for education and workforce training.

BACKGROUND & RATIONALE

One of the foremost challenges in skill development is the need for a strategic approach to workforce training that aligns with the integration of AI. Companies are recognizing the importance of investing in skill development strategies to harness the benefits of AI effectively. For instance, organizations are actively adopting comprehensive skill development frameworks to prepare their workforce for the AI-driven future (Babashahi, 2024). This proactive approach is essential, as it enables employees to adapt to new technologies and enhances their productivity. However, the challenge lies in ensuring that these training programs are accessible and relevant to all employees, not just a select few.

Moreover, the integration of AI in business organizations necessitates a shift in the skill set required from employees. The future workforce will need not only technical expertise but also strong interpersonal and cognitive skills to collaborate effectively with AI systems (Bobitan, 2024). This dual requirement underscores the complexity of skill development in the AI era, as employees must cultivate both hard and soft skills to thrive in an increasingly automated environment. The challenge for educational institutions and training programs is to design curricula that encompass this broad spectrum of skills.

In the realm of education, the incorporation of AI literacy into teaching practices is becoming increasingly vital. argue that experiential learning activities and AI pedagogies are crucial for enhancing students' technical skills, creativity, critical thinking, and problem-solving abilities (Yetişensoy & Rapoport, 2023). This perspective aligns with the need for educational frameworks that not only teach students how to use AI tools but also encourage them to think critically about the implications of AI in society. However, the challenge remains in effectively implementing these pedagogical strategies across diverse educational settings, particularly in under-resourced areas.

Furthermore, the global landscape of AI skills policy reveals significant disparities in readiness among different countries. Systematic review indicates that nations with lower AI readiness scores often adopt narrow approaches to skill development, limiting opportunities for broader population engagement (Rigley, 2023). This situation exacerbates inequalities in access to AI education and training, highlighting the urgent need for inclusive policies that promote equitable skill development across all demographics. The challenge for policymakers is to create frameworks that not only foster innovation but also ensure that all individuals have the opportunity to participate in the AI economy.

Figure 1. Relative AI Skill penetration rate by Country, 2015-23

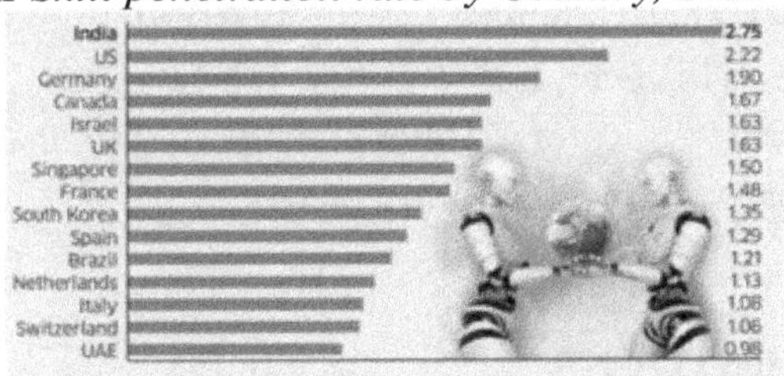

The evolving nature of work due to AI integration also raises concerns about job displacement and the need for upskilling and reskilling. emphasize that organizations must implement strategies to guide employees through the transition process, addressing the costs associated with training and ensuring fairness in access to skill development opportunities (Morandini et al., 2023). This challenge is particularly pronounced in industries where AI is expected to automate routine tasks, necessitating a shift in the skill sets required for various roles. Organizations must therefore prioritize continuous learning and adaptability to remain competitive in the face of technological advancements.

In addition to technical skills, the importance of critical thinking and ethical considerations in the context of AI cannot be overstated. argues that as AI continues to disrupt various professions, the ability to think critically will become increasingly essential for workers to navigate the complexities of an AI-driven job market (Dumitru, 2023). This perspective highlights the need for educational programs to emphasize not only technical proficiency but also the development of ethical frameworks that guide the responsible use of AI technologies. The challenge lies in integrating these critical thinking components into existing curricula while ensuring that students are equipped to address the ethical dilemmas posed by AI.

Moreover, the role of AI in enhancing specific professional skills, such as those in healthcare, is becoming more pronounced. For instance, discuss the potential of simulation-based education in medical training, which can be enhanced through AI technologies to improve skill acquisition and patient safety (Komasawa & Yokohira, 2023). However, the challenge remains in ensuring that healthcare professionals are adequately trained to work alongside AI systems, recognizing both the benefits and limitations of these technologies. This necessitates a reevaluation of training programs to incorporate AI literacy and collaborative skills.

As organizations and educational institutions strive to adapt to the demands of the AI era, the need for a cohesive strategy that encompasses both skill development and ethical considerations becomes increasingly apparent. The integration of AI into various sectors presents a unique opportunity to redefine skill sets and enhance workforce capabilities. However, it also poses significant challenges that require a collaborative effort from educators, policymakers, and industry leaders to ensure that individuals are prepared for the future of work.

RESEARCH OBJECTIVES

1) To analyse the Skill development challenges for the developing countries like India, to be technically capable to handle AI related initiatives
2) To relate through facts and figures the challenges posed against available resources versus skill development initiatives for the challenges posed by AI.
3) To evaluate the strengths and weaknesses of the current policy framework against the required development for creating skill development initiatives for the entire growing India's Young Working Population.
4) To suggest practical and possible suggestions for implementation of planned activities, and to predict on the possible outcomes, with the augmenting, of training initiatives to reskill, rightskill and align those skills for the emerging jobs.

LITERATURE REVIEW

The integration of Artificial Intelligence (AI) into Human Resource (HR) management presents both significant opportunities and formidable challenges for HR leaders. As organizations increasingly adopt AI technologies, HR professionals must navigate a complex landscape characterized by the need for technical proficiency, ethical considerations, and strategic alignment with business goals.

One of the primary challenges for HR leaders is the necessity to prepare their workforce for the changes that AI will bring. This preparation involves not only familiarizing employees with AI-driven tools but also fostering a culture that embraces technological change. emphasizes the importance of integrating AI into business models and hiring technology-savvy staff to mitigate resistance and drive innovation (Dima, 2024). Furthermore, highlight that HR professionals must possess both technical capabilities and a strong understanding of business processes to effectively implement AI in HR practices (Agustono et al., 2023). This dual expertise is crucial as organizations face the risk of alienating employees who may feel threatened by AI technologies if not adequately supported (Baki, 2023).

Another significant challenge is the ethical implications of AI in HR. As AI systems are increasingly used for recruitment, performance management, and employee engagement, concerns about bias and transparency in AI algorithms have emerged. discusses the ethical landscape that organizations must navigate when implementing AI-ML systems, emphasizing the need for transparent and explainable algorithms to avoid perpetuating biases (Basnet, 2024). Similarly, points out that while AI can enhance decision-making processes, HR leaders must prioritize ethical considerations to ensure that AI technologies align with organizational values and employee welfare (Vaddepalli, 2023). This ethical framework is essential for maintaining trust and engagement among employees, particularly in an era where algorithmic decision-making is becoming commonplace.

Moreover, the effective management of data is critical for leveraging AI in HR. underscores the foundational importance of data quality, privacy, and governance in AI-driven HR analytics, which are vital for deriving accurate and actionable insights (Nyathani, 2023). The ability to manage and analyze large volumes of employee data can significantly enhance HR decision-making. The role of data analytics is important in providing insights into workforce dynamics (Ore & Sposato, 2021). However, the challenge lies in ensuring that HR teams are equipped with the necessary skills to interpret and utilize this data effectively, as highlighted by Chen (2022), who notes the importance of AI in streamlining onboarding processes through data-driven insights.

In addition to these challenges, HR leaders must also focus on the strategic implementation of AI technologies. emphasizes that digital leaders in HR must inspire and guide their teams in augmenting AI capabilities rather than allowing technology to replace human judgment (Singh, 2024). This approach requires a shift in mindset among HR professionals, who must view AI as a tool for enhancing human capabilities rather than a substitute for them. Furthermore, the integration of AI into HR functions necessitates a holistic approach, which involves collaboration between HR professionals and AI experts to address both technical and ethical challenges (Baki, 2023).

While the integration of AI into HR management offers substantial benefits, it also presents significant challenges that require careful navigation. HR leaders must prioritize workforce preparation, ethical considerations, data management, and strategic implementation to harness the full potential of AI technologies. By addressing these challenges, HR professionals can ensure that AI not only enhances operational efficiency but also contributes positively to employee experiences and organizational culture.

AI research across the countries in the world including India shows it is far more analytics oriented, where softwares are using history and algorithms, with data getting smarter and smarter over time. The Investment challenges: The investments in AI are very exponential, and are growing at a consistent rate from $ 12.5 billion since 2017, to $ 46 billion by 2020. A Mckinsey report suggests that the automation could accelerate the production capacity to the level of 0.8 to 1.4 percent of the global GDP annually, and the human labor will be replaced by the automation, AI that takes into account the technical, economic and social factors that affects the pace and the extent of automation. The McKinsey estimates that by 2030, almost 30 percent of the current work activities or tasks that human beings are doing will be displaced.

AI impact on the Blue collar Jobs/White collar Jobs: Almost 6.4 million retail sales people jobs are at risk in advanced countries like the U.S. with the impact of AI, and the threat is for the 1.8 million truck drivers, 1.2 Million construction workers, 4.3 million cooks and waiters, 3.8 million cleaners, and 2.4 million movers and warehouse workers. The predictions are strong that the new wave of AI infused expert automation and augmentation softwares(EAAS), will steer to the new era of AI assisted or AI enhanced productivity (C. Karthikeyan 2019).Even the white collar jobs are under scanner for the impact on professions like lawyers, HR professionals, Teachers, Marketing and Sales personnel, researchers, accountants as well as software developers' needs to be reskilled (Soslau and Bell 2018).

The Skill Development Initiatives by HRD Department of Government of India

The skill development initiatives by the Human Resource Development (HRD) departments of the Government of India are pivotal in addressing the evolving demands of the workforce in an increasingly competitive global landscape. These initiatives aim to enhance employee capabilities, foster innovation, and ensure that the workforce is equipped with the necessary skills to thrive in a rapidly changing economic environment.

One of the primary objectives of HRD initiatives in India is to cultivate a culture of continuous learning and skill enhancement. HRD activities significantly contribute to the development of employee creativity and innovation, which are essential for organizational growth (Kahfi, 2022). By implementing training programs and workshops, HRD departments can help employees broaden their skill sets and adapt to new challenges, thereby fostering a more innovative work environment. This aligns with the findings of Katou (2017), who emphasizes that organizations can achieve substantial operational benefits by investing in skill-enhancing policies and practices. Such investments not only improve individual performance but also enhance overall organizational productivity.

Moreover, the integration of modern technologies, including Artificial Intelligence (AI), into skill development initiatives is crucial. As noted by Mustopa (2024), there is a pressing need for skill development in AI and related fields to address the shortages of proficient human resources in India. This is particularly relevant in the context of the Fourth Industrial Revolution (4IR), where digital skills are paramount. The Government of India has recognized this need and has initiated various programs aimed at upskilling the workforce in digital competencies and AI technologies ("Role of Modern Technology in Industry 4.0: An Empirical Study in the Context of Artificial Intelligence", 2023). These programs are designed to prepare workers for the demands of the digital economy, ensuring that they remain competitive in the job market.

The challenges faced by HRD initiatives, particularly in the context of technological advancements, cannot be overlooked. As highlighted by Chuang & Graham (2018), the rapid evolution of technology necessitates a reevaluation of HRD practices to focus on upskilling employees in areas that are resistant to automation. This includes fostering critical thinking, creativity, and interpersonal skills—capabilities that are essential in an AI-driven workplace. Furthermore, the emphasis on green HRD practices, as discussed by Osolase et al., (2023), indicates a growing recognition of the need for sustainable development within HRD frameworks. This approach not only addresses environmental concerns but also aligns with global trends towards sustainability in business practices.

In addition to technological and environmental considerations, HRD initiatives in India must also address the socio-cultural dynamics that influence skill development. points out that globalization and changing work environments present unique challenges in managing diversity and promoting gender equality within organizations (Ghosh, 2015). HRD professionals are tasked with creating inclusive training programs that cater to diverse employee backgrounds, ensuring equitable access to skill development opportunities.

Furthermore, the effectiveness of HRD initiatives is often contingent upon the active involvement of management and employees in the training process. The perceived effectiveness of HRD activities is significantly influenced by how engaged both management and employees are in these initiatives (Manohar et al., 2023). This highlights the importance of fostering a collaborative environment where employees feel empowered to participate in their own development.

Training Programs Conducted

As of 31st March 2015, across 28 sectors, standards for 1319 job roles pegged at NSQF levels 1 to 8 have been defined by the Sector Skill Councils (SSCs). Fourteen SSCs have covered development of 80% of entry level workforce QPs. The system of multi-entry and multi-exit will enable students to acquire some skills after finishing compulsory general schooling, then enter the labour market and gain some work experience and return to the vocational education and training system to continue their vocational education/training. It would be particularly beneficial for relatively poor students, since it would enable them to continue in either the vocational education stream of the secondary system or the ITI system, rather than dropping out from the educational or vocational training space altogether. Skill India mission was launched by Government of India in the year 2015 with an aim of training over 40 crore Indians in market related skills in different industry related jobs. Skilled India vision was materialized with initiatives likes setting up of National Skill Development Agency (NSDA), National Skill Development Corporation (NSDC), National Skill Development Fund (NSDF) and 33 Sector Skill Councils (SSCs) as well as 187 training partners registered with NSDC. It is estimated that by about 2025, India will have the 25% of the total global workforce (Singh 2020).

Table 1. Details of Training organized and trainees trained for the month pf April 1, 2022 to December 31,2022

Sl. No	Programmes	Achievement	No of Persons Trained							
			SC	ST	W	PH	Minority	OBC	Others	Total
			SC	ST	W	PH	Minority	OBC	Others	Total
1	EDPs	32	10	64	228	1	18	198	84	356
2	SDP/ESDPs	718	886	19118	14463	65	66	982	854	21840
4	Others	33	218	528	1160	3	86	477	284	1507
	Total	783	1114	19710	15851	69	170	1657	1222	23703

Source. Ministry of Skill Development & Entrepreneurship Annual Report 2022-23

The Problem Statement: Fear of mass unemployment, technology related to AI, skill shift and employment displacement are the concerns now with almost all the countries in the world including India. Very large employment shifts accompanying the process of structural transformation and large shifts of workers across occupations and industries are very huge. The impact of AI in the Right Skilling, Re-Skilling, for countries like India, where the structural unemployment is higher, catering to the next level requirements is a wicked problem.Most of the daily routine tasks like the paper work or paper movements across files and offices, scheduling duties or shifts, timesheets for the work allocation by HR, Accounting tasks, where the tasks are repetitive will be replaced by the digital assistants or automated software's supported by AI.

The obvious challenge is the HR development index of majority of countries that in turn puts pressure on the training demands of the HRD ministries or MHRDs in the country like India. Automate, Augment, Amplify will be the mantra to boost human activities towards the competing global work culture across the world to keep up productivity. Hence the HRD movement needs to happen for the countries like India where the skill development initiatives are the primary requirements to reorient and reskill the entire country's working population, which this papers looks at length. India has the world's youngest work force with a median age way below that of China and OECD countries. Half the population of India was younger than 25 in 2010. It will change to half the population being under 28 in 2030, making India a very young country for the next 20 years. The current focus of skill development has shifted to the learner and his/her needs and expectations from vocational education and training (VET). To empower the working population, is it essential to start from the source, i.e., the learner. India has the advantage of the "demographic dividend" (younger population compared to the ageing population of developed countries), which can be cultivated to build a skilled workforce in the near future.

A need for intensive efforts in achieving the skilling target of 500 million workers by 2022 exists which is a very big challenge coupled with other challenges which are dealt in this study.

Ministries Working for Skill Development

The Government of India has established various ministries that play a crucial role in promoting skill development across the nation. These ministries are integral to implementing policies and programs aimed at enhancing the employability of the workforce, particularly in light of the demographic dividend that India possesses. The following discussion synthesizes the contributions of key ministries involved in skill development initiatives.

1) Ministry of Skill Development and Entrepreneurship (MSDE) is the primary body responsible for coordinating skill development efforts across the country. Established in 2014, the MSDE oversees the implementation of the Skill India Mission, which aims to train over 400 million people by 2022. The mission focuses on providing skill training in various sectors, including manufacturing, services, and agriculture, thereby addressing the skill gap in the labor market (Akther, 2023). The ministry also promotes entrepreneurship among the youth, particularly in rural areas, by facilitating access to training programs and resources necessary for starting businesses (Akther, 2023).
2) Ministry of Education (MoE) plays a significant role in integrating skill development into the educational framework. The New Education Policy (NEP) 2020 emphasizes vocational education and skill training at all levels of education, aiming to create a more skilled workforce that meets the demands of the economy (Gandhi, 2022). The MoE collaborates with the MSDE to implement programs that enhance the quality of vocational education and training (VET) in India, ensuring that students acquire relevant skills before entering the job market (Pilz & Regel, 2021).
3) Ministry of Labour and Employment (MoLE) is also pivotal in skill development initiatives, particularly through its various schemes aimed at enhancing employability. The MoLE implements programs that focus on the formalization of the workforce and the provision of skill training to marginalized groups, including women and youth (Asuyama, 2019). By promoting labor market policies that support skill development, the ministry aims to reduce unemployment and underemployment in the country (Sharma, 2018).
4) Ministry of Rural Development (MoRD) addresses skill development in rural areas, focusing on empowering rural youth through skill training programs. The MoRD implements schemes like the Deen Dayal Upadhyaya Grameen

Kaushalya Yojana (DDU-GKY), which aims to enhance the employability of rural youth by providing them with market-relevant skills (Akther, 2023). This initiative is crucial for fostering entrepreneurship and self-employment in rural regions, thereby contributing to overall economic development (Akther, 2023).

5) Ministry of Women and Child Development (MWCD) also contributes to skill development by focusing on women's empowerment through vocational training. The MWCD implements programs that aim to enhance women's skills in various sectors, thereby promoting gender equality in the workforce (Sheshadri et al., 2021). Initiatives under this ministry are designed to address the specific barriers that women face in accessing skill training and employment opportunities (Sheshadri et al., 2021).
6) Ministry of Micro, Small and Medium Enterprises (MSME) plays a vital role in promoting skill development among entrepreneurs and small business owners. The MSME ministry provides training programs that equip individuals with the skills necessary to start and manage small enterprises, thereby fostering a culture of entrepreneurship (Akther, 2023). This is particularly important in a country where small businesses contribute significantly to employment and economic growth (Akther, 2023).

METHODOLOGY

Meta Analysis on the secondary data and facts and figures released by government sources and related literature. It also includes Reviewing of Literature on the growth and development initiatives by MHRD in India.

DISCUSSION

The problem of Planned policies and Available resources and its utility are discussed in detail.

Challenge 1; **Skilled Workforce**- With the formally skilled workforce is less than 3 percent of total workforce; unfortunately, the current size of India's formally skilled workforce is very small. As per the latest survey by the Labour Bureau for 2013-14, only 6.8 percent of persons aged 15 years and above have received or were receiving vocational training, of which only 2.8 percent was through formal channels while 4 percent was through the informal system. In contrast, skilled workforce in other countries is much higher – Korea (96%), Germany (75%), Japan (80%) and United Kingdom (68%). Poor literacy levels impede skilling through normal channels; Amongst the formally skilled labour force, 74% have higher secondary or higher education levels, and amongst the labour force with informal skills, 78% of the workforce has completed only middle or lower education. Such skewed nature of skilling can be attributed to two factors – a) the education level entry requirements in the current skill set-up makes it difficult for workers with minimal education to access formal skills training; and b) lack of education also impedes the ability to absorb higher level of skills. Inadequate training capacities ; The number of people who enter the work force age group every year is estimated to be 26 million. With average labour participation rate of 90% for male and 30% for female, at least 16.16 million will enter the workforce and would need to acquire skills. However, current annual skilling capacity, including training for the farm sector, in India is estimated at only 7 million. The table below highlights the dismal state of training capacities at the ITIs, which are a key source of skill training in India. Enrolments in vocational training are way below the enrolments in formal education. As against the enrolment of 23.76 million students in higher education, the skill training capacities in ITIs is mere 1.69 million. Training partners of NSDC have collectively trained 3.4 million youths in 2015-16 (Shrotriya, Dhir and Sushil 2018)

Table 2. Number of it is with total seating capacity (as of Sept. 8 2024)

Region	No. of Govt. ITIs	Seating capacity (Govt.)	Number of private ITIs	Seating capacity (private)	Total ITIs	Total seating capacity at ITIs
North India	813	130818	3757	458837	4570	589655
South India	437	100828	3056	347926	3493	448754
East India	209	58250	1569	250301	1778	308551
West India	825	208474	1298	137402	2123	345876
GRAND TOTAL	**2284**	**498370**	**9680**	**1194466**	**11964**	**1692836**

Source: Labour Bureau, Ministry of Labour and Employment

Challenge 2; Inadequate training capacities- The number of people who enter the work force age group every year is estimated to be 26 million. With average labour participation rate of 90% for male and 30% for female, at least 16.16 million will enter the workforce and would need to acquire skills. However, current annual skilling capacity, including training for the farm sector, in India is estimated at only 7 million. The table below highlights the dismal state of training capacities at the ITIs, which are a key source of skill training in India. Enrolments in vocational training are way below the enrolments in formal education. As against the enrolment of 23.76 million students in higher education, the skill training capacities in ITIs is mere 1.69 million. Training partners of NSDC have collectively trained 3.4 million youths in 2015-16 (Dash and Dash 2020).

Table 3. Enrollment in Higher Education in India

Level	Enrollment in University Departments Colleges	Enrollment in affiliated colleges	Total	% Share
Graduate	2,125,559	18,104,033	20,229,592	85.12
Post Graduate	774,557	2,160,432	2,934,989	12.35
Research	156,845	43,885	200,730	0.85
Diploma/ Certificate	156,909	242,740	399,649	1.68
Grand Total	3,213,870	20,551,090	23,764,960	100

Challenge 3; Categories of Services Based on their Productivity Growth- An ongoing productivity research study funded by the Reserve Bank of India shows that from 1980 to 2008, TFP growth in India was highest in the service sector at 1.58% per annum followed by agriculture at 1.06% and manufacturing at 0.3%. Economy-wide estimates recorded an annual labor productivity growth rate of around 4.5% from 1980 to 2008 while the growth rates in labor productivity for services, agriculture, and manufacturing were 3.52%, 1.94%, and 5.45%, respectively. The study further found that labor productivity rates for services increased from 2.69% per annum from 1980 to 1999 to 6% from 2000 to 2008 due to growth in post and telecommunications, hotels and restaurants, and trade. Healthcare and social work, other services, and education registered lower rates which is a cause for concern. It is expected that the high productivity is largely driven by telecommunications since the postal service in India is still a government monopoly that suffers from over-employment. The service sector has been the highest and that communication services are one of the major propellers of growth in sector productivity in India.

Challenge 4; India's economic growth- slowed to 6.9% in 2012; nevertheless, it is projected to grow at 7.3% in 2013 which is higher than the 6% average projected growth rate for emerging and developing economies. The share of the middle class in the total population will increase to 41% in 2025, and they will account for 59% of the country's total consumption. With the increase in incomes, there has also been an increase in the literacy rate which is expected to improve further. Moreover India has one of the youngest populations in the world with 54% below 25 years of age. All this is leading to a change in consumption patterns with an increase in demand for discretionary services like education, private healthcare providers, personal care, and hotels and restaurants. The Indian market is large and unsaturated, and most services have been opened up for foreign investment. India wants to be a knowledge-based hub, and the government is promoting exports of services. Only 10% of the total workforce in the country receives some kind of skill training (2% with formal training and 8% with informal training). Further, 80% of the entrants into the workforce do not have the opportunity for skill training.

Challenge 5; Investments- In the post-liberalization period, the service sector has attracted significant foreign investment due to the availability of skilled labor at lower wages and the large and unsaturated domestic market. According to the A.T. Kearney Global Services Location Index, in 2011 India was the leading outsourcing destination among 50 countries followed by the PRC. India's rank is high due to human resources (2nd), but it ranked poorly in terms of business environment (43rd).According to the A.T. Kearney FDI Confidence Index, in 2012 India was the second most attractive destination for FDI after the PRC; however, the Inward FDI Performance Index of the United Nations Conference on Trade and Development (UNCTAD)19 which compares the relative performance of 141 countries in attracting FDI found that India has performed poorly compared with other developing countries.

Challenge 6; Future prospects of Service Sector -The bulk of FDI in India is routed through Mauritius. Other important investing countries include Japan, Singapore, the UK, and the US. At present, FDI is allowed in most but not all services in the sector. In the post liberalization period, the overall sector has been the largest recipient of FDI with a share of over 50% between 2000 and 2011. Financial services, telecommunication services, and computer software and hardware were large recipients. In FY2010, India's FDI outflow in the service sector was $10.3 billion out of the total outflow of $14.6 billion.23 In FY2011, 62.1% of India's outward investments were in services followed by the manufacturing sector at 31.4%. Within the sector, financial, insurance, real estate, and business services accounted for 29% of total outward investments followed by transport, communication, and storage (15.3%) and wholesale and retail trade and restaurants.

Challenge 7; Confusing Service Sector Policy- There is no government policy on how the sector can lead to inclusive growth. This is partly because the focus is on agriculture and manufacturing, and the service sector has largely been left to grow on its own. There is no nodal ministry for services like retailing while for others like transport and energy there are multiple ministries with conflicting interests. The quasi-federal governance structure has led to multiple regulatory bodies, numerous regulations, and multiple clearance requirements. For example, there are around 13 regulatory bodies for higher education, and each of them functions in isolation. This can be done with the help of technology such as computerizing check posts at state borders and with regulations such as implementing single goods and service taxes. In the case of industries like energy, various government departments should work together to design a policy that will facilitate equitable access at affordable prices. The policy should lay down a short-term strategy (5 years coinciding with the 5-year plans) and a long-term strategy (10–15 years) for development.

Challenge 8; Governing regulatory reforms- Some regulations do not take into account technological developments while others are outdated or do not follow international best practices. In areas like transportation, there is a lack of comprehensive regulations enabling integrated door-to-door service which increases waste in the supply chain. In addition, existing regulations do not take into account the characteristics of new services such as the Service Sector in India direct selling and express delivery. Lack of prescribed standards and common accreditation also adversely affect services like construction and education. While deregulation and removing regulatory barriers are often necessary for service sector growth (Hoekman and Mattoo 011, Jain and Ninan 2010),

In India it may not necessarily be true. For example, the **privatization of Indian airports** led to an arbitrary increase in tariffs prior to the appointment of the Airport Economic Regulatory Authority. Since many services have erstwhile been public monopolies, the vested interests of the government and of public sector units adversely affect performance as they get preferential prices in commodities like energy. Moreover, government procurement is not always transparent, e.g., private companies working for the railways have to procure materials from vendors selected by the railways. In many services, especially infrastructure, it is often difficult for the private sector to enter and operate due to a lack of third party access and of transparent procedures for sharing scare resources among other problems.

Challenge 9; Service sector employment and education- Employment opportunities and quality education are both necessary for inclusive growth. There is a skill shortage in ICT and organized retail. According to the Electronic and Computer

Software Export Promotion Council, approximately 5,000 people are needed every year to meet the demand of the ICT industry, but the total available from educational and training institutes is only a third of this number. This is leading to a rise in salaries (average salary increase was 11% in 2012), high attrition rates, and a high cost of operations. Studies (Mukherjee and Goyal 2012) have shown that although employees prefer to work in the formal sector for better salaries and job security, skill requirements are different, and it is not easy for employees to shift from the informal to the formal sector. In many cases companies have to invest substantially in training employees. Critics have argued that the government's education policy and funding have focused on higher education and have neglected primary education (Kochhar et al. 2006). There are reserved seats for the so-called backward classes in higher education but not in primary education; this is not based on income. Also, labor productivity is lower in social services like healthcare and education which affects inclusive growth. To create quality employment in the service sector, it is important to encourage growth in the formal sector.

Challenge 10; Access and availability of infrastructure- Indian government investment in infrastructure is low and has not been able to meet demand. For instance, most ICT companies have to invest in power units due to the erratic power supply. This increases their costs. Companies in construction, ICT, hospital services, and retail, among others, find it difficult to acquire property due to the lack of urban planning, restrictive zoning regulations, outdated laws related to land conversion, and the lack of clear ownership and titles to land. This causes delays in project implementation. In addition, due to poor infrastructure planning, the full benefits of existing investments cannot be reaped. The government needs to act as a facilitator so that private developers have access to basic facilities like land. There is a need for proper urban and infrastructure planning. The focus should not only be on creating new infrastructure but also on efficiently using existing infrastructure.

Therefore, the rise of Artificial Intelligence (AI) presents a vast range of opportunities for India to become a global leader in technology and innovation. As the country embraces digital transformation, it opens doors for individuals and organizations to develop skills that are in high demand. The AI-driven future is creating a landscape where Indian professionals can leverage their technical prowess and creativity to excel. Here are some of the key opportunities available:

Advantages of Large Youth Population; Within the next several years, India's population is expected to exceed that of China. Unlike China, however, India's population structure is still relatively young overall, and the population keeps growing rapidly, with 28 million youth being added every year! Of India's total population of 1.21 billion according to the 2011 Census (Government of India (GOI) 2011b), more than 672 million people are of working age (15 to 59). Of these, 253 million are youth aged 15 to 24, accounting for 21 % of the total population in 2011. With a continued decline in the dependency ratio estimated over the next 30 years, India is expected to enjoy a large "demographic dividend" for the coming decades. With 12.8 million young people newly entering the labor market every year (GOI 2011a), the government recognizes that the country faces a serious skills shortage, as the majority of these new labor market entrants are likely to remain unskilled. It has also as Calculated from the data on total population from the provisional 2011 Census Data and the 2001 Census Data available from the Office of the Registrar General and Census Commissioner, Ministry of Home Affairs, Government of India. In fact, the government ambitiously envisages that India could become a supplier of skilled workers "exportable" to other countries, given four factors: the vast size of the youth population, their limited domestic employment opportunities, the shortage of skilled workers in developed countries, and the growing global practice of outsourcing. At the same time, India's demographic profile poses serious pressure on government and society to invest in education and training. Indeed, in 2005, roughly 413 million people were in the school-going age group 6 to 24 years accounting for 35% of the total population. Since then, this figure has surely increased. Thus, expanding education and training for them and ensuring its quality will seriously challenge the government, which will have to build more schools, train and hire more teachers, and provide them with more textbooks, educational materials, and equipment. Despite India's projected demographic dividend and its abundant labor supply, it suffers from a serious shortage of skilled workers, because of their limited access to education and skills training and a large skills mismatch in the labor market.

Table 4. Budget Allocation

Demand No. 92- Ministry of Skill Development and EntrepreneurshipDetails of Budget Allocated to Ministry (₹ in Cr.)												
	BE 2022-23			RE 2022-23			Actual Expenditure 2022-23 (upto 31.12.2022)			BE 2023-24		
	Revenue	Capital	Total	Revenue	Capital	Total	Revenue	Capital	Total	Revenue	Capital	Total
	2847.54	151.46	2999.00	1829.64	72.07	1901.71	584.70	19.53	604.23	3418.07	99.24	3517.31

GENDER BUDGET

Table no. 2 & 3

(i) 100% provision towards Women

(₹ In Cr)

Details of Scheme	BE 2022-23	RE 2022-23	BE 2023-24
National Skill Training Institutes **(Women Training)**	65.85	64.28	68.00

(ii) Pro-women (at least 30% of provision)

(₹ In Cr)

Details of Scheme	BE 2022-23	RE 2022-23	BE 2023-24
Skill India Programme*	—	—	2278.37

* Although there is no Gender specific budget provisions under the scheme but the training programs being run have some dedicated women oriented programs/incentives to encourage women participation in the skill ecosystem.

Distribution of Rural and Urban Workers in India; 1980s and more seriously in the 1990s, employment growth stagnated in the 1990s and 2000s, making those two decades a period of "jobless growth." Thus, even the growing Indian economy has failed to generate sufficient jobs to accommodate its new young entrants into the labor market. Unlike the experience of East Asian countries, growth in the Indian economy has largely been led by its service sector, whose relative importance has been growing. While the agriculture sector's contribution to GDP has gradually declined and that of the industrial sector has grown slightly, the share of the service sector has grown quite rapidly. In 2010, it accounted for 55% of India's GDP. Looking at the amount of employment in each sector, however, agriculture is still the largest, accounting for 54%, while the industry and service sectors accounted for 18% and 25%, respectively, in 2008. In rural areas,non-farm employment also increased to 35% of the rural workforce in 2009/10, up from 30% in 2004/05. Looking at the employment structures in non-agricultural sectors, we see that apart from manufacturing (26% of non-agricultural employment), some subsectors of the service sector such as wholesale and retail, and personal service have been growing. They now account for 48.6% and 35.6%, respectively, of non-agricultural employment (GOI

2008a). In manufacturing, almost all firms belong to the informal sector. Formal sector firms account for only 0.7% of total manufacturing firms. The majorities of informal sector firms are small, and located in rural areas (see Table 3). Size also accounts for large differentials in wages and productivity. Small firms have 12% of the productivity on average and pay 19% of the wages of large firms. This high prevalence of informality suggests that the majority of India's manufacturing workers, including youth, work in low-productivity, low-wage jobs, with little access to opportunities for formal skills development.

Skills Development Opportunities outside the Formal Education System Outside of the formal education system is a well-established vocational training system, the Craftsman Training Scheme (CTS), established in 1951. The public Industrial Training Institutes (ITI) and private Industrial Training Centers (ITCs), under the Directorate General of Employment and Training (DGE&T) of the Ministry of Labor and Employment, provide pre-employment vocational training as key post lower secondary institutions to train the technical workforce. Under CTS, nationwide, 8,306 ITIs/ITCs (2140 public ITIs and 6166 private ITCs) in 114 trades in 44 engineering and 24 non-engineering courses offer six months to three years of vocational training for those who have completed 8 to 10 years of schooling. Each state government is responsible for overseeing its ITIs. In total, over 740,000 trainees are enrolled in training courses at it is and ITCs. At ITIs, tuition was free until 2006. Trainees also received fixed monthly stipends based on government norms. Despite this orientation, the demand for vocational training has generally been low even among the socially disadvantaged. Both parents and youths prefer general education, partly because it is considered to better prepare students for examinations for the government jobs. Moreover, because of India's traditional hierarchical social structure based on the centuries-old caste system, society has not generally highly appreciated or valued craft and trade skills. Students prefer white-collar jobs in their search for upward mobility. Vocational training has largely been seen as a second-choice option for economically disadvantaged and/or academically less capable. In addition to the Directorate General of Employment and Training, more than 17 ministries/departments of the Indian government, along with their related agencies, provide and/or sponsor formal/non-formal TVET programs for specific groups, covering about 2.5 million people annually (Ministry of Home Affairs 2011). However, these TVET programs vary in many ways, including duration, target groups, entry qualifications, testing and certification, and curriculum. The result is overlap and duplication, and little unified recognition of qualifications and equivalence. In recent years, however, private training firms such as NIIT have been offering a wide range of IT-related training courses, providing young people with practical and general skills that are in high demand in the labor market. (Okada 2012)

First, it set up the Prime Minister's National Skills Development Council (NSDC) to coordinate various schemes provided by various ministries. The Office of the Advisor to Prime Minister for Skills Development serves as an apex coordinating body and as a secretariat for the NSDC. Second, the National Skills Development Board (NSDB) was set up under the Planning Commission to coordinate 17 relevant ministries. Third, the National Skill Development Corporation (NSDC) was created, operating as a public-private partnership (PPP) involving industry associations and industry representatives to upgrade training institutions and deliver vocational training. Fourth, Sector Skills Councils have been set up for about two dozen sub-sectors involving various interested industrial associations to identify skills gaps and enhance skills training in each sub-sector. These organizations are responsible for developing policies, setting priorities and strategies, and overseeing and coordinating the various stakeholder initiatives and efforts. These Councils also try to involve employers more in establishing skills standards and assessing training performance. The creation of the NCSD in charge of skills development directly under the Prime Minister's Office helped show that the government was seriously committed to promoting skills development and raising awareness about skills development among policymakers, industry leaders, training institutions, and the general public (Grover and Kapoor 2020).

The development of NVEQF has led to a closer partnership and collaboration of government with industry to 6 For example, courses in plumbing are popular among people wishing to work in the Middle East and Australia. They develop courses, curriculum, assessment, certification, and placement. Also, to improve the quality of training, the government introduced the concepts of competency-based training and training modules. These have changed the basis for certifying vocational training from duration to competence. Now individuals can have their skills recognized regardless of their educational and employment paths. India is experiencing an acute sense of urgency, given its serious shortage of skilled labor in the face of the potential "demographic dividend," the need to sustain rapid economic growth, and an interest in making its young skilled workforce "exportable" to global labor markets. Some advanced countries, especially Australia and Western European countries, are keenly interested in India's potential skilled labor, and have started offering attractive incentives and generous support to India's TVET and higher education sectors. Such external support and pressure has helped the Indian government make institutional reforms. Moreover, the private sector, particularly key industrial associations such as the Confederation of Indian Industries (CII), and the Federation of Indian Chambers of Commerce and Industry (FICCI), have played key roles in increasing public awareness about skills development--organizing workshops and seminars and lobbying the government to promote institutional reforms (Kapur 2016). These associations are now represented and actively participate in various committees of tertiary and training institutions as well as national boards. Industry has also felt an urgent need to promote skills development given their frequent problems in finding workers with adequate skills. Thus, they have also demanded a well-designed skills development system with greater involvement on the part of the private sector. Projecting that by 2022, India's working-age population will reach 700 million, of whom, 500 million will need to be skilled, the government set a national target of skilling 500 million people by then, allocating increased budgets for skills development. Thus, it ambitiously plans to increase the capacity of training institutions to 15 million (currently 2.5 million), by setting up more ITIs, encouraging the private sector to engage in vocational training, and expanding tertiary education.

Innovative Reforms at Training Institutes; Reflecting the changing policy environment for skills development, training institutions have recently introduced several new initiatives. Supported by the World Bank, the government selected 500 ITIs as Centers of Excellence (COE) to offer "advanced module" training, and upgrade their facilities, equipment, and machinery to the same standard used in industry. Under the COE scheme, each ITI must establish an institute management committee (IMC) of 8 to 10 members. The IMC chair is selected from the private sector, often from a leading local private firm, and has power to approve major decisions about the ITI's management. Operating as a public-private partnership, the IMC is expected to forge partnerships between ITIs and the private sector to: share labor market information, especially on the types of skills in demand; develop curriculum; and seek donations of equipment and tools from the private sector to upgrade ITI facilities and equipment. Also, the creation of IMCs has increased industry participation in decision making around the ITIs, to greater autonomy for ITIs, more channels to send trainees for internships, and improved facilities through more donations from industry (Kanchan and Varshney 2015). These closer linkages with employers and increased autonomy may help ITIs meet industry demands. In fact, COE courses achieved close to 100% job placements of their trainees at many ITIs.

Recognizing the importance of involving industry, some ITIs recently created partnerships with leading firms such as Toyota, Tata Motors, and Suzuki to offer training courses to cater to the firm. For example, four ITIs in Karnataka offer a Motor Mechanic Tool and Maintenance (MMTM) course jointly with Toyota located in Bangalore. The curriculum follows NCVT norms, but Toyota decides on the topics to cover in the syllabus so it can teach firm-specific skills. Toyota takes all the students in their second year as apprentices and places them at its dealers. The courses enjoy 100% placement rates as all the trainees who pass all the requirements are placed as regular employees at Toyota dealerships on the completion of training. This tailor-made arrangement in close collaboration with particular firms has helped make training more relevant, better able to respond to industry needs, and has significantly improved placement rates. Many it is are keen to work with leading firms to create such firm-specific courses and to increase opportunities for both apprenticeships and instructors' training with these firms. The leadership levels at education institutions, and various supporting sectors needs to get on this serious social malice.

Suggestive Measures to Counter the Challenges

Today, India faces complex and enormous challenges in fostering skills development for youth. A fraction of economically well-off middle classes get good education, and, training and well-paid jobs in the organized sector. Meanwhile, the great majority of youth from economically and socially disadvantaged groups get very limited education and little access to vocational training. They work in the unorganized sector. The majority of Indian youth enter the labor market without adequate vocational skills, leading to unstable, informal, low-wage employment, such as casual labor and various forms of self-employment. In India, the bulk of employment is in rural areas and in the unorganized sector, and almost all manufacturing firms are in the informal sector. Given the highly-stratified and segmented nature of the labor market, Indian youths must acquire education, training, and skills if they are to find decent jobs and experience any social mobility. Thus, with rapid economic growth, demand for education is likely to grow further at all levels in coming years. However, access to education, training, and employment opportunities is still largely determined by youth's socioeconomic backgrounds, gender, and geographic locations (Johansson and Van 2004).

Training institutes now have more autonomy and private-sector involvement, and have improved their governance and curriculum. These changes are too recent to examine the effects on training outcomes. But it will be interesting to see how these reforms improve access to and demand for vocational training among youths as well as the outcomes of training. Based on the discussion above, some suggestions for policy may be offered here. First, for India to promote industrial development and achieve sustainable growth, it must increase its investment in education and training for youth. In particular, to move further into a knowledge-based economy and move up the value chain, it is indispensable for India to improve the quality of education at every level. Second, the focus of India's skills development system does not correspond to either the level of skills demanded by industry or the overall levels of education of most young people. Thus, the government must ensure that most young people at least finish lower secondary school (i.e., 10th grade). Third, to open training opportunities for youths who have not completed secondary education, it would be helpful to create more courses at ITIs with lower levels of educational requirements. Fourth, training for the informal sector needs to be strengthened. Generally, it is difficult to reorient formal training institutions toward the informal sector. Given the vast size of the informal sector, however, it is critically important to institutionalize some training for work in the informal sector. Rather than the current somewhat ad-hoc delivery of training such as the MES, more institutionalized and structured settings may help offer more effective and streamlined training for the informal sector. Formal and informal apprenticeships and other types of training by enterprises with public private partnerships, Training for self-employment/entrepreneurial development, Adult learning, retraining of retired or retiring, Employees and lifelong learning, Non-formal training, including training by civil society organizations, E-learning, web-based learning and distance learning, Institutional framework: The policy lays down three the institutional framework comprising; Prime Minister's National Council on Skill Development, National Skill Development Co-ordination Board, National Skill Development Corporation (NSDC), National Council for Vocational Training (NCVT) The policy states the roles and responsibilities of stakeholders, which include the government, industry, trade unions, local governments, civil society institutions and all skill providers. Promotes the expansion of outreach, equity and access under the skill development initiative.

The skill development initiative requires key components. Automate, Augment, Align and Assimilate is the formulae that can work for the countries like India. A nodal agency can be identified for each service and given the responsibility to see that the strategies are implemented. To standardize policies across states, the central government can come up with model regulations that the state governments can implement. It is important to note that there are disparities in performance across states and that poor states seem to do badly in service infrastructure and in delivering public services like healthcare andeducation. For inclusive growth, policies have to focus on state-specific requirements. Today, private organizations can operate only as not-for-profit institutions in education. The government may consider allowing for-profit education while putting in place a regulatory framework to ensure that participants meet a required standard. This will facilitate private investment. Focusing on vocational training and developing appropriate curricula will increase the employability of students in the service sector (Kuruvilla, Erickson and Hwang 2002).

The quality of education can be improved through proper accreditation at international standards. Cross-subsidization and inappropriate subsidies have led to misallocations of resources. In railways the average passenger tariff in India is 55% lower than in the PRC while the average freight tariff is 66% higher. Similarly, while the commercial sector has to pay a higher power tariff, the agriculture sector, irrespective of land size, is highly subsidized.

CONCLUSION

The challenges of skill development in the era of artificial intelligence are multifaceted, encompassing the need for strategic workforce training, the integration of diverse skill sets, and the promotion of ethical considerations. As organizations and educational institutions navigate this complex landscape, it is imperative to adopt inclusive and forward-thinking approaches that empower individuals to thrive in an AI-driven world. By addressing these challenges collaboratively, stakeholders can foster a workforce that is not only skilled in the use of AI technologies but also equipped to navigate the ethical implications of their integration into society.

REFERENCES

Agustono, D., Nugroho, R., & Fianto, A. (2023). *Artificial intelligence in human resource management practices*. Kne Social Sciences., DOI: 10.18502/kss.v8i9.13409

Akther, F. (2023). Role of skill india programs in fostering entrepreneurship among rural youth in india. *Formosa Journal of Science and Technology*, 2(10), 2891–2902. DOI: 10.55927/fjst.v2i10.6678

Alshorman, S. (2024). The readiness to use ai in teaching science: Science teachers' perspective. *Journal of Baltic Science Education*, 23(3), 432–448. DOI: 10.33225/jbse/24.23.432

Amdan, M. (2024). Advancement of ai-tools in learning for technical vocational education and training (tvet) in malaysia (empowering students and tutor). *International Journal of Scientific Research.*

Asuyama, Y. (2019). Skill sorting and production linkages: Evidence from india. *The Developing Economies*, 57(2), 125–158. DOI: 10.1111/deve.12193

Babashahi, L. (2024). Ai in the workplace: A systematic review of skill transformation in the industry. *Administrative Sciences*, 14(6), 127. DOI: 10.3390/admsci14060127

Baki, N. (2023). Integrating artificial intelligence in human resource functions: Challenges and opportunities. *International Journal of Academic Research in Business & Social Sciences*, 13(8). Advance online publication. DOI: 10.6007/ijarbss/v13-i8/18071

Basnet, S. (2024). Navigating the ethical landscape: Considerations in implementing ai-ml systems in human resources. *International Journal of Research Publication and Reviews*, 5(3), 3436–3447. DOI: 10.55248/gengpi.5.0324.0755

Bobitan, N. (2024). Shaping tomorrow: Anticipating skills requirements based on the integration of artificial intelligence in business organizations—a foresight analysis using the scenario method. *Electronics (Basel)*, 13(11), 2198. DOI: 10.3390/electronics13112198

Cacciamani, G., Anvar, A., Chen, A., Gill, I., & Hung, A. (2021). How the use of the artificial intelligence could improve surgical skills in urology: State of the art and future perspectives. *Current Opinion in Urology*, 31(4), 378–384. DOI: 10.1097/mou.0000000000000890

Cao, W., Ye, X., & Chen, X. (2023). Exploration and research on employment guidance system in universities from the perspective of artificial intelligence. *Ozean Journal of Applied Sciences*, 13(06), 934–940. DOI: 10.4236/ojapps.2023.136075

Chen, L. (2023). Research on the impact of artificial intelligence on the development of the accounting industry. *Frontiers in Business Economics and Management*, 11(3), 262–266. DOI: 10.54097/fbem.v11i3.13328

Chen, Z. (2022). Artificial intelligence-virtual trainer: Innovative didactics aimed at personalized training needs. *Journal of the Knowledge Economy*, 14(2), 2007–2025. DOI: 10.1007/s13132-022-00985-0

Chuang, S., & Graham, C. (2018). Embracing the sobering reality of technological influences on jobs, employment and human resource development. *European Journal of Training and Development*, 42(7/8), 400–416. DOI: 10.1108/ejtd-03-2018-0030

CII, and Peoplestrong. (2019). India Skill Report. Wheebox.

Dash, D. C. S., & Dash, S. (2020). Skill Development Mission and the Skill Landscape. International Journal of Innovative Science and Research Technology, 34-37.

Dima, J. (2024). The effects of artificial intelligence on human resource activities and the roles of the human resource triad: Opportunities and challenges. *Frontiers in Psychology*, 15. Advance online publication. DOI: 10.3389/fpsyg.2024.1360401

Dumitru, D. (2023). Critical thinking: Creating job-proof skills for the future of work. *Journal of Intelligence*, 11(10), 194. DOI: 10.3390/jintelligence11100194

Gandhi, R. (2022). Significance of new education policy (nep) 2020 for adult education and lifelong learning program. International Journal of Management Technology and Social Sciences, 79-95. https://doi.org/DOI: 10.47992/ijmts.2581.6012.0179

Ghosh, R. (2015). Gender and diversity in india. *Advances in Developing Human Resources*, 18(1), 3–10. DOI: 10.1177/1523422315614929

Grover, M., & Kapoor, R. (2020). *Skill Development in India:A study of key success factors and challenges*. CLIO An Interdisciplinary Journal.

Holmes, A., & Douglass, A. (2021). Artificial intelligence: Reshaping the accounting profession and the disruption to accounting education. *Journal of Emerging Technologies in Accounting*, 19(1), 53–68. DOI: 10.2308/jeta-2020-054

Ibrahim, A. (2024). Assessing the knowledge and perception of artificial intelligence for teaching and research among lecturers in the faculties of arts in nigeria. *Journal of Global Research in Education and Social Science*, 18(2), 25–33. DOI: 10.56557/jogress/2024/v18i28671

Johanson, R. K., & Adams, A. V. (2004). *Skills development in sub-Saharan Africa*. World Bank Publications.

Kahfi, F. (2022). The existence of human resource development (hrd) on the development of employee creativity. *Journal of Management and Administration Provision*, 2(2), 51–57. DOI: 10.55885/jmap.v2i2.178

Kanchan, S., & Varshney, S. (2015). Skill development initiatives and strategies. *Asian Journal of Management Research*, 5(4), 666–672.

Kapur, H. (2016). Skill India programme: A compliment to Make in India campaign. *Global Journal for Research Analysis*, •••, 84–86.

Karthikeyan, C. (2019). A Meta analytical descriptive study on evolving concepts of Human Capital and its application in the age of Artificial intelligence(AI). *International Journal of Research and Analytical Reviews*, •••, 361–373.

Katou, A. (2017). How does human resource management influence organisational performance? an integrative approach-based analysis. *International Journal of Productivity and Performance Management*, 66(6), 797–821. DOI: 10.1108/ijppm-01-2016-0004

Komasawa, N., & Yokohira, M. (2023). Simulation-based education in the artificial intelligence era. *Cureus*. Advance online publication. DOI: 10.7759/cureus.40940

Kuruvilla, S., Erickson, C. L., & Hwang, A. (2002). An Assessment of the Singapore Skills Development System:Does it constitute a viable model for other Developing countries? *World Development*, •••, 1461–1467.

Manohar, P., Rayel, J., & Sause, L. (2023). Efficacy of management and employees' involvement in hrd initiatives: The case of png power limited. *Business Ethics and Leadership*, 7(2), 35–46. DOI: 10.21272/bel.7(2).35-46.2023

Ministry of Home Affairs, GOI. (2011). "Census of India 2011." Provisional population totals.

Morandini, S., Fraboni, F., Angelis, M., Puzzo, G., Giusino, D., & Pietrantoni, L. (2023). The impact of artificial intelligence on workers' skills: upskilling and reskilling in organisations. Informing Science the International Journal of an Emerging Transdiscipline, 26, 039-068. https://doi.org/DOI: 10.28945/5078

Mustopa, M. (2024). Challenges in artificial intelligence development in higher education in china, india, and indonesia: International students' perspectives. *International Journal of Learning Teaching and Educational Research*, 23(2), 354–373. DOI: 10.26803/ijlter.23.2.17

Nyathani, R. (2023). Ai-driven hr analytics: Unleashing the power of hr data management. *Journal of Technology and Systems*, 5(2), 15–26. DOI: 10.47941/jts.1513

Okada, A. (2012). Skill development for Youth in India:Challenges & Opportunities. *Kokusai Kyoiku Kyoryoku Ronshu*, •••, 169–193.

Ore, O., & Sposato, M. (2021). Opportunities and risks of artificial intelligence in recruitment and selection. *The International Journal of Organizational Analysis*, 30(6), 1771–1782. DOI: 10.1108/ijoa-07-2020-2291

Osolase, E., Rasdi, R., & Mansor, Z. (2023). Developing awareness of green human resource development practices in the hotel industry. *Advances in Developing Human Resources*, 25(2), 116–122. DOI: 10.1177/15234223231155503

Pilz, M., & Regel, J. (2021). Vocational education and training in india: Prospects and challenges from an outside perspective. *Margin - the Journal of Applied Economic Research*, 15(1), 101–121. DOI: 10.1177/0973801020976606

Rigley, E. (2023). Evaluating international ai skills policy: A systematic review of ai skills policy in seven countries. *Global Policy*, 15(1), 204–217. DOI: 10.1111/1758-5899.13299

Sharma, H. (2018). Skill development policies in india: Implications and challenges. *Journal of Social and Development Sciences*, 8(4), 43–50. DOI: 10.22610/jevr.v8i4.2159

Sheshadri, S., Pradeep, A., & Chandran, M. (2021). Towards gender inclusive skill development in rural India: Factors that inhibit and facilitate skill women's enrolment in vocational training. *Environment-Behaviour Proceedings Journal*, 6(SI4), 239–243. DOI: 10.21834/ebpj.v6isi4.3032

Shrotriya, S., & Dhir, S. (2018). Innovation driven ecosystem for quality skill development in India. *Benchmarking*, 25(8), 2997–3020.

Singh, A. (2024). Artificial intelligence adoption in extended hr ecosystems: Enablers and barriers. an abductive case research. *Frontiers in Psychology*, 14. Advance online publication. DOI: 10.3389/fpsyg.2023.1339782

Singh, S. (2020). Emergence of Skill Universities in India. In *Emerging Issues in Business Management* (pp. 133–138). National Press Associates.

Soslau, E., & Bell, N. (2018). The Challenges of Supporting Equity Literacy Skill Development in White Teacher Candidates: A Self-Study of Two White Field Instructors, Studying Teacher Education. *Studying Teacher Education*, •••, 156–173.

Vaddepalli, D. (2023). The future of work: implications of artificial intelligence on hr practices. tjjpt, 44(3), 1711-1724. https://doi.org/DOI: 10.52783/tjjpt.v44.i3.562

Yetişensoy, O. and Rapoport, A. (2023). Artificial intelligence literacy teaching in social studies education. Journal of Pedagogical Research. https://doi.org/DOI: 10.33902/jpr.202320866

Chapter 10
Artificial Intelligence Innovations in Visual Arts and Design Education

Hanjun Su
https://orcid.org/0000-0002-7106-1455
Universiti Sains Malaysia, Malaysia

Jingru Zhang
https://orcid.org/0009-0002-6537-2334
Universiti Sains Malaysia, Malaysia

Shiqing Tang
Nanjing Chengxin Primary School, China

ABSTRACT

Visual arts and design education is an important area in higher education, and artificial intelligence (AI), which can provide personalised learning experiences, plays a pivotal role in facilitating the learning process and student creativity within it. This chapter provides an insight into the current use of AI technologies in the teaching of visual arts and design, highlighting their impact on student engagement. Through the integration of current research findings as well as detailed case studies, it reveals how AI can be effective in fostering creativity and meeting specific pedagogical needs in the field of visual arts and design. In addition, the article explores the role of AI in visual arts and design education and highlights the ethical issues encountered when integrating technology into educational frameworks. Finally, the chapter looks at future research trends and calls for further studies to improve the quality of teaching and learning in visual arts and design education and to prepare students for a technology-led future.

DOI: 10.4018/979-8-3693-6745-2.ch010

1 INTRODUCTION

Over the last few decades, accelerated development in the field of information technology has significantly contributed to advancing Artificial Intelligence in myriad ways. In education, technological innovation continuously informs ways of delivering teaching materials and enriches the subject's learning experience. Since AI is becoming widely available, the world of art and accordingly its education are just beginning to look more closely at the possibilities. At the higher level of arts education, among the fields that could benefit from AI's innovative outcomes are visual arts and design education. Undergraduate arts education in various countries is typically viewed as a form for fostering creativity and learning acquisition in this aspect. These fields are, by nature, creative and expressive in ways that the approaches to teaching must then create a learning context in which to reach creativity and a personal expression of technical ability. Higher education institutions need to provide students with personalised learning experiences to meet their diverse needs and abilities. Artificial intelligence, with its ability to analyse data and adapt to individual learning patterns, is a powerful tool to achieve this.

By providing features such as sources of inspiration, compositional references, and style transitions, AI art generators make the creation of art easy. Artificial intelligence is thought to represent a turning point in fine art (Cotroneo & Hutson, 2023). As the creative industry increasingly adopts AI tools in design, animation, and other visual arts applications, it becomes imperative to equip students with AI knowledge and skills. Understanding and utilising AI will not only enhance students' creativity but will also improve their employability in a technology-driven job market. However, these technologies and capabilities have yet to be fully integrated into actual higher art education.

Visual arts and design education has traditionally relied on direct student-teacher interaction, hands-on practice, and iterative feedback. These approaches face challenges of scalability, accessibility, and resource constraints. Artificial intelligence can address these challenges by providing scalable, personalised and adaptive learning solutions. By leveraging AI technologies, educators can provide customised learning paths, real-time feedback and enhanced creativity tools that enrich the learning experience and prepare students for a future where technology plays a key role in the creative industries.

This chapter aims to explore the multifaceted impact of AI on visual arts and design education. The main research questions are as follows:

1. How can AI be applied in visual arts and design education?
2. What are the ethical issues that need to be considered when integrating AI into visual arts and design education?

3. What are the future directions of AI innovations in visual arts and design education?

This chapter aims to provide a comprehensive analysis of AI innovations in visual arts and design education. Following the introduction, the second part of the literature review section explores existing research on AI in education, focusing on its application and impact in visual arts and design and the shortcomings of the research findings. Parts three and four discuss specific types of applications as well as specific case studies. Subsequently, Part Five discusses the ethical issues related to integrating AI into art education. Finally, part six discusses future research directions and identifies potential areas for further exploration and innovation. The chapter also provides recommendations for educators and policymakers on how to effectively integrate AI into visual arts and design education to improve teaching quality and student learning outcomes.

2 LITERATURE REVIEW

2.1 AI in Education

AI is the general term for the science of artificial intelligence, including learning, reasoning, problem-solving, perception, and language understanding. AI can be broadly classified into two categories: narrow AI, which is specifically designed to perform a particular task (e.g., facial recognition or Internet searching); and general-purpose AI, which is designed to perform any intellectual task that humans can perform. Artificial intelligence is developing rapidly, with remarkable results in many application areas such as speech recognition, image processing, natural language processing, automatic theorem proving, and intelligent robotics (Zhang & Lu, 2021). These fields explore different aspects of replicating or augmenting human cognitive functions, respectively, driving the rapid development and widespread application of AI in various industries. In the area of speech recognition, AI algorithms are being developed to interpret and transcribe language with increasing accuracy, driving the creation of virtual assistants such as Siri and Alexa. In image processing, AI techniques are used for facial recognition, medical imaging, and navigation in self-driving cars. Natural language processing (NLP) enables machines to understand, interpret and generate human language, fuelling the development of chatbots and translation services. Automated theorem proving involves the use of AI to solve mathematical problems and prove complex theorems, contributing to advances in various scientific fields. Intelligent robotics combines AI with robotics to create machines capable of performing tasks in dynamic environments, ranging from manufacturing to healthcare.

With the remarkable advancements in AI technology, its potential in the field of education has attracted a lot of attention. Educational Artificial Intelligence (AIED), or Educational Artificial Intelligence (EAI), refers to the use of AI in education to support personalised, automated feedback and instruction (Song & Wang, 2020). Applications of AI have been widely explored in different educational contexts, especially in the areas of chatbots, expert systems, intelligent tutors, machine learning, personalised learning systems, visualizations, and virtual learning environments, which have received much attention (Zhang & Aslan, 2021).

For example, chatbot is one of the most well-known AI applications in education today. These AI-powered systems interact with students in a conversational manner, answering questions, providing resources, and guiding students through the learning process; personalized learning systems use AI algorithms to customize educational content based on individual learning styles, pacing, and preferences; and intelligent tutors provide students with instant feedback and personalised guidance for students through intelligent tutors that mimic the experience of a human tutor and streamline administrative operations such as grading and attendance management; and expert systems that aim to replicate the decision-making capabilities of human experts, providing guidance based on a large knowledge base. These systems use sophisticated algorithms to assess student performance and adapt instructional materials, ensuring that each student receives the support they need. Despite these advances, current research on the use of AI in education leaves much to be desired. Many studies focus on specific technologies or applications without considering the broader implications of integrating AI into the education system. In addition, more comprehensive research is needed to explore the long-term impact of AI on teaching and learning in specific disciplines.

2.2 Visual Arts and Design Education

Arts education is a discipline that fosters creativity, critical thinking, and cultural awareness and plays a vital role in the overall development of students (Anderson & Milbrandt, 2018). Unlike other disciplines that emphasise standardisation, arts education encourages exploration, self-expression, and the development of individual voices (Aguilera & Revilla, 2021). It provides students with unique opportunities to engage with materials, concepts, and practices. Arts are related to all aspects of personal growth and have long been recognised as a bridge between the human heart and the Art can convey feelings emotions, perceptions, and perceptions without the language barrier; at the same time, art records and perpetuates human values and beliefs. Perpetuates human values and beliefs (Amini & Laghabdoost, 2021). Art education also provides a way of understanding and critiquing the world, allowing students to explore complex issues in both visual and tangible forms.

Visual arts and design education is a branch of arts education in the broad sense, characterised by an emphasis on creative expression and practical application. Programmes typically include a variety of courses in drawing, painting, sculpture, digital media, and design principles, and are designed to develop students' technical skills as well as their understanding of concepts (Marshall, 2014). Shared practices across visual arts and design educational pedagogies include studio-based teaching and project-based learning, which provide for active students' participation, accompanied by critique sessions, and support collaborative learning (Cunliffe & Morris, 2019).

Although there are many strengths in visual arts and design education, there are several challenges that are current in the educational environment. One such challenge is the continued marginalization of arts curriculum through the prioritization of STEM education—science, technology, engineering, and mathematics—in the classroom and with the reduced funding and support for arts programs this shift in focus brings (Parks, 2018). Furthermore, there is a fear of access to quality arts education since most of the time, a disparity in socio-economic conditions means that students have differential access to participating in the arts. Also, because of the increase in student size, means that many students cannot get timely feedback and personalized guidance on their learning process, hence preventing them from solving problems they encounter on time. The digital technological revolution offers visual arts education many opportunities and challenges that call for continuous updating of curriculum content, including the integration of new tools and platforms (Sweeny & Mason, 2019). It will be worth continuing the evolution of pedagogical approaches to innovate and promote the importance of arts education as part of the well-rounded curriculum.

Whereas some research exists on emergent technologies integration for arts education, little investigation exists to shed light on how these technologies enhance or detract from the learning experience of the student within current research (Choi & Lee, 2017). Although there is now a fast-growing interest in the junction between the arts and design thinking, much research remains to be done in understanding how to effectively integrate these practices within educational contexts. Potential future research direction might be the long-term impact of arts education on the cognitive and emotional development of students (Winner et al., 2018).

3 APPLICATIONS OF AI IN VISUAL ARTS AND DESIGN EDUCATION

3.1 Personalized Learning Experiences

Conventional methods of teaching in visual art and design do not labour under the restrictions of personal learning where the differing needs of students are typically not satisfied. Too standardized teaching methodology will limit students' creativity in art design. It can easily access a lot of student information: learning progress and quality of homework submissions. Through data analysis and machine learning, these technologies are used to tailor the educational experience to any given student's interests, abilities, and progress, dynamically adapting each specific student's needs and hosting their individual experience to create a learning path that will substantially augment their engagement and educational outcomes. An AI-driven recommendation system would also suggest art projects according to students' strengths and areas of weakness, thus keeping the learning experience relevant and challenging. For instance, Kovanovic et al. illustrate that predictive analytics can be used to track student progress and intervene at the right time, counting for much where the creative discipline could see great improvements in the student's development with a high level of individual support.

Getting personalized, real-time feedback compared to traditional teacher guidance is another big benefit of AI. For instance, in digital art projects, AI can be used by Plein (2021) to run systematic analyses of elements, such as colour harmony and compositions, and go to the extent of providing immediate suggestions for alterations. This real-time feedback hastens skill development and keeps students motivated.

3.2 AI Assistance in the Creative Process

Artificial intelligence is changing the process of creation into a new scenario in which creativity traditionally has been based on intuition and experience. However, AI opens tremendous possibilities for innovating those very traditional forms of creativity. Technologies like Generative Adversarial Networks provide an artist with options for exploration and creation in ways never thought possible before (Goodfellow et al., 2020). Generative Artificial Intelligence Models like GANs make new images by learning from pre-existing datasets. For example, Elgammal et al. designed a GAN-based system for automatically generating new art styles through style deviations, allowing artists to browse new visual styles with AI-assisted suggestions in the creation of new inspirations.

It is further seen that AI can also assess already designed pieces of art, offer design recommendations, and help artists draw the mechanism better or find alternate styles. McCosker and Wilken, 2020. On the contrary, it can automate everything from the design process to color matching, and composition optimization so that time-saving and creativity are the key. Such tools allow designers to be innovative while AI acts as a tool that maintains high standards at all works (Sims and Hampson, 2018)

In sectors like fashion and architecture, AI-augmented design processes have increased productivity and enriched the creative industries operated by humans with improved outcomes in innovation as well as more ideas generated by the students (Lee & Chang, 2019). The use of AI in the design process within visual arts allows students to generate new ideas and be empowered to develop a high level of autonomy in the workflow process and to realize that they can pose more questions about what might be done creatively.

3.3 Student Engagement and Interaction

Student engagement and interaction make effective learning. In the case where students never feel engaged and interested, it may result in them being less involved. AI technology comes in to create interactive learning environments and gamified experiences for learning that offer increased student engagement and motivation.

Some AI-based, interactive, next-generation learning platforms leverage technologies such as virtual and augmented reality to make learning interactive and experiential. These platforms help students approach subjects related to art and design more interactively, making in-depth understanding and retention of material feasible. For example, Wang et al. conclude that an AI-driven VR platform furthers an enhanced spatial understanding of architectural designs and leads to better learning outcomes by students. Such platforms give real-time feedback and virtual instructions, making students active participants and collaborators. In other words, it makes learning more engaging and effective.

There is a need for empirical and applied studies on effectiveness to determine the reality regarding the promises made. For example, Hwang and Chiu conducted a study about educational gaming, driven by AI, and found that students who were engaged in the gamified learning process were able to achieve better results in these assessments compared to the ones who obtained traditional instruction. These findings continue to underscore that AI can reshape the student experience for learning visual arts and design through interactive, personally oriented, and enjoyable learning experiences.

4 CASE STUDIES

Case Study 1: Artificial Intelligence-Supported Art Education: A Deep Learning-Based System for Promoting University Students' Artwork Appreciation and Painting Outcomes

In the study by Chiu et al. (2022), the authors describe how a Deep Learning-based Art Learning System (DL-ALS) was developed and adopted to elevate the ability of University Students to Appreciate and Create Works of Art (Figure 1). Personalized feedback and instruction are crucial elements of a conventional arts education, but in large classes, it becomes difficult to achieve this in a timely manner because teachers cannot provide instant responses. The AI-powered DL-ALS bridges this gap using trained models fine-tuned from ResNet50, which will be helpful for students to identify and classify works of art.

It further refines the model regarding an art educational problem that suffers from a limited amount of training data and even complexity in accurately classifying different styles of art. The user interface is developed in such a way that the user, especially students, can easily insert their artwork and receive feedback easily and simply, hence not constrained by space, time, or device. It does not only provide instant feedback but also provides personalized guidance, similar to expert commentary, hence a powerful tool for learning to appreciate and create an art piece.

Figure 1. System architecture of DL-ALS (Chiu et al., 2022)

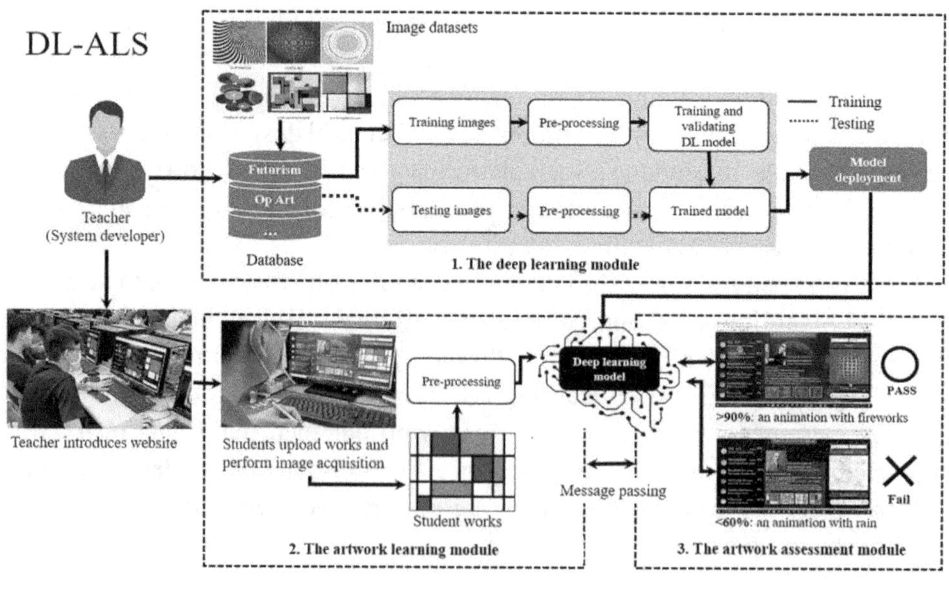

Secondly, the DL-ALS system is incorporated with animated feedback, which gamifies the learning process. For example, in those cases the artwork of a student shows a similarity with some particular art style, it will show a congratulating animation to reinforce the student's positive behaviour. On the contrary, if the artwork does not meet expected standards, it tells services and links pointing to what should be additionally done.

This research was conducted in quasi-experiment settings between two university student groups, taking an art appreciation course: an experimental group using the DL-ALS system and a control group using traditional technology-supported arts learning (CT-AL). A comparative investigation suggested that substantially better performance represented most outcomes for the students using the DL-ALS.

This suggests that AI could allow quick, accurate feedback and tremendously enhance the arts education experience, a precept central to the development of artistic skills and appreciation of arts. This indicates that adaptive learning environments set up with the help of expert feedback from AI can bridge the gap between traditional modes of teaching and the felt need for personalized, instructive modalities combined with immediate feedback. The fact that the DL-ALS system enhanced such an astute comprehensive range of educational output proves that AI could be a significant add-on to art and design education towards breaking through innovative and more effective modes of instruction.

Case Study 2: Application of Artificial Intelligence Technology in Computer-Aided Art Teaching

The study by He and Sun (2021) proposed a model for an artificial intelligence-assisted art teaching system (Figure 2). This design helped the students to understand clearly what they are taught through simulating real-life scenarios created through the virtual environment. That is, the student is immersed in the learning scenario, and thus, there is collaborative learning between students.

In the case of arts learning, a student can only learn how to better do it by creating and doing it. This stimulates students during their creative process, creating extensive interaction and peer-to-peer assessment, hence deepening the exploration and learning of students. It supports a range of teaching and learning activities, including online exercises, tests, and practical work, whereas at the same time – through learning to learn from the specific students' levels – the system gives customized advice and support accordingly to help students to address difficulties and enhance their performances. The research findings have put the AI-assisted model of teaching art at odds with other traditional models of teaching through which art has been passed down. In this manner, the study found that it taught students to be much more creative, deeper in their understanding of design concepts, and dedicated to art projects. The fact is, this difference emanates from the fact that the AI system gives instant feedback and directed instruction.

Figure 2. Intelligent computer-assisted teaching system

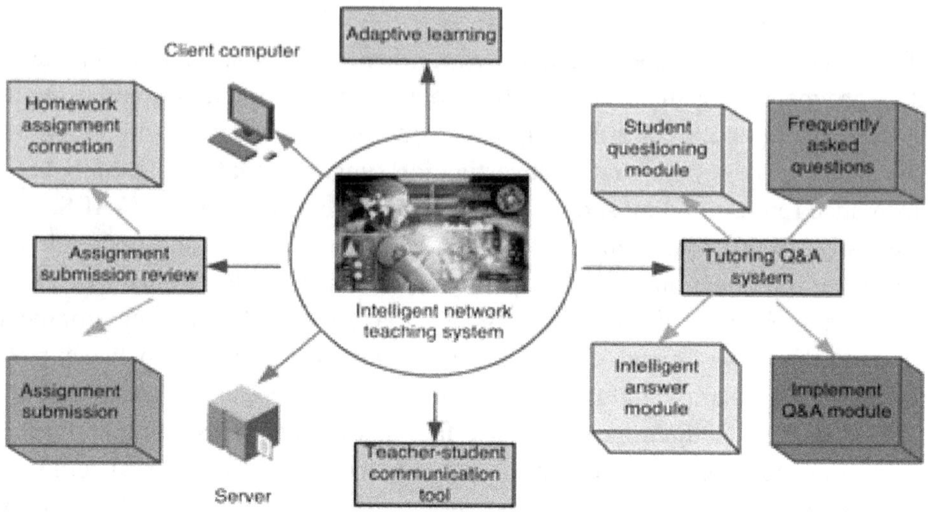

Generally, the level of creativity among students taught using real-time AI in art rose up and was a more guided and supported approach. The AI system supports the students with personal guidance and collaborative projects to get better outcomes and be better prepared for real-life problems in art and design.

Case Study 3: New Strategies and Practices of Design Education Under the Background of Artificial Intelligence Technology: Online Animation Design Studio

Tang et al. (2022) delved into the practice of artificial intelligence (AI) in online animation design studios, analysing the potential of AI technology to enhance pedagogy, enhance learning, and improve the overall efficiency of design education by comparing traditional design education methods with a new educational model that incorporates AI technology.

This paper explored the effective integration of technology, pedagogy and content knowledge, centred on the TPACK model (Technological Pedagogical Content Knowledge). Specifically, the research methodology is based on the traditional design studio model and integrates the TPACK model to create an online design studio. This online design studio not only provides traditional design pedagogical content but also incorporates AI technology to enable pedagogical activities and design project practices to take place in an online environment (Figure 3). The specific application of AI technology focuses on two key areas: personalised learning and collaborative learning, where AI technology is used to customise the learning content and project practices, tailoring them to the student's interests and learning needs. In addition to this, online design studios use AI tools to support collaboration between students, simulating real-life design challenges and teamwork. This collaborative environment not only enables students to communicate creatively in a virtual space but also provides them with hands-on opportunities for interdisciplinary cooperation and helps students adapt to future work patterns. The application of AI tools in collaboration not only aims to improve design efficiency but also develops the ability of students to work effectively in teams. During the study, the authors selected 40 animation design students to experiment to determine its effectiveness.

Figure 3. TPACK model and implementation integration of online design studio

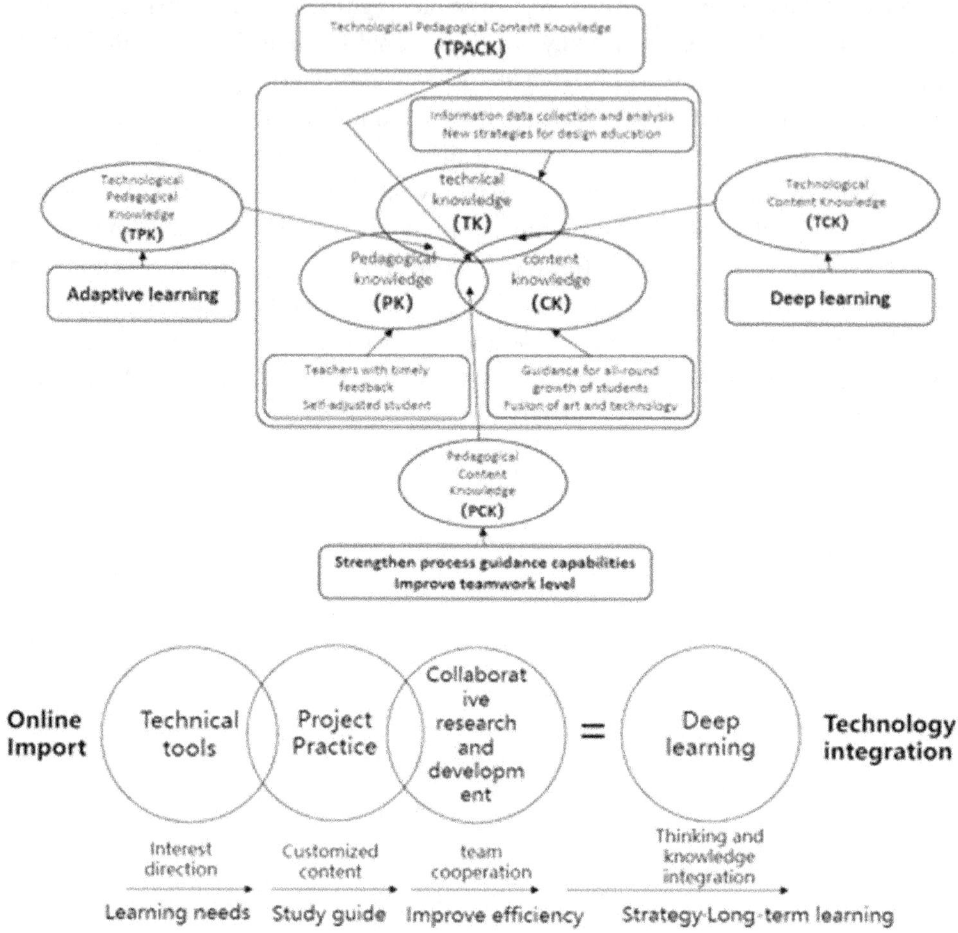

In summary, this research described in detail the design of the study, the methodology, and how the educational effects of the online design studio were constructed and evaluated by combining the TPACK model and AI technology.

5 ETHICAL CONSIDERATIONS IN AI-ENHANCED ART EDUCATION

5.1 Data Privacy and Security

The use of AI in art education demonstrates great opportunities to enhance the learning experience and effectiveness. However, it also brings potential ethical issues. Su and Yang (2023) mentioned in the theoretical framework for using generative AI in education that ethical considerations are emphatically needed (Figure 4).

Figure 4. The theoretical framework for using generative AI in education (Su & yang, 2023)

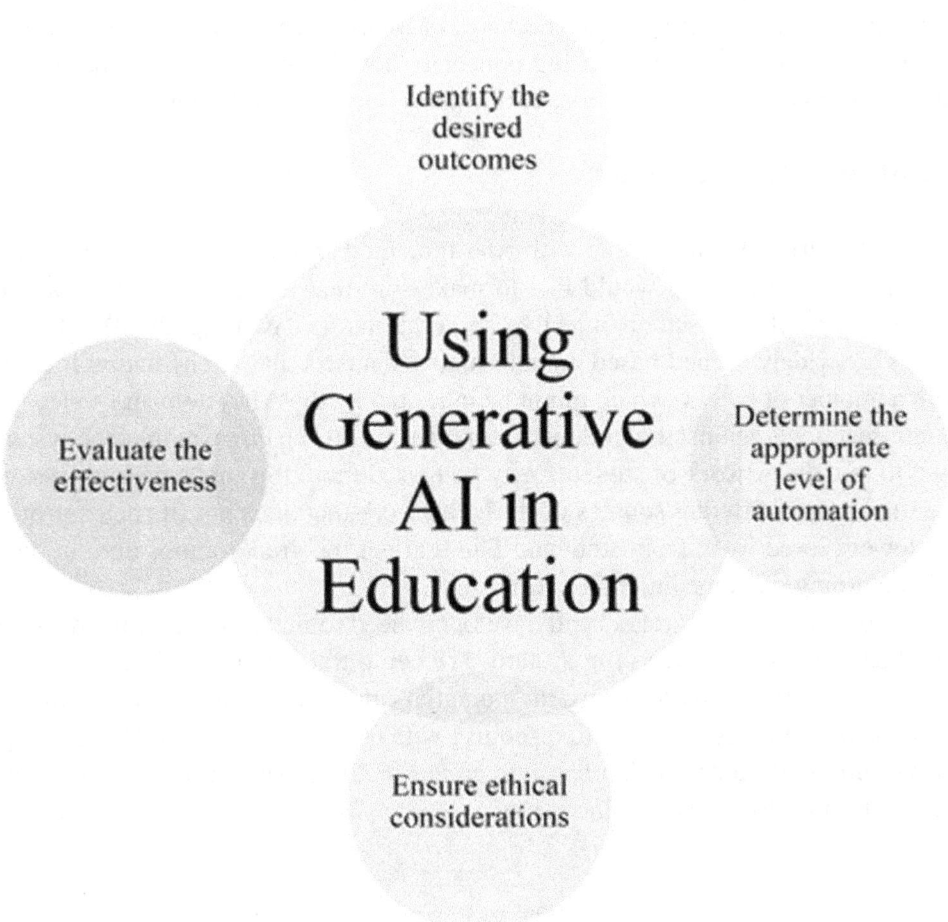

AI systems to achieve personalised learning, recommendation of educational resources and other functions cannot be achieved without the processing and operation of a large number of data sets. This cannot be done without sensitive student information including student study habits, personal preferences, and even biometric data (Ferguson, 2019). The collection, processing, and use of this data raises potential privacy and security concerns. If this data is not handled properly, there can be serious implications. For example, unauthorized personnel could gain access to student information, which would then result in identity theft or other exploitations related to the data exposed in the learning environment (Baker & Gow, 2020), or worse still, the data could be re-used and applied in a manner that violates their privacy rights (Varkey, 2020).

Therefore, experts and technologists designing AI systems need to particularly consider data privacy and security concerns, including issues involving encryption, secure data storage solutions, and strict access control. Second, ensure students pay full attention to what data are being collected, how it would be used, and who is allowed access to it to cut cuts risk in this part (Buchanan & McPherson, 2019).

5.2 AI Bias and Fairness

Another critical ethical issue with AI-augmented art education is the challenge of bias in AI systems. "I would like to make sure that the generated feedback is unbiased and solely based on objective observations" (Su & Yang, 2023). AI algorithms are widely trained based on voluminous datasets that are by nature imbued with a number of biases, which might be inherited by the AI system and so lead to unfair treatments against the student (Mehrabi et al., 2021). For example, the system used to rate the artwork of students may be biased more towards a certain style or situation due to different sources of data, and work that does not fit such a profile has lower scored work from students. These affect the grade ratings and, in turn, affect learning outcome and motivation.

To address this, researchers and developers need to make sure that the datasets on which the AI-based learning systems are being trained are sufficiently varied and representative, thus lowering the potential impact of biased results, while at the same time engaging in careful discourse with teachers on how to flexibly adapt the system to the content being learnt to create an AI-assisted arts learning system that contributes to equity and inclusion.

5.3 Teacher Roles and Student Dependency

Dependency on AI tools in the process of arts learning by students is a matter not to be neglected. The older way of doing things on learning had long made the teacher become the center point of directing and coaching students to achieve good critical thinking and problem-solving skills. Nevertheless, if the trend in the use of AI in arts education continues, the roles of the teachers and the level of student dependency may change. The real role of teachers might be pushed into the background with the use of AI systems in teaching more and more, and this actually might lead to overdependence on technology (Williamson & Eynon, 2020). If AI systems are used to automate feedback and assessment, the human element of teaching - such as providing nuanced, context-specific instruction - may be neglected.

One concern is that students may become overly reliant on AI tools for the creative process, which is especially important in the arts. For example, students use AI tools to assist in the creative process, generating ideas or refining artwork. This in itself can help students open their minds and inspire them. However, inappropriate use can also hinder the development of their creative skills and limit their ability to think independently (Selwyn, 2019). For example, the direct adoption of generated ideas, or even the direct use of generated images for their work, can be extremely detrimental to students' learning and growth, preventing them from getting the training in art-making that they need to truly develop their own abilities.

To combat these issues, it is crucial to find a balance between the use of AI and the traditional role of the teacher. AI should be viewed as a tool that enhances, rather than replaces, the role of the teacher in the classroom. Teachers can use AI to enhance their teaching methods and provide more personalised support to students while still promoting critical thinking and creativity (Luckin, 2018). Additionally, educators should focus on helping students develop a healthy relationship with AI by encouraging them to view these tools as aids rather than dependencies.

Such ethical considerations in AI-enhanced arts education are numerous and multi-faceted. Guarantees of data privacy and security, dealing with bias and fairness in AI, and careful management of teacher roles and student dependencies are called for if AI is to be responsibly used within education. As AI continues to evolve and become more widely integrated into educational practice, educators, developers, and policymakers must collaborate to develop ethical guidelines that prioritise the well-being and equitable treatment of all students.

6 FUTURE RESEARCH DIRECTIONS

6.1 Potential Areas of Research

Since artificial intelligence is still growing, with its integration into visual arts and design education this provides a wide range of possibilities for improving the teaching-learning process further. Now, looking at the potential areas for research in the future, first of all, one is the development and incorporation of particular AI capabilities suited to art education. Currently, AI applications are focused on STEM educational tools ., there is a need to create AI capabilities that answer the unique needs of education in art. For instance, AI-assisted teaching of color theory, tools that offer real-time composition feedback, or simulating various artistic techniques. Research should focus on the practical application of these AI tools in the art classroom, using research to assess their effectiveness in improving student outcomes and engagement.

Secondly, consider integrating teaching theories and methods into AI art education. Traditional teaching methods, such as constructivism and experiential learning, have been shown to be effective in fostering creativity and critical thinking. The challenge is how these theories can be adapted or enhanced through AI to create more dynamic and interactive learning environments. Research should explore how AI can be used as a bridge between theoretical frameworks and practical teaching strategies, ensuring effective application of the technology (Durall & Gros, 2020).

Third, future research also needs to explore how AI can be used as a teaching assistant in arts education to help teachers support students more effectively in the classroom. AI has the potential to automate everyday tasks, such as grading assignments or providing basic instructional guidance, allowing teachers to devote more time and energy to creative and interactive teaching. However, this needs to be carefully designed to ensure that AI tools are complementary to teachers' teaching, not replacements (Holmes & Porayska-Pomsta, 2020). Research can examine how AI can support teachers in personalizing feedback, classroom management, or providing complementary lessons to enhance the overall teaching process.

In addition, the use of AI to promote visual arts and design education in resource-limited areas is also a potential research area to watch. AI technology can provide high-quality educational content and tools to help fill the gap in arts education in resource-poor areas (Knox, Wang, & Gallagher, 2020). Ai-powered online platforms can provide access to virtual art studios, interactive classes, and a global arts community, helping to bridge the education gap between resource-rich and resource-poor regions. Research should focus on the practical challenges of implementing these technologies in different educational contexts and assess their impact on educational equity and student outcomes.

6.2 Technological Trends

In terms of technology trends, one of the future trends for AI in visual arts and design education is the development of immersive learning environments combined with augmented reality (AR) and virtual reality (VR). These environments can provide students with hands-on experiences that are difficult to achieve in a traditional classroom.

At the same time, it simplifies the use and development of AI tools and lowers the barrier to entry. Currently, the complexity of AI technology can be a significant barrier for educators, especially those who lack technical expertise. Future AI tools should be designed to be more user-friendly, enabling teachers to easily integrate them into their curriculum without in-depth technical knowledge to meet their specific teaching needs.

As AI algorithms continue to advance, they will play a key role in enhancing personalized learning experiences. Advanced machine learning algorithms can analyze vast amounts of student data to customize educational content that matches individual learning styles, needs, and preferences. Future research should focus on the improvement of algorithms to improve their accuracy and effectiveness in predicting student needs and delivering personalized educational experiences, thereby promoting deeper learning and greater engagement in visual arts and design education.

6.3 Strategies for Improving Teaching Quality

In order to improve the quality of teaching in visual arts and design education, AI models designed specifically for the art field can be integrated into the curriculum. For example, AI models that simulate artistic techniques or generate works of art can be used to teach students different styles and approaches. Research should explore how these models can be effectively integrated into teaching practices that not only enhance students' technical skills but also encourage creative exploration.

With a blended learning model that combines AI-driven tools with traditional teaching methods, by using AI to deliver personalized content and assessments, teachers can focus on facilitating discussions and providing practical guidance, creating a more holistic learning experience for students. Research can explore best practices for implementing blended learning in visual arts and design education to optimize its effectiveness.

Finally, ensuring that teachers can effectively use AI technology is critical to improving the quality of teaching. Professional development programs should be developed that train teachers in how to effectively integrate the use of AI into their teaching practice. Specific policies, such as grants or incentives for AI integration, and standardized guidelines for AI usage, should be developed to support educators.

Furthermore, training programs must provide clear certifications for teachers to boost their confidence in applying AI.

7 CONCLUSION

The use of AI in education is bound to be highly instrumental to both personalized learning and creativity, keeping the learner engaged. This chapter is, therefore, an attempt at an all-inclusive overview of the current state and potential future of AI in visual arts and design education. This chapter aims to provide a comprehensive overview of the current state and future potential of AI in visual arts and design education. Through a detailed analysis of existing research, case studies, and ethical considerations, it seeks to offer valuable insights and recommendations for educators, researchers, and policymakers. By embracing AI innovations, we can prepare students for a future where technology and creativity intersect, equipping them with the skills and knowledge needed to thrive in a rapidly evolving world.

REFERENCES

Aguilera, D., & Revilla, J. O. (2021). STEM vs. STEAM Education and Student Creativity: A Systematic Literature Review. *Education Sciences*, 11(7), 331. DOI: 10.3390/educsci11070331

Amini, M., & Laghabdoost, M. (2021). Representation of teachers' lived experiences of functions implementation and challenges of art education in primary schools. *Research in Teaching*, 9(4), 29–1.

Anderson, T., & Milbrandt, M. K. (2018). *Art for life: Authentic instruction in art.* McGraw-Hill Education.

Baker, T., & Gow, G. A. (2020). Privacy and surveillance: AI ethics in education. *Journal of Educational Technology & Society*, 23(4), 31–41.

Bower, M. (2019). Technology-mediated learning theory. *British Journal of Educational Technology*, 50(3), 1030–1042. DOI: 10.1111/bjet.12771

Buchanan, T., & McPherson, S. (2019). Ethical considerations in the use of AI in education. *Journal of Information Ethics*, 28(2), 15–27.

Chiu, M., Hwang, G., Hsia, L., & Shyu, F. (2022). Artificial intelligence-supported art education: A deep learning-based system for promoting university students' artwork appreciation and painting outcomes. *Interactive Learning Environments*, 32(3), 824–842. DOI: 10.1080/10494820.2022.2100426

Choi, S., & Lee, J. (2017). The impact of digital technology on art education. *International Journal of Art & Design Education*, 36(3), 363–377.

Cotroneo, P., & Hutson, J. (2023). Generative AI tools in art education: Exploring prompt engineering and iterative processes for enhanced creativity. *Metaverse*, 4(1), 14. DOI: 10.54517/m.v4i1.2164

Cunliffe, L., & Morris, M. (2019). Collaborative art education and its role in fostering social skills. *Art Education*, 72(4), 24–31.

Durall, E., & Gros, B. (2020). Learning and creativity in the age of artificial intelligence: Challenges for education. *Technology. Knowledge and Learning*, 25(3), 555–568. DOI: 10.1007/s10758-019-09417-7

Elgammal, A., Liu, B., Elhoseiny, M., & Mazzone, M. (2017). CAN: Creative adversarial networks, generating "art" by learning about styles and deviating from style norms. *arXiv preprint arXiv:1706.07068.*

Ferguson, R. (2019). Ethical Challenges of AI in Education. *AI & Society*, 34(1), 25–33.

Goodfellow, I., Pouget-Abadie, J., Mirza, M., Xu, B., Warde-Farley, D., Ozair, S., Courville, A., & Bengio, Y. (2020). Generative adversarial networks. *Communications of the ACM*, 63(11), 139–144. DOI: 10.1145/3422622

He, C., & Sun, B. (2021). Application of artificial intelligence technology in computer aided art teaching. *Computer-Aided Design and Applications*, 18(S4), 118–129. DOI: 10.14733/cadaps.2021.S4.118-129

Holmes, W., & Porayska-Pomsta, K. (2020). The ethics of AI in education: Who cares? *British Journal of Educational Technology*, 51(3), 981–983. DOI: 10.1111/bjet.13045

Hwang, G. J., & Chiu, L. Y. (2020). Applying an inquiry-based learning approach to flipped classrooms: A study on learning effects in STEM and non-STEM subjects. *Journal of Educational Technology & Society*, 23(1), 26–40.

Knox, J., Wang, Y., & Gallagher, M. (2020). Artificial intelligence and inclusive education: Speculative futures and emerging practices. *Learning, Media and Technology*, 45(3), 226–238. DOI: 10.1080/17439884.2020.1761641

Kovanović, V., Joksimović, S., Gašević, D., Siemens, G., & Hatala, M. (2019). Predictive analytics in education: Towards a unified framework. *Learning Analytics & Knowledge*, 2019, 82–91. DOI: 10.1145/2723576.2723580

Lee, S. H., & Chang, M. J. (2019). AI and fashion design: How artificial intelligence is reshaping the industry. *International Journal of Fashion Design, Technology and Education*, 12(4), 372–381.

Luckin, R. (2018). *Machine learning and human intelligence: The future of education for the 21st century*. Routledge.

Marshall, J. (2014). Transdisciplinarity and art integration: Toward a new understanding of art-based learning across the curriculum. *Studies in Art Education*, 55(2), 104–127. DOI: 10.1080/00393541.2014.11518922

McCosker, A., & Wilken, R. (2020). AI for artists: Transformative practices in creative industries. *Media International Australia*, 177(1), 71–84. DOI: 10.1177/1329878X20937694

Mehrabi, N., Morstatter, F., Saxena, N., Lerman, K., & Galstyan, A. (2021). A survey on bias and fairness in machine learning. *ACM Computing Surveys*, 54(6), 1–35. DOI: 10.1145/3457607

Parks, M. (2018). The decline of arts education in the era of STEM: A critical analysis. *Arts Education Policy Review*, 119(2), 82–92.

Petrides, L., & Ogawa, R. (2020). Integrating design thinking and arts education: Lessons from a cross-disciplinary approach. *Journal of Design Education*, 12(1), 45–63.

Plein, C. (2021). AI-powered creativity: Exploring the implications of AI-driven tools for creative practice in the arts. *Leonardo*, 54(3), 275–283. DOI: 10.1162/leon_a_01953

Selwyn, N. (2019). Should robots replace teachers? AI and the future of education. *Polity*.

Sims, J. G., & Hampson, G. (2018). AI in architecture: Tools for creative design. *Design Studies*, 54(2), 26–38.

Song, P., & Wang, X. (2020). A bibliometric analysis of worldwide educational artificial intelligence research development in recent twenty years. *Asia Pacific Education Review*, 21(3), 473–486. DOI: 10.1007/s12564-020-09640-2

Su, J., & Yang, W. (2023). Unlocking the power of ChatGPT: A framework for applying generative AI in education. *ECNU Review of Education*, 209653112311684. Advance online publication. DOI: 10.1177/20965311231168423

Sweeny, R. W., & Mason, C. L. (2019). Digital media in art education: Prospects and challenges. *Journal of Art & Design Education*, 38(2), 148–159.

Tang, T., Li, P., & Tang, Q. (2022). New Strategies and Practices of Design Education Under the Background of Artificial Intelligence Technology: Online Animation Design Studio. *Frontiers in Psychology*, 13, 767295. DOI: 10.3389/fpsyg.2022.767295 PMID: 35651576

Varkey, B. (2020). AI and student data: Protecting privacy in the age of big data. *Journal of Education Policy*, 35(3), 407–426.

Wang, F., Liu, M., & Dun, L. (2021). Augmented and virtual reality in art education: Exploring new frontiers with AI. *Computers & Graphics*, 92, 26–35. DOI: 10.1016/j.cag.2020.12.005

Williamson, B., & Eynon, R. (2020). Automation in education: Rethinking the roles of teachers and technology. *Learning, Media and Technology*, 45(2), 115–128.

Winner, E., Goldstein, T. R., & Vincent-Lancrin, S. (2018). *Art for art's sake? The impact of arts education*. OECD Publishing.

Zawacki-Richter, O., Marín, V. I., Bond, M., & Gouverneur, F. (2019). Systematic review of research on artificial intelligence applications in higher education–Where are the educators? *International Journal of Educational Technology in Higher Education*, 16(1), 39. DOI: 10.1186/s41239-019-0171-0

Zhang, C., & Lu, Y. (2021). Study on artificial intelligence: The state of the art and future prospects. *Journal of Industrial Information Integration*, 23, 100224. DOI: 10.1016/j.jii.2021.100224

Zhang, K., & Aslan, A. B. (2021). AI technologies for education: Recent research & future directions. *Computers and Education Artificial Intelligence*, 2, 100025. DOI: 10.1016/j.caeai.2021.100025

Zou, J., & Schiebinger, L. (2018). AI can be sexist and racist—It's time to make it fair. *Nature*, 559(7714), 324–326. DOI: 10.1038/d41586-018-05707-8 PMID: 30018439

Chapter 11 Revolutionizing Education: The Transformative Power and Challenges of Artificial Intelligence in Learning

Zeenat Shafiq
University of Kashmir, India

ABSTRACT

This abstract examines the many facets of artificial intelligence, outlining its reach, development, and effects, with an emphasis on how it can be used in education. The study explores the evolutionary history of artificial intelligence, which has been fueled by exponential gains in computer power, data availability. The research looks at how AI is changing teaching, learning, and administrative procedures in educational institutions. The abstract explores the ways in which artificial intelligence is transforming education, outlining the nature, uses, implications, difficulties, and importance of AI. It explores how artificial intelligence technologies which include learning, reasoning and self-correction are revolutionizing traditional teaching methods and administrative procedures. It also facilitates automatic grading, data-driven decision-making, and lifelong learning. AI has significant ramifications that highlight its critical role in transforming educational paradigms internationally, helping both students and educators, despite its limitations.

DOI: 10.4018/979-8-3693-6745-2.ch011

INTRODUCTION

Artificial Intelligence (AI) is a major force in the current technological innovation landscape, transforming economies, industries, and societies in general. AI is defined as the emulation of human intelligence processes by machines. It includes a wide range of subfields, from robotics and from processing natural languages and deep learning to computer vision. Driven by exponential increase in computer power, huge volumes of data, and improvements in algorithmic sophistication, its evolution over the past few decades has been characterized by impressive achievements. Artificial intelligence is a rapidly developing sector of technology that has the power to fundamentally alter human communication. Artificial intelligence is generating novel teaching and learning approaches in the field of education, which are being tested in multiple settings. When one hears the word artificial intelligence, they instantly picture a supercomputer. These robots have the cognitive and functional abilities of humans when sensors and other features are added. They can also exhibit adaptive behavior and have massive computing power. Supercomputers can even communicate with humans more successfully thanks to these features. In actuality, a number of films have been produced to highlight the promise of artificial intelligence. One such instance is how smart buildings control the music, temperature and air quality according on how the occupants perceive their mood. More uses of artificial intelligence (AI) in education have been found, extending beyond the traditional conception of AI as a supercomputer to encompass embedded computer systems. In fact, it is clear that artificial intelligence (AI) has impacted many facets of society, especially education, as the United Nations Educational Scientific and Cultural Organization (UNESCO) noted, citing examples such as instructional strategies, instruments and instructions. Because of alterations in the surrounding environment, artificial intelligence has also been functional in the fields of learning and administration. Wartman and Combs assert that the addition of artificial intelligence (AI) into instruction and learning is imperative, as changes in the professional and employment landscape are also impacting education. Artificial Intelligence (AI) has settled into an authoritative force in recent years, drastically altering many facets of modern civilization (Norvig & Russell, 2022). Because AI technologies are being widely used in the 21st century, our way of life, our jobs, and how we interact with the world around us have drastically altered. AI is now closely associated with innovation and development, from the easy incorporation of virtual assistants into our daily lives to the revolutionary developments in driverless cars (Haenlein & Kaplan, 2019). According to Nilsson (2014), artificial intelligence (AI) is a paradigm change in the way we understand and use computing power to mimic human intelligence (Nilsson, 2014). Artificial intelligence (AI) systems have demonstrated remarkable abilities in various fields such as natural language processing, image identification, and decision-making by creating intricate algorithms and machine learning methods (LeCun et al., 2015). These developments could lead to increased productivity, better quality of life, and global economic growth (Brynjolfsson & McAfee, 2017). Artificial intelligence (AI) has had a revolutionary journey, from its early conception in the 1950s, when pioneers like Alan Turing raised important questions about machine intelligence, to the current period defined by neural networks and deep learning architectures. Over time, as computer and information transmission technology have advanced continuously, artificial intelligence has grown. Artificial intelligence, according to Coppin, is the capability of a computer to learn from experience, deal with unfamiliar circumstances, resolve problems, reply to questions, formulate plans of action, and do a wide range of other tasks necessitating a level of intelligence often displayed by humans (Coppin, 2004). Whitby defines artificial intelligence as the study of intelligent behavior in machines, humans, and animals with the goal of incorporating that behavior into technological objects like computers (Whitby, 2008). Using these standards, it is evident that artificial intelligence is the outcome of the convergence of computers, machines, and information communication technological breakthroughs, allowing computers to perform jobs that are nearly human-like. In mark with the acceptance and usage of new machineries in the industry, artificial intelligence has been applied broadly in the education sector. Applications of AI are significantly changing the systems and procedures related to learning and education. In reality, a number of administrative and academic tasks—such as the admissions process, counseling, library services, evaluation, feedback, and tutoring have seen significant changes due to artificial intelligence (AI). Moreover, AI tools facilitate administrative tasks in educational institutions, from automated grading and assessment to optimizing scheduling and resource allocation (Molnar, 2022). Owing to its significance, artificial intelligence (AI) has become a prevalent research matter overall and an evolving ground in education. AI-powered adaptive learning platforms, for instance, analyze student performance data to provide personalized learning experiences, thereby addressing individual learning styles and pace (Chen, 2020). Several procedures were built in harmony with the aims since Artificial Intelligence has a strong correlation with both administrative and academic tasks. Through the Artificial Intelligence, one can gain and receive assistance with various assessment kinds, behavior patterns, and many other factors. In addition to being used to analyze job applications, the AI-based technology supports the human resources department in effectively supervising the applications. These technologies mechanically establish requirements for the ideal aspirants and information collection, which offers directives for interviews and other processes. It should be emphasized that AI tools and applications support current faculty members at educational institutions rather than replacing them. AI technologies like machine learning and natural language processing are increasingly integrated into educational settings to cater to diverse learner needs and improve outcomes (HolonIQ, 2021). AI technologies and apps are also beneficial for any educational institution's admissions procedure. The online application submitted to the admission department starts the admissions process. In addition, the admission form is accompanied by a series of repeated questions from candidates and their parents, which are challenging to answer quickly. Education institutions are employing AI tools, such as chat boxes and other forms of inquiry management, to tackle the problem of managing a large volume of queries during the admissions process. The use of AI applications in the form of chatbots and other applications is greatly assisting educational institutions with the admissions process. It not only helps with the admissions process but also lessens the workload of the department and admissions staff in addressing questions. It works without human support, offering services continuously. Learning analytics also makes use of AI. As a means of understanding and improving learning and its settings, learning analytics (LA) is defined as the measurement, gathering, analysis, and reporting of data on learners and their circumstances. Analytics plays a substantial and indispensable part in the education and learning sector at many levels, including departments, universities, classrooms, and the regional, national, and global levels. Different outcomes are obtained for the improvement of education at each level. It provides details about a student's interests, social networks, IQ, grades, and much more in a classroom setting, at the department level, it provides statistics on risk, interpolation, support services, and macro and meso level guidelines for actions. Depending on the objectives and contexts different kinds of data sets are required for each level. It provides guidance for educational policy, funding, etc. at both the national and international levels. The phrase "micro objectives and contexts of the analytics" describes it. Artificial Intelligence encompasses a range of technologies such as machine learning, natural language processing, and computer vision, which are increasingly integrated into educational settings to cater to diverse learner needs and improve educational outcomes (Holmes, 2020). Artificial Intelligence Assistant can help parents and students with the admissions process and offer feedback. Additionally, it can assist educators in a range of difficult duties, like managing courses, budgets, student enrollment, application or data administration, etc., freeing up more time for teachers to teach. In addition, AI technologies help with facilities management, lower operating incidentals for institutions, and increase their receptiveness. Furthermore, these systems lessen biases in a variety of situations when credibility is important and human influence is strong. Artificial intelligence (AI) technologies are leading the way in improving efficiency and productivity in a variety of industries. AI-driven systems free up human resources by automating repetitive operations, freeing people up to focus on more complex, inventive, and creative endeavors. It fosters worker morale and job satisfaction in addition to increasing efficiency. Predictive analytics and decision support systems enabled by artificial intelligence enable firms to utilize data-driven insights to make well-informed decisions. AI algorithms help with resource allocation optimization, growth opportunity detection, and risk avoidance by analyzing big datasets at a surprising speed and accuracy (Brynjolfsson & McAfee, 2017).

NATURE OF ARTIFICIAL INTELLIGENCE

Artificial intelligence is usually closely related to computers (AI). The expression "artificial intelligence" (AI) states to the capability of computers, specifically, to mimic human intellectual purposes. These processes comprise learning (gaining knowledge and using that knowledge through rules), self-correction, and reasoning (using rules to arrive at approximations or strong conclusions). Although the concept of artificial intelligence may have originated with computers, a review of the various articles—especially those pertaining to the education sector—indicates that the focus is now more on the hardware and software that make up the device than it is on the actual computer. It is now simpler to incorporate artificial intelligence into machines and other items, such as robots and structures by the development of advanced technology such as sensors and embedded computers. Actually, there are two aspects to the concept and description of artificial intelligence provided by Chassignol et al. They characterize AI as both a discipline and a concept. By meaning, artificial intelligence (AI) is a subfield of computer science that aims to address a variety of cognitive problems, such as learning, pattern recognition, and problem solving that are commonly associated with human intelligence. Chassignol et al. define artificial intelligence (AI) as a theoretical framework that directs the creation and application of computer systems possessing human like qualities, particularly intelligence and the capacity to carry out activities requiring human intelligence, like language translation, speech recognition, visual perception, and decision-making. Other academics have emphasized similar aspects or characteristics of artificial intelligence in other research that build upon the idea that has been provided. Sharma et al. well defined artificial intelligence as computers that can mimic human mental processes. Pokrivcakova also defined and discussed artificial intelligence (AI) in relation to the field of education. The system designer, data scientist, product designer, statistician, linguist, cognitive scientist, psychologist, education expert, and many others worked for decades to create educational systems that are intelligent enough to carry out a variety of tasks, such as assisting educators and learners in expanding their knowledge and developing flexible abilities in light of a world that is changing all the time. She stated that AI is the outcome of these periods of research and development. As per the author's assertion, artificial intelligence (AI) utilizes improved software and program abilities, including algorithmic machine learning, to do diverse tasks that require human-like understanding and the ability to adapt to the present surroundings. Wartman et al. reported similar results, defining artificial intelligence as computers and other technology capacity to simulate human thought and behavior. These definitions and explanations state that artificial intelligence is commonly defined as the expansion of robots that possess specific level of intelligence and the capability to accomplish tasks that are similar to those of humans, such as knowledge, decision-making, cognitive processes, and environment variation. Consequently, a few characteristics, ideas stand out as essential to AI. This description and clarification of AI highlights intelligence as a key component of the technology, the machine's ability to exhibit a certain degree of intelligence and carry out a variety of tasks requiring human-like skills. Systems that use artificial intelligence (AI) make use of a variety of techniques and approaches, including machine learning, deep learning, computer vision, and natural language dispensation. Large datasets can be used to train these systems to recognize patterns, predict results, and perform tasks with varying levels of autonomy. Artificial intelligence (AI) technologies have been widely applicable in several industries such as healthcare, banking, entertainment, and transportation. The way we live, work, and engage with technology could all be completely transformed by AI.

THE APPLICATION OF ARTIFICIAL INTELLIGENCE IN EDUCATION

An increasing amount of research is being done on the application of artificial intelligence (AI) in education to improve instruction, create smart campuses, and achieve intelligent teaching, learning, and administration. Numerous advancements in the field of education have resulted from the application in AI technologies, including face recognition, picture recognition and adaptive learning (Cui, Thai & Xue, 2019). These advancements have also increased teacher and student productivity (Kuo, 2020). Furthermore, the integration of AI technology with big data enables the comprehensive exploration and analysis of educational data, hence facilitating the advancement of teaching restructuring and elevating caliber of instruction (Williamson, 2018). Artificial Intelligence (AI) has transformed education in the modern world by improving teaching techniques, course materials, and other aspects, just like it has done in other domains. Education is no longer only done in classrooms. Artificial Intelligence has enhanced education, even within classrooms. AI has various potential applications in the arena of education. It can help instructors, forecast student performance, assess and grade students, and enhance course materials, among other things. Virtual reality and other online learning resources, like MOOCs, are becoming more and more popular and artificial intelligence aids educators in delivering content. Teachers should expect an acceleration of the shift from published textbooks to audio and digital scripts and media in the future, given the recent and rapid advancements in technology. Conferring to an examination of the scholarly foundations selected for the study, artificial intelligence (AI) actually has been applied in educational institutions in a number of means, comprising curriculum and content development, instruction, student learning processes, and administrative tasks and procedures automation. AI has increased productivity in administrative activities by automating processes with internet-based systems or software, like grading, reviewing, giving feedback on assignments. Artificial intelligence has also been used in the education sector in curriculum and content development and also in instructional design. By utilizing tools such as web-based platforms, robots, video conferencing, audio visual files, virtual reality, and 3-D technology, these applications have enhanced student learning. Teachers are more operative and productive and learners gain from a more customized and thorough educational experience. Additional noteworthy findings from more complete investigation of the foundations include the possibility to bypass the physical obstacles delivered by national and international borders by analyzing artificial intelligence (AI) in education, as learning resources now are stored on the Internet and the World Wide Web. By utilizing online learning platforms or web-based learning, students have accessibility to the course materials from any location in the globe. Through the use of AI capabilities, such as language translation tools, students can tailor their education to best suit their individual learning preferences. The results of the study do, in fact, prove that management, training, and education are more effective as well as efficient, as is noticeable in the section devoted to discussing the research results of AI's effects on education. Numerous lessons deliberated and provided examples of AI's application in education. The introduction and changes that have characterized the use of AI in education are given by Chassignol et al. He claimed that the development of processors and computer related technologies, such as the Internet and the World Wide Web, allowed AI needs to be incorporated into education. It appears that the transition from computers to online intelligent (AI) systems and web technologies has been happening gradually, keeping up with developments in the macro operating environment. AI in education is touching beyond just computers to implanted systems, including robots or colleague robots (cobots), which can slog autonomously and in tandem with teachers to carry out teacher like tasks. Although Timms acknowledged that artificial intelligence in education (AIED) takes many systems, there is signal that artificial intelligence and computers are not the same thing, or that the emphasis is on thoughtful and utilizing AI as computers alone, which includes the use of computer embedded systems like cobots and smart classrooms. Artificial Intelligence has evolved beyond just computers, desktops, and other traditional computer applications. As seen by the publication of results from previous investigations, it has continued to incorporate additional components.

AI is already being applied creatively in a variety of industries. We are still in the early stages of the education sector; there are a lot of active experiments and some rudimentary "commercial" applications available, but they are not being used much. AI is hidden and entangled in a broader trend in education, particularly the use of ICT and computers. The expansion of AI in novel application domains, including education, is gentler than the technology's progress because most developmental researches focus on AI technologies relatively than their relevant or applied elements. Along with the numerous ongoing improvements, artificial intelligence technology has seen major achievements. In terms of education, schools are adapting to the varied needs of their students by providing online option to each and every student. Recent studies indicate that students may receive individualized tutoring from artificial intelligence tutors and classmates as an outcome of advancements in educational technology, including educational analytics, personalised education, and student valuation of learning requirements. A variety of instructional resources are available, such as up-to-date textbooks and materials and cloud-based online learning tools. A technology idea known as Intelligent Tutoring Systems (ITS) has successfully moved from the lab to the classroom and is currently in widespread usage. Both the online language learning platform Duolingo and the app Carnegie Speech, which helps users improve their voices and accents, use automatic speech recognition (training in foreign languages). Furthermore, ITS provides artificial intelligence-driven tools like Carnegie Intellectual Tutor, that helps learners learn mathematics and SHERLOCK82 which trains air force workers to recognize electrical system problems, equips people to interact tactfully with people from different sociocultural backgrounds. Virtual reality and other online learning resources, like MOOCs, are becoming more and more popular and artificial intelligence aids educators in delivering content. Teachers should expect an acceleration of the shift from published textbooks to audio and digital scripts and media in the future, given the recent and rapid advancements in technology. A number of important artificial intelligence technologies have emerged recently, including machine learning, computer vision, natural language processing, context aware computing, and querying approaches. Artificial intelligence is being driven by a lack of trained teachers in education and a lack of communication between patients and professionals in healthcare. AI-Assisted and AI-Led are the two tiers of artificial intelligence that will support education in the future. The majority of the work in schools is still done by human teachers. Duolingo states that 34 hours on Duolingo's app is equivalent to one semester of language study at a university, analyzing current actions and promoting its accomplishment. MOOCs and cloud-based solutions are starting to take center stage. Professional and lifetime continuing education, in addition to traditional education, are disproportionately impacted by this problem. The platform has a large user base, which makes it feasible to leverage data from it for machine learning, which would otherwise be unable to fully restructure the system. Artificial Intelligence has become more pervasive in the classroom and in school instruction. The significance of this technology in the field of education is becoming increasingly apparent to a rising number of people. Teaching and classroom management have been significantly impacted by the extensive application of AI in education, which has demonstrated significant application benefits (Chassignol, Bilyatdinova, Khoroshavin & Klimova, 2018; Roll & Wylie, 2016). AI may spark student's enthusiasm, initiative, and creativity while constantly improving and optimizing the learning environment (Aldabbagh, Alghazzawi, Colchester & Hagras, 2017; Bai & Yang, 2020). Furthermore, this may significantly improve teacher's proficiency in classroom organization that ensure further logical as well as efficient classroom management (Tuomi, 2018; Wang, 2020).The development of technologies for sensing, hearing, augmented reality and virtual reality (VR) can be used to transform the educational understanding. To develop virtual classrooms and virtual laboratories, use ubiquitous computing technologies to realize the merging of physical and virtual environment (Encalada & Sequera, 2017; Krumm, 2018). Virtual technology can be used in a smart classroom to portray natural occurrences or changes in things that are hard or impossible to see in real life, giving pupils a contextual learning environment. The way that learning content is presented engages student's senses auditory, visual, tactile, and other improving instructional results, helps students grasp abstract concepts and theories more clearly, and helps them develop a strong sense of reality. The hybrid virtual classroom holds significant promise for enabling flexibility in course attendance, as it allows students to watch lectures at home or on campus (Bateman, Bédard & Lakhal, 2017).

Impact of Artificial Intelligence in Education

The technology known as artificial intelligence (AI) remains continually developing and also finding wide applications in a variety of fields, including education. Artificial intelligence mimics a variety of human functions, including hearing (Delić et al., 2019), speech synthesis, human-computer dialogue, watching (computer vision, image recognition, text recognition), thinking (Theorem Proving) (Hay & Sarma, 2017), learning (machine learning, intelligent adaptive learning) (Colchester et al., 2017), and acting (robot) (Khandelwal et al., 2017). Particularly, AI technologies have altered traditional education and teaching methods, particularly in the areas of computer visualisation, natural language processing, and intelligent adaptive learning (Abdullah, Jiahui, Saleh & Yufei, 2020). These innovations also gives educators and institutions fresh concepts for teaching reform. AI's ability to support individualized teaching and learning is one of its many benefits for education. AI has altered both how pupils learn and how professors instruct to help students become more competent and capable learners. According to their needs and learning environment, it might create a personalized learning plan (Dishon, 2017), offer an immersive learning environment (Ip et al., 2019) and make use of tracking intelligence in learning. Another advantage of implementing AI in education is that it may reduce the responsibilities of educators and allow them to focus more on providing humanistic care. Amending homework assignments in addition to exam papers takes up significant portion of instructor's time these days. Teacher's time is taken up by these uninteresting chores, which also interfere with their research and teaching time with student interaction. A lot of mechanically repetitive daily tasks, like editing homework and test papers, can be completed by educators with the aid of intelligent tutoring systems (Aleven, Holstein & McLaren, 2017), intelligent assessment systems (CUI & LI, 2019), educational robots (Chevalier, Mondada & Riedo, 2016), and other AIs. By utilizing these AIs, teachers can also receive some relief from their workload. Du, Meng and Gao (2016) claim that encouraging the development of smart campuses is the third method AI advances education. Traditional approaches to teaching and learning have evolved as a result of the emergence of artificial intelligence technology. Building smart campuses is made possible by technical advancements in face recognition, text recognition, augmented reality, voice interaction, human body recognition, and other AI applications (Kwet & Prinsloo, 2020). AI can help with a variety of campus administration and service tasks, including school attendance, classroom effect monitoring, and campus safety (Muhamad et al., 2017). In addition to lowering administrative expenses, this will enhance instruction for both teachers and students. Qiu (2020) asserts that artificial intelligence (AI) technology helps attain educational fairness. Because of topographical issues or variances in commercial progress, there are educational disparities among various nations and areas. Geographically based disparities in educational resources between pupils in large cities and those in rural areas can be bridged by artificial intelligence (AI) technology. Personalized remote instruction is possible with the integration of AI and the Internet (Karen Hao, 2019). One teacher can promote the sharing of outstanding teachers resources in remote areas where there aren't enough teachers, offer students the opportunity to interact with and learn from remarkable teachers and deliver remote online education for students in many locations.

Challenges of AI in Education

Although AI has numerous positive effects on instruction, it will also present specific never-before-seen problems. In addition to the potential benefits that artificial intelligence (AI) offers, there are also considerable hazards and difficulties that must be resolved. There is a growing concern about job displacement as AI systems become increasingly adept at activities that people normally perform. Artificial intelligence (AI) driven automation is having the potential to replace certain work roles, leading to job losses and economic instability (Autor, 2015). As AI systems usually depend on huge datasets, including sensitive peculiar information, to function properly, worries about data security and privacy are raised by the increasing deployment of AI technologies. Nonetheless, insufficient security measures and weaknesses in AI systems may result in privacy violations and unapproved access to confidential information (Gartner, 2019).The creation of extremely clever AI systems has existential hazards. With the advancement of AI technology, it is possible that AI systems will outsmart humans, develop unpredictable, self-governing decision-making abilities (Bostrom, 2014). People will be better equipped to propose ahead and enrich the forthcoming use of AI in education if they have a greater understanding of the possible matters that could arise. The following are the primary areas of difficulty:

First priority should be given to guaranteeing fairness while integrating AI in education. As AI improves, developing countries face possibility that new technologies will widen educational gaps. Comparable to how the digital divide has split those with access to internet from those without increasing the algorithmic obstacle now poses a danger to several of the educational occasions made possible by AI. To establish compulsory conditions for artificial intelligence (AI) in order to improve learning, the education sector needs to overcome major obstacles, including inadequate technology and infrastructure.

Second, we need to be aware of the ethical and security concerns that arise from accumulating, using, and disclosing data. AI has raised several ethical questions about providing students with individualized advice, accumulating peculiar data, safeguarding data privacy, allocating responsibilities, data feed algorithms (Bodó et al., 2017; Southgate, 2020).

Third, it assists educationalists in getting arranged for instruction aided by AI. To effectively engage AI to support classroom change, educators need to acquire new digital instruction procedures. When developing an AI teaching product, developers also need to have a thorough understanding of how teachers operate.

Fourth, because learning methods are changing, it is becoming more and more crucial for kids to be able to learn on their own. AI-era education will be learner driven, with learners taking initiative in learning tasks (Chang & Lu, 2019; Fu,

2020). Apprentices can design their own adapted learning plans, select course content on their own, schedule their progress, and follow the guidelines of the intelligent teaching system when engaging in group cooperative learning (Fang et al., 2019; Bernacki & Walkington, 2020; Yilmaz, 2018).

Fifth, there has to be more emphasis on student-to-student contact. If students utilize AI podiums for learning and converse with the robots rather than with one another, their societal communication abilities will deteriorate. Students should stimulate group education. To explain this problem, AI education programs establishes a distant learning paradigm that values sociability. Learners can learn online in addition to engaging with peers in a wide range of social settings, such as camps.

In conclusion, the full improvement of commercial and technical globalization is the reason behind the budding importance of artificial intelligence (AI) technology in education. Furthermore, many countries is prioritizing the enlargement of AI technology. The cutting edge ecosystem of AI-based education is characterized by the precision, adaptability, and flexibility of instructive services and organisations. Schools, educators, and students are juggling a range of AI-related worries and challenges while trying to establish a cutting-edge learning environment. To solve these problems and achieve the best possible integration of AI technology with education, educators, learners and other stakeholders in the education ecosystems must work together.

Types of Artificial Intelligence

Narrow AI (weak AI): denotes that AI systems that have been taught and developed for particular domains or tasks. While lacking broad intelligence, these systems are excellent at completing a limited number of tasks within predetermined boundaries or cognitive capacities similar to those of humans. Narrow AI applications include language translation software, commendation appliances, image recognition algorithms, virtual personal assistants (like Siri and Alexa).

General AI (strong AI): refers to the artificial intelligence (AI) systems that possess cognitive skills similar to those of humans and are able to comprehend, learn, and reason in a variety of contexts and tasks. Artificial general intelligence (AGI) would be capable to do any intellectual work that a human can since it would be capable of self-awareness, abstract thought, creativity, and adaptability.

Artificial Super intelligence (ASI): symbolizes an even greater degree of AI power that is superior to human intelligence in every way. The intellectual competence of ASI would surpass even that of the most brilliant human minds, with the ability to bring about profound changes in science, technology, and society. Instead of being used in real-world applications, ASI is still a theoretical notion that is frequently debated in theoretical settings. Significant existential, societal, and ethical issues are brought up by its growth.

Reactive AI: describes artificial intelligence (AI) systems that lack the capacity for learning or adaptation and instead function according to preset rules and preprogrammed responses. These systems are quite good at certain jobs, but they are not able to learn or get better with time through experience. Reactive AI is the foundation for chess-playing programs like Deep Blue and expert systems in certain fields.

Limited Memory AI: denotes that artificial intelligence (AI) systems having memory capacity as well as duration restrictions but can learn from historical data or prior experiences to make decisions. Though they might not be able to store a lot of information or long-term memory, these systems can use past experiences to improve decision-making. Limited memory AI is a technique which is used by self-driving cars to predict and react to traffic patterns based on prior observations and learning.

Theory of Mind AI: refers to artificial intelligence (AI) systems with the capacity to comprehend and simulate human feelings, thoughts, intentions, and mental states. These technologies can replicate and infer other people's mental states, which opens up new possibilities for advanced human collaboration and interaction. Research and conjecture on Theory of Mind AI are still ongoing, with advances in natural language understanding, affective computing, and social robotics influencing this topic.

Significance of AI in Education

Education could be revolutionized in numerous ways by artificial intelligence (AI), which has great promise. The mechanisation of academic and administrative work, personalised learning, intelligent material, and persistent accessibility are the primary purposes of artificial intelligence in education. Some noteworthy implications are as follows:

Personalized learning: AI is able to provide personalized learning practices by regulating to each student's distinctive learning style and pace. This maximizes learning results by ensuring that every student receives instruction that is specific to their requirements, strengths and weaknesses.

Enhanced teaching: AI-driven resources can help educators produce and deliver superior instructional materials. Teachers can devote more of their time to teaching and mentoring students by using these tools, which can automate administrative work, give insights into student performance, and promote instructional tactics.

Augmented Reality and Virtual Reality: When AI is integrated with AR and VR technology, it may produce immersive knowledge settings that let students perform experiments, discover virtual worlds, and interact more interactively and engagingly with difficult subjects.

Intelligent Tutoring Systems: AI-driven tutoring programs can give students immediate feedback and direction, assisting them in understanding complex ideas and overcoming obstacles to learning. Based on the answers from the students, these systems can modify their instruction and offer focused assistance where it is required.

Automated Grading and Assessment: By automating grading and evaluation, AI algorithms can free up teachers time and give students feedback more quickly. This frees up teachers to concentrate on other important facets of teaching, such guiding class discussions and giving specific comments.

Lifelong Learning and Skill Development: Through the provision of individualized learning routes catered to each person's interests and professional goals, AI-powered adaptive learning platforms can promote lifelong learning and skill development. This allows students to pick up new information and abilities at their own convenience and speed.

Data analysis and predictive analytics: Large scale educational data can be analyzed by AI to check trends, forms and perceptions that can monitor instructional decision making. By identifying kids who are at danger of falling behind or who require more support, educators can use predictive analytics to provide individualized intervention tactics and early intervention.

Language translation and accessibility: Students from different linguistic backgrounds can have greater access to educational resources thanks to AI-powered dialectal transformation technologies that can overwhelm language obstacles. In a similar vein, AI can help disabled students by offering customized learning support and alternate content delivery forms.

In general, artificial intelligence (AI) has great potential to advance learning outcomes, increase the usefulness of teachers and make education more individualized, accessible and interesting for students of all ages and backgrounds. While AI presents difficulties that demand careful thought and responsible development, it also has the potential to generate substantial improvements across a variety of domains. Its revolutionary ability to change industries, boost productivity and tackle difficult societal issues is what gives it relevance.

REFERENCES

Ahmad, K., Qadir, J., Al-Fuqaha, A., Iqbal, W., El-Hassan, A., Benhaddou, D., & Ayyash, M. (2020). Artificial intelligence in education: a panoramic review. DOI: . io/zvu2n.DOI: <ALIGNMENT.qj></ALIGNMENT>10.35542/osf

Ahmad, S. F., Alam, M. M., Rahmat, M. K., Mubarik, M. S., & Hyder, S. I. (2022). Academic and administrative role of artificial intelligence in education. *Sustainability (Basel)*, 14(3), 1101. DOI: 10.3390/su14031101

Alam, A. (2021, November). Possibilities and apprehensions in the landscape of artificial intelligence in education. In *2021 International Conference on Computational Intelligence and Computing Applications (ICCICA)* (pp. 1-8). IEEE. DOI: 10.1109/ICCICA52458.2021.9697272

Autor, D. H. (2015). Why are there still so many jobs? The history and future of workplace automation. *The Journal of Economic Perspectives*, 29(3), 3–30. DOI: 10.1257/jep.29.3.3

Bird, J. J., Ekart, A., & Faria, D. R. (2018). Learning from interaction: An intelligent networked-based human-bot and bot-bot chatbot system. In *Advances in Computational Intelligence Systems* (1st ed., pp. 179–190). Springer.

Bostrom, N. (2014). *Super intelligence: Paths, dangers, strategies*. Oxford University Press.

Brynjolfsson, E., & McAfee, A. (2017). The business of artificial intelligence. *Harvard Business Review*, 95(1), 62–71.

Chassignol, M., Khoroshavin, A., Klimova, A., & Bilyatdinova, A. (2018). Artificial Intelligence trends in education: A narrative overview. *Procedia Computer Science*, 136, 16–24. DOI: 10.1016/j.procs.2018.08.233

Chassignol, M., Khoroshavin, A., Klimova, A., & Bilyatdinova, A. (2018, January). Artificial intelligence trends in education: A narrative overview. *Procedia Computer Science*, 136, 16–24. DOI: 10.1016/j.procs.2018.08.233

Chen, L., Chen, P., & Lin, Z. (2020). Artificial intelligence in education: A review. *IEEE Access : Practical Innovations, Open Solutions*, 8, 75264–75278. DOI: 10.1109/ACCESS.2020.2988510

Chen, N.-S., Yin, C., Isaias, P., & Psotka, J. (2020). Educational big data: Extracting meaning from data for smart education. *Interactive Learning Environments*, 28(2), 142–147. DOI: 10.1080/10494820.2019.1635395

Chevalier, M., Riedo, F., & Mondada, F. (2016). Pedagogical Uses of Thymio II: How Do Teachers Perceive Educational Robots in Formal Education? *IEEE Robotics and Automation Magazine*.

Chiba, Y., Nose, T., Kase, T., Yamanaka, M., & Ito, A. (2019). *An Analysis of the Effect of Emotional Speech Synthesis on Non-Task-Oriented Dialogue System.*

Colchester, K., Hagras, H., Alghazzawi, D., & Aldabbagh, G. (2017). A Survey of Artificial Intelligence Techniques Employed for Adaptive Educational Systems within E-Learning Platforms. [De Gruyter Open Ltd.]. *Journal of Artificial Intelligence and Soft Computing Research*, 7(1), 47–64. DOI: 10.1515/jaiscr-2017-0004

Coppin, B. (2004). *Artificial Intelligence Illuminated.* Jones and Bartlett.

Delić, V., Perić, Z., Sečujski, M., Jakovljević, N., Nikolić, J., Mišković, D., Simić, N., Suzić, S., & Delić, T. (2019). Speech Technology Progress Based on New Machine Learning Paradigm. *Computational Intelligence and Neuroscience*, 2019, 1–19. DOI: 10.1155/2019/4368036 PMID: 31341467

Dishon, G. (2017). New data, old tensions: Big data, personalized learning, and the challenges of progressive education. *Theory and Research in Education*, 15(3), 272–289. DOI: 10.1177/1477878517735233

Du, S., Meng, F., & Gao, B. (2016). Research on the Application System of Smart Campus in the Context of Smart City. 2016 8th *International Conference on Information Technology in Medicine and Education (ITME)* (pp. 714– 718). IEEE.

Encalada, W. L., & Castillo Sequera, J. L. (2017). Model to implement virtual computing labs via cloud computing services. *Symmetry*, 9(7), 117. DOI: 10.3390/sym9070117

Gartner. (2019). Gartner identifies top 10 data and analytics technology trends for 2019. Retrieved from https://www.gartner.com/en/newsroom/press-releases/2019-02-18-

Gobert, J. D., Sao Pedro, M. A., Baker, R. S., Toto, E., & Montalvo, O. (2012). Leveraging educational data mining for real-time performance assessment of scientific inquiry skills within microworlds. J. *Educ. Data Min.*, 4, 104–143.

Goksel, N., & Bozkurt, A. (2019). Artificial intelligence in education: Current insights and future perspectives. In Sisman-Ugur, S., & Kurubacak, G. (Eds.), *Handbook of Research on Learning in the Age of Transhumanism* (pp. 224–236). IGI Global. DOI: 10.4018/978-1-5225-8431-5.ch014

Hao, K. (2019). *China has started a grand experiment in AI education. It could reshape how the world learns*. MIT Technology Review.

Holstein, K., McLaren, B. M., & Aleven, V. (2017). Intelligent tutors as teachers' aides: Exploring teacher needs for real-time analytics in blended classrooms. *ACM International Conference Proceeding Series*. DOI: 10.1145/3027385.3027451

Huang, J., Saleh, S., & Liu, Y. (2021). A review on artificial intelligence in education. *Academic Journal of Interdisciplinary Studies, 10(3).*

Ip, H. H. S., Li, C., Leoni, S., Chen, Y., Ma, K. F., Wong, C. H., & Li, Q. (2019). Design and Evaluate Immersive Learning Experience for Massive Open Online Courses (MOOCs). *IEEE Transactions on Learning Technologies*, 12(4), 503–515. DOI: 10.1109/TLT.2018.2878700

Kaplan, A. M., & Haenlein, M. (2019). Siri, Siri, in my hand: Who's the fairest in the land? On the interpretations, illustrations, and implications of artificial intelligence. *Business Horizons*, 62(1), 15–25. DOI: 10.1016/j.bushor.2018.08.004

Khandelwal, P., Zhang, S., Sinapov, J., Leonetti, M., Thomason, J., Yang, F., Gori, I., Svetlik, M., Khante, P., Lifschitz, V., Aggarwal, J. K., Mooney, R., & Stone, P. (2017). BWIBots: A platform for bridging the gap between AI and human–robot interaction research. *The International Journal of Robotics Research*, 36(5–7), 635–659. DOI: 10.1177/0278364916688949

Krumm, J. (Ed.). (2018). Ubiquitous Computing Fundamentals. (John Krumm, Ed.) Ubiquitous Computing Fundamentals. *Chapman and Hall/CRC.*

Kuo, T. H. (2020). The Current Situation of AI Foreign Language Education and Its Influence on College Japanese Teaching. Lecture Notes in Computer Science (including subseries Lecture Notes in Artificial Intelligence and Lecture Notes in Bioinformatics) (Vol. 12193 LNCS, pp. 315–324). *Springer.* DOI: 10.1007/978-3-030-49913-6_27

Kwet, M., & Prinsloo, P. (2020). The 'smart' classroom: A new frontier in the age of the smart university. *Teaching in Higher Education*, 25(4), 510–526. DOI: 10.1080/13562517.2020.1734922

Lakhal, S., Bateman, D., & Bédard, J. (2017). Blended Synchronous Delivery Modes in Graduate Programs: A Literature Review and How it is Implemented in the Master Teacher Program. *Collected Essays on Learning and Teaching*, 10, 47–60. DOI: 10.22329/celt.v10i0.4747

LeCun, Y., Bengio, Y., & Hinton, G. (2015). Deep learning. *Nature*, 521(7553), 436–444. DOI: 10.1038/nature14539 PMID: 26017442

Muhamad, W., & Kurniawan, N. B., Suhardi, & Yazid, S. (2017). Smart campus features, technologies, and applications: A systematic literature review. 2017 International Conference on Information Technology Systems and Innovation (ICITSI) (pp. 384–391). *IEEE*. DOI: 10.1109/ICITSI.2017.8267975

Nilsson, N. J. (2014). *Artificial intelligence: A new synthesis*. Morgan Kaufmann.

Paglen, T. (2019). Invisible Images: Your Pictures Are Looking at You. *Architectural Design*, 89(1), 22–27. DOI: 10.1002/ad.2383

Pedro, F., Subosa, M., Rivas, A., & Valverde, P. (2019). Artificial intelligence in education: Challenges and opportunities for sustainable development.

Pokrivcakova, S. (2019, December). Preparing teachers for the application of AI-powered technologies in foreign language education. *J. Lang. Cultural Edu.*, 7(3), 135–153. DOI: 10.2478/jolace-2019-0025

Powell, S., & MacNeill, S. (2012). Institutional readiness for analytics. *Cetis Anal. Ser.*, 1, 1–11.

Qiu, Y. (2020). Education Informationization. *Proceedings of the 2020 6th International Conference on Education and Training Technologies* (pp. 40–43). New York, NY, USA: ACM. DOI: 10.1145/3399971.3399978

Reid, J. M. (1995). *Learning Styles in the ESL/EFL Classroom*. Heinle & Heinle Publishers.

Roll, I., & Wylie, R. (2016). Evolution and Revolution in Artificial Intelligence in Education. [Springer New York LLC.]. *International Journal of Artificial Intelligence in Education*, 26(2), 582–599. DOI: 10.1007/s40593-016-0110-3

Russell, S., & Norvig, P. (2022). Artificial intelligence: A modern approach (4th esd.).

Sarma, G. P., & Hay, N. J. (2017). Robust Computer Algebra, Theorem Proving, and Oracle AI. SSRN *Electronic Journal*. DOI: 10.2139/ssrn.3038545

Shah, H., Warwick, K., Vallverdú, J., & Wu, D. (2016). Can machines talk? Comparison of Eliza with modern dialogue systems. *Computers in Human Behavior*, 58, 278–295. DOI: 10.1016/j.chb.2016.01.004

Strickland, J. How Virtual Reality Military Applications Work. Available online: howstuffworks.com/virtual-military (accessed on 15 April 2021).

Tuomi, I. (2018). *The Impact of Artificial Intelligence on Learning, Teaching, and Education. Policies for the future*. EUR - Scientific and Technical Research Reports.

Wang, Y. (2020). An improved machine learning and artificial intelligence algorithm for classroom management of English distance education. *Journal of Intelligent & Fuzzy Systems*, •••, 1–12. DOI: 10.3233/JIFS-179615

Wartman, S. A., & Combs, C. D. (2018, August). Medical education must move from the information age to the age of artificial intelligence. *Academic Medicine*, 93(8), 1107–1109. DOI: 10.1097/ACM.0000000000002044 PMID: 29095704

Whitby, B. (2008). *Artificial Intelligence: A Beginner's Guide*. Oneworld.

Williamson, B. (2018). The hidden architecture of higher education: Building a big data infrastructure for the 'smarter university.'. *International Journal of Educational Technology in Higher Education*, 15(1), 12. DOI: 10.1186/s41239-018-0094-1

Yang, S., & Bai, H. (2020). The integration design of artificial intelligence and normal students' Education. *Journal of Physics: Conference Series*, 1453(1), 012090. DOI: 10.1088/1742-6596/1453/1/012090

Yufei, L., Saleh, S., Jiahui, H., & Abdullah, S. M. S. (2020). Review of the application of artificial intelligence in education. *International Journal of Innovation. Creativity and Change*, 12(8), 548–562.

KEY TERMS AND DEFINITIONS

John McCarthy: "Artificial intelligence is the science and engineering of making intelligent machines, especially intelligent computer programs. It is related to the similar task of using computers to understand human intelligence, but AI does not have to confine itself to methods that are biologically observable."

Herbert A. Simon: "AI is the science of making machines do things that would require intelligence if done by humans."

Forbes: "Artificial intelligence (AI) refers to the simulation of human intelligence in machines programmed to think and act like humans."

Cambridge Dictionary: "Artificial intelligence is the study of how to produce machines that have some of the qualities that the human mind has, such as the ability to understand language, recognize pictures, solve problems, and learn."

World Health Organization (WHO): "Artificial intelligence refers to the ability of machines to perform tasks that would normally require human intelligence."

IEEE (Institute of Electrical and Electronics Engineers): "Artificial intelligence is the branch of computer science that is concerned with the automation of intelligent behavior."

Merriam-Webster Definition: "The capability of a machine to imitate intelligent human behavior."

Oxford Languages Definition: "The theory and development of computer systems able to perform tasks that normally require human intelligence, such as visual perception, speech recognition, decision-making, and translation between languages."

Sir Anthony Seldon: "AI has the potential to revolutionize education by offering personalized learning experiences, automating administrative tasks, and augmenting the role of teachers as mentors and facilitators of learning."

Vikas Pota: "Artificial intelligence in education encompasses the development of intelligent tutoring systems, adaptive learning platforms, and data-driven insights to optimize learning experiences and outcomes for students."

Chapter 12

The Implementation of Virtual Reality Technology in Enhancing University Student Learning Engagement:
A Five-Year Systematic Literature Review

Jingru Sun
Universiti Sains Malaysia, Malaysia

Kien Tsong Chau
https://orcid.org/0000-0003-1896-7239
Universiti Sains Malaysia, Malaysia

Mariam Binti Mohamad
Universiti Sains Malaysia, Malaysia

ABSTRACT

Virtual reality has a lot of potential, and researchers are becoming increasingly interested in using it in the classroom. However, there is little systematic work on how researchers can apply VR to higher education for the purpose of improving student engagement. Therefore, we propose to use systematic mapping to investigate how VR can be used to improve engagement in higher education. The review synthesizes the results of various studies conducted over the past five years, highlights the effectiveness of VR in creating immersive and interactive learning environments, and provides

DOI: 10.4018/979-8-3693-6745-2.ch012

a literature review of related studies. The results of the study show that students who use VR technology are more engaged and motivated to learn. The demand for virtual reality technology is surging as a means to enhance student engagement in educational settings. Consequently, the future development of effective tools that promote student involvement is imperative. Nevertheless, it is crucial to meticulously consider design, accessibility, and pedagogical strategies to optimize its efficacy.

1. INTRODUCTION

A wide range of information is necessary for effective teaching, but so is the capacity to raise student interest in and engagement levels. Since the turn of the twenty-first century, VR technology has been progressively incorporated into a variety of fields thanks to the quick advancement of information technology. One of its main areas of application has progressively evolved into higher education. With its immersive qualities and cutting-edge interactive techniques, VR technology has expanded the possibilities for traditional education. VR technology is pushing the boundaries of education by providing more individualized and engaging learning experiences among the difficulties faced by traditional classroom formats. The purpose of this article is to examine how VR technology is used in higher education and how it enhances students' learning engagement. We can better comprehend VR technology's impact on educational innovation and how to optimize its potential to enhance students' learning engagement and overall learning experience by conducting thorough study on the subject. diversity in the classroom.

1.1. VR Applications

With the rapid progress of information and communication technologies, numerous new platforms and tools aimed at improving social and collaborative learning have emerged (Oliveira et al., 2019). Virtual reality (VR) is among the most prominent of these technologies, offering immense potential to transform education (Oumaima et al., 2023). VR refers to a deeply immersive, interactive experience that relies on computer-generated, real-time, 3D images (Petersen et al., 2022). This technology allows users to interact with virtual spaces dynamically, creating a sense of presence that replicates real-life experiences (Hamad & Jia, 2022). VR can be classified in different ways, such as by its application, interaction mode, or degree of immersion (Yin et al., 2021). This study comprehensively examines all forms of VR, including head-mounted displays and desktop systems, to provide an in-depth analysis of the technology and its various uses across platforms.

The introduction of VR technology into education has significantly revolutionized instructional methods, necessitating the creation of comprehensive guidelines for utilizing information technology (Marougkas et al., 2023). It is crucial for both educators and students to navigate the complexities of integrated digital platforms. VR's innovative pedagogical approach not only broadens the scope of educational applications but also enhances interactivity and realism in simulations compared to traditional offline learning (Asad et al., 2021). Moreover, various artificial environments designed specifically for virtual education using VR technology have emerged, categorized as VR-based teaching environments. This shift in educational practices marks a move toward immersive learning, reshaping teaching and learning processes (Lege & Bonner, 2020). These advanced environments significantly reduce training costs while faithfully replicating real-world scenarios. VR has transformed the traditional teacher-centered classroom into a dynamic setting with interactive exchanges between students and instructors (Chen et al., 2021). This method enhances learners' proficiency and practical knowledge through immersive interaction. The VR immersive environment breaks down traditional barriers to learning, enabling authentic experiential engagement for students. VR technology immerses users in virtually real environments with three-dimensional visualizations (Petersen et al., 2022), facilitated by equipment like helmets, headsets, and hand controllers, allowing them to process multi-sensory information simultaneously, including visual, auditory, and tactile inputs. The adoption of VR in education has increased due to its unique attributes (Hodgson et al., 2019). In educational contexts, VR fosters a deeper level of engagement than traditional video-based learning (Marougkas et al., 2021). This heightened interactivity helps students engage with educational resources, boosts their intrinsic interest in learning, and enriches the overall educational experience (Xin, 2022).

VR is an effective educational tool that significantly enhances student engagement and motivation. As a result, many educational institutions are considering substantial investments in financial resources, human capital, and advanced technology for developing and implementing VR systems. The focus is especially on immersive VR, which differs greatly from the traditional VR formats previously used in virtual environments. Immersive VR has been shown to improve learning outcomes in higher education (Makransky et al., 2019), making research into its potential applications in this field particularly important. Among various teaching methods, the use of simulated environments and virtual laboratories has been revolutionary (Hirshfield & Koretsky, 2021). Virtual labs not only address the limitations of traditional labs—such as time, cost, and safety concerns—but also offer students a richer experimental experience (Alvarez, 2021). While traditional labs often face logistical challenges that limit experimentation, VR technologies allow students to conduct a wide array of experiments in a simulated setting. This immersive experience enables learners to interact with virtual tools and materials, simulating real-world workflows (Tibaldi et al., 2020). Additionally, the real-time feedback provided in these virtual environments enhances the learning process, helping students refine their skills and deepen their understanding in ways that traditional methods may not allow (Liu et al., 2022).

Teachers can create realistic scenes using VR technology in subjects like literature, history, and art to immerse pupils in the storylines of books, the context of historical events, and even the creative process of artistic creations (Yan, 2023). Pupils can become fully immersed in virtual environments, experience the work's atmosphere, and improve their comprehension of the subject matter and emotional resonance. One valuable tool that VR technology offers students is virtual conferences. Students can interact online in real-time with peers, teachers, and experts from around the globe by using virtual conferences (Onyema et al., 2019). Students' perspectives are broadened and they gain a deeper understanding of cutting-edge research and development trends in various sectors as a result of this engagement, which also encourages interdisciplinary thinking and knowledge exchange (Yan, 2023).

VR systems are well-known for their strong interactive features, allowing users to maintain a continuous flow of real-world information and receive operational feedback while in virtual environments (Dincelli & Yayla, 2022). This capability enables educational settings to replicate materials and phenomena that are often difficult to observe in everyday life (Marougkas et al., 2023). As a result, both educators and students are increasingly adopting VR-based learning methods, particularly in fields that emphasize hands-on learning, such as mechanical testing and geotechnical experimentation. Students can take on significant roles in virtual environments, actively participating in the learning process, which boosts their engagement, enhances learning efficiency, and helps them develop skills (Mystakidis, 2020). The immersive and interactive nature of VR is key to this process. Unlike traditional methods that rely heavily on textbooks, VR offers more realistic and dynamic learning environments (Mulders et al., 2020). With advanced VR technology, students can gain and experience new knowledge and skills in ways that go far beyond passive learning. Therefore, it is essential to explore and design innovative teaching models that increase student motivation in VR-based learning, maximizing educational outcomes (Xin, 2022).

1.2 Student Learning Engagement

Since 1980, educational research has centered on how actively students engage in their learning. This focus is likely driven by the potential impact of engagement on academic performance and motivation (Sun et al., 2021). In their study, Skinner and Belmont (1993) described student engagement as an ongoing interaction characterized by active behavior and often accompanied by enjoyment or satisfaction. They identified two related but distinct types of involvement: behavioral engagement, which refers to students' visible actions in educational activities, and emotional engagement, which involves their feelings and emotional reactions toward the learning process. Building on these ideas, Fredricks et al. (2004) emphasized that student engagement is multifaceted, with the cognitive aspect being central to the overall framework. Later research recognized engagement as occurring in three dimensions: cognitive, behavioral, and emotional (Brophy, 2004). These dimensions reflect how students behave and feel while learning. Cognitive engagement represents the transition from rote memorization to self-directed learning and deep analytical thinking. It includes key skills like sustained attention, effective recall, and innovative problem-solving, which are vital for mastering complex academic challenges (Chai et al., 2015). Behavioral engagement involves students' active participation in learning activities, including their attentiveness in class and involvement in extracurricular activities. It also refers to their ability to complete tasks effectively, adhere to the instructional guidelines, and demonstrate this through the quality and timeliness of their work. Furthermore, it is indicative of the degree to which students engage in various interactive activities within the classroom setting, revealing their overall involvement in the learning process (Zhang et al., 2023). The term "behavioral engagement" describes how involved students are in the classroom, particularly how focused they are when they are engaging in class. Students' positive and negative emotional reactions to school, the learning process, their peers, and their teachers are referred to as emotional engagement. These reactions, which can include happiness, irritation, and boredom, indicate how willing they are to engage in learning activities (Fredricks et al., 2004). Additional research suggests that a social component should be included in students' learning involvement. The term "social engagement" refers to the extent of a student's participation within a community, reflecting how much they interact with their learning environment, peers, and individual learners (Wang et al., 2016). Recent research has increasingly emphasized the importance of learning engagement as a crucial intermediary variable that enhances student performance (Xu et al., 2020). For instance, Li et al. explored the complex relationship between academic success and learning engagement using structural equation modeling (SEM). Their study found a strong positive correlation between academic achievement and student involvement in the learning process (Wilder,

2023). In addition, peer, instructor, and parental support play essential roles in promoting learner engagement, which subsequently improves student achievement (Jelas et al., 2016). The level of learning engagement also significantly shapes the overall quality of educational experiences for both students and educators. Zhang and Liu's research, based on a survey of 520 educators, examined the connections between task value, learning engagement, motivational regulation, and self-efficacy. Their findings revealed direct correlations among these factors, with educators' engagement indirectly affecting their perception of task value through motivational regulation strategies. Thus, a major factor influencing student success is their level of engagement in the learning process (Wilder, 2023).

Learning engagement encompasses the dimensions of students' cognitive and emotional investment, as it relates to their attention, interest, and effort dedicated to various educational activities (Marks et al., 2000). This concept represents a crucial element in shaping learning outcomes and serves as a vital, enduring factor necessary for nurturing meaningful learning experiences (Loveless et al., 2012). Recent research within the realm of educational environments has revealed that these settings can enhance students' creativity by positively influencing their levels of engagement (Richardson & Mishra, 2018). Additionally, the design of social learning spaces has the potential to transform learners' enthusiasm, interactions, and sense of belonging, which are all instrumental in impacting overall learning engagement (Wenger-Trayner et al., 2020). The Interactive Feedback Effect posits that the educational environment can effectively cater to the diverse needs of learners through fostering human connections and organizing information in a coherent manner, thereby significantly amplifying learners' engagement in the learning process (Wang & He, 2020). Furthermore, the diversity of learning environments leads to a multitude of inputs from students, subsequently influencing their academic achievements (Hodson & Sander, 2019). Research indicates that student engagement in learning is significantly more positively linked to educational outcomes when situated within a social network-based learning context compared to traditional in-person classroom settings. This underscores the importance of considering the dynamics of various learning environments in educational research and practice, as they can play a crucial role in shaping student success (Zhang et al., 2022).

Besides, contemporary research examining the engagement within VR settings has unearthed significant effects on both learning outcomes and overall engagement levels (Dubovi, 2022). Additionally, the cognitive involvement of students in VR environments has emerged as a prominent theme within the field of educational research, particularly in the context of higher education. This topic has garnered substantial interest and investigation, reflecting the growing recognition of the potential benefits that immersive technologies can offer to enhance college student engagement and learning processes (Baxter & Hainey, 2024).

VR environments that promote cognitive engagement have garnered significant interest within the community of educational researchers. This burgeoning scholarly focus arises from the correlation between student participation in higher education and positive learning outcomes, which encompasses not only improved academic grades but also enhanced critical thinking skills (Hartikainen et al., 2019). Furthermore, indicators of student success, such as academic performance and the overall quality of education have been linked to levels of engagement. In recent years, several studies have emerged that delve into the dynamics of cognitive involvement within VR contexts. One empirical investigation revealed that student engagement levels in a VR learning environment substantially surpassed those observed in conventional asynchronous learning platforms (Grant et al., 2021). The research concluded that heightened levels of student engagement in these immersive VR platforms could indeed lead to improved educational outcomes, suggesting the potential transformative power of such environments in the realm of higher education. Brondi et al. (2015) conducted a thorough evaluation of the effects of immersive VR technology on the sense of presence and overall engagement in a related research study. The researchers subjected test participants to a collaborative gaming experience within a VR realm, which featured multiple configurations that varied in their levels of immersion. Their findings revealed that VR environments characterized by a high degree of immersion significantly enhance participant engagement compared to those with lower immersion levels (Hudson et al., 2019). Research findings demonstrated that students who participated in immersive virtual reality experiences, particularly those utilizing advanced head-mounted display systems, exhibited significantly higher levels of engagement and involvement compared to their counterparts who interacted with traditional, non-VR learning environments. This highlights the potential of virtual reality as a transformative educational tool, capable of enhancing student engagement and fostering deeper learning experiences (Bueno-Vesga et al., 2021).

1.3 Research Questions

In order to effectively design a tailored VR experience, the aspect of immersion—which encompasses both physical sensations and mental engagement—emerges as the most essential element of virtual reality. This immersion, pivotal in creating a personalized experience, serves as the cornerstone of effective VR applications. Over recent years, the integration of VR technology into educational settings has increased significantly, reflecting a growing trend aimed at enhancing student interest and participation in learning activities (Chen, Li, & Wang, 2024; López-Banet, Martínez-Carmona, & Reis, 2024; Prayogo, Khotimah, Istiqomah, & Maharsi, 2024). The incorporation of three-dimensional visuals plays a critical role in enriching students' perception of their contextualized learning environment, thereby facilitating a deeper comprehension of complex concepts and materials (Cappello & Lafferty, 2015). This study aims to investigate the effects of employing VR applications on boosting student engagement in learning processes, thereby analyzing the significant role these applications fulfill in promoting enhanced student interaction and participation. Furthermore, it intends to address pertinent questions regarding the efficacy and impact of these innovative educational tools.

> Question 1: Which areas of higher education have used VR for teaching in the past five years? Sample?
> Question 2: What research designs have been used in higher education research in the past five years?
> Question 3: What are the learning outcomes of higher education research in the past five years?

2. METHOD

2.1 Data Collection and Processing

This research provides a systematic review of the literature focusing on utilizing VR to enhance student engagement in learning. The systematic review encompasses the research question, selection of scholarly journals, criteria for inclusion and exclusion, search methodology, databases utilized, tools and techniques for data collection, and criteria for analyzing the research findings. This systematic review strictly follows the recommendations outlined in the PRISMA (Preferred Reporting Items for Systematic Reviews and Meta-Analyses) statement (Moher et al., 2009).

Although the research question has been identified, defining the scope and keywords has been challenging due to the vastness of VR studies and the large number of papers in this field. The researchers followed the recommended procedures by Webster and Watson (Webster & Watson, 2002), starting with selecting keyword search strategies in relevant digital libraries. The IEEE Xplore Digital Library, Scopus, and Google Scholar proved to be the appropriate online databases for the search. IEEE Xplore offers a comprehensive collection focusing on computer science, information technology, engineering, multimedia, and other software-related articles. Scopus provides access to a wide array of publication domains, spanning technology, natural sciences, information technologies, social sciences, and medical fields. Google Scholar, as a search engine, hosts a wealth of academic resources across various disciplines, ensuring thorough coverage. Using Boolean logic, the researchers defined the following search string for our database search. ("virtual reality" OR VR in subject terms) AND ("Learning Engagement" OR "Educational

Engagement" in subject terms") AND ("University" OR "Higher education" OR "College" in abstract") Only peer-reviewed journal articles with complete texts accessible have been included to guarantee accuracy and quality. And the publication year was constrained, covering only papers authored in English and covering the years 2019 through 2024. The inclusion and exclusion criteria are displayed in Table 1:

Table 1. Inclusion and Exclusion Criteria.

Inclusion Criteria	Exclusion criteria
Students used VR devices to learn Measuring Student Learning Engagement The participants were university students Indexed Journal (research articles) Written in English Between 2020-2024	**Not use VR treatment as an independent variable** **The dependent variable does not include student learning engagement** **For preschool children, primary or secondary school or high school students, special education, teachers, other adult learners** **Non-indexed journals, Systematic review journals, chapters in books.** **Written in other languages** **Less than 2020**

Based on the aforementioned information, the researchers undertook a comprehensive PRISMA review process (Figure 1). We meticulously followed the Preferred Reporting Items for Systematic Reviews and Meta-Analyses (PRISMA) guidelines to ensure that their review was thorough, transparent, and reproducible, thus enhancing the reliability of their findings in the context of scientific literature (Moher et al., 2009). 13 papers that met the requirement were eventually kept after multiple screening rounds.

Figure 1. Literature selection process

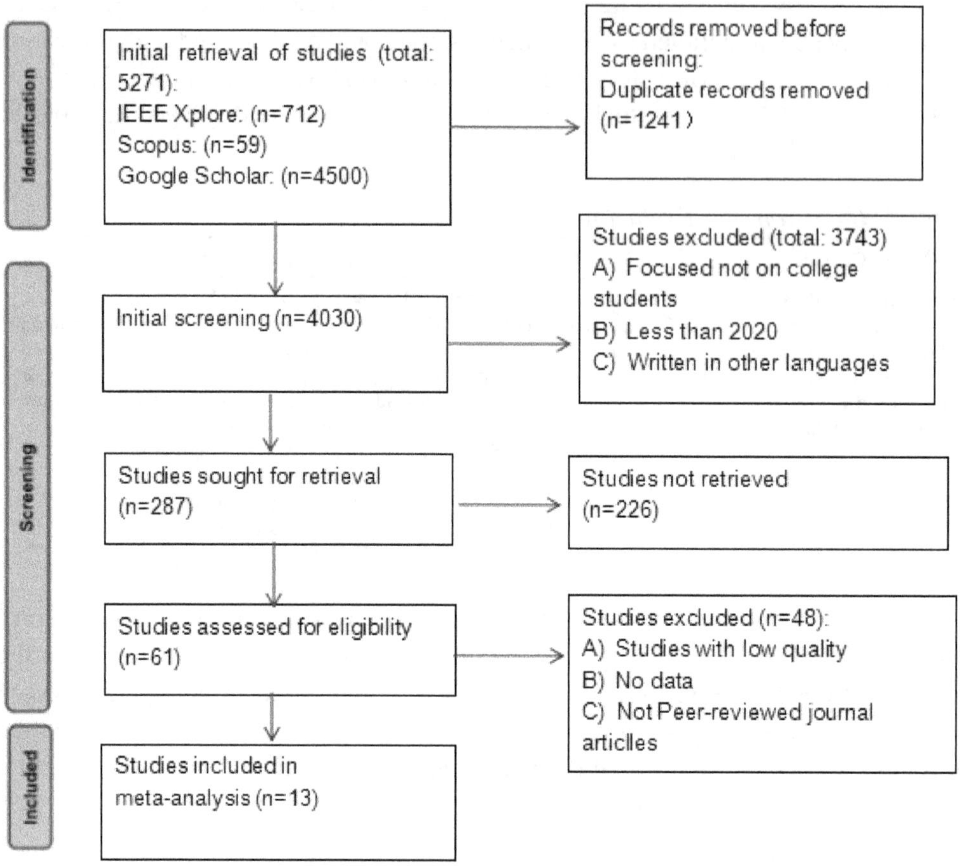

3. RESULT

In order to identify and analyze a selection of published articles that specifically address significant advancements within the realms of VR and learning engagement, a systematic review was meticulously conducted. This comprehensive search was strategically concentrated on the theme of learning engagement in the context of virtual reality environments. As illustrated in Table 2, the reviewed papers encompass research published from 2020 to 2024, providing insights and findings pertinent to the evolving field of learning engagement within VR.

Table 2. Paper Reviewed from 2020 - 2024 in the field of Learning Engagement in VR.

No.	Sample	Subject area	Method	Outcome
1	College students from Zhejiang:36	college English for Geography course	• Pre-Test • Post-Test • quasi-experimental design • Experimental group learned English vocabulary through VR-based instruction. • Control group learned English vocabulary through video-based instruction. • Questionnaire	• Students who used a VR-based approach to learning performed better in incidental vocabulary acquisition as well as cognitive, behavioral, and social engagement • Students employing VR-based methods demonstrated improved learning experiences, greater success and enjoyment.
2	College students in their second or third year from Henan (aged 21): 82	Engineering Structure	• Experimental • immediate test • one-week-later test • Experimental group utilized VR-based experiential teaching in the virtual simulation training facility. • The traditional offline, in-person PowerPoint teaching approach was used with the control group. • Questionnaire	• The VR-based instruction could increase students' engagement in their studies. • The results of the experiment show that learning in a VR environment can maintain or even improve students' knowledge retention rates. This phenomenon can also help students apply their knowledge to new situations or problems, which will strengthen their ability to memorize and retrieve information.
3	College students in their second year from China: 134	University English course	• Empirical research • The experimental group adopted the wisdom teaching approach, which blends offline and online, virtual and entity learning. • Control group uses traditional teaching models • Questionnaire • Semi-structured interviews.	• Students engage in teaching tasks across various dimensions within immersive VR environments, significantly enhancing their motivation and efficiency in acquiring English language skills. This innovative approach not only fosters a heightened interest in learning but also leads to a marked increase in their overall engagement in the learning process.

continued on following page

Table 2. Continued

No.	Sample	Subject area	Method	Outcome
4	Electrical engineering students and electronic engineering students (aged 18-20): 36	Vocational education	• Experimental • The experimental group (electronic engineering students) focused on VR for robots • Control group (electrical engineering students) focused on power plants. • Questionnaire	• Students who learn in a VR-based manner enjoy the learning process because of the excitement of playing the games, the higher level of student engagement in learning, and the engaging descriptions of the materials provided.
5	College students from USA: 62 24 males (39%) and 38 females (61%)	Digital media website development	• Pre-test • Post-test • The VR module took up one of the rigorous course's eight weeks, and all activities lasted three. • Questionnaire • Semi-structured interviews.	• VR-based learning will have a significant positive impact on students' cognitive engagement • Developing methods to reduce students' frustration and boost their effort levels will probably raise their engagement and, thus, improve learning outcomes.
6	Engineering students (aged 20-25):12	Industrial engineering branch.	• Qualitative and case study • Observation-To observe the learners' interactions in the virtual environment. • Individual and focus group interviews	• The findings demonstrate how VR technology, by fostering deeper learning immersion and the creation of efficient social structures, may support collaboration and learner engagement.
7	Non-English majors students from Wenzhou University:69	Daily English learning	• Experimental • Pre-test • Post-test • Experimental Group use high reality scenes and Control group use low reality scenes. • The learning method consists of listening to and reading dialogue, as well as role simulation. • Questionnaire	• The more realistic the scene in the virtual environment, the more engaged the student is in the learning process. • Under VR-based learning, there is a significant correlation between learning engagement and learning effects.

continued on following page

Table 2. Continued

No.	Sample	Subject area	Method	Outcome
8	Students from the Department of Computer and Systems Sciences (DSV) of Stockholm University: 10	Computer Programming Courses	• Experimental • Experimental group use VR application and control group use desktop application. • Mixed data were obtained through questionnaires and observations. • The body language, facial expressions, and verbal expressions of the participants are the main subjects of the research observations. • Semi-structured interview	• The application of VR provides students with a higher level of interest and engagement in learning. • The outcome suggests that there is a great deal of promise for using VR in education, particularly in programming.
9	Students from Mukachevo State University, Ukraine: 48 (28 females, 20 males)	Human anatomy learning	• Theoretical and empirical methods • Pre-test • Post-test • Experimental group use VR system and control group use traditional (reading material style) mode. • Empirical part contained observations and questionnaires for determining the effectiveness of student engagement and learning outcomes.	• Comparing the VR mode to the traditional learning mode, participants' engagement scores and learning performance improved. • Positive feelings were higher and negative emotions were lower in the emotional self-ratings conducted in the VR mode before and after the learning period. • When compared to traditional learning approaches, participants in the VR mode demonstrated a better learning experience.
10	Students from Midwest R1 institution: 67 and Southeast R2 institution: 22	Architectural Engineering Disciplines	• Pilot study • Pre-test • Post-test • The entire duration of the project was three weeks • Semi-structured interview • The data collected for analysis in this paper were student responses to items and their comments on the project	• VR-based course activities provide a more realistic engineering experience, keeping students engaged and helping them persist in their engineering courses.

continued on following page

Table 2. Continued

No.	Sample	Subject area	Method	Outcome
11	Undergraduate business students from Hong Kong (mean age was 20.51 years): 321	Undergraduate business students	• Experimental • Pre-test • Post-test • Questionnaire related engagement in VR-based learning and learning effectiveness	• VR technology is often seen as a helpful training tool by students who have an open mind about trying new things. • Learning engagement was higher among students who had more favorable opinions of VR technology-assisted instruction.
12	Freshmen nursing students from Israeli university (mean age was 23 years): 61	Medical Nursing Courses	• Prospective study-Students used the VR-based simulation learning course for an average of 41.18 (±13.7) minutes. • Pre-test • Post-test • Questionnaire	• As a re-engaging learning activity, the VR procedural learning phase causes a higher mental effort and more joyful facial expressions.
13	Students come from both campuses of Tecnológico de Monterrey:104	Industrial engineering courses	• Mixed—Using data collection through surveys, observation and document analysis (academic activities). • VR case and traditional case in two weeks	• Students attest that having access to this technology in the classroom helps them understand the actual issues at hand and formulate collaborative proposal ideas. • They agree to the fact that it makes learning more engaging and permits absorption in the situation, as though they were there.

This collection of 13 research publications meticulously investigates the implementation of VR across a range of academic disciplines, scrutinizing its influence on student learning outcomes and engagement levels. Through a comprehensive evaluation of the potential and actual impacts that VR can have within educational settings, diverse experimental methodologies and data collection strategies are employed. The research draws from a heterogeneous sample of college students, representing various age demographics, academic specializations, and geographic regions, thereby enriching the findings and conclusions regarding the efficacy of VR integration in educational practices.

3.1 Application Domain (RQ1: Which Areas of Higher Education Have Used VR for Teaching in the Past Five Years? Sample?)

The research comprehensively addressed a total of seven distinct topic areas. According to 31% of the publications, the most common application area was engineering (see Fig. 2). Among these, it included two specific domains pertaining to computer programming, one focused on digital media education, one concentrated on vocational education, three encompassing various aspects of business, and finally, two dedicated to the fields of medical and nursing education. The sample population are all college students, aged 18-25 years old.

Figure 2. Application domain

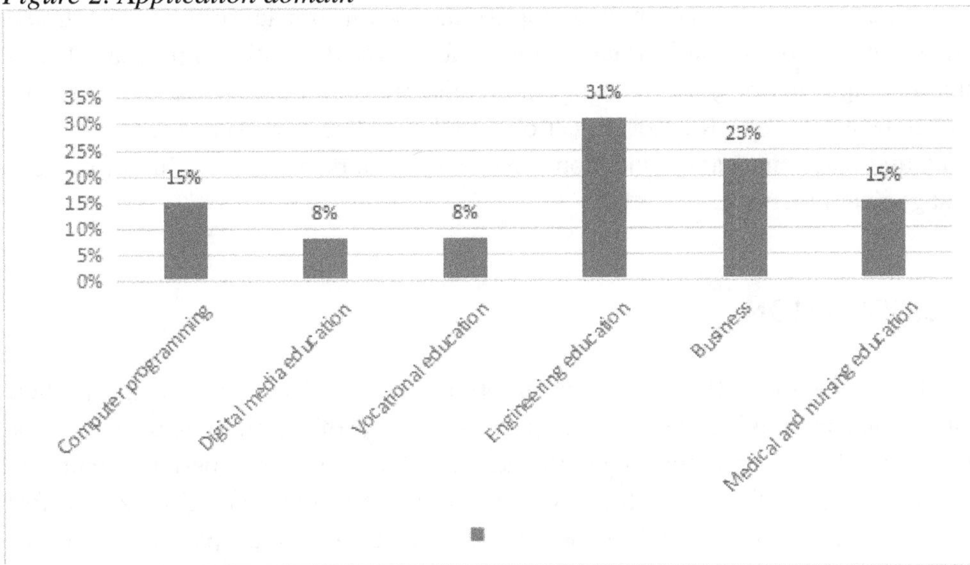

3.2 Research designs (RQ2: What Research Designs Have Been Used in Higher Education Research in the Past Five Years?)

The table presents a comprehensive overview of the various data analysis techniques employed in the research. Both quantitative and qualitative data analysis methods were systematically applied to ensure a robust interpretation of the findings. The average range of articles that incorporated mixed research methodologies, including focus group discussions and observational studies, varied from one to three. Furthermore, pre- and post-test questionnaires, along with comparative analyses between experimental and control groups, emerged as the predominant quantitative research methodologies in this context. This evidence suggests that the most frequently encountered types of research contents encompassed design-oriented studies, empirical quantitative research, and empirical qualitative investigations, reflecting the diverse approaches taken in the field.

3.3 Learning Outcomes (RQ3: What are the Learning Outcomes of Higher Education Research in the Past Five Years?)

Based on the findings of various studies, VR exhibits a broad spectrum of promising applications within the field of education. Notably, it has the potential to significantly enhance students' engagement with the learning process, improve their retention of information, and amplify the overall impact of their educational experiences. Furthermore, VR technology offers a transformative approach to learning, making it not only more engaging but also more immersive for students. The beneficial effects of VR as an educational tool have been evidenced across diverse academic disciplines and educational contexts, underscoring its value in modern pedagogical practices.

4. DISCUSSION

The commitment, time, and concentration that an individual dedicates to their educational pursuits is encapsulated within the concept of learning engagement. This term not only encompasses the depth and breadth of learning experiences but also integrates critical factors such as motivation, concentration, and dedicated effort (Chen et al., 2024). Research recognizes the existence of multiple dimensions of learning engagement, specifically highlighting two, three, and four distinct frameworks. Among these, the notion of investment in cognitive, emotional, and behavioral dimensions of engagement in three-dimensional learning is particularly prominent and widely accepted. Cognitive engagement pertains to the mental exertion that learners undertake throughout the educational process. This includes activities such as understanding, memorizing, analyzing, and effectively solving problems (López-Banet et al., 2024). On the other hand, emotional engagement refers to the emotional responses that learners experience, which can encompass a range of feelings including curiosity, enthusiasm, frustration, and satisfaction. Lastly, behavioral engagement is characterized by the observable actions and participation of learners (Prayogo et al., 2024). This encompasses various activities such as active participation in classroom discussions, leading group dialogues, conducting independent research beyond the curriculum, among other forms of engagement (Pan, 2023).

Higher education is certainly not immune to the extraordinary transformational impact of VR technology, which is reshaping a wide array of industries due to the relentless advancement of technological capabilities. With its unique interactive components, deeply immersive experiences, and innovative pedagogical approaches, VR technology is progressively establishing itself as a vital tool within the educational landscape. This article delves into the integration of VR technology in the realm of higher education, highlighting strategies for leveraging this technology to enhance student engagement within academic settings. It also focuses on fostering the comprehensive skill sets required to thrive in an increasingly complex and fast-paced societal landscape.

To enhance student engagement and participation, it is essential for educators to design and implement VR courses. By harnessing the capabilities of VR technology, teachers can cultivate a more immersive and captivating educational experience that allows students to grasp complex concepts in a manner that feels both intuitive and dynamic. VR classes not only hold the promise of elevating students' enthusiasm and motivation towards learning but also provide invaluable real-world simulations that facilitate the application of acquired knowledge in practical contexts. Moreover, VR technology can recreate authentic scenarios, enabling students to delve into explorative and experimental activities within a controlled virtual environment. Ultimately, this pedagogical approach has the potential to foster more profound learning experiences and knowledge application, driven by heightened student interest and active participation in the learning process. A case study from an Indonesian polytechnic shows the researchers using three research approaches in a classroom setting, including total simulation with VR Oculus Rift technology and data analysis using desktop computer theme analysis. Students from engineering departments participated in the study, which used virtual reality to increase student learning engagement. According to the statistics, VR appears to be relatively straightforward to use, and students believe it improves their knowledge and engagement. Consequently, educators are encouraged to actively develop VR courses.

When developing VR courses, it is crucial for educators to take into account not only the content being delivered but also the valuable feedback provided by students, alongside the availability of technological infrastructure. VR as an advanced educational technology, VR has promoted students' interest and participation in learning. Educators hope to use the immersive features of today's technology in college classroom teaching. Despite the growing interest, many educators still face major challenges when trying to apply VR technology to the classroom on a large scale. The first is the limitation of technical knowledge. Most teachers have no knowledge reserve for the development of technology and do not have clear design and development considerations when planning to implement VR systems. The second is the more obvious budget challenge. Colleges and universities need to invest a lot of money in infrastructure construction, equipment procurement, software development and personnel training for VR immersive teaching, which to some extent limits its widespread application in the field of education. Therefore, adequate technical and financial support plays a key role in ensuring the smooth operation and overall effectiveness of VR projects. In parallel, the prompt collection and thorough analysis of student feedback can significantly assist educators in their continuous pursuit to refine and enhance course design, ultimately aiming to align more closely with the unique needs and preferences of their learners. By adopting this iterative approach to improvement, instructors can significantly enrich the educational journey of their students, foster greater engagement, and stimulate creative thought, paving the way for the emergence of innovative educational paradigms.

In summary, the development of VR courses specifically designed for educators represents a noteworthy strategy that not only enhances student involvement but also marks a substantial progression in the field of educational technology. By implementing VR technology effectively, teachers are empowered to cultivate a more stimulating, interactive, and productive educational atmosphere. This innovative approach ultimately contributes to the holistic growth and development of students, equipping them with the skills and experiences necessary for their future endeavors.

The current research also has its limitations. To assure quality, for instance, we purposefully selected journal articles from reputable databases for the study rather than adding conference papers or theses. This means that the review was quite selective. Another drawback was that, in an effort to keep the study tighter and more focused, the citation or reference network analysis was excluded. In order to perform a more thorough review, future study may broaden its coverage and make use of knowledge mapping technologies to create complex presentations that highlight research hotspots and trends.

5. CONCLUSION

This research is centered on a comprehensive systematic review of the existing literature. Based on the review results, it appears that there is a lot of interest in immersive VR technologies for educational purposes, as seen by the wide range of study fields that have used this technology in the classroom. In summary, the research findings strongly indicate that the utilization of VR applications has the potential to significantly enhance student learning engagement. This enhancement manifests through immersive and interactive experiences that facilitate deeper understanding and retention of educational material, showcasing the transformative power of technology in contemporary educational practices. The comprehensive results obtained from the study consistently highlight the significant impact of these university course subjects when employed as educational tools within VR contexts. This suggests that the implementation of VR learning environments for educational training can lead to substantial improvements in student learning outcomes and significantly enhance student engagement with academic activities. In addition, these VR settings contribute positively to the development of knowledge and the overall performance of students. In other words, incorporating virtual reality into educational practices presents innovative opportunities for effective teaching methodologies.

The advent of VR technology is increasingly becoming interwoven into a multitude of industries, propelled by the rapid growth and advancements within the information technology sector. One of the most significant arenas where this technology is finding its application is in the realm of higher education. The immersive qualities and state-of-the-art interactive methods offered by VR have greatly expanded the horizons of conventional educational frameworks. In the face of various challenges posed by traditional classroom settings, VR technology is redefining the educational landscape by delivering more personalized and captivating learning experiences. This essay aims to delve into the various implementations of VR technology in higher education and to analyze how it substantially enhances student engagement in the learning process. Engaging in comprehensive research on the implications of VR technology in the realm of educational innovation enables us to gain a deeper understanding of its effects and identify methods to maximize its capabilities to boost students' engagement in learning as well as their overall educational experiences. This article provides insights for future improvements, especially for VR application developers and higher education instructors, to enhance classroom design for instructors developing VR systems, as VR technology matures into a promising higher education learning tool. Ultimately, the incorporation of VR technology within higher education has afforded students a richer and more tailored learning journey, thus laying the groundwork for a future characterized by diversity, creativity, and practical application in educational contexts.

REFERENCES

Akbari, E., Naderi, A., & Simons, R.-J., & K. J. A.-P. J. o. S. (2016). Student engagement and foreign language learning through online social networks. *Journal of Social Sciences*, 1(1), 4. DOI: 10.11648/j.jss.2016.01.11

Alvarez, K. S. (2021). Using virtual simulations in online laboratory instruction and active learning exercises as a response to instructional challenges during COVID-19. *Journal of Microbiology & Biology Education*, 22(1), 10–1128. DOI: 10.1128/jmbe.v22i1.2503 PMID: 33884091

Asad, M. M., Naz, A., Churi, P., & Tahanzadeh, M. M. (2021). Virtual reality as pedagogical tool to enhance experiential learning: A systematic literature review. *Education Research International*, 2021(1), 7061623. DOI: 10.1155/2021/7061623

Baxter, G., & Hainey, T. (2024). Using immersive technologies to enhance the student learning experience. *Interactive Technology and Smart Education*, 21(3), 403–425. DOI: 10.1108/ITSE-05-2023-0078

Brondi, R., Alem, L., Avveduto, G., Faita, C., Carrozzino, M., Tecchia, F., & Bergamasco, M. (2015). Evaluating the impact of highly immersive technologies and natural interaction on player engagement and flow experience in games. In Chorianopoulos, K., Divitini, M., Baalsrud Hauge, J., Jaccheri, L., & Malaka, R. (Eds.), *Entertainment Computing – ICEC 2015* (pp. 169–181). Springer., DOI: 10.1007/978-3-319-24589-8_13

Brophy, J. (2004). *Motivating students to learn* (2nd ed.). Routledge. DOI: 10.4324/9781410610218

Bueno-Vesga, J. A., Xu, X., & He, H. (2021, March). *The effects of cognitive load on engagement in a virtual reality learning environment. In 2021 IEEE Virtual Reality and 3D User Interfaces (VR)*. IEEE., DOI: 10.1109/VR48863.2021.00086

Cappello, M., & Lafferty, K. E. (2015). The roles of photography for developing literacy across the disciplines. *The Reading Teacher*, 69(3), 287–295. DOI: 10.1002/trtr.1418

Carini, R. M., Kuh, G. D., & Klein, S. P. (2006). Student engagement and student learning: Testing the linkages. *Research in Higher Education*, 47(1), 1–32. DOI: 10.1007/s11162-005-8150-9

Chai, C. S., Deng, F., Tsai, P. S., Koh, J. H. L., & Tsai, C. C. (2015). Assessing multidimensional students' perceptions of twenty-first-century learning practices. *Asia Pacific Education Review*, 16(3), 389–398. DOI: 10.1007/s12564-015-9379-4

Chang, S. C., Hsu, T. C., & Jong, M. S. Y. (2020). Integration of the peer assessment approach with a virtual reality design system for learning earth science. *Computers & Education*, 146, 103758. DOI: 10.1016/j.compedu.2019.103758

Chang, S. C., Hsu, T. C., Kuo, W. C., & Jong, M. S. Y. (2020). Effects of applying a VR-based two-tier test strategy to promote elementary students' learning performance in a geology class. *British Journal of Educational Technology*, 51(1), 148–165. DOI: 10.1111/bjet.12790

Chen, M., Chai, C. S., Jong, M. S. Y., & Jiang, M. Y. C. (2021). Teachers' conceptions of teaching Chinese descriptive composition with interactive spherical video-based virtual reality. *Frontiers in Psychology*, 12, 591708. DOI: 10.3389/fpsyg.2021.591708 PMID: 33613380

Chen, S., Li, Q., & Wang, T. (2024). Smart campus and student learning engagement. [IJICTE]. *International Journal of Information and Communication Technology Education*, 20(1), 1–22. DOI: 10.4018/IJICTE.2024010101

Chien, S. Y., Hwang, G. J., & Jong, M. S. Y. (2020). Effects of peer assessment within the context of spherical video-based virtual reality on EFL students' English-speaking performance and learning perceptions. *Computers & Education*, 146, 103751. DOI: 10.1016/j.compedu.2019.103751

Christenson, S. L., Reschly, A. L., & Wylie, C. (Eds.). (2012). *Handbook of research on student engagement*. Springer. DOI: 10.1007/978-1-4614-2018-7

Claman, F. L. (2015). The impact of multiuser virtual environments on student engagement. *Nurse Education in Practice*, 15(1), 13–16. DOI: 10.1016/j.nepr.2014.11.006 PMID: 25532889

Dincelli, E., & Yayla, A. (2022). Immersive virtual reality in the age of the Metaverse: A hybrid-narrative review based on the technology affordance perspective. *The Journal of Strategic Information Systems*, 31(2), 101717. DOI: 10.1016/j.jsis.2022.101717

Dubovi, I. (2022). Cognitive and emotional engagement while learning with VR: The perspective of multimodal methodology. *Computers & Education*, 183, 104495. DOI: 10.1016/j.compedu.2022.104495

Ekman, J. (2023). Comparing engagement of VR and non-VR games for programming learning purposes. *Unpublished manuscript.*

Erdogmus, E., Ryherd, E., Diefes-Dux, H. A., & Armwood-Gordon, C. (2021, October). Use of virtual reality to improve engagement and self-efficacy in architectural engineering disciplines. In *2021 IEEE Frontiers in Education Conference (FIE)* (pp. 1-7). IEEE. DOI: 10.1109/FIE49875.2021.9637182

Fredricks, J. A., Blumenfeld, P. C., & Paris, A. H. (2004). School engagement: Potential of the concept, state of the evidence. *Review of Educational Research*, 74(1), 59–109. DOI: 10.3102/00346543074001059

Grant, L. L., Opperman, M. J., Schiller, B., Chastain, J., Richardson, J. D., Eckel, C., & Plawecki, M. H. (2021). Medical student engagement in a virtual learning environment positively correlates with course performance and satisfaction in psychiatry. *Medical Science Educator*, 31(3), 1133–1140. DOI: 10.1007/s40670-021-01287-x PMID: 33868773

Hamad, A., & Jia, B. (2022). How virtual reality technology has changed our lives: An overview of the current and potential applications and limitations. *International Journal of Environmental Research and Public Health*, 19(18), 11278. DOI: 10.3390/ijerph191811278 PMID: 36141551

Hartikainen, S., Rintala, H., Pylväs, L., & Nokelainen, P. (2019). The concept of active learning and the measurement of learning outcomes: A review of research in engineering higher education. *Education Sciences*, 9(4), 276. DOI: 10.3390/educsci9040276

Hirshfield, L. J., & Koretsky, M. D. (2021). Cultivating creative thinking in engineering student teams: Can a computer-mediated virtual laboratory help? *Journal of Computer Assisted Learning*, 37(2), 587–601. DOI: 10.1111/jcal.12509

Hodgson, P., Lee, V. W., Chan, J. C., Fong, A., Tang, C. S., Chan, L., & Wong, C. (2019). Immersive virtual reality (IVR) in higher education: Development and implementation. *Augmented reality and virtual reality: The power of AR and VR for business*, 161-173.

Hodson, C. B., & Sander, H. A. (2019). Relationships between vegetation in student environments and academic achievement across the continental US. *Landscape and Urban Planning*, 189, 212–224. DOI: 10.1016/j.landurbplan.2019.04.027

Huang, Y. M., Wang, W. S., Lee, H. Y., Lin, C. J., & Wu, T. T. (2024). Empowering virtual reality with feedback and reflection in hands-on learning: Effect of learning engagement and higher-order thinking. *Journal of Computer Assisted Learning*, 40(4), 1413–1427. Advance online publication. DOI: 10.1111/jcal.12959

Hudson, S., Matson-Barkat, S., Pallamin, N., & Jegou, G. (2019). With or without you? Interaction and immersion in a virtual reality experience. *Journal of Business Research*, 100, 459–468. DOI: 10.1016/j.jbusres.2018.10.062

Jelas, Z. M., Azman, N., Zulnaidi, H., & Ahmad, N. A. (2016). Learning support and academic achievement among Malaysian adolescents: The mediating role of student engagement. *Learning Environments Research*, 19(2), 221–240. DOI: 10.1007/s10984-015-9202-5

Korniienko, I. A., & Barchi, B. V. (2020). Influence of virtual reality tools on human anatomy learning. *Unpublished manuscript*.

Lege, R., & Bonner, E. (2020). Virtual reality in education: The promise, progress, and challenge. *The JALT CALL Journal*, 16(3), 167–180. DOI: 10.29140/jaltcall.v16n3.388

Li, Y., Lerner, J. V., & Lerner, R. M. (2010). Personal and ecological assets and academic competence in early adolescence: The mediating role of school engagement. *Journal of Youth and Adolescence*, 39(8), 801–815. DOI: 10.1007/s10964-010-9535-4 PMID: 20407920

Li, Y., Ying, S., Chen, Q., & Guan, J. (2022). An experiential learning-based virtual reality approach to foster students' vocabulary acquisition and learning engagement in English for geography. *Sustainability (Basel)*, 14(22), 15359. DOI: 10.3390/su142215359

Liu, X., Sun, D., & Zhao, B. (2022). Research on the impact of virtual reality technology on student classroom participation. *Shanxi Youth, 19*, 39-41. https://www.cqvip.com/QK/87921X/202219/1010237166.html

López-Banet, L., Martínez-Carmona, M., & Reis, P. (2024). Effects of an intervention on emotional and cognitive engagement in teacher education: Scientific practices concerning greenhouse gases. *Frontiers in Education*, 9, 1307847. DOI: 10.3389/feduc.2024.1307847

Loup, G., Serna, A., Iksal, S., & George, S. (2016). Immersion and persistence: Improving learners' engagement in authentic learning situations. In Verbert, K., Sharples, M., & Klobučar, T. (Eds.), *Adaptive and Adaptable Learning* (pp. 410–415). Springer., DOI: 10.1007/978-3-319-45153-4_35

Loveless, T. (2012). *How well are American students learning?* Brookings Institution.

Makransky, G., Terkildsen, T. S., & Mayer, R. E. (2019). Adding immersive virtual reality to a science lab simulation causes more presence but less learning. *Learning and Instruction*, 60, 225–236. DOI: 10.1016/j.learninstruc.2017.12.007

Marks, H. M. (2000). Student engagement in instructional activity: Patterns in the elementary, middle, and high school years. *American Educational Research Journal*, 37(1), 153–184. DOI: 10.3102/00028312037001153

Marougkas, A., Troussas, C., Krouska, A., & Sgouropoulou, C. (2023). Virtual reality in education: A review of learning theories, approaches and methodologies for the last decade. *Electronics (Basel)*, 12(13), 2832. DOI: 10.3390/electronics12132832

Matthews, K. E., Andrews, V., & Adams, P. J. H. E. R. (2011). Social learning spaces and student engagement. *Assessment & Evaluation in Higher Education*, 30(2), 105–120. DOI: 10.1080/02602930903500170

Moher, D., Liberati, A., Tetzlaff, J., & Altman, D. G.PRISMA Group. (2009). Preferred reporting items for systematic reviews and meta-analyses: The PRISMA statement. *Annals of Internal Medicine*, 151(4), 264–269. DOI: 10.7326/0003-4819-151-4-200908180-00135 PMID: 19622511

Mulders, M., Buchner, J., & Kerres, M. (2020). A framework for the use of immersive virtual reality in learning environments. [iJET]. *International Journal of Emerging Technologies in Learning*, 15(24), 208–224. DOI: 10.3991/ijet.v15i24.16615

Mystakidis, S. (2020, July). Distance education gamification in social virtual reality: A case study on student engagement. In *2020 11th International Conference on Information, Intelligence, Systems and Applications (IISA)* (pp. 1-6). IEEE. DOI: 10.1109/IISA50023.2020.9284417

Oliveira, A., Feyzi Behnagh, R., Ni, L., Mohsinah, A. A., Burgess, K. J., & Guo, L. (2019). Emerging technologies as pedagogical tools for teaching and learning science: A literature review. *Human Behavior and Emerging Technologies*, 1(2), 149–160. https://doi.org/xx.xxx/yyyy. DOI: 10.1002/hbe2.141

Onyema, E. M., Deborah, E. C., Alsayed, A. O., Noorulhasan, Q., & Sanober, S. (2019). Online discussion forum as a tool for interactive learning and communication. *International Journal of Recent Technology and Engineering*, 8(4), 4852–4859. DOI: 10.35940/ijrte.D8062.118419

Oumaima, E., Abdelhak, C., & Youssef, S. (2023, December). Exploring social learning through virtual reality: How technology can enhance collaboration and learner engagement. In *2023 7th IEEE Congress on Information Science and Technology (CiSt)* (pp. 442-444). IEEE. https://doi.org/DOI: 10.1109/CiSt58110.2023.00103

Pan, X. (2023). Online learning environments, learners' empowerment, and learning behavioral engagement: The mediating role of learning

Papanastasiou, G., Drigas, A., Skianis, C., Lytras, M., & Papanastasiou, E. (2019). Virtual and augmented reality effects on K-12, higher and tertiary education students' twenty-first century skills. *Virtual Reality (Waltham Cross)*, 23(4), 425–436. DOI: 10.1007/s10055-018-0363-2

Petersen, G. B., Petkakis, G., & Makransky, G. (2022). A study of how immersion and interactivity drive VR learning. *Computers & Education*, 179, 104429. DOI: 10.1016/j.compedu.2021.104429

Piovesan, S. D., Passerino, L. M., & Pereira, A. S. (2012). Virtual reality as a tool in the education. *International Association for Development of the Information Society*. https://www.researchgate.net/publication/292838721_Virtual_Reality_as_a_Tool_in_the_Education

Prayogo, A., Khotimah, K., Istiqomah, L., & Maharsi, I. (2024). Students' emotional engagement in online classes: A conceptual framework. *International Journal of Information and Learning Technology*, 41(1), 61–72. DOI: 10.1108/IJILT-04-2023-0052

Rafiq, A. A., Triyono, M. B., & Djatmiko, I. W. (2022). Enhancing student engagement in vocational education by using virtual reality. *Waikato Journal of Education*, 27(3), 175–188. DOI: 10.15663/wje.v27i3.964

Richardson, C., & Mishra, P. (2018). Learning environments that support student creativity: Developing the SCALE. *Thinking Skills and Creativity*, 27, 45–54. DOI: 10.1016/j.tsc.2017.11.004

Robinson, C. C., & Hullinger, H. (2008). New benchmarks in higher education: Student engagement in online learning. *Journal of Education for Business*, 84(2), 101–109. DOI: 10.3200/JOEB.84.2.101-109

Ruiz-Cantisani, M. I., del Carmen Lima-Sagui, F., Aceves-Campos, N., Ipiña-Sifuentes, R., & Flores, E. G. R. (2020, April). Virtual reality as a tool for active learning and student engagement: Industrial engineering experience. In *2020 IEEE Global Engineering Education Conference (EDUCON)* (pp. 1031-1037). IEEE. DOI: 10.1109/EDUCON45650.2020.9125225

Skinner, E. A., & Belmont, M. J. (1993). Motivation in the classroom: Reciprocal effects of teacher behavior and student engagement across the school year. *Journal of Educational Psychology*, 85(3), 571–581. DOI: 10.1037/0022-0663.85.4.571

Sun, C., Yao, Y., Wang, R., & Ye, X. (2020, June). A study on the influence of scene reality of VR environment on English learners' learning engagement and learning effectiveness. In *2020 IEEE 2nd International Conference on Computer Science and Educational Informatization (CSEI)* (pp. 181-185). IEEE. https://doi.org/DOI: 10.1109/CSEI49390.2020.00044

Sun, F. R., Pan, L. F., Wan, R. G., Li, H., & Wu, S. J. (2021). Detecting the effect of student engagement in an SVVR school-based course on higher level competence development in elementary schools by SEM. *Interactive Learning Environments*, 29(1), 3–16. DOI: 10.1080/10494820.2018.1558258

Tibaldi, A., Bonali, F. L., Vitello, F., Delage, E., Nomikou, P., Antoniou, V., Becciani, U., de Vries, B. V. W., Krokos, M., & Whitworth, M. (2020). Real world–based immersive Virtual Reality for research, teaching and communication in volcanology. *Bulletin of Volcanology*, 82(5), 1–12. DOI: 10.1007/s00445-020-01376-6

Trowler, V. (2010). Student engagement literature review. *Higher Education Academy*. https://www.heacademy.ac.uk/system/files/student_engagement_literature_review.pdf

Wang, L., & He, Y. (2020). Online learning engagement assessment based on multimodal behavioral data. In *Transactions on Edutainment XVI* (pp. 256–265). Springer., DOI: 10.1007/978-3-662-61510-2_25

Wang, M. T., Fredricks, J. A., Ye, F., Hofkens, T. L., & Linn, J. S. (2016). The math and science engagement scales: Scale development, validation, and psychometric properties. *Learning and Instruction*, 43, 16–26. DOI: 10.1016/j.learninstruc.2016.01.008

Webster, J., & Watson, R. T. (2002). Analyzing the past to prepare for the future: Writing a literature review. *Management Information Systems Quarterly*, 26(2), xiii–xxiii. https://www.jstor.org/stable/4132319

Wenger-Trayner, E., Wenger, E., & Wenger-Trayner, B. (2020). *Learning to make a difference: Value creation in social learning spaces*. Cambridge university press. DOI: 10.1017/9781108677431

Wilder, S. (2023). Effects of parental involvement on academic achievement: a meta-synthesis. In *Mapping the field* (pp. 137–157). Routledge. DOI: 10.4324/9781003403722-12

Wong, E. Y. C., Hui, R. T. Y., & Kong, H. (2023). Perceived usefulness of, engagement with, and effectiveness of virtual reality environments in learning industrial operations: The moderating role of openness to experience. *Virtual Reality (Waltham Cross)*, 27(3), 2149–2165. DOI: 10.1007/s10055-023-00793-0 PMID: 37360804

Xin, Y. (2022). Influence of learning engagement on learning effect under a virtual reality (VR) environment. [iJET]. *International Journal of Emerging Technologies in Learning*, 17(5), 226–237. DOI: 10.3991/ijet.v17i05.29451

Xu, B., Chen, N. S., & Chen, G. (2020). Effects of teacher role on student engagement in WeChat-based online discussion learning. *Computers & Education*, 157, 103956. DOI: 10.1016/j.compedu.2020.103956

Yan, S. (2023). The application of virtual reality technology in higher education and its impact on student learning performance. *The Educational Review, USA*, 7(11), 1808–1812. DOI: 10.26855/er.2023.11.032

Yin, K., He, Z., Xiong, J., Zou, J., Li, K., & Wu, S. T. (2021). Virtual reality and augmented reality displays: Advances and future perspectives. *JPhys Photonics*, 3(2), 022010. DOI: 10.1088/2515-7647/abf02e

Yuan, J., Liu, Y., Han, X., Li, A., & Zhao, L. (2023). Educational metaverse: An exploration and practice of VR wisdom teaching model in Chinese open university English course. *Interactive Technology and Smart Education*, 20(3), 403–421. DOI: 10.1108/ITSE-10-2022-0140

Zhang, H., Yu, L., Ji, M., Cui, Y., Liu, D., Li, Y., & Wang, Y. (2023). Investigating high school students' perceptions and presences under VR learning environment. In *Cross Reality (XR) and Immersive Learning Environments (ILEs) in Education* (pp. 97–117). Routledge. DOI: 10.4324/9781003457121-8

Zhang, J., Ding, Y., Yang, X., Zhong, J., Qiu, X., Zou, Z., Xu, Y., Jin, X., Wu, X., Huang, J., & Zheng, Y. (2022). COVID-19's impacts on the scope, effectiveness, and interaction characteristics of online learning: A social network analysis. *PLoS One*, 17(8), e0273016. DOI: 10.1371/journal.pone.0273016 PMID: 35998175

Zhang, S., & Liu, Q. (2019). Investigating the relationships among teachers' motivational beliefs, motivational regulation, and their learning engagement in online professional learning communities. *Computers & Education*, 134, 145–155. DOI: 10.1016/j.compedu.2019.02.013

Chapter 13
A Systematic Literature Review of Creative Metacognition (CMC) and Its Impact on Students' Creative Performance

Lin Chuxuan
https://orcid.org/0009-0006-3941-2290
Centre for Instructional Technology and Multimedia, Universiti Sains Malaysia, Malaysia

Wan Ahmad Jaafar Wan Yahaya
https://orcid.org/0000-0002-8605-0062
Centre for Instructional Technology and Multimedia, Universiti Sains Malaysia, Malaysia

ABSTRACT

This systematic review analyzes research up to 2024 on the effects of creative metacognition on creative performance. Following PRISMA guidelines, the study screened and examined 30 high-quality journal articles, focusing on creative metacognition, divergent thinking, metacognitive monitoring skills, their application in educational settings, and the effectiveness of various assessment methods and tools. Key findings highlight a significant increase in research interest in creative metacognition, which positively affects creative performance. Most studies currently use subjective or indirect objective measurement methods. The crucial role of metacognitive monitoring skills is emphasized, supporting the hypothesis that creative metacognition can enhance creative performance. This review identifies gaps in

DOI: 10.4018/979-8-3693-6745-2.ch013

applying creative metacognition theory in educational practice. It suggests future research directions, emphasizing the need for in-depth exploration to promote the development of students' creative abilities.

1. INTRODUCTION

Since 2012, research on creative metacognition and creative performance has been emerging. Studies within the framework of creative metacognition theory have explored the factors influencing metacognition and how this theory enhances creative performance. A growing body of research demonstrates that creative performance is critical for innovation and problem-solving (Bowen et al., 2018; Dori et al., 2018; Giacumo & Savenye, 2020; Imran, 2019; Karwowski et al., 2020; Khasanah et al., 2017; Rominger et al., 2022; M. Urban & Urban, 2021). Moreover, metacognition plays a positive role in promoting creativity, and creative metacognition has become a frontier topic (de Acedo Lizarraga & de Acedo Baquedano, 2013; Jia et al., 2019; Mevarech & Paz-Baruch, 2022). It is believed that by improving learners' creative metacognition through preparation, better creative performance can be achieved.

Creativity refers to the novelty and appropriateness of creative ideas or solutions (Runco & Acar, 2012). Simonton (2012) defines creativity as the product of originality and appropriateness: creativity = originality * appropriateness. If something is neither appropriate nor novel, it cannot be considered creative. This formula underscores that originality and appropriateness positively influence creativity. Beghetto and Kaufman (2014) further elaborated Simonton's (2012) formula: C = [O * A] context, emphasizing that what is considered original or appropriate is determined by specific social, cultural, and historical contexts (Plucker et al., 2004). Beghetto and Kaufman (2013) found that teachers prefer students to produce appropriate creativity at an appropriate time and in line with context, and proposed a theoretical framework of creative metacognition. This framework combines self-knowledge (knowing one's creative strengths and limitations) and situational knowledge (knowing when, where, how, and why to be creative).

In higher education, *creativity* is commonly defined as either a thought process that requires both novelty and practicality (Greene et al., 2019) or as a practical process, often called creative expression (Cropley, 2000). Recent research and practice on higher-order cognitive processes, such as creative expression, have shown that students' creative performance is essential for innovation and problem-solving (Khasanah et al., 2017; Bowen et al., 2018; Imran, 2019; Giacumo & Savenye, 2020; Dori et al., 2018; Karwowski et al., 2020; Rominger et al., 2022; Urban & Urban, 2021). In higher education, particularly in art and design programs focused on fostering creative expression, researchers have found that cultivating students' self-regulated learning skills enhances their creative expression and creative design abilities (Greene et al., 2019). Additionally, research consistently demonstrates a strong correlation between creative performance and metacognition (Hargrove & Nietfeld, 2015; Kaufman et al., 2013; Pesut, 1990). As a metacognitive concept within the broader realm of cognition, metacognition positively contributes to the development of creativity (Jia et al., 2019). Furthermore, creative metacognition has emerged as a critical area of interest, with studies suggesting that enhancing learners' creative metacognition through structured preparation can lead to improved creative performance (Forgeard & Mecklenburg, 2013; Jia et al., 2019; Sanz et al., 2013; Mevarech & Paz-Baruch, 2022).

Creative metacognition refers to the integration of self-knowledge—understanding one's creative strengths and limitations—and situational knowledge, which involves recognizing when, where, how, and why to be creative (Kaufman & Beghetto, 2013, p. 160). This concept encompasses both metacognitive knowledge—awareness of creativity and its processes—and metacognitive judgment, which includes planning, monitoring, and evaluating creative activities. It is considered a crucial factor in enhancing students' creative performance (Kaufman & Beghetto, 2013, p. 160). Beghetto and Kaufman (2013) found that educators tend to value creativity that is both appropriate and contextually relevant, delivered at the right time. Cognitive theories, such as metacognition theory and creative metacognition theory, play a foundational role in the study of creative metacognition. Research has demonstrated that the application of creative metacognition theory in educational settings can significantly improve students' creative abilities and performance. Therefore, it is essential to ensure that creative metacognition theory is effectively integrated into curriculum design to maximize its impact on student learning outcomes.

An increasing number of empirical studies have explored the impact of divergent thinking abilities on creative metacognition (Karwowski, 2021; Zielińska et al., 2021, 2022; Urban & Urban, 2021), as well as the role of metacognitive monitoring skills, which have been tested and validated in various contexts (Mevarech & Paz-Baruch, 2022; Pesout & Nietfeld, 2021; Sidi et al., 2020; Steele et al., 2021; Urban & Urban, 2021).

Divergent thinking plays a critical role in the creative production process and is equally vital to creative metacognition, with the two processes influencing one another (Urban & Urban, 2021). Research indicates that enhancing learners' divergent thinking abilities, improving the accuracy of metacognitive regulation skills, and fostering more fluent and original creative ideas can significantly enhance creative performance in educational settings (Kavousi et al., 2020; Ji & Xue, 2022; Liu, 2023; McVeigh et al., 2023; Chou et al., 2023). Several researchers have thoroughly examined three key factors influencing divergent thinking: semantic association, risk-taking propensity, and openness to experience. Five studies have analyzed the interrelated processes by which these factors affect creative metacognition.

The study by Sidi et al. (2020) points out that persistent efforts to generate more ideas in a given task can improve originality, demonstrating the significant impact of divergent thinking on the originality of creative performance. Suppose individuals perceive their ideas to be highly original. In that case, they are likely to terminate the idea-generating process earlier and produce fewer ideas than if they perceive them to be less original. If people underestimate the originality of their ideas, they will persist with the creative process longer. Putting more effort into finding additional solutions can increase originality but may reduce the attention resources devoted to elaborating and developing the idea and ensuring its usefulness. By exploring the metacognitive processes inherent in creating ideas, researchers address the timely but understudied question of what influences originality judgments. Subsequently, Kenett et al. (2023) replicated the findings of Sidi et al. (2020) that people tend to underestimate their originality while also reliably judging their initial ideas to be more creative than their later ones (sequential effects). However, another experiment by Kennett et al. showed that people sometimes rely too strongly on sequential order and too weakly on semantic association and that examples of originality and semantic distance influence people's creative processes. Kennett et al.'s findings suggest that a higher ability to judge originality may lead to better predicting subsequent responses, promoting more creative thinking, i.e., divergent thinking. Anderson and Graham (2021) used the two-channel model theory to measure the influence of divergent thinking's fluency, flexibility, and originality on creative metacognition. The two-channel model identifies two processes of creative production: the cognitive flexibility approach and the persistence approach. The flexibility approach refers to flexible ideas switching between different categories, overcoming "functional fixation." The persistence approach involves systematically, thoroughly, and actively exploring possibilities within a few categories or a single problem, exhausting possibilities, and focusing on the task to obtain more creative ideas. The results show that the fluency of divergent thinking improves the level of creative metacognition, originality affects the improvement of flexibility and fluency, and the improvement of flexibility affects the further improvement of fluency. Originality in divergent thinking contributes to increased creative performance (especially in the visual arts), creative self-efficacy, and creative self-belief. PuenteDiaz et al. (2022) used a metacognitive approach to assess the relationship between experience and its two aspects and ideas' generation, evaluation, and selection. People with "high openness to experience" often show an interest in and sensitivity to new things, are more open to new experiences, are imaginative, and seek variety in their lives. By examining two indicators of metacognition—the correlation of advantages and disadvantages and the accuracy of idea selection—, the research shows that the degree of openness to experience significantly impacts creative performance and is positively correlated with the presentation of the ideas generated. Openness to experience is the most important predictor of creative performance, and its contribution to ideas is crucial. The researchers also found that intelligence had no significant effect on thoughts compared to openness to experience. Woo and Lee's (2024) study revealed the relationship between risk-taking, creative metacognition, and creative performance in the school environment. They empirically investigated the relationship between creative metacognitive knowledge and creative metacognitive regulation on two kinds of risk-taking (daily and content-specific risk-taking) and various aspects of creative performance (general creativity and original usefulness) for junior high school students.

Metacognitive monitoring skills are critical to creative metacognitive measurement, encompassing intra- and inter-individual monitoring. Accurate metacognitive monitoring skills indicate superior creative metacognitive ability, which, in turn, influences creative performance (Karwowski et al., 2020). Intra-individual monitoring involves numerous complex factors and has been studied extensively under various terminologies, including self-judgment, self-evaluation, and self-assessment. Key factors influencing intra-individual monitoring include creative potential, creative ability, creative thinking ability, intelligence, age, and the ease with which ideas are generated.

Multiple studies have demonstrated significant positive correlations between creative potential, creative ability, and creative thinking ability with different subscales of creative metacognition, suggesting mutual reinforcement among these variables. For instance, de Acedo Lizarraga and de Acedo Baquedano (2013) compared the effects of narrative, graphic, and holistic creative potential on creative metacognition, revealing that the predictive power of metacognition was significant, albeit inconsistent. The predictive power was moderate (approximately 40%) for narrative and overall creative potential and low (17%) for graphic creative potential. These findings imply that metacognition may have a more substantial impact on linguistic creativity than on graphic creativity. Kaufman et al. (2016) also found that children demonstrated accurate self-assessment abilities in both verbal and visual domains; however, children tended to underestimate their creativity. Mevarech and Paz-Baruch (2022) further explored how students with varying creativity levels employ metacognitive skills during creative production, comparing creative metacognition to general metacognition. Their study found that differences in creativity levels were attributable to variations in creative metacognition, with high and medium-creative students scoring significantly higher than low-creative students. No significant difference was observed in general metacognition.

Contrasting with other studies, Puente-Diaz and Cavazos-Arroyo (2018) proposed that creative metacognitive emotion influences creative self-efficacy and subsequently impacts creative potential by affecting individuals' self-confidence. Creative self-efficacy also influences idea generation, and Puente-Diaz et al. (2021) demonstrated that creative self-efficacy positively affects originality and the ease of idea generation.

Urban and Urban (2021) conducted a comparative study on self-judgment and comparative judgment bias among students across four educational stages: preschool, primary school, middle school, and undergraduate. Urban classified students into three categories: skilled but unconscious, unskilled unconscious, and unskilled but conscious. They investigated the effects of lack of proficiency and ignorance in self-assessments of creative performance and linked these findings to creative metacognition (CMC) research. Their study revealed that poor performers overestimate their performance, while high performers underestimate theirs. Similarly, Rominger et al. (2022) investigated the accuracy of creativity assessment within and between individuals and, for the first time, examined creative metacognitive monitoring skills on a neurophysiological basis. Their study distinguished between creative metacognitive monitoring skills (level 2) and performance (level 1), suggesting that creative metacognitive monitoring occurs both during explicit evaluation and the creative idea generation process (Guo et al., 2022; Kleinmintz et al., 2019; Sidi et al., 2020). They also found that participants with higher metacognitive monitoring skills exhibited reduced cognitive control and working memory load during the creative assessment process.

Karwowski et al. (2020) indicated that intelligence enhances the positive effect of creativity on the self-rating of creative ideas. Intelligence is not only related to idea generation (e.g., Beaty et al., 2014; Beaty & Silvia, 2012) and creative achievement (Karwowski et al., 2017) but is also associated with accurate self-assessment of creative ideas. These findings suggest that more creative individuals are better at identifying their creative ideas, and those with more creative ideas are more adept at evaluating them (e.g., Benedek et al., 2016; Runco & Dow, 2004; Runco & Smith, 1992). Conversely, individuals with lower intelligence significantly overestimated their creativity.

In addition to exploring various variables related to creative metacognition, many researchers focus on applying creative metacognition theory within educational environments to enhance students' creative performance in courses. Researchers integrate creative metacognition theory and frameworks into instructional design to improve student outcomes.

In a study by Kavousi et al. (2020), researchers applied metacognitive knowledge and process monitoring from creative metacognition theory to teaching architectural design. They developed an instructional exercise involving reflection and thinking aloud, enabling students to independently judge and monitor their strategies, ideas, results, and emotional states. The results indicated a significant improvement in students' creative performance. Ji and Xue (2022) developed two ability tests using creative metacognition theory: the Creative Metacognition Test and the Creative Thinking Ability Test. They found that students' creative metacognition played a regulatory and monitoring role in the design process, with knowledge and experience allowing them to identify critical constraints or viewpoints and continually optimize their solutions. The results demonstrated that creative metacognition knowledge and monitoring are crucial to creative thinking and promoting creative metacognition development. Liu (2023) applied metacognitive monitoring skills from creative metacognition theory to students' self-analysis of visual artworks, examining four aspects: the nature of creativity, the cost and benefit of creativity, creative self-cognition, and the context of creative performance. The results showed that a self-analysis method integrated with creative metacognitive theory effectively improved the accuracy of intra-individual monitoring. McVeigh et al. (2023) designed a creative self-development model based on the creative metacognitive framework to help undergraduate students in an art screenwriting program develop creative performance, self-efficacy, and self-belief. Finally, Chou et al. (2023) integrated creative metacognition theory, entrepreneurship education, and BIG6 teaching strategies into undergraduate creative marketing courses to enhance students' creativity and metacognitive ability. The results showed that the experimental group significantly improved the specialized course's innovation motivation, creativity, and metacognition.

Although creative metacognition is considered to be at the forefront of current educational trends (Mevarech & Paz-Baruch, 2022), the number of relevant review articles remains relatively small. Lebuda and Benedek (2023) proposed a systematic framework for the metacognitive process of creative thinking. In their paper, they distinguished between core cognitive processes and metacognitive processes, identifying three components: metacognitive monitoring, control, and knowledge.

The influencing factors of divergent thinking and metacognitive monitoring skills are crucial in studying creative metacognition and creative performance. Various measurements have been used in these studies to analyze these two factors. Unlike previous review studies, this study analyzes the two key factors affecting creative performance and focuses on the design and application of creative metacognition in instructional design.

Creative metacognition is widely considered to have a significant impact on creative performance. However, researchers must pay more attention to creative metacognition's influence in the teaching environment. This review further explores the influencing factors and measurement methods of creative metacognition and the application and measurement methods of creative metacognition in teaching. To analyze the characteristics and shortcomings of the reviewed studies, we examined the data according to the following research questions:

RQ1. What are the characteristics of the studies on creative metacognition and creative performance published before 2024?

Divergent thinking and metacognitive monitoring skills are two essential topics in exploring the influential factors of creative metacognition. Fluency, flexibility, and originality in divergent thinking can directly affect metacognitive knowledge in creative metacognition, which also refers to originality in Simonton's (2012) definition of creativity. Appropriateness in Simonton's (2012) definition and contextual and situational knowledge (Kaufman & Beghetto, 2013), emphasized by Beghetto and Kaufman (2014), are related to metacognitive monitoring skills. The ability of self-assessment in metacognitive monitoring has a significant effect on creative metacognition and creative performance. With this in mind, we pose the following research question:

RQ 2. What influence factors are considered when studying creative metacognition and expression?

The combination of creative metacognition theory and education is an important research direction. Unlike other studies on influencing factors, this research must combine creative metacognition with the educational environment, instructional design, and teaching strategies (Ji & Xue, 2022) to analyze the correlation with students' creative performance. Research in this direction is crucial to advancing the body of knowledge in this field. The purpose of this survey is to provide suggestions for the application of creative metacognition in teaching by addressing the following questions:

RQ 3. How can creative metacognition be applied in teaching to improve students' creative performance?

In empirical studies examining creative metacognition, many different variables are discussed. Divergent thinking has been explored in many studies (Sidi et al., 2020; Kenett et al., 2023; Benedek & Lebuda, 2024; Woo & Lee, 2024) and metacognitive monitoring skills (de Acedo Lizarraga & de Acedo Baquedano, 2013; Kaufman et al., 2016; Karwowski et al., 2020; Urban & Urban, 2021; Rominger et al., 2022) influence creative metacognition. Similarly, many studies have also explored the impact of creative metacognition on students' creative performance (Kavousi et al., 2020; Ji & Xue, 2022; Liu, 2023; McVeigh et al., 2023; Chou et al., 2023). Researchers used different data collection tools and methods to collect data on these variables. For research questions 4 and 5, the aim is to examine data collection tools in detail:

RQ 4. How are the variables affecting creative metacognition measured?

RQ 5. How are the variables associated with creative metacognition measured in the study?

In conclusion, this systematic review provides a detailed analysis of creative metacognition and its significant impact on students' creative performance. By offering educators and researchers valuable insights into the development and application of creative metacognition, this review aims to support fostering creativity in educational settings and contribute to the broader goal of helping students adapt to the needs of the 21st century.

2. METHODOLOGY

This study aims to explore and summarize the relationship between creative metacognition and creative performance through a systematic literature review, inspired by the previous work of Kaufman and Beghetto (2013) and Karwowski and Lebuda (2016). Following the rigorous PRISMA guidelines (Moher et al., 2009, 2015), this study seeks not only to provide a fresh perspective and deep understanding of the current research field but also to define and elaborate on the topic in a broader academic context, as highlighted by Kaufman et al. (2016).

The review process was carefully divided into two stages to ensure comprehensiveness and precision. The first stage focused on the construction of a document atlas (Hallinger, 2013; Hallinger & Kovačević, 2019), involving extensive data collection on the country distribution of the application of affective design methods in multimedia learning, data sources (covering various databases and repositories), language diversity, publication volume, and trends in the topic over time. Key descriptors and specific criteria for document inclusion and exclusion were defined, and an efficient search and classification strategy was developed, using a combination of Boolean operators to accurately locate the target documents.

The second phase involved a more in-depth thematic analysis (Crowe et al., 2015), where the selected literature was carefully evaluated and selected according to rigorous peer review criteria (Sarthou, 2016). This process ensured the academic rigor and reliability of the review content.

The core objective of this study is to clearly define and elaborate on the concept of emotional design in multimedia learning through a systematic review. To this end, five key research questions were designed as a guide, and the research process was refined into three closely linked stages: planning, execution, and reporting. In the planning stage, evaluation indicators were carefully selected, and clear criteria for inclusion and exclusion of literature were established, laying a solid foundation for the subsequent work. In the implementation phase, the literature was meticulously screened and reviewed in strict accordance with established criteria to ensure that each included document could provide valuable insights for the review. Finally, in the reporting stage, the selected literature was comprehensively analyzed and discussed, and the relevant research results on emotional design in multimedia learning were systematically presented. The paper comprehensively summarizes the research characteristics, participant characteristics, multimedia learning materials, learning fields, research methods, emotional state parameters, emotional design techniques, emotional measurement tools, and data collection methods.

Through this systematic and comprehensive review process, this study not only contributes new knowledge to the field of emotional design in multimedia learning but also provides valuable references and insights for subsequent research.

2.1 Search Sources

We selected six well-known and comprehensive academic databases to search the literature for the most significant research on emotional design in multimedia learning: Web of Science, ERIC, Scopus, Google Scholar, and CNKI. These databases are renowned for their extensive literature coverage, high-quality content, advanced search capabilities, interdisciplinary nature, and high recognition in the academic community, making them indispensable reference tools for researchers seeking primary sources (Frankel et al.). Given the constraints of time and the complexity of comprehensively reviewing all historical research, our systematic review strategy focuses on these selected high-quality databases to ensure timeliness and depth of analysis.

Keywords such as "creative metacognition," "student," "creative performance," and "education" were used in the literature search (de Acedo Lizarraga & de Acedo Baquedano, 2013; Puente-Diaz & Cavazos-Arroyo, 2018; Kavousi et al., 2020; Sidi et al., 2020; Urban & Urban, 2023). The studies included in the review were selected based on criteria such as relevance to the topic, empirical research design, and publication in peer-reviewed journals. Both qualitative and quantitative research were considered to ensure a holistic view of the topic. The analysis involved synthesizing research findings to identify common themes and disagreements in the literature. The search strategy strictly followed the guidelines of the Preferred Reporting Items for Systematic Reviews and Meta-Analyses (PRISMA) (Moher et al., 2009), which provide a standardized and structured framework for the development and reporting of systematic reviews, effectively improving the transparency, integrity, and reliability of the results.

The records retrieved from the above databases were rigorously screened according to pre-established inclusion and exclusion criteria (see Table 1). This screening process was designed to ensure that only studies meeting specific criteria were included in the review, namely original and empirical studies in multimedia learning that involve emotional design. Non-empirical literature, such as conference papers, dissertations/abstracts, book chapters, review articles, meta-analyses, or reviews, were excluded to ensure the review content's direct relevance and research depth. Through this detailed process, we selected high-quality studies closely related to emotional design in multimedia learning, laying a solid foundation for the subsequent systematic review.

2.2 Study Selection Process

After an extensive literature search, we initially collected 126 articles on the influence of creative metacognition on creative performance from six authoritative databases: Web of Science, ERIC, Scopus, Google Scholar, and CNKI (see Figure 1). This preliminary screening provided a substantial database for further analysis.

Table 1. Inclusion and exclusion criteria

Inclusion criteria	Exclusion criteria
The studies must be conducted on creative metacognition and student's creative performance	The research work is not be related to the creative metacognition and student's creative performance.
The studies must be original and empirical	The studies must not be conference papers, dissertations/ thesis, book chapters, review, meta-analysis, or commentary article.
The research area of the articles should focus on education.	The research area of the articles should not be outside of education, such as engineering or marketing.
The articles must be full-text	The full version of the publication is not available.
The articles should have been published in journals that WOS, Scopus, Google Scholar, CNKI databases indexed	The study is listed in another database.

However, a closer examination of the literature collection revealed the presence of 25 duplicated articles, likely due to cross-inclusion between different databases or multiple publications of the same study. To ensure the efficiency of the review, these duplicates were excluded, resulting in 101 articles for further screening (see Fig. 1).

Figure 1. **PRISMA flow diagram (Moher et al., 2009)**

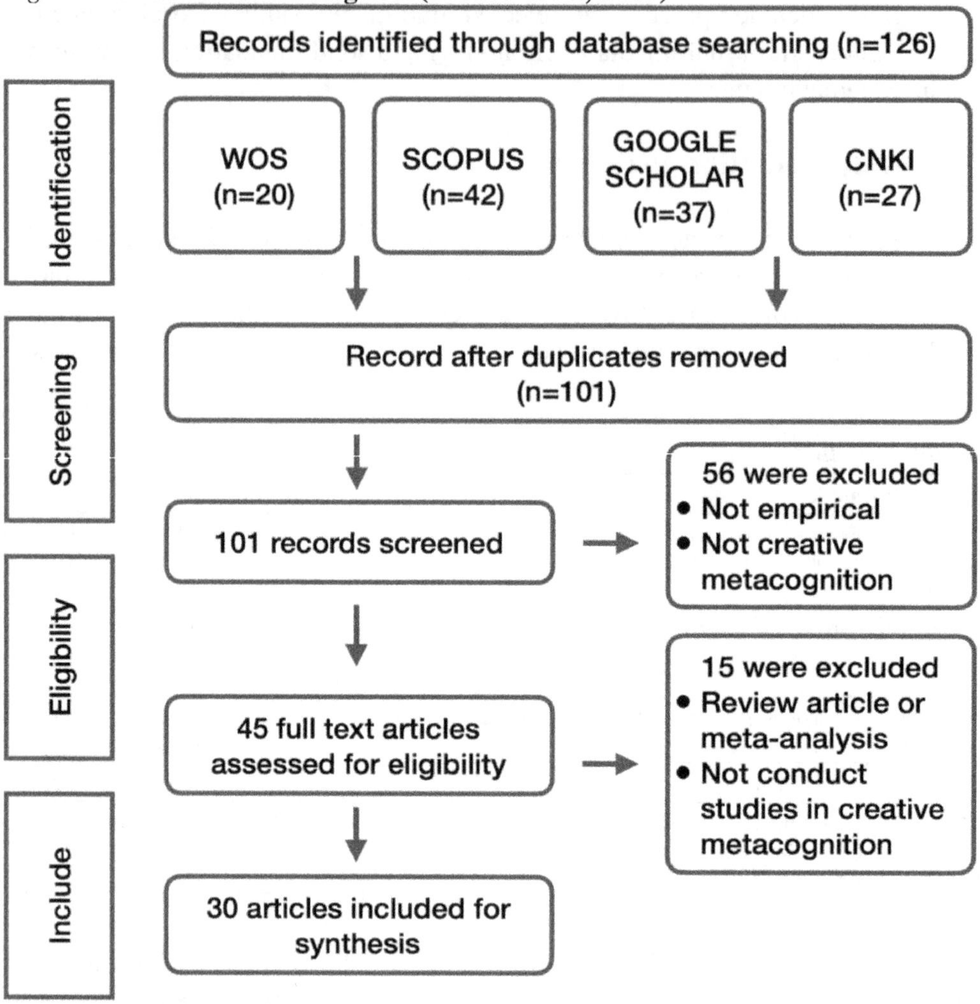

The remaining 101 articles were meticulously evaluated in the subsequent review phase according to the preset inclusion and exclusion criteria (see Table 2). This rigorous screening led to the elimination of 56 ineligible articles that either did not fall under the category of empirical research or did not directly address the application of emotional design to multimedia learning. This ensured that the articles included in the review were closely aligned with the research topic.

Following this selection process, 45 articles remained for final inspection. At this stage, more stringent review standards were applied to ensure that each article provided valuable insights for the review. Consequently, another 15 articles were excluded: 5 for not exploring creative metacognition in depth and ten for being review articles or meta-analyses rather than direct empirical studies.

To ensure the comprehensiveness and completeness of the literature search, backward and forward search techniques were employed to trace and search the citations and follow-up studies of the remaining articles. However, this search yielded only some new articles that met the inclusion criteria.

In summary, after several rounds of rigorous screening and evaluation, 30 articles were ultimately selected for the systematic review (see Fig.1). These articles represent the latest research findings on the impact of creative metacognition on creative performance and provide robust data support for further exploration of this topic.

Table 2. The countries where research articles on creative metacognition and creative performance are conducted

Continent	Country	*N*
America 36.67%	United States	6
	Mexico	5
Europe 33.32%	Czech	4
	Austria	3
	Turkey	1
	Spain	1
	Poland	1
Asia 26.67%	China	2
	South Korea	2
	India	1
	Israel	3
Oceania 3.33%	Australia	1

3. RESULTS

3.1 Study Characteristics

In addressing the first research question, the characteristics of studies examining the influence of creative metacognition theory on creative performance are analyzed. The results encompass the year of publication, country of study, participant characteristics, type of measurement, and study methodology.

3.1.1 Year

The influence of creative metacognition theory on creative performance was first investigated in 2013. Most studies (N=19) have been published within the last five years, with the highest number of papers published in 2023 (see Fig. 2).

3.1.2 Countries

Most studies on the impact of creative metacognition theory on creative performance have been conducted in the Americas (37%), followed by Europe (32%), Asia (17%), and Oceania (3%) (see figure; Table 2). The United States is not only the first country to study creative metacognition but also has the most significant number of studies on the topic (Anderson et al., 2020; Anderson & Graham, 2021; Anderson & Haney, 2021; Kaufman et al., 2016; Kavousi et al., 2020; Liu, 2023) (see Fig. 3).

3.1.3 Participant Characteristics

In the reviewed literature, the smallest number of participants was 23, and the largest was 500. Most studies involved college students (n=18). Participants in the other studies included secondary school students (13.3%), primary school students (10%), adults (10%), teachers (3.3%), and kindergarten children (3.3%) (see Fig. 4). The educational level of the participants is predominantly at the university level.

3.1.4 Research Content

The factors influencing creative metacognition theory on creative performance are numerous and complex.

Figure 2. **The distribution of creative metacognition and creative performance by year**

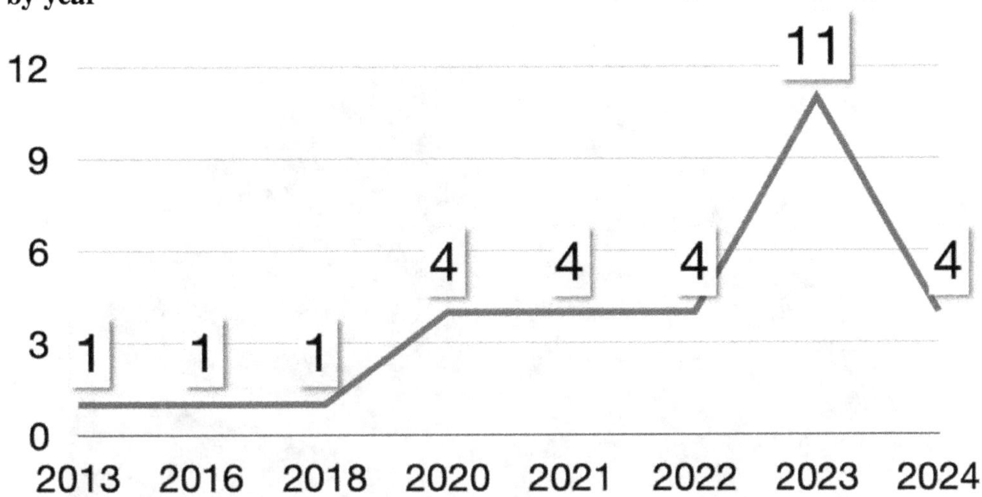

Figure 3. **The countries where research articles on creative metacognition and creative performance are conducted**

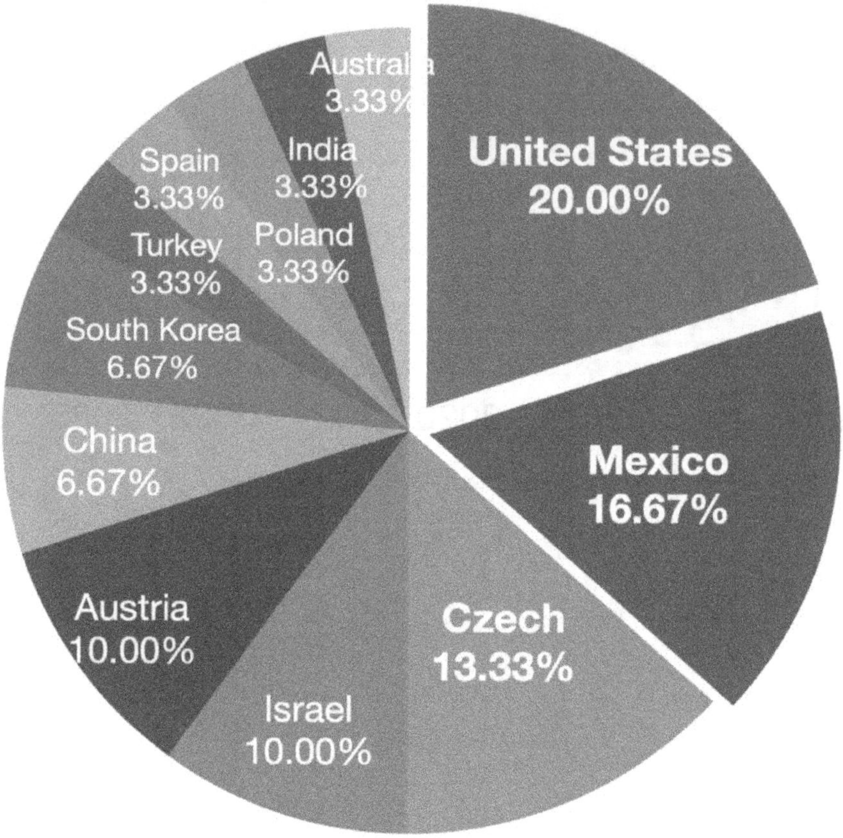

Figure 4. **The education level of participants in the reviewed studies**

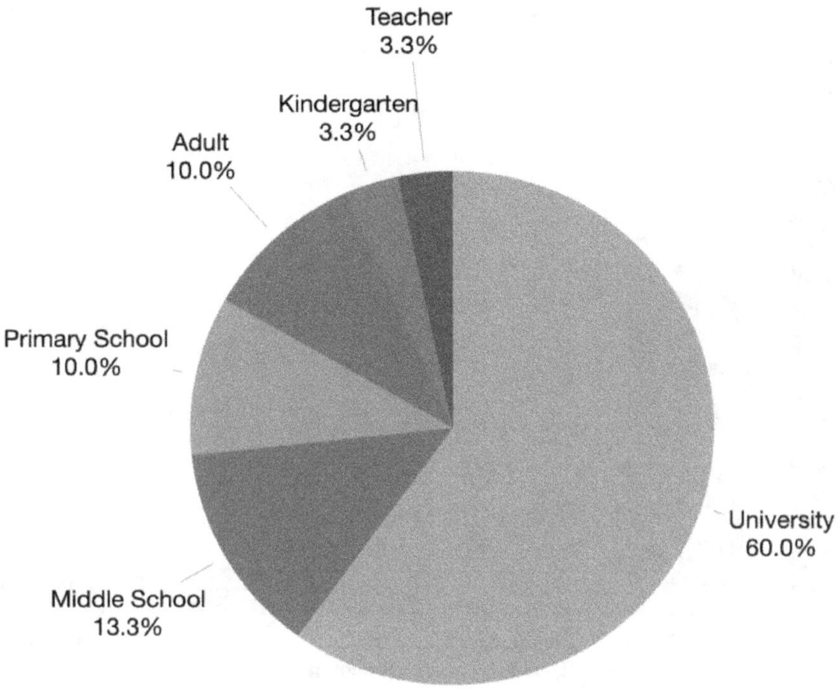

When creative metacognition theory is treated as an independent or dependent variable, it directly or indirectly influences creative performance. Most papers discussed the direct impact of creative metacognition on creative performance (n=12)

Figure 5. **Creative metacognition and creative performance variables in the reviewed studies**

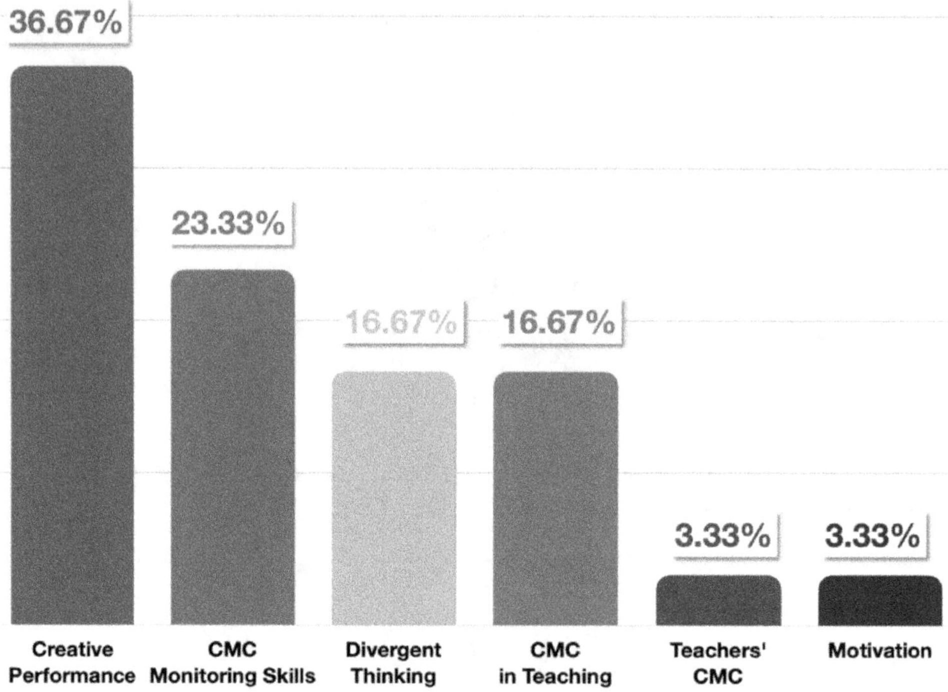

and the effect of the accuracy of metacognitive monitoring skills on creative metacognition and creative performance (n=7). Other studies examined the effect of divergent thinking on creative metacognition and creative performance (n=5). The indirect effects on creative performance were also explored. A few articles investigated how creative metacognition enhances students' creative performance in educational settings (n=5), the influence of teachers with creative metacognition on students' creative performance (n=1), and the impact of intrinsic and extrinsic motivation (n=1) (see Fig. 5).

3.2 Creative Metacognitive State Parameters

In the study of the influence of creative metacognition theory on creative performance, creative metacognition theory is considered both an independent and a dependent variable. The second research question analyzes the variables influencing creative metacognition and creative performance. When creative metacognition is taken as the dependent variable, parameters such as divergent thinking, semantic association, risk-taking spirit, and openness to experience are examined for their effects on creative metacognition. Five articles have specifically explored the impact of divergent thinking on creative metacognition by measuring these parameters.

Conversely, when creative metacognition is used as an independent variable, it primarily focuses on its influence on creative performance. Researchers predominantly emphasize metacognitive monitoring skills, which can directly affect creative performance. These skills encompass parameters such as creative potential, creative ability, creative thinking ability, intelligence, age, and ease of idea generation. A total of 11 studies have investigated the direct and indirect effects of these parameters on creative performance.

3.3 Creative Metacognition in Teaching

This section addresses the third research question by presenting findings on applying creative metacognition in teaching. The reviewed studies demonstrate that metacognitive knowledge and metacognitive monitoring within creative metacognition significantly influence course design (n = 5). Researchers have implemented creative training programs ranging from 2 to 4 weeks, primarily targeting art and design disciplines. These programs include architectural design (Kavousi et al., 2020), information design (Ji & Xue, 2022), creative screenwriting (McVeigh, 2023), innovation courses (Chou et al., 2023), and visual art appreciation (Liu, 2023). Five studies applied creative metacognition theory in educational settings, testing the effects of metacognitive knowledge and metacognitive judgment skills on students' creative performance.

Creative design exercises conducted before class have been analyzed and discussed (Kavousi et al., 2020; McVeigh, 2023), enabling students to reflect on creative knowledge and content, fostering an understanding and appreciation of their creativity. Students can enhance their metacognitive judgment skills by analyzing and introducing the creative process's stages, essential elements, and fundamental concepts. Such pre-class tests allow teachers to provide feedback to students, and positive, accurate feedback can influence students' self-belief and self-efficacy, thereby impacting their subsequent creative performance in the course. One strategy researchers employ involves administering creative-level tests and creative-thinking-level tests before class (Ji & Xue, 2022). This approach encourages students to consciously utilize creative metacognition's regulatory and monitoring roles, reflecting on and understanding their creative potential and creative thinking abilities through the level tests. Students can then use their acquired knowledge and experience to identify their creative perspectives, continually optimizing their creative performance.

Similarly, employing concise and open guidance strategies, along with "thinking out loud" strategies in teaching, enables students to consciously or unconsciously monitor the outcomes of each strategy in the creative process. This helps them identify successful strategies and the contexts in which each strategy is most suitable (Kavousi et al., 2020). Developing theme-based exercises for students is also a crucial aspect of instructional design. By reminding students that they can complete relevant exercises in various ways (Kavousi et al., 2020), teachers can provide ample practice time for students to maximize the use of strategies such as divergent thinking and brainstorming (Chou et al., 2023), generating more creative ideas.

Moreover, students' self-analysis and self-assessment after completing relevant exercises are linked to the level of metacognitive skills within creative metacognition theory. Requiring students to submit an assessment report after completing the exercises (McVeigh et al., 2023) can positively influence their creative metacognitive abilities and creative performance. Some studies have adopted a more detailed metacognitive analysis method of creativity (Liu, 2023), enabling a comprehensive self-analysis of creative works from four perspectives: the nature of creativity, the costs and benefits of creativity, self-awareness of the advantages and limitations of creativity, and situational awareness of creative performance. The greater the nature and scope of creativity's influence, the greater the benefits and costs of creativity. This comprehensive self-reflection on creative works effectively enhances students' creative metacognitive knowledge and abilities (Liu, 2023).

3.4 Measurement of Relevant Parameters Affecting Creative Metacognition

In the reviewed studies on creative metacognition and creative performance, participants' parameters were measured through various tests. The test methods for divergent thinking and creative performance used in the study are shown in Figure 7.

The Alternate Use Task (AUT) is the most widely employed measure of divergent thinking (n = 9; Guilford, 1967). This method is based on Guilford's (1950) three-dimensional model of intelligence, which primarily assesses four elements of divergent thinking: originality, fluency, flexibility, and elaboration. Participants were asked to generate as many unusual or creative uses for everyday objects (e.g., bricks, paper clips) as possible within a given timeframe, either orally (M. Urban & Urban, 2023) or in writing (Kenett et al., 2023; Rominger et al., 2022), with feedback provided on their ideas. Additionally, the Creative Imagination Test (n = 1; Artola Gonz ez et al., 2012) assessed participants' imagination levels through storytelling, drawing, and problem-solving activities. Nine studies indicated that divergent thinking ability can enhance creative metacognitive monitoring ability and positively impact creative performance.

A total of 16 articles asked participants to rate their creative ideas, and the consensus assessment technique (CAT) (n = 16; Amabile, 1996) required experts to rate these ideas on a specified scale (Anderson & Haney, 2021). Both participants and experts rated works on a scale of 1 (low creativity) to 5 (high creativity), with some studies using a scale of 0 (poor) to 10 (excellent) (Puente-D z et al., 2022). All 16 studies demonstrated that while students tended to underestimate their creative abilities, expert assessments provided a more objective measure of creativity.

Five articles utilized the Torrance Tests of Creative Thinking (TTCT; Torrance, 1974), which primarily examine individual divergent thinking achievements, including divergent thinking ability, imagination, and the ability to break conventions. The TTCT consists of three sets of creativity scales: verbal creativity tests, product transformation tests, and the unusual uses test. The drawing creativity test required participants to complete an unfinished pattern or create a composition based on a specific figure. Finally, the creative thinking mode involving sounds and words was assessed through audio tapes, where participants were asked to write down the objects or activities they associated with the sounds.

3.5 Measurement of Creative Metacognition in Teaching

Of the 30 studies reviewed, 11 focused on teaching-related, student-related research that examined creative performance by measuring relevant concepts within the metacognitive theory of creativity. The specific scales of these related concepts include the Creative Metacognition Scale, Creative Self-Summary Scale (SSCS) (McVeigh et al., 2023), Creativity Scale (Chou et al., 2023), Metacognition Scale (Chou et al., 2023), Creative Motivation Scale (Taylor & Kaufman,2021), Metacognition Scale (MP) Questionnaire (Mevarech & Paz-Baruch, 2022), and OSF Questionnaire (Lebuda & Benedek, 2024). One-third of the studies investigated the effects of these parameters on creative metacognition and creative performance. Results from three studies indicated that creative metacognitive feelings had both direct and indirect positive effects by enhancing creative self-efficacy. Additionally, it was found that children's self-assessments demonstrated accurate discriminative abilities in both verbal and visual domains, enabling them to distinguish between different levels of creativity. One study found no relationship between gender and creativity or metacognition.

Two studies employed various scales to measure creative self-efficacy. One study utilized the Creative Self-Efficacy component of the Creative Self Simple Scale developed by Karwowski (2012). Another study developed four items for assessment, using a 0-100 scale to evaluate individuals' judgment of their ideas. The results showed that enhancing students' creative self-efficacy in teaching positively impacted creative performance.

Creative metacognition data from 10 studies were collected through offline testing and data collection before and after offline courses or with students. Two studies collected data via online web testing, and one study employed EEG testing for analysis. Research indicated that during creative evaluation (compared to creative generation), participants with higher monitoring skills exhibited reduced cognitive control or working memory load.

Four studies examined and measured creative metacognitive knowledge and creative metacognitive monitoring. In two of these studies, self-developed scales were used to design OSF lists and creative metacognitive level tests, measured using a four-item, 5-point Likert scale (Ji & Xue, 2022). One of these studies utilized the Metacognitive Scale developed by Song et al. (2020), which evaluated metacognitive activity through six measures. Participants indicated the extent to which they had engaged in the following activities in the past 3 to 4 days (1 = I have never done this, 5 = I have always done this): guiding and monitoring student behavior, contemplating strategies to enhance student skills, and analyzing interviews to improve subsequent performance.

4. DISCUSSION AND CONCLUSION

In recent years, there has been growing interest in the research of creative metacognition and creative performance. This interest has resulted in numerous studies with varying outcomes by applying creative metacognition theory (Anderson et al., 2020; Rominger et al., 2022; Liu, 2023; Woo & Lee, 2024; Lebuda & Benedek, 2024; Urban & Urban, 2024).

Addressing the first research question, an overarching perspective is presented through the characteristics of the studies examined in this review. These characteristics are analyzed in terms of year of publication, continent and country, participants, research methods, materials, and areas of study. The year 2023 is noted to have the highest number of published papers. The analysis indicates a growing interest in creative representation within creative metacognition, particularly in recent years. The increase in published papers since 2020 suggests that this is an emerging area of research with potential implications for educational practice and theory. Most creative metacognition and creative performance reviews have been conducted in the Americas, Europe, and Asia. The United States has the largest number of studies on the impact of creative metacognition theory on creative performance (Kaufman et al., 2016; Anderson et al., 2020; Kavousi et al., 2020; Anderson & Haney, 2021; Anderson & Graham, 2021; Liu, 2023). Urban and Urban have extensively discussed the issue of creative metacognition in several articles in the Czech Republic (Urban & Urban, 2021; Urban & Urban, 2023; Urban & Urban, 2024). The predominance of studies conducted in the Americas, followed by Europe and Asia, underscores the global nature of creative metacognition research. However, the concentration of studies in specific regions or countries, notably the United States, Mexico, and the Czech Republic, raises questions about the generalizability of the findings across different cultural contexts. This highlights the need for more diverse representation in future studies. The regional focus of these studies limits the ability to make cross-cultural comparisons or interpret the findings broadly. Conducting research in various regions and cultural contexts will be crucial for expanding the scope of future investigations.

In the study of creative metacognition and creative performance, college students are the predominant participants, indicating a focus on higher education backgrounds and learning environments. However, studies involving preschool children, elementary school students, middle school students, and adults suggest that the research encompasses a broader and more diverse group of learners. Almost all reviewed studies emphasize the creative performance of research content. Notably, there are few studies on teachers' creative metacognition and motivation. Future research could explore creative metacognition in other target populations, such as teachers, to more fully understand the effects of creative metacognition on different subjects.

The second research question of this study focuses on analyzing the parameters of creative metacognition and creative performance. Divergent thinking and metacognitive monitoring skills emerge as the two most significant parameters. Notably, the parameters related to divergent thinking in the literature also encompass semantic association, risk-taking spirit, and openness to experience. Skills associated with metacognitive monitoring include creative potential, creative ability, creative thinking ability, intelligence, age, and the ease of idea generation. These concepts or parameters vary in structure, scope, and limits. The parameters examined in the study of creative metacognition and creative performance are not uniform, necessitating a detailed explanation of the definitions, concepts, and applications of divergent thinking and metacognitive monitoring skills. Divergent thinking is a fundamental element in the process of creative production. Studies have shown that divergent thinking, creative metacognition, and creative performance are closely related (Kaufman et al., 2016). The analysis of divergent thinking parameters underscores its measurement's complexity. Using assessment techniques such as the Alternate Use Task, Torrance Tests of Creative Thinking, consensus assessment techniques, and creative imagination tests indicates a reliance on divergent thinking measures. Future research could explore the validity and reliability of different measurement tools and their impact on understanding creative metacognition and creative performance.

Various techniques were employed to examine the accuracy of metacognitive monitoring skills. The primary methods used in the reviewed studies were in vivo and interindividual monitoring. Among the parameters that affect intra-individual monitoring are creative potential, creative ability, creative thinking ability, intelligence, age, and the ease with which ideas are generated. Creative potential and creative ability refer to the level of an individual's creative capability, reflected through a series of self-assessments. Creative thinking ability can be divided into growth and fixed mindsets. The cultivation of these mindsets is closely related to participants' metacognitive experiences. Participants need to perceive the importance of evaluation, encouraging more individuals to adopt a growth mindset. Studies have shown that a growth mindset and metacognitive experiences, such as creative self-efficacy, positively impact creative metacognition. Research related to intelligence has indicated that more creative individuals are better at recognizing their creative ideas and possess higher metacognitive monitoring skills. At the same time, less intelligent subjects significantly overestimate their creativity. Research suggests that intelligence is related not only to the production of ideas (e.g., Beaty & Silvia, 2012; Beaty et al., 2014) and creative achievement (Karwowski et al., 2017) but also to sufficiently accurate self-assessments of the creativity of ideas. Creative metacognition theory demonstrates different results in various teaching environments. Several studies on integrating creative metacognition and education have pointed out that incorporating creative metacognition theory into instructional design positively impacts students' creative performance. For example, students should engage in in-depth discussions about the nature of creativity before instruction and conduct self-assessments of their creative levels (Ji & Xue, 2022). Direct guidance should be provided during instruction, along with timely feedback, and the teaching strategy of thinking aloud should be adopted (McVeigh et al., 2023), enabling students to learn to self-monitor the creative process. Post-instruction, students should analyze and evaluate their work (Chou et al., 2023) to clearly understand their creative strengths and weaknesses and the suitability of the strategies and techniques used in their work in context (Liu, 2023).

In addressing the fourth research question, an analysis of measures used in creative metacognition studies reveals several key findings. The review article explores the effects of creative performance by assessing divergent thinking, metacognitive monitoring skills, and creative metacognition in educational settings. For divergent thinking, multipurpose tasks, developed based on Guilford's (1950) three-dimensional model of intelligence, are the most frequently utilized measure in the reviewed studies, followed by the Torrance Tests of Creative Thinking. Nearly half of the studies also employed consensus assessment techniques to evaluate metacognitive monitoring skills. The most frequently selected variables were creative performance, creative metacognitive monitoring skills, and divergent thinking. Results from nine studies indicate that divergent thinking ability can enhance learners' creative metacognitive ability. Sixteen project research results suggest that learners' intra-monitoring skills may depend on their intelligence, creative thinking ability, and creative potential, with younger students more likely to underestimate their creativity (Kaufman et al., 2016). Some studies propose that age does not significantly affect learners' monitoring skills (Mevarech & Paz-Baruch). Conversely, other research indicates that preschool children overestimate their poor performance. This situation improves with educational development up to the university level, where undergraduates are likelier to underestimate their performance (Urban & Urban, 2021). Five studies demonstrate that intra-monitoring skills can effectively enhance learners' creative metacognition (Rominger et al., 2022), positively impacting creative performance (Lebuda & Benedek, 2024). One study found no relationship between gender and creativity and metacognition.

The effect of creative performance in educational environments is examined using various scales and measurement methods, including the Creative Metacognition Scale, the Creative Self-Summary Scale (SSCS), the Creativity Scale, the Metacognition Scale, the Innovation Motivation Scale, the Meta-process (MP) questionnaire, and the OSF questionnaire. Measurement methods primarily include pre- and post-course offline tests, online web tests, and EEG tests and analyses. These scales and measures assist researchers in understanding the effectiveness of creative metacognition in educational settings on aspects of students' creative performance, such as creative metacognition emotion, creative self-efficacy, creative thinking, and creative level. The research conclusions indicate that creative metacognitive feelings can enhance students' creative metacognitive emotions, such as creative self-belief and creative self-efficacy, as measured by the Creative Self-Summary Scale and the Creative Metacognition Scale. These metacognitive emotions can positively affect students' creative performance (Anderson & Haney, 2021). One study found that courses incorporating creative metacognition theory can impact students' creative performance, not their creative self-efficacy. Two studies suggest that the application of creative metacognition theory significantly affects students' creative performance in subjects related to visual and language arts (Kaufman et al., 2016; Jamal et al., 2023). Additionally, a study using EEG monitoring indicated that visual content better stimulates brain activation associated with creative potential (Rominger et al., 2022).

5. IMPLICATION FOR FUTURE RESEARCH

Many studies have emphasized the influence of creative metacognition on creative performance. This section provides suggestions for future research. This study systematically reviews creative metacognition and creative performance, identifying research gaps. Most of the studies reviewed were conducted with higher education students. Studying the knowledge-building processes of young learners is crucial, as their characteristics differ from those of adults. It is believed that metacognitive monitoring skills in creative metacognition have a more significant impact on young learners. A limitation of the current research on creative metacognition is the predominant focus on higher education students, which complicates the generalization of findings to other populations. Repeating these studies across different age groups is necessary (de Acedo Lizarraga & de Acedo Baquedano, 2013; Urban & Urban, 2023). The self-judgment ability of younger age groups differs from that of older age groups, with the former being more influenced by external factors. Research on younger age groups will significantly contribute to understanding creative metacognition. Additionally, investigating the learning characteristics of different groups, including those with learning disabilities, is suggested. Research on creative metacognition is primarily conducted in the Americas and Europe (Mevarech & Paz-Baruch, 2022). As students' creativity is influenced by culture and environment, future research conducted in diverse cultural contexts will be essential to assess variations in research findings. Conducting research in different regions and cultural contexts is valuable for broadening the scope of future studies.

Future research should incorporate more empirical studies examining the integration of instructional design related to creative metacognition in educational settings. Additionally, it is recommended that in-line measures be employed for assessing creative metacognition (Mevarech & Paz-Baruch, 2022). There is also a need to investigate the impact of digital technology on creative metacognition and creative expression. Although some studies have utilized digital tools such as tablets, digital courseware (Zhou et al., 2024), and web-based games (Wang et al., 2022), these studies have primarily demonstrated that digital games can achieve various STEM learning objectives, enhance students' motivation, and improve their conceptual understanding, while also fostering problem-solving skills (Hwang et al., 2012). However, further research is required to explore the role of educational technology, particularly within digital and blended learning environments, in enhancing creative metacognition and performance.

REFERENCES

Amabile, T. M. (1996). *Creativity and innovation in organizations* (Vol. 5). Harvard Business School Boston. https://edisciplinas.usp.br/pluginfile.php/4927750/mod_resource/content/0/Creativity%20and%20Innovation%20in%20Organizations.pdf

Anderson, R. C., & Graham, M. (2021). Creative potential in flux: The leading role of originality during early adolescent development. *Thinking Skills and Creativity*, 40, 100816. DOI: 10.1016/j.tsc.2021.100816

Anderson, R. C., & Haney, M. (2021). Reflection in the creative process of early adolescents: The mediating roles of creative metacognition, self-efficacy, and self-concept. *Psychology of Aesthetics, Creativity, and the Arts*, 15(4), 612–626. DOI: 10.1037/aca0000324

Anderson, R. C., Haney, M., Pitts, C., Porter, L., & Bousselot, T. (2020). "Mistakes Can be Beautiful": Creative Engagement in Arts Integration for Early Adolescent Learners. *The Journal of Creative Behavior*, 54(3), 662–675. DOI: 10.1002/jocb.401

Artola González, T., Barraca, J., Mosteiro Pintor, P., Ancillo Gómez, I., Poveda, B., & Sánchez, N. (2012). *PIC-A Prueba de Imaginación Creativa para Adultos*. http://repositorio.ucjc.edu/handle/20.500.12020/435

Beaty, R. E., Benedek, M., Wilkins, R. W., Jauk, E., Fink, A., Silvia, P. J., Hodges, D. A., Koschutnig, K., & Neubauer, A. C. (2014). Creativity and the default network: A functional connectivity analysis of the creative brain at rest. *Neuropsychologia*, 64, 92–98. DOI: 10.1016/j.neuropsychologia.2014.09.019 PMID: 25245940

Beaty, R. E., & Silvia, P. J. (2012). Why do ideas get more creative across time? An executive interpretation of the serial order effect in divergent thinking tasks. *Psychology of Aesthetics, Creativity, and the Arts*, 6(4), 309–319. DOI: 10.1037/a0029171

Benedek, M., Nordtvedt, N., Jauk, E., Koschmieder, C., Pretsch, J., Krammer, G., & Neubauer, A. C. (2016). Assessment of creativity evaluation skills: A psychometric investigation in prospective teachers. *Thinking Skills and Creativity*, 21, 75–84. DOI: 10.1016/j.tsc.2016.05.007

Bowen, R. S., Picard, D. R., Verberne-Sutton, S., & Brame, C. J. (2018). Incorporating Student Design in an HPLC Lab Activity Promotes Student Metacognition and Argumentation. *Journal of Chemical Education*, 95(1), 108–115. DOI: 10.1021/acs.jchemed.7b00258

Chou, C.-M., Shen, T.-C., Shen, T.-C., & Shen, C.-H. (2023). The impact of CIE education integrated with the BIG 6 teaching strategy on students' innovative motivation, creativity, metacognition, and self-perceived employability. *Thinking Skills and Creativity*, 48, 101287. DOI: 10.1016/j.tsc.2023.101287

Crowe, M., Inder, M., & Porter, R. (2015). Conducting qualitative research in mental health: Thematic and content analyses. *The Australian and New Zealand Journal of Psychiatry*, 49(7), 616–623. DOI: 10.1177/0004867415582053 PMID: 25900973

de Acedo Lizarraga, M. L. S., & de Acedo Baquedano, M. T. S. (2013). How creative potential is related to metacognition. *European Journal of Education and Psychology*, 6(2), 69–81.

Dori, Y. J., Avargil, S., Kohen, Z., & Saar, L. (2018). Context-based learning and metacognitive prompts for enhancing scientific text comprehension. *International Journal of Science Education*, 40(10), 1198–1220. DOI: 10.1080/09500693.2018.1470351

Giacumo, L. A., & Savenye, W. (2020). Asynchronous discussion forum design to support cognition: Effects of rubrics and instructor prompts on learner's critical thinking, achievement, and satisfaction. *Educational Technology Research and Development*, 68(1), 37–66. DOI: 10.1007/s11423-019-09664-5

Guilford, J. P. (1950). *Fundamental statistics in psychology and education*. https://psycnet.apa.org/record/1950-04974-000

Guilford, J. P. (1967). Creativity: Yesterday, Today and Tomorrow. *The Journal of Creative Behavior*, 1(1), 3–14. DOI: 10.1002/j.2162-6057.1967.tb00002.x

Guo, Y., Lin, S., Acar, S., Jin, S., Xu, X., Feng, Y., & Zeng, Y. (2022). Divergent Thinking and Evaluative Skill: A Meta-Analysis. *The Journal of Creative Behavior*, 56(3), 432–448. DOI: 10.1002/jocb.539

Hallinger, P. (2013). A conceptual framework for systematic reviews of research in educational leadership and management. *Journal of Educational Administration*, 51(2), 126–149. DOI: 10.1108/09578231311304670

Hallinger, P., & Kovačević, J. (2019). A Bibliometric Review of Research on Educational Administration: Science Mapping the Literature, 1960 to 2018. *Review of Educational Research*, 89(3), 335–369. DOI: 10.3102/0034654319830380

Imran, M. (2019). Analysis of learning and teaching strategies in Surgery Module: A mixed methods study. *JPMA. The Journal of the Pakistan Medical Association*, 69(9), 1287–1292. PMID: 31511713

Ji, Y., & Xue, M. (2022). Relationship Between Design Metacognition and Design Thinking. *School of Information and Communication Engineering, Beijing University of Posts and Telecommunications, 24*(01), 85-94+112.

Jia, X., Li, W., & Cao, L. (2019). The Role of Metacognitive Components in Creative Thinking. *Frontiers in Psychology*, 10, 2404. DOI: 10.3389/fpsyg.2019.02404 PMID: 31708842

Karwowski, M., Czerwonka, M., & Kaufman, J. C. (2020). Does intelligence strengthen creative metacognition? *Psychology of Aesthetics, Creativity, and the Arts*, 14(3), 353–360. DOI: 10.1037/aca0000208

Kaufman, J. C., & Beghetto, R. A. (2013). In Praise of Clark Kent: Creative Metacognition and the Importance of Teaching Kids When (Not) to Be Creative. *Roeper Review*, 35(3), 155–165. DOI: 10.1080/02783193.2013.799413

Kaufman, J. C., & Beghetto, R. A. (2014). Creativity in the schools: Renewed interest and promising new directions. In *Handbook of positive psychology in schools* (pp. 165–175). Routledge., https://api.taylorfrancis.com/content/chapters/edit/download?identifierName=doi&identifierValue=10.4324/9780203106525-13&type=chapterpdf

Kaufman, J. C., Beghetto, R. A., & Watson, C. (2016). Creative metacognition and self-ratings of creative performance: A 4-C perspective. *Learning and Individual Differences*, 51, 394–399. DOI: 10.1016/j.lindif.2015.05.004

Kavousi, S., Miller, P. A., & Alexander, P. A. (2020). Modeling metacognition in design thinking and design making. *International Journal of Technology and Design Education*, 30(4), 709–735. DOI: 10.1007/s10798-019-09521-9

Kenett, Y. N., Gooz, N., & Ackerman, R. (2023). The Role of Semantic Associations as a Metacognitive Cue in Creative Idea Generation. *Journal of Intelligence*, 11(4), 59. DOI: 10.3390/jintelligence11040059 PMID: 37103244

Khasanah, A. N., Widoretno, S., & Sajidan, S. (2017). Effectiveness of Critical Thinking Indicator-Based Module in Empowering Student's Learning Outcome in Respiratory System Study Material. *Jurnal Pendidikan IPA Indonesia*, 6(1). Advance online publication. DOI: 10.15294/jpii.v6i1.8490

Kleinmintz, O. M., Ivancovsky, T., & Shamay-Tsoory, S. G. (2019). The two-fold model of creativity: The neural underpinnings of the generation and evaluation of creative ideas. *Current Opinion in Behavioral Sciences*, 27, 131–138. DOI: 10.1016/j.cobeha.2018.11.004

Liu, M. (2023). A self-case study of the female doctoral student's own creative metacognition on art expressions: Based on the theory of creative metacognition (CMC). *Thinking Skills and Creativity*, 48, 101292. DOI: 10.1016/j.tsc.2023.101292

McVeigh, M. (2023). A Creative Thinking and Writing Tool. The Creativity Metacognitive Framework. In M. McVeigh, *Screenwriting from the Inside Out* (pp. 179–186). Springer International Publishing. DOI: 10.1007/978-3-031-40520-4_9

Mevarech, Z. R., & Paz-Baruch, N. (2022). Meta-creativity: What is it and how does it relate to creativity? *Metacognition and Learning*, 17(2), 427–441. DOI: 10.1007/s11409-022-09290-2

Moher, D., Liberati, A., Tetzlaff, J., & Altman, D. G.PRISMA Group. (2009). Preferred reporting items for systematic reviews and meta-analyses: The PRISMA statement. *PLoS Medicine*, 6(7), e1000097. DOI: 10.1371/journal.pmed.1000097 PMID: 19621072

Pesout, O., & Nietfeld, J. L. (2021). How creative am I?: Examining judgments and predictors of creative performance. *Thinking Skills and Creativity*, 40, 100836. DOI: 10.1016/j.tsc.2021.100836

Plucker, J. A., Beghetto, R. A., & Dow, G. T. (2004). Why Isn't Creativity More Important to Educational Psychologists? Potentials, Pitfalls, and Future Directions in Creativity Research. *Educational Psychologist*, 39(2), 83–96. DOI: 10.1207/s15326985ep3902_1

Puente-Diaz, R., & Cavazos-Arroyo, J. (2018). Creative Metacognitive Feelings as a Source of Information for Creative Self-efficacy, Creativity Potential, Intrapersonal Idea Selection, and Task Enjoyment. *The Journal of Creative Behavior*, 54(3), 499–507. DOI: 10.1002/jocb.384

Puente-Díaz, R., Cavazos-Arroyo, J., Puerta-Sierra, L., & Vargas-Barrera, F. (2022). The contribution Openness to Experience and its two aspects to the explanation of idea generation, evaluation and selection: A metacognitive perspective. *Personality and Individual Differences*, 185, 111240. DOI: 10.1016/j.paid.2021.111240

Puente-Díaz, R., Cavazos-Arroyo, J., & Vargas-Barrera, F. (2021). Metacognitive feelings as a source of information in the evaluation and selection of creative ideas. *Thinking Skills and Creativity*, 39, 100767. DOI: 10.1016/j.tsc.2020.100767

Ritter, S. M., Damian, R. I., Simonton, D. K., van Baaren, R. B., Strick, M., Derks, J., & Dijksterhuis, A. (2012). Diversifying experiences enhance cognitive flexibility☆. *Journal of Experimental Social Psychology*, 48(4), 961–964. DOI: 10.1016/j.jesp.2012.02.009

Rominger, C., Benedek, M., Lebuda, I., Perchtold-Stefan, C. M., Schwerdtfeger, A. R., Papousek, I., & Fink, A. (2022). Functional brain activation patterns of creative metacognitive monitoring. *Neuropsychologia*, 177, 108416. DOI: 10.1016/j.neuropsychologia.2022.108416 PMID: 36343705

Runco, M. A., & Acar, S. (2012). Divergent Thinking as an Indicator of Creative Potential. *Creativity Research Journal*, 24(1), 66–75. DOI: 10.1080/10400419.2012.652929

Runco, M. A., & Dow, G. T. (2004). Assessing the Accuracy of Judgments of Originality on Three Divergent Thinking Tests. *Korean Journal of Thinking & Problem Solving*, 14(2), 5–14.

Runco, M. A., & Smith, W. R. (1992). Interpersonal and intrapersonal evaluations of creative ideas. *Personality and Individual Differences*, 13(3), 295–302. DOI: 10.1016/0191-8869(92)90105-X

Sarthou, N. F. (2016). Key Points of Discussion in Scientific Research Evaluation: Peer Review, Bibliometrics and Relevance. *Revista de Estudios Sociales*, 58(58), 76–86. DOI: 10.7440/res58.2016.06

Sidi, Y., Torgovitsky, I., Soibelman, D., Miron-Spektor, E., & Ackerman, R. (2020). You may be more original than you think: Predictable biases in self-assessment of originality. *Acta Psychologica*, 203, 103002. DOI: 10.1016/j.actpsy.2019.103002 PMID: 32004640

Song, L., Shi, J., Luo, P., Wei, W., Fang, Y., & Wang, Y. (2020). More Time Spent, More Job Search Success?: The Moderating Roles of Metacognitive Activities and Perceived Job Search Progress. *Journal of Career Assessment*, 28(1), 147–164. DOI: 10.1177/1069072719841575

Torrance, E. P. (1974). Differences Are Not Deficits. *Teachers College Record*, 75(4), 1–14. DOI: 10.1177/016146817407500403

Urban, K., & Urban, M. (2024). "I know my idea is original!" Creative metacognitive monitoring and regulation in kindergarten children. *Thinking Skills and Creativity*, 52, 101541. DOI: 10.1016/j.tsc.2024.101541

Urban, M., & Urban, K. (2021). Unskilled But Aware of It? Cluster Analysis of Creative Metacognition from Preschool Age to Early Adulthood. *The Journal of Creative Behavior*, 55(4), 937–945. DOI: 10.1002/jocb.499

Urban, M., & Urban, K. (2023). Orientation Toward Intrinsic Motivation Mediates the Relationship Between Metacognition and Creativity. *The Journal of Creative Behavior*, 57(1), 6–16. DOI: 10.1002/jocb.558

Woo, J., & Lee, S.-Y. (2024). The moderating effect of creative metacognition on adolescents' risk-taking in creative performance. *Asia Pacific Education Review*, 25(1), 99–115. DOI: 10.1007/s12564-024-09927-8

Zielińska, A., Forthmann, B., Lebuda, I., & Karwowski, M. (2023). Self-Regulation for Creative Activity: The Same or Different Across Domains? *Psychology of Aesthetics, Creativity, and the Arts*. Advance online publication. DOI: 10.1037/aca0000540

Chapter 14
Do Anthropomorphic Graphics in Multimedia Learning Materials Help Learning by Capturing Learners' Attention?

Jinya Liu
https://orcid.org/0009-0008-2433-4060
Universiti Sains Malaysia, Malaysia

Mageswaran Sanmugam
https://orcid.org/0000-0003-3313-4462
Universiti Sains Malaysia, Malaysia

ABSTRACT

This article explores the impact of using anthropomorphic graphics in multimedia learning materials on learners' attention allocation and learning outcomes. Anthropomorphic graphics refer to images that possess human-like characteristics, meaning they are described and conceived based on human traits(Salles et al., 2020). In the context of multimedia education, the integration of anthropomorphic graphics has been widely discussed as a means to enhance learners' attention and overall learning outcomes. This paper reviews multiple studies, summarizing the role of anthropomorphic graphics in attracting and maintaining students' attention, and whether this can improve learning outcomes. The authors hold that while the effect of anthropomorphic graphics on final learning outcomes is unclear, they positively influence student attention, deepen understanding, and facilitate knowledge transfer. Despite the uncertain impact on outcomes, their potential to enhance learning

DOI: 10.4018/979-8-3693-6745-2.ch014

effectiveness should not be overlooked.

I. INTRODUCTION

Artificial Intelligence (AI) has become a transformative force in today's world, bringing revolutionary changes to various fields, including education. The COVID-19 pandemic accelerated the shift towards remote and hybrid learning models, leading educational institutions to increasingly adopt digital tools and mobile applications to facilitate online education (Waang, 2023). These digital platforms, driven by AI, provide learning experiences that are significantly different from traditional methods, enhancing both accessibility and engagement for students.

AI is a broad field that encompasses subfields such as Human-Computer Interaction (HCI), intelligent systems, machine learning, deep learning, and more. Among these, HCI plays a crucial role in shaping the way intelligent systems interact with human users, including the design of intuitive and user-friendly interfaces (Zhang et al., 2018). In educational contexts, AI-driven tools need to focus on user interface design principles, visual learning variables, and overall user experience to ensure smooth interaction and engagement (Gong et al., 2017). The success of AI-based educational platforms relies not only on their technical sophistication but also on how effectively they engage students through well-designed interfaces (Guney, 2019).

One of the key concepts in interface design is ‘anthropomorphic design,’ where non-human elements are imbued with human-like characteristics (Lee et al., 2018). Anthropomorphism is not only prevalent in interface design but is also reflected in various ways across AI applications. For instance, robots and virtual assistants are often designed with human-like features to create a more intuitive and emotionally engaging user experience (Salles et al., 2020). This growing trend of anthropomorphism has raised important questions regarding its impact on user engagement, especially in the educational field. Research suggests that anthropomorphic elements can help build emotional connections with users, improving both user emotional experience, cognitive processes and learning outcomes (Blut et al., 2021; Y. Wang & Zheng, 2022).

Despite the widespread use of anthropomorphism in AI applications, there is relatively little research focusing on its impact within the field of education, specifically in multimedia learning environments. This study aims to fill that gap by exploring how anthropomorphic graphics influence learners' attention allocation in multimedia teaching materials. Attention allocation is critical to the learning process, as sustained attention is necessary for effective information processing and knowledge retention.

Therefore, this study seeks to address the following research question:

RQ1: Does the attention drawn by anthropomorphic graphics in multimedia learning materials help with learning?
RO1: Explore the impact of anthropomorphic graphics on learners' attention allocation in multimedia teaching materials.

The use of anthropomorphism in the interactive interfaces of education can partly be attributed to cognitive tools, which are intended to help students and users better understand complex concepts and technological devices. As the interaction between humans and computers becomes increasingly close and complex, the role of anthropomorphism in cognitive and behavioral processes becomes more important (Chamberlain et al., 2018).

Cognition involves a series of processes the brain undergoes when perceiving, understanding, processing, and storing information (Y. Wang & Zheng, 2022), with learning being a significant cognitive process. However, unlike traditional learning models, multimedia teaching is a form of instruction that integrates various media and technological means to support learning. As multimedia materials become more deeply integrated into the learning process, research on multimedia learning has also become increasingly refined. Researchers generally agree that adhering to cognitive principles of multimedia learning and designing multimedia learning experiences accordingly can improve learning (Mayer, 2009; Mayer & Fiorella, 2021; Renkl & Scheiter, 2017).

When researchers have sought to improve instruction by leveraging affective-motivational factors (Abrami et al., 1982; Garner et al., 1992; Kaplan & Pascoe, 1977; Yeager & Walton, 2011), the principle of affective design emerged, complementing the cognitive principles of multimedia learning (Brom, Stárková, et al., 2018). Currently, adding facial anthropomorphism to non-human graphic elements and/or incorporating pleasing colors in instructional presentations, animations, and web pages are popular affective design principles (Brom, Stárková, et al., 2018). A series of research findings indicate that integrating human characteristics and emotional elements into multimedia learning materials not only significantly enhances learners' emotional experiences but also improves memory retention and understanding of knowledge (Brom, Stárková, et al., 2018). These findings provide valuable information and support for our understanding and explanation of the widespread application of anthropomorphism in multimedia teaching.

II. LITERATURE REVIEW

2.1 Anthropomorphism in Multimedia Education

Anthropomorphism refers to attributing human-like characteristics, such as emotions, thoughts, and behaviors, to non-human objects or entities (Airenti, 2015; Epley et al., 2007). In the context of multimedia education, anthropomorphic design is used to enhance the learning experience by adding human-like features to graphics, characters, language, and even voice elements. This study summarises research related to the exploration of anthropomorphic graphics in multimedia education, without the inclusion of speech elements, etc.Anthropomorphic graphics, specifically, are a form of emotional design that can engage learners by making the educational content more relatable and memorable (Brom Stárková et al., 2018).

Regarding the definition of anthropomorphism in multimedia learning materials, Brom and Stárková, et al. (2018) argue that a key defining feature is that anthropomorphic elements should be depicted on existing non-anthropomorphic graphic objects (i.e., it is not a new graphic object).According to Moremoholo and de Lange (2018), the key advantage of using human-like elements in graphics is their ability to make learning experiences more memorable, thus improving knowledge retention. By establishing an emotional connection between learners and multimedia content, anthropomorphic designs can influence the emotional state of the user, encouraging deeper engagement with the material (Mayer & Estrella, 2014; Um et al., 2012). For example, research by Um et al. (2012) and Park et al. (2015) found that warm, bright colors combined with anthropomorphic elements improved learners' comprehension and emotional engagement.

However, while these designs often improve memory retention, they are not always effective in facilitating the transfer of knowledge to new contexts. Park et al. (2015) showed that although anthropomorphic designs improved comprehension, they did not enhance transfer outcomes in their study. Similarly, a study by Brom and Hannemann, et al. (2018) found that the use of anthropomorphic graphics in multimedia learning environments significantly improved retention but had little effect on deep conceptual learning or knowledge transfer.

A study by Bautista (2015) has shown that primary pupils' interest and attitudes towards anthropomorphic images decline with age.They attribute the anthropomorphic tendency to age and it diminishes through learning experience and the progressive ability to comprehend phenomena better. Another research among primary school students by Slabbert et al. (2022) showed that anthropomorphised graphics had no significant effect on participants' recall or comprehension. they conclude that some anthropomorphised graphics could merely be decorative graphic elements and may not always improve learning outcomes. It is only when a graphic becomes instructional and moves away from being decorative that it acquires the potential to facilitate learning.

2.2 Emotional Design and Motivation in Multimedia Learning

Emotional design refers to the strategic use of visual and interactive elements that evoke specific emotional responses in learners. These emotions are used to enhance the learning experience by creating a positive learning environment that stimulates engagement, interest, and motivation. In the context of multimedia learning, emotional design often involves the use of colors, shapes, facial expressions, and anthropomorphic graphics to influence learners' emotional states. The aim is to evoke positive emotions, such as enjoyment, curiosity, or empathy, which can help students remain attentive and engaged with the learning material. Studies have shown that emotional responses play a significant role in shaping cognitive processes during learning. For instance, Um et al. (2012) found that integrating warm colors and anthropomorphic graphics into learning materials can improve students' emotional experiences, which in turn enhances their motivation to engage with the content. This phenomenon is closely related to the Affective-Motivational Theory, which suggests that learners who experience positive emotions are more likely to engage deeply with the learning material, leading to better cognitive outcomes, such as comprehension and retention (Mayer & Estrella, 2014).

One of the most prominent strategies in emotional design is the use of anthropomorphic features,to evoke empathy and social connection, thereby fostering a more engaging learning environment (Schneider et al., 2018). For example, adding a smiling face to an instructional animation or interactive avatar can make the learning process feel more personal and relatable, which encourages learners to invest more effort and attention in the material (Park et al., 2015). Motivation is a critical factor that determines the success of any learning experience. The Self-Determination Theory (SDT), developed by Deci and Ryan, categorizes motivation into two types: intrinsic motivation and extrinsic motivation. Intrinsic motivation refers to the internal desire to learn or engage in an activity for its own sake, driven by curiosity, enjoyment, or interest. Extrinsic motivation, on the other hand, involves engaging in an activity due to external rewards or pressures, such as grades or praise (Ryan & Deci, 2020). In the context of multimedia learning, emotional design can play a pivotal role in fostering intrinsic motivation. By making the learning materials more emotionally engaging, learners are more likely to experience positive emotional states that encourage them to explore the content out of genuine interest rather than obligation (Mayer & Fiorella, 2021). These types of emotional design features help learners stay more engaged and willing to persevere through difficult tasks, leading to improved learning outcomes (Park et al., 2015).

While emotional design has clear benefits, it is also important to avoid overloading learners with too many emotional stimuli. Excessive or overly complex emotional designs can increase cognitive load and detract from learning, particularly if learners are distracted by the visual or emotional elements rather than focusing on the instructional content (Schneider et al., 2019).

2.3 The Role of Anthropomorphic Graphics in Attention Allocation and Cognitive Processing

Attention is a limited cognitive resource, meaning learners must allocate their attention wisely when faced with multiple stimuli (Chang et al., 2011). In multimedia learning environments, attention allocation is a key factor influencing learning outcomes. It is a prerequisite for students to maintain their attention in the learning process to learn effectively (Gao & Li, 2022)——only when students pay attention to the knowledge points can they subsequently engage in deeper analysis, understanding, synthesis, and memory processing of the information. In other words, capturing students' attention is the precondition for effective learning. However, the capacity limits of working memory directly affect attention allocation. Among them, Visual attention and visual working memory exert severe capacity limitations on cognitive processing (Y. V. Jiang et al., 2014). Anthropomorphic graphics can help optimize attention allocation by capturing learners' attention through vivid and emotionally engaging designs (Mayer & Fiorella, 2021). These designs not only draw attention but also help learners focus on the most important aspects of the educational material.Research by Park et al. (2015) and X. Wang et al. (2023) has shown that anthropomorphic graphics capture learners' attention more effectively than non-anthropomorphic visuals, leading to longer fixation durations on learning materials and improved focus on key content. This suggests that the use of anthropomorphism in multimedia learning environments can facilitate better learning outcomes by guiding learners' attention toward essential information.

Throughout the prolonged course of human evolution, anthropomorphism is a way of human cognition where people attribute humanlike mental capacities to inanimate objects (Epley, 2018). Anthropomorphism is a human innate tendency to facilitate understanding and explanation of their behavior and intentions (Pfeuffer et al., 2019). In many situations, graphics can ease cognitive load, helping people grasping the essence of the information communicated (Tseng, 2022). Adding anthropomorphic faces to multimedia graphics and using pleasant colors in learning improves retention, comprehension, and transfer, with larger effects for children (Brom, Stárková, et al., 2018). A study on the attractiveness of anthropomorphic app icons (Cao et al., 2021), surveyed adults aged 18-24 and found that anthropomorphic app icons are more attractive and garner more attention than non-anthropomorphic app icons. From a deeper processing perspective, anthropomorphic graphics help students establish clearer mental representations by presenting information in a contextualized and concrete manner, reducing intrinsic cognitive load and improving information processing efficiency. Graphic decision aids can improve decision performance at high levels of task complexity by shifting some cognitive burden to our visual perception system (Lohse, 1997). Comprehension was enhanced by the independent and combined effects of warm colors and round, face-like shapes. Additionally, the use of round, face-like shapes in conjunction with neutral colors facilitated transfer(Plass et al., 2014). Mayer and Fiorella (2021) highlighted that anthropomorphic graphics can attract students' attention and enhance their understanding and memory of information through personalized interaction and feedback. Visual designs that simplify complex concepts can enhance learners' sense of competence, as they help students feel more capable of mastering the material.

However, not all studies agree on the effectiveness of anthropomorphic graphics in enhancing learning outcomes. For instance, a study by Stárková et al. (2019) found that while anthropomorphic graphics significantly impacted learners' initial attention allocation during the first two seconds of viewing, they had little to no impact on overall learning outcomes. The researchers concluded that the anthropomorphic elements served more as decorative aids than as instructional tools, emphasizing the need for careful design to avoid unnecessary distractions. The research among primary school students by Slabbert et al. (2022) showed that anthropomorphised graphics had no significant effect on participants' recall or comprehension. they conclude that some anthropomorphised graphics could merely be decorative graphic elements and may not always improve learning outcomes. It is only when a graphic becomes instructional and moves away from being decorative that it acquires the potential to facilitate learning. Münchow and Bannert (2019) adopted the experiment's emotional design elements (such as bright and saturated colours, rounded shapes, and anthropomorphic figures) from other studies which used then successfully (Plass et al., 2014), but found that there is no significant effect on comprehension and transfer.

In summary, while existing research generally supports the idea that anthropomorphic designs can improve attention and emotional engagement, their impact on deeper learning outcomes, such as knowledge transfer, remains inconsistent. Therefore, further research is needed to explore the specific mechanisms through which anthropomorphism influences cognitive processing in multimedia learning environments.

III. THEORY

3.1 Anthropomorphic Graphics and Emotional Motivation Theory

Emotions and motivation play a crucial role in student engagement and academic performance. Affective-Motivational Theory suggests that positive emotional experiences directly stimulate learning motivation, which improves attention and deep learning processes (Niu et al., 2021). Mega et al. (2014) emphasize the link between emotions, self-regulated learning, and motivation, which can influence academic success. Students with high motivation tend to focus better and participate more in learning tasks, leading to better outcomes (Chen et al., 2016). Studies show that increasing the level of anthropomorphism in digital learning materials significantly impacts intrinsic motivation, learning outcomes, and emotional engagement (Schneider et al., 2019). Anthropomorphic images in learning materials can boost cognitive performance and influence both motivation and emotional responses (Schneider et al., 2018). Meyer and Turner (2006) highlight how intrinsic motivation promotes deeper engagement and long-term knowledge retention, while extrinsic rewards, if excessive, can undermine intrinsic motivation.

Anthropomorphic graphics that simulate human behavior and emotions can trigger emotional responses, grabbing learners' attention and enhancing how they process key information. Positive facial expressions on anthropomorphic characters, such as smiles, can make learning more enjoyable, leading to increased engagement with the content (Xiao et al., 2023). Studies have used facial expressions to predict emotional engagement, finding that they are effective at maintaining learner focus (Gupta et al., 2023; Psaltis et al., 2018). According to Affective-Motivational Theory, anthropomorphic graphics—through emotional expressions and body language—enhance emotional engagement and motivation. Smiling and encouraging graphics can make students feel supported, increasing motivation to learn. Anthropomorphic elements in multimedia materials have been shown to improve retention, comprehension, and knowledge transfer while positively influencing intrinsic motivation and reducing perceived task difficulty (Brom, Stárková, et al., 2018; Schneider et al., 2018). Particularly for younger learners, these features significantly enhance both performance and motivation (Gong et al., 2017; Shangguan et al., 2020). Research also suggests that anthropomorphic graphics expressing positive emotions provide personalized interactions, fostering engagement and improving learning outcomes (Park et al., 2014). When designed effectively, such materials encourage students' emotional involvement and intrinsic motivation, helping them focus better and optimize attention allocation.

3.2 Anthropomorphic Graphics and Theory of Attention Allocation

Attention is a limited mental resource meaning that humans cannot always focus on simultaneous presentations of information (Chang et al., 2011). Attention Allocation Theory emphasizes the importance of capturing and sustaining attention during the learning process, especially when learners are faced with competing stimuli in digital environments. When faced with multiple stimuli, the human brain develops a selective attention mechanism. This attention mechanism helps people focus mainly on the most useful information during perception (Z. Jiang et al., 2021). Visual explanations, including anthropomorphic images, can enhance student learning by leveraging the brain's powerful visual processing capabilities (Schmidt, 2009). Anthropomorphic graphics, with their vivid and engaging visual features, can play a crucial role in optimizing attention allocation by drawing learners' focus to key elements of the educational content (Mayer & Fiorella, 2021). Anthropomorphic elements, such as human-like faces, gestures, and body language, naturally attract visual attention because humans are biologically predisposed to notice and respond to social cues (Cao et al., 2021).

In multimedia learning contexts, learners' attention allocation is one of the key factors affecting learning outcomes. As a visual feature in multimedia learning materials, anthropomorphic graphics can attract and focus learners' attention through their vivid and interesting appearance and emotional expressions. So as enhances learners' focus on and processing of key information, thereby improving overall learning effectiveness. Therefore, the reasonable use of anthropomorphic graphic design can help optimize attention allocation in multimedia learning contexts, promoting learners' deep engagement and effective learning.

However, the effectiveness of anthropomorphic graphics in improving learning outcomes is not always consistent. Some studies suggest that while anthropomorphic features are effective in capturing initial attention, they may not always result in deeper conceptual learning or knowledge transfer (Stárková et al., 2019). This discrepancy could be due to differences in the design complexity or the instructional context in which these graphics are used. Graphics that are too complex or distracting may cause learners to misallocate cognitive resources, focusing more on the anthropomorphic features themselves rather than on the instructional content they are meant to highlight (Niu et al., 2021). To optimize attention allocation, it is essential to design anthropomorphic graphics that are visually prominent yet functionally supportive of the learning objectives. The goal should be to strike a balance between visual appeal and instructional clarity, ensuring that anthropomorphic elements serve as cues that enhance rather than detract from the learning experience.

IV. UTILITY ANALYSIS

After a class begins, the learning process can typically be divided into multiple stages, which together form the path for students to fully grasp and apply knowledge. The learning process includes information acquisition, information comprehension, memory and encoding, application and practice, as well as reflection and summary, knowledge integration, and knowledge transfer. These stages do not proceed linearly in a single sequence; rather, they are intertwined and cyclical, forming a complex cognitive process network that collectively influences learning outcomes. Specifically, information acquisition is the foundational stage of learning and the starting point of the entire learning process. It involves the process of perceiving and receiving information. At this stage, students receive external information through sensory channels such as vision and hearing, converting it into initial cognitive material. In the context of modern multimedia teaching, this stage mainly manifests as the synchronous output from the screen and input from students. For example, students acquire new knowledge by watching instructional videos, reading e-textbooks, or participating in interactive exercises. Effective information acquisition relies not only on the quality of the information itself but also on students' attention, cognitive load, and prior knowledge reserves. This multisensory engagement can enhance students' attention to and understanding of the information, thereby laying a solid foundation for subsequent learning.

Information comprehension is the process of interpreting and understanding the acquired information. This stage is crucial as it involves not just simple information reception but also connecting new information with existing knowledge to form a deep understanding of concepts, principles, or processes. In this process, students need to concretize abstract knowledge and integrate scattered information into a coherent cognitive system through thinking activities such as analysis, reasoning, and induction. The depth and breadth of information comprehension directly determine the effectiveness of subsequent learning stages.

In the memory and encoding stage, students need to store the understood information in long-term memory so that it can be effectively retrieved and applied when needed in the future. This process involves encoding the information into a form that can be retrieved when needed and using strategies such as repetition or association to strengthen memory. The quality of information encoding directly affects students' efficiency in storing and retrieving information (Ji, 2023; Naveh-Benjamin et al., 1998), that is, their ability to recall and apply knowledge later.

In the stages mentioned above, the use of anthropomorphic graphics plays an important role. In multimedia teaching, anthropomorphic graphics, with their vivid and friendly visual effects, can significantly capture students' attention, thereby improving the efficiency of information acquisition. Additionally, anthropomorphic graphics, by giving abstract concepts concrete images and emotional characteristics, can help students more easily understand complex knowledge content. More importantly, anthropomorphic graphics help encode information into more visually and emotionally appealing forms, which can enhance students' memory, especially when it comes to recalling and applying knowledge.

Table 1.The effects of anthropomorphic graphics on memory, comprehension, attention and learning outcomes

Type	Title	Year	Author	Finding
Helps to capture attention	Emotional design and positive emotions in multimedia learning: An eyetracking study on the use of anthropomorphisms	2015	Park, B., Knörzer, L., Plass, J. L., & Brünken, R.	Learners in a positive emotional state who learned with the learning environment that included anthropomorphisms showed the highest learning outcome and longest fixation on the relevant information of the multimedia instruction.
	Eye Tracking in Emotional Design Research: What are its Limitations?	2016	Brom, C., Stárková, T., Lukavský, J., Javora, O., & Bromová, E.	In the debriefing, learners clearly indicated their awareness of anthropomorphisms and eyes captured more attention compared to the sechematic version.
	Anthropomorphisms in multimedia learning: Attract attention but do not enhance learning?	2019	Stárková, T., Lukavský, J., Javora, O., & Brom, C.	Anthropomorphisms significantly affected attention distribution during initial fixations but not overall.
	Two Emotional Design Features Are More Effective Than One in Multimedia Learning	2023	Wang, X., Mayer, R. E., Han, M., & Zhang, L.	suggesting that the positive emotional design—in the colorful & anthropomorphizing emotional design group—was helpful for guiding learners' attention to the emotional design areas.

continued on following page

Table 1. Continued

Type	Title	Year	Author	Finding
Facilitates comprehension and retention	Children's anthropomorphic and anthropocentric ideas about micro-organisms	2009	Byrne, J., Grace, M., & Hanley, P.	Anthropomorphic ideas seem to help children to explain their understanding of some aspects of micro-organisms
	Emotional design in multimedia learning	2012	Um, E. "Rachel", Plass, J. L., Hayward, E. O., & Homer, B. D.	Controlling for the germane load of the materials, the internal induction of positive emotions through design of the materials increased comprehension and transfer, whereas the external induction of positive emotions through mood induction enhanced transfer but not comprehension.
	Emotional design in multimedia learning: Effects of shape and color on affect and learning	2014	Plass, J. L., Heidig, S., Hayward, E. O., Homer, B. D., & Um, E.	Comprehension was facilitated by warm colors and round face-like shapes, independently as well as together.
	The effects of emotional design on multimedia learning	2017	Gong, S., Shangguan, C., Zhai, K., & Guo, Y.	Chromatic design and anthropomorphic design facilitated transfer performance independently as well as together.
	How effective is emotional design? A meta-analysis on facial anthropomorphisms and pleasant colors during multimedia learning	2018	Brom, C., Stárková, T., & D'Mello, S. K.	Found significant positive meta-analytic effects for retention (k = 18, d+ = 0.387), comprehension (k = 14, d+ = 0.317), and transfer (k = 27, d+ = 0.327) under a random-effects model.
	Anthropomorphism in decorative pictures: Benefit or harm for learning?	2018	Schneider, S., Nebel, S., Beege, M., & Rey, G. D.	Results show that both human faces and anthropomorphic labels were able to increase the learning performance on cognitive assessments.
	Anthropomorphic Faces and Funny Graphics in an Instructional Animation May Improve Superficial Rather than Deep Learning: A Quasi-Experimental Study	2018	Brom, C., Hannemann, T., Stárková, T., Bromová, E., & Děchtěrenko, F.	The two groups did not differ in state engagement (flow: d = -0.16; positive affect: d = 0.03) and transfer test scores (d = 0.13), but there was a small trend favoring the enhanced graphics in the retention test, when corrected for pretest scores ($\eta 2 = 0.038$; p = .095). Qualitative data suggest that the graphical enhancements might serve as memory cues during the test phase for some participants. The small effect of the enhanced graphics on retention may thus be of cognitive, rather than of affective, origin.
	Anthropomorphisms in multimedia learning: Do they facilitate learning in primary school learners?	2022	Slabbert, C., De Lange, R. W., & Mason, H.	Anthropomorphic shapes yielded a statistically significant effect (g+ = .55) on retention, as did anthropomorphic shapes plus color (g+ = .28), and color alone (g+ = .46), while shape (roundness) did not have a relationship with retention.
Not conducive to understanding and retention	Feeling good, learning better? Effectivity of an emotional design procedure in multimedia learning	2019	Münchow & Bannert,	Exploring the effect of color and anthropomorphism on learning outcomes found no significant differences between the two groups for recall, knowledge, or transfer
No improvement in learning outcomes	Anthropomorphisms in multimedia learning: Attract attention but do not enhance learning?	2019	Stárková, T., Lukavský, J., Javora, O., & Brom, C.	Found no significant effect of anthropomorphisms on learning outcomes.

Research shows that anthropomorphic graphics aid in knowledge retention and comprehension. Although they may not significantly improve final learning outcomes, several studies have indicated that anthropomorphism excels in capturing and holding students' attention (Table 1). It is well known that understanding knowledge is the cornerstone of effective learning, and deep understanding and knowledge transfer are important indicators of learning effectiveness, while academic performance is a comprehensive reflection of learning outcomes. Although in some studies, anthropomorphic graphics have not directly led to significant improvements in academic performance, they have demonstrated unique advantages in capturing and maintaining students' attention. Focused attention is a prerequisite for effective learning, making anthropomorphic graphics a crucial element in improving learning efficiency and quality. Furthermore, research has indicated that even if anthropomorphic graphics do not significantly enhance final learning outcomes, they still have a positive effect on promoting students' deep understanding and knowledge transfer.

In summary, the various stages of the learning process are interconnected; information acquisition, comprehension, memory and encoding, application and practice, as well as reflection and summary, are all important components that contribute to learning outcomes. Anthropomorphic graphics play a vital role in this process, effectively promoting students' learning motivation and knowledge comprehension. Although their impact on final learning outcomes may not be significant, their potential in enhancing learning effectiveness should not be overlooked

V. CONCLUSION

This study investigates the effects of anthropomorphic graphics on learning, with a focus on emotional design, attention allocation, and motivation. The results confirm that emotional design elements, such as anthropomorphic graphics, effectively capture learners' attention and foster emotional engagement. These features enhance intrinsic motivation, leading to better retention and comprehension of learning materials. The integration of Affective-Motivational Theory and Attention Allocation Theory demonstrates that anthropomorphic graphics play a crucial role in improving cognitive processes in multimedia learning environments. The study emphasizes how anthropomorphic graphics enhance the learning process by improving information acquisition, comprehension, and memory encoding. Anthropomorphic elements reduce cognitive load by transforming abstract concepts into visually engaging and emotionally relatable forms. This not only captures students' attention but also aids in long-term retention of knowledge. The findings highlight that anthropomorphic graphics are particularly effective in early stages of learning, where emotional engagement helps maintain focus and motivates learners to persist through challenging material.

5.1 Future Prospects

The study presents promising prospects for integrating anthropomorphic graphics into multimedia learning materials, particularly in terms of enhancing emotional engagement and motivation. Future research could explore ways to fine-tune the balance between emotional design and cognitive load to optimize learning outcomes across various educational contexts and age groups. Additionally, further investigation into how anthropomorphic graphics can be tailored to different subjects, content complexity, and learner demographics would provide deeper insights into maximizing their effectiveness.

5.2 Limitations

Despite the positive outcomes, this study also reveals some limitations. While anthropomorphic graphics effectively capture attention and boost motivation, their impact on deep conceptual learning and knowledge transfer remains less consistent. The overuse or excessive complexity of anthropomorphic elements can lead to cognitive overload, potentially distracting learners from core content. Moreover, the effects of anthropomorphic graphics may diminish with older learners, as emotional engagement may be less critical for attention maintenance.

In conclusion, the potential of anthropomorphic graphics in multimedia learning is evident, but further research is needed to explore how to balance their emotional appeal with instructional clarity. By addressing these limitations, future studies could develop more refined design strategies to improve learning outcomes for diverse learner populations.

Funding

This research was funded by the Ministry of Higher Education Malaysia for Fundamental Research Grant Scheme with Project Code: FRGS/1/2020/SSI0/USM/02/23 awarded to Mageswaran Sanmugam.

REFERENCES

Abrami, P. C., Leventhal, L., & Perry, R. P. (1982). Educational Seduction. *Review of Educational Research*, 52(3), 446–464. DOI: 10.3102/00346543052003446

Airenti, G. (2015). The Cognitive Bases of Anthropomorphism: From Relatedness to Empathy. *International Journal of Social Robotics*, 7(1), 117–127. DOI: 10.1007/s12369-014-0263-x

Bautista, R. G. (2015). Students' affordance of teleologic explanations and antrhropomorphic language in eliciting concepts in physics. *Journal of Technology and Science Education*, 5(1), 31–40. DOI: 10.3926/jotse.137

Blut, M., Wang, C., Wünderlich, N. V., & Brock, C. (2021). Understanding anthropomorphism in service provision: A meta-analysis of physical robots, chatbots, and other AI. *Journal of the Academy of Marketing Science*, 49(4), 632–658. DOI: 10.1007/s11747-020-00762-y

Brom, C., Hannemann, T., Stárková, T., Bromová, E., & Děchtěrenko, F. (2018). *Anthropomorphic Faces and Funny Graphics in an Instructional Animation May Improve Superficial Rather than Deep Learning: A Quasi-Experimental Study.*

Brom, C., Stárková, T., & D'Mello, S. K. (2018). How effective is emotional design? A meta-analysis on facial anthropomorphisms and pleasant colors during multimedia learning. *Educational Research Review*, 25, 100–119. DOI: 10.1016/j.edurev.2018.09.004

Cao, Y., Zhang, Y., Ding, Y., Duffy, V. G., & Zhang, X. (2021). Is an anthropomorphic app icon more attractive? Evidence from neuroergonomomics. *Applied Ergonomics*, 97, 103545. DOI: 10.1016/j.apergo.2021.103545 PMID: 34352470

Chamberlain, R., Mullin, C., Scheerlinck, B., & Wagemans, J. (2018). Putting the art in artificial: Aesthetic responses to computer-generated art. *Psychology of Aesthetics, Creativity, and the Arts*, 12(2), 177–192. DOI: 10.1037/aca0000136

Chang, T.-W., Hsu, J.-M., & Yu, P.-T. (2011). A Comparison of Single- and Dual-Screen Environment in Programming Language: Cognitive Loads and Learning Effects. *Journal of Educational Technology & Society*, 14, 188–200.

Chen, W., Zhu, W., Mason, S., Hammond-Bennett, A., & Colombo-Dougovito, A. (2016). Effectiveness of quality physical education in improving students' manipulative skill competency. *Journal of Sport and Health Science*, 5(2), 231–238. DOI: 10.1016/j.jshs.2015.04.005 PMID: 30356505

Epley, N. (2018). A Mind like Mine: The Exceptionally Ordinary Underpinnings of Anthropomorphism. *Journal of the Association for Consumer Research*, 3(4), 591–598. DOI: 10.1086/699516

Epley, N., Waytz, A., & Cacioppo, J. T. (2007). On seeing human: A three-factor theory of anthropomorphism. *Psychological Review*, 114(4), 864–886. DOI: 10.1037/0033-295X.114.4.864 PMID: 17907867

Gao, Q., & Li, S. (2022). Impact of Online Courses on University Student Visual Attention During the COVID-19 Pandemic. *Frontiers in Psychiatry*, 13, 848844. DOI: 10.3389/fpsyt.2022.848844 PMID: 35422723

Garner, R., Brown, R., Sanders, S., & Menke, D. (1992). *'Seductive details' and learning from text.*https://api.semanticscholar.org/CorpusID:200060851

Gong, S., Shangguan, C., Zhai, K., & Guo, Y. (2017). The effects of emotional design on multimedia learning. *Acta Psychologica Sinica*, 49(6), 771. DOI: 10.3724/SP.J.1041.2017.00771

Guney, Z. (2019). Considerations for human–computer interaction: User interface design variables and visual learning in IDT. *Cypriot Journal of Educational Sciences*, 14(4), 731–741. DOI: 10.18844/cjes.v14i4.4481

Gupta, S., Kumar, P., & Tekchandani, R. (2023). A Multimodal Facial Cues Based Engagement Detection System in E-Learning Context Using Deep Learning Approach. *Multimedia Tools and Applications*, 82(18), 28589–28615. DOI: 10.1007/s11042-023-14392-3 PMID: 36789011

Ji, L. (2023). The Validity of the Specific Coding Principle: The Explanations from Cognitive Psychology and Psychoanalysis. *Journal of Education. Humanities and Social Sciences*, 8, 1259–1263. DOI: 10.54097/ehss.v8i.4460

Jiang, Y. V., Capistrano, C. G., & Palm, B. E. (2014). Spatial Working Memory in Children With High-Functioning Autism: Intact Configural Processing But Impaired Capacity. *Journal of Vision (Charlottesville, Va.)*, 14(10), 42–42. DOI: 10.1167/14.10.42 PMID: 24661175

Jiang, Z., Wang, Y., Shi, C., Wu, Y., Hu, R., Chen, S., Hu, S., Wang, X., & Qiu, B. (2021). *Attention module improves both performance and interpretability of 4D fMRI decoding neural network.*

Kaplan, R. M., & Pascoe, G. C. (1977). Humorous lectures and humorous examples: Some effects upon comprehension and retention. *Journal of Educational Psychology*, 69(1), 61–65. DOI: 10.1037/0022-0663.69.1.61

Lee, J. M., Baek, J., & Ju, D. Y. (2018). Anthropomorphic Design: Emotional Perception for Deformable Object. *Frontiers in Psychology*, 9, 1829. DOI: 10.3389/fpsyg.2018.01829 PMID: 30333773

Lohse, G. L. (1997). The role of working memory on graphical information processing. *Behaviour & Information Technology*, 16(6), 297–308. DOI: 10.1080/014492997119707

Mayer, R. E. (2009). *Multimedia Learning* (2nd ed.). Cambridge University Press., DOI: 10.1017/CBO9780511811678

Mayer, R. E., & Estrella, G. (2014). Benefits of emotional design in multimedia instruction. *Learning and Instruction*, 33, 12–18. DOI: 10.1016/j.learninstruc.2014.02.004

Mayer, R. E., & Fiorella, L. (Eds.). (2021). *The Cambridge Handbook of Multimedia Learning* (3rd ed.). Cambridge University Press., DOI: 10.1017/9781108894333

Mega, C., Ronconi, L., & Béni, R. D. (2014). What Makes a Good Student? How Emotions, Self-Regulated Learning, and Motivation Contribute to Academic Achievement. *Journal of Educational Psychology*, 106(1), 121–131. DOI: 10.1037/a0033546

Meyer, D. K., & Turner, J. C. (2006). Re-Conceptualizing Emotion and Motivation to Learn in Classroom Contexts. *Educational Psychology Review*, 18(4), 377–390. DOI: 10.1007/s10648-006-9032-1

Moremoholo, T. P., & de Lange, R. W. (2018). *Anthropomorphic graphics: How useful are they as an instructional aid to facilitate learning? 13.*

Münchow, H., & Bannert, M. (2019). Feeling good, learning better? Effectivity of an emotional design procedure in multimedia learning. *Educational Psychology*, 39(4), 530–549. DOI: 10.1080/01443410.2018.1524852

Naveh-Benjamin, M., Craik, F. I. M., Guez, J., & Dori, H. (1998). Effects of divided attention on encoding and retrieval processes in human memory: Further support for an asymmetry. *Journal of Experimental Psychology. Learning, Memory, and Cognition*, 24(5), 1091–1104. DOI: 10.1037/0278-7393.24.5.1091 PMID: 9747524

Niu, Z., Zhong, G., & Yu, H. (2021). A review on the attention mechanism of deep learning. *Neurocomputing*, 452, 48–62. DOI: 10.1016/j.neucom.2021.03.091

Park, B., Knörzer, L., Plass, J. L., & Brünken, R. (2015). Emotional design and positive emotions in multimedia learning: An eyetracking study on the use of anthropomorphisms. *Computers & Education*, 86, 30–42. DOI: 10.1016/j.compedu.2015.02.016

Park, B., Plass, J. L., & Brünken, R. (2014). Cognitive and affective processes in multimedia learning. *Learning and Instruction*, 29, 125–127. DOI: 10.1016/j.learninstruc.2013.05.005

Pfeuffer, N., Benlian, A., Gimpel, H., & Hinz, O. (2019). Anthropomorphic Information Systems. *Business & Information Systems Engineering*, 61(4), 523–533. DOI: 10.1007/s12599-019-00599-y

Plass, J. L., Heidig, S., Hayward, E. O., Homer, B. D., & Um, E. (2014). Emotional design in multimedia learning: Effects of shape and color on affect and learning. *Learning and Instruction*, 29, 128–140. DOI: 10.1016/j.learninstruc.2013.02.006

Psaltis, A., Apostolakis, K. C., Dimitropoulos, K., & Daras, P. (2018). Multimodal Student Engagement Recognition in Prosocial Games. *IEEE Transactions on Games*, 10(3), 292–303. DOI: 10.1109/TCIAIG.2017.2743341

Renkl, A., & Scheiter, K. (2017). Studying Visual Displays: How to Instructionally Support Learning. *Educational Psychology Review*, 29(3), 599–621. DOI: 10.1007/s10648-015-9340-4

Ryan, R. M., & Deci, E. L. (2020). Intrinsic and extrinsic motivation from a self-determination theory perspective: Definitions, theory, practices, and future directions. *Contemporary Educational Psychology*, 61, 101860. DOI: 10.1016/j.cedpsych.2020.101860

Salles, A., Evers, K., & Farisco, M. (2020). Anthropomorphism in AI. *AJOB Neuroscience*, 11(2), 88–95. DOI: 10.1080/21507740.2020.1740350 PMID: 32228388

Schmidt, S. J. (2009). Development and Use of Visual Explanations: Harnessing the Power of the "Seeing" Brain to Enhance Student Learning. *Journal of Food Science Education*, 8(3), 68–72. DOI: 10.1111/j.1541-4329.2009.00076.x

Schneider, S., Nebel, S., Beege, M., & Rey, G. D. (2018). Anthropomorphism in decorative pictures: Benefit or harm for learning? *Journal of Educational Psychology*, 110(2), 218–232. DOI: 10.1037/edu0000207

Schneider, S., Wirzberger, M., & Rey, G. D. (2019). The moderating role of arousal on the seductive detail effect in a multimedia learning setting. *Applied Cognitive Psychology*, 33(1), 71–84. DOI: 10.1002/acp.3473

Shangguan, C., Gong, S., Guo, Y., Wang, X., & Lu, J. (2020). The effects of emotional design on middle school students' multimedia learning: The role of learners' prior knowledge. *Educational Psychology*, 40(9), 1076–1093. DOI: 10.1080/01443410.2020.1714548

Slabbert, C., De Lange, R. W., & Mason, H. (2022). Anthropomorphisms in multimedia learning: Do they facilitate learning in primary school learners? *Cogent Education*, 9(1), 2034390. DOI: 10.1080/2331186X.2022.2034390

Stárková, T., Lukavský, J., Javora, O., & Brom, C. (2019). Anthropomorphisms in multimedia learning: Attract attention but do not enhance learning? *Journal of Computer Assisted Learning*, 35(4), 555–568. DOI: 10.1111/jcal.12359

Tseng, H. (2022). Patterns of basic knowledge. *iScience*, 25(2), 103803. DOI: 10.1016/j.isci.2022.103803 PMID: 35198869

Um, E., Plass, J. L., Hayward, E. O., & Homer, B. D. (2012). Emotional design in multimedia learning. *Journal of Educational Psychology*, 104(2), 485–498. DOI: 10.1037/a0026609

Waang, G. P. (2023). Maximizing the Potential of Multimedia in Indonesia: Enhancing Engagement, Accessibility, and Learning Outcomes. *Academic Society for Appropriate Technology*, 9(3), 235–245. DOI: 10.37675/jat.2023.00409

Wang, X., Mayer, R. E., Han, M., & Zhang, L. (2023). Two Emotional Design Features Are More Effective Than One in Multimedia Learning. *Journal of Educational Computing Research*, 60(8), 1991–2014. DOI: 10.1177/07356331221090845

Wang, Y., & Zheng, L. (2022). A Novel Deep Framework for English Communication Based on Educational Psychology Perspective. *Frontiers in Public Health*, 10, 916101. DOI: 10.3389/fpubh.2022.916101 PMID: 35801240

Xiao, J., Jiang, Z., Wang, L., & Yu, T. (2023). What Can Multimodal Data Tell Us About Online Synchronous Training: Learning Outcomes and Engagement of in-Service Teachers. *Frontiers in Psychology*, 13, 1092848. Advance online publication. DOI: 10.3389/fpsyg.2022.1092848 PMID: 36687926

Yeager, D. S., & Walton, G. M. (2011). Social-Psychological Interventions in Education: They're Not Magic. *Review of Educational Research*, 81(2), 267–301. DOI: 10.3102/0034654311405999

Zhang, X., Lyu, F., & Cheng, S. (2018). Interaction paradigm in intelligent systems. *SCIENTIA SINICA Informationis*, 48(4), 406–418. DOI: 10.1360/N112017-00217

Chapter 15
Integrating Social Media in Education to Explore Benefits, Challenges, Theories, and Strategies for Enhanced Learning

Nusratul Islam
University of Kashmir, India

Syed Ishfaq Ahmad Shah
University of Kashmir, India

ABSTRACT

In recent years, the integration of social media into educational settings has emerged as a significant trend, revolutionizing traditional teaching and learning practices. Social media integration into learning environments is becoming more and more common, providing innovative ways to improve teaching and learning. This book chapter presents a detailed analysis of the role, benefits, challenges, and strategies associated with social media integration in teaching and learning. It aims to discuss the effective utilization of social media platforms, such as Facebook, Twitter, Instagram, YouTube, and other applications, to promote student and teacher engagement, collaboration, and knowledge sharing. The chapter explores various theoretical frameworks such as connectivism and constructivism, which support the integration of social media in fostering active learning environments. However, there are challenges as well, like maintaining academic integrity, protecting data privacy, and managing distractions.

DOI: 10.4018/979-8-3693-6745-2.ch015

INTRODUCTION

A broad definition of social media is a variety of interactive web resources that facilitate users' individual or group creation, curation, and sharing of user-generated content. Examples of social media platforms are numerous. These consist of YouTube, Instagram, Facebook, Friendster, Wikipedia, Craigslist, and recipe-sharing websites like all-recipes.com. While social media platforms all have the aforementioned traits, they differ greatly from one another as well. Specifically, the designs, structures, norms, and user bases of different platforms tend to differ. Social network sites are web-based services that let users: (1) create a public or semi-public profile inside a system; (2) list other users they are connected to; and (3) browse and view both their list of connections and those made by other users inside the system (Boyd and Ellison, 2007).

A collection of web-based tools known as social media creates a technological framework and facilitates information sharing. Through social media platforms, people can share thoughts, emotions, private information, images, and videos. Social media promotes constant and unrestricted idea-sharing (Allen, Ryan., Gray., McInerney, and Waters, 2014), and its impact on education is enormous. Social media interactions between shy and introverted people and their coworkers are more comfortable than in-person interactions. It facilitates interpersonal communication, information sharing, message sending, blogging, and face-to-face interactions. Through social media, students can engage with peers, professionals, and resources worldwide, expanding their global connectivity beyond the confines of the traditional classroom. Beyond what is possible with traditional methods alone, this connectivity makes cross-cultural exchanges, collaborative projects, and real-time discussions possible. Social media platforms present special chances for interaction and communication outside of the classroom. With their assistance, teachers can establish engaging learning environments in which students can share resources, work together in real time on projects, and take an active part in class discussions. The degree to which websites integrate novel information and communication technologies, like blogging, mobile connectivity, and photo and video sharing, also differs (Boyd and Ellison, 2007).

Social media includes not only social network sites but also discussion forums or publishing platforms (Pan., Coleman., Manago, and Goodof, 2019). According to one definition, social media refers to electronically mediated technologies that make it easier for people to share and create ideas, interests, and information. Given that today's digitalized world revolves around the Internet and technology, social media can play a pivotal role in the educational system. As such, educators must recognize the significance of social networking. The way we teach, learn, and communicate has changed as a result of technology. College students in this generation have never experienced life without a computer or a cell phone. Their lives are significantly impacted by social media. Students' expectations for a learning experience are evolving along with technology. This experience transcends the limitations of the conventional classroom. Social media technology has become an essential part of personal life as users generate content, share photos, and choose to "like", or interact in a game.

The Internet has developed into one of the innovations that people in today's society use the most frequently in recent years. Among Internet users, social media is one aspect of the network that has grown to be indispensable. Students of the current generation are showing signs of diminished interest, engagement, and participation in the various subject areas that are being taught to them. One of the main reasons why students are portraying learning in a negative light is because of traditional teaching methods. This is partly because active learning and stimulation are no longer prioritized in traditional methods. Due to their upbringing in a fast-paced setting, students require stimulation to fully comprehend the material. Students can stay engaged and stimulated with the help of social media. Students' daily routines hold a considerable amount of time for social media usage; therefore, further integration into the classroom could rekindle the participation, engagement, and interest once held by students.

Technology has changed education in ways that go far beyond simple integration. These days, they are an integral part of students' daily lives, offering fresh chances for engagement, information sharing, and the formation of social viewpoints. Learners enjoy an active, social, and digital environment and their expectations lie within the vast scope of available rapidly developing technologies for online and face-to-face instruction. We want to change the way students learn by entering social media into the classroom. We want to make learning more dynamic, more collaborative, and relevant to the generation that grew up with technology. Social media may mean enhanced class discussions, enable more dynamic teacher-student idea exchanges, and increase the amount of learning that can be done outside traditional classroom settings. Social media has gained popularity as a tool for information and sharing private details of one's life. Many educational institutions have employed the use of social media to facilitate teaching and learning. Research has calculated that more than 90% of college students use social networks (Ellison., Steinfeld., and Lampe, 2007). Social media incorporation in education makes it easier for parents, teachers, and students to access information, communicate with other learning communities, and even comprehend the global education system. Students nowadays are familiar with a variety of platforms. Teachers, parents, and students all benefit from using social media for communication, question and answer sessions, and marking and commenting on student work. Social media for use in communications, question and answer sessions, and marking and commenting on student work must be embraced as imperative parts of modern pedagogy.

Every student has a unique way of learning. Students can typically be taught using a combination of writing, auditory, visual, kinesthetic, and reading strategies. The use of new technologies in education is surpassing the adoption of antiquated methods. The new technologies of the twenty-first century are essential to their education. Social media can be used to enhance traditional teaching methods. Teachers can use social media platforms as an effective tool to engage these students in learning activities. Due to their interactive features, which enable teachers to interact with students, social media platforms such as WhatsApp, Facebook (FB), and Twitter appear to hold great promise in the field of education (Javaeed, Kibria, Khan, & Ghauri, 2020). Furthermore, social media significantly affects how students view other people and themselves. Social media exposes the students' learning scope to be so broad, from messages to images, and views and comments from others that may greatly influence their self-identity, values, and the norms and expected behaviors they expect to adhere to. Even though traditional teaching techniques are still more effective, they are said to be encouraged or supported by the use of social media. Use of social media in combination with asynchronous and synchronous learning approaches for instance, FaceTime, or real-time commenting/messaging and those with delayed responses to group posts can, on its own, help to understand better other people's intentions and manage behavior by and large. Using the strengths of the digital platform can better engage students, improve teaching, and prepare students for success in an increasingly connected world.

BACKGROUND

At the dawn of the 21st Century, social networking sites were launched. These sites enable users to share information, photos, private journals, hobbies, and interests with networks of mutual friends. Web 2.0 gave rise to social networks in the late 1990s, and websites like sixdegrees.com (1997), which let users create profiles and friends, offered blogging and posting features. Later, new features emerged, and in 2003, linkedin.com and myspace.com gave rise to a new face for social networks, but in the same year, facebook.com and orkut.com completely changed the definition of social networks in the annals of social media and web sciences. Social networks saw significant advancements in functionality after 2003. One such feature was the ability for users to modify the website's front end entirely through their profile, which is an evolutionary step (Tariq., Mehboob., Khan and Ullah, 2012).

Nowadays, technology forms an essential part of daily life. As compared to traditional marketing, social media is a technology that offers more opportunities for the institution to market itself and attract more students. Since social media platforms like Instagram, Twitter, Facebook, Edmodo, and Google Classroom have been very popular within the school setting, the integration of social media in education changed a lot.

Here's a brief overview of its background and evolution:

1. **Early Adoption and Experimentation (2000s):** The first attempts to use social media, with the view of optimizing the learning conditions for students, began among educators in the early 2000s. They tried to apply several online facilities like blogs, forums, and wikis, among others that would give students and teachers the ability to work together and discuss various topics. As early as the mid-2000s, educators started to realize the potential of social media sites like Facebook, Twitter, and YouTube as additional resources for instruction (Saini and Mir, 2023).
2. **Emergence of Dedicated Educational Platforms (2010s):** 2010 saw the emergence of photo-dominant platforms, beginning with Pinterest (Streets, 2023). By the 2010s, platforms specifically designed for educational purposes, such as Edmodo (2010) and Schoology (2009), began to gain traction. These platforms offered features tailored to the needs of teachers and students, such as assignment management, discussion forums, and grading tools. Google also entered the education space with Google Classroom in 2014, integrating seamlessly with Google's suite of productivity tools.
3. **Benefits Recognized:** Social media integration in education was recognized for its ability to enhance communication between educators, students, and parents. It provided a platform for instant feedback, collaboration on projects, and discussion beyond the confines of the classroom. It also fostered digital literacy skills as students learned to navigate and interact responsibly on these platforms. Upon conducting a comprehensive analysis of various social media platforms, it has been determined that these resources offer numerous educational benefits to educators and learners alike, thereby facilitating opportunities for lifelong learning (Faizi, Afia, and Chiheb, 2013).
4. **Challenges and Concerns:** Alongside the benefits, concerns arose regarding privacy, digital distraction, and the need for moderation to ensure appropriate use. Educators had to navigate issues such as maintaining professionalism on public platforms like Twitter and managing digital footprints. Teachers battle with the extra workload that comes with using social media, which includes working after hours and privacy issues. The absence of certain software features contributes to some of this work. Social media lacks features that would facilitate teaching, such as file size restrictions, a lack of a presentation mode, and a poor language translator. Additionally, teachers lack the necessary social media training. Some educators were hesitant to use social media to enhance

their instruction because of these difficulties (Jaffer, Davids, and Seymour, 2023).

5. **Current Trends (2020s):** As of the early 2020s, social media integration in education continues to evolve. Educators are exploring ways to leverage newer platforms and features, such as Instagram Stories for educational content, TikTok for short educational videos, and LinkedIn for career-focused networking and learning. The COVID-19 pandemic accelerated the adoption of social media and digital tools for remote and hybrid learning, highlighting their role in maintaining educational continuity. The closing of the school to stop the spread of COVID-19 has flown the adoption of technology-based learning activities (Riady, et al.2022).
6. **Future Outlook:** Social media has only been around for a couple of decades, but it has already undergone several evolutions. As end users change, so do the ways they use these platforms. In response to these behavioral shifts, technology adapts to offer new features and ways to connect (Streets, 2023). Looking ahead, social media integration in education is likely to become more sophisticated, with advancements in artificial intelligence potentially enabling personalized learning experiences and automated feedback mechanisms. However, ongoing concerns about data privacy and digital well-being will need to be addressed to ensure the safe and effective use of social media in educational contexts. Overall, social media integration in education has transformed how teachers teach and students learn, offering new opportunities for collaboration, engagement, and personalized learning experiences both inside and outside the classroom. A combination of new avenues for interaction and content sharing, emerging technologies like virtual reality (VR) and augmented reality (AR) have the potential to completely change the world of social media (Saini and Mir, 2023).

OBJECTIVES

To explore the meaning and concept of social media integration into education.

To define the role and benefits of social media in education and its potential to enhance teaching-learning experiences.

To discuss and explain the use of various social media applications in education.

To understand the challenges in integrating social media into education.

Review of Related Literature

This book chapter examines social media from a theoretical point of view, emphasizing studies that have integrated social media as a teaching and learning tool in education using theory as a support. **Navneet and Sajad (2023)** a study on Social Media: Usage and the impact on Education. This study emphasized how the adoption of social media platforms like Facebook, Twitter, and Instagram, has revolutionized the ways students and educators interact and learn. Social media improves educational experiences by enabling instantaneous communication, information sharing, and teamwork. Students can interact with peers and experts worldwide, participate in online discussions, and access educational resources. This study mentions numerous benefits, but it also presents challenges such as distractions, privacy concerns, and the spread of misinformation.

Yulian & Asdlori (2023) a research article on "The Role of Social Media in Students' Social Perception and Interaction: Implications for Learning and Education". The article's main focus was on how social media apps like Facebook, Instagram, and Twitter have altered how students interact with one another and with others, thereby influencing students' perceptions of social interactions and their effects on education and learning. This study drew upon a literature review employing a qualitative method approach, whereby data will be analyzed and interpreted through a combination of textual and informational sources. The results of the study showed how social media has changed how students interact with one another. Social pressure and psychological effects are potential outcomes for students who use social media. Given the role of social media, educators must teach students how to use it responsibly for education, that they receive the necessary psychological support, and that they learn social media literacy. It's also essential to include parents in their children's social media literacy education.

Georgios et al. (2022) a paper on Social media in Education: A Case Study Regarding Higher Education Students' Viewpoints. Through investigating and comprehending the experiences and opinions of higher education students regarding the use of social media in education, the study was aimed at investigating this digital shift. The study involved 130 students in total. According to the findings, most students had a positive opinion of social media's role in education and saw it as a way to improve group projects, communication, collaboration, and the exchange of ideas and knowledge between students and teachers. Additionally, students believed that social media was a priceless teaching tool that could enhance the teaching and learning process and boost student productivity, engagement, motivation, and academic performance when used in a student-centered way.

Kwaku et al. (2021) a study on Integration of social media for smart pedagogy: initial perceptions of senior high school students in Ghana. For this study, a questionnaire was used to collect data using the descriptive survey design. Using basic and purposive random sampling methods, 200 seniors from a high school were chosen. For analysis, statistical tools like regression, analysis of variance (ANOVA), means, and standard deviation were used. According to the study, the majority of students thought that social media integration improved teaching and learning.

Kam and Billy Tak (2021) a literature review conducted on "The Opportunities and Challenges of Social Media in Higher Education". The paper reviews the applications of social media for teaching and learning in higher education, highlighting the positive as well as negative aspects that have been identified. For analysis, 77 relevant case studies that were published between 2010 and 2019 were gathered from Scopus and Google Scholar. The findings demonstrated that social media was typically utilized to improve learner engagement and as a learning management system. Due to social media's widespread use among students and ability to facilitate two-way communication, simple knowledge sharing, community building, and collaborative learning, all of which improve the educational experience for students it has created opportunities for educational practices. The case studies highlight various challenges, including the insufficiency of instructors' pedagogical and technological skills, the lack of integration with instructional design, and the blurring of boundaries between students' private and public lives as well as between students' relationships with instructors. Additionally, the effectiveness of this approach for knowledge construction is questionable.

Amandeep et al. (2018) a study on the relationship between psychological health and social media fatigue online examination of fear of missing out, depression, anxiety, fatigue, and compulsive behavior. This study examines the relationship between social media fatigue and anxiety, depression, and psychosocial well-being measures like compulsive media use and fear of missing out, by using the stressor-strain-outcome framework (SSO). To test the research model, data from two waves of Indian adolescent social media users (N = 1554 and 1144) were gathered using a repeated cross-sectional methodology. The results of the study showed that social media fatigue was largely caused by compulsive media use, which in turn raised anxiety and depressive symptoms. Fear of missing out on something indirectly predicted social media use through the medium of compulsive social media use.

METHODOLOGY

This book chapter is based on the existing source of knowledge regarding the subject of interest social media integration in education. Data is mainly from secondary sources including scholarly journals, books, research documents, and related articles.

Role and Benefit of Social Media Integration in Education

Social media platforms have been proven to improve student learning when used in the classroom. Teachers who have effectively integrated social media into their lesson plans have observed an increase in student motivation, engagement, and participation. (Drylie, 2013). It's crucial to remember that social media enhances formal education in ways beyond simply "going online." Time and location mobility are undoubtedly added to a course when blended or online components are added to a program via the use of an LMS. Also, there are some limited opportunities for digital literacy advancement as a result of this use (Anderson, 2019).

1. **Enhances Participation and Engagement**: When students use social media to learn actively rather than passively, it increases their participation in the classroom. Students who read the articles of others might connect with the topic and other knowledgeable people. Videos have a special way of delivering information that makes it more engaging than traditional learning methods. With the help of a video editor, educators can create engaging, interactive content that keeps students engaged and learning. Students consider social media to be an invaluable teaching tool that when used in a student-centered manner can increase their productivity, engagement, motivation, and academic performance as well as improve the teaching and learning process (Lampropoulos., Makkonen and Siakas, 2022).
2. **Personalized Learning**: Social media tools can be utilized to personalize learning experiences, catering to individual student needs and learning preferences. Support learning at students' own pace and convenience. Adjust content difficulty based on student performance. Social media can take a lot of different forms. Everyone now has the chance to select the social media platform that most closely suits their tastes (Drylie, 2013). The use of technology in education has greatly increased the potential for personalized learning and created new opportunities for learners to receive it (Nandigam, Tirumala, and Baghaei, 2014).
3. **Resource Accessibility**: Students can access several lectures and courses from within the comfort of their homes. Because social media is so accessible, students can access a greater number of resources, which enhances their under-

standing of the material. They can consult the experts if they would like a clear understanding. Social media sites offer updated information on trends, events, and advancements in many sectors. The most important manner through which social media has transformed education is by increasing information accessibility. People can access the vast amount of knowledge available on the internet, which has developed into the modern library, through social media (Saini and Mir,2023).

4. **Content Sharing and Distribution:** Teachers can use social media platforms to distribute instructional materials, videos, and articles to their students. This facilitates a variety of learning styles and makes resources easily accessible. Users can exchange content with other members of their network, including articles, videos, images, messages, and status updates. Other users may like, share, and comment on this content (Purnama and Asdlori, 2023). Social media users can interact with like-minded individuals by joining communities, groups, and forums. This makes the exchange of knowledge and experiences in particular fields possible (Siddiqui and Singh, 2016).
5. **Flexibility in Learning:** Education can occur at any time or location; it is not limited to traditional classroom settings. The use of social media in the classroom facilitates a more flexible teaching-learning process. Making use of play, forward, rewind, and rewatch functions, students can view recorded lectures at their own pace (Islam et al., 2020). Students are free to learn at their own speed. Students can study and move through content at their own pace because of social media platforms, which give them access to learning resources whenever they need them. Through e-learning, students can select their own material, time, location, and study phases while learning at their own pace (Kumar and Nanda, 2022).
6. **Feedback and Discussion:** Teachers can use social media to initiate discussions, gather feedback on lessons, and engage students in conversations that extend beyond traditional classroom boundaries. Discussions on social media can reach a broader audience beyond the immediate classroom, inviting perspectives from individuals with varied backgrounds and experiences. Social media can help with quick evaluation and feedback. Online surveys, tests, and discussion forums can be used by teachers to assess their students' understanding and pinpoint any areas that need more explanation. Because of this real-time feedback loop, teachers can adjust their pedagogy as needed to keep students interested and informed (Saini and Mir, 2023).
7. **Professional Development:** By connecting with colleagues worldwide, sharing best practices, and taking part in online forums, educators can use social media for professional development. Social media platforms offer educators a wealth of professional development resources, such as webinars, online courses, and

articles. Teachers can create a community of practice where ideas and innovations are shared by sharing lesson plans, effective teaching strategies, and classroom activities on social media. To promote a positive learning environment, educators can participate in online communities and groups on social media sites such as Facebook and LinkedIn to talk about problems, trends, and solutions in the field of education. Social media provides educators with the opportunity to establish professional networks and connect with colleagues across the globe. Faculty members can now participate in professional learning through professional learning networks (PLNs) and online learning communities of practices (CoPs), which are made possible by social media (Luo, Freeman, and Stefaniak, 2020).

8. **Enhanced Communication and Collaboration:** Social media provides a forum for better collaboration and communication between educators, parents, and students. It is possible to have discussions, feedback, and updates in real time. These features can improve learning outcomes and student engagement. Using social media as a teaching tool naturally utilizes collaboration (Kalia, 2013). Learners can access and exchange resources and information from internal and external collaboration networks through a multitude of social media tools. Thus, online learners who could be students, teachers, or anybody else in the community can create their learning materials and benefit from the body of knowledge that exists. Social media can thus be a useful tool for establishing pathways for student-teacher and student-student collaboration. Both nonverbal and verbal communication play significant roles in interpersonal or group social interactions. This includes face-to-face conversations, texts, phone calls, emails, body language, facial expressions, and more (Purnama and Asdlori, 2023).
9. **Global Learning:** Students can interact with other classmates from any region of the world, learn about different cultures, and gain multiple types of perspectives. Social networking sites allow for the exchange of useful information and facilitate the sharing of ideas across geographic boundaries (Siddiqui and Singh, 2016). The media will also be used by the teachers as a tool to invite international guest lecturers and topic experts who will conduct online seminars and workshops to expose the students to many areas of viewpoints and expertise. Global connectivity, apart from making improvements in education, exposes people to many viewpoints and cultural diversity (Saini and Mir, 2023). By providing students with up-to-date information on social movements, global events, and cultural advancements, social media facilitates discussions and critical analysis of contemporary issues as part of the educational process. By engaging with native speakers worldwide on social media, students can improve their language skills and become more fluent in other languages.

10. **Project-Based Learning:** In the current environment, projects are crucial because they facilitate the development of higher-order thinking abilities. These days, the focus of the educational system is on helping students acquire metacognitive abilities. With project-based learning requiring group interaction outside of the classroom, social media tools can be crucial to its continuation (Sain and Abraham, 2015).
11. **Social Interaction:** Social interaction refers to all forms of communication, information exchange, and contact between individuals or groups within a society (Anna, 2020). Social media platforms enable users to communicate with one another through private messages, comments, and responses to content shared by others. Through social media, users can establish online friendship networks that they can use for communication and information sharing with friends, family, coworkers, and even strangers (Purnama and Asdlori, 2023). With sites like group chats, discussion boards, and collaborative tools, students can interact, share ideas, and work together on assignments and projects. Social networking sites give people the chance to get in touch with previous coworkers, friends, and lovers. Additionally, it facilitates to making of new friends and the sharing of documents, images, audio files, and videos. Social media impacts society's ways of life (Siddiqui and Singh, 2016).
12. **Inclusivity in Learning:** Students with different needs can access educational resources more easily thanks to social media platforms, which can host a variety of multimedia content (text, audio, and video) that caters to different learning styles and preferences. Digital technologies can help integrate diverse student groups into the classroom in several ways, including by increasing the accessibility of course materials, enhancing customization, and providing opportunities for distance learning (Gottschalk, 2023). Social media integration ensures that all students have access to educational materials, information, and support services, irrespective of their circumstances or background. Because social networks offer opportunities for inclusive learning, they are becoming indispensable to education. Social networks provide channels for communication, collaboration, and information access, which makes them crucial for educational inclusion. When inclusive education is well-supported and schools, teachers, parents, and students have access to digital resources that can remove obstacles to education, everyone wins (Thanavathi, 2020). According to research, kids in Europe are most comfortable using smartphones and tablets, which is probably true everywhere since kids these days use smartphones the most (Chaudron, Gioia, and Gemo, 2018). Technology can present challenges for particular student groups if it is not designed with a diverse user base in mind.

Applications, online learning environments, and digital curricula must make broad assumptions about the interests, experiences, and viewpoints of their users (Gottschalk, 2023).

Due to social media's widespread use among students and its ability to facilitate two-way communication, simple knowledge sharing, community building, and collaborative learning all of which improved the educational experience for students, has created opportunities for educational practices (Cheong Li and Ming Wong, 2021). By encouraging student participation and teamwork, social media integration in the classroom is essential to changing traditional learning settings. It facilitates flexible learning formats that accommodate individual schedules and preferences while also improving accessibility to a wide range of learning resources. Social media integration also makes it possible for students and teachers to communicate easily and quickly, fostering a vibrant and encouraging learning community. To sum up, social media integration improves education by encouraging participation, customization, global connectedness, professional development, inclusivity, and efficient communication. This improves the learning process for all parties involved.

Theoretical Foundations for Social Media Integration in Education

Many theoretical frameworks that emphasize the ability of social networks to improve communication, collaboration, and learning can be used to support the integration of social media into education. The following are some fundamental theories that help explain how social media is incorporated into education:

1. **Constructivist Learning Theory:** This theory highlights how learners actively create their knowledge and comprehension of the world by engaging in experiences and critically analyzing those experiences. Students can participate in active learning through social media platforms by exchanging ideas with peers, working together on projects, and sharing their points of view. Students can co-construct knowledge through interactions on collaborative documents, blogs, and discussion forums. Constructivist theory is greatly supported by social media resources. A plethora of relevant and helpful online learning resources can be shared via social networking sites. This aids the pupils in deriving their interpretations. The collaborative aspect of learning and the importance of the social and cultural context for that learning are both heavily emphasized in social constructivist theory (Sain and Abraham, 2015). Social media exchanges foster interactions that open doors for knowledge to grow. Opportunities to interact in online social networks or through computer and/or mobile technologies mediate the cognitive equilibration processes of assimilation and accommodation

of new experiences to one's knowing system or the sociocultural appropriation of new skills. Knowledge is created in a community of shared activity through dialogue, communication, and community engagement (Schrader, 2015).

2. **Connectivism:** This theory believes that knowledge is found in networks and that learning is the process of incorporating nodes, or information sources. Social media helps create networked learning environments where students can interact with peers, experts, and a variety of information sources. With the help of websites such as Twitter, LinkedIn, or specialized educational networks, students can follow trends, explore interests, and join communities of practice that are related to their learning objectives (Sain and Abraham, 2015). Part of connectivism comes from the networked Web 2.0, which is the participatory architect and uses collective memory. The majority of Web 2.0 features are connected to learners' growth. Web 2.0 technologies such as blogs, wikis, and social media platforms serve as the foundation for the development of connectivism, enabling students and teachers to work together and communicate freely and openly at any time, regardless of the transactional distance of time or space (Hendricks, 2019).
3. **Social Learning Theory**: This theory highlights how important it is to observe, emulate, and imitate the actions, attitudes, and feelings of others. Social media platforms offer chances for behavior modeling and observational learning. For example, peer engagement with educational content, discussion participation, and feedback-giving can all be observed by students, and this can have an impact on their learning behaviors and strategies. According to the social learning theory (SLT), learning takes place in a social context through cognitive processes used for observation (Barfi., Bervell., and Arkorful, 2021). SLT describes how a person's learning and behavior patterns are influenced by their surroundings. In this way, people create their content and distribute it to others (Ainin., Naqshbandi., Moghavvemi., and Jaafar, 2015). Social media use has an impact on users' learning outcomes and experiences. Ainin., Naqshbandi., Moghavvemi., and Jaafar, (2015), who underlined that people's behavior is influenced by observing and interacting with others, lend support to this. Individuals' interactions with their surroundings are what lead to changes in their behavior. Consequently, interactions people have with others on social media platforms lead to behavioral consequences that can either positively or negatively impact the individual.
4. **Digital Citizenship and Ethical Considerations**: To encourage knowledgeable and considerate participation in online communities, digital citizenship refers to the ethical and responsible use of technology, particularly social media. Teaching students about digital citizenship concepts including online safety, privacy protection, polite communication, and intellectual property rights is a

key component of integrating social media into the classroom. Teachers can engage students in meaningful learning experiences by modeling and reinforcing these principles through social media platforms. Teachers can teach good digital citizenship and how to use the Internet for productivity by having access to social media (Siddiqui and Singh, 2016).

5. **Active Learning Theory**: This theory encourages participation by having students engage with peers, teachers, and course material through interactive activities. Social media sites give students the chance to produce, share, and discuss content in real time, which can support active learning. Live chats, group projects, and interactive surveys on social media sites like Instagram, TikTok, and Snapchat can promote engagement and a deeper comprehension of academic ideas. Because of its increased interactivity and time-saving benefits, technology-based education has seen a general upsurge in popularity in recent years (Wang, Wang, and Li, 2022).
6. **Self-Determination Theory**: According to this theory, people seek to satisfy their fundamental psychological needs for autonomy, competence, and connection. By giving students more control over how they engage with the materials and other students, social media in the classroom can increase motivation. Students who have access to flexible learning environments, like project-based learning or personalized learning pathways, may feel more competent and independent. Instructors and instructional designers can also find more effective online learner support strategies with the aid of the SDT framework (Chen and Jang, 2010). By putting these concepts into practice, educators can design social media-based learning activities that encourage student participation, collaboration, and critical thinking in virtual environments. Social media in education is suitable for developing students' sense of competence, autonomy, and relatedness to boost their affective learning involvement, according to the self-determination theory (Alturki, and Aldraiweesh, 2024).

Commonly Used Social Media Applications

Applied to education, these platforms leave a very positive note on the student's learning. Teachers who had managed to successfully integrate social media into their teaching methods noted that students were more engaged, participating, and motivated. Many of these social media applications gained popularity and can be integrated into ground or online classrooms to further achievement. These platforms thus enable users to create digital personas that elude physical confines and create forms of sociality that transcend cultural, temporal, and spatial categories (Hasan,2023).

Social media platforms are now essential teaching tools because they give teachers a variety of ways to interact with students and promote learning.

1. **Instagram**: Educators share photos and short videos of classroom activities, projects, and educational resources on Instagram. Many students are already familiar with Instagram, making it a comfortable platform for interaction. Teachers can create class accounts or hashtags to encourage discussions, sharing of ideas, and peer collaboration.
2. **Facebook**: Many educational institutions have Facebook pages or groups, which help them connect with students and parents. They use these platforms to share news and details. Facebooks also offer live-streaming options for online courses and events. The site is considered to be one of the most influential mediums when it comes to building networks in the educational sector.
3. **Twitter**: Used for sharing instructional content, making announcements, and providing rapid updates. Using hashtags associated with courses or topics can help promote networking and more extensive conversations. Teachers use Twitter to stay informed about current events, educational policies, and trends in teaching and learning, which can enrich classroom discussions and lesson planning.
4. **LinkedIn**: Concentrated on networking and professional growth. It is used in higher education to exchange academic and career-related content and establish connections with resources for career planning. An extensive selection of online tutorials and courses covering a variety of subjects, such as academic subjects, technical skills, and professional development, are available from LinkedIn Learning. Many educational institutions provide access to LinkedIn learning as part of their student services. LinkedIn was the original business networking tool and has maintained its social position throughout the last 20 years (Streets, 2023).
5. **Pinterest**: Perfect for discovering and sharing lesson plans, project ideas, and educational materials. Useful for discovering and sharing educational resources, lesson plans, and project ideas. Teachers can create boards for different subjects or projects.
6. **Edmodo:** An e-learning platform that combines social media components with classroom management tools. Instructors and students may discuss and share tasks, assessments, and content. Edmodo can be integrated with other educational apps and platforms, which improves its functionality and lets teachers use other resources for particular teaching needs. Jeff O'Hara and Nic Borg established Edmodo in September 2008 to utilize a cutting-edge social learning platform

to facilitate communication and collaboration between educators and students on a global scale (Gurleen and Sarabjit, 2018).

7. **Flipgrid:** This platform for video discussions enables educators and students to create and share brief videos for topic discussion, question-answering, and interactive, peer-to-peer learning. With Flipgrid, educators can ask students questions or provide prompts, and the students can reply by making quick videos. Students are encouraged to express themselves both orally and visually in this format, which fosters self-expression and communication skills.
8. **Reddit**: Reddit offers many educational communities, where teachers and students can exchange resources, have discussions on particular subjects, and pose questions. Reddit can be used to organize and collaborate on projects.
9. **WhatsApp**: A platform for parent-student and teacher communication. Group chats are useful for announcements, document sharing, and discussion facilitation. WhatsApp allows teachers and students to communicate outside of the classroom to clarify doubts, discuss assignments, and share important updates. Teachers can create WhatsApp groups for their classes to send announcements, reminders about deadlines, and information about upcoming events or exams.
10. **TikTok**: Though TikTok is primarily known as an entertainment platform, there is a growing number of educational content creators offering quick tutorials, practical advice, and engaging lessons. TikTok's visual and interactive elements make it incredibly captivating. Each video post lets users like, comment, save, and share. Users can also layer saved audio tracks over their videos, which helps users find related content (Streets, 2023). Teachers can use this to get pupils interested in a variety of subjects and increase their enjoyment of learning.
11. **Zoom**: Zoom is a popular platform for virtual classrooms, webinars, meetings, and remote collaboration in education. Screen sharing, breakout spaces, and interactive elements that support synchronous learning are supported. Zoom is a platform for virtual classrooms where teachers can hold live online lectures, seminars, and workshops. Teachers can interact with students in real time in a synchronous learning environment by using features like screen sharing, chat, audio, and video.
12. **YouTube:** The primary source for instructional videos, tutorials, and lectures. Instructors can set up channels on which they can post playlists and other materials related to the subjects they teach. An inventive substitute for traditional written work is student-produced videos that cover the material covered in class. Furthermore, a student has the option to review material that they may have missed in class or that they may have misinterpreted. If students have the option to go back and review the material as it was presented in class, they can ultimately do so as many times as necessary to feel comfortable with the concepts.

13. **Padlet:** Teachers and students can collaborate on Padlet, a virtual whiteboard, by exchanging notes, photos, videos, and links. It is adaptable and useful for group projects, brainstorming sessions, presentations, and discussions. Students' creativity and interactive learning are encouraged by it.

Each of these platforms offers different features and benefits based on the particular needs and preferences of educators as well as their requirements and preferences. However, when incorporating social media into educational settings, it's crucial to take privacy, security, and appropriate use policies into account.

Challenges in Using Social Media in Education

The rapid movement of social media through today's schools can be a problem. The biggest downfall to social media use in education is its tempting appeal to students as a distraction. Allowing students to use social media in the classroom is like giving them permission to play on Facebook and aimlessly surf the web. Giving students the ability to use social media platforms during instruction detracts from the learning taking place. The constant pings, notifications, and the urge to check one's feed can significantly impede their concentration, ultimately leading to reduced productivity. Consequently, students may struggle to complete assignments, retain information, or perform well in examinations. The main reason people continue to use social media actively is not because they feel safe and at ease, but rather because they value the benefits or services the platform offers (Anderson,2019).

Integrating social media into education comes with its challenges, despite the potential benefits it offers. Some of the challenges are as:

1. **Privacy issues:** The frequent gathering and utilization of students' private information on social media raises concerns concerning the privacy and security of data. In such conditions, there stands a chance that social media will store information related to the student's private and browsing information; this no doubt raises concerns about the security of data and whether there will be possible breaches. Information shared on social networking sites can be vulnerable to security threats and privacy invasion (Saini and Mir, 2023). Quite probably, teachers and students are knowingly disclosing their personal information through social networking websites since they generally remain unaware of or lack control over the privacy settings.
2. **Distraction:** Social media may be a significant distraction for students, potentially reducing their focus on educational content. It would be comparable to giving students permission to play on Facebook and browse the internet aimlessly if social media was permitted in the classroom. Allowing students to use social

media sites while receiving instruction diminishes the quality of learning that occurs (Sain and Abraham, 2015). The tendency for distraction that social media creates is one of the most obvious negative effects on education (Siddiqui and Singh, 2016). Particularly for students, it can be difficult to resist the lure of social media sites when doing homework or studying (Saini, and Mir, 2023). Engaging in social media discussions or browsing unrelated content can lead to a loss of concentration on educational material, hindering comprehension and retention. Access to social media platforms may tempt students to procrastinate on academic tasks, delaying the completion of assignments or preparation for exams.

3. **Quality control:** There are differences in the credibility, applicability, and caliber of content on social media. It can be difficult to evaluate the quality of educational resources due to the wealth of content on social media, which could result in discrepancies in content standards and learning objectives.
4. **Information overload:** The wealth of information that is easily accessible on social media may terrify educators and students. Students may become less focused as a result of being constantly distracted by notifications, updates, and conversations on social media instead of paying attention to their academic work.
5. **Training and support:** Adequate training and assistance are necessary for social media integration in education to be successful. A considerable skill gap in digital literacy may exist, necessitating extensive training programs. Not every teacher or student has the same level of expertise in using social media sites for learning. Technical expertise is needed on the part of teachers to effectively integrate Social Media into the teaching-learning process. Moreover, before using social media as a learning tool, students should also be trained. Lack of training will only complicate the teaching-learning process rather than fully exploiting its potential for learning purposes (Sain and Abraham, 2015).
6. **Miscommunication:** Students who learn online do not have the same opportunity for clarification and explanation as they would in person. While many students prefer to express their ideas orally a method they have used for years during their studies they encounter some difficulty when using social networking sites to put their views and ideas into writing. On the other hand, users of e-education must develop writing skills to freely express their ideas and opinions. In-person communication enables people to read nonverbal cues like tone, inflection, and body language; these are absent in an online setting.
7. **Lack of Control:** Teachers have little influence over what appears on social media sites, where offensive or irrelevant content may appear. Setting up policies and keeping an eye on platforms is essential to mitigate risks.

8. **Social Media Addiction:** One of the negative effects of social media is that it makes people addicted. People spend lots of time on social networking sites which can divert their concentration and focus from a particular task (Siddiqui and Singh, 2016). Social ties like family ones also weaken as people spend more time connecting to new people.
9. **Psychological effects of using social media among students:** Excessive use of social media has been connected to several mental health problems, such as social isolation, depression, and anxiety. Pupils who use social media extensively may feel more inadequate, compare themselves to others, and worry about missing out on things. These psychological issues may have an effect on their general well-being and, consequently, on their capacity for learning and academic success (Saini and Mir, 2023). Research shows that more usage of social media, the number of social networking sites, and too much time spent on social networking sites are affecting students' mental health such as depression and anxiety (Rajesh and Priya, 2020). One of the research studies shows that female students have low self-esteem and are more depressed than male students regarding social media usage. Students who had a low level of social media usage are better at their psychosocial well-being than those students who had a high and moderate level of media usage (Yimer, 2021). Study showed that students with poor mental health may be greater users of Social Networking Sites (Sampasa-Kanyinga and Lewis, 2015). There is evidence to suggest a direct relationship between Social Media Usage and impaired mental health status, including depression, anxiety, loneliness, and narcissism (Pantic, 2014). Prior research has defined social media fatigue as a situation whereby social media users suffer from mental exhaustion after experiencing various technological, informative, and communicative overloads through their participation and interactions on different online social media platforms (Bright, Kleiser, & Grau, 2015; Lee, Son, & Kim, 2016; Ravindran, Kuan, Chua, & Hoe Lian, 2014; Zhang, Zhao, Lu, & Yang, 2016). Social media clearly has detrimental effects on people's lives, as it encourages young people to overanalyze and criticize their issues as well as themselves (Damota, 2019).
10. **Cyberbullying:** By directing students to engage further in social media during school time, harm to student learning may arise in the form of bullying. Students are also put at risk when interacting with strangers over the web. The age group of learners makes them an easy target for cyberbullying (Sain and Abraham, 2015). Social media provides constant access to communication channels, which means cyberbullying can occur outside of school hours and beyond the control of educators, potentially affecting students' mental well-being. Cyberbullying can create a hostile or unsafe learning environment, affecting students' academic performance, attendance, and overall well-being. Some people use their images

or videos on social sites which can encourage others to use it false fully. Social media can easily affect kids, the reason is sometimes people share photos, and videos on media that contain violence and negative things which can affect the behavior of kids or teenagers. (Siddiqui and Singh, 2016). Many scholars are concerned about certain insidious aspects of cyberbullying. Firstly, because victims can receive unwarranted texts and emails from the comfort of their own homes, cyberbullying may be more pervasive than bullying. Moreover, victims may feel belittled in front of a larger audience since materials posted online have the potential to reach thousands or even millions of people. Because offensive material is hard to eradicate from the internet, victims may need to relive unpleasant experiences over and over again (Van Geel and Vedder, 2019).

11. **Digital divide:** The term "digital divide" was first used in the second half of the 20th century, referring to those people who had access to cell phones and those who did not. Defined from there, it referred to having the financial means and technology to access the internet and use current technology. Still, due to the constant evolution of technology, the "digital divide" remains in flux as it changes (Taylor, 2024). The vast majority of studies on this subject have focused on the "digital divide," or the difference between those with access to technology and the skill to operate it, versus those who do not (Bolt & Crawford, 2000). The Digital divide between urban and rural areas, between the developed and developing worlds, and between the wealthy and the poor is getting wider (Afzal, Khan, Daud, and Ahmed, 2023).

Careful planning is required to get around these challenges and consider the advantages of integrating social media in the classroom. Because social comparison can lead to anxiety, depression, and a lowered sense of self-worth, it has a detrimental psychological impact that is particularly dangerous for students' mental health. These emotional struggles may significantly hinder a person's ability to focus on their studies, which may lower their academic performance. Social media platforms can be the venue for cyberbullying and online harassment. Due to their frequent and heavy usage of these platforms, students are vulnerable to threats, derogatory remarks, and personal attacks. These interactions could have a major impact on their mental health and, consequently, their academic achievement. The content that each user is exposed to on a unique basis is chosen by the big, centralized social media companies using exclusive algorithms. Users cannot possibly comprehend the algorithm's workings to generate their personalized information feed, much less exercise direct control over it. The algorithm chooses the content that is presented to me (Anderson, 2019).

Effective Strategies for Social Media Integration in Education

Social media integration in the classroom can improve instruction, encourage teamwork, and engage students in fresh ways. Here are a few successful methods for doing so:

1. **Promote Collaborative Projects:** Students can engage with peers, professionals, and educators worldwide through social media platforms. This wide network allows for different viewpoints and makes it easier for people to collaborate across geographical boundaries. Students can more easily share project components, like presentations, drafts, or research findings, between themselves thanks to social media's support for sharing different media types, including documents, videos, and images.
2. **Create Class Groups and Pages:** Provide precise instructions on how to participate, behave in conversation, and exhibit expected behaviors. Place a strong emphasis on following school rules, maintaining academic integrity, and polite communication. Invite students and, if appropriate, their guardians, to join the group. Give precise directions on how to sign up and take part in the activity.
3. **Integrate Multimedia Content:** Incorporate multimedia elements such as images, videos, and embedded links to external resources to enhance engagement and understanding. Engage students actively with quizzes, polls, or surveys embedded directly into social media platforms, promoting participation and feedback. Align multimedia content with learning objectives and curriculum standards to reinforce key concepts effectively.
4. **Promote Peer-to-Peer Learning:** Using platforms like Turnitin or Google Docs, students can provide feedback on each other's work, fostering critical thinking and constructive criticism. Students can organize and lead workshops or study sessions on social media platforms, sharing knowledge and expertise with peers. Students can publish articles or blog posts on platforms like Medium or LinkedIn, sharing their knowledge and experiences with peers.
5. **Use Blogs:** Blogs provide a platform for students to reflect on their learning experiences, express their thoughts, and articulate their understanding of concepts. A single person typically writes blogs about a specific subject, and they are typically updated frequently with entries shown in reverse chronological order (Faizi, Afia, and Chiheb, 2013). Writing for blogs encourages students to practice writing skills in a more informal and engaging format. Educators can encourage students to publish polished pieces or multimedia-rich content, demonstrating their learning progress and achievements.

6. **Encourage Reflection and Critical Thinking:** Prompt students to reflect on their social media experiences, analyze information critically, evaluate sources, and consider the impact of their online presence. Use social media as a platform for discussing digital citizenship and ethical considerations.
7. **Digital literacy:** Digital literacy is just one of the foundational skills that will ensure students' success in their future lives in the current digital age. A review of how technology is being used and also provided in the classroom helps to identify gaps in digital literacy skills and work out strategies for enhancing such skills. This would make sure that students are well equipped with abilities to face contemporary workforce demands in a world that is increasing its tendency towards becoming technologically driven (Afzal, Khan, Daud, and Ahmed, 2023). Students need to be equipped with skills in using technology in learning, from curriculum integration to training programs. Topics for teaching learners include digital collaboration, literacy information, online safety, and critical thinking. When equipped with the above-mentioned digital literacy skills, they will be well-equipped to prosper in the digital age (Afzal, Khan, Daud, and Ahmed, 2023).
8. **Reducing Adverse Effects of Social Media on Education:** There is no denying the negative impact of social media on education, from misinformation and cyberbullying to distractions and decreased productivity. However, these unfavorable effects can be reduced with knowledge and proactive steps, ensuring that social media stays a tool for education and personal development rather than a barrier. Promoting digital literacy is one of the best strategies to lessen the detrimental effects of social media on education (Saini and Mir, 2023). Many students use social media without considering all of the possible consequences that could occur. The student who takes digital literacy classes will be able to wade through information found online, determine sources, and differentiate between fact and misinformation. These are very vital skills in living at a time when wrong information goes virally on social media. Spending time on social media can be a major waste of time that further affects productivity and academic achievement. The educational institutions should therefore incorporate time management skills into their curriculum.

Utilizing social media is beneficial but it should be done carefully to avoid addiction (Siddiqui and Singh, 2016). Instead of merely using this tool for texting or messaging, students should learn how to use media for positive purposes in their educational classes (Kalia, 2013).

Parental and Community Involvement in Social Media Integration in Education

For social media integration in education to be successful, parental and community involvement is essential.

1. **Parent-Teacher Communication through Social Media:** Techniques for enabling frequent updates, announcements, and conversations between educators and parents through the use of social media sites such as Facebook groups, Twitter, or specialized apps. Plan and organize parent-teacher conferences with the help of social media sites.
2. **Educating Parents on Social Media Use:** Outlining guidelines for parents to encourage their kids to use social media for learning and reiterating the values of digital citizenship. Describe the various social media sites that young people are interested in, like Facebook, Instagram, TikTok, and Snapchat. Describe their characteristics and objectives. Talk about the risks that come with using social media, such as exposure to offensive content, cyberbullying, and privacy issues.
3. **Encouraging Parental Participation:** Establishing channels via which parents can offer suggestions, materials, and comments on learning projects supported by social media. Inform parents about how social media is utilized in the classroom to improve student learning. Parents should be invited to participate in the decision-making process when it comes to integrating social media. To make sure that policies, guidelines, and social media-related activities are in line with parents' expectations and concerns, get their feedback.
4. **Workshops and Webinars:** Putting on parent workshops or webinars on subjects like digital literacy, online safety, and efficient use of social media in the classroom. Techniques for integrating social media into curriculums and lesson plans.
5. **Involving Parents in School Activities:** Make use of social media to extend invitations to parents for volunteer work, parent-teacher conferences, and school functions. Provide parents a way to voice their opinions and pose inquiries regarding their children's social media education. Keep lines of communication open and transparent with parents about the school's social media integration strategy. Spread the word about the goals, rules, and regulations surrounding the use of social media in educational settings.
6. **Transparent Communication**: Create open lines of communication with parents to outline the goals, advantages, and rules surrounding the use of social media in the classroom. Give details about the platforms that will be used, the

methods for utilizing social media, and the measures taken to protect the safety and privacy of students.

> Social media integration in education can improve student learning and build stronger ties with parents and the larger community when educators and administrators create a positive learning environment.

Curriculum Integration Strategies for Social Media Use in Education

Start by figuring out which competencies or curriculum-based learning objectives can be enhanced with the help of social media. Consider how social media can support critical thinking, creativity, teamwork, communication, and digital literacy, among other abilities. Choose social media platforms for your pupils according to their learning goals and age. Consider using Twitter for brief discussions or news updates, LinkedIn for professional networking and career exploration, and Instagram for visual storytelling, or art projects. Develop curriculum-aligned activities that capitalize on the unique features of social media platforms. Examples include collaborative work on projects, online discussions, multimedia presentations, and involvement in global discussions about curriculum topics. Students must be taught how to use social media critically and purposefully to maximize learning outcomes if social media is to be successfully incorporated into the course curriculum (Abe and Jordan, 2014).

Use social media to relate what is being taught in the classroom to current affairs and issues. Examine social media campaigns, research online, or follow hashtags related to current events to gain an understanding of their significance and impact. Make assessments to determine how well students are using social media for education. Examples of assessments include analyses of digital projects, social media presentations of findings, and evaluations of the quality of contributions to online forums. Pay attention to how well the curriculum's objectives are being met by social media integration. To enhance and adapt practices over time, gather student feedback, monitor engagement metrics, and consider instructional strategies. By putting these strategies into practice, educators can make better use of social media as a teaching tool that boosts student engagement, promotes collaboration, and gives students the skills they need. Social networking sites also conduct online examinations which play an important role in enhancing the student's knowledge (Siddiqui and Singh, 2016).

DISCUSSION

Social media's influence on education is a complex and dynamic phenomenon with positive as well as negative implications. Social media helps in participation, engagement, and content sharing. These discussions align with how social media platforms have become an integral part of our daily lives, reshaping how we communicate, share information, and learn (Saini and Mir, 2023). Educators need to understand that, in today's world, social media is starting to replace traditional classroom instruction for students. Students are motivated, engaged, and captivated by social media. Because of the integration, there has been a rise in the amount of active student participation in those classes, and students no longer feel shy about asking questions or expressing their opinions (Drylie, 2013). Curriculum integration strategies can be helpful in effective social media integration in education which is supported by Saini and Mir's 2023 study in which they emphasized that Social media platforms can be incorporated by teachers into their lesson plans through sharing resources, interacting with students, and starting conversations. A multifaceted approach that brings together educators, parents, and students will help to lessen the negative impacts. We can ensure that instead of being a hindrance in education, social media becomes a source for positive online communities, critical thinking, responsible screen time, and digital literacy. For multiple participants to make the most of social media's helpful educational influence and the least of its negative impacts, it must be involved. This includes teaching children social media literacy and guiding responsible usage by parents. Also, schools need to work together with social media companies as well as experts in social media literacy to enhance their safe use guidelines. Teachers and parents can monitor their kids' social media use to ensure that they don't encounter any offensive or harmful material or cyberbullying (Purnama and Asdlori, 2023).

CONCLUSION

The use of social media as a teaching tool has advantages and disadvantages. The four main issues with social networking education are privacy, genuine friendship, time commitment, and misconceptions. On the other hand, social networking's application in education is greatly influenced by factors like repeatability, flexibility, ease of use, and accessibility. Teachers need to start learning about and getting comfortable with social media tools to integrate them with ease. Rather than throwing out their outdated teaching strategies entirely, educators should modify them to better suit the needs of today's students. Additionally, social media has a big impact on how students view other people and themselves in larger social contexts. Students' self-image, values, and adherence to societal norms may be significantly impacted by the wide range of content they encounter on social media, which includes messages, images, and comments from peers and other users. There is constant pressure on social media to present the "ideal" version of oneself, which can significantly alter one's self-perception and encourage social comparisons. Teachers and educational institutions need to be aware of how important social media is to students' lives and take proactive steps to incorporate it into the classroom in a seamless manner. Giving students a thorough understanding of social media literacy is crucial to give them the tools they need to successfully navigate this digital environment. This entails educating people about the advantages and disadvantages of social media and offering advice on how to use it responsibly. While there are social media tools that are better than others, teachers must consider what works and what doesn't for their students and the curriculum. However, social media use is becoming commonplace, and educators must provide the best learning environment possible so that their students can thrive. Recognizing that social media can have significant psychological and emotional effects on students is important. In addition to the constant pressure to maintain a flawless online persona, the prevalence of cyberbullying, and the fierce social competition, students may suffer from higher levels of stress and anxiety. Beyond the immediate emotional effects, there are long-term issues that affect students' academic performance, interpersonal relationships, and mental health. The need for resources and support systems to assist students in navigating the complex psychological terrain that their interactions with technology have shaped is growing for both educational institutions and society at large.

ACKNOWLEDGMENT

Thanks to the reviewers for their valuable suggestions. Learned a lot from their analysis of this book chapter. Tried to follow those suggestions which will be useful for future writing endeavors. Thanks to the editors and the whole team.

REFERENCES

Abe, P. & Jordan, N. A. (2014). Integrating Social Media Into the Classroom Curriculum. Integrating-Social-Media-Into-the-Classroom-Curriculum.pdf (ubc.ca)

Afzal, A., Khan, S., Daud, S., & Ahmed, Z. (2023). Addressing the Digital Divide: Access and Use of Technology in Education. *Journal of Social Sciences Review*, 3(2), 883–895. DOI: 10.54183/jssr.v3i2.326

Ahmed, R. (2016). Social Media Integration in Secondary Education in Pakistan. *Journal of Education and Educational Development*, 3(1), 74. DOI: 10.22555/joeed.v3i1.712

Ainin, S., Naqshbandi, N. M., Moghavvemi, S., & Jaafar, N. I. (2015). Facebook usage, socialization, and academic performance. *Computers & Education*, 83, 64–73. DOI: 10.1016/j.compedu.2014.12.018

Allen, K., Ryan, T., Gray, D., McInerney, D., & Waters, L. (2014). Social media use and social connectedness in adolescents: The positives and the potential pitfalls. *Australian Educational and Developmental Psychologist*, 31(1), 18–31. DOI: 10.1017/edp.2014.2

Alturki, U. & Aldraiweesh, A. (2024). The impact of self-determination theory: the moderating functions of social media (SM) use in education and affective learning engagement | Humanities and Social Sciences Communications (nature.com)

Anderson, T. (2019). Challenges and Opportunities for Use of Social Media in Higher Education. *Journal of Learning for Development*, 6(1), 6–19. DOI: 10.56059/jl4d.v6i1.327

Bandura, A. (1997). *Self-efficacy: The exercise of control*. Macmillan.

Barfi, K. A., Bervell, B., & Arkorful, V. (2021). Integration of social media for smart pedagogy: Initial perceptions of senior high school students in Ghana. *Education and Information Technologies*, 26(3), 3033–3055. DOI: 10.1007/s10639-020-10405-y

Bolt, D., & Crawford, R. (2000). *Digital divide: Computers and our children's future*. TV Books LLC.

Boyd, D. M., & Ellison, N. B. (2007). Social Network Sites: Definition, History, and Scholarship. *Journal of Computer-Mediated Communication*, 13(1), 210–230. DOI: 10.1111/j.1083-6101.2007.00393.x

Bright, L. F., Kleiser, S. B., & Grau, S. L. (2015). Too much Facebook? An exploratory examination of social media fatigue. *Computers in Human Behavior*, 44(44), 148–155. DOI: 10.1016/j.chb.2014.11.048

Cao, X., Guo, X., Liu, H., & Gu, J. (2015). The role of social media in supporting knowledge integration: A social capital analysis. *Information Systems Frontiers*, 17(2), 351–362. DOI: 10.1007/s10796-013-9473-2

Chen, K. C., & Jang, S. J. (2010). Motivation in online learning: Testing a model of self-determination theory. *Computers in Human Behavior*, 26(4), 741–752. DOI: 10.1016/j.chb.2010.01.011

Cheong Li, K., & Ming Wong, B. T. (2021). The Opportunities and Challenges of Social Media in Higher Education: A Literature Review. SN Computer Science, https://link.springer.com/article/10.1007/s42979-021-00857-5#citeas

Damota, M. D. (2019). Effects of Social Media on Society. *New Media and Mass Communication*, 78, 7–11. DOI: 10.7176/NMMC

Dhir, A., Yossatorn, Y., Kaur, P., & Chen, S. (2018). Online social media fatigue and psychological wellbeing—A study of compulsive use, fear of missing out, fatigue, anxiety and depression. *International Journal of Information Management*, 40, 141–152. DOI: 10.1016/j.ijinfomgt.2018.01.012

Drylie, D. (2013). Social Media in Education Assessing the Benefits of Integration. content (snhu.edu)

Ellison, N. B., Steinfield, C., & Lampe, C. (2007). The Benefits of Facebook "Friends:" Social Capital and College Students' Use of Online Social Network Sites. *Journal of Computer-Mediated Communication*, 12(4), 1143–1168. DOI: 10.1111/j.1083-6101.2007.00367.x

Faizi, R., El Afia, A., & Chiheb, R. (2013). Exploring the potential benefits of using social media in education. *International Journal of Engineering Pedagogy*, 3(4), 50–53. DOI: 10.3991/ijep.v3i4.2836

Ferguson, C., DiGiacomo, M., Gholizadeh, L., Ferguson, L. E., & Hickman, L. D. (2017). The integration and evaluation of a social-media facilitated journal club to enhance the student learning experience of evidence-based practice: A case study. *Nurse Education Today*, 48, 123–128. DOI: 10.1016/j.nedt.2016.10.002 PMID: 27810629

Garelli, G., & Ranu, S. K. (2018). The attitude of university students towards educational networking through social media about academic satisfaction and study habits. http://hdl.handle.net/10603/218795

Gottschalk, F. (2023). Digital equity and inclusion in education: An overview of practice and policy in OECD countries. oecd.org

Greenhow, C., & Lewin, C. (2019). Social media and education: Reconceptualizing the boundaries of formal and informal learning. In *social media and education* (pp. 6-30). Routledge.

Hamadi, M., El-Den, J., Narumon Sriratanaviriyakul, C., & Azam, S. (2021). A social media adoption framework as pedagogical instruments in higher education classrooms. *E-Learning and Digital Media*, 18(1), 55–85. DOI: 10.1177/2042753020950869

Hasan, M. I. (2023). The Impact of Social Media on Mental Health and Well-Being on Students. researchgate.net

Hendricks, G. (2019). Connectivism as a Learning Theory and Its Relation to Open Distance Education. *Progressio South African Journal for Open and Distance Learning Practice*, 41(1), 1–13. DOI: 10.25159/2663-5895/4773

Islam, M., Kim, D. A., & Kwon, M. (2020). A comparison of two forms of instruction: Pre-recorded video lectures vs. Live ZOOM lectures for education in the business management field. *Sustainability (Basel)*, 12(19), 8149–8160. DOI: 10.3390/su12198149

Ismail, N. (2015). The Integration of New Media in Schools: Comparing Policy with Practice. *International Education Studies*, 8(12), 231–240. DOI: 10.5539/ies.v8n12p231

Jaffer, R., Davids, Z., & Seymour, L. F. (2023). Challenges of Using Social Media as a Teaching Tool in Secondary Schools. *European Conference on e-Learning*, 22(1), 131-138. DOI: 10.34190/ecel.22.1.1657

Javaeed, A., Kibria, Z., Khan, Z., & Ghauri, S. K. (2020). Impact of social media integration in teaching methods on exam outcomes. *Advances in Medical Education and Practice*, 11, 53–61. DOI: 10.2147/AMEP.S209123 PMID: 32021544

Kalia, G. (2013). A Research Paper on Social Media: An Innovative Educational Tool. *Issues and Ideas in Education*, 1(1), 1-8.

Kumar, V., & Nanda, P. (2022). Social Media as a Learning Tool: A Perspective on Formal and Informal Learning. *International Journal of Educational Reform*, 33(3), 1–26. DOI: 10.1177/10567879221094303

Labus, A., Simic, K., Barac, D., Despotovic-Zrakic, M., & Radenkovic, M. (2012). Integration of social network services in the e-education process. *Metalurgia International*, 17(7), 161.

Lampropoulos, G., Makkonen, P., & Siakas, K. (2022). Social Media in Education: A Case Study Regarding Higher Education Students' Viewpoints | SpringerLink.

Lee, A.R., Son, S.M., Kim K.K. (2016). Information and communication technology overload and social networking service fatigue: A stress perspective. *Computers in Human Behavior*, 55 (A), 51-61.

Luo, T., Freeman, C., & Stefaniak, J. (2020). "Like, comment, and share"—professional development through social media in higher education: A systematic review. *Educational Technology Research and Development*, 68(1), 1659–1683. Advance online publication. DOI: 10.1007/s11423-020-09790-5

Marzulina, L., Habibi, A., Mukminin, A., Desvitasari, D., Yaakob, M. F. M., & Ropawandi, D. (2018). The integration of social networking services in higher education: Benefits and barriers in teaching English. *International Journal of Virtual and Personal Learning Environments*, 8(2), 46–62. DOI: 10.4018/IJVPLE.2018070104

Moran, M., Seaman, J., & Tinti-Kane, H. (2011). *Teaching, learning, and sharing: How Today's higher education faculty use social media*. Babson Survey Research Group.

Nandigam, D., Tirumala, S. S., & Tirumala, N. (2014). Personalized Learning: Current Status and Potential. *IEEE Conference on E-Learning, E-Management, and E-Services*. DOI:DOI: 10.1109/IC3e.2014.7081251

Okoro, E. (2012). Integrating social media technologies in higher education: Costs-benefits analysis. *Journal of International Education Research*, 8(3), 255–262. DOI: 10.19030/jier.v8i3.7107

Pan, Y., Coleman, L., Manago, S., & Goodof, D. (2019). Effects of social media usage on social integration of university students. *International Journal of Technology in Teaching and Learning*, 15(1), 1–17. DOI: 10.37120/ijttl.2019.15.1.01

Pantic, I. (2014). Online social networking and mental health. *Cyberpsychology, Behavior, and Social Networking*, 17(10), 652–657. DOI: 10.1089/cyber.2014.0070 PMID: 25192305

Pulido, C. M., Redondo-Sama, G., Sorde-Marti, T., & Flecha, R. (2018). Social impact in social media: A new method to evaluate the social impact of research. *PLoS One*, 13(8), e0203117. DOI: 10.1371/journal.pone.0203117 PMID: 30157262

Purnama, Y., & Asdlori, A. (2023). The role of social media in students' social perception and interaction: Implications for learning and education. *Technology and Society Perspectives*, 1(2), 45–55. DOI: 10.61100/tacit.v1i2.50

Rajesh, D., & Priya, V. K. (2020). Impact of Social Media on Mental Health of Students. *International Journal of Scientific & Technology Research*, 9(3), 3796–3800.

Ravindran, T., Kuan, Y., Chua, A., & Hoe Lian, D. G. (2014). Antecedents and effects of social network fatigue. *Journal of the Association for Information Science and Technology*, 65(11), 2306–2320. DOI: 10.1002/asi.23122

Riady, Y., Alqahtany, T. M., Habibi, A., Sofyan, S., & Albelbisi, N. A. (2022). Factors affecting teachers' social media use during covid-19. *Cogent Social Sciences*, 8(1), 2115658. Advance online publication. DOI: 10.1080/23311886.2022.2115658

Saini, N., & Mir, S. A. (2023). Social media: Usage and the impact on Education. *Journal of Namibian Studies*, 33(3), 4670–4689. DOI: 10.59670/jns.v33i.4041

Sainil, C., & Abraham, J. (2015). Using Social Media for Educational Purposes: Approaches and Challenges. *International Education Conference 2015 on Learning Technologies in Education,* Excel India Publishers, 484-489.

Sampasa-Kanyinga, H., & Lewis, R. F. (2015). Frequent use of social networking sites is associated with poor psychological functioning among children and adolescents. *Cyberpsychology, Behavior, and Social Networking*, 18(7), 380–385. DOI: 10.1089/cyber.2015.0055 PMID: 26167836

Schrader, D. E. (2015). Constructivism and Learning in the Age of Social Media: Changing Minds and Learning Communities. *New Directions for Teaching and Learning*, 144(144), 23–35. DOI: 10.1002/tl.20160

Shepherd, H., & Lane, J. (2019). In the mix: Social integration and social media adoption. *Social Science Research*, 82, 1–17. DOI: 10.1016/j.ssresearch.2019.02.004 PMID: 31300070

Siddiqui, S. & Singh, T. (2016). Social Media Its Impact with Positive and Negative Aspects. International Journal of Computer Applications Technology and Research, 5(2), 71-75.

Snethen, G., & Zook, P. (2016). Utilizing social media to support community integration. *American Journal of Psychiatric Rehabilitation*, 19(2), 160–174. DOI: 10.1080/15487768.2016.1171176

Streets, M. (2023). The history and evolution of social media explained. techtarget.com

Tariq, W., Mehboob, M., Khan, M. A., & Ullah, F. (2012).. . *International Journal of Computational Science*, 9(4), 407–411.

Taylor, K. (2024). The Digital Divide: What It Is, and What's Being Done to Close It. The Digital Divide: What It Is, and What's Being Done to Close It. investopedia.com

Tess, P. A. (2013). The role of social media in higher education classes (real and virtual)–A literature review. *Computers in Human Behavior*, 29(5), A60–A68. DOI: 10.1016/j.chb.2012.12.032

Thanavath, C. (2020). Digital tools with inclusive education. *Inclusive Education*, International Research Foundations, Konchnadu Publications, 320-326.

Van Geel, M., & Vedder, P. (2020). Does cyberbullying predict internalizing problems and conduct problems when controlled for traditional bullying? *Scandinavian Journal of Psychology*, 61(2), 307–311. DOI: 10.1111/sjop.12601 PMID: 31802517

Wang, H., Wang, M. & Li, G. (2022). The use of social media inside and outside the classroom to enhance students' engagement in EFL contexts – PMC. nih.gov

Yeh, E., & Swinehart, N. (2018). A model for mobile social media integration in constructivist ESL classrooms. In *Social Media in Education: Breakthroughs in Research and Practice* (pp. 258–278). IGI Global. DOI: 10.4018/978-1-5225-5652-7.ch014

Yimer, B. L. (2021). Social media usage, psychosocial well-being and academic performance. *Community Health Equity Research & Policy*, 43(4), 399–404. DOI: 10.1177/0272684X211033482 PMID: 34275379

Yohanna, A. (2020). The influence of social media on social interactions among students. *Indonesian Journal of Social Sciences*, 12(2), 34–48. DOI: 10.20473/ijss.v12i2.22907

Zaidieh, A. J. Y. (2012). The use of social networking in education: Challenges and opportunities. *World of Computer Science and Information Technology Journal*, 2(1), 18–21.

Zhang, S., Zhao, L., Lu, Y., & Yang, J. (2016). Do you get tired of socializing? An empirical explanation of discontinuous usage behavior in social network services. *Information & Management*, 53(7), 904–914. DOI: 10.1016/j.im.2016.03.006

Chapter 16
Innovative Approaches to Problem-Solving Through Educational Technology Integration

Piyal Roy
https://orcid.org/0009-0007-5378-2789
West Bengal State University, India

Rajat Pandit
West Bengal State University, India

Sudip Kumar Naskar
Jadavpur University, India

ABSTRACT

Society is currently going through major changes in the educational field due to technological changes. The impact of EdTech on teaching methods, learner commitment, and effectiveness is explored in this paper. Adaptive learning systems differentiate students, utilizing technology like VR and AR for immersive learning, encouraging participation, understanding, and empowering students with control over their learning. We emphasize the need to employ technology judiciously and cautiously to find the right balance between implementing modern technology and using traditional instructional techniques. The future of EdTech also looking bright with such developments as AI adding a more personalized element and metaverse allowing everyone to go to school online. The effective implementation of EdTech allows for the development of a promising future for everyone since education should be open and engaging for all students and transform education into a lifelong process.

DOI: 10.4018/979-8-3693-6745-2.ch016

1. INTRODUCTION

It goes beyond the mere use of computers in the classrooms. It indicates a science that is constantly changing and transforming, and involves the strategic combination of ever-developing technologies – from hardware and software to related practices – with traditional education principles and pedagogical strategies to facilitate learning. EdTech offers a vast and dynamic toolkit for educators, encompassing:

- **Digital and online learning platforms:** Distance learning: MOOCs, Interactive Learning Environments and Learning apps for flexible and inclusive learning.
- **Learning Management Systems (LMS):** Learning management systems – online software platforms that are designed to help better organize courses and track student performance and the delivery of content so that instructors can focus on teaching.
- **Mobile learning (m-learning):** Institutionalizing learning through utilizing ubiquitous devices such as smartphones and tablets in schools to enhance the availability of learning opportunities on the go and personalization of the learning process.
- **Gamification:** Gamification is the practice of incorporating game mechanics into something that is not a game. It is widely used in education to engage students in learning and improve memory retention.
- **Adaptive learning systems:** When technological devices are employed, the learning content may be directed to a specific student in accordance with his or her preferences and needs as to the level of difficulty and the speed of work, which helps to increase the success rate of the learning process in general.
- **AR and VR:** Creation of educational simulations that may allow the students to be sent to different places and visualize the ideas as well as engage more in the content.
- **Data analytics and big data**: Taking personal notes to individualize students based on their needs, areas of deficiencies, and strengths to improve instructional techniques to achieve learning outcomes.
- **Social and collaborative learning platforms:** These are the tools that will assist in creating a more engaging and dynamic classroom environment through the facilitation of peer interchange communication and group projects.

It is also important to understand that EdTech is not only relevant for formal classrooms, but it can also be used in informal learning environments. It finds use in several areas of education like the corporate sector, K-12 segment, higher education, career training, and personal growth projects. Online teaching helps teachers to meet the needs of their students and make the classroom more inclusive.

It is safe to say that the instructional technology is a very dynamic field. New methods and technology are continually being invented and this is useful to teachers because they have enabled teachers to have useful techniques and resources to enhance their teaching and improve students' performance. There are several compelling reasons for it to continue to stay abreast with these developments.

- **Enhanced Learning Outcomes:** New technologies have the potential to make learning more personalized and tailored to different learning styles as well as to increase the role of an interactive nature in the learning process. This can translate to demonstrable enhancements in terms of the knowledge acquisition and retention, critical thinking skills, and problem-solving abilities of students.
- **Increased Student Engagement:** There are a number of innovations which are based on the game, simulation, and interactive approaches to education that can considerably increase the motivation of the students and attract their attention. Thus, learning environment becomes dynamic and students are actual participants of the process instead of being just 'consumers' of information.
- **Preparing Students for the Future:** Technology is now prevalent in the world, and preparing students to use and evaluate the technological tools in the real world is crucial for their future career (Sarkar et al., 2024). Adopting various EdTechs in the classroom can ensure that students are equipped with the skills they need to be successful in the future workplace.
- **Addressing Diverse Learner Needs:** EdTech presents a wide variety of imparting and learning tools and techniques than the traditional ones. This ability enables educators to plan instruction according to the learning styles, ability, and level of each learner. For instance, students with dyslexia can use text-to-speech applications and video and audio recordings of lessons, while visual learners can use interactive simulations and AR/VR environments.
- **Efficiency and Accessibility:** The use of technology in the management of administrative activities could increase the time that educators spend in the classrooms and performing individualized instruction and relating with students. Also, EdTech tools can present very valuable learning opportunities for students in inaccessible geographies or with a complicated schedule.

It is possible that educators will use EdTech to expand educational opportunities for children to become more inclusive and effective, as well as more engaging, so that they can achieve success in the digital world by keeping abreast of new trends.

This article will seek to address this need for the effective understanding of the developing trends in the field of educational technology. It describes the current situation of EdTech, explains the most promising trends that are developing in the field and reveals the ways these technologies affect education and learning.

2. HISTORICAL CONTEXT AND EVOLUTION

EdTech has a history in the ancient times such as the cave paintings and writing systems before it can develop into modern EdTech such as the computer-aided instruction systems. These tools facilitate open learning environments where learners can learn in an interactive way and learn on their own while they share information. Differentiated instruction is geared towards varying learning styles and adapts the level of difficulty as well as the learning pace of the students. The online platforms, social media tools, and web tools make it easier to achieve the culture of collaboration, game-based learning, and provide multimedia content. EdTech also makes it easier and more flexible for the students too.

2.1. Brief History of Educational Technology

The history of the EdTech can be traced from the first time man developed tools for learning. For example, cave paintings indicated the existence of a medium through which information and narratives could be passed from one generation to another. The development of writing systems such as cuneiform and hieroglyphic also helped to transform education as information can now be kept and made accessible to more people.

The article also explains that in the past, there have been different advancements that contributed to the development of educational practices. The oldest of them is the abacus, which is a calculating device and was used in teaching math principles even in the ancient times. The invention of the printing press by Johannes Gutenberg in the fifteenth century represents an important milestone in history. It facilitated the development of technology that saw mass production of books and spread of knowledge and also the invention of standardized curricula.

The vast progress of the 20th century in the area of learning technologies. The 20th century marks the dawn of the instructional films, radio shows, and overhead projector that gave a new way of teaching inside the classroom. Computer-assisted instruction: The idea was created in the 1950s and introduced by B. F. Skinner under the label of programmed instruction.

2.2. Key Milestones in the Evolution of Educational Tools and Methods

Several key milestones stand out in the evolution of educational tools and methods, each one building upon the last to create a richer learning experience:

- **1800s: Invention of the Blackboard:** This simple yet effective tool revolutionized classroom instruction by providing a space for visual presentations, note-taking, and collaborative learning. It became a mainstay in classrooms for over a century.
- **1920s & 1930s:** Introduction of Educational Films and Radio Broadcasts- These technologies brought multimedia elements into the classroom for the first time. Educational films exposed students to diverse locations, historical events, and scientific phenomena that would have been difficult or impossible to experience first hand. Radio broadcasts offered a captivating way to deliver lectures, dramatizations, and educational programs to a wide audience.
- **1945:** Vannevar Bush's Memex Concept- This visionary proposal for a hypertext system, outlined in Bush's essay "As We May Think," laid the groundwork for the development of the World Wide Web and its subsequent impact on education. Memex (Park, 2014) envisioned a device that would allow users to store information on microfilm and then retrieve it through a network of associative links, foreshadowing the non-linear information access that the web would provide.
- **1950s:** Programmed Instruction and Teaching Machines- B.F. Skinner's work on programmed learning paved the way for individualized instruction and the use of technology in delivering educational content. Teaching machines, based on Skinner's principles, presented learners with information in small, sequential steps and provided immediate feedback on their responses. While these machines faced limitations, they marked a significant step towards personalized learning.
- **1960s & 1970s:** Computer Technology and Education – The personal computer as a learning tool emerged in the late twentieth century and gave rise to such innovations as simulation games and the first CAI (Computer-aided instruction). These programs, though often text-focused and used in drills, represented a higher degree of student involvement with learning content.
- **1980s & 1990s:** Educational Software and the Internet- The history of the educational software and the invention of the World Wide Web and the web-based learning tools considerably facilitated and significantly enhanced the process of the access to information. The first one is educational software that offered a more engaging and interactive way for the students to learn the

different subjects while the other one is the internet that opened the students to a whole universe of learning materials and online learning.

- **2000s & Onwards:** New technological improvements in the field of educational technology- Field of educational technology has been changing due to the new technological advancements like increased use of mobile devices, social media in classrooms, and new technologies like big data, AR, and AI. Mobile learning also has an advantage of allowing the students to access the course materials and do assignments at the convenience of their time and place. The social media has the potential to promote group work, share of ideas and even peer teaching both in and out of the classroom. New technologies have the power to address some of the most critical problems in education today, such as the personalization of learning, the development of virtual classrooms, and the generation of quantitative data to guide instruction.

These are significant because they demonstrate the fact that EdTech is a constantly changing and developing field, in which every new development is a further development of the previous one.

2.3. Transition from Traditional to Modern Educational Technologies

The historical development of educational technology therefore clearly denotes a historical shift in learning methods. The traditional classrooms were characterized by teacher-centered instruction with the focus on mere learning through memorizing and passing instructions through lectures. Although suitable for delivering certain information, the use of this approach to teaching has its shortcomings in cultivating critical skills, problem-solving techniques, and the practical use of knowledge.

On the other hand, today's technology gives instructors the ability to develop engaging and learner-focused classroom models. Interactive learning systems, simulations, and games help the learners to find information on their own, perform experiments through a simulation, and work in groups to solve a given task. This allows the student to have a better grasp of the subject and how to utilize knowledge outside of the classroom. Besides, EdTech allows learners to be engaged in differentiated learning, which is a core concept of modern learning theories. Assessment systems for adaptive learning measure student performance to make adjustments to the pace and difficulty of instruction. Students are ensured of intellectual stimulation in this way and, therefore, spared from unnecessary work on too complicated contents and unnecessary repetitiveness of assignments. Additionally a wide variety of electronic media addresses variable learning styles. Websites that are suitable for visual learners include those with infographics and simulations; the ones that are usable for auditory learners include podcasts and audiobooks; and the ones that are good for kinesthetic learners include interactive exercises and simulations. EdTech ensures that every student has the best opportunity to meet their full potential based on their desires and needs.

The capacity to interact and share information is equally important in the current learning system. Social media tools and other websites do not have geographical boundaries and therefore students can reach peers and exchange ideas and projects from a distance. It promotes and develops teamwork, peer learning review and also the use of media communication – all vital for the modern working environment.

Rising EdTech software also helps in the crucial engagement and motivation issues. They can also be used in an intrinsic manner by including some aspects of gamification like points, badges, and leaderboards, among others. This appeals to students' sense of competitiveness and their need to achieve, turning what used to be a tedious exercise into a learning activity they actually enjoy. Moreover, videos, simulations, as well as interactive activities engage students' minds, and help them to perceive connections between the theory they study, and the reality outside. One of the technologies that have revolutionized learning is the educational technology. The distance learning and customised e-learning support have the ability to provide high-quality education to those who cannot attend classes physically due to geographical limitations, disabilities, or non-traditional scheduling. Learners can go through the curriculum at their own convenience and repeat concepts that they may not have understood at the first instance; it is also personal as learners have control and can decide what they would like to learn. This new flexibility is beneficial to different learning styles and also offers access to education benefits to more people.

3. CURRENT TRENDS IN EDUCATIONAL TECHNOLOGY

The current state of educational technology presents incredible opportunities and trends that are changing the face of learning and instruction. These trends provide adaptability, availability and a plethora of opportunities in learning from diverse needs to different learning styles.

3.1. MOOCs and Digital and Online Learning Platforms

Today it is easy to see that digital and online education platforms are a trend that is capable of completely changing and improving the sphere of education (Bates, 2019).

Massive Open Online Courses (MOOCs): A MOOC allows one to benefit from high-quality educational content provided by the best universities and other institutions in the world. They provide more flexibility and are much more affordable for a learner to gain new knowledge and skills based on his or her location, nationality, or financial background (Zarghami, 2022). This democratization of education enables people to learn more and earn additional qualifications thus enhancing their career opportunities. The National Bureau of Economic Research recently conducted a study that showed that the employment of MOOCs can result in better wages and employment opportunities (Majerowicz & Zárate, 2023).

Microlearning platforms: Such channels are suitable to the learner who seeks quick and easy access to information. They offer just-in-time lessons which emphasize on specific skills or subjects to provide learners with concentrated knowledge or enable learners to complete training tasks in short periods of time (Emerson & Berge, 2018). It is especially beneficial for people who can't get much time for continuous learning and busy professionals who can easily fit microlearning modules into ordinary tasks and do them during commuting or breaks. Recent research conducted by the Institute for Corporate Learning reveals that microlearning techniques can increase knowledge recall by up to 25% compared to generic training and learning strategies (Redondo et al., 2020).

Adaptive learning platforms: Such systems base their operation on algorithms for individualizing learning for every learner. They also transcend the one-size-fits-all approach by conducting pre-assessments to identify strengths and weaknesses, facilitating the observation of performance throughout the course of the study, and identifying knowledge gaps (Marienko et al., 2020). Adaptive learning systems enhance the learner's experience by modifying the level of complexity of content and the rate at which it is presented, and by offering new routes to complete the same learning objective. A research conducted by the Bill & Melinda Gates Foundation on adaptive learning suggested that it can help to improve student achievement (Aliyeva, 2022).

Interactive learning environments: The era of boring static presentations is over. Interactive learning environments are the use of multimedia elements, simulations, and gamified activities to present an interesting and engaging learning content (Lange et al., 2022). These platforms help students to shift from passive knowledge acquisition to active learning and seek to engage learners in interactive practices and discovery learning. NRC research also notes that interactive learning environments are instrumental in developing critical thinking and scientific inquiry skills.

3. 2. Learning Management Systems

It is therefore not a surprise that LMS have evolved into one of the most prominent and fundamental components of learning technology. Such platforms become the central place for organizing course work, providing content, tracking progress, and interacting (Turnbull et al., 2020).

Streamlined Course Management: LMSs offer all the required course contents, assignments, assessments, and communications in one place. This provides an easy means of course structuring for instructors while sparing them unnecessary organizational responsibilities.

Enhanced Accessibility and Flexibility: It is via LMS that educators can deliver course materials online making it easier for students to access the course materials anytime and anywhere. This supports the individual learning styles and schedules and allow students to learn at their own time and repeat if necessary (Bates, 2019).

Effective Communication and Collaboration: Some LMSs have incorporated discussion forums, messaging functions, and group projects among other communication features. This helps students to communicate and work as a group in sharing lessons as well as improving their teamwork skills.

Performance Tracking and Assessment: LMSs provide useful data on how students are progressing through the course, the rates of completion and performance on quizzes and assignments. This data enables the educators to determine which areas need to be boosted, enhance learning and improve the feedback given to the students (Turnbull et al., 2020).

3.3. Mobile Learning (M-Learning)

Mobile phones and tablets have made way for the adoption of mobile learning (m-learning) (Cavanaugh, 2018). M-learning involves the use of these portable devices to present learning content, activities, and assessments just about anywhere and anytime. This provides for more flexibility and availability of learning for the learners with busy schedules.

Increased Accessibility and Flexibility: Students can access learning materials and activities on their mobile devices and study during the trip, at a time when it is convenient for them. This accommodates the short time and the need to customize learning according to student needs (Ally, 2009).

Microlearning Opportunities: Mobile learning is very suitable for the very brief nature of microlearning. Students can use short learning modules or practice sessions during their five to ten minutes free time at work or school to improve learning (Emerson & Berge, 2018).

Engaging and Interactive Learning: Smartphones are well suited to interactive learning. These features may include using AR, gamification aspects, and location-based learning to develop learning solutions that are engaging and suitable for different types of learners (Cavanaugh, 2018).

Personalized Learning Paths: The learning applications can be made for mobiles, which can utilize the adaptive learning system that adjusts the content and pace of learning depending on the performance of the learner. This enables learners to be exposed to tasks that match their ability levels while also allowing them to go through learning materials at their own speed (Marienko et al., 2020).

3.4. Gamification in Education

The application of games or game design elements and principles in contexts outside of games is called gamification. Educators may incorporate elements like challenges, leaderboards, narratives, points, and badges in a way that encourages students to engage in greater efforts and feel a sense of achievement in the learning process.

Increased Engagement and Motivation: One of the strongest points of gamification is that it works with the competition, achievement and progress instincts that students have. Achievements like point accumulation, badges awarded, and ranking on leader boards allow students to feel a sense of achievement and keep going through difficult tasks (Riopel et al., 2019).

Enhanced Learning Through Play: Game-based learning can turn mundane tasks like learning and practicing into a more entertaining and engaging activity. Games create a safe environment for students to test their ideas and try out strategies and solutions (Prensky, 2003).

Personalized Learning Opportunities: Gamification can be tailored to the individual student needs and preferences. Various types of challenges, badges, and rewards work for differing learners and encourage the development of intrinsic motivation and the construct of agency in the learning process (Kim & Castelli, 2021).

Assessment and Feedback: Gamified learning platforms are sources of data on student progress through gameplay metrics. Teachers can use this data to highlight topics that students have difficulty with and design lesson plans specifically for those topics (Rivera et al., 2021).

On the other hand, some negative aspects of gamification in education must be mentioned. High pressure can also turn out to be frustrating and discouraging to some learners. An emphasis on points and badges might distract from more meaningful learning goals. Thus, gamification should be carried out deliberately to achieve effective learning and motivation outcomes for students (Rivera et al., 2021).

4. EMERGING TRENDS IN EDUCATIONAL TECHNOLOGY

The era of information technology has revolutionized the education sector by introducing new advancements constantly. These emerging trends are ripe with opportunities to create more personalized learning environments, enhance the learning experience with virtual reality and augmented reality, deliver actionable data to educators, and ultimately increase engagement and performance among students.

4. 1. The Power of AI and Machine Learning

Artificial intelligence and machine learning programs are playing a significant role in the development of education by providing numerous possibilities that can change teaching and learning.

4. 1. 1. Adaptive Learning Systems

The adaptive learning systems employ AI algorithms to personalize each student's learning experience.

- Quizzes and assignment scores
- Duration of topics studied
- Strengths and weaknesses of the organization

Among them is the ability for the system to dynamically vary the difficulty and speed of teaching, suggest learning materials, and detect weak spots in knowledge. This means that any student is challenged at a level they can handle and is prevented from being bored from doing a task repetitively or feeling frustrated from working with material that is beyond their capabilities.

Personalized Learning Paths: An AI system might suggest more practice problems on a concept if a student does not answer a specific question in a quiz well. On the other hand, if the system discovers that a student is continuously doing well, it can recommend that the student skips over material to a higher level (Baker, 2017).

Differentiated Instruction: Learning platforms can be tuned for different needs by providing content in various formats such as video, simulations, and interactive activities. Students may select the learning modality that suits them most in order to learn better and enhance the knowledge that they have acquired.

Real-world example: DreamBox[1] Learning is a K-12[2] adaptive learning software for math that uses AI to determine the learning path of students. The platform assesses students' levels of ability, adapts the levels of difficulty of the problems and tasks, and offers interesting tasks for strengthening the material. Research has established that DreamBox can produce major gains in math proficiency levels for students.

4. 1. 2. AI-Based Assistance and Teaching

Chatbots and virtual tutors powered by AI provide individualized feedback and tutorial help after school.

- **24/7 Availability:** Students can always learn from AI tutors on concepts that they do not understand whenever and wherever they are. This helps to completely eliminate the constraints of regular class schedules and also allows for immediate access to the teacher when required.
- **Personalized Feedback:** AI tutors can identify the learning problems the students have and give individual feedback accordingly. This individualized instruction enables students to spot knowledge misconceptions and gaps in time to correct them.
- **Scalability and Accessibility**: AI tutors can handle many students at a time meaning that they are of great importance to schools which have few teachers or very huge classes of learners.

Case Study: Knewton[3] is a personal online tutoring service that uses artificial intelligence for teaching math, science and writing. It employs AI algorithms to evaluate student's answers and find the topics they struggle with. Knewton then offers skill-specific tutorials and other exercises to assist struggling learners. Research indicates that Knewton can lead to improvements in student learning outcomes.

4. 2. Augmented Reality and Virtual Reality

AR and VR will change the way people get educated by helping them have immersive and shared learning experiences.

4.2.1. Immersive Learning Experiences

AR and VR technologies offer students the opportunity to visit various places and even different historical periods in a safe way – to walk through the jungles of Africa, observe historical events or even get inside the human body.

- **Virtual Field Trips:** VR technology will remove geographical boundaries and expose students to virtual environments. Students can be taken to the Great Wall of China or the coral reefs – VR will allow them to virtually see and touch these places and learn about the peculiarities of life in different countries or natural processes (Durukan et al., 2020).
- **Interactive Learning Activities:** Students can experience virtual interactions with 3D models of complex structures, observe scientific processes, and perform virtual experiments with the help of AR (Kljun et al., 2020). For example, students can use AR applications to learn how the engine works from the inside or to look at a person's skeleton on a virtual model.

Real-world example: Google Expeditions is a VR application that can be used to conduct virtual school trips to different places around the world. Students can incorporate the use of the VR headsets to view historical buildings, natural wonders and cultural sites from their classrooms.

4.2.2. Practical Applications and Case Studies

AR and VR are not the scenes of some idealized future, it is already taking place in classrooms all over the world (Figure 1).

Figure 1. Practical Applications of AR & VR

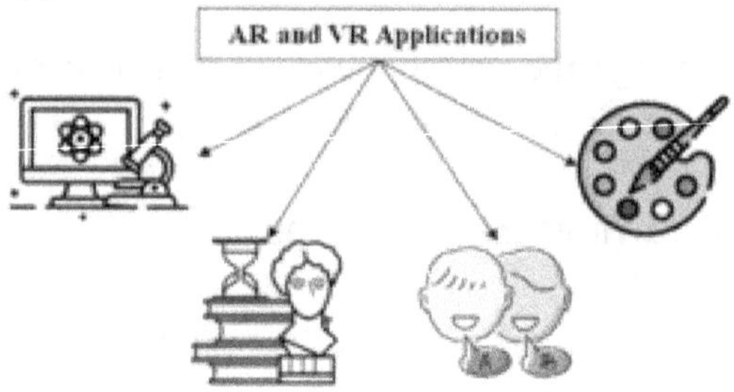

- **Science:** Students may operate a scalpel in a virtual reality environment to surgically dissect a frog, explore the Solar System, or observe the process of cellular respiration in real-time (van et al., 2023). AR apps can also be used to superimpose digital information over objects to explain complex biological processes or molecular structures (Facer & Sandford, 2010).
- **History:** Students for example may be taken through history such as the Battle of Gettysburg or an ancient city of Rome virtually. AR apps can make the history virtual or mix the history with reality at the right places (Facer & Sandford, 2010).
- **Language Learning:** The learners can locate additional tools for translation of texts in the real time for practicing their conversation skills in foreign languages in the AR environments. In this way, such VR simulations can allow students to experience the diversity of countries and cultures, which in turn can help in the learning of language and communication.
- **Art and Design:** Such examples of AR usage are the ability of students to see the 3D copies of the sculptures or paintings in the classroom (Kljun et al., 2020). VR simulations can place learners in a virtual art gallery or empower them to learn how to use design models in a three-dimensional sphere.

Case Study: The Mars Curriculum uses the VR method to enable learners to visualize Mars landscape (Durukan et al., 2020). Students can explore the world by walking and flying over the planet Mars and do virtual experiments and get familiar with space exploration. Research has shown that this VR experience is useful in improving student interest and motivation toward learning science.

4.3. Blockchain Technology

The process of validating the credentials and documentation for educational purposes might undergo a paradigm shift because of the blockchain technology, which is known for its decentralized and secure digital ledger. Here is a deeper look at its possible applications:

4. 3. 1. Building Trust Through Credentialing and Certification

Schools can then create a record on the blockchain for academic records/ transcripts/certificates. This makes it possible to securely store and protect these records from any form of distortion or forgery (Sidiqui et al. 2021). It means that the students who are using this platform can control the access of their verified credentials to only selected potential employers or educational institutions and keep their data private.

Benefits:

- **Reduced Fraud:** Blockchain technology makes it virtually impossible to alter or forge academic credentials stored on the ledger.
- **Improved Efficiency:** Verification of credentials becomes a streamlined process, as employers or educational institutions can access secure and verifiable records on the blockchain.
- **Empowering Learners:** Students own and control their credentials, allowing them to share them easily with relevant parties without relying on third-party verification services.

Challenges:

- **Standardization**: Still in the works is the creation of a blockchain-based digital credentialing system that will provide standardization for issuing and validating credentials.
- **Accessibility**: Further adoption of the blockchain in education can only happen if the necessary distribution of decentralization has been made equally available to everyone.

4. 3. 2. Academic Record Keeping

Blockchain can be used to transform the way students' records are managed and retrieved. A decentralised ledger can help in recording a student's complete journey in school with records for their grades, course completion certificates and even badges from micro-credential programs (Siddiqui et al., 2021).

Benefits:

- **Secure and Transparent Records:** Blockchain prevents unwanted changes or data loss by guaranteeing the validity and integrity of academic records.
- **Improved Data Sharing:** Students can easily share their complete academic records with potential employers or educational institutions, streamlining the application process (Biswas et al., 2024e).
- **Lifelong Learning:** A blockchain-based record system can track and store all learning experiences, including micro-credentials and informal learning activities, providing a comprehensive overview of a student's skills and knowledge.

Challenges:

- **Privacy Concerns:** It is crucial to protect student privacy and control over their academic records while using blockchain technology in the classroom.
- **Regulation and Governance:** It is critical to create precise rules and frameworks for governance when it comes to using blockchain technology to manage academic records.

4.4. Internet of Things (IoT)

Anything in the physical world that has sensors, applications, and connectivity to the Internet is referred to as the IoT. These networked gadgets can create an intelligent system of information that is huge and proliferated across several systems. This is the way the IoT is affecting education:

4. 4. 1. Smart Rooms

Picture classrooms fitted with interactive whiteboards, information screens and environmental monitoring devices. They may include either separate or integrated devices which can be used to offer personalized learning.

- **Personalized Learning Experiences:** Smart devices can measure details such as classroom temperature, lighting, and noise levels. The effect is that the learning environment can be personalized so that it is comfortable and distracting for the student.
- **Interactive Learning Activities:** Interactive classroom technologies such as smart boards and interactive displays can be used to create interactive and collaborative learning opportunities in the classroom. Students can click and swipe to navigate and touch or click to answer questions or participate in

polls and quizzes and the content can be shared and manipulated together in projects in real-time.

- **Real-time Data and Feedback**: The IoT devices may be used in tracking students' engagement, participation as well as progress in learning. Educators on the other hand would use this information to monitor student progress and to determine if there are certain areas in which the students need extra assistance so they can help them while teaching.

Challenges:

- **Cost and Implementation:** Equipping classrooms with the necessary IoT devices and infrastructure can be expensive, potentially creating an equity gap between schools with varying financial resources.
- **Data Security and Privacy:** Ensuring the security and privacy of student data collected through IoT devices is crucial (Sarkar et al., 2023).

4.4.2. Connected Learning Environments

The integration of IoT devices extends beyond the physical classroom walls. Imagine a network of learning resources and tools accessible to students anytime, anywhere.

- **Personalized Learning Paths:** Students can access learning materials, tutorials, and interactive activities tailored to their individual learning pace and style through connected learning platforms.
- **Blended Learning Opportunities:** IoT can facilitate seamless integration of online and offline learning experiences. For example, students can participate in online lectures and then use VR simulations or interactive labs in the classroom to solidify their understanding.
- **Global Collaboration:** Connected learning environments can connect students from different classrooms and countries, fostering collaboration, peer learning, and cultural exchange.

Challenges:

- **Digital Divide:** Participation in linked educational activities may be hampered by unequal access to technology and dependable internet connectivity.
- **Support and Training for Teachers:** Teachers require support and training to successfully incorporate IoT devices and connected learning platforms into their lesson plans.

4.5. Data Analytics and Big Data

The current trend in the use of large volumes of education data offers opportunities for learning personalization and better performance. Here is how big data and learning analytics are transforming education:

4. 5.1. Personalization of Learning Experiences

Schools and other educational facilities can produce huge amounts of data, including results of quiz and assignment tests, and other activities done online and on learning resource platforms. Learning analytics tools leverage this data to personalize learning experiences for each student (Aivaloglou et al., 2023):

- **Identifying Learning Gaps:** Educators can also use data to compare student achievements and find out where they are facing challenges so as to offer them intervention.
- **Recommending Learning Materials:** Learning analytics platforms can automatically identify pertinent reading materials that focus on articles, videos, or even online courses related to each individual student's needs and interests.
- **Predicting Student Success:** Predictive analytics based on the past history of a student may identify the students who are in danger of becoming laggards or dropouts. This advantage helps in early intervention to empower all students with the needed support.

Challenges:

- **Data Privacy Concerns:** There is a need to ensure that the information collected about the student is ethically obtained, stored, and used. It is also important to have consent from the students and clear rules pertaining to the collection of data.
- **Algorithmic Bias:** algorithms employed during data analysis can be biased and this can lead to perpetuation of biases. These tools should also strive for equity and providing equal education to students.

4.5.2. Predictive Analytics for Student Performance

Educational data can be mined for insights about student performance and to predict performance setbacks.

- **Early Intervention Strategies:** Knowing which students are at risk of failing in school early helps the teaching staff develop programs for the intervention of those problems.

- **Customized Learning paths:** Learning paths that are individually designed to meet each student's needs and preferences might also be forecasted based on predictive analytics. This proactive strategy will enable students to attain their full potential.
- **Formative Assessment and Feedback:** Teachers could also significantly benefit from real-time data analysis to know how well students are grasping the course. This makes it possible to make changes in the teaching process and feed children back effectively and help them to correct their mistakes before they become ingrained.

4. 6. Discussion Boards and Other Social Learning Tools

The development of such media as SM and VC has led to the shift in emphasis from the purely competitive and even aggressive forms of learning to cooperative and social ones. Supported by a class or group with open communication and group projects, these platforms enhance learning through deeper thinking and knowledge generation.

4.6.1. Tools for Collaborative Learning

A variety of online platforms and tools are transforming the way students learn collaboratively (Figure 2).

Figure 2. Collaborative Learning Tools

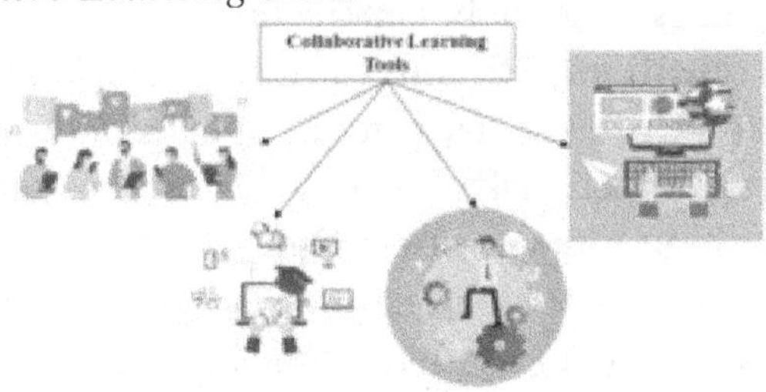

- **Discussion Forums:** The members of an online forum use computers to post questions, add references, and engage in asynchronous dialogue when they are not in class. This makes the pupils discuss what they understand and benefits from their fellow group members.
- **Wikis and Collaborative Documents:** Wikis facilitate the students to share and share resources together to create and edit documents simultaneously on

the same platform a great way to teach students teamwork, research skills and critical thinking.

- **Project Management Tools:** Online project management may help the student group to complete specific collaborative tasks or projects by letting the student assign tasks and record progress as well as communicate with the groups (van et al., 2023).
- **Gamified Learning Platforms:** These platforms: The former includes game elements such as points, badges, and leader boards into collaborative learning activities to engage students.

Benefits

- **Development of Soft Skills:** Cooperative learning is beneficial for learning communication skills, listening skills, the ability to work in a group, solve problems, and think critically.
- **Diverse Perspectives:** They learn from the perspectives of other students and their exposure and end up grasping the concepts better.
- **Increased Engagement:** There are also incentives resulting from creating a more stimulating and engaging social environment for learning.

4. 6. 2 Influence of Social Networking Sites on Education

Social media platforms, while often associated with distraction, can be harnessed for educational purposes:

- **Connecting Learners Beyond Classrooms:** Social media can allow students in different classrooms and countries to share experiences in cultural exchange and global interaction.
- **Sharing Educational Resources:** Instructors and learners can post educational content on social media channels and exchange articles and news about it, which makes the learning process rather dynamic.
- **Microlearning Opportunities:** Quizzes, short video explanations, infographics, and discussion questions are among the activities that can be applied for the microlearning format in social media. These are short units of learning that can be used to refresh the concepts and get learners active.

Challenges of Social Media Integration:

- **Digital Divide:** Participation in social media-based learning activities may be hampered by unequal access to technology and internet connectivity.
- **Cyberbullying and Online Safety:** It is critical to protect students online and provide a polite learning environment.

- **Distraction and Time Management:** Social media can provide distractions. Teachers must mentor students in the efficient use of social media for educational objectives.

Planning ahead and integrating social and collaborative learning platforms into the curriculum are essential for their effective utilization. Teachers must set clear expectations for behavior on the internet and construct a welcoming, safe classroom where all kids may participate and benefit from one another.

5. IMPACT OF EMERGING TECHNOLOGIES ON EDUCATION

The developments in the world today continue to present many opportunities for innovators in the education field, especially for teachers and learners. Such developments can help in the improvement of teaching styles, increased participation of students and in the achievement of the set learning goals. Nevertheless, it is important to understand how technology integration may have implications for learners and education access and make sure that these aspects won't be negative.

5. 1. Enhancements in Teaching Methods

Personalized Learning: Universal education is no longer being experienced. Educational technology can now help teachers to address students' needs and styles of learning (Chen et al., 2020). Learning analytics technologies provide instructors with a unique set of data-driven insights that allow instructors to make effective instructional decisions; adaptive learning systems focus on detecting gaps in knowledge and prompting students to use particular resources (Aivaloglou et al., 2023). The individualized instruction may also allow the students to be taught at a faster pace and finish topics easily before being challenged by tougher activities.

Immersion-Based Learning Settings: VR and AR are no longer the sole goods manufactured for the science fiction domain. Using these technologies schools are gradually transforming into the Interactive classroom in which learning is done in virtual reality with the help of which students get immersed in the human body or other historical events and places (Kljun et al., 2020). Think of virtually dissecting a frog or going for a tour in the pyramids of ancient Egypt. The explanations that can be adopted for occurrences in these subjects cannot be adequately presented by written text-based textbooks. This means students will be involved in more participative exercises, practical lessons, and deeper learning and remembering of the concepts being taught.

Empowering and Engaging Instructional Tools: Many technology resources exist to help teachers convert boring and passive instruction into engaging and interactive learning. For example, gamification means that games are incorporated into learning, for example, the ordinary tasks for students are given in the form of quests, levels, quests, rewards (medals, points), rankings and others. Digital simulations can help students develop their critical thinking and problem-solving abilities by allowing them to explore difficult subjects in a secure and controlled setting.

Cooperation and Social Learning: Thanks to technology, which cuts beyond the traditional classroom boundaries, cooperation and social learning are promoted globally. Wikis and discussion boards are examples of online platforms and tools that allow students to interact with classmates from other backgrounds, exchange ideas, collaborate on projects, and gain insight from different points of view. This collaborative approach promotes communication skills, teamwork, and critical thinking, preparing students for success in an increasingly interconnected world.

5.2. Improvement in Student Engagement and Learning Outcomes

Increased Motivation and Interest: The rote learning methods are also limited as they can be quite boring to the students. However, with the development of new technologies, it is possible to make learning an exciting and interactive process. Intuitive programs and interactive games can trigger student desire and establish interest in the subject.

Enhanced Feedback and Assessment: Feedback can be delivered to the students in a way that technology can transform. Formative assessment technologies can also offer real-time feedback on student progress and enable teachers to recognize students' areas of weakness in order to switch to more effective way of teaching. In addition, students may monitor their progress toward learning goals and identify knowledge deficiencies through the help of quiz games that provide immediate feedback on what students have learned.

Boosting Self-Directed Learning: It is easier today for students to become owners of their learning due to technology. Students may explore themes beyond the curriculum boundaries and delve deeper into topics that appeal to them thanks to the numerous resources available to them on the Internet such as informative videos, articles, and lessons. This helps to ready children for lifelong learning and fosters their interest in learning that surpasses their school years.

5. 3. Challenges and Limitations

Privacy and Security Concerns: There are considerable privacy concerns and security risks associated with collecting and storing student data on a massive scale. This is only possible by having effective security systems in place and student data privacy policies that forbid illegal data access or misuse. Another ethical consideration in the use of personal data is the need to obtain informed consent from students and their parents if the technology being used collects data on them.

Digital Divide and Accessibility Issues: Disparities in education may also be perpetuated by the allocation of limited online resources and technology and fewer well-trained teachers to some students. It may also be that rural or low-income households cannot afford some of the materials required for technology-driven learning activities. Additional efforts to overcome the digital gap and provide all students with access to the technological resources necessary for their success in the twenty-first century are required to achieve greater equality.

Teacher Training and Support: To use technology in the curriculum effectively the teachers need continuous professional learning. Educators also require professional development in the use of these tools in their classrooms, including technical support when issues arise. Effective use also entails establishing an open environment for learning that encourages trying and learning new technologies.

Overdependence on Technology: Technology is a brilliant idea but should not replace high-quality teaching even though it has many upsides. The learner over relies on technology and thus fails to develop critical thinking, problem-solving and interpersonal skills which are all very essential. Teachers need to identify the ways to incorporate technology in the classroom and those that can help promote these essential skills.

5.4. Case Studies and Real-World Applications

- **The Mars Curriculum:** This VR program allows students to travel to Mars, to walk on the Martian surface and to test the simulations of experiments on the planet Mars and to learn about the possibilities and difficulties of space flight (Durukan et al., 2020). This VR experience positively affects students' interest and motivation in science learning.

- **Google Expeditions:** This VR platform enables students to take virtual tours to a wide range of destinations around the world. Students can also visit historical places, natural wonders, and cultural destinations by sitting in their classrooms through the use of virtual reality glasses (Durukan et al., 2020).

These are just a few examples of how new technologies are revolutionizing learning. These technologies will, therefore, have an even more positive impact on education as they are refined further. It is possible to create the future in which learning is accessible, attractive, and helps all students develop the skills they need to act successfully in a dynamic world by embracing while addressing the challenges of educational technologies possibilities.

6. CONCLUSION & FUTURE SCOPE

Current trends in technology have a significant impact on learning by offering personalization, engagement, and improved results. Technologies as varied as virtual reality simulators and adaptive learning environments provide a vast range of possibilities for taking education to the next level. But issues like making sure everyone has access when there are privacy concerns, and how to use these technologies alongside traditional ones, continue to pose problems.

The future of educational technology holds much promise. Artificial intelligence will continue to provide more and more individualized learning environments as well as be used in creating more immersive learning environments through VR and AR. The metaverse also offers a futuristic outlook for global virtual classrooms. If we manage to wisely adopt these innovations, we will be able to craft a future where education is open, interesting, and powerful to all. Our mission is to engage students through their curiosities and support them in becoming lifelong learners and successful citizens. One of the defining frontiers of a world of unlimited learning would be EdTech.

REFERENCES

Aivaloglou, E., Fletcher, G., & Miedema, D. International Workshop on Data Systems Education: Bridging Education Practice with Education Research,(DataEd) 2023.

Aliyeva, V. (2022). The Impact of Personalized Learning on Student Achievement. *Journal of Informatics Education and Research*, 2(1).

Ally, M. (Ed.). (2009). *Mobile learning: Transforming the delivery of education and training*. Athabasca University Press. DOI: 10.15215/aupress/9781897425435.01

Bates, T. (2019). Teaching in a digital age: Guidelines for designing teaching and learning. BCcampus Open Education.

Biswas, D., Dutta, A., Ghosh, S., & Roy, P. (2024). Future Trends and Significant Solutions for Intelligent Computing Resource Management. In Computational Intelligence for Green Cloud Computing and Digital Waste Management (pp. 187-208). IGI Global. DOI: 10.4018/979-8-3693-1552-1.ch010

Cavanaugh, C., Maor, D., & McCarthy, A. (2018). Mobile learning. In *Handbook of Research on K-12 Online and Blending Learning* (pp. 575–591). Carnegie Mellon University: ETC Press.

Chen, L., Chen, P., & Lin, Z. (2020). Artificial intelligence in education: A review. *IEEE Access : Practical Innovations, Open Solutions*, 8, 75264–75278. DOI: 10.1109/ACCESS.2020.2988510

Durukan, A., Artun, H., & Temur, A. (2020). Virtual reality in science education: A descriptive review. Journal of science learning, 3(3), 132-142.

Emerson, L. C., & Berge, Z. L. (2018). Microlearning: Knowledge Management Applications and Competency-Based Training in the Workplace. *Knowledge Management & E-Learning*, 10(2), 125–132.

Facer, K., & Sandford, R. (2010). The next 25 years?: Future scenarios and future directions for education and technology. *Journal of Computer Assisted Learning*, 26(1), 74–93. DOI: 10.1111/j.1365-2729.2009.00337.x

Kim, J., & Castelli, D. M. (2021). Effects of gamification on behavioral change in education: A meta-analysis. *International Journal of Environmental Research and Public Health*, 18(7), 3550. DOI: 10.3390/ijerph18073550 PMID: 33805530

Kljun, M., Geroimenko, V., & Čopič Pucihar, K. (2020). Augmented reality in education: Current status and advancement of the field. Augmented Reality in Education: A New Technology for Teaching and Learning, 3-21.

Lange, K. P., Korevaar, G., Oskam, I. F., & Herder, P. M. (2022). Re-organise: Game-based learning of circular business model innovation. *Frontiers in Sustainability*, 3, 809700. DOI: 10.3389/frsus.2022.809700

Majerowicz, S., & Zárate, R. A. (2023). Massive Open Online Courses and Labor Market Outcomes: Experimental Evidence from Colombia. Available at *SSRN* 4643591.

Marienko, M., Nosenko, Y., & Shyshkina, M. (2020). Personalization of learning using adaptive technologies and augmented reality. arXiv preprint arXiv:2011.05802. DOI: 10.31812/123456789/4418

National Research Council. Division of Behavioral, Board on Behavioral, Sensory Sciences, Committee on Developments in the Science of Learning with additional material from the Committee on Learning Research, & Educational Practice. (2000). How people learn: Brain, mind, experience, and school: Expanded edition (Vol. 1). National Academies Press.

Park, H. (2014). Memex and Beyond: A Design Trajectory from Vannevar Bush's Memex (Doctoral dissertation).

Platonova, R. I., Orekhovskaya, N. A., Dautova, S. B., Martynenko, E. V., Kryukova, N. I., & Demir, S. (2022, July). Blended learning in Higher Education: Diversifying models and practical recommendations for researchers. [). Frontiers Media SA.]. *Frontiers in Education*, 7, 957199. DOI: 10.3389/feduc.2022.957199

Prensky, M. (2003). Digital game-based learning. Computers in entertainment (CIE), 1(1), 21-21.

Redondo, R. P. D., Ktena, A., Kunicina, N., Zabasta, A., Patlins, A., & Mele, D. E. (2020, November). Advanced practices: micro learning, practice oriented teaching and gamified learning. In 2020 IEEE 61th International Scientific Conference on Power and Electrical Engineering of Riga Technical University (RTUCON) (pp. 1-7). IEEE. DOI: 10.1109/RTUCON51174.2020.9316555

Riopel, M., Nenciovici, L., Potvin, P., Chastenay, P., Charland, P., Sarrasin, J. B., & Masson, S. (2019). Impact of serious games on science learning achievement compared with more conventional instruction: An overview and a meta-analysis. *Studies in Science Education*, 55(2), 169–214. DOI: 10.1080/03057267.2019.1722420

Rivera, E. S., & Garden, C. L. P. (2021). Gamification for student engagement: A framework. *Journal of Further and Higher Education*, 45(7), 999–1012. DOI: 10.1080/0309877X.2021.1875201

Sarkar, S. K., Podder, A., & Roy, P. (2023). An Analysis of the Privacy and Security Related Problem with Social Networks.

Sarkar, S. K., Roy, P., Ghosh, S., Podder, A., & Paul, S. (2024). Impact of Frequency and Consistency in Preparing Students for Career Paths. In *Preparing Students From the Academic World to Career Paths: A Comprehensive Guide* (pp. 267–292). IGI Global. DOI: 10.4018/978-1-7998-7999-2.ch012

Siddiqui, S. T., Fakhreldin, M., & Alam, S. (2021, August). Blockchain technology for IoT based educational framework and credentials. In 2021 International Conference on Software Engineering & Computer Systems and 4th International Conference on Computational Science and Information Management (ICSECS-ICOCSIM) (pp. 194-199). IEEE. DOI: 10.1109/ICSECS52883.2021.00042

Turnbull, D., Chugh, R., & Luck, J. (2020). Learning management systems, an overview. Encyclopedia of education and information technologies, 1052-1058. DOI: 10.1007/978-3-030-10576-1_248

van der Meer, N., van der Werf, V., Brinkman, W. P., & Specht, M. (2023). Virtual reality and collaborative learning: A systematic literature review. *Frontiers in Virtual Reality*, 4, 1159905. DOI: 10.3389/frvir.2023.1159905

Zarghami, S. A. (2022). Forecasting project duration in the face of disruptive events: A resource-based approach. *Journal of Construction Engineering and Management*, 148(5), 04022016. DOI: 10.1061/(ASCE)CO.1943-7862.0002257

ENDNOTES

1. https://www.dreambox.com/
2. https://www.k12.com/
3. https://knewton.edu.my/

Chapter 17
The Preliminary Study of a Multi-User Collaborative Musical Instrument Application for Middle School Students

Xiyu Cheng
Universiti Sains Malaysia, Malaysia

Mariam Binti Mohamad
Universiti Sains Malaysia, Malaysia

ABSTRACT

With its interactive and captivating learning experiences, touchscreen technology has become a particularly promising new direction for music learning in recent years. This paper reports the preliminary study which investigates the impact of a touchscreen-technology-based multi-user collaborative musical instrument application in middle school students' music learning. Four secondary school students were chosen as participants and participated in interviews and non-participant observation. The evaluation revealed that this application fulfilled the usability aspect; it was confirmed to be easy to use and contributes to fostering collaborative skills and increasing student engagement in music learning. As there is no existing mobile music instrument application for multi-users to support middle school students in music learning, this study would be considered a groundbreaking attempt. The insights provide valuable implications for educators and developers aiming to

DOI: 10.4018/979-8-3693-6745-2.ch017

integrate touchscreen technology into music curricula, promoting more interactive and collaborative learning environments

INTRODUCTION

Sometimes rigid and less interactive, traditional teaching methods can lower student engagement (Lan, 2022). Instead of engaging in group activities that promote creativity and teamwork, students frequently work alone in traditional music classrooms. Teacher-led ensembles in the classroom, which are top-down, and students follow instructions from the teacher to complete tasks, may not provide enough opportunities to develop students' musical understanding or allow them to participate in any decision-making process (Webster, 2011). In research on the psychology of music learning, musical engagement has been defined as an intense social activity (Jorgensen, 1993). Jorgensen stated in his article "Music Education as Community" that one prevalent music education model is the community model (1995). A few years later, Luce (2001) surveyed the literature on collaborative learning in music education and concluded in his article that music as "essential creative communication permeates all cultures as a collaborative, communally-based expression of humanity" (p. 24). In the event that interactive and collaborative components are absent, students may become less motivated and interested in music because they will not be able to participate in the social aspects of music-making which can push students to cooperate, exchange ideas, and gain knowledge from one another (Luce, 2001). When it comes to retaining students' interest and encouraging a deeper understanding of music, creative methods that include interactive and collaborative components are frequently more successful.

The advent of new technologies has given music education a new focus in this age of rapid technological advancement. Technology is continually changing how people collaborate on music and is also making up for some of the flaws of traditional educational approaches. Like mobile and touchscreen technology, their convenience and interactivity bring infinite possibilities to music-collaborative learning (Courage, 2020). With its interactive and captivating learning experiences, touchscreen technology has become a particularly promising new direction for music instruction in recent years (Huang, 2021). The touchscreen technology inherent in tablets and smartphones provides an intuitive and engaging interface for music learning (Courage, 2020). According to research by Liu et al. (2023), in the discipline of music education, tablet computers are the most often used mobile device while other mobile devices are used less frequently. Compared with smartphones, tablets are equipped with larger screens, which makes them more practical in music education. Students can engage in interactive learning experiences with touchscreen technology, which improves their learning outcomes and creativity (Liu et al., 2023). Because touchscreen technology offers interactive, user-friendly, and collaborative tools, it has the potential to revolutionize the way that music education is taught (Ren, 2024).

It can be seen that investigating the application of touchscreen technology in music education is an extremely worthwhile area of study. However, the software or applications used in previous studies were all for one user, and there was no research on multi-user music learning on the same mobile touchscreen device. Therefore, researchers developed a Multi-User Collaborative Musical Instrument (MCMI) application designed for middle school students to fill the gap in music education. This preliminary study focused on evaluating the usability of the MCMI app, with an emphasis on understanding its user interface, functionality, and overall user experience. The goal was to identify potential usability issues that could hinder the app's effectiveness in promoting student collaboration and engagement and to gather initial feedback to inform further development of the app.

LITERATURE REVIEW

Collaborative Learning in Music Education

In music education, collaborative learning is also an important method. In research on the psychology of music learning, musical engagement has been defined as an intense social activity (Jorgensen, 1993). Jorgensen stated in his article "Music Education as Community" that one prevalent music education model is the community model (1995). A few years later, Luce (2001) surveyed the literature on collaborative learning in music education and concluded in his article that music as "essential creative communication permeates all cultures as a collaborative, communally-based expression of humanity" (p. 24).

In 2008, Mantie and Tucker mentioned two main points of view in their research on the connection between school music experience and lifelong music learning: "Students do not view their learning as co-participating in a real, in-the-world social practice" (p. 220) and "Teachers do not view their teaching as leading toward the goal of life-long participation" (p. 223). Teacher-led ensembles in the classroom, which are top-down and students follow instructions from the teacher to complete tasks, may not provide enough opportunities to develop students' musical understanding or allow them to participate in any decision-making process (Webster, 2011). The method of collaborative musical work is quite different, in which students need to reflect and process their ideas and then verbalize their thoughts to their peers. In 2008, Green studied bringing informal learning practices into the music classroom. In this study, Green pointed out that when students can structure their learning independently and seek help from teachers only when needed, they can learn music with deep understanding and ownership. This research helps us understand that downplaying the teacher's role in music learning and allowing students to practice collaboratively with their peers is conducive to the development of students' lifelong music learning and problem-solving skills. Collaborative activities require communication among students. When students must explain and articulate their views or defend their positions to others, deeper learning is more likely to occur.

In addition, many previous studies have shown that engaging in collaborative musical exercises can positively influence students' social growth and classroom environment. In a 2002 study, Hallam argued that music could enhance classroom atmosphere and improve social skills. In the article, she acknowledges that various factors can influence a student's decision to learn an instrument or join a music group. However, the most critical factor affecting a student's enthusiasm for learning is the environment, including their social interactions. In later research, Hallam (2010) found that music activities can promote students' self-worth. She states that when students can express themselves in collaborative groups, their relationships are more robust, and through musical collaboration, they learn to respect and trust their peers. In Gooding's (2009) study, she found that the interaction in the music classroom enhanced the social contact between students and made students more motivated to participate in future musical activities. Since collaborative musical tasks are a natural requirement in the music classroom, it is an appropriate environment for the development of social competence.

These studies highlight the positive impact of collaboration on music education, making it an essential component of contemporary music pedagogy. The research above supports the premise that for students to acquire autonomous musical cognition and foster the creative expression of musical ideas, they might require opportunities for collaboration in the music classroom. From the existing research, interactive and student-centered learning methods are of great importance in music education.

Touchscreen Technology in Music Education

Since Apple first launched the iPhone in 2007 and the iPad in 2010, it set off a technology boom, and mobile technology has become a commonly used tool in music education (Buchborn & Treß, 2023). According to research by Liu et al. (2023), in the discipline of music education, tablet computers are the most often used mobile device while other mobile devices are used less frequently. Tablets have many benefits, such as excellent connectivity, portability, and interactivity (Schrock, 2015). The touchscreen interface offers a better function for human-computer interaction than the mouse, increasing the likelihood that users will interact with gestures. Compared with smartphones, tablets are equipped with larger screens, which makes them more practical in music education (Liu et al., 2023). For example, iPads are used as analog instruments for musicians to perform in ensembles (Williams, 2014); tablets are used as analog instruments for practice, virtual scores for viewing, or editable music creation tools (Chou & Chu, 2017); Middle school students use GarageBand for iPad to create original music in music class (Sabet, 2020). In these cases, tablets with large screens are more popular among music educators and musicians.

Based on his music production practice, Koszolko (2019) studied the various affordances of iOS applications in the field of electronic music production. Koszolko's analysis shows that portable touchscreen technology facilitates the acquisition of musical knowledge, enables tactile interaction, and provides a new and innovative approach to music performance and production. Sabet (2020) organized a survey on high school students' experiences in using GarageBand for iPads to create original music in music technology classes. The results of this survey show that using GarageBand applications for music creation in music classes dramatically promotes the development of students' creative thinking.

Eusterbrock (2023) points out that such instrument applications can guide musicians freely to find specific places for music creation using applications, allowing them to enter the mindset required for the creative process. Therefore, Eusterbrock calls music applications a kind of music technology of the self, which "involve a complex interplay between music, place, and various aspects of the self, and they not only function as self-care and self-constitution but also as a creative strategy" (2023, p. 61). This portability and flexibility of mobile musical instrument applications enable users to find their creative inspiration anytime and anywhere. The application of mobile touchscreen technology in music education can innovate music production and learning methods in non-traditional ways (Koszolko, 2019), but also effectively stimulate students' creativity and collaboration in the music education environment (NG, et al., 2022), playing a constructive function in the development of music education.

NG, et al. (2022) studied students' use of the instrumental application "Muyu" for creative music composition in an online flipped classroom, thereby providing an innovative set of teaching methods during the COVID-19 pandemic's challenging periods. instruments. Muyu is a mobile music app that offers a variety of virtual instruments. It allows users to perform a variety of music activities, such as playing virtual instruments and composing and arranging music, directly on their mobile devices or tablets. The app incorporates gamification features such as badges, points, and levels, and allows students to work in groups, share their work and provide feedback to each other. This app's interactivity and gamification features increase students' enthusiasm for music learning and promote student-centered learning. It also provides a customized learning experience where students can learn at their own pace, enhancing the traditional music education experience. This study confirms the view that incorporating mobile technology into music education improves students' collaborative music learning experiences and aids in skill-based learning processes through touch-based interaction.

In a study exploring the impact of mobile technology on sixth graders' learning outcomes and experiences, researchers set up an experimental group and a control group (Uludağ & Satir, 2023). The students in the experimental group used mobile apps such as NoteWorks, Rhythm Cat, GarageBand, and Kids Piano over 8 weeks, while the control group received traditional music instruction. The software selected by this study has a high degree of completeness and usage. NoteWorks uses an interactive interface to help students learn music notation, such as the name of the note, its corresponding letter symbol, and its location on the piano.Rhythm Cat uses game elements to teach students different rhythmic patterns and help them practice and play rhythms. GarageBand provides virtual instruments, multi-track recording, and editing capabilities, allowing students to play instruments, record melodies, and arrange music using a touchscreen interface, simulating a music studio environment. Kids Piano uses a simplified virtual keyboard with visual cues and audio feedback to help students practice playing songs. These apps all use mobile technology on smartphones and tablets, combined with an interactive touchscreen interface. In addition, these apps use visual and audio feedback to provide real-time responses to students and incorporate some gamification elements to motivate and engage students. After downloading, most of their features can be used offline, but some still require an Internet connection. The study found that students in the experimental group had significantly better grades than those in the control group, their learning engagement also increased and they were willing to learn outside the classroom. This demonstrates that mobile technology can effectively enhance students' learning outcomes in music education and has the potential to make learning more engaging and interactive.

Despite the positive results, both studies by Uludağ and Satir (2023) and NG et al. (2022) showed that there are still some challenges in using mobile technology in music education. Certain usability challenges within the application, like sporadic technical snags or lags, could hinder the overall efficiency of the real-time interactive classroom setting. And the limited screen size may make it difficult for students to interact with certain elements of complex instruments or limit detailed tasks such as reading music scores. In addition, both students and teachers need time to familiarize themselves with the new technology, which may cause some obstacles to classroom activities. The lack of resources is also one of the major challenges in using mobile technology in music education. The high prices associated with acquiring mobile devices and apps can hinder students from under-resourced schools from having the advantages of mobile technology in music education.(Kleopatra et al., 2023). This can also lead to unequal access to technology-enhanced music education for students in different regions and schools. Globally, music education is moving towards integrating digital tools and technologies to foster creativity, collaboration, and engagement. However, these challenges show that balancing these new technologies with traditional approaches and addressing technical issues and equity of access remains critical to realizing music education's full potential in mobile technologies.

MCMI APPLICATION

The recommended Integrated Development Environment for the Swift program is called Xcode, which is used to develop the iPad-based Multi-User Collaborative Musical Instrument (MCMI) application in this study. Xcode is a proprietary program made available by Apple to program iOS apps and makes coding easier by giving users a place to write, test, and debug code quickly. The MCMI application includes four different instruments: i) piano, ii) guitar, iii) bass, iv) drums (as shown in Figure 1). This application includes four user operation areas, which 2-4 users can use to collaborate on music creation freely.

Drums and bass have become a very common combination that can be incorporated into many settings and styles. The combination of these two elements can create a powerful and engaging listening experience. The exploration of new sounds and genres in this combination has been made easier by technological advancements. Drums and bass can develop together in a live setting, for example, by using systems that modify drum patterns to correspond with the rhythm of other instruments like guitars. This enhances the overall musical interaction (Zhang et al., 2022).

The note range of piano and guitar is c1 to b2. These two instruments are the higher-pitched instruments in this app and can play the main melody. The range of bass chords is from c to b, as a low-pitched instrument played in chord form, it can be used as a harmony in an ensemble. The drum instrument is composed of a bass drum, two Tom-Tom Drums, and a Crash Cymbal which mainly plays the role of accompaniment.

Figure 1. The Main Interface in the MCMI Application

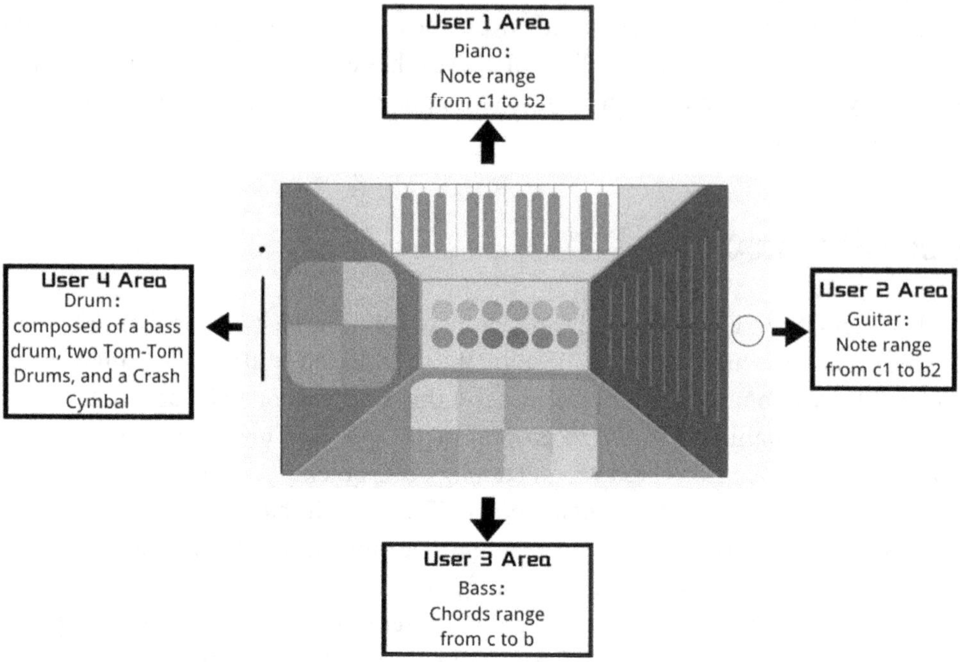

METHODOLOGY

Research Design

This study's design was qualitative, and it used a case study methodology to investigate how secondary music teachers used the MCMI app. Using a qualitative research approach, the study examined how well participants used the MCMI app. This allowed for direct quotes from participant statements, a more thorough examination of the nature of the issue, and the addition of various examples to the findings, all of which the researcher felt were more pertinent to the study's objectives. Data collection included observations during the use of the mobile app as well as interviews with the participants.

Participants of the Study

This study used semi-structured interviews and non-participant observation to collect data. According to Patton (2002) using a smaller sample size in the study facilitates in-depth interviews and observations to gain a deeper understanding of the respondents' experiences and perceptions. Four middle school music teachers and four middle school students from different schools in Guangdong Province, China participated in the preliminary study. These teachers' degrees of experience in incorporating technology into the music curriculum varied. Teachers were chosen based on their experience in using digital technologies and their willingness to participate. The students' musical levels vary, but they all receive additional instrumental training outside of class and have a high passion for music. To enable comprehensive qualitative feedback, which is essential in the early phases of product development, a small sample size was chosen. Purposeful sampling is considered appropriate in qualitative research because it aims to generate deep understanding rather than empirical generalizations (Patton, 2002). To maintain anonymity, participants used pseudonyms, and the teacher participant numbers were: T1, T2, T3, and T4, while the student participant numbers were: S1, S2, S3, and S4.

Table 1. Preliminary Study Teacher Participants

Participants	Teaching Experience	Technologies Teaching Experience
T1	7 Years	Known for integrating traditional Chinese instruments into the curriculum
T2	5Years	Has actively incorporated digital tools in music lessons
T3	12Years	Has limited experience with digital tools but is open to exploring new methods
T4	6Years	Interested in using technology to enhance student engagement

Table 2. Preliminary Study Student Participants

Participants	Grade	Extracurricular Music Learning Experience
S1	Seventh Grade	5 years of piano learning experience
S2	Seventh Grade	3 years of guitar learning experience
S3	Eighth Grade	6 years of jazz drum learning experience
S4	Eighth Grade	8 years of piano learning experience

Non-Participant Observation

According to Muzari et al. (2022), observation is a data generation method used in qualitative research, which is to observe the behavior of something or someone to gain information. In this preliminary study, the purpose of the observation was to observe teachers using the app, identify usability issues with the MCMI app, understand user behavior, and collect qualitative data that could be used to improve the app. The observations were conducted in a controlled environment that simulated a typical classroom setting. In this study, the researcher conducted two observation sessions, one with four teachers and one with four students. Before the observation session, the researcher briefly briefed participants on the nature of the observation and the objectives of the study and obtained informed consent, ensuring that participants knew they had the right to withdraw from the study at any time. The participants used the MCMI app on a touchscreen device provided for the study, ensuring that every participant had a uniform experience. During the observation period, all four participants worked together in the same space, using the MCMI app to self-organize and collaborate on music creation. The researcher created an observation checklist to guide the process, focusing on important usability factors like functional accessibility and user engagement. This checklist ensured that the observations were thorough and addressed all relevant aspects.

The researcher used a non-participant observation method during the observation session. This approach allowed the researchers to see how participants interacted with the MCMI application without engaging with or influencing their activities. The observation process was as follows:

i) Introduction: The researcher briefly explained the process and the study objectives before the session began, and encouraged participants to use the MCMI app as usual during the observation session to avoid being influenced by potential participant bias.
ii) Navigation: The researcher carefully watched as the participants used the app to find their way. Also, the researcher focused on how easy it was for them to find features, understand the icons, and move between different parts of the app without getting lost.
iii) Interacting with Features: The researcher recorded how the participants used the main features of the MCMI application.
iv) Non-verbal cues: The researchers also looked at nonverbal cues during the meetings, including participants' facial expressions, body language, and pauses. These could indicate different emotions for participants, such as satisfaction, frustration, or confusion.

Throughout the observation sessions, the researcher took detailed notes on the participants' behaviors, reactions, and any issues encountered. These notes were later used to supplement the data obtained from the semi-structured interviews.

Figure 2. Participants Used the MCMI App During Observation Session

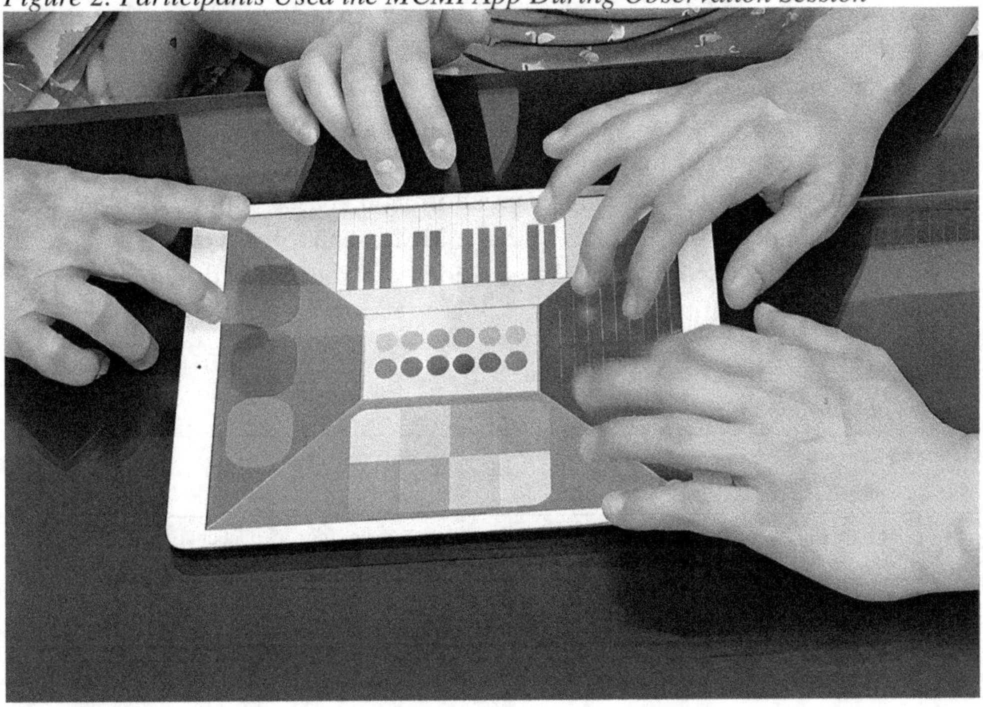

Semi-Structured Interview

Following the observation session, each participant had an interview with the researcher. This allowed them to explain their behaviors during the observation session so that the researcher could quickly understand how they felt about the experience and discuss any usability issues they encountered. According to Borg(2006), interviews are a common qualitative survey method that participants use to provide verbal comments about their thoughts and perceptions. The purpose of the semistructured interviews was to obtain feedback from teachers on their use of the MCMI app.

Topics such as the app's functionality, ease of use, and potential implementation issues in a classroom setting were included in the interviews.

To allow the researcher ample opportunity to engage in in-depth conversation with the participants, interviews lasted approximately 45 minutes for each participant. The researcher gave a brief introduction before each interview, restating the focus of the investigation and the reason for the interview. In order to obtain the most authentic data, the researchers also assured the participants that their honest feedback was very important and would help improve the MCMI app. In the semi-structured interview, the researcher was guided by a pre-planned set of core questions so that each interviewee covered the same areas. However, as the interview progresses, interviewees could provide more relevant information based on their own perspectives. The respondents' experiences with the MCMI app formed the central theme of the interviews. The purpose of the questions was to explore different facets of functionality and usability.

Table 3. Interview Questions for Teachers

Interview Questions	
Introduction and General Feedback	
Q1	How do you generally perceive the idea of using a digital application for collaborative music learning in a middle school setting?
Usability	
Q2	What are your first impressions of the MCMI app's user interface? Is it intuitive and user-friendly?
Q3	Were there any features of the app that you found confusing or difficult to use?
Q4	How would you describe the process of setting up and starting a collaborative session using the app?
Functionality	
Q5	How effectively do you think the MCMI app facilitates collaboration between students?
Q6	Do you believe the app's features align well with the goals of your music curriculum? Why or why not?
Q7	Are there any additional features you would suggest to improve the app's functionality?
Implementation in the Classroom	
Q8	How do you envision using this app in your classroom? What challenges might you face?
Q9	How do you think students would respond to using this app for collaborative music creation?
Overall Experience	
Q10	Based on your experience, what are the app's strongest points?
Q11	What improvements do you think are necessary before the app can be effectively integrated into classroom teaching?

Table 4. Interview Questions for Students

Interview Questions	
Introduction and General Feedback	
Q1	Can you describe your overall experience using the MCMI app for creating music?
Usability	
Q2	How easy or difficult was it for you to learn how to use the app?
Q3	Did you find the touch interface intuitive? Were there any specific elements that were confusing or hard to navigate?
Q4	Did you experience any technical issues (such as lags, crashes, or errors) while using the app? If so, how did this impact your experience?
Functionality	
Q5	Did you find it easier to collaborate with your peers using the app compared to traditional classroom methods? Why or why not?
Q6	Did using the app make you feel more engaged in music class? If so, how?
Suggestions for Improvement	
Q7	Were there any additional features you would like to see in the app that could make it more useful or enjoyable?
Personal Reflection	
Q8	How do you feel about using technology like the MCMI app in music education? Do you think it adds value to the learning experience?
Q9	Would you recommend the app to other students? Why or why not?
Closing	
Q10	Is there anything else you would like to share about your experience with the MCMI app that we haven't discussed?

Following the interview, participants were given the chance to ask questions or express any other thoughts that might not have occurred to them during the interview. The researcher then thanked the participants for their time and contributions and emphasized the value of their feedback in the app development process.

Data Analysis

Non-participant observation and semi-structured interviews for this study yielded a wealth of qualitative data, which required classification and analysis to develop valid interpretations. According to Bogdan and Biklen (1998), data analysis is the process of systematically managing data in various forms and presenting them in a way that researchers and readers can understand. When analyzing data in qualitative research, an inductive examination of the data is frequently conducted to find recurrent themes, patterns, or concepts. These categories are then described and interpreted (Nassaji, 2015). According to Cleland (2017), we can determine that qualitative data analysis aims to find new themes, patterns, ideas, realizations, and insights. The main steps in qualitative data analysis are data processing, organization, and division into manageable chunks; following this, encoding, synthesizing, and pattern recognition are performed (Bogdan & Biklen, 1998).

In this peilimininary study, the researchers began by transcribing the audio recordings of the interviews by software exactly as they were spoken, enabling a detailed examination of what the participants said. After that, the transcripts were coded to find common themes, patterns, and key insights related to the usability of the MCMI app.Text passages related to key themes such as "ease of use", "collaborative features", "engagement", and "suggestions for improvement" were given codes. Finally, the researcher categorized the coded data into more general themes that represented the main conclusions of the study. The feedback from the participants was sorted into useful categories with the aid of this thematic analysis, which guided the app's development. Lastly, a comparison and integration between the observational data and the interview findings were made. This triangulation of data sources improved the findings' validity and gave rise to a more thorough comprehension of the usability of the app.

Findings

Through non-participant observation and semi-structured interviews, the researcher gained valuable insights into the usability of the MCMI app. During the activity, all participants showed great interest and gave positive feedback on the research questions.

All four teachers thought that the interface of the app was visually appealing and generally easy to operate. However, there were concerns that buttons and icons were not sufficiently obvious and that some students might not have understood them immediately. Therefore, some teachers suggested that a short tutorial could be provided to guide first-time users. In terms of functionality and features, teachers felt that the collaborative nature of the app was excellent and should increase student engagement. Music teachers believe that the combination of the four instruments in the app is in line with musical instrumentation and can be played together. In addition, some teachers believe that the timely feedback and visual prompts of the sound when the instrument button is triggered also help to improve students' participation in the process of use. All four teachers made a common suggestion: adding different instrument versions for users to choose freely. In terms of implementation, the teachers were enthusiastic about integrating the app into the classroom, but they also expressed concerns about the uneven digital literacy levels of their students. Therefore, they also suggested providing some additional resources, such as tutorial videos or manuals, to support teachers and students in maximizing the potential of the application. Another issue mentioned by some teachers is that the limited availability of tablets or touchscreen devices in some schools could impede their widespread use. In terms of the overall usability of the MCMI app, these music educators generally felt that the app had great potential for improving collaborative music learning. The participating teachers also thought that continued research and updates to address usability issues identified in the study were important.

For the four participating students, they found the touch interface very intuitive after a short familiarization period, however, some icons were difficult to identify immediately, which caused some confusion at first. One student who had less exposure to digital tools found that he needed more time to understand the navigation and functions when he first started using the app. Therefore, this student suggested adding some labels to make the layout more intuitive to reduce initial confusion. Regarding usability, all four students agreed that the app was easy to learn and use, and no technical issues were reported. In terms of functionality, the students agreed that the app effectively promoted collaboration and expressed their enjoyment of being able to interact in real time and create music together on the same device. Students said that the app made them more motivated to participate in music activities. Three of the four students expressed their desire to use the app regularly in music class because they believed it would make the lessons more engaging. In addition, the students also made a suggestion similar to the teachers', which was to add more instrument options to enable more diverse music creation.

In conclusion, the MCMI application received positive feedback from participants regarding its usability, ability to facilitate collaboration, and ability to engage learners. The findings suggest that the app has the potential to enhance music education by integrating technology to create an interactive and collaborative learning environment. Participants also made suggestions for improvements to the user interface and an expansion of instrument selection that could further enhance its effectiveness. These feedback will provide the refinement for the improvement of the application and subsequent research.

DISCUSSION AND CONCLUSION

The purpose of this preliminary study was to investigate the Multi-User Collaborative Musical Instrument (MCMI) application's usability in a secondary music education context. Four middle school music teachers and four middle school students participated in the study and offered their opinions on the usability, functionality, and potential of incorporating the application into lessons. This section of the discussion ties the findings back to the initial research and the core concepts driving the study. It also takes a close look at the results in the context of the broader objectives of the research.

Evaluating the usability of the MCMI app from the perspectives of experienced music educators and middle school students was one of the primary goals of this preliminary study. According to Nielsen (1993), there are a number of important factors that contribute to usability, such as learnability, efficiency, memorability, errors, and satisfaction. While the application received generally positive reviews from participants in terms of usability, the feedback indicated that there was room for further improvement in its functionality and interface to meet additional usability criteria. Participating teachers highly rated the MCMI app's ability to facilitate collaboration between two to four users playing different instruments. They felt that this feature directly contributed to the app's goal of encouraging collaborative music-making, which was the main research question. On the other hand, students stated that the interactive features and digital instruments of the MCMI app attracted their interest and increased their willingness to participate in music activities, and they also agreed that this app effectively promoted collaboration. The educational technology literature has established the importance of interactive feedback in enhancing learning outcomes. It is considered a crucial element in sustaining student engagement and fostering a deeper comprehension of the subject matter (Hui et al., 2022). These components enable the MCMI app to integrate more effectively with instructional models that emphasize active learning and provide rapid feedback.

Although the participants had a generally positive view of the MCMI app's potential, they also pointed out several obstacles that might prevent its use in a regular secondary school classroom. It was especially concerning how different the students' levels of digital literacy were. Some students were initially confused when navigating the app's features, which was related to their lack of experience with similar music apps or mobile touchscreen tools. Effective use of digital tools is a component of digital literacy, which is becoming more and more acknowledged as a necessary ability in contemporary education (Peng & Yu, 2022). Peng and Yu did point out, though, that disparities in digital literacy may make it more difficult for technology to be used effectively in the classroom, particularly in cases where students may not have much access to or experience with digital devices. To address this challenge, participants suggested adding navigation labels to the app and developing tutorials and support materials as potential solutions. Ideas from Vygotsky's 1978 social constructivism theory contend that it's critical to give students short-term support structures so they can finish assignments they might not be able to finish on their own. When it comes to the MCMI application, instructional videos or guides can take the form of clear instructions, step-by-step tutorials, or guided practice sessions that step-by-step guide students through becoming familiar with and using the application.

Initial findings suggest that the MCMI app has strong potential to support collaborative music learning, particularly through the creative use of touchscreen technology to facilitate real-time collaboration among students, according to participants feedback from this preliminary study, which also provided important insights into the usability of the app and a foundational understanding of how middle school music teachers and students perceived it. Participants feedback on the collaborative features of the app suggests that the app is well aligned with the goal of promoting collaboration and engagement in music education. However, ongoing improvements to the usability issues identified are necessary to better realize the app's potential. Through a thorough analysis of the preliminary study's findings, the researcher can implement specific enhancements to improve the app's usability and efficacy in promoting collaborative music learning.

LIMITATIONS OF THE STUDY

There are still some limitations of this preliminary study that need to be recognized and considered. The first is the limitation of methodology and sample. The method of this study is a case study of qualitative research. However, the results of the study evaluation may be affected by the background and individual differences of the participants, which may limit the generalizability of the results. Due to resource and time constraints, we selected four different schools from the same region as the sample, which may also lead to a lack of diversity in cultural, socioeconomic, and educational backgrounds. Although we obtained a large amount of data through in-depth case studies, the findings cannot be directly generalized to other secondary schools with different geographical, economic, or cultural backgrounds. There may be some differences in the usability and acceptance of the MCMI app in schools with different resources, student demographics, or educational focus.

The second limitation is because the preliminary study was completed in a comparatively short amount of time, participants might not have had enough time to thoroughly explore and comprehend the app's functionality. More thorough insights into how the app was incorporated into routine teaching practices and how students eventually became accustomed to using it might have been obtained with a longer study period.

The third limitation is potential participant bias. The preliminary study participants knew they were being watched, and they also knew their input would affect how the app was developed. This knowledge might have caused participants to exhibit a social desirability bias, in which case they might have given more positive feedback than usual or, on the other hand, might have been unduly critical in an attempt to be helpful. Both biases might have had an impact on the study's findings.

The fourth limitation is technology. Although the researchers are designing a musical instrument app for collaborative learning, the implementation of the app is limited by technology. Touchscreen technology has made significant progress in music simulation, but there is still room for improvement in the accurate simulation and timbre of the instruments in the MCMI app. In addition, the balance between music theory education and actual performance is also a challenge, and the types of instruments we provide in the app may not meet the needs of all middle school students.

The fifth limitation is the influence of environmental variables. The study was carried out in particular classroom environments that might have special features, like a particular teaching methodology, class size, or technology setup. Some external factors might affect how useful and easy to use the MCMI app is. For example, the app could be more beneficial in classrooms with better technology compared to those with fewer devices or less internet access.

The sixth limitation is the limited scope of the non-participant observation. The part of the study that involved observing only looked at specific aspects of using the MCMI app or just a few interactions. This limited observation might not adequately convey the intricacy of using the MCMI app in various teaching and learning environments. Important details about how students interact, work together, or get involved might be overlooked.

Although the aforementioned constraints, this preliminary study sheds light on the promising role of touchscreen technology in enhancing music education for middle schoolers. These limitations provide directions for future investigations aimed at unlocking the full potential of collaborative musical tools in the realm of music learning.

FUTURE DIRECTIONS FOR RESEARCH

This preliminary study of the MCMI app provided important information into its usability and potential as a collaborative learning tool for secondary music education, while also identifying areas for further research to optimize the app's functionality and ensure it can be useful in educational settings. Given the many impacts that the rapid development of new technologies has on the field of music education, future research should focus on expanding the scope of this study, addressing the issues mentioned, and exploring new ways to improve the pedagogical value of MCMI applications.

One of the main limitations of the preliminary study was the small sample size, which included only four secondary music teachers and students from a single geographic area. This means that, although the findings provide detailed qualitative data, they may not be generalizable to a larger population. Future research should aim to include a larger and more diverse sample of participants, including not only a wider range of teachers but also students from different cultural backgrounds and geographical regions. Therefore, the researchers will continue to collect more comprehensive data on how different users use the app and explore any potential usability issues that may arise in different educational settings.

This preliminary study focused solely on the usability of the MCMI app, but there is still much research to be done on how it affects students' long-term learning outcomes. Future research should consider this by doing more detailed long-term studies to observe the effects of the app over a longer period. These studies could look into how students' musical skills, creativity, and collaboration are affected when they use the MCMI app regularly. On the other hand, a longitudinal research approach would allow the researcher to examine whether the app's benefits are sustainable and identify any potential challenges that may arise over time. For example, it would be important to find out if users' original excitement for the app stays the same as time goes by or if it decreases when the newness of the app wears off.

While preliminary research provides some insights into the potential of the MCMI app to promote student engagement and collaboration, further research is needed to more fully evaluate these aspects. To understand how the app influences student behavior and learning results, future studies could use a mixed methods approach. This means combining numerical data (like scores on collaboration and measures of engagement) with descriptive data (such as interviews with students and instructors).To better understand how the app impacts students' overall learning experience, various aspects of student engagement (e.g., cognitive, affective, and behavioral engagement) should be studied in the future. Furthermore, analyzing the specific features of the app that best facilitate collaborative music learning among students may provide insightful information on how to improve the app's functionality and design.

In the future, related research also could be conducted regarding the role of cultural relevance in music education. Given that participating teachers in the initial study encouraged the development of more versions of the app for different instruments, future research could consider exploring the role of different cultural relevance in music education and how it impacts students' learning experiences. This might entail contrasting the MCMI app's efficacy when it comes to musical instruments that are culturally appropriate for students versus those that they are less acquainted with. Teachers and developers may be able to create more inclusive and stimulating learning environments that speak to the experiences and backgrounds of their students if they have a better understanding of cultural dynamics in music education. Future research could also explore how student motivation and interest in music education are affected by culturally relevant content, particularly in classrooms with culturally diverse student populations.

Future research could also delve deeper into how the app impacts students' musical creative processes and outcomes. Using a case study approach, an in-depth study of the creative journeys of students using the app, as well as the development and testing of specific metrics for assessing creativity in music composition, could potentially be part of future research. The researcher could also look at how various aspects of the app, like tool selection, collaborative tools, and interactive elements, support creativity; comprehension of the relationship between these aspects and students' creative expression could lead to improvements in app design to better support creative learning.

Future research on the MICMI app in music education should also consider the availability of resources to ensure its effective implementation and sustainability. These resources include technological infrastructure, such as devices that are compatible with it and stable internet connections. As well as human resources, such as training teachers to gain support for using the app, and initiatives to improve students' digital literacy. And financial resources are also crucial, including funding for equipment procurement, especially for schools in disadvantaged areas and with insufficient resources. By addressing these resource availability issues, future research can increase the scalability and effectiveness of the MCMI app in promoting collaborative and creative music education.

In terms of the MCMI app's functionality and its promise as a collaborative educational resource for secondary music education, this initial investigation has established a strong groundwork for future studies and provided valuable insights. Still, there is a lot of uncharted territory to cover in order to deepen our understanding of the ways in which digital technologies are transforming music education. The MCMI app can be further improved and made into an effective tool to encourage student collaboration, engagement, and creativity by addressing the issues raised in the first study and broadening the research's focus. In order to accomplish this and support the ongoing advancement of music education in the digital era, future research will be crucial.

REFERENCES

Bogdan, R. C., & Biklen, S. K. (1998). *Qualitative research for education an introduction to theory and methods* (3rd ed.). Nancy Forsyth.

Borg, S. (2006). Teacher cognition and language education: Research and practice. *Continuum*.

Buchborn, T., & Treß, J. (2023). Acting self-determinedly and critically in a post-digital future? A critical review on digitalisation in music education. *Culture, Education, and Future*, 1(1), 66–82. Advance online publication. DOI: 10.70116/298027415

Chen, J. C. W. (2020). Mobile composing: Professional practices and impact on students' motivation in popular music. *International Journal of Music Education*, 38(1), 147–158. DOI: 10.1177/0255761419855820

Chou, C., & Chu, Y. (2017). Interactive rhythm learning system by combining tablet computers and robots. *Applied Sciences (Basel, Switzerland)*, 7(3), 258. Advance online publication. DOI: 10.3390/app7030258

Cleland, J. A. (2017). The qualitative orientation in medical education research. *Korean Journal of Medical Education, 29*(2), 61–71. NCBI. DOI: 10.3946/kjme.2017.53

Courage, M. L. (2020). Interactive technologies: Tablets, smartphones, and learning. In *Encyclopedia of Infant and Early Childhood Development* (2nd ed., pp. 194–201). Elsevier., DOI: 10.1016/B978-0-12-809324-5.23561-X

Eusterbrock, L. (2023). Mobile safe spaces and preset emotions: Making music with apps as a digital technology of the self. *Popular Music and Society*, 46(1), 50–69. DOI: 10.1080/03007766.2022.2155029

Forsman, M. (2015). The pros and cons of iPad : The evaluation process and its results. In *Paducation: An EU-based method-advancement project by German and Swedish teachers working with iPad* (pp. 35–55). Södertörns högskola.

Gooding, L. (2009). Enhancing social competence in the music classroom. *General Music Today*, 23(1), 35–38. DOI: 10.1177/1048371309342531

Green, L. (2008). *Music, informal learning and the school: A new classroom pedagogy*. Ashgate.

Hallam, S. (2002). Musical motivation: Towards a model synthesising the research. *Music Education Research*, 4(2), 225–244. DOI: 10.1080/1461380022000011939

Hallam, S. (2024). 21st century conceptions of musical ability. *Psychology of Music*, 38(3), 308–330. DOI: 10.1177/0305735609351922

Huang, Y. (2021). Research on interactive creation of computer-aided music teaching. *Solid State Technology*, 64(01), 577–587.

Hui, B. Björn Rudzewitz, & Detmar Meurers. (2022). Learning processes in interactive CALL systems: Linking automatic feedback, system logs, and learning outcomes. *Computer Science, Education, Linguistics*. https://api.semanticscholar.org/CorpusID:245872345

Jorgensen, E. (1993). On building social theories of music education. *Bulletin of the Council for Research in Music Education*, 116(Spring).

Jorgensen, E. R. (1995). Music education as community. *Journal of Aesthetic Education, 29*(3), 71–84. JSTOR. DOI: 10.2307/3333542

Kleopatra, N., Vasilis, G., & Konstantinos, L. (2023). Mobile learningtechnology barriers in school education: Teachers' views. *Technology, Pedagogy and Education*, 32(1), 29–44. DOI: 10.1080/1475939X.2022.2121314

Koszolko, M. (2019). The tactile evolution — electronic music production and affordances of iOS apps. In *Proceedings of the 12th Art of Record Production Conference: Mono: Stereo: Multi* (pp. 187–204). Stockholm: Royal College of Music (KMH) & Art of Record Production.

Lan, X. (2022). Construction of a music education model based on internet big data. *Wireless Communications and Mobile Computing*, 2022, 1–6. DOI: 10.1155/2022/3732776

Liu, C., Hwang, G., Tu, Y., Yin, Y., & Wang, Y. (2023a). Research advancement and foci of mobile technology supported music education: A systematic review and social network analysis on 20082019 academic publications. *Interactive Learning Environments*, 31(7), 4535–4554. DOI: 10.1080/10494820.2021.1974890

Liu, C., Hwang, G., Tu, Y., Yin, Y., & Wang, Y. (2023b). Research advancement and foci of mobile technology supported music education: A systematic review and social network analysis on 20082019 academic publications. *Interactive Learning Environments*, 31(7), 4535–4554. DOI: 10.1080/10494820.2021.1974890

Luce, D. W. (2001). Collaborative learning in music education: A review of the literature. *Update - University of South Carolina. Dept. of Music*, 19(2), 20–25. DOI: 10.1177/87551233010190020105

Mantie, R., & Tucker, L. (2008). Closing the gap: Does musicmaking have to stop upon graduation? *International Journal of Community Music*, 1(2), 217–227. DOI: 10.1386/ijcm.1.2.217_1

Muzari, T., Shava, G. N., & Shonhiwa, S. (2022). Qualitative research paradigm, a key research design for educational researchers, processes and procedures: A theoretical overview. *Indiana Journal of Humanities and Social Sciences, 03*(01).

Nassaji, H. (2015). Qualitative and descriptive research: Data type versus data analysis. *Language Teaching Research*, 19(2), 129–132. DOI: 10.1177/1362168815572747

Ng, D. T., Ng, E. H., & Chu, S. K. (2022). Engaging students in creative music making with musical instrument application in an online flipped classroom. *Education and Information Technologies*, 27(1), 45–64.

Nielsen, J. (1993). *Usability engineering*. Morgan Kaufmann. DOI: 10.1016/B978-0-08-052029-2.50007-3

Patton, M. Q. (2002). Two decades of developments in qualitative inquiry. *Qualitative Social Work: Research and Practice*, 1(3), 261–283. DOI: 10.1177/1473325002001003636

Peng, D., & Yu, Z. (2022). A Literature Review of Digital Literacy over Two Decades. *Education Research International*, 2022, 1–8. DOI: 10.1155/2022/2533413

Ren, D. (2024). Research on the application of computer music technology in solfeggio teaching in universities. *International Journal of Social Sciences and Public Administration*, 2(1), 200–207. DOI: 10.62051/ijsspa.v2n1.26

Sabet, S. (2020). Composing with mobile technology: High school students and garageband for iPad. *Journal of Popular Music Education*, 4(3), 349–369. Advance online publication. DOI: 10.1386/jpme_00032_1

Schrock, A. R. (2015). Communicative affordances of mobile media: Portability, availability, locatability, and multimediality. *International Journal of Communication*, 9, 18. https://api.semanticscholar.org/CorpusID:31064350

Uludağ, A. K., & Satir, U. K. (2023). Seeking alternatives in music education: The effects of mobile technologies on students' achievement in basic music theory. *International Journal of Music Education*, 02557614231196972. Advance online publication. DOI: 10.1177/02557614231196972

Vygotsky, L. (1978). *Mind in society: The development of higher psychological processes*. Harvard University Press.

Webster, P. R. (2011). Construction of music learning. In *MENC handbook of research on music learning* (pp. 35–83). Oxford University Press. DOI: 10.1093/acprof:osobl/9780195386677.003.0002

Williams, D. A. (2014). Another perspective. *Music Educators Journal*, 101(1), 93–98. DOI: 10.1177/0027432114540476

Zhang, Y. T., Cheng, Y. L., Wu, H. X., & Liao, Y. P. (2022). Intelligent music accompaniment system based on discrete wavelet transform. *Journal of Physics: Conference Series*, 2345(1), 012021–012021. DOI: 10.1088/1742-6596/2345/1/012021

APPENDIX

Participant Informed Consent

Chapter 18
Unified Threat Modeling:
Strategies for Comprehensive Risk Assessment in Modern Systems

Rasmita Kumari Mohanty
https://orcid.org/0000-0002-5828-5649
Vallurupalli Nageswara Rao Vignana Jyothi Institute of Engineering and Technology, India

Chinimilli Venkata Rama Padmaja
Institute of Aeronautical Engineering, India

Suresh Kumar Kanaparthi
https://orcid.org/0000-0003-4945-6554
SRM University, India

Anusha Rajan
Mallareddy University, India

ABSTRACT

Today, in the digital world, the security of systems is crucial because, with continuous information exchange and huge quantities of data being processed, the protection of operation processes and data assets becomes paramount. Threat modeling is an important part of cybersecurity management methodology that looks for any possible threats or weaknesses that can break the system or endanger the environment. This paper is an attempt to analyze all the models of threat modeling by taking STRIDE, PASTA, DREAD, TREK, VAST and Attack Trees as references. An integrated model is suggested that combines the benefits of existing approaches, which includes the adoption of a comprehensive frame to deal with cyber threats. This methodology emphasizes iterative refinement and rigorous testing to ensure the effectiveness of threat mitigation strategies. By incorporating user-friendly web portals and the

DOI: 10.4018/979-8-3693-6745-2.ch018

integration of new technologies, this framework enhances usability and addresses emerging threats.

1. INTRODUCTION

As it is today, making the systems, computers, and data safe from hackers and such threats is a matter of great importance since they are preventing interruptions and protecting data that has a huge value. Against the backdrop of the threat and being armed with an arsenal of sophisticated tools and techniques, organizations in different sectors face such critical challenges. While these entities are not the same and face other threats, each one should develop purposeful defense strategies. Achieving the necessary environment of anticipating and handling these threats is an essence for effective cyber security, and therefore threat modeling is a critical part of this quest. Threat modeling implicates a methodical procedure of studying and analyzing threats, vulnerabilities, and risks in a certain system or environment. By looking at the assets, the associated weaknesses, and the possible intrusion paths, organizations will be able to start addressing these security concerns and will also strengthen their defenses. The strategic planning model which falls within the framework comprises such steps as scoping and goal definition, threat identification, environment characterization, threat evaluation, their selection, and implementing evaluated solutions. Many legacy threat modeling frameworks combine structure methodologies into one to make sure that the threat analyses performed in certain contexts are complete. STRIDE, for instance, categorizes threats into six distinct types: the types of attacks that cause spoofing, result in tampering, service DoS, denial of service, data exhilaration, and escalation. By delineating these threat categories, STRIDE provides valuable insights into potential attack vectors, aiding organizations in identifying and prioritizing security measures effectively.

As opposed to this PASTA a risk-based strategy takes up a direction that enhances the Know- how crashing business operations. Such a strategy paves the way for organizations to ensure that resources are distributed effectively by primarily concentrating on minimizing the effects of those risks that will probably cause the greatest disruption to the continuity of their operations. On the other hand, DREAD sticks to both a novel grading scenario and offers an evaluative framework that assesses threats according to Damage, Reproducibility, Exploitability, Affected users, and Discoverability. Threat modeling gains strength through digitalization with visualization techniques. VAST (Visualization and Sensory Training) improves comprehension and communication of threats and vulnerabilities. Ultimately, TRIKE brings together the aspects of attack trees with passengers under the general classification of transportation. Connecting these models into one form, there is a broad range of analyzing methods in threat discussing, which enable companies to reinforce the level of their cyber security reliably. Common Threat Models are:

Asset-centric Perspective:

- An asset standpoint should form the fulcrum of the system, whereby a comprehensive inventory of assets and their order of importance should be prepared.
- Offer a wide range of rationales for the allocation of assets because of high-value assets always comes first.

Attack-centric Perspective

- They elaborate on different ways by which attackers gain access to the computer system and the methods they use for the purpose of exploitation.
- Ensures the advantageous environment of recognizing the adversary's attack techniques and plans and hence, the prompt rebuttal planning.

Software-centric Perspective

- Magnifies existing software applications and systems deficiencies and misuses by exposing the developers and implementation of the possibility.
- Risk identification in software-related domains such as code errors, design flaws, and insecure configurations is the intended purpose of this activity.

Such a research project aims to score the highest marks in the threat modeling practices field, which is a rich source of existing methodologies, using them as a basis and adding to them a novel unlike anything seen before. An integrated threat model is proposed, which builds upon the strong points of already existing approaches and also eliminates their negative aspects. It will provide the challenge of cyber security from a holistic and adaptable view. The framework is designed iteratively to be regularly checked and tested so that organizations can strategically save on false alarms and predict, and deal with threats, effectively while enhancing their security stance in a continually changing threat atmosphere.

2. LITERATURE REVIEW

Some of the Existing Threat Models are:

Microsoft Threat Modeling Tool (TMT): TMT is a free, open-source tool that helps users identify and mitigate security threats to their systems. It is based on the STRIDE methodology, which considers six types of threats: spoofing, tampering, repudiation, information disclosure, elevation of privilege, and denial of service. TMT is relatively easy to use and provides a visual interface for creating and managing threat models. However, it is important to note that TMT only supports the STRIDE methodology, so it may not be suitable for more complex systems or requirements.

Threat Dragon: Threat Dragon is a cloud-based threat modeling tool that supports a variety of threat modeling methodologies, including STRIDE, PASTA, and VAST. It offers a number of features to help users create and manage complex threat models, such as collaboration features, risk assessment tools, and integration with other security tools. However, Threat Dragon is a paid subscription service, so it may not be suitable for all organizations.

OWASP ASVS Threat Modeling Tool: The OWASP ASVS Threat Modeling Tool is a free, open-source tool that helps users identify and mitigate security vulnerabilities in web applications. It is based on the OWASP Application Security Verification Standard (ASVS), which is a comprehensive list of known web application vulnerabilities. However, the OWASP ASVS Threat Modeling Tool is not as versatile as some other threat modeling tools, as it only supports the STRIDE methodology.

Cairis: Cairis is a free, open-source threat modeling tool that provides a comprehensive set of features for creating and managing threat models. It supports a variety of threat modeling methodologies, including STRIDE, PASTA, and VAST. Cairis also offers several features to help users assess the risk of threats and identify appropriate mitigations. However, Cairis is a complex tool, so it may not be suitable for users who are new to threat modeling (Nweke and Wolthusen, 2020).

Many researchers, whose contribution has been instrumental in the foundation of the threat modeling practice, have been looking into the specific domains of the problem that have been pinpointed and working to fill up those gaps. For instance, while STRIDE, PASTA, and attack tree approaches are highlighted other advanced approaches are discovered, however, a combined methodology that pulls them from where they are good is created from them. Therefore, this framework looks into creating a platform for the improvement of the strengths of general threat modeling approaches while at the same time discarding their weaknesses - which in turn enhances the method for threat modeling in the real world (Viswanathan, 2021). The first method concentrates on increasing IT systems' robustness to cyber threats via the application of attack simulation toolkits together with developers' traditional methodology of danger modeling (Potteiger, Martins, and Koutsoukos, 2016). This technique can be accomplished by building multiple attack scenarios and subsequently applying them to the specific system that is being examined thus, analysts are able to determine the vulnerabilities and possible consequences of different scenarios. But the fact is that this approach may require the developers to become specialists concerning the use of attack simulation tools, and the method's exactitude is entirely dependent on the quality and accuracy of the data that is given into the system, including any assumptions about the attackers' behavior and abilities (Xiong, 2021).

The use of a security approach that fits perfectly into agile and DevSecOps approaches (Martelleur and Hamza, 2022) is one of the methods that are embraced. This comprises a pragmatic risk modelling methodology specifically designed for the rapid development model and which allows security duties to being encompassed in the quick sprints. A general line that collaboration is often the key to development where security thinking cuts through the entire development process is portrayed. Security being the core design of systems is being executed at this point. This is a contradiction, though, tight deadlines might be insufficient to cover every authentication within it and the company has to bring up its technologies and culture along with the accelerating development of web security.

The researcher thoroughly and systematically digs into what such popularly used threat modeling tools provide. This assessment will be done on the parameter of whether the tool has the required capabilities, whether it is user-friendly or not, and to what level it can be integrated into development processes (Yeng, D., and Yang, 2020)Even though tools examination could be dulled by the speed of change of threat mapping technologies currently exploding into the market effectiveness of it may vary from one organization to another based on their unique requirements.

The adaptation of the threat modeling existing frameworks for existing IoT devices addressed in one paper (Liebl, 2023)is considered with the less processing power and communication protocols taken into further detail. Supported this with the cutting-edge development of the IoT to the point of obsolescence of areas that have been covered, leaving recommendations worthless.

A hybrid strategy is designed (Eng, 2017) which combines different threat modelling techniques that are appropriate for different activities. Comprising various approaches into a single threat model is the concept of the model - illustrating its application in a cloud solution case study. On the other hand, combining several methodologies may result in the need for complicated procedures.

The automation hybrid technique is suggested, which will adopt the most suitable methods according to the respective organizational function's needs. Constraints, for example, highly complex interactions inherent to the mixing of different methods; cost varies from time and workload and advanced equipment skills need are those which present the main limitations (Mohanty and Jyothi, 2015)

The STRIDE(Mohanty et al., 2023) threat model is renowned for its effectiveness in identifying and categorizing threats into six distinct types of attacks: masking, tampering, denial of service (DoS), data exfiltration (to alternative entities), service

DoS, and escalation. Another factor, that contributes to its popularity, is its ability to identify critical systems, devices, and networks and ensure the protection of the same from possible attacks. Accomplishing this kind of input-based modelling, STRIDE makes it possible to see the security weaknesses allowing for preventive actions to be put into place and posture to be improved.

PASTA (Mohanty, Sahoo, and Kabat, 2023) which is an acronym for Pasteurize Attack Scenario and Stress Analysis Procedure, translates to a risk-focused procedure for threat modeling. First and foremost, giving a main focus to risk means PASTA will identify the specific risk factors that can potentially disrupt business operations. The addressing of IT infrastructure as a tool for achieving the goals of general business conduct implies the possibility of solving the issue of risk management accordingly. With risk assessment as its main principle, PASTA helps organizations direct their security processes from the viewpoint of business purposes successfully.

Attack trees (Mohanty, Sahoo, and Kabat, 2023) are useful graphical representations of how low-level attack activities of threats often interact and hence converge to achieve certain malicious objectives that are mostly harmful to victims. Reflecting the notions of roots symbolizing power and the branches down below covering subordinate activities, such trees are depicted as the framework for oppositional movements. In the form of a head node, the aim or goal of the attacker is specified at the base (root), whereas leaf nodes indicate particular activities the adversary is involved. Intermediate items represent the states or sub goals, while the AND/OR items indicate that certain activities are either in conjunction or in conflict with others. Frequently de-escalation is brought about by the attack which is after to be graver as one move further up the tree. Performing visual risk analysis and identifying dependence and attack paths, attack trees make threat assessment comprehensive. They also play a vital role in developing up-to-date defense measures to prevent or reduce risks.

Our modeling method will be set by the mixture of the previously mentioned approaches. They assist us in deleting the extraneous which we have in the different types of models. Thus, a complex and end-to-end risk model is developed that leads us to discover the threats that the software applications, assets and systems turn into by leaking in their vulnerabilities.

3. SOFTWARE REQUIREMENTS

3.1 Functional Requirements

- **User Authentication:** The system must authenticate users to allow access to the threat modeling functionalities.

- **Threat Model Management**: The system must provide functionality to create new threat models. Users must be able to define the scope and details of each threat model.
- **Technology Association:** Users must be able to add technologies to a threat model.

  The system should allow association of technologies with their respective threat models.
- **Security Details Specification**: The system must allow users to add security details and controls to each threat model. Users should be able to specify policies and measures for threat mitigation.
- **Threat Generation:** The system must be capable of generating threats based on the defined threat model and associated technologies and security details.
- **Model Deletion:** Users must be able to delete threat models. The system should confirm deletions and update the state accordingly.
- **State Management:** After any addition or deletion of threat models, the system must update its local state to reflect these changes.

4. PROPOSED METHODS

4.1 Testcase-1

We evaluated the layout of an average healthcare network represented in Fig 4.1. By connecting a research hospital with separate inpatient facilities which include intensive care units, burns units, and more. Our investigation uncovered 20,000 devices within the environments which we categorized into IT, IoMT, OT and IoT. They fulfill a huge variety of tasks, like exchange highly sensitive data and finances, connecting and monitoring patients.

Figure 1. Healthcare Network Architecture diagram

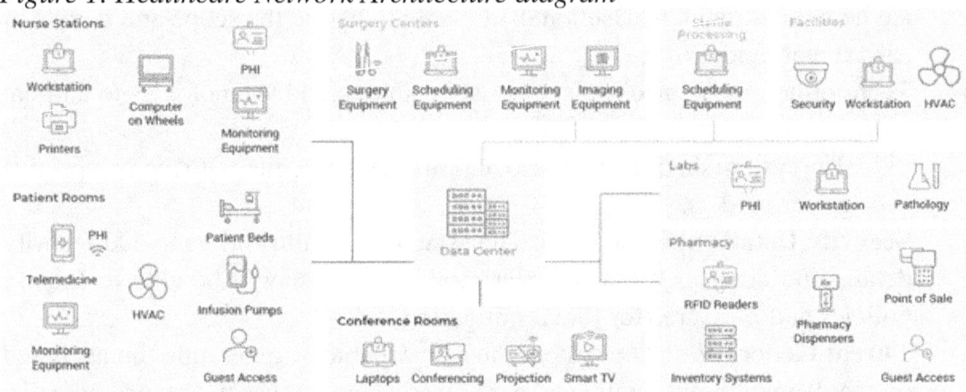

Our testing approach encompasses two main sections: here, we are going analyze the most common devices in healthcare network and we will try to see if these networks are vulnerable in any way. The first thing that we do is explore the heart of the network, which is a data center with both Electronic Health Records (EHR) and Electronic Medical Records (EMR) systems. Regarding targets of such systems, they store critical data like personal health information (PHI) and card payment details that are most wanted by attackers to exploit.

In addition, we conduct examinations of the different medical devices that are connected in many different facilities such patient rooms, nurse stations, surgicenters and pharmacies. This equipment covers everything from life-saving devices used for servicing such as insulin pumps and heart defibrillators to patient monitors and laboratory equipment. Besides, we parameterize the medical Internet of Things devices, like cafeteria and medicinal point-of-sale systems, vending machines and smart-building power and energy management systems.

As a result of a testing performed, we found out several possible threats for delivery healthcare organizations, which are shown in Figure 2. These threats include external threats such as a malicious actor purposely breaching a system and which then financialize the said weaknesses for their own benefits or other meddlesome purposes. As far as internal threats are concerned there always exists the danger of machines being exposed to risks like dangers involved in vendor and contractor access. These constitute an equally big challenge to network security. Furthermore, the number of legacy systems, used equipment that is not secured, and default passwords is in constant growth, which makes the healthcare organizations' position more complicated.

Figure 2. Potential Threats of Healthcare organisation

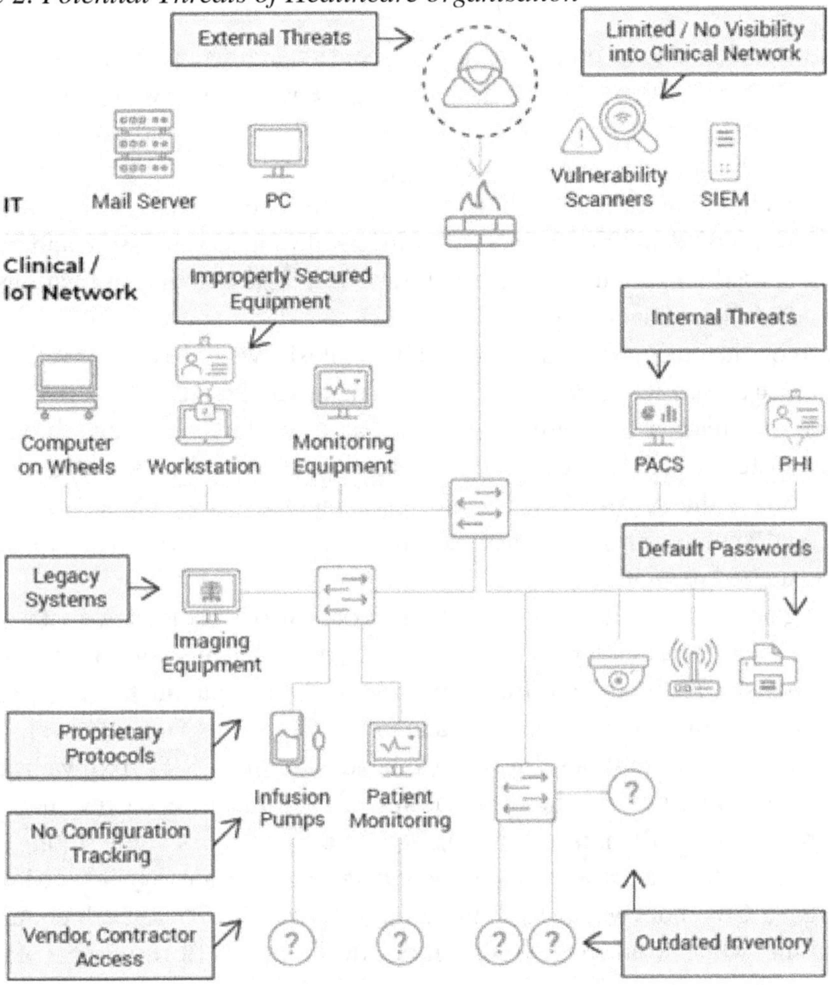

To face these threats, our campaign is designed by incorporating the framework in our project which is designed in this case. Nevertheless, healthcare might be the most problematic area that we are going to face up with because of the proprietary protocols, outdated inventory, and the absence of the visibility into the clinical network. These obstacles complicate the task of discovery of the gaps in security, ergo the lack of segmentation and the attacks which are not complete, therefore, strengthening the need for comprehensive threat modeling and risk assessment strategies.

In a nutshell, test case report describes the testing procedure implemented in the project with special emphasis put on breakdown of the structure of healthcare networks, detection of threats and proposing counter-measures to increase network security and resilience.

4.2 Testcase-2

In our project focused on enhancing the security architecture of the VNRVJIET website (https: For this, we used //vnrvjiet.ac.in/ website, where we systematized the whole process to check the possible risks, find critical assets, and give the efficient mitigation. This was accomplished through the implementation of our black box testing technique where-in the architectural elements of the website were researched, the assets identified and the threats and critical information assessed, and a model designed, based on which the vulnerabilities were assessed and mitigations were suggested(Mohanty, Sahoo, and Kabat, 2022).

Based on the outcome of the architecture analysis, we have discovered some of the key assets, potential threats, and important details about the VNRVJIET website. Sensitive information belonging to students and the staff had been stored in the software system which in turn faced risks like unauthorized access, data breaches and spoofing of the website. Critical information includes login credentials, contact details, and specific program information necessary to operate veraciously and maintain a good reputation.

Taking on the task of analyzing, we singled out various parameters that would be utilized in the website such as user inputs, or the data transmission channels as well as an administrative module of functions. We used those parameters as essentially the base for identifying vulnerabilities and mitigating them (Mohanty et al., 2023).

The vulnerability tool developed for the website, the VNRVJIET website was tested for potential security holes accordingly. As a result of our evaluation, we discovered inherent dilemmas, including SQL injections, cross-site scripting (XSS), weak authentication methods and incomplete data protection among others. Moreover, we assigned Common Weakness Enumeration (CWE) scores to each enumerated vulnerability which would help to concentrate the remedial efforts wisely (Mohanty, Sahoo, and Kabat 2024).

Figure 3. VNR VJIET

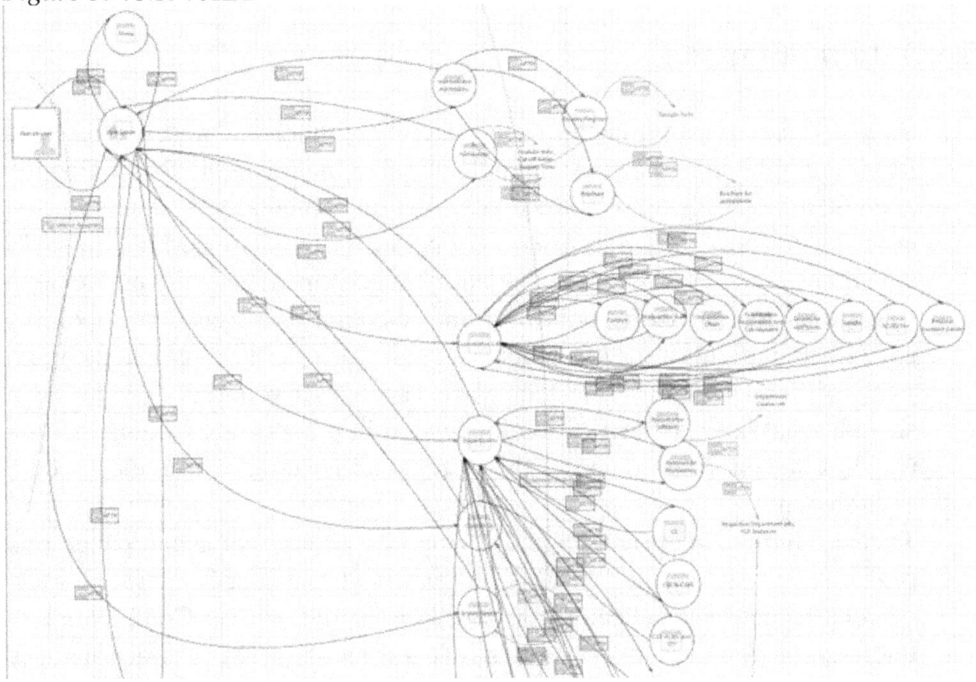

Analyzing the discovered vulnerabilities and their corresponding CWE scores, we recommended solutions to close security holes so that they will not pose potential threats which is shown in Fig 4.3. This measure included member verification (Multi-factor Authentication), encryption of sensitive data packets, encrypting in transit and at rest, and performing software components updating on regular basis to Patch known vulnerabilities (Mohanty, Kumar, Padmaja, and Prashanthi, 2024).

This cut through the examination process of the website architecture at VNRVJIET, showing the present weaknesses and suggesting curatives to reduce potential danger against the security; in conclusion, it revealed the loopholes in the security architecture and clearly outlined the decisions to be taken in the future. The technique that was utilized it was a systematic approach and the models that were proven together was used to be identified the weaknesses of the security and, in fact, made a positive contribution to the posture of security of the website as a whole and assets and information are also secured.

5. RESULTS

5.1 Output Screens

Sign-in Page: The sign-in page is the gateway to the threat modeling tool, offering multiple authentication options for the user, including Microsoft, Google, and GitHub. This level of access control is fundamental to system security, ensuring that only authorized users can operate the tool. It underlines the tool's compliance with best practices in identity management and data protection.

Account Selection Page: Following the selection of a sign-in method, this page likely presents a list of accounts associated with the chosen authentication provider. Users must select the correct account to proceed. This step adds an additional layer of verification in the sign-in process, confirming that the user has the authority to access the system and is acting within their secure environment.

Threat Models Overview Page: Serving as a central command panel, this page displays an overview of all the threat models a user has created. Each model is tagged with indicators for security priorities, such as Confidentiality, Integrity, and Availability—key pillars of cyber security. The interface includes functions to add new threats, edit existing models, and possibly delete them. This page is instrumental in managing the various threat scenarios the user needs to address, facilitating an organized approach to threat modeling.

Add Technology Stack Page: Here, users are presented with the ability to define and build upon the technological framework of their system within the threat model. By adding elements like APIs, programming languages, database tables, and file storage solutions, users can create a comprehensive model of their system's architecture. This is a critical step in threat modeling, as it lays the groundwork for identifying where vulnerabilities may exist and how they can be exploited.

Add Security Tech Page: This interface is designed for users to enhance their system's defenses by adding specific security technologies. Each technology—Authentication, Access Control Lists, Load Balancers, Web Application Firewalls—is presented as a solution to particular security challenges. The page likely explains the purpose of each technology and its role in safeguarding the system, thus guiding users in selecting the appropriate security layers that align with their threat model.

Vulnerability Identification Page: This particular page appears to function as an informational hub for users to understand the potential vulnerabilities that could impact their systems. It provides a list of common vulnerabilities, likely drawn from an authoritative source like the Common Weakness Enumeration (CWE) list. Each listed vulnerability, such as 'OS Command Injection' or 'Cross-site Scripting', includes a brief description, which details how the vulnerability manifests and potentially impacts a system. This information is crucial for developers and security analysts to understand the security landscape of the technology stack they are using and to prepare appropriate defenses.

Recommendations and Vulnerabilities Summary Page: On this page, the tool aggregates the findings from its analysis and presents the user with a snapshot of the security health of their system. It enumerates the number of potential vulnerabilities detected alongside a count of security recommendations. This summary offers a high-level view of the system's security posture, enabling users to quickly grasp the severity and breadth of their security concerns, which is essential for prioritizing remediation efforts.

Together, these pages form an interactive environment designed to streamline the threat modeling process, guiding users through each step—from identifying potential vulnerabilities and enhancing system security to managing an array of threat scenarios in a user-friendly manner.The threat modeling is performed the same way as we framework as the guide to conduct the iterative assessments to see if the security solution is effective. Stats of accuracy have been done on several runs of the model and are depicted below as Fig. 2. To this end, our examination has shown that the precision is steadily increasing. Precision increased from 78% to 83%, next to it 87%, and at the last stage reached 92% easing our way and achieving the goal. I admit that it was okay initially but the performance deteriorated after that and there were just marginal changes in the following versions which were called insignificant. Contrasting this, the RAT model achieved the accuracy of 94.2% at the seventh crop. Certainly, it lead us to the truth that our way seems to work quickly at first but its impact is low when it is measured after a few repetitions. On this chip, the fourth iteration performance is responsible for and therefore the framework has successfully handled the major categories of security threats which finally lead to a good performance very close to perfect. An evaluation of our threat modelling framework was definitely performed at the last stage of the iterative refinement but it contributed to the gradual development of system security at all the points of mission execution.

Attack Trees (7), TRIKE (9), and VAST (8). The findings of the scenario support the adequacy of our model to address security risks in their holistic approach. By developing a more effective shield with a higher number of mitigation recommendations, our framework will practically eliminate the risk of successful attacks. The outcomes of our established threat modelling framework not only prove the superiority of our approach but also demonstrate the practical applicability in the real-world security problems.

Our framework reached 94.2% in its seventh iteration when tested on our local computing environment, as presented in figure 5. Concerning the results, the accuracy score of 92% significantly outperforms many other well- renowned frameworks, for instance, STRIDE (89%), DREAD (81%), PASTA (86%), Attack Trees (87%), TRIKE (83%), and VAST (74%) shown in Fig 5.1.

The great accuracy, in itself, is an embodiment of the efficiency and excellency of the framework that we have in place to determine and counter the existing network threats. Iterative method lie at the core of the proposed framework and ensures continuous refinement and betterment with time. The developed method of threat modeling and analysis can be adapted easily to different types of threats that arise in future and changing networks conditions The cyclic return leads to process of learning and improvement, which in turn hold the threat analysis, more accurate at each iteration.

Figure 4. Accuracy achieved by different threat modeling frameworks

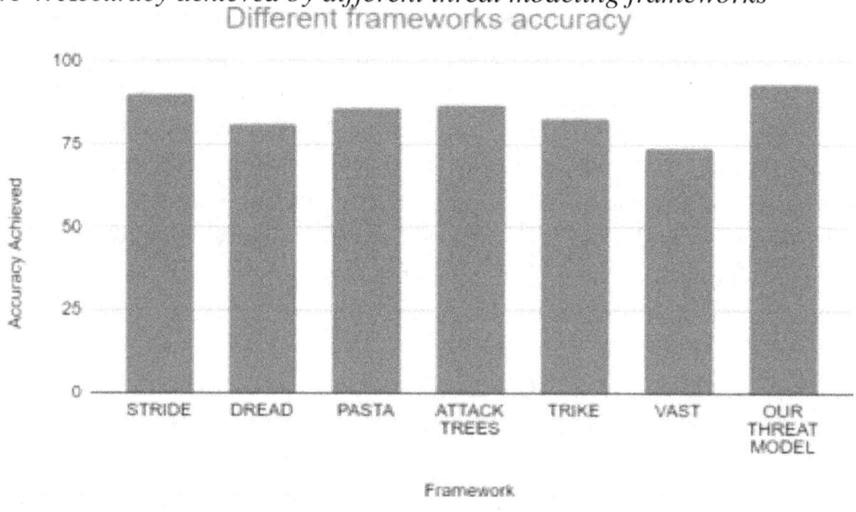

The fact that our methodology did top the other frameworks which includes STRIDE (11), DREAD, (7) PASTA (15), Attack Trees (10), TRIKE (5), and VAST (5) that is shown in figure 5 clearly reveals how powerful and progressive our proposal is. Through multi-factor analysis and in-depth exploration, our framework turns the inherited system defenses inside-out and exposes latent flaws. Part two, a mitigating phase appears in each iteration because as a result of that the identified vulnerabilities become less likely to be revealed overtime and we can be certain that we are building a more secure network. Stressed strategically the frameworks will secure the network through identifying and eliminating vulnerabilities which in turn will build the security culture within the organization teaching the need to be always updated and ever adaptable. After all, our framework which shows up the vulnerable areas fast and determines the most suitable measures of attempts to create secure and unwavering environment shown in Figure 5.

Figure 5. Number of Vulnerabilities Identified by different threat modelling frameworks

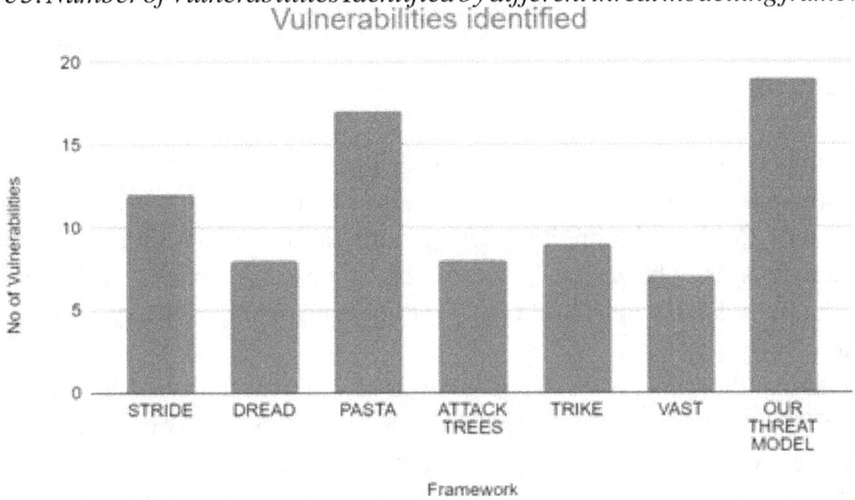

6. CONCLUSION

The cyber security world is in constant flux, but our framework is a portrayal of the interaction between scalability and human-centricity. We admit that any successful security system should be not only strong but also relevant and user-friendly. We adhere to this principle; therefore, our way begins from simplicity and directly influences security measures also for small or medium-sized organizations.

We first start with small systems and applications, aiming at creating a basis that can lead to the progressive implementation of high security measures in other networks and systems. This cycle approach provides suitable time for comprehensive and detailed appraisal of upgrade and improvement programs making sure that all the iterations of the framework are thoroughly developed and fulfilled.The testing web portal of our system performs the streamlining of threat modeling even if the users are less knowledgeable in cybersecurity. In addition, this affordability of CIS makes it easier to use and motivates the companies to do active cybersecurity actions.

On top of that, we are devoted to being ahead of the technology curve, and that is possible through constant updates of our framework which makes us stable and responsive to risks that come with time. We achieve this through tackling the critical weaknesses and gaining the upper hand over the threat universe within the various constraints relating to our platform. Consequently, our resource management and operational effectiveness are enhanced.The ultimate aim is to improve the framework integration with various web portal modules and operate applications in different fields. Through we evaluate its interoperability with different organizations ecosystems, we wish to lay a solid basis for their digital transition path.

6.1 Summary

The importance of system security in the digital age cannot be overstated as it is essentially based on the continuous exchange of information and processing of massive data. As a result, threat modeling comes as a crucial tool in managing the cybersecurity system because it helps to evaluate possible threats or vulnerabilities present in the system which could lead to the undermining of the system integrity or data security.

The aim of this paper is a detailed analysis of different threat modeling methods such as STRIDE, PASTA, DAST, TREK, (VAST) Attack Trees. To each methodology belongs its own particular bent of thought and approaches, which might happen to be useful in various types of organizations working in different threat environments.

The paper thus argues that the approach to cybersecurity threat management should be holistic, and the paper suggests an integrated model that merges the strengths of the disciplines. By joining parts of STRIDE's systemic thinking, PASTA's risk oriented approach, DREAD's hazard assessment, TREK's adaptability, VAST's global vision, and Attack Tree's structured representation, the integrated system encloses a strong tool that may help deal with the present cybersecurity challenges.

One of the driving factors of the proposed framework is the emphasis on refining iteratively and running strict checks on the used strategies, which ensures their effectiveness. The framework does this by including user-friendly web-portals as well as using new technologies so that the framework can provide a higher level of usability and adaptability so as organizations can keep up with evolving threats.

Furthermore, there is a trifecta approach that help detect and protect against different threats ranging from hardware, software, and direct attacks. This triad means that the framework addresses not only the vulnerabilities of software but also considers the most possible ways of attack as well as the possible means of gaining access.

The rat model (Risk Assessment Threat Modelling) put forward is the most comprehensive and comprehension model by making the revision iterative and exhaustive. through the use of comparing and contrasting the model proves itself as effective having an amazing accuracy of 94.2% in containing and neutralizing the threat.

Finally, this is integrated threat modeling framework proposed is very dynamic and strong approach in cybersecurity. Through the utilization of inherent methodologies and also integrating new technologies, framework establishes a way to enhance system resistance as well as resilience against ongoing cyber threats. This paper adds to the debate about cybersecurity management, because it gives a straightforward and useful information for the organizations seeking to protect themselves from cybersecurity entry.

6.2 Further Work

Proceeding onwards, a wide range of possibilities arise, granting plenty of space for future development and improvement. undefined

- **Advanced Threat Detection Mechanisms:** Implementing edge-of-the-curve technologies such as machine learning and artificial intelligence to improve the monitoring ability. This advanced detection mechanism will facilitate the near real- time identification and neutralization of emerging hazards, thus strengthening the framework's aim of doing the utmost in preserving organizational assets.
- **Expanded Integration Capabilities:** Ensuring the framework's capacity for integration becomes more robust and advanced to detect and properly transfer data or services to other elements of the digital ecosystem. Through this expanded integration, the collaboration and information sharing between different systems and organizations will be made smoother and much more effective, thus improving cyberspace resilience in general.
- **Comprehensive User Training Resources:** Developing informative training materials to ensure that by the end the user has an understanding and the right skills for effective tackling of cybersecurity threats. The resources would feature tutorials, simulations as well as materials for people in different roles and with various levels of proficiency.
- **Regulatory Compliance Features:** Integrating features to cater for industry policies, rules and standards. By putting regulatory compliance procedures and controls within the framework it is possible for the organizations to carry out this process more efficiently and reduce regulatory risks more effectively.
- **Feedback-Driven Continuous Improvement:** Introducing the feedback-based framework which enables the periodic check to be performed considering the user experience, emerging threats, and the industry standards. By implementing an iterative improvement process, the framework will be made responsive and more competent in countering the evolving cybersecurity threats.

- **Enhanced Threat Intelligence Sharing**: The utilization of multilateral body framework to enhance partnerships and information exchange among organisations through ethically binding guidelines for threat intelligence sharing. This can be done through the involvement in the sector-specific ISACs (Information Sharing and Analysis Centers) or by establishing the succesful partnerships with peer organizations for mutual exchange of intelligence and security best practices.
- **Behavioral Analytics and User Behavior Monitoring:** Integrating sophisticated behavioral analytics and user tracking approach to detect suspicious behavior that could be due to outsider threats or unpermitted access. Through human behavior patterns analysis and determining abnormal behavior of entity employee responsible for the management of the company's confidential data, organizations can forward/take action on such deviations in a timely manner.
- **Automated Vulnerability Management:** The automation of vulnerability scanning, assessment, and remediation tasks should be used for greater effectiveness of vulnerability management processes. This may, for instance, include applying vulnerability management solutions and tools which parody the vulnerabilities based on their intensity and impact on the security situation of the organization.
- **Enhanced Endpoint Security:** Implementing strong end-point security measures to prevent occasional sophisticated threats like Trojans and virus-writings. This can be through the application of upgraded endpoint detection and response (EDR) tools, and implementing application whitelisting, as well as micro-segmentation techniques. And finally, these measures must provide for the device encryption and remote wipe features.
- **Continuous Threat Hunting:** Setting up the continuous threat hunting services to preventively detect and block the existing (prior known), and other new unknown risks inside the organization's network, sharply. This can be carried out by operations of threat hunting platforms and the techniques that include log analysis, network traffic analysis, and threat intelligence correlation, for early detection and neutralization of potential risk that is about to grow.
- **Enhanced Supply Chain Security:** Taking up measures to increase the robustness of supply chain security mechanisms for dealing with the risk factors related to third party vendors and suppliers. It should involve performing detailed security scans of the third-party suppliers' services, establishing the supply chain risk management specifications, and forcing compliance with security contractual requirements, ensuring the security of the whole supply chain eco-system.

We therefore want to reinforce our model as an ultimate choice for preemptive cybersecurity management by giving precedence to those areas in need of development. With innovation and teamwork always in mind, our goal is to facilitate a safe digital space for companies of every sector and size.

REFERENCES

Eng, D. (2017). *Integrated threat modelling* (Master's thesis, University of Oslo). Retrieved from http://hdl.handle.net/10852/55699

Liebl, S. (2023). *Threat modelling for Internet of Things devices*.

Manzoor, S., Zhang, H., & Suri, N. (2018, April). Threat modeling and analysis for the cloud ecosystem. In *2018 IEEE International Conference on Cloud Engineering (IC2E)* (pp. 278-281). IEEE. DOI: 10.1109/IC2E.2018.00056

Martelleur, J., & Hamza, A. (2022). *Security tools in DevSecOps: A systematic literature review* (Master's thesis). Retrieved from https://urn.kb.se/resolve?urn= urn:nbn:se:lnu:diva-118400

Meng, B., Smith, W., & Durling, M. (2021). Security threat modeling and automated analysis for system design. *SAE International Journal of Transportation Cybersecurity and Privacy, 4*(11-04-01-0001), 3-17.

Mohanty, R. K., & Jyothi, N. (2015). A secured framework for protecting sensitive information from unauthorized users.

Mohanty, R. K., Kumar, A. P., Padmaja, R., & Prashanthi, V. (2024). Deep Learning for Analyzing User and Entity Behaviors: Techniques and Applications. In *Consumer and Organizational Behavior in the Age of AI* (pp. 219–250). IGI Global. DOI: 10.4018/979-8-3693-8850-1.ch008

Mohanty, R. K., Motupalli, R. K., Manju, D., Gangappa, M., Gouthami, B., & Mounika, G. (2023, December). Energy-efficient cluster based routing protocol to enhance the lifetime of wearable wireless body area networks (WBAN). In **2023 OITS International Conference on Information Technology (OCIT)** (pp. 71-76). IEEE. DOI: 10.1109/OCIT59427.2023.10431071

Mohanty, R. K., Motupalli, R. K., Manju, D., Gangappa, M., Gouthami, B., & Mounika, G. (2023, December). Energy-efficient cluster based routing protocol to enhance the lifetime of wearable wireless body area networks (WBAN). In **2023 OITS International Conference on Information Technology (OCIT)** (pp. 71-76). IEEE. DOI: 10.1109/OCIT59427.2023.10431071

Mohanty, R. K., Sahoo, S. P., & Kabat, M. R. (2022, October). A survey on emerging technologies in wireless body area network. In *2022 13th International Conference on Computing Communication and Networking Technologies (ICCCNT)* (pp. 1-5). IEEE.

Mohanty, R. K., Sahoo, S. P., & Kabat, M. R. (2023). Sustainable remote patient monitoring in wireless body area network with multi-hop routing and scheduling: A four-fold objective based optimization approach. *. *Wireless Networks*, 29(5), 1–15. DOI: 10.1007/s11276-023-03276-x

Mohanty, R. K., Sahoo, S. P., & Kabat, M. R. (2023, June). A network reliability based secure routing protocol (NRSRP) for secure transmission in wireless body area network. In *2023 8th International Conference on Communication and Electronics Systems (ICCES)* (pp. 663-668). IEEE.

Mohanty, R. K., Sahoo, S. P., & Kabat, M. R. (2024). Thermal-energy-efficient-secured-link reliable and delay-aware routing protocol (TESLDAR) for wireless body area networks. *. *International Journal of Computers and Applications*, 46(9), 1–13. DOI: 10.1080/1206212X.2024.2380675

Myagmar, S., Lee, A. J., & Yurcik, W. (2005). Threat modeling as a basis for security requirements.

Nweke, L. O., & Wolthusen, S. (2020). A review of asset-centric threat modelling approaches.

Potteiger, B., Martins, G., & Koutsoukos, X. (2016, April). Software and attack-centric integrated threat modeling for quantitative risk assessment. In **Proceedings of the Symposium and Bootcamp on the Science of Security** (pp. 99-108). DOI: 10.1145/2898375.2898390

Sion, L., Yskout, K., Van Landuyt, D., & Joosen, W. (2018). Solution-aware data flow diagrams for security threat modeling. In **Proceedings of the 33rd Annual ACM Symposium on Applied Computing** (pp. 1425-1432). DOI: 10.1145/3167132.3167285

UcedaVelez. T., & Morana, M. M. (2015). Risk Centric Threat Modeling: process for attack simulation and threat analysis. John Wiley & Sons.

Viswanathan, G. (2021). *A hybrid threat model for system-centric and attack-centric for effective security design in SDLC. *Web Intelligence, 19*(1-2), 1-11.* IOS Press.

Xiong, W. (2021). *Enhancing IT systems cyber resilience through threat modeling: Cyber security analysis of enterprise systems and connected vehicles* (Doctoral dissertation, KTH Royal Institute of Technology). Retrieved from https://urn.kb.se/resolve?urn=urn:nbn:se:kth:diva-300046

Yeng, P. K., D., S., & Yang, B. (2020). Comparative analysis of threat modeling methods for cloud computing towards healthcare security practice. *International Journal of Advanced Computer Science and Applications, 11*(11).

Compilation of References

Abdullaev, Z. K. (2021). Second Language Learning. *Mental Enlightenment Scientific-Methodological Journal*, 2021(06), 1–11.

Abe, P. & Jordan, N. A. (2014). Integrating Social Media Into the Classroom Curriculum. Integrating-Social-Media-Into-the-Classroom-Curriculum.pdf (ubc.ca)

Abrami, P. C., Leventhal, L., & Perry, R. P. (1982). Educational Seduction. *Review of Educational Research*, 52(3), 446–464. DOI: 10.3102/00346543052003446

Abt, C. C. (1987). Serious games. University press of America.

Abujaber, A. A., Abd-Alrazaq, A., Al-Qudimat, A. R., & Nashwan, A. J. (2023). A strengths, weaknesses, opportunities, and threats (SWOT) analysis of ChatGPT integration in nursing education: A narrative review. *Cureus*, 15(11). Advance online publication. DOI: 10.7759/cureus.48643 PMID: 38090452

Adipat, S., Laksana, K., Busayanon, K., Asawasowan, A., & Adipat, B. (2021). Engaging Students in the Learning Process with Game-Based Learning: The Fundamental Concepts. *International Journal of Technology in Education*, 4(3), 542–552. DOI: 10.46328/ijte.169

Adnan, N. H., Norman, H., & Nordin, N. M. (2020). Instructor-generated hand-drawn 2D animations for ESL vocabulary learning in secondary education. *The Asian ESP Journal, 16*(1.2), 67-81. https://www.elejournals.com/asian-esp-journal/aesp-february-2020-16-1-2/

Afzal, A., Khan, S., Daud, S., & Ahmed, Z. (2023). Addressing the Digital Divide: Access and Use of Technology in Education. *Journal of Social Sciences Review*, 3(2), 883–895. DOI: 10.54183/jssr.v3i2.326

Aguilera, D., & Revilla, J. O. (2021). STEM vs. STEAM Education and Student Creativity: A Systematic Literature Review. *Education Sciences*, 11(7), 331. DOI: 10.3390/educsci11070331

Agustono, D., Nugroho, R., & Fianto, A. (2023). *Artificial intelligence in human resource management practices*. Kne Social Sciences., DOI: 10.18502/kss.v8i9.13409

Ahmad, C. V. (2021). Causes of students' reluctance to participate in classroom discussions. ASEAN Journal of Science and Engineering Education, 1(1), 47-62. https://ejournal.upi.edu/index.php/AJSEE/

Ahmad, K., Qadir, J., Al-Fuqaha, A., Iqbal, W., El-Hassan, A., Benhaddou, D., & Ayyash, M. (2020). Artificial intelligence in education: a panoramic review. DOI: . io/zvu2n.DOI: <ALIGNMENT.qj></ALIGNMENT>10.35542/osf

Ahmad, S. F., Alam, M. M., Rahmat, M. K., Mubarik, M. S., & Hyder, S. I. (2022). Academic and administrative role of artificial intelligence in education. *Sustainability (Basel)*, 14(3), 1101. DOI: 10.3390/su14031101

Ahmad, S., Umirzakova, S., Jamil, F., & Whangbo, T. K. (2022). Internet-of-things-enabled serious games: A comprehensive survey. *Future Generation Computer Systems*, 136, 67–83. DOI: 10.1016/j.future.2022.05.026

Ahmed, A. A. A., Ampry, E. S., Komariah, A., Hassan, I., Thahir, I., Hussein Ali, M., Fawzi Faisal, A., & Zafarani, P. (2022). Investigating the effect of using game-based learning on EFL learners' motivation and anxiety. *Education Research International*, 2022, 1–9. DOI: 10.1155/2022/6503139

Ahmed, R. (2016). Social Media Integration in Secondary Education in Pakistan. *Journal of Education and Educational Development*, 3(1), 74. DOI: 10.22555/joeed.v3i1.712

Aibar-Almazán, A., Castellote-Caballero, Y., Carcelén-Fraile, M. del C., Rivas-Campo, Y., & González-Martín, A. M. (2024). Gamification in the classroom: Kahoot! As a tool for university teaching innovation. *Frontiers in Psychology*, 15(March), 1–8. DOI: 10.3389/fpsyg.2024.1370084 PMID: 38646120

Ainin, S., Naqshbandi, N. M., Moghavvemi, S., & Jaafar, N. I. (2015). Facebook usage, socialization, and academic performance. *Computers & Education*, 83, 64–73. DOI: 10.1016/j.compedu.2014.12.018

Airenti, G. (2015). The Cognitive Bases of Anthropomorphism: From Relatedness to Empathy. *International Journal of Social Robotics*, 7(1), 117–127. DOI: 10.1007/s12369-014-0263-x

Aivaloglou, E., Fletcher, G., & Miedema, D. International Workshop on Data Systems Education: Bridging Education Practice with Education Research,(DataEd) 2023.

Akbari, E., Naderi, A., & Simons, R.-J., & K. J. A.-P. J. o. S. (2016). Student engagement and foreign language learning through online social networks. *Journal of Social Sciences*, 1(1), 4. DOI: 10.11648/j.jss.2016.01.11

Akter, S. N., Wu, Z., Muhamed, A., Ou, T., Bäuerle, A., Cabrera, Á. A., Dholakia, K., Xiong, C., & Neubig, G. (2023). An in-depth look at Gemini's language abilities. *ArXiv*. https://doi.org//arXiv.2312.11444DOI: 10.48550

Akther, F. (2022). English for personal and career development and its importance for better employment opportunities. *Journal of Languages. Linguistics and Literary Studies*, 2(3), 95–100.

Akther, F. (2023). Role of skill india programs in fostering entrepreneurship among rural youth in india. *Formosa Journal of Science and Technology*, 2(10), 2891–2902. DOI: 10.55927/fjst.v2i10.6678

Alam, A. (2021, November). Possibilities and apprehensions in the landscape of artificial intelligence in education. In *2021 International Conference on Computational Intelligence and Computing Applications (ICCICA)* (pp. 1-8). IEEE. DOI: 10.1109/ICCICA52458.2021.9697272

Alexander, B., Becker, S. A., Cummins, M., & Giesinger, C. H. (2017). *Digital literacy in higher education, Part II: An NMC Horizon project strategic brief.* The New Media Consortium.

Al-Hafdi, F. S., & Alhalafawy, W. S. (2024). Ten Years of Gamification-Based Learning: A Bibliometric Analysis and Systematic Review. [IJIM]. *International Journal of Interactive Mobile Technologies*, 18(07), 188–212. DOI: 10.3991/ijim.v18i07.45335

Ali, H. H. H. (2022). The importance of the four English language skills: Reading, writing, speaking, and listening in teaching Iraqi learners. *Humanitarian and Natural Sciences Journal*, 3(2), 155–165. DOI: 10.53796/hnsj3210

Aliyeva, V. (2022). The Impact of Personalized Learning on Student Achievement. *Journal of Informatics Education and Research*, 2(1).

Allamanis, M., & Brockschmidt, M. (2021, December 8). Finding and fixing bugs with deep learning. *Microsoft Research.* https://www.microsoft.com/research/blog/finding-and-fixing-bugs-with-deep-learning/

Allamanis, M., Jackson-Flux, H., & Brockschmidt, M. (2021). Self-supervised bug detection and repair. *Advances in Neural Information Processing Systems*, 34, 27865–27876.

Allen, K., Ryan, T., Gray, D., McInerney, D., & Waters, L. (2014). Social media use and social connectedness in adolescents: The positives and the potential pitfalls. *Australian Educational and Developmental Psychologist*, 31(1), 18–31. DOI: 10.1017/edp.2014.2

Ally, M. (Ed.). (2009). *Mobile learning: Transforming the delivery of education and training*. Athabasca University Press. DOI: 10.15215/aupress/9781897425435.01

Alsawaier, R S. (2018, January 2). The effect of gamification on motivation and engagement. Emerald Publishing Limited, 35(1), 56-79. https://doi.org/DOI: 10.1108/IJILT-02-2017-0009

Alshorman, S. (2024). The readiness to use ai in teaching science: Science teachers' perspective. *Journal of Baltic Science Education*, 23(3), 432–448. DOI: 10.33225/jbse/24.23.432

Altaie, M. A., & Jawawi, D. N. A. (2021). Adaptive Gamification to Promote Computational Thinking. *Journal of E-Learning and Knowledge Society*, 17(3), 89–100.

Alturki, U. & Aldraiweesh, A. (2024). The impact of self-determination theory: the moderating functions of social media (SM) use in education and affective learning engagement | Humanities and Social Sciences Communications (nature.com)

Alvarez, K. S. (2021). Using virtual simulations in online laboratory instruction and active learning exercises as a response to instructional challenges during COVID-19. *Journal of Microbiology & Biology Education*, 22(1), 10–1128. DOI: 10.1128/jmbe.v22i1.2503 PMID: 33884091

Amabile, T. M. (1996). *Creativity and innovation in organizations* (Vol. 5). Harvard Business School Boston. https://edisciplinas.usp.br/pluginfile.php/4927750/mod_resource/content/0/Creativity%20and%20Innovation%20in%20Organizations.pdf

Amdan, M. (2024). Advancement of ai-tools in learning for technical vocational education and training (tvet) in malaysia (empowering students and tutor). *International Journal of Scientific Research*.

Amin, A. M., Adiansyah, R., & Hujjatusnaini, N. (2023). The contribution of communication and digital literacy skills to critical thinking. [Indonesian Journal of Science Education]. *Jurnal Pendidikan Sains Indonesia*, 11(3), 697–712. DOI: 10.24815/jpsi.v11i3.30838

Amini, M., & Laghabdoost, M. (2021). Representation of teachers' lived experiences of functions implementation and challenges of art education in primary schools. *Research in Teaching*, 9(4), 29–1.

Amo, L., Liao, R., Rao, H R., & Walker, G. (2018, June 18). Effects of Leaderboards in Games on Consumer Engagement. https://doi.org/DOI: 10.1145/3209626.3209708

Anak Yunus, C. C., & Hua, T. K. (2021). Exploring a gamified learning tool in the ESL classroom: The case of Quizizz. *Journal of Education and e-learning Research*, 8(1), 103–108. DOI: 10.20448/journal.509.2021.81.103.108

Anderson, R. C., & Graham, M. (2021). Creative potential in flux: The leading role of originality during early adolescent development. *Thinking Skills and Creativity*, 40, 100816. DOI: 10.1016/j.tsc.2021.100816

Anderson, R. C., & Haney, M. (2021). Reflection in the creative process of early adolescents: The mediating roles of creative metacognition, self-efficacy, and self-concept. *Psychology of Aesthetics, Creativity, and the Arts*, 15(4), 612–626. DOI: 10.1037/aca0000324

Anderson, R. C., Haney, M., Pitts, C., Porter, L., & Bousselot, T. (2020). "Mistakes Can be Beautiful": Creative Engagement in Arts Integration for Early Adolescent Learners. *The Journal of Creative Behavior*, 54(3), 662–675. DOI: 10.1002/jocb.401

Anderson, T. (2019). Challenges and Opportunities for Use of Social Media in Higher Education. *Journal of Learning for Development*, 6(1), 6–19. DOI: 10.56059/jl4d.v6i1.327

Anderson, T., & Milbrandt, M. K. (2018). *Art for life: Authentic instruction in art*. McGraw-Hill Education.

An, Y. (2020, February 21). Designing Effective Gamified Learning Experiences. *Designing Effective Gamified Learning Experiences.*, 3(2), 62–62. DOI: 10.46328/ijte.v3i2.27

An, Y., Zhu, M., Bonk, C. J., & Lin, L. (2021). Exploring instructors' perspectives, practices, and perceived support needs and barriers related to the gamification of MOOCs. *Journal of Computing in Higher Education*, 33(1), 64–84. DOI: 10.1007/s12528-020-09256-w

Arnab, S., Lim, T., Carvalho, M. B., Bellotti, F., De Freitas, S., Louchart, S., Suttie, N., Berta, R., & De Gloria, A. (2015). Mapping learning and game mechanics for serious games analysis. *British Journal of Educational Technology*, 46(2), 391–411. DOI: 10.1111/bjet.12113

Arnaoudova, V., Di Penta, M., & Antoniol, G. (2016). Linguistic antipatterns: What they are and how developers perceive them. *Empirical Software Engineering*, 21(1), 104–158. DOI: 10.1007/s10664-014-9350-8

Artola González, T., Barraca, J., Mosteiro Pintor, P., Ancillo Gómez, I., Poveda, B., & Sánchez, N. (2012). *PIC-A Prueba de Imaginación Creativa para Adultos*. http://repositorio.ucjc.edu/handle/20.500.12020/435

Asad, M. M., Naz, A., Churi, P., & Tahanzadeh, M. M. (2021). Virtual reality as pedagogical tool to enhance experiential learning: A systematic literature review. *Education Research International*, 2021(1), 7061623. DOI: 10.1155/2021/7061623

Asuyama, Y. (2019). Skill sorting and production linkages: Evidence from india. *The Developing Economies*, 57(2), 125–158. DOI: 10.1111/deve.12193

Autor, D. H. (2015). Why are there still so many jobs? The history and future of workplace automation. *The Journal of Economic Perspectives*, 29(3), 3–30. DOI: 10.1257/jep.29.3.3

Ayewah, N., Pugh, W., Hovemeyer, D., Morgenthaler, J. D., & Penix, J. (2008). Using static analysis to find bugs. *IEEE Software*, 25(5), 22–29. DOI: 10.1109/MS.2008.130

Aziz, A. A., & Kashinathan, S. (2021). ESL learners' challenges in speaking English in Malaysian classroom. *Development*, 10(2), 983–991. DOI: 10.6007/IJARPED/v10-i2/10355

Babashahi, L. (2024). Ai in the workplace: A systematic review of skill transformation in the industry. *Administrative Sciences*, 14(6), 127. DOI: 10.3390/admsci14060127

Bai, S., Hew, K F., & Huang, B. (2020, June 1). Does gamification improve student learning outcomes? Evidence from a meta-analysis and synthesis of qualitative data in educational contexts. Elsevier BV, 30, 100322-100322. https://doi.org/.DOI: 10.1016/j.edurev.2020.100322

Baker, T., & Gow, G. A. (2020). Privacy and surveillance: AI ethics in education. *Journal of Educational Technology & Society*, 23(4), 31–41.

Baki, N. (2023). Integrating artificial intelligence in human resource functions: Challenges and opportunities. *International Journal of Academic Research in Business & Social Sciences*, 13(8). Advance online publication. DOI: 10.6007/ijarbss/v13-i8/18071

Bala, Y. Z., Samat, P. A., Sharif, K. Y., & Manshor, N. (2023). Improving cross-project software defect prediction method through transformation and feature selection approach. *IEEE Access : Practical Innovations, Open Solutions*, 11, 2318–2326. DOI: 10.1109/ACCESS.2022.3231456

Bandura, A. (1997). *Self-efficacy: The exercise of control*. Macmillan.

Barbosa, M. W., de Avila, ´., & Rodrigues, C. (2020). Project portfolio management teaching: Contributions of a gamified approach. *International Journal of Management Education*, 18(2), 100388. DOI: 10.1016/j.ijme.2020.100388

Barfi, K. A., Bervell, B., & Arkorful, V. (2021). Integration of social media for smart pedagogy: Initial perceptions of senior high school students in Ghana. *Education and Information Technologies*, 26(3), 3033–3055. DOI: 10.1007/s10639-020-10405-y

Basnet, S. (2024). Navigating the ethical landscape: Considerations in implementing ai-ml systems in human resources. *International Journal of Research Publication and Reviews*, 5(3), 3436–3447. DOI: 10.55248/gengpi.5.0324.0755

Bates, T. (2019). Teaching in a digital age: Guidelines for designing teaching and learning. BCcampus Open Education.

Bautista, R. G. (2015). Students' affordance of teleologic explanations and antrhropomorphic language in eliciting concepts in physics. *Journal of Technology and Science Education*, 5(1), 31–40. DOI: 10.3926/jotse.137

Baxter, G., & Hainey, T. (2024). Using immersive technologies to enhance the student learning experience. *Interactive Technology and Smart Education*, 21(3), 403–425. DOI: 10.1108/ITSE-05-2023-0078

Beaty, R. E., Benedek, M., Wilkins, R. W., Jauk, E., Fink, A., Silvia, P. J., Hodges, D. A., Koschutnig, K., & Neubauer, A. C. (2014). Creativity and the default network: A functional connectivity analysis of the creative brain at rest. *Neuropsychologia*, 64, 92–98. DOI: 10.1016/j.neuropsychologia.2014.09.019 PMID: 25245940

Beaty, R. E., & Silvia, P. J. (2012). Why do ideas get more creative across time? An executive interpretation of the serial order effect in divergent thinking tasks. *Psychology of Aesthetics, Creativity, and the Arts*, 6(4), 309–319. DOI: 10.1037/a0029171

Benedek, M., Nordtvedt, N., Jauk, E., Koschmieder, C., Pretsch, J., Krammer, G., & Neubauer, A. C. (2016). Assessment of creativity evaluation skills: A psychometric investigation in prospective teachers. *Thinking Skills and Creativity*, 21, 75–84. DOI: 10.1016/j.tsc.2016.05.007

Bennani, S., Maalel, A., & Ben Ghezala, H. (2022). Adaptive gamification in E-learning: A literature review and future challenges. *Computer Applications in Engineering Education*, 30(2), 628–642. DOI: 10.1002/cae.22477

Bilohur, Vlada, & Andriukaitiene, Regina (2020). Sports culture as a means of improving the integrity of sports personality: philosophicalcultural and anthropological analysis. Humanities studies. N° 6 (83). P. 136–152.

Bird, J. J., Ekart, A., & Faria, D. R. (2018). Learning from interaction: An intelligent networked-based human-bot and bot-bot chatbot system. In *Advances in Computational Intelligence Systems* (1st ed., pp. 179–190). Springer.

Biswas, D., Dutta, A., Ghosh, S., & Roy, P. (2024). Future Trends and Significant Solutions for Intelligent Computing Resource Management. In Computational Intelligence for Green Cloud Computing and Digital Waste Management (pp. 187-208). IGI Global. DOI: 10.4018/979-8-3693-1552-1.ch010

Blalock, L. D. (2015). Stimulus familiarity improves consolidation of visual working memory representations. *Attention, Perception & Psychophysics*, 77(4), 1143–1158. DOI: 10.3758/s13414-014-0823-z PMID: 25720758

Blau, I., Shamir-Inbal, T., & Avdiel, O. (2020). How does the pedagogical design of a technology-enhanced collaborative academic course promote digital literacies, self-regulation, and perceived learning of students? *The Internet and Higher Education*, 45, 100722. DOI: 10.1016/j.iheduc.2019.100722

Blut, M., Wang, C., Wünderlich, N. V., & Brock, C. (2021). Understanding anthropomorphism in service provision: A meta-analysis of physical robots, chatbots, and other AI. *Journal of the Academy of Marketing Science*, 49(4), 632–658. DOI: 10.1007/s11747-020-00762-y

Bobitan, N. (2024). Shaping tomorrow: Anticipating skills requirements based on the integration of artificial intelligence in business organizations—a foresight analysis using the scenario method. *Electronics (Basel)*, 13(11), 2198. DOI: 10.3390/electronics13112198

Bogdan, R. C., & Biklen, S. K. (1998). *Qualitative research for education an introduction to theory and methods* (3rd ed.). Nancy Forsyth.

Boghian, I., Cojocariu, V.-M., Popescu, C. V., & Mat , L. (2019). Game-based learning. Using board games in adult education. *J. Educat. Sci. Psychol.*, 9, 51–57.

Bolt, D., & Crawford, R. (2000). *Digital divide: Computers and our children's future*. TV Books LLC.

Bond, M., Marín, V. I., Dolch, C., Bedenlier, S., & Zawacki-Richter, O. (2018). Digital transformation in German higher education: Student and teacher perceptions and usage of digital media. *International Journal of Educational Technology in Higher Education*, 15(1), 1–20. DOI: 10.1186/s41239-018-0130-1

Bonfield, C. A., Salter, M., Longmuir, A., Benson, M., & Adachi, C. (2020). Transformation or evolution?: Education 4.0, teaching and learning in the digital age. *Higher Education Pedagogies*, 5(1), 223–246. DOI: 10.1080/23752696.2020.1816847

Borg, S. (2006). Teacher cognition and language education: Research and practice. *Continuum.*

Bostrom, N. (2014). *Super intelligence: Paths, dangers, strategies*. Oxford University Press.

Botra, A., Rerselman, M., & Ford, M. (2014, May 1). Gamification beyond badges. https://doi.org/DOI: 10.1109/ISTAFRICA.2014.6880651

Bowen, R. S., Picard, D. R., Verberne-Sutton, S., & Brame, C. J. (2018). Incorporating Student Design in an HPLC Lab Activity Promotes Student Metacognition and Argumentation. *Journal of Chemical Education*, 95(1), 108–115. DOI: 10.1021/acs.jchemed.7b00258

Bower, M. (2019). Technology-mediated learning theory. *British Journal of Educational Technology*, 50(3), 1030–1042. DOI: 10.1111/bjet.12771

Boyce, A. K. (2014). *Deep gamification: Combining game-based and play-based methods*. North Carolina State University.

Boyd, D. M., & Ellison, N. B. (2007). Social Network Sites: Definition, History, and Scholarship. *Journal of Computer-Mediated Communication*, 13(1), 210–230. DOI: 10.1111/j.1083-6101.2007.00393.x

Brandl, L. C., & Schrader, A. (2024). Serious Games in Higher Education in the Transforming Process to Education 4.0—Systematized Review. *Education Sciences*, 14(3), 281. DOI: 10.3390/educsci14030281

Breien, F. S., & Wasson, B. (2021). Narrative categorization in digital game-based learning: Engagement, motivation & learning. *British Journal of Educational Technology*, 52(1), 91–111. DOI: 10.1111/bjet.13004

Bright, L. F., Kleiser, S. B., & Grau, S. L. (2015). Too much Facebook? An exploratory examination of social media fatigue. *Computers in Human Behavior*, 44(44), 148–155. DOI: 10.1016/j.chb.2014.11.048

Brom, C., Hannemann, T., Stárková, T., Bromová, E., & Děchtěrenko, F. (2018). *Anthropomorphic Faces and Funny Graphics in an Instructional Animation May Improve Superficial Rather than Deep Learning: A Quasi-Experimental Study.*

Brom, C., Stárková, T., & D'Mello, S. K. (2018). How effective is emotional design? A meta-analysis on facial anthropomorphisms and pleasant colors during multimedia learning. *Educational Research Review*, 25, 100–119. DOI: 10.1016/j.edurev.2018.09.004

Brondi, R., Alem, L., Avveduto, G., Faita, C., Carrozzino, M., Tecchia, F., & Bergamasco, M. (2015). Evaluating the impact of highly immersive technologies and natural interaction on player engagement and flow experience in games. In Chorianopoulos, K., Divitini, M., Baalsrud Hauge, J., Jaccheri, L., & Malaka, R. (Eds.), *Entertainment Computing – ICEC 2015* (pp. 169–181). Springer., DOI: 10.1007/978-3-319-24589-8_13

Brophy, J. (2004). *Motivating students to learn* (2nd ed.). Routledge. DOI: 10.4324/9781410610218

Brynjolfsson, E., & McAfee, A. (2017). The business of artificial intelligence. *Harvard Business Review*, 95(1), 62–71.

Buchanan, T., & McPherson, S. (2019). Ethical considerations in the use of AI in education. *Journal of Information Ethics*, 28(2), 15–27.

Buchborn, T., & Treß, J. (2023). Acting self-determinedly and critically in a post-digital future? A critical review on digitalisation in music education. *Culture, Education, and Future*, 1(1), 66–82. Advance online publication. DOI: 10.70116/298027415

Bueno-Vesga, J. A., Xu, X., & He, H. (2021, March). *The effects of cognitive load on engagement in a virtual reality learning environment. In 2021 IEEE Virtual Reality and 3D User Interfaces (VR).* IEEE., DOI: 10.1109/VR48863.2021.00086

Byusa, E., Kampire, E., & Mwesigye, A. R. (2022). Game-based learning approach on students' motivation and understanding of chemistry concepts: A systematic review of literature. *Heliyon*, 8(5), 1–10. DOI: 10.1016/j.heliyon.2022.e09541 PMID: 35663764

Cacciamani, G., Anvar, A., Chen, A., Gill, I., & Hung, A. (2021). How the use of the artificial intelligence could improve surgical skills in urology: State of the art and future perspectives. *Current Opinion in Urology*, 31(4), 378–384. DOI: 10.1097/mou.0000000000000890

Camilleri, V. (2023, October). *Designing GBL for Higher Education: Pitfalls & Recommendations*, In European Conference on Games Based Learning, *17*(1), 869-875. https://papers.academic-conferences.org/index.php/ecgbl/article/view/1900

Cao, W., Ye, X., & Chen, X. (2023). Exploration and research on employment guidance system in universities from the perspective of artificial intelligence. *Ozean Journal of Applied Sciences*, 13(06), 934–940. DOI: 10.4236/ojapps.2023.136075

Cao, X., Guo, X., Liu, H., & Gu, J. (2015). The role of social media in supporting knowledge integration: A social capital analysis. *Information Systems Frontiers*, 17(2), 351–362. DOI: 10.1007/s10796-013-9473-2

Cao, Y., Zhang, Y., Ding, Y., Duffy, V. G., & Zhang, X. (2021). Is an anthropomorphic app icon more attractive? Evidence from neuroergonomomics. *Applied Ergonomics*, 97, 103545. DOI: 10.1016/j.apergo.2021.103545 PMID: 34352470

Cappello, M., & Lafferty, K. E. (2015). The roles of photography for developing literacy across the disciplines. *The Reading Teacher*, 69(3), 287–295. DOI: 10.1002/trtr.1418

Carini, R. M., Kuh, G. D., & Klein, S. P. (2006). Student engagement and student learning: Testing the linkages. *Research in Higher Education*, 47(1), 1–32. DOI: 10.1007/s11162-005-8150-9

Carrillo, E. (2019). *Digital game-based learning: An analysis of teacher preparation* (Doctoral dissertation, University of West Georgia). https://www.proquest.com/docview/2234237055?pq-origsite=gscholar&fromopenview=true&sourcetype=Dissertations%20&%20Theses

Caserman, P., Hoffmann, K., Müller, P., Schaub, M., Straßburg, K., Wiemeyer, J., Bruder, R., & Göbel, S. (2020). Quality criteria for serious games: Serious part, game part, and balance. *JMIR Serious Games*, 8(3), e19037. DOI: 10.2196/19037 PMID: 32706669

Catacutan, A. B., Malbas, M. H., Valiente, M. P. M., Moneva, J. C., & Mauring, L. (2022). Social disconnectedness and anxiety. *Asian Education, 2022*, 3-3. https://www.lynnp.org

Cavanaugh, C., Maor, D., & McCarthy, A. (2018). Mobile learning. In *Handbook of Research on K-12 Online and Blending Learning* (pp. 575–591). Carnegie Mellon University: ETC Press.

Cavus, N., Ibrahim, I., Ogbonna Okonkwo, M., Bode Ayansina, N., & Modupeola, T. (2023). The Effects of Gamification in Education: A Systematic Literature Review. *BRAIN.Broad Research in Artificial Intelligence and Neuroscience*, 14(2), 211–241. DOI: 10.18662/brain/14.2/452

Cazco, G. H. O., González, M. C., Abad, F. M., Altamirano, J. E. D., & Mazón, M. E. S. (2016). Determining factors in acceptance of ICT by the university faculty in their teaching practice. In: *Proceedings of the Fourth International Conference on Technological Ecosystems* DOI: 10.1145/3012430.3012509

Cecotti, H. (2023, June). A Serious Game Based on Hidden Objects for Art History in Fully Immersive Virtual Reality. In International Conference on Immersive Learning (pp. 223-238). Cham: Springer Nature Switzerland.

Chai, C. S., Deng, F., Tsai, P. S., Koh, J. H. L., & Tsai, C. C. (2015). Assessing multidimensional students' perceptions of twenty-first-century learning practices. *Asia Pacific Education Review*, 16(3), 389–398. DOI: 10.1007/s12564-015-9379-4

Chamberlain, R., Mullin, C., Scheerlinck, B., & Wagemans, J. (2018). Putting the art in artificial: Aesthetic responses to computer-generated art. *Psychology of Aesthetics, Creativity, and the Arts*, 12(2), 177–192. DOI: 10.1037/aca0000136

Chang, S. C., Hsu, T. C., & Jong, M. S. Y. (2020). Integration of the peer assessment approach with a virtual reality design system for learning earth science. *Computers & Education*, 146, 103758. DOI: 10.1016/j.compedu.2019.103758

Chang, S. C., Hsu, T. C., Kuo, W. C., & Jong, M. S. Y. (2020). Effects of applying a VR-based two-tier test strategy to promote elementary students' learning performance in a geology class. *British Journal of Educational Technology*, 51(1), 148–165. DOI: 10.1111/bjet.12790

Chang, T.-W., Hsu, J.-M., & Yu, P.-T. (2011). A Comparison of Single- and Dual-Screen Environment in Programming Language: Cognitive Loads and Learning Effects. *Journal of Educational Technology & Society*, 14, 188–200.

Chassignol, M., Khoroshavin, A., Klimova, A., & Bilyatdinova, A. (2018). Artificial Intelligence trends in education: A narrative overview. *Procedia Computer Science*, 136, 16–24. DOI: 10.1016/j.procs.2018.08.233

Checa, D., & Bustillo, A. (2020). A review of immersive virtual reality serious games to enhance learning and training. *Multimedia Tools and Applications*, 79(9), 5501–5527. DOI: 10.1007/s11042-019-08348-9

Chen, J., & Yang, W. H. (2023). Research on the project teaching method of landscape design courses in higher vocational colleges. *Modern Gardening, 24*, 197–200. https://doi.org/DOI: 10.14051

Chen, X. Y. (2024). The reform and exploration of project teaching methods in the course of graphic design software: Taking the direction of visual communication as an example. *Shoes, 13*, 15–17.

Chen, J. C. W. (2020). Mobile composing: Professional practices and impact on students' motivation in popular music. *International Journal of Music Education*, 38(1), 147–158. DOI: 10.1177/0255761419855820

Chen, K. C., & Jang, S. J. (2010). Motivation in online learning: Testing a model of self-determination theory. *Computers in Human Behavior*, 26(4), 741–752. DOI: 10.1016/j.chb.2010.01.011

Chen, L. (2023). Research on the impact of artificial intelligence on the development of the accounting industry. *Frontiers in Business Economics and Management*, 11(3), 262–266. DOI: 10.54097/fbem.v11i3.13328

Chen, L., Chen, P., & Lin, Z. (2020). Artificial intelligence in education: A review. *IEEE Access : Practical Innovations, Open Solutions*, 8, 75264–75278. DOI: 10.1109/ACCESS.2020.2988510

Chen, M., Chai, C. S., Jong, M. S. Y., & Jiang, M. Y. C. (2021). Teachers' conceptions of teaching Chinese descriptive composition with interactive spherical video-based virtual reality. *Frontiers in Psychology*, 12, 591708. DOI: 10.3389/fpsyg.2021.591708 PMID: 33613380

Chen, N.-S., Yin, C., Isaias, P., & Psotka, J. (2020). Educational big data: Extracting meaning from data for smart education. *Interactive Learning Environments*, 28(2), 142–147. DOI: 10.1080/10494820.2019.1635395

Chen, S., Li, Q., & Wang, T. (2024). Smart campus and student learning engagement. [IJICTE]. *International Journal of Information and Communication Technology Education*, 20(1), 1–22. DOI: 10.4018/IJICTE.2024010101

Chen, W., Zhu, W., Mason, S., Hammond-Bennett, A., & Colombo-Dougovito, A. (2016). Effectiveness of quality physical education in improving students' manipulative skill competency. *Journal of Sport and Health Science*, 5(2), 231–238. DOI: 10.1016/j.jshs.2015.04.005 PMID: 30356505

Chen, Y. (2022, July). Research on comprehensive management of digital literacy education in the era of big data. In *Proceedings of the 6th International Conference on Education and Multimedia Technology* (pp. 421-427). DOI: 10.1145/3551708.3551766

Chen, Z. (2022). Artificial intelligence-virtual trainer: Innovative didactics aimed at personalized training needs. *Journal of the Knowledge Economy*, 14(2), 2007–2025. DOI: 10.1007/s13132-022-00985-0

Cheong Li, K., & Ming Wong, B. T. (2021). The Opportunities and Challenges of Social Media in Higher Education: A Literature Review. SN Computer Science, https://link.springer.com/article/10.1007/s42979-021-00857-5#citeas

Chevalier, M., Riedo, F., & Mondada, F. (2016). Pedagogical Uses of Thymio II: How Do Teachers Perceive Educational Robots in Formal Education? *IEEE Robotics and Automation Magazine*.

Chiba, Y., Nose, T., Kase, T., Yamanaka, M., & Ito, A. (2019). *An Analysis of the Effect of Emotional Speech Synthesis on Non-Task-Oriented Dialogue System.*

Chien, S. Y., Hwang, G. J., & Jong, M. S. Y. (2020). Effects of peer assessment within the context of spherical video-based virtual reality on EFL students' English-speaking performance and learning perceptions. *Computers & Education*, 146, 103751. DOI: 10.1016/j.compedu.2019.103751

Chiu, M., Hwang, G., Hsia, L., & Shyu, F. (2022). Artificial intelligence-supported art education: A deep learning-based system for promoting university students' artwork appreciation and painting outcomes. *Interactive Learning Environments*, 32(3), 824–842. DOI: 10.1080/10494820.2022.2100426

Choi, S., & Lee, J. (2017). The impact of digital technology on art education. *International Journal of Art & Design Education*, 36(3), 363–377.

Chou, C., & Chu, Y. (2017). Interactive rhythm learning system by combining tablet computers and robots. *Applied Sciences (Basel, Switzerland)*, 7(3), 258. Advance online publication. DOI: 10.3390/app7030258

Chou, C.-M., Shen, T.-C., Shen, T.-C., & Shen, C.-H. (2023). The impact of CIE education integrated with the BIG 6 teaching strategy on students' innovative motivation, creativity, metacognition, and self-perceived employability. *Thinking Skills and Creativity*, 48, 101287. DOI: 10.1016/j.tsc.2023.101287

Christenson, S. L., Reschly, A. L., & Wylie, C. (Eds.). (2012). *Handbook of research on student engagement*. Springer. DOI: 10.1007/978-1-4614-2018-7

Christopoulos, A., & Mystakidis, S. (2023). Gamification in education. *Encyclopedia*, 3(4), 1223–1243. DOI: 10.3390/encyclopedia3040089

Chuang, S., & Graham, C. (2018). Embracing the sobering reality of technological influences on jobs, employment and human resource development. *European Journal of Training and Development*, 42(7/8), 400–416. DOI: 10.1108/ejtd-03-2018-0030

CII, and Peoplestrong. (2019). India Skill Report. Wheebox.

Claman, F. L. (2015). The impact of multiuser virtual environments on student engagement. *Nurse Education in Practice*, 15(1), 13–16. DOI: 10.1016/j.nepr.2014.11.006 PMID: 25532889

Clark, J. S., Porath, S., Thiele, J., & Jobe, M. (2020)... *Action Research*.

Cleland, J. A. (2017). The qualitative orientation in medical education research. *Korean Journal of Medical Education, 29*(2), 61–71. NCBI. DOI: 10.3946/kjme.2017.53

Codepal.ai. (2022). *Bug Detector*. https://codepal.ai/bug-detector

Colchester, K., Hagras, H., Alghazzawi, D., & Aldabbagh, G. (2017). A Survey of Artificial Intelligence Techniques Employed for Adaptive Educational Systems within E-Learning Platforms. [De Gruyter Open Ltd.]. *Journal of Artificial Intelligence and Soft Computing Research*, 7(1), 47–64. DOI: 10.1515/jaiscr-2017-0004

Colquhoun, H. L., Levac, D., O'Brien, K. K., Straus, S., Tricco, A. C., Perrier, L., Kastner, M., & Moher, D. (2014). Scoping reviews: Time for clarity in definition, methods, and reporting. *Journal of Clinical Epidemiology*, 67(12), 1291–1294. DOI: 10.1016/j.jclinepi.2014.03.013 PMID: 25034198

Connolly, T. M., Boyle, E. A., MacArthur, E., Hainey, T., & Boyle, J. M. (2012). A systematic literature review of empirical evidence on computer games and serious games. *Computers & Education*, 59(2), 661–686. DOI: 10.1016/j.compedu.2012.03.004

Coppin, B. (2004). *Artificial Intelligence Illuminated*. Jones and Bartlett.

Cotroneo, P., & Hutson, J. (2023). Generative AI tools in art education: Exploring prompt engineering and iterative processes for enhanced creativity. *Metaverse*, 4(1), 14. DOI: 10.54517/m.v4i1.2164

Courage, M. L. (2020). Interactive technologies: Tablets, smartphones, and learning. In *Encyclopedia of Infant and Early Childhood Development* (2nd ed., pp. 194–201). Elsevier., DOI: 10.1016/B978-0-12-809324-5.23561-X

Cowley, B., Ravaja, N., & Heikura, T. (2013). Cardiovascular physiology predicts learning effects in a serious game activity. *Computers & Education*, 60(1), 299–309. DOI: 10.1016/j.compedu.2012.07.014

Creswell, J. W., & Plano Clark, V. L. (2018). *Designing and Conducting Mixed Methods Research* (3rd ed.). Sage Publications.

Cronbach, L. J. (1951). Coefficient alpha and the internal structure of tests. psychometrika, 16(3), 297-334.

Crowe, M., Inder, M., & Porter, R. (2015). Conducting qualitative research in mental health: Thematic and content analyses. *The Australian and New Zealand Journal of Psychiatry*, 49(7), 616–623. DOI: 10.1177/0004867415582053 PMID: 25900973

Cui, L. B. (2021). The research of mixed work order classroom teaching practice based on CDIO. *Master's Dissertation, Shandong Normal University*. https://doi.org/DOI: 10.27767

Cunico, G., Aivazidou, E., & Mollona, E. (2022). System dynamics gamification: A proposal for shared principles. *Systems Research and Behavioral Science*, 39(4), 723–733. DOI: 10.1002/sres.2805

Cunliffe, L., & Morris, M. (2019). Collaborative art education and its role in fostering social skills. *Art Education*, 72(4), 24–31.

Cyberspace Administration of the CPC Central Committee. Ministry of Education, Ministry of Industry and Information Technology, Human Resources and Social Security(2024).*Key points of work to upgrade digital literacy and skills for all by 2024*.https://bit.ly/3Y7cP0e

Dabbous, M., Kawtharani, A., Fahs, I., Hallal, Z., Shouman, D., Akel, M., Rahal, M., & Sakr, F. (2022). The role of game-based learning in experiential education: Tool validation, motivation assessment, and outcomes evaluation among a sample of pharmacy students. *Education Sciences*, 12(7), 434. DOI: 10.3390/educsci12070434

Damota, M. D. (2019). Effects of Social Media on Society. *New Media and Mass Communication*, 78, 7–11. DOI: 10.7176/NMMC

Daoudi, I. (2022). Learning analytics for enhancing the usability of serious games in formal education: A systematic literature review and research agenda. *Education and Information Technologies*, 27(8), 11237–11266. DOI: 10.1007/s10639-022-11087-4 PMID: 35528757

Daoudi, I., Chebil, R., Tranvouez, E., Chaari, W. L., & Espinasse, B. (2021). Improving learners' assessment and evaluation in crisis management serious games: An emotion-based educational data mining approach. *Entertainment Computing*, 38, 100428. DOI: 10.1016/j.entcom.2021.100428

Dash, D. C. S., & Dash, S. (2020). Skill Development Mission and the Skill Landscape. International Journal of Innovative Science and Research Technology, 34-37.

David, L., & Weinstein, N. (2024). Using technology to make learning fun: Technology use is best made fun and challenging to optimize intrinsic motivation and engagement. *European Journal of Psychology of Education*, 39(2), 1441–1463. DOI: 10.1007/s10212-023-00734-0

de Acedo Lizarraga, M. L. S., & de Acedo Baquedano, M. T. S. (2013). How creative potential is related to metacognition. *European Journal of Education and Psychology*, 6(2), 69–81.

De Freitas, S. (2018). Are games effective learning tools? A review of educational games. *Journal of Educational Technology & Society*, 21(2), 74–84.

De Gloria, A., Bellotti, F., & Berta, R. (2012). Building a comprehensive R&D community on serious games. *Procedia Computer Science*, 15, 1–3. DOI: 10.1016/j.procs.2012.10.051

De Sousa Borges, S., Durelli, V. H. S., Reis, H. M., & Isotani, S. (2014). A systematic mapping on gamification applied to education. Proceedings of the 29th Annual ACM Symposium on Applied Computing - SAC '14, (Icmc), 216e222. DOI: 10.1145/2554850.2554956

Delić, V., Perić, Z., Sečujski, M., Jakovljević, N., Nikolić, J., Mišković, D., Simić, N., Suzić, S., & Delić, T. (2019). Speech Technology Progress Based on New Machine Learning Paradigm. *Computational Intelligence and Neuroscience*, 2019, 1–19. DOI: 10.1155/2019/4368036 PMID: 31341467

Denden, M., Tlili, A., Essalmi, F., Jemni, M., Chen, N. S., & Burgos, D. (2021). Effects of gender and personality differences on students' perception of game design elements in educational gamification. *International Journal of Human-Computer Studies*, 154(May), 102674. DOI: 10.1016/j.ijhcs.2021.102674

Deng, G. (2023). The vocational college double division team innovates the mechanism and path of "Post Course Competition Certificate." *University, 35*, 7–10.

Deterding, S., Dixon, D., Khaled, R., & Nacke, L. (2011). From game design elements to gamefulness: Defining "gamification." *Proceedings of the 15th International Academic MindTrek Conference: Envisioning Future Media Environments, MindTrek 2011,* March 2014, 9–15. DOI: 10.1145/2181037.2181040

Dhir, A., Yossatorn, Y., Kaur, P., & Chen, S. (2018). Online social media fatigue and psychological wellbeing—A study of compulsive use, fear of missing out, fatigue, anxiety and depression. *International Journal of Information Management*, 40, 141–152. DOI: 10.1016/j.ijinfomgt.2018.01.012

Dicheva, D., & Dichev, C. (2016). An Active Learning Model Employing Flipped Learning and Gamification Strategies. *13th International Conference on Intelligent Tutoring Systems (ITS 2016), July*, 7.

Dicheva, D., Dichev, C., Agre, G., & Angelova, G. (2015). Gamification in education: A systematic mapping study. *Journal of Educational Technology & Society*, 18(3), 75–88.

Dichev, C., & Dicheva, D. (2017, February 20). Gamifying education: what is known, what is believed and what remains uncertain: a critical review. *International Journal of Educational Technology in Higher Education*, 14(1), 9. Advance online publication. DOI: 10.1186/s41239-017-0042-5

Dima, J. (2024). The effects of artificial intelligence on human resource activities and the roles of the human resource triad: Opportunities and challenges. *Frontiers in Psychology*, 15. Advance online publication. DOI: 10.3389/fpsyg.2024.1360401

Dincelli, E., & Yayla, A. (2022). Immersive virtual reality in the age of the Metaverse: A hybrid-narrative review based on the technology affordance perspective. *The Journal of Strategic Information Systems*, 31(2), 101717. DOI: 10.1016/j.jsis.2022.101717

Dishon, G. (2017). New data, old tensions: Big data, personalized learning, and the challenges of progressive education. *Theory and Research in Education*, 15(3), 272–289. DOI: 10.1177/1477878517735233

Dori, Y. J., Avargil, S., Kohen, Z., & Saar, L. (2018). Context-based learning and metacognitive prompts for enhancing scientific text comprehension. *International Journal of Science Education*, 40(10), 1198–1220. DOI: 10.1080/09500693.2018.1470351

Drylie, D. (2013). Social Media in Education Assessing the Benefits of Integration. content (snhu.edu)

Du, L. N. (2021). Higher vocational pre-school art education to carry out project-based teaching. *China Educational Technology & Equipment, 13*, 48–49.

Du, X. M. (2015). Research on project-driven practical teaching reform of digital media design major. *China Packaging, 11*, 65–68.

Dubovi, I. (2022). Cognitive and emotional engagement while learning with VR: The perspective of multimodal methodology. *Computers & Education*, 183, 104495. DOI: 10.1016/j.compedu.2022.104495

Dumitru, D. (2023). Critical thinking: Creating job-proof skills for the future of work. *Journal of Intelligence*, 11(10), 194. DOI: 10.3390/jintelligence11100194

Durall, E., & Gros, B. (2020). Learning and creativity in the age of artificial intelligence: Challenges for education. *Technology. Knowledge and Learning*, 25(3), 555–568. DOI: 10.1007/s10758-019-09417-7

Durukan, A., Artun, H., & Temur, A. (2020). Virtual reality in science education: A descriptive review. Journal of science learning, 3(3), 132-142.

Du, S., Meng, F., & Gao, B. (2016). Research on the Application System of Smart Campus in the Context of Smart City. 2016 8th *International Conference on Information Technology in Medicine and Education (ITME)* (pp. 714– 718). IEEE.

Dyck, J., Pinelle, D., Brown, B., & Gutwin, C. (2003). *Learning from games: HCI design innovations in entertainment software*. Graphics Interface.

Dyulicheva, Y. Y., & Glazieva, A. O. (2021). Game based learning with artificial intelligence and immersive technologies: An overview. CS&SE@ SW, 146-159.

Ekman, J. (2023). Comparing engagement of VR and non-VR games for programming learning purposes. *Unpublished manuscript.*

Elgammal, A., Liu, B., Elhoseiny, M., & Mazzone, M. (2017). CAN: Creative adversarial networks, generating "art" by learning about styles and deviating from style norms. *arXiv preprint arXiv:1706.07068.*

Ellison, N. B., Steinfield, C., & Lampe, C. (2007). The Benefits of Facebook "Friends:" Social Capital and College Students' Use of Online Social Network Sites. *Journal of Computer-Mediated Communication*, 12(4), 1143–1168. DOI: 10.1111/j.1083-6101.2007.00367.x

Elshamy, N., AbouElenen, A., & Elmougy, S. (2023). Automatic detection of software defects based on machine learning. *International Journal of Advanced Computer Science and Applications*, 14(3). Advance online publication. DOI: 10.14569/IJACSA.2023.0140340

Elshareif, E., & Mohamed, E. (2021). The effects of e-learning on students' motivation to learn in higher education. *Online Learning : the Official Journal of the Online Learning Consortium*, 25(3), 128–143. DOI: 10.24059/olj.v25i3.2336

Emerson, L. C., & Berge, Z. L. (2018). Microlearning: Knowledge Management Applications and Competency-Based Training in the Workplace. *Knowledge Management & E-Learning*, 10(2), 125–132.

Encalada, W. L., & Castillo Sequera, J. L. (2017). Model to implement virtual computing labs via cloud computing services. *Symmetry*, 9(7), 117. DOI: 10.3390/sym9070117

Eng, D. (2017). *Integrated threat modelling* (Master's thesis, University of Oslo). Retrieved from http://hdl.handle.net/10852/55699

Epley, N. (2018). A Mind like Mine: The Exceptionally Ordinary Underpinnings of Anthropomorphism. *Journal of the Association for Consumer Research*, 3(4), 591–598. DOI: 10.1086/699516

Epley, N., Waytz, A., & Cacioppo, J. T. (2007). On seeing human: A three-factor theory of anthropomorphism. *Psychological Review*, 114(4), 864–886. DOI: 10.1037/0033-295X.114.4.864 PMID: 17907867

Erdogmus, E., Ryherd, E., Diefes-Dux, H. A., & Armwood-Gordon, C. (2021, October). Use of virtual reality to improve engagement and self-efficacy in architectural engineering disciplines. In *2021 IEEE Frontiers in Education Conference (FIE)* (pp. 1-7). IEEE. DOI: 10.1109/FIE49875.2021.9637182

Eshet, Y. (2004). Digital literacy: A conceptual framework for survival skills in the digital era. *Journal of Educational Multimedia and Hypermedia*, 13(1), 93–106.

European Commision. (2006). Recommendation on key competences for lifelong learning. Council of 18 December 2006 on key competences for lifelong learning, 2006/962/EC, L. 394/15. Retrieved December 7, 2017, from http://eur-lex.europa .eu/legal-content/ en/TXT/?uri=CELEX:32006H0962&qid= 1496720114366.

EUROPEAN UNION (EU).Digital Education Action Plan (2021 -2027) [EB/OL]. [2023- 02-13].https: / / education.ec.europa.eu /node /1518

Eusterbrock, L. (2023). Mobile safe spaces and preset emotions: Making music with apps as a digital technology of the self. *Popular Music and Society*, 46(1), 50–69. DOI: 10.1080/03007766.2022.2155029

Facer, K., & Sandford, R. (2010). The next 25 years?: Future scenarios and future directions for education and technology. *Journal of Computer Assisted Learning*, 26(1), 74–93. DOI: 10.1111/j.1365-2729.2009.00337.x

Faizi, R., El Afia, A., & Chiheb, R. (2013). Exploring the potential benefits of using social media in education. *International Journal of Engineering Pedagogy*, 3(4), 50–53. DOI: 10.3991/ijep.v3i4.2836

Fan, Q. Q. (2023). Research on the "deep learning" strategy of higher vocational art students' informationization based on project-based teaching. *Dazhongwenyi, 10*, 127–129. https://doi.org/DOI: 10.20112/j.cnki.issn1007-5828.2023.10.044

Farrokhnia, M., Banihashem, S. K., Noroozi, O., & Wals, A. (2024). A SWOT analysis of ChatGPT: Implications for educational practice and research. *Innovations in Education and Teaching International*, 61(3), 460–474. DOI: 10.1080/14703297.2023.2195846

Ferguson, C., DiGiacomo, M., Gholizadeh, L., Ferguson, L. E., & Hickman, L. D. (2017). The integration and evaluation of a social-media facilitated journal club to enhance the student learning experience of evidence-based practice: A case study. *Nurse Education Today*, 48, 123–128. DOI: 10.1016/j.nedt.2016.10.002 PMID: 27810629

Ferguson, R. (2019). Ethical Challenges of AI in Education. *AI & Society*, 34(1), 25–33.

Fokides, E. (2018). Digital educational games and mathematics. Results of a case study in primary school settings. *Education and Information Technologies*, 23(2), 851–867. DOI: 10.1007/s10639-017-9639-5

Forsman, M. (2015). The pros and cons of iPad : The evaluation process and its results. In *Paducation: An EU-based method-advancement project by German and Swedish teachers working with iPad* (pp. 35–55). Södertörns högskola.

Fraga-Varela, F., Vila-Couñago, E., & Martínez-Piñeiro, E. (2021). The impact of serious games in mathematics fluency: A study in Primary Education. *Comunicar*, 29(69), 125–135. DOI: 10.3916/C69-2021-10

Framework of Educational Innovation. *Comunicar: Media Education Research Journal, 28*(65), 9-20. DOI: 10.3916/C65-2020-01

Fredricks, J. A., Blumenfeld, P. C., & Paris, A. H. (2004). School engagement: Potential of the concept, state of the evidence. *Review of Educational Research*, 74(1), 59–109. DOI: 10.3102/00346543074001059

Fromm, J., Radianti, J., Wehking, C., Stieglitz, S., Majchrzak, T. A., & vom Brocke, J. (2021). More than experience?-On the unique opportunities of virtual reality to afford a holistic experiential learning cycle. *The Internet and Higher Education*, 50, 100804. DOI: 10.1016/j.iheduc.2021.100804

Fuchs, M. (2015). *Total Gamification*.

Furdu, I., Tomozei, C., & Köse, U. (2017, January 1). Pros and cons gamification and gaming in classroom. Cornell University. https://doi.org/DOI: 10.48550/arXiv.1708

Fürst, H., & Nylander, E. (2023). *The value of art education: Cultural engagements at the Swedish folk high schools*. Springer Nature. DOI: 10.1007/978-3-031-14061-7

Gabe, J. (2020). Does educational gamification improve students' motivation? *Proceedings of the Second International Conference on Technological Ecosystems for Enhancing Multiculturality*, 701-707.

Galloway, N., & Rose, H. (2021). English medium instruction and the English language practitioner. *ELT Journal*, 75(1), 33–41. DOI: 10.1093/elt/ccaa063

Gandhi, R. (2022). Significance of new education policy (nep) 2020 for adult education and lifelong learning program. International Journal of Management Technology and Social Sciences, 79-95. https://doi.org/DOI: 10.47992/ijmts.2581.6012.0179

Gao, Q., & Li, S. (2022). Impact of Online Courses on University Student Visual Attention During the COVID-19 Pandemic. *Frontiers in Psychiatry*, 13, 848844. DOI: 10.3389/fpsyt.2022.848844 PMID: 35422723

García-Barrios, V. M., Mödritscher, F., & Gütl, C. (2005). Personalisation versus Adaptation? A User-centred Model Approach and its Application. *International Conference on Knowledge Management (I-Know), Iicm*, 120–127.

Garelli, G., & Ranu, S. K. (2018). The attitude of university students towards educational networking through social media about academic satisfaction and study habits. http://hdl.handle.net/10603/218795

Garner, R., Brown, R., Sanders, S., & Menke, D. (1992). *'Seductive details' and learning from text.*https://api.semanticscholar.org/CorpusID:200060851

Gartner. (2019). Gartner identifies top 10 data and analytics technology trends for 2019. Retrieved from https://www.gartner.com/en/newsroom/press-releases/2019-02-18-

Gee, J. P. (2006). Are video games good for learning? *Nordic Journal of Digital Literacy*, 1(3), 172–183. DOI: 10.18261/ISSN1891-943X-2006-03-02

Gee, J. P. (2009). Deep learning properties of good digital games: How far can they go? In Ritterfeld, U., Cody, M., & Vorderer, P. (Eds.), *Serious games: Mechanisms and effects* (pp. 67–82). Routledge.

Ge, H., & Wu, Y. (2023). An Empirical Study of Adoption of ChatGPT for Bug Fixing among Professional Developers. *Innovation & Technology Advances*, 1(1), 21–29. DOI: 10.61187/ita.v1i1.19

Ghazy, A., & Wajdi, M. Ikhsanudin, & Sada, C. (2021). The use of game-based learning in English class. *Journal of Applied Studies in Language, 5*(1), 67—78. https://ojs.pnb.ac.id/index.php/JASL

Ghosh, R. (2015). Gender and diversity in india. *Advances in Developing Human Resources*, 18(1), 3–10. DOI: 10.1177/1523422315614929

Giacumo, L. A., & Savenye, W. (2020). Asynchronous discussion forum design to support cognition: Effects of rubrics and instructor prompts on learner's critical thinking, achievement, and satisfaction. *Educational Technology Research and Development*, 68(1), 37–66. DOI: 10.1007/s11423-019-09664-5

Gil-Aciron, L. A. (2024). The gamer psychology: A psychological perspective on game design and gamification. *Interactive Learning Environments*, 32(1), 183–207. DOI: 10.1080/10494820.2022.2082489

Girard, C., Ecalle, J., & Magnan, A. (2013). Serious games as new educational tools: How effective are they? A meta-analysis of recent studies. *Journal of Computer Assisted Learning*, 29(3), 207–219. DOI: 10.1111/j.1365-2729.2012.00489.x

Gobert, J. D., Sao Pedro, M. A., Baker, R. S., Toto, E., & Montalvo, O. (2012). Leveraging educational data mining for real-time performance assessment of scientific inquiry skills within microworlds. J. *Educ. Data Min.*, 4, 104–143.

Goksel, N., & Bozkurt, A. (2019). Artificial intelligence in education: Current insights and future perspectives. In Sisman-Ugur, S., & Kurubacak, G. (Eds.), *Handbook of Research on Learning in the Age of Transhumanism* (pp. 224–236). IGI Global. DOI: 10.4018/978-1-5225-8431-5.ch014

Goli, A., Teymournia, F., Naemabadi, M., & Garmaroodi, A. A. (2022). Architectural design game: A serious game approach to promote teaching and learning using multimodal interfaces. *Education and Information Technologies*, 27(8), 11467–11498. DOI: 10.1007/s10639-022-11062-z PMID: 35578701

Gómez, R. L., & Suárez, A. M. (2021). Gaming to succeed in college: Protocol for a scoping review of quantitative studies on the design and use of serious games for enhancing teaching and learning in higher education. *International Journal of Educational Research Open*, 2, 100021. DOI: 10.1016/j.ijedro.2020.100021

Gong, S., Shangguan, C., Zhai, K., & Guo, Y. (2017). The effects of emotional design on multimedia learning. *Acta Psychologica Sinica*, 49(6), 771. DOI: 10.3724/SP.J.1041.2017.00771

González, C. S. G. (2022). *Unplugged Gamification : towards a definition. September.*

Goodfellow, I., Pouget-Abadie, J., Mirza, M., Xu, B., Warde-Farley, D., Ozair, S., Courville, A., & Bengio, Y. (2020). Generative adversarial networks. *Communications of the ACM*, 63(11), 139–144. DOI: 10.1145/3422622

Gooding, L. (2009). Enhancing social competence in the music classroom. *General Music Today*, 23(1), 35–38. DOI: 10.1177/1048371309342531

Google. (2023). *Google Gemini*. https://gemini.google.com/app

Gottschalk, F. (2023). Digital equity and inclusion in education: An overview of practice and policy in OECD countries. oecd.org

Graeske, C., & Sjöberg, S. A. (2021). VR-Technology in Teaching: Opportunities and Challenges. *International Education Studies*, 14(8), 76–83. DOI: 10.5539/ies.v14n8p76

Grant, L. L., Opperman, M. J., Schiller, B., Chastain, J., Richardson, J. D., Eckel, C., & Plawecki, M. H. (2021). Medical student engagement in a virtual learning environment positively correlates with course performance and satisfaction in psychiatry. *Medical Science Educator*, 31(3), 1133–1140. DOI: 10.1007/s40670-021-01287-x PMID: 33868773

Greenhow, C., & Lewin, C. (2019). Social media and education: Reconceptualizing the boundaries of formal and informal learning. In *social media and education* (pp. 6-30). Routledge.

Green, L. (2008). *Music, informal learning and the school: A new classroom pedagogy*. Ashgate.

Grover, M., & Kapoor, R. (2020). *Skill Development in India:A study of key success factors and challenges*. CLIO An Interdisciplinary Journal.

Gu, J., & Ding, R. (2022). Digital Literacy of Chinese Normal Students: A Literature Review. Digital Literacy for Teachers, 191-210.

Guay, F. (2022). Applying self-determination theory to education: Regulations types, psychological needs, and autonomy supporting behaviors. *Canadian Journal of School Psychology, 37*(1), 75-92. s://DOI: 10.1177/08295735211055355

Guilford, J. P. (1950). *Fundamental statistics in psychology and education*. https://psycnet.apa.org/record/1950-04974-000

Guilford, J. P. (1967). Creativity: Yesterday, Today and Tomorrow. *The Journal of Creative Behavior*, 1(1), 3–14. DOI: 10.1002/j.2162-6057.1967.tb00002.x

Guney, Z. (2019). Considerations for human–computer interaction: User interface design variables and visual learning in IDT. *Cypriot Journal of Educational Sciences*, 14(4), 731–741. DOI: 10.18844/cjes.v14i4.4481

Guo, J. Q. (2023). Research on the construction of project teaching methods in art design teaching. *Grand Spectacle, 5*, 153–155.

Guo, Y. (2024). *An investigation into the practice of blended teaching in English courses based on the BOPPPS model*. Applied Mathematics and Nonlinear Sciences. DOI: 10.2478/amns.2023.1.00336

Guo, Y., Lin, S., Acar, S., Jin, S., Xu, X., Feng, Y., & Zeng, Y. (2022). Divergent Thinking and Evaluative Skill: A Meta-Analysis. *The Journal of Creative Behavior*, 56(3), 432–448. DOI: 10.1002/jocb.539

Gupta, S., Kumar, P., & Tekchandani, R. (2023). A Multimodal Facial Cues Based Engagement Detection System in E-Learning Context Using Deep Learning Approach. *Multimedia Tools and Applications*, 82(18), 28589–28615. DOI: 10.1007/s11042-023-14392-3 PMID: 36789011

Gurjanow, I., Oliveira, M., Zender, J., Santos, P. A., & Ludwig, M. (2019). Shallow and deep gamification in mathematics trails. *Lecture Notes in Computer Science (Including Subseries Lecture Notes in Artificial Intelligence and Lecture Notes in Bioinformatics), 11385 LNCS*(3), 364–374. DOI: 10.1007/978-3-030-11548-7_34

Hainey, T., Connolly, T. M., Boyle, E. A., Wilson, A., & Razak, A. (2016). A systematic literature review of games-based learning empirical evidence in primary education. *Computers & Education*, 102, 202–223. DOI: 10.1016/j.compedu.2016.09.001

Hallam, S. (2002). Musical motivation: Towards a model synthesising the research. *Music Education Research*, 4(2), 225–244. DOI: 10.1080/1461380022000011939

Hallam, S. (2024). 21st century conceptions of musical ability. *Psychology of Music*, 38(3), 308–330. DOI: 10.1177/0305735609351922

Hallifax, S., Serna, A., Marty, J. C., Lavoué, G., & Lavoué, E. (2019). Factors to consider for tailored gamification. *CHI PLAY 2019 - Proceedings of the Annual Symposium on Computer-Human Interaction in Play*, 559–572. DOI: 10.1145/3311350.3347167

Hallifax, S., Jean, U., & Lyon, M. (2020). *Adaptive gamification of digital learning environments*.

Hallinger, P. (2013). A conceptual framework for systematic reviews of research in educational leadership and management. *Journal of Educational Administration*, 51(2), 126–149. DOI: 10.1108/09578231311304670

Hallinger, P., & Kovačević, J. (2019). A Bibliometric Review of Research on Educational Administration: Science Mapping the Literature, 1960 to 2018. *Review of Educational Research*, 89(3), 335–369. DOI: 10.3102/0034654319830380

Hamad, A., & Jia, B. (2022). How virtual reality technology has changed our lives: An overview of the current and potential applications and limitations. *International Journal of Environmental Research and Public Health*, 19(18), 11278. DOI: 10.3390/ijerph191811278 PMID: 36141551

Hamadi, M., El-Den, J., Narumon Sriratanaviriyakul, C., & Azam, S. (2021). A social media adoption framework as pedagogical instruments in higher education classrooms. *E-Learning and Digital Media*, 18(1), 55–85. DOI: 10.1177/2042753020950869

Hamari, J., Koivisto, J., & Sarsa, H. (2014, January 6). Does Gamification Work? A Literature Review of Empirical Studies on Gamification. https://www.semanticscholar.org/paper/Does-Gamification-Work-A-Literature-Review-of-on-Hamari-Koivisto/0768149ce1170691bcde8b4539153a282f0cc74c

Hamari, J., Shernoff, D. J., Rowe, E., Coller, B., Asbell-Clarke, J., & Edwards, T. (2016). Challenging games help students learn: An empirical study on engagement, flow and immersion in game-based learning. *Computers in Human Behavior*, 54, 170–179. DOI: 10.1016/j.chb.2015.07.045

Han, R. (2024). The application research of project teaching methods in electronic and electrical engineering teaching of higher vocational education. *Theoretical and Practice of Innovation and Entrepreneurship, 8*, 161–163.

Hanus, M., & Fox, J. (2015, January 1). Assessing the effects of gamification in the classroom: A longitudinal study on intrinsic motivation, social comparison, satisfaction, effort, and academic performance. Elsevier BV, 80, 152-161. DOI: 10.1016/j.compedu.2014.08.019

Hao, K. (2019). *China has started a grand experiment in AI education. It could reshape how the world learns*. MIT Technology Review.

Hartikainen, S., Rintala, H., Pylväs, L., & Nokelainen, P. (2019). The concept of active learning and the measurement of learning outcomes: A review of research in engineering higher education. *Education Sciences*, 9(4), 276. DOI: 10.3390/educsci9040276

Hartt, M., Hosseini, H., & Mostafapour, M. (2020). Game on: Exploring the effectiveness of game-based learning. *Planning Practice and Research*, 35(5), 589–604. DOI: 10.1080/02697459.2020.1778859

Hasan, M. I. (2023). The Impact of Social Media on Mental Health and Well-Being on Students. researchgate.net

Hassan, M. A., Habiba, U., Majeed, F., & Shoaib, M. (2021). Adaptive gamification in e-learning based on students' learning styles. *Interactive Learning Environments*, 29(4), 545–565. DOI: 10.1080/10494820.2019.1588745

Heaps, J., Slavin, R., & Wang, X. (2018). Toward A Code Pattern Based Vulnerability Measurement Model. *InProceedings of the 23rd ACM on Symposium on Access Control Models and Technologies (SACMAT '18)* (pp. 209–211). Association for Computing Machinery. DOI: 10.1145/3205977.3208948

He, C., & Sun, B. (2021). Application of artificial intelligence technology in computer aided art teaching. *Computer-Aided Design and Applications*, 18(S4), 118–129. DOI: 10.14733/cadaps.2021.S4.118-129

Heldal, I., Helgesen, C., Ali, Q., Patel, D., Geitung, A. B., & Pettersen, H. (2021). Supporting school aged children to train their vision by using serious games. *Computers*, 10(4), 53. DOI: 10.3390/computers10040053

Hendricks, G. (2019). Connectivism as a Learning Theory and Its Relation to Open Distance Education. *Progressio South African Journal for Open and Distance Learning Practice*, 41(1), 1–13. DOI: 10.25159/2663-5895/4773

Hicks, A., Zhi, R., Dong, Y., & Barnes, T. (2011). *Applying "Deep Gamification"*. Principles to Improve Quality of User-Designed Levels.

Hirshfield, L. J., & Koretsky, M. D. (2021). Cultivating creative thinking in engineering student teams: Can a computer-mediated virtual laboratory help? *Journal of Computer Assisted Learning*, 37(2), 587–601. DOI: 10.1111/jcal.12509

Ho, D. G., Sa'adi, M., He, D., & Hoon, C.-Y. (2023). Silence over the wire: Student verbal participation and the virtual classroom in the digital era. *Asia Pacific Education Review*, 24(4), 599–615. DOI: 10.1007/s12564-023-09834-4

Hodgson, P., Lee, V. W., Chan, J. C., Fong, A., Tang, C. S., Chan, L., & Wong, C. (2019). Immersive virtual reality (IVR) in higher education: Development and implementation. *Augmented reality and virtual reality: The power of AR and VR for business*, 161-173.

Hodson, C. B., & Sander, H. A. (2019). Relationships between vegetation in student environments and academic achievement across the continental US. *Landscape and Urban Planning*, 189, 212–224. DOI: 10.1016/j.landurbplan.2019.04.027

Holly, M., Pirker, J., Resch, S., Brettschuh, S., & Gütl, C. (2021). Designing VR experiences–expectations for teaching and learning in VR. *Journal of Educational Technology & Society*, 24(2), 107–119.

Holmes, A., & Douglass, A. (2021). Artificial intelligence: Reshaping the accounting profession and the disruption to accounting education. *Journal of Emerging Technologies in Accounting*, 19(1), 53–68. DOI: 10.2308/jeta-2020-054

Holmes, W., & Porayska-Pomsta, K. (2020). The ethics of AI in education: Who cares? *British Journal of Educational Technology*, 51(3), 981–983. DOI: 10.1111/bjet.13045

Holstein, K., McLaren, B. M., & Aleven, V. (2017). Intelligent tutors as teachers' aides: Exploring teacher needs for real-time analytics in blended classrooms. *ACM International Conference Proceeding Series*. DOI: 10.1145/3027385.3027451

Hong, Y., Saab, N., & Admiraal, W. (2024). Approaches and game elements used to tailor digital gamification for learning: A systematic literature review. *Computers & Education*, 212(January), 105000. DOI: 10.1016/j.compedu.2024.105000

Ho, P. H., Fleitas, Y. B., & González-gonzález, C. S. (2023). Unplugged Versus Plugged Gamification - A Comparative Study in Higher Education on Engagement, Motivation and Teachers '. *Perception*, 1(1).

Huang, J., Saleh, S., & Liu, Y. (2021). A review on artificial intelligence in education. *Academic Journal of Interdisciplinary Studies, 10(3).*

Huang, S. D. (2022). The application of project teaching methods in the construction of top-quality online open courses in electrical and electronic technology. *China Educational Technology & Equipment, 20*, 54–57.

Huang, S., Xu, J., Sang, Q., & Shao, Z. (2023, September). Research on the digital literacy model construction and practice of higher vocational students in the digital era. In *Proceedings of the 15th International Conference on Education Technology and Computers* (pp. 370-377). DOI: 10.1145/3629296.3629356

Huang, W. H.-Y., & Soman, D. (2013). A Practitioner's Guide To Gamification Of Education. *Early Child Development and Care*, 189(3), 392–404. DOI: 10.1080/03004430.2017.1324434

Huang, W., Li, X., & Shang, J. (2023). Gamified Project-Based Learning: A Systematic Review of the Research Landscape. *Sustainability (Basel)*, 15(2), 940. Advance online publication. DOI: 10.3390/su15020940

Huang, Y. (2021). Research on interactive creation of computer-aided music teaching. *Solid State Technology*, 64(01), 577–587.

Huang, Y. M., Wang, W. S., Lee, H. Y., Lin, C. J., & Wu, T. T. (2024). Empowering virtual reality with feedback and reflection in hands-on learning: Effect of learning engagement and higher-order thinking. *Journal of Computer Assisted Learning*, 40(4), 1413–1427. Advance online publication. DOI: 10.1111/jcal.12959

Hudson, S., Matson-Barkat, S., Pallamin, N., & Jegou, G. (2019). With or without you? Interaction and immersion in a virtual reality experience. *Journal of Business Research*, 100, 459–468. DOI: 10.1016/j.jbusres.2018.10.062

Hui, B. Björn Rudzewitz, & Detmar Meurers. (2022). Learning processes in interactive CALL systems: Linking automatic feedback, system logs, and learning outcomes. *Computer Science, Education, Linguistics*. https://api.semanticscholar.org/CorpusID:245872345

Hunter, K. W. dan. (2012). *How Game Thinking Can Revolutionize Your Business*. Wharton Digital Press.

Hussain, M. S., Salam, A., & Farid, A. (2020). Students' motivation in English language learning (ELL): An exploratory study of motivation-al factors for EFL and ESL adult learners. *International Journal of Applied Linguistics and English Literature*, 9(4), 15–28. DOI: 10.7575/aiac.ijalel.v.9n.4p.15

Hwang, G. J., & Chiu, L. Y. (2020). Applying an inquiry-based learning approach to flipped classrooms: A study on learning effects in STEM and non-STEM subjects. *Journal of Educational Technology & Society*, 23(1), 26–40.

Hwang, G. J., Chiu, M. C., Hsia, L. H., & Chu, H. C. (2023). Promoting art appreciation performances and behaviors in effective and joyful contexts: A two-tier test-based digital gaming approach. *Computers & Education*, 194, 104706. DOI: 10.1016/j.compedu.2022.104706

Ibáñez, M. B., Serio, Á. D., & Kloos, C. D. (2014, July 1). Gamification for Engaging Computer Science Students in Learning Activities: A Case Study. *IEEE Transactions on Learning Technologies*, 7(3), 291–301. DOI: 10.1109/TLT.2014.2329293

Ibrahim, A. (2024). Assessing the knowledge and perception of artificial intelligence for teaching and research among lecturers in the faculties of arts in nigeria. *Journal of Global Research in Education and Social Science*, 18(2), 25–33. DOI: 10.56557/jogress/2024/v18i28671

Ibrahim, N., & Ali, N. M. (2018). A conceptual framework for designing virtual heritage environment for cultural learning. [JOCCH]. *Journal on Computing and Cultural Heritage*, 11(2), 1–27. DOI: 10.1145/3117801

Imran, M. (2019). Analysis of learning and teaching strategies in Surgery Module: A mixed methods study. *JPMA. The Journal of the Pakistan Medical Association*, 69(9), 1287–1292. PMID: 31511713

International Society for Technology in Education. (2007). *National educational technology standards for students. ISTE*. Interntl Soc Tech Educ.

International Society for Technology in Education. (2017). *ISTE standards for educators*. International Society for Technology in Education.

Ip, H. H. S., Li, C., Leoni, S., Chen, Y., Ma, K. F., Wong, C. H., & Li, Q. (2019). Design and Evaluate Immersive Learning Experience for Massive Open Online Courses (MOOCs). *IEEE Transactions on Learning Technologies*, 12(4), 503–515. DOI: 10.1109/TLT.2018.2878700

Irkinovich, N. R. (2022). The importance of role-playing game in teaching English in a non-linguistic university. *International Journal of Pedagogics*, 2(09), 29–32. https://theusajournals.com/index.php/ijp/article/view/376

Islam, M., Kim, D. A., & Kwon, M. (2020). A comparison of two forms of instruction: Pre-recorded video lectures vs. Live ZOOM lectures for education in the business management field. *Sustainability (Basel)*, 12(19), 8149–8160. DOI: 10.3390/su12198149

Ismail, N. (2015). The Integration of New Media in Schools: Comparing Policy with Practice. *International Education Studies*, 8(12), 231–240. DOI: 10.5539/ies.v8n12p231

Ismaizam, N. M., Rahman, S. F. A., Ahmad, S. N. S. M., Nazri, N. I. I. M., Idris, N. A. A., & Ali, N.

Ismaizam, N. M., Rahman, S. F. A., Ahmad, S. N. S. M., Nazri, N. I. I. M., Idris, N. A. A., Ali, N. A., & Aldaba, A. M. A. (2022). An integration of game-based learning in a classroom: An overview (2016-2021). *International Journal of Academic Research in Progressive Education and Development*, 11(1).

Jääskä, E., & Aaltonen, K. (2022). Teachers' experiences of using game-based learning methods in project management higher education. *Project Leadership and Society, 3*, 100041. https://www.sciencedirect.com/science/article/pii/S2666721522000011

Jääskä, E., Aaltonen, K., & Kujala, J. (2021). Game-based learning in project sustainability management education. *Sustainability (Basel)*, 13(15), 8204. DOI: 10.3390/su13158204

Jaccard, D., Bonnier, K.E., & Hellstrom, M. (2022). How might serious games trigger a

Jaffer, R., Davids, Z., & Seymour, L. F. (2023). Challenges of Using Social Media as a Teaching Tool in Secondary Schools. *European Conference on e-Learning*, 22(1), 131-138. DOI: 10.34190/ecel.22.1.1657

Järvelä, S., & Renninger, K. A. (2014). Designing for learning: interest, motivation, and engagement. In Sawyer, R. K. (Ed.), *The Cambridge Handbook of the Learning Sciences, Cambridge Handbooks in Psychology* (pp. 668–685). Cambridge University Press., DOI: 10.1017/CBO9781139519526.040

Jatmoko, D., Suyitno, S., Rasul, M. S., Nurtanto, M., Kholifah, N., Masek, A., & Nur, H. R. (2023). The Factors Influencing Digital Literacy Practice in Vocational Education: A Structural Equation Modeling Approach. *European Journal of Educational Research*, 12(2), 1109–1121. DOI: 10.12973/eu-jer.12.2.1109

Javaeed, A., Kibria, Z., Khan, Z., & Ghauri, S. K. (2020). Impact of social media integration in teaching methods on exam outcomes. *Advances in Medical Education and Practice*, 11, 53–61. DOI: 10.2147/AMEP.S209123 PMID: 32021544

Jelas, Z. M., Azman, N., Zulnaidi, H., & Ahmad, N. A. (2016). Learning support and academic achievement among Malaysian adolescents: The mediating role of student engagement. *Learning Environments Research*, 19(2), 221–240. DOI: 10.1007/s10984-015-9202-5

Ji, Y., & Xue, M. (2022). Relationship Between Design Metacognition and Design Thinking. *School of Information and Communication Engineering,Beijing University of Posts and Telecommunications, 24*(01), 85-94+112.

Jia, R. (2020). Research on the status quo and problems of digital media talent training in higher vocational colleges. *Journalists Cradle, 10*, 51–52.

Jian, B., & Sun, X. J. (2024). The reform and practice of the teaching mode of digital media art in colleges and universities. *Journal of Taiyuan Urban Vocational College, 5*, 86–90. https://doi.org/DOI: 10.16227/j.cnki.tycs.2024.0279

Jiang, Z., Wang, Y., Shi, C., Wu, Y., Hu, R., Chen, S., Hu, S., Wang, X., & Qiu, B. (2021). *Attention module improves both performance and interpretability of 4D fMRI decoding neural network.*

Jiang, S. (2016, January 1). A Review of the Effectiveness of Gamification in Education. RELX Group (Netherlands). DOI: 10.2139/ssrn.3163896

Jiang, Y. V., Capistrano, C. G., & Palm, B. E. (2014). Spatial Working Memory in Children With High-Functioning Autism: Intact Configural Processing But Impaired Capacity. *Journal of Vision (Charlottesville, Va.)*, 14(10), 42–42. DOI: 10.1167/14.10.42 PMID: 24661175

Jiao, Z. X., Yuan, G. H., & Wu, C. Z. (2024). Practice of project teaching methods in the course of electrical machinery and electrical control. *Electronic Technology & Software Engineering, 1*, 88–89.

Jia, X., Li, W., & Cao, L. (2019). The Role of Metacognitive Components in Creative Thinking. *Frontiers in Psychology*, 10, 2404. DOI: 10.3389/fpsyg.2019.02404 PMID: 31708842

Ji, L. (2023). The Validity of the Specific Coding Principle: The Explanations from Cognitive Psychology and Psychoanalysis. *Journal of Education. Humanities and Social Sciences*, 8, 1259–1263. DOI: 10.54097/ehss.v8i.4460

Jin, T. (2024). Master of practical research on project-based teaching methods in digital audio-visual editing and synthesis. *Dissertation*. https://link.cnki.net/doi/10.27280/d.cnki.gsdsu.2024.001504

Johanson, R. K., & Adams, A. V. (2004). *Skills development in sub-Saharan Africa*. World Bank Publications.

Jorgensen, E. R. (1995). Music education as community. *Journal of Aesthetic Education, 29*(3), 71–84. JSTOR. DOI: 10.2307/3333542

Jorgensen, E. (1993). On building social theories of music education. *Bulletin of the Council for Research in Music Education*, 116(Spring).

Kahfi, F. (2022). The existence of human resource development (hrd) on the development of employee creativity. *Journal of Management and Administration Provision*, 2(2), 51–57. DOI: 10.55885/jmap.v2i2.178

Kalia, G. (2013). A Research Paper on Social Media: An Innovative Educational Tool. *Issues and Ideas in Education*, 1(1), 1-8.

Kanchan, S., & Varshney, S. (2015). Skill development initiatives and strategies. *Asian Journal of Management Research*, 5(4), 666–672.

Kaplan, A. M., & Haenlein, M. (2019). Siri, Siri, in my hand: Who's the fairest in the land? On the interpretations, illustrations, and implications of artificial intelligence. *Business Horizons*, 62(1), 15–25. DOI: 10.1016/j.bushor.2018.08.004

Kaplan, R. M., & Pascoe, G. C. (1977). Humorous lectures and humorous examples: Some effects upon comprehension and retention. *Journal of Educational Psychology*, 69(1), 61–65. DOI: 10.1037/0022-0663.69.1.61

Kapur, H. (2016). Skill India programme: A compliment to Make in India campaign. *Global Journal for Research Analysis*, •••, 84–86.

Kara, N. (2024). A mixed-methods study of cultural heritage learning through playing a serious game. *International Journal of Human-Computer Interaction*, 40(6), 1397–1408. DOI: 10.1080/10447318.2022.2125627

Karthikeyan, C. (2019). A Meta analytical descriptive study on evolving concepts of Human Capital and its application in the age of Artificial intelligence(AI). *International Journal of Research and Analytical Reviews*, •••, 361–373.

Karwowski, M., Czerwonka, M., & Kaufman, J. C. (2020). Does intelligence strengthen creative metacognition? *Psychology of Aesthetics, Creativity, and the Arts*, 14(3), 353–360. DOI: 10.1037/aca0000208

Katou, A. (2017). How does human resource management influence organisational performance? an integrative approach-based analysis. *International Journal of Productivity and Performance Management*, 66(6), 797–821. DOI: 10.1108/ijppm-01-2016-0004

Kaufman, J. C., & Beghetto, R. A. (2013). In Praise of Clark Kent: Creative Metacognition and the Importance of Teaching Kids When (Not) to Be Creative. *Roeper Review*, 35(3), 155–165. DOI: 10.1080/02783193.2013.799413

Kaufman, J. C., & Beghetto, R. A. (2014). Creativity in the schools: Renewed interest and promising new directions. In *Handbook of positive psychology in schools* (pp. 165–175). Routledge., https://api.taylorfrancis.com/content/chapters/edit/download?identifierName=doi&identifierValue=10.4324/9780203106525-13&type=chapterpdf

Kaufman, J. C., Beghetto, R. A., & Watson, C. (2016). Creative metacognition and self-ratings of creative performance: A 4-C perspective. *Learning and Individual Differences*, 51, 394–399. DOI: 10.1016/j.lindif.2015.05.004

Kavousi, S., Miller, P. A., & Alexander, P. A. (2020). Modeling metacognition in design thinking and design making. *International Journal of Technology and Design Education*, 30(4), 709–735. DOI: 10.1007/s10798-019-09521-9

Kenett, Y. N., Gooz, N., & Ackerman, R. (2023). The Role of Semantic Associations as a Metacognitive Cue in Creative Idea Generation. *Journal of Intelligence*, 11(4), 59. DOI: 10.3390/jintelligence11040059 PMID: 37103244

Khaitova, N. F. (2021). History of Gamification and Its Role in the Educational Process. *International Journal of Multicultural and Multireligious Understanding*, 8(5), 212. DOI: 10.18415/ijmmu.v8i5.2640

Khaldi, A., Bouzidi, R., & Nader, F. (2023). Gamification of e-learning in higher education: A systematic literature review. *Smart Learning Environments*, 10(1), 10. DOI: 10.1186/s40561-023-00227-z

Khaleel, F L., Ashaari, N S., Wook, T S M T., & Ismail, A. (2015, April 1). User-enjoyable learning environment based on Gamification elements. DOI: 10.1109/I4CT.2015.7219570

Khandelwal, P., Zhang, S., Sinapov, J., Leonetti, M., Thomason, J., Yang, F., Gori, I., Svetlik, M., Khante, P., Lifschitz, V., Aggarwal, J. K., Mooney, R., & Stone, P. (2017). BWIBots: A platform for bridging the gap between AI and human–robot interaction research. *The International Journal of Robotics Research*, 36(5–7), 635–659. DOI: 10.1177/0278364916688949

Khasanah, A. N., Widoretno, S., & Sajidan, S. (2017). Effectiveness of Critical Thinking Indicator-Based Module in Empowering Student's Learning Outcome in Respiratory System Study Material. *Jurnal Pendidikan IPA Indonesia*, 6(1). Advance online publication. DOI: 10.15294/jpii.v6i1.8490

Kilpatrick, W. H. (1918). The Project Method. *Teachers College Record*, •••, 318–330.

Kim, J. T., & Lee, W. H. (2015). Dynamical model for gamification of learning (DMGL). *Multimedia Tools and Applications*, 74(19), 8483–8493. DOI: 10.1007/s11042-013-1612-8

Kim, J., & Castelli, D. M. (2021). Effects of gamification on behavioral change in education: A meta-analysis. *International Journal of Environmental Research and Public Health*, 18(7), 3550. DOI: 10.3390/ijerph18073550 PMID: 33805530

Klašnja-Milićević, A., Ivanović, M., & Budimac, Z. (2017). Data science in education: Big data and learning analytics. *Computer Applications in Engineering Education*, 25(6), 1066–1078. DOI: 10.1002/cae.21844

Kleinmintz, O. M., Ivancovsky, T., & Shamay-Tsoory, S. G. (2019). The two-fold model of creativity: The neural underpinnings of the generation and evaluation of creative ideas. *Current Opinion in Behavioral Sciences*, 27, 131–138. DOI: 10.1016/j.cobeha.2018.11.004

Kleopatra, N., Vasilis, G., & Konstantinos, L. (2023). Mobile learningtechnology barriers in school education: Teachers' views. *Technology, Pedagogy and Education*, 32(1), 29–44. DOI: 10.1080/1475939X.2022.2121314

Kljun, M., Geroimenko, V., & Čopič Pucihar, K. (2020). Augmented reality in education: Current status and advancement of the field. Augmented Reality in Education: A New Technology for Teaching and Learning, 3-21.

Klock, A. C. T., Gasparini, I., Pimenta, M. S., & Hamari, J. (2020). Tailored gamification: A review of literature. *International Journal of Human Computer Studies, 144*(September 2019). DOI: 10.1016/j.ijhcs.2020.102495

Knox, J., Wang, Y., & Gallagher, M. (2020). Artificial intelligence and inclusive education: Speculative futures and emerging practices. *Learning, Media and Technology*, 45(3), 226–238. DOI: 10.1080/17439884.2020.1761641

Kolb, A. Y., & Kolb, D. A. (2005). Learning styles and learning spaces: Enhancing experiential learning in higher education. *Academy of Management Learning & Education*, 4(2), 193–212. DOI: 10.5465/amle.2005.17268566

Komasawa, N., & Yokohira, M. (2023). Simulation-based education in the artificial intelligence era. *Cureus*. Advance online publication. DOI: 10.7759/cureus.40940

Korniienko, I. A., & Barchi, B. V. (2020). Influence of virtual reality tools on human anatomy learning. *Unpublished manuscript*.

Koszolko, M. (2019). The tactile evolution — electronic music production and affordances of iOS apps. In *Proceedings of the 12th Art of Record Production Conference: Mono: Stereo: Multi* (pp. 187–204). Stockholm: Royal College of Music (KMH) & Art of Record Production.

Kovanović, V., Joksimović, S., Gašević, D., Siemens, G., & Hatala, M. (2019). Predictive analytics in education: Towards a unified framework. *Learning Analytics & Knowledge*, 2019, 82–91. DOI: 10.1145/2723576.2723580

Krath, J., Schürmann, L., & Von Korflesch, H. F. (2021). Revealing the theoretical basis of gamification: A systematic review and analysis of theory in research on gamification, serious games and game-based learning. *Computers in Human Behavior*, 125, 106963. DOI: 10.1016/j.chb.2021.106963

Krohn, F. W. (2005). *Foundations of Pedagogy*. Educational Science Press.

Krumm, J. (Ed.). (2018). Ubiquitous Computing Fundamentals. (John Krumm, Ed.) Ubiquitous Computing Fundamentals. *Chapman and Hall/CRC*.

Kucher, T. (2021, March 17). Principles and Best Practices of Designing Digital Game-Based Learning Environments. *Principles and Best Practices of Designing Digital Game-Based Learning Environments.*, 5(2), 213–223. DOI: 10.46328/ijtes.190

Kumar, P., & Venkatesan, R. (2020). Improving software defect prediction using generative adversarial networks. *International Journal of Science and Engineering Applications*, 9(9), 117–120. DOI: 10.7753/IJSEA0909.1001

Kumar, V., & Nanda, P. (2022). Social Media as a Learning Tool: A Perspective on Formal and Informal Learning. *International Journal of Educational Reform*, 33(3), 1–26. DOI: 10.1177/10567879221094303

Kumar, V., & Rewari, M. (2022). A responsible approach to higher education curriculum design. *International Journal of Educational Reform*, 31(4), 422–441. DOI: 10.1177/10567879221110509

Kuo, T. H. (2020). The Current Situation of AI Foreign Language Education and Its Influence on College Japanese Teaching. Lecture Notes in Computer Science (including subseries Lecture Notes in Artificial Intelligence and Lecture Notes in Bioinformatics) (Vol. 12193 LNCS, pp. 315–324). *Springer.* DOI: 10.1007/978-3-030-49913-6_27

Kuruvilla, S., Erickson, C. L., & Hwang, A. (2002). An Assessment of the Singapore Skills Development System:Does it constitute a viable model for other Developing countries? *World Development*, •••, 1461–1467.

Kwet, M., & Prinsloo, P. (2020). The 'smart' classroom: A new frontier in the age of the smart university. *Teaching in Higher Education*, 25(4), 510–526. DOI: 10.1080/13562517.2020.1734922

Laamarti, F., Eid, M., & El Saddik, A. (2014). An overview of serious games. *International Journal of Computer Games Technology*, 2014, 358152. DOI: 10.1155/2014/358152

Labus, A., Simic, K., Barac, D., Despotovic-Zrakic, M., & Radenkovic, M. (2012). Integration of social network services in the e-education process. *Metalurgia International*, 17(7), 161.

Laine, T. H., & Lindberg, R. S. N. (2020, October 1). Designing Engaging Games for Education: A Systematic Literature Review on Game Motivators and Design Principles. *IEEE Transactions on Learning Technologies*, 13(4), 804–821. DOI: 10.1109/TLT.2020.3018503

Lakhal, S., Bateman, D., & Bédard, J. (2017). Blended Synchronous Delivery Modes in Graduate Programs: A Literature Review and How it is Implemented in the Master Teacher Program. *Collected Essays on Learning and Teaching*, 10, 47–60. DOI: 10.22329/celt.v10i0.4747

Lamprinou, D., & Fotini, P. (2015, November 1). Gamification design framework based on SDT for student motivation. DOI: 10.1109/IMCTL.2015.7359631

Lampropoulos, G., Makkonen, P., & Siakas, K. (2022). Social Media in Education: A Case Study Regarding Higher Education Students' Viewpoints | SpringerLink.

Lampropoulos, G., & Kinshuk. (2024). Virtual reality and gamification in education: A systematic review. *Educational Technology Research and Development*, •••, 1–95.

Landers, R. N. (2014, December 1). Developing a Theory of Gamified Learning. *Simulation & Gaming*, 45(6), 752–768. DOI: 10.1177/1046878114563660

Lange, K. P., Korevaar, G., Oskam, I. F., & Herder, P. M. (2022). Re-organise: Game-based learning of circular business model innovation. *Frontiers in Sustainability*, 3, 809700. DOI: 10.3389/frsus.2022.809700

Lan, X. (2022). Construction of a music education model based on internet big data. *Wireless Communications and Mobile Computing*, 2022, 1–6. DOI: 10.1155/2022/3732776

Law, N. W. Y., Woo, D. J., De la Torre, J., & Wong, K. W. G. (2018). A global framework of reference on digital literacy skills for indicator 4.4. 2.

Lazonder, A. W., Walraven, A., Gijlers, H., & Janssen, N. (2020). Longitudinal assessment of digital literacy in children: Findings from a large Dutch single-school study. *Computers & Education*, 143, 103681. DOI: 10.1016/j.compedu.2019.103681

LeCun, Y., Bengio, Y., & Hinton, G. (2015). Deep learning. *Nature*, 521(7553), 436–444. DOI: 10.1038/nature14539 PMID: 26017442

Lee, A.R., Son, S.M., Kim K.K. (2016). Information and communication technology overload and social networking service fatigue: A stress perspective. *Computers in Human Behavior*, 55 (A), 51-61.

Lee, J. J., & Hammer, J. (2011, January 1). Gamification in Education: What, How, Why Bother? Rapid Intellect Group, 15(2). https://www.uwstout.edu/soe/profdev/resources/upload/Lee-Hammer-AEQ-2011.pdf

Lee, J. M., Baek, J., & Ju, D. Y. (2018). Anthropomorphic Design: Emotional Perception for Deformable Object. *Frontiers in Psychology*, 9, 1829. DOI: 10.3389/fpsyg.2018.01829 PMID: 30333773

Lee, L. K., Wei, X., Chui, K. T., Cheung, S. K., Wang, F. L., Fung, Y. C., Lu, A., Hui, Y. K., Hao, T., U, L. H., & Wu, N. I. (2024). A Systematic Review of the Design of Serious Games for Innovative Learning: Augmented Reality, Virtual Reality, or Mixed Reality? *Electronics (Basel)*, 13(5), 890. DOI: 10.3390/electronics13050890

Lee, S. H., & Chang, M. J. (2019). AI and fashion design: How artificial intelligence is reshaping the industry. *International Journal of Fashion Design, Technology and Education*, 12(4), 372–381.

Lege, R., & Bonner, E. (2020). Virtual reality in education: The promise, progress, and challenge. *The JALT CALL Journal*, 16(3), 167–180. DOI: 10.29140/jaltcall.v16n3.388

Leitão, R., Maguire, M., Turner, S., & Guimarães, L. (2022). A systematic evaluation of game elements effects on students' motivation. *Education and Information Technologies*, 27(1), 1–23. DOI: 10.1007/s10639-021-10651-8

Lester, D., Skulmoski, G. J., Fisher, D. P., Mehrotra, V., Lim, I., Lang, A., & Keogh, J. W. (2023). Drivers and barriers to the utilisation of gamification and game-based learning in universities: A systematic review of educators' perspectives. *British Journal of Educational Technology*, 54(6), 1748–1770. DOI: 10.1111/bjet.13311

Li, X. Y. (2023). *An empirical study on the application of project-based teaching methods in technical environmental monitoring courses in secondary vocational education* (Master's thesis, Shandong Normal University). https://doi.org/DOI: 10.27280/d.cnki.gsdsu.2023.001113

Liang, G., Wang, J., Li, S., & Chang, R. (2014). PatBugs: A pattern-based bug detector for cross-platform mobile applications. In *2014 IEEE International Conference on Mobile Services* (pp. 84-91). https://doi.org/DOI: 10.1109/MobServ.2014.21

Liang, W. L.. (2024). Research on the application of project-based teaching methods in Tea Art Association courses from the perspective of curriculum ideology and politics. *Guangdong Tea Industry*, 01, 65–69.

Liberati, A., Altman, D. G., Tetzlaff, J., Mulrow, C., Gøtzsche, P. C., Ioannidis, J. P., & Moher, D. (2009). The PRISMA statement for reporting systematic reviews and meta-analyses of studies that evaluate health care interventions: Explanation and elaboration. *Annals of Internal Medicine*, 151(4), W-65. DOI: 10.7326/0003-4819-151-4-200908180-00136 PMID: 19622512

Liebl, S. (2023). *Threat modelling for Internet of Things devices*.

Lim, D., Sanmugam, M., & Jaafar, W. A. (2023). *The Effect of Gamified Depth on Malaysian Higher Education Students ' Intrinsic Motivation Level and Achievement Level*. 1–14.

Lindland, K. (2021). *Gaming as a Tool in English Language Teaching What is Game-based Learning, and how do teachers experience digital games as an educational tool?* (Master's thesis, University of South-Eastern Norway).

Li, Q., Wang, P., Liu, Z., Zhang, H., Song, Y., & Zhang, Y. (2024). Using scaffolding theory in serious games to enhance traditional Chinese murals culture learning. *Computer Animation and Virtual Worlds*, 35(1), e2213. DOI: 10.1002/cav.2213

Liu, J. Y. (2020). Reform and practice of the project-driven mode of cultivating innovative and enterprising talents through school-enterprise cooperation. *Education Teaching Forum, 12*, 8–9.

Liu, X., Sun, D., & Zhao, B. (2022). Research on the impact of virtual reality technology on student classroom participation. *Shanxi Youth, 19*, 39-41. https://www.cqvip.com/QK/87921X/202219/1010237166.html

Liu, C., Hwang, G., Tu, Y., Yin, Y., & Wang, Y. (2023a). Research advancement and foci of mobile technology supported music education: A systematic review and social network analysis on 20082019 academic publications. *Interactive Learning Environments*, 31(7), 4535–4554. DOI: 10.1080/10494820.2021.1974890

Liu, L. (2024). On the development of digital media art education in the context of art science and technology integration. *University*, 11, 134–137.

Liu, M. (2023). A self-case study of the female doctoral student's own creative metacognition on art expressions: Based on the theory of creative metacognition (CMC). *Thinking Skills and Creativity*, 48, 101292. DOI: 10.1016/j.tsc.2023.101292

Liu, R., Wang, L., Koszalka, T. A., & Wan, K. (2022). Effects of immersive virtual reality classrooms on students' academic achievement, motivation and cognitive load in science lessons. *Journal of Computer Assisted Learning*, 38(5), 1422–1433. DOI: 10.1111/jcal.12688

Liu, W., Wang, Z., Liu, X., Zeng, N., Liu, Y., & Alsaadi, F. E. (2017). A survey of deep neural network architectures and their applications. *Neurocomputing*, 234, 11–26. DOI: 10.1016/j.neucom.2016.12.038

Liu, Y. (2001). A Brief Overview of Higher Teacher Education Reform in the United States. *Educational Researcher*, 10, 74–77.

Liu, Z. Y., Shaikh, Z., & Gazizova, F. (2020). Using the concept of game-based learning in education. [iJET]. *International Journal of Emerging Technologies in Learning*, 15(14), 53–64. DOI: 10.3991/ijet.v15i14.14675

Li, Y., Lerner, J. V., & Lerner, R. M. (2010). Personal and ecological assets and academic competence in early adolescence: The mediating role of school engagement. *Journal of Youth and Adolescence*, 39(8), 801–815. DOI: 10.1007/s10964-010-9535-4 PMID: 20407920

Li, Y., Ying, S., Chen, Q., & Guan, J. (2022). An experiential learning-based virtual reality approach to foster students' vocabulary acquisition and learning engagement in English for geography. *Sustainability (Basel)*, 14(22), 15359. DOI: 10.3390/su142215359

Lohse, G. L. (1997). The role of working memory on graphical information processing. *Behaviour & Information Technology*, 16(6), 297–308. DOI: 10.1080/014492997119707

Lomas, J. D., Koedinger, K., Patel, N., Shodhan, S., Poonwala, N., & Forlizzi, J. L. (2017). Is difficulty overrated? The effects of choice, novelty and suspense on intrinsic motivation in educational games. In: *Proceedings of the 2017 CHI Conference on Human Factors in Computing Systems,* CHI '17. Association for Computing Machinery, New York, NY, USA, pp. 1028–1039. DOI: 10.1145/3025453.3025638

Long, W. L. (2022). *Based on the idea of project management: PBL teaching method in secondary vocational "Dynamic web design" course of practical research* (Master's thesis, Jiangxi Science and Technology Normal University). DOI: 10.27751/d.cnki.gjxkj.2022.000050

Lopez, C. E., & Tucker, C. S. (2021). Adaptive Gamification and Its Impact on Performance. *Lecture Notes in Computer Science (Including Subseries Lecture Notes in Artificial Intelligence and Lecture Notes in Bioinformatics), 12789 LNCS,* 327–341. DOI: 10.1007/978-3-030-77277-2_25

López-Banet, L., Martínez-Carmona, M., & Reis, P. (2024). Effects of an intervention on emotional and cognitive engagement in teacher education: Scientific practices concerning greenhouse gases. *Frontiers in Education*, 9, 1307847. DOI: 10.3389/feduc.2024.1307847

Loria, E., & Marconi, A. (2018). Player types and player behaviors: Analyzing Correlations in an On-the-field Gamified System. *CHI PLAY 2018 - Proceedings of the 2018 Annual Symposium on Computer-Human Interaction in Play Companion Extended Abstracts, October*, 531–538. DOI: 10.1145/3270316.3271526

Loup, G., Serna, A., Iksal, S., & George, S. (2016). Immersion and persistence: Improving learners' engagement in authentic learning situations. In Verbert, K., Sharples, M., & Klobučar, T. (Eds.), *Adaptive and Adaptable Learning* (pp. 410–415). Springer., DOI: 10.1007/978-3-319-45153-4_35

Loveless, T. (2012). *How well are American students learning?* Brookings Institution.

Low, J. Y., Balakrishnan, B., & Yaacob, M. I. H. (2023). Game-Based Learning: Current Practices and Perceptions of Secondary School Physics Teachers in Malaysia. *The international journal of science, mathematics and technology learning, 31*(1), 1-21. DOI: 10.18848/2327-7971/CGP/v31i01/1-21

Luce, D. W. (2001). Collaborative learning in music education: A review of the literature. *Update - University of South Carolina. Dept. of Music*, 19(2), 20–25. DOI: 10.1177/87551233010190020105

Luckin, R. (2018). *Machine learning and human intelligence: The future of education for the 21st century*. Routledge.

Lu, J. (2019). Research on the status quo and problems of digital media art professional training in higher vocational colleges. *Home Drama*, 01, 172–174.

Luo, T., Freeman, C., & Stefaniak, J. (2020). "Like, comment, and share"—professional development through social media in higher education: A systematic review. *Educational Technology Research and Development*, 68(1), 1659–1683. Advance online publication. DOI: 10.1007/s11423-020-09790-5

Mac Namara, D., & Murphy, L. (2017). Online versus offline perspectives on gamified learning. *CEUR Workshop Proceedings*, 1857, 47–52.

Madariaga, L., Allendes, C., Nussbaum, M., Barrios, G., & Acevedo, N. (2023). Offline and online user experience of gamified robotics for introducing computational thinking: Comparing engagement, game mechanics and coding motivation. *Computers and Education, 193*(July 2022), 1–24. DOI: 10.1016/j.compedu.2022.104664

Majerowicz, S., & Zárate, R. A. (2023). Massive Open Online Courses and Labor Market Outcomes: Experimental Evidence from Colombia. Available at *SSRN* 4643591.

Makransky, G., Terkildsen, T. S., & Mayer, R. E. (2019). Adding immersive virtual reality to a science lab simulation causes more presence but less learning. *Learning and Instruction*, 60, 225–236. DOI: 10.1016/j.learninstruc.2017.12.007

Malegiannaki, I., & Daradoumis, T. (2017). Analyzing the educational design, use and effect of spatial games for cultural heritage: A literature review. Computers &amp. *Education*, 108, 1–10.

Manohar, P., Rayel, J., & Sause, L. (2023). Efficacy of management and employees' involvement in hrd initiatives: The case of png power limited. *Business Ethics and Leadership*, 7(2), 35–46. DOI: 10.21272/bel.7(2).35-46.2023

Mantie, R., & Tucker, L. (2008). Closing the gap: Does musicmaking have to stop upon graduation? *International Journal of Community Music*, 1(2), 217–227. DOI: 10.1386/ijcm.1.2.217_1

Manzoor, S., Zhang, H., & Suri, N. (2018, April). Threat modeling and analysis for the cloud ecosystem. In *2018 IEEE International Conference on Cloud Engineering (IC2E)* (pp. 278-281). IEEE. DOI: 10.1109/IC2E.2018.00056

Marczewski, A. (2020). *Analogue vs Digital Gamification*. Gamified UK. https://www.gamified.uk/2020/01/17/analogue-vs-digital-gamification-2/

Marienko, M., Nosenko, Y., & Shyshkina, M. (2020). Personalization of learning using adaptive technologies and augmented reality. arXiv preprint arXiv:2011.05802. DOI: 10.31812/123456789/4418

Marks, H. M. (2000). Student engagement in instructional activity: Patterns in the elementary, middle, and high school years. *American Educational Research Journal*, 37(1), 153–184. DOI: 10.3102/00028312037001153

Marougkas, A., Troussas, C., Krouska, A., & Sgouropoulou, C. (2023). Virtual reality in education: A review of learning theories, approaches and methodologies for the last decade. *Electronics (Basel)*, 12(13), 2832. DOI: 10.3390/electronics12132832

Marshall, J. (2014). Transdisciplinarity and art integration: Toward a new understanding of art-based learning across the curriculum. *Studies in Art Education*, 55(2), 104–127. DOI: 10.1080/00393541.2014.11518922

Martelleur, J., & Hamza, A. (2022). *Security tools in DevSecOps: A systematic literature review* (Master's thesis). Retrieved from https://urn.kb.se/resolve?urn=urn:nbn:se:lnu:diva-118400

Marzulina, L., Habibi, A., Mukminin, A., Desvitasari, D., Yaakob, M. F. M., & Ropawandi, D. (2018). The integration of social networking services in higher education: Benefits and barriers in teaching English. *International Journal of Virtual and Personal Learning Environments*, 8(2), 46–62. DOI: 10.4018/IJVPLE.2018070104

Matthews, K. E., Andrews, V., & Adams, P. J. H. E. R. (2011). Social learning spaces and student engagement. *Assessment & Evaluation in Higher Education*, 30(2), 105–120. DOI: 10.1080/02602930903500170

Mayer, R. E. (2009). *Multimedia Learning* (2nd ed.). Cambridge University Press., DOI: 10.1017/CBO9780511811678

Mayer, R. E., & Estrella, G. (2014). Benefits of emotional design in multimedia instruction. *Learning and Instruction*, 33, 12–18. DOI: 10.1016/j.learninstruc.2014.02.004

Mayer, R. E., & Fiorella, L. (Eds.). (2021). *The Cambridge Handbook of Multimedia Learning* (3rd ed.). Cambridge University Press., DOI: 10.1017/9781108894333

McCall, J. (2016). Teaching history with digital historical games. *Simulation & Gaming*, 47(4), 517–542. DOI: 10.1177/1046878116646693

McCosker, A., & Wilken, R. (2020). AI for artists: Transformative practices in creative industries. *Media International Australia*, 177(1), 71–84. DOI: 10.1177/1329878X20937694

McVeigh, M. (2023). A Creative Thinking and Writing Tool. The Creativity Metacognitive Framework. In M. McVeigh, *Screenwriting from the Inside Out* (pp. 179–186). Springer International Publishing. DOI: 10.1007/978-3-031-40520-4_9

Mee, R. W. M., Pek, L. S., Von, W. Y., Ghani, K. A., Shahdan, T. S. T., Ismail, M. R., & Rao, Y. S. (2021). A Conceptual Model of Analogue Gamification to Enhance Learners' Motivation and Attitude. *International Journal of Language Education*, 5(2), 40–50.

Mega, C., Ronconi, L., & Béni, R. D. (2014). What Makes a Good Student? How Emotions, Self-Regulated Learning, and Motivation Contribute to Academic Achievement. *Journal of Educational Psychology*, 106(1), 121–131. DOI: 10.1037/a0033546

Mehrabi, N., Morstatter, F., Saxena, N., Lerman, K., & Galstyan, A. (2021). A survey on bias and fairness in machine learning. *ACM Computing Surveys*, 54(6), 1–35. DOI: 10.1145/3457607

Meng, B., Smith, W., & Durling, M. (2021). Security threat modeling and automated analysis for system design. *SAE International Journal of Transportation Cybersecurity and Privacy, 4*(11-04-01-0001), 3-17.

Menzies, T., & Marcus, A. (2008). Automated severity assessment of software defect reports. *2008 IEEE International Conference on Software Maintenance*, 346–355. DOI: 10.1109/ICSM.2008.4658083

Mevarech, Z. R., & Paz-Baruch, N. (2022). Meta-creativity: What is it and how does it relate to creativity? *Metacognition and Learning*, 17(2), 427–441. DOI: 10.1007/s11409-022-09290-2

Meyer, D. K., & Turner, J. C. (2006). Re-Conceptualizing Emotion and Motivation to Learn in Classroom Contexts. *Educational Psychology Review*, 18(4), 377–390. DOI: 10.1007/s10648-006-9032-1

Microsoft. (2022). *Copilot*. https://copilot.microsoft.com/

Ministry of Education, National Development and Reform Commission, Ministry of Industry and Information Technology, et al. (2020). *Action Plan for Improving the Quality and Excellence of Vocational Education (2020-2023)*. The Chinese Ministry of Education, National Development and Reform Commission, Ministry of Industry and Information Technology, et al. https://bit.ly/3WaFHSJ

Ministry of Home Affairs, GOI. (2011). "Census of India 2011." Provisional population totals.

Mohamadbahuldin, U. Q. (2022). Challenge of Way of Teaching. *Journal of Arts, Literature, Humanities, and Social Sciences*, 80, 144–165. DOI: 10.33193/JALHSS.80.2022.687

Mohanty, R. K., & Jyothi, N. (2015). A secured framework for protecting sensitive information from unauthorized users.

Mohanty, R. K., Sahoo, S. P., & Kabat, M. R. (2022, October). A survey on emerging technologies in wireless body area network. In *2022 13th International Conference on Computing Communication and Networking Technologies (ICCCNT)* (pp. 1-5). IEEE.

Mohanty, R. K., Sahoo, S. P., & Kabat, M. R. (2023, June). A network reliability based secure routing protocol (NRSRP) for secure transmission in wireless body area network. In *2023 8th International Conference on Communication and Electronics Systems (ICCES)* (pp. 663-668). IEEE.

Mohanty, R. K., Kumar, A. P., Padmaja, R., & Prashanthi, V. (2024). Deep Learning for Analyzing User and Entity Behaviors: Techniques and Applications. In *Consumer and Organizational Behavior in the Age of AI* (pp. 219–250). IGI Global. DOI: 10.4018/979-8-3693-8850-1.ch008

Mohanty, R. K., Motupalli, R. K., Manju, D., Gangappa, M., Gouthami, B., & Mounika, G. (2023, December). Energy-efficient cluster based routing protocol to enhance the lifetime of wearable wireless body area networks (WBAN). In *2023 OITS International Conference on Information Technology (OCIT)* (pp. 71-76). IEEE. DOI: 10.1109/OCIT59427.2023.10431071

Mohanty, R. K., Sahoo, S. P., & Kabat, M. R. (2023). Sustainable remote patient monitoring in wireless body area network with multi-hop routing and scheduling: A four-fold objective based optimization approach. *. *Wireless Networks*, 29(5), 1–15. DOI: 10.1007/s11276-023-03276-x

Mohanty, R. K., Sahoo, S. P., & Kabat, M. R. (2024). Thermal-energy-efficient-secured-link reliable and delay-aware routing protocol (TESLDAR) for wireless body area networks. *. *International Journal of Computers and Applications*, 46(9), 1–13. DOI: 10.1080/1206212X.2024.2380675

Moher, D., Liberati, A., Tetzlaff, J., & Altman, D. G.PRISMA Group. (2009). Preferred reporting items for systematic reviews and meta-analyses: The PRISMA statement. *Annals of Internal Medicine*, 151(4), 264–269. DOI: 10.7326/0003-4819-151-4-200908180-00135 PMID: 19622511

Moher, D., Liberati, A., Tetzlaff, J., & Altman, D. G.PRISMA Group. (2009). Preferred reporting items for systematic reviews and meta-analyses: The PRISMA statement. *PLoS Medicine*, 6(7), e1000097. DOI: 10.1371/journal.pmed.1000097 PMID: 19621072

Morandini, S., Fraboni, F., Angelis, M., Puzzo, G., Giusino, D., & Pietrantoni, L. (2023). The impact of artificial intelligence on workers' skills: upskilling and re-skilling in organisations. Informing Science the International Journal of an Emerging Transdiscipline, 26, 039-068. https://doi.org/DOI: 10.28945/5078

Moran, M., Seaman, J., & Tinti-Kane, H. (2011). *Teaching, learning, and sharing: How Today's higher education faculty use social media*. Babson Survey Research Group.

Moremoholo, T. P., & de Lange, R. W. (2018). *Anthropomorphic graphics: How useful are they as an instructional aid to facilitate learning? 13.*

Morris, T. H. (2020). Experiential learning–a systematic review and revision of Kolb's model. *Interactive Learning Environments*, 28(8), 1064–1077. DOI: 10.1080/10494820.2019.1570279

Mozelius, P. (2021). Deep and Shallow Gamification in Higher Education, What Is the Difference? *INTED2021 Proceedings, 1*(March 2021), 3150–3156. DOI: 10.21125/inted.2021.0663

Muhamad, W., & Kurniawan, N. B., Suhardi, & Yazid, S. (2017). Smart campus features, technologies, and applications: A systematic literature review. 2017 International Conference on Information Technology Systems and Innovation (ICITSI) (pp. 384–391). *IEEE.* DOI: 10.1109/ICITSI.2017.8267975

Muhridza, N. H., Rosli, N. A., Sirri, A., & Abdul Samad, A. (2018). Using Game-based Technology, kahoot! for Classroom Engagement. *LSP International Journal*, 5(2). Advance online publication. DOI: 10.11113/lspi.v5n2.77

Mukaromah, D., Mutoharoh, A., Pramudwiatmoko, A., Tsutoh, S., Gutmann, G., Konagaya, A., & Cahyono, T. D. (2019). Digital quiz as media to review material for English education students. *Script Journal: Journal of Linguistic and English Teaching*, 4(2), 88–100. DOI: 10.24903/sj.v4i2.319

Mulders, M., Buchner, J., & Kerres, M. (2020). A framework for the use of immersive virtual reality in learning environments. [iJET]. *International Journal of Emerging Technologies in Learning*, 15(24), 208–224. DOI: 10.3991/ijet.v15i24.16615

Münchow, H., & Bannert, M. (2019). Feeling good, learning better? Effectivity of an emotional design procedure in multimedia learning. *Educational Psychology*, 39(4), 530–549. DOI: 10.1080/01443410.2018.1524852

Munisa, I., & Mohinur, S. (2024). Teaching English To Elementary School Students Through Different Games. *Western European Journal of Linguistics and Education*, 2(5), 4–8. https://westerneuropeanstudies.com/index.php/2

Murillo-Zamorano, L. R., López-Sánchez, J. Á., López-Rey, M. J., & Bueno-Muñoz, C. (2023). Gamification in higher education: The ECOn+ star battles. *Computers and Education, 194*(March 2022). DOI: 10.1016/j.compedu.2022.104699

Mustopa, M. (2024). Challenges in artificial intelligence development in higher education in china, india, and indonesia: International students' perspectives. *International Journal of Learning Teaching and Educational Research*, 23(2), 354–373. DOI: 10.26803/ijlter.23.2.17

Muzari, T., Shava, G. N., & Shonhiwa, S. (2022). Qualitative research paradigm, a key research design for educational researchers, processes and procedures: A theoretical overview. *Indiana Journal of Humanities and Social Sciences, 03*(01).

Myagmar, S., Lee, A. J., & Yurcik, W. (2005). Threat modeling as a basis for security requirements.

Mystakidis, S. (2020, July). Distance education gamification in social virtual reality: A case study on student engagement. In *2020 11th International Conference on Information, Intelligence, Systems and Applications (IISA)* (pp. 1-6). IEEE. DOI: 10.1109/IISA50023.2020.9284417

Nah, F. F. H., Zeng, Q., Telaprolu, V. R. A., Ayyappa, S., & Eschenbrenner, B. (2014). Gamification of education: a review of literature. *Proceedings of the 1st international conference on HCI in business*, 401-409. DOI: 10.1007/978-3-319-07293-7_39

Nandigam, D., Tirumala, S. S., & Tirumala, N. (2014). Personalized Learning: Current Status and Potential. *IEEE Conference on E-Learning, E-Management, and E-Services*. DOI:DOI: 10.1109/IC3e.2014.7081251

Nascimento, I. M. do. (2023). *UnplugGamify : a didactic material to support user-centered unplugged gamification.*

Nassaji, H. (2015). Qualitative and descriptive research: Data type versus data analysis. *Language Teaching Research*, 19(2), 129–132. DOI: 10.1177/1362168815572747

National Research Council. Division of Behavioral, Board on Behavioral, Sensory Sciences, Committee on Developments in the Science of Learning with additional material from the Committee on Learning Research, & Educational Practice. (2000). How people learn: Brain, mind, experience, and school: Expanded edition (Vol. 1). National Academies Press.

Naul, E., & Liu, M. (2020). Why story matters: a review of narrative in serious games.

Naul, E., & Liu, M. (2020, June). Why Story Matters: A Review of Narrative in Serious Games. *Journal of Educational Computing Research*, 58(3), 687–707. DOI: 10.1177/0735633119859904

Naveh-Benjamin, M., Craik, F. I. M., Guez, J., & Dori, H. (1998). Effects of divided attention on encoding and retrieval processes in human memory: Further support for an asymmetry. *Journal of Experimental Psychology. Learning, Memory, and Cognition*, 24(5), 1091–1104. DOI: 10.1037/0278-7393.24.5.1091 PMID: 9747524

Ng, D. T., Ng, E. H., & Chu, S. K. (2022). Engaging students in creative music making with musical instrument application in an online flipped classroom. *Education and Information Technologies*, 27(1), 45–64.

Ng, S. C., Lee, L. K., Lui, A. K. F., Wong, K. F., Chan, W. Y., & Tam, H. H. (2020). Using immersive reality in training nursing students. *International Journal of Innovation and Learning*, 27(3), 324–343. DOI: 10.1504/IJIL.2020.106815

Nguyen, L. A. T., & Habók, A. (2024). Tools for assessing teacher digital literacy: A review. *Journal of Computers in Education*, 11(1), 305–346. DOI: 10.1007/s40692-022-00257-5

Nielsen, J. (1993). *Usability engineering*. Morgan Kaufmann. DOI: 10.1016/B978-0-08-052029-2.50007-3

Nilsson, N. J. (2014). *Artificial intelligence: A new synthesis*. Morgan Kaufmann.

Niu, Z., Zhong, G., & Yu, H. (2021). A review on the attention mechanism of deep learning. *Neurocomputing*, 452, 48–62. DOI: 10.1016/j.neucom.2021.03.091

Noyes, J., Booth, A., Moore, G., Flemming, K., Tunçalp, Ö., & Shakibazadeh, E. (2019). Synthesising quantitative and qualitative evidence to inform guidelines on complex interventions: clarifying the purposes, designs and outlining some methods. *BMJ global health, 4*(Suppl 1).

Nusi, A., Dewirahmadanirwati, D., Novia, N., & Ardi, H. (2024). Factors and Challenges in Using Gamification In Teaching ESP. *Jurnal Ilmiah Pendidikan Scholastic, 8*(1), 15-25. https://e-journal.sastra-unes.com/index.php/JIPS

Nweke, L. O., & Wolthusen, S. (2020). A review of asset-centric threat modelling approaches.

Nyathani, R. (2023). Ai-driven hr analytics: Unleashing the power of hr data management. *Journal of Technology and Systems*, 5(2), 15–26. DOI: 10.47941/jts.1513

O'Sullivan, D., Stavrakakis, I., Gordon, D., Curley, A., Tierney, B., Murphy, E., Collins, M., & Becevel, A. (2021). "You Can't Lose a Game If You Don't Play the Game": Exploring the Ethics of Gamification in Education. *International Journal for Infonomics*, 14(1), 2035–2045. DOI: 10.20533/iji.1742.4712.2021.0211

Okada, A. (2012). Skill development for Youth in India:Challenges & Opportunities. *Kokusai Kyoiku Kyoryoku Ronshu*, •••, 169–193.

Okan, Z. (2011). Edutainment and learning. In Seel, N. M. (Ed.), *Encyclopedia of the Sciences of learning (pp. 1080e1082)*. Springer.

Okoro, E. (2012). Integrating social media technologies in higher education: Costs-benefits analysis. *Journal of International Education Research*, 8(3), 255–262. DOI: 10.19030/jier.v8i3.7107

Oliveira, W., Hamari, J., Joaquim, S., Toda, A. M., Palomino, P. T., Vassileva, J., & Isotani, S. (2022). The effects of personalized gamification on students' flow experience, motivation, and enjoyment. In *Smart Learning Environments* (Vol. 9, Issue 1). DOI: 10.1186/s40561-022-00194-x

Oliveira, W., Hamari, J., Shi, L., Toda, A. M., Rodrigues, L., Palomino, P. T., & Isotani, S. (2022). Tailored gamification in education : A literature review and future agenda. In *Education and Information Technologies* (Issue 0123456789). Springer US. DOI: 10.1007/s10639-022-11122-4

Oliveira, A., Feyzi Behnagh, R., Ni, L., Mohsinah, A. A., Burgess, K. J., & Guo, L. (2019). Emerging technologies as pedagogical tools for teaching and learning science: A literature review. *Human Behavior and Emerging Technologies*, 1(2), 149–160. https://doi.org/xx.xxx/yyyy. DOI: 10.1002/hbe2.141

Oliveira, W. M., Toda, A. T., Palomino, P., Rodrigues, L., & Isotani, S. (2020). Which one is the best? A quasi-experimental study comparing frameworks for unplugged gamification. *Renote*, 18(1). Advance online publication. DOI: 10.22456/1679-1916.105971

Onyema, E. M., Deborah, E. C., Alsayed, A. O., Noorulhasan, Q., & Sanober, S. (2019). Online discussion forum as a tool for interactive learning and communication. *International Journal of Recent Technology and Engineering*, 8(4), 4852–4859. DOI: 10.35940/ijrte.D8062.118419

Open, A. I. (2021). *ChatGPT*. https://chatgpt.com/

Ore, O., & Sposato, M. (2021). Opportunities and risks of artificial intelligence in recruitment and selection. *The International Journal of Organizational Analysis*, 30(6), 1771–1782. DOI: 10.1108/ijoa-07-2020-2291

Ortiz, S. A., Bowers, C., & Cannon-Bowers, J. (2015). Video game self-efficacy and its effect on training performance. International Journal of Serious Games, 2(3), 63e75.

Osheim, D. E. (2013). "THIS COULD BE A GAME!": DEFINING GAMIFICATION FOR THE CLASSROOM. *Journal of Chemical Information and Modeling*, 53(9), 1689–1699.

Osolase, E., Rasdi, R., & Mansor, Z. (2023). Developing awareness of green human resource development practices in the hotel industry. *Advances in Developing Human Resources*, 25(2), 116–122. DOI: 10.1177/15234223231155503

Oumaima, E., Abdelhak, C., & Youssef, S. (2023, December). Exploring social learning through virtual reality: How technology can enhance collaboration and learner engagement. In *2023 7th IEEE Congress on Information Science and Technology (CiSt)* (pp. 442-444). IEEE. https://doi.org/DOI: 10.1109/CiSt58110.2023.00103

Outeda, C. C. (2024). European Education Area and Digital Education Action Plan (2021–2027): One More Step Towards the Europeanisation of Education Policy. In *E-Governance in the European Union: Strategies, Tools, and Implementation* (pp. 187–206). Springer Nature Switzerland. DOI: 10.1007/978-3-031-56045-3_13

Paglen, T. (2019). Invisible Images: Your Pictures Are Looking at You. *Architectural Design*, 89(1), 22–27. DOI: 10.1002/ad.2383

Pan, X. (2023). Online learning environments, learners' empowerment, and learning behavioral engagement: The mediating role of learning

Pantic, I. (2014). Online social networking and mental health. *Cyberpsychology, Behavior, and Social Networking*, 17(10), 652–657. DOI: 10.1089/cyber.2014.0070 PMID: 25192305

Pan, Y., Coleman, L., Manago, S., & Goodof, D. (2019). Effects of social media usage on social integration of university students. *International Journal of Technology in Teaching and Learning*, 15(1), 1–17. DOI: 10.37120/ijttl.2019.15.1.01

Papanastasiou, G., Drigas, A., Skianis, C., Lytras, M., & Papanastasiou, E. (2019). Virtual and augmented reality effects on K-12, higher and tertiary education students' twenty-first century skills. *Virtual Reality (Waltham Cross)*, 23(4), 425–436. DOI: 10.1007/s10055-018-0363-2

Pardim, V. I., Contreras Pinochet, L. H., Viana, A. B. N., & Souza, C. A. (2023). Where is the student who was here? Gamification as a strategy to engage students. *The International Journal of Information and Learning Technology*, 40(2), 177–192. DOI: 10.1108/IJILT-05-2022-0122

Park, H. (2014). Memex and Beyond: A Design Trajectory from Vannevar Bush's Memex (Doctoral dissertation).

Park, B., Knörzer, L., Plass, J. L., & Brünken, R. (2015). Emotional design and positive emotions in multimedia learning: An eyetracking study on the use of anthropomorphisms. *Computers & Education*, 86, 30–42. DOI: 10.1016/j.compedu.2015.02.016

Park, B., Plass, J. L., & Brünken, R. (2014). Cognitive and affective processes in multimedia learning. *Learning and Instruction*, 29, 125–127. DOI: 10.1016/j.learninstruc.2013.05.005

Parks, M. (2018). The decline of arts education in the era of STEM: A critical analysis. *Arts Education Policy Review*, 119(2), 82–92.

Partovi, T., & Razavi, M. R. (2019). The effect of game-based learning on academic achievement motivation of elementary school students. *Learning and Motivation*, 68, 101592. DOI: 10.1016/j.lmot.2019.101592

Passalacqua, M., Sénécal, S., Frédette, M., Nacke, L. E., Pellerin, R., & Léger, P.-M. (2021). Should Gamification be Personalized? A Self- deterministic Approach. *AIS Transactions on Human-Computer Interaction*, 13(3), 265–286. DOI: 10.17705/1thci.00150

Patton, M. Q. (2002). Two decades of developments in qualitative inquiry. *Qualitative Social Work: Research and Practice*, 1(3), 261–283. DOI: 10.1177/1473325002001003636

Pedro, F., Subosa, M., Rivas, A., & Valverde, P. (2019). Artificial intelligence in education: Challenges and opportunities for sustainable development.

Pelegro, R. (2022). Gamification in Online Education. SSRN *Electronic Journal, January*. DOI: 10.2139/ssrn.4054977

Pellas, N., Fotaris, P., Kazanidis, I., & Wells, D. (2019). Augmenting the learning experience in primary and secondary school education: A systematic review of recent trends in augmented reality game-based learning. *Virtual Reality (Waltham Cross)*, 23(4), 329–346. https://surl.li/qxcdw. DOI: 10.1007/s10055-018-0347-2

Peng, D., & Yu, Z. (2022). A Literature Review of Digital Literacy over Two Decades. *Education Research International*, 2022, 1–8. DOI: 10.1155/2022/2533413

Pérez, J., Castro, M., & López, G. (2023). Serious games and ai: Challenges and opportunities for computational social science. *IEEE Access : Practical Innovations, Open Solutions*, 11, 62051–62061. DOI: 10.1109/ACCESS.2023.3286695

Pesout, O., & Nietfeld, J. L. (2021). How creative am I?: Examining judgments and predictors of creative performance. *Thinking Skills and Creativity*, 40, 100836. DOI: 10.1016/j.tsc.2021.100836

Petersen, G. B., Petkakis, G., & Makransky, G. (2022). A study of how immersion and interactivity drive VR learning. *Computers & Education*, 179, 104429. DOI: 10.1016/j.compedu.2021.104429

Petrides, L., & Ogawa, R. (2020). Integrating design thinking and arts education: Lessons from a cross-disciplinary approach. *Journal of Design Education*, 12(1), 45–63.

Pfeiffer, A., Bezzina, S., König, N., & Kriglstein, S. (2020). Beyond classical gamification: in-and around-game gamification for education.

Pfeuffer, N., Benlian, A., Gimpel, H., & Hinz, O. (2019). Anthropomorphic Information Systems. *Business & Information Systems Engineering*, 61(4), 523–533. DOI: 10.1007/s12599-019-00599-y

Pichai, S. (2023). *Google Gemini AI: A new era of intelligence.*

Pilz, M., & Regel, J. (2021). Vocational education and training in india: Prospects and challenges from an outside perspective. *Margin - the Journal of Applied Economic Research*, 15(1), 101–121. DOI: 10.1177/0973801020976606

Piovesan, S. D., Passerino, L. M., & Pereira, A. S. (2012). Virtual reality as a tool in the education. *International Association for Development of the Information Society*. https://www.researchgate.net/publication/292838721_Virtual_Reality_as_a_Tool_in_the_Education

Plano-Clark, V., & Ivankova, N. (2016). What is mixed methods research?: considering how mixed methods research is defined. In Plano-Clark, V., & Ivankova, N. (Eds.), *Mixed methods research: A guide to the field* (pp. 55–78). Sage., DOI: 10.4135/9781483398341.n6

Plass, J. L., Heidig, S., Hayward, E. O., Homer, B. D., & Um, E. (2014). Emotional design in multimedia learning: Effects of shape and color on affect and learning. *Learning and Instruction*, 29, 128–140. DOI: 10.1016/j.learninstruc.2013.02.006

Platonova, R. I., Orekhovskaya, N. A., Dautova, S. B., Martynenko, E. V., Kryukova, N. I., & Demir, S. (2022, July). Blended learning in Higher Education: Diversifying models and practical recommendations for researchers. [). Frontiers Media SA.]. *Frontiers in Education*, 7, 957199. DOI: 10.3389/feduc.2022.957199

Plein, C. (2021). AI-powered creativity: Exploring the implications of AI-driven tools for creative practice in the arts. *Leonardo*, 54(3), 275–283. DOI: 10.1162/leon_a_01953

Plucker, J. A., Beghetto, R. A., & Dow, G. T. (2004). Why Isn't Creativity More Important to Educational Psychologists? Potentials, Pitfalls, and Future Directions in Creativity Research. *Educational Psychologist*, 39(2), 83–96. DOI: 10.1207/s15326985ep3902_1

Pnevmatikos, D., Christodoulou, P., Georgiadou, T., & Lithoxoidou, A. (2023). Undergraduate students' conceptualization of critical thinking and their ideas for critical thinking acquisition. *Education Sciences*, 13(4), 416. DOI: 10.3390/educsci13040416

Pokrivcakova, S. (2019, December). Preparing teachers for the application of AI-powered technologies in foreign language education. *J. Lang. Cultural Edu.*, 7(3), 135–153. DOI: 10.2478/jolace-2019-0025

Polizzi, G. (2020). Digital literacy and the national curriculum for England: Learning from how the experts engage with and evaluate online content. *Computers & Education*, 152, 103859. DOI: 10.1016/j.compedu.2020.103859

Potteiger, B., Martins, G., & Koutsoukos, X. (2016, April). Software and attack-centric integrated threat modeling for quantitative risk assessment. In **Proceedings of the Symposium and Bootcamp on the Science of Security** (pp. 99-108). DOI: 10.1145/2898375.2898390

Potyrała, K., & Tomczyk, Ł. (2021). Teachers in the lifelong learning process: Examples of digital literacy. *Journal of Education for Teaching*, 47(2), 255–273. DOI: 10.1080/02607476.2021.1876499

Powell, S., & MacNeill, S. (2012). Institutional readiness for analytics. *Cetis Anal. Ser.*, 1, 1–11.

Pradel, M., & Sen, K. (2018). Deepbugs: A learning approach to name-based bug detection. *Proceedings of the ACM on Programming Languages, 2*(OOPSLA), 1–25. DOI: 10.1145/3276517

Prakash, B. V. A., Ashoka, D. V, & Aradya, V. N. M. (2015). Application of data mining techniques for defect detection and classification. *Advances in Intelligent Systems and Computing*, 387–395. DOI: 10.1007/978-3-319-11933-5_42

Prayogo, A., Khotimah, K., Istiqomah, L., & Maharsi, I. (2024). Students' emotional engagement in online classes: A conceptual framework. *International Journal of Information and Learning Technology*, 41(1), 61–72. DOI: 10.1108/IJILT-04-2023-0052

Prensky, M. (2003). Digital game-based learning. Computers in entertainment (CIE), 1(1), 21-21.

Price, C. B. (2008). Unreal PowerPointTM: Immersing PowerPoint presentations in a virtual computer game engine world. *Computers in Human Behavior*, 24(6), 2486–2495. DOI: 10.1016/j.chb.2008.03.009

Psaltis, A., Apostolakis, K. C., Dimitropoulos, K., & Daras, P. (2018). Multimodal Student Engagement Recognition in Prosocial Games. *IEEE Transactions on Games*, 10(3), 292–303. DOI: 10.1109/TCIAIG.2017.2743341

Puente-Diaz, R., & Cavazos-Arroyo, J. (2018). Creative Metacognitive Feelings as a Source of Information for Creative Self-efficacy, Creativity Potential, Intrapersonal Idea Selection, and Task Enjoyment. *The Journal of Creative Behavior*, 54(3), 499–507. DOI: 10.1002/jocb.384

Puente-Díaz, R., Cavazos-Arroyo, J., Puerta-Sierra, L., & Vargas-Barrera, F. (2022). The contribution Openness to Experience and its two aspects to the explanation of idea generation, evaluation and selection: A metacognitive perspective. *Personality and Individual Differences*, 185, 111240. DOI: 10.1016/j.paid.2021.111240

Puente-Díaz, R., Cavazos-Arroyo, J., & Vargas-Barrera, F. (2021). Metacognitive feelings as a source of information in the evaluation and selection of creative ideas. *Thinking Skills and Creativity*, 39, 100767. DOI: 10.1016/j.tsc.2020.100767

Pulido, C. M., Redondo-Sama, G., Sorde-Marti, T., & Flecha, R. (2018). Social impact in social media: A new method to evaluate the social impact of research. *PLoS One*, 13(8), e0203117. DOI: 10.1371/journal.pone.0203117 PMID: 30157262

Purba, F. A., & Katemba, C. V. (2022). English Teachers Perception of Using Game-Based Learning (GBL) to Enhance Students' Vocabulary. *8ISC Proceedings: Arts and Education*, 35-46.

Purnama, Y., & Asdlori, A. (2023). The role of social media in students' social perception and interaction: Implications for learning and education. *Technology and Society Perspectives*, 1(2), 45–55. DOI: 10.61100/tacit.v1i2.50

Putz, L. M., Hofbauer, F., & Treiblmaier, H. (2020). Can gamification help to improve education? Findings from a longitudinal study. *Computers in Human Behavior*, 110(April), 106392. DOI: 10.1016/j.chb.2020.106392

Qiusi, M. (2022). Research on the improvement method of music education level under the background of AI technology. *Mobile Information Systems*, 2022(1), 7616619. DOI: 10.1155/2022/7616619

Qiu, Y. (2020). Education Informationization. *Proceedings of the 2020 6th International Conference on Education and Training Technologies* (pp. 40–43). New York, NY, USA: ACM. DOI: 10.1145/3399971.3399978

Quaicoe, J. S., & Pata, K. (2020). Teachers' digital literacy and digital activity as digital divide components among basic schools in Ghana. *Education and Information Technologies*, 25(5), 4077–4095. DOI: 10.1007/s10639-020-10158-8

Quraishi, T.Helena ULUSIAsma MUHIDMusawer HAKIMIMohammad Reshad OLUSI. (2024). Empowering students through digital literacy: A case study of successful integration in a higher education curriculum. *Journal of Digital Learning and Distance Education*, 2(9), 667–681. DOI: 10.56778/jdlde.v2i8.208

Qu, S. L., Yang, J. J., & Xie, Z. H. (2023). The application of project teaching methods in the teaching of environmental art design in colleges and universities. *Journal of Shanxi University of Finance and Economics*, S1, 181–183.

Radianti, J., Majchrzak, T. A., Fromm, J., & Wohlgenannt, I. (2020). A systematic review of immersive virtual reality applications for higher education: Design elements, lessons learned, and research agenda. *Computers & Education*, 147, 103778. DOI: 10.1016/j.compedu.2019.103778

Rafiq, A. A., Triyono, M. B., & Djatmiko, I. W. (2022). Enhancing student engagement in vocational education by using virtual reality. *Waikato Journal of Education*, 27(3), 175–188. DOI: 10.15663/wje.v27i3.964

Rajesh, D., & Priya, V. K. (2020). Impact of Social Media on Mental Health of Students. *International Journal of Scientific & Technology Research*, 9(3), 3796–3800.

Ramírez-Montoya, M.S., & Lugo-Ocando, J. (2020). Systematic Review of Mixed Methods in the

Ravindran, T., Kuan, Y., Chua, A., & Hoe Lian, D. G. (2014). Antecedents and effects of social network fatigue. *Journal of the Association for Information Science and Technology*, 65(11), 2306–2320. DOI: 10.1002/asi.23122

Ray, B., Posnett, D., Filkov, V., & Devanbu, P. (2014). A large scale study of programming languages and code quality in github. *Proceedings of the 22nd ACM SIGSOFT International Symposium on Foundations of Software Engineering*, 155–165. DOI: 10.1145/2635868.2635922

Redondo, R. P. D., Ktena, A., Kunicina, N., Zabasta, A., Patlins, A., & Mele, D. E. (2020, November). Advanced practices: micro learning, practice oriented teaching and gamified learning. In 2020 IEEE 61th International Scientific Conference on Power and Electrical Engineering of Riga Technical University (RTUCON) (pp. 1-7). IEEE. DOI: 10.1109/RTUCON51174.2020.9316555

Reid, J. M. (1995). *Learning Styles in the ESL/EFL Classroom*. Heinle & Heinle Publishers.

Ren, D. (2024). Research on the application of computer music technology in solfeggio teaching in universities. *International Journal of Social Sciences and Public Administration*, 2(1), 200–207. DOI: 10.62051/ijsspa.v2n1.26

Renkl, A., & Scheiter, K. (2017). Studying Visual Displays: How to Instructionally Support Learning. *Educational Psychology Review*, 29(3), 599–621. DOI: 10.1007/s10648-015-9340-4

Resnick, M. (2004). Edutainment? No thanks. I prefer playful learning. Associazione civita report on edutainment.

Reyes, V. C.Jr, Reading, C., Doyle, H., & Gregory, S. (2017). Integrating ICT into teacher education programs from a TPACK perspective: Exploring perceptions of university lecturers. *Computers & Education*, 115, 1–19. DOI: 10.1016/j.compedu.2017.07.009

Riady, Y., Alqahtany, T. M., Habibi, A., Sofyan, S., & Albelbisi, N. A. (2022). Factors affecting teachers' social media use during covid-19. *Cogent Social Sciences*, 8(1), 2115658. Advance online publication. DOI: 10.1080/23311886.2022.2115658

Ricci, F., Shapira, B., & Rokach, L. (2015). Recommender systems handbook, Second edition. In *Recommender Systems Handbook, Second Edition*. DOI: 10.1007/978-1-4899-7637-6

Richardson, C., & Mishra, P. (2018). Learning environments that support student creativity: Developing the SCALE. *Thinking Skills and Creativity*, 27, 45–54. DOI: 10.1016/j.tsc.2017.11.004

Ridzaimi, S. (2022). *Education Minister: Schools to continue banning smartphones to curb gaming addiction among students*. TechNave. https://technave.com/gadget/Education-Minister-Schools-to-continue-banning-smartphones-to-curb-gaming-addiction-among-students-29174.html

Rigley, E. (2023). Evaluating international ai skills policy: A systematic review of ai skills policy in seven countries. *Global Policy*, 15(1), 204–217. DOI: 10.1111/1758-5899.13299

Riopel, M., Nenciovici, L., Potvin, P., Chastenay, P., Charland, P., Sarrasin, J. B., & Masson, S. (2019). Impact of serious games on science learning achievement compared with more conventional instruction: An overview and a meta-analysis. *Studies in Science Education*, 55(2), 169–214. DOI: 10.1080/03057267.2019.1722420

Ritterfeld, U., & Weber, R. (2006). Video games for entertainment and education. In Vorderer, P., & Bryant, J. (Eds.), *Playing video games: Motives, responses, and consequences* (pp. 399–413). Lawrence Erlbaum Associates.

Ritter, S. M., Damian, R. I., Simonton, D. K., van Baaren, R. B., Strick, M., Derks, J., & Dijksterhuis, A. (2012). Diversifying experiences enhance cognitive flexibility☆. *Journal of Experimental Social Psychology*, 48(4), 961–964. DOI: 10.1016/j.jesp.2012.02.009

Rivera, E. S., & Garden, C. L. P. (2021). Gamification for student engagement: A framework. *Journal of Further and Higher Education*, 45(7), 999–1012. DOI: 10.1080/0309877X.2021.1875201

Robinson, C. C., & Hullinger, H. (2008). New benchmarks in higher education: Student engagement in online learning. *Journal of Education for Business*, 84(2), 101–109. DOI: 10.3200/JOEB.84.2.101-109

Rodrigues, L., Toda, A. M., Oliveira, W., Palomino, P. T., Avila-Santos, A. P., & Isotani, S. (2021). Gamification Works, but How and to Whom?: An Experimental Study in the Context of Programming Lessons. *SIGCSE 2021 - Proceedings of the 52nd ACM Technical Symposium on Computer Science Education, March*, 184–190. DOI: 10.1145/3408877.3432419

Rodrigues, L., Palomino, P. T., Toda, A. M., Klock, A. C. T., Oliveira, W., Avila-Santos, A. P., Gasparini, I., & Isotani, S. (2021). Personalization Improves Gamification: Evidence from a Mixed-methods Study. *Proceedings of the ACM on Human-Computer Interaction, 5*(CHIPLAY). DOI: 10.1145/3474714

Rodrigues, L., Toda, A. M., Oliveira dos Santos, W., Palomino, P. T., Vassileva, J., & Isotani, S. (2022). Automating Gamification Personalization to the User and Beyond. *IEEE Transactions on Learning Technologies*, 15(2), 1–1. DOI: 10.1109/TLT.2022.3162409

Roll, I., & Wylie, R. (2016). Evolution and Revolution in Artificial Intelligence in Education. [Springer New York LLC.]. *International Journal of Artificial Intelligence in Education*, 26(2), 582–599. DOI: 10.1007/s40593-016-0110-3

Rominger, C., Benedek, M., Lebuda, I., Perchtold-Stefan, C. M., Schwerdtfeger, A. R., Papousek, I., & Fink, A. (2022). Functional brain activation patterns of creative metacognitive monitoring. *Neuropsychologia*, 177, 108416. DOI: 10.1016/j.neuropsychologia.2022.108416 PMID: 36343705

Rosenthal, S., & Ratan, R. A. (2022). Balancing learning and enjoyment in serious games: Kerbal Space Program and the communication mediation model. *Computers & Education*, 182, 104480. DOI: 10.1016/j.compedu.2022.104480

Ruiz-Cantisani, M. I., del Carmen Lima-Sagui, F., Aceves-Campos, N., Ipiña-Sifuentes, R., & Flores, E. G. R. (2020, April). Virtual reality as a tool for active learning and student engagement: Industrial engineering experience. In *2020 IEEE Global Engineering Education Conference (EDUCON)* (pp. 1031-1037). IEEE. DOI: 10.1109/EDUCON45650.2020.9125225

Runco, M. A., & Acar, S. (2012). Divergent Thinking as an Indicator of Creative Potential. *Creativity Research Journal*, 24(1), 66–75. DOI: 10.1080/10400419.2012.652929

Runco, M. A., & Dow, G. T. (2004). Assessing the Accuracy of Judgments of Originality on Three Divergent Thinking Tests. *Korean Journal of Thinking & Problem Solving*, 14(2), 5–14.

Runco, M. A., & Smith, W. R. (1992). Interpersonal and intrapersonal evaluations of creative ideas. *Personality and Individual Differences*, 13(3), 295–302. DOI: 10.1016/0191-8869(92)90105-X

Russell, S., & Norvig, P. (2022). Artificial intelligence: A modern approach (4th esd.).

Ryan, R. M., & Deci, E. L. (2000). Self-determination Theory and the Facilitation of Intrinsic Motivation, Social Development, and Well-Being. *The American Psychologist*, 55(1), 68–78. DOI: 10.1037/0003-066X.55.1.68 PMID: 11392867

Ryan, R. M., & Deci, E. L. (2020). Intrinsic and extrinsic motivation from a self-determination theory perspective: Definitions, theory, practices, and future directions. *Contemporary Educational Psychology*, 61, 101860. DOI: 10.1016/j.cedpsych.2020.101860

Sabet, S. (2020). Composing with mobile technology: High school students and garageband for iPad. *Journal of Popular Music Education*, 4(3), 349–369. Advance online publication. DOI: 10.1386/jpme_00032_1

Sadkoğlu, E., Gök, M., & Mjwl, M. M., & Kösesoy, \.Irfan. (2023). The Evolution and Impact of Large Language Model Chatbots in Social Media: A Comprehensive Review of Past, Present, and Future Applications. *Veri Bilimi*, 6(2), 67–76.

Saha, M., Islam, S., Akhi, A. A., & Saha, G. (2024). Factors affecting success and failure in higher education mathematics: Students' and teachers' perspectives. *Heliyon*, 10(7), e29173. DOI: 10.1016/j.heliyon.2024.e29173 PMID: 38601642

Sainil, C., & Abraham, J. (2015). Using Social Media for Educational Purposes: Approaches and Challenges. *International Education Conference 2015 on Learning Technologies in Education,* Excel India Publishers, 484-489.

Saini, N., & Mir, S. A. (2023). Social media: Usage and the impact on Education. *Journal of Namibian Studies*, 33(3), 4670–4689. DOI: 10.59670/jns.v33i.4041

Saleem, A. N., Noori, N. M., & Ozdamli, F. (2021). Gamification Applications in E-learning: A Literature Review. *Technology. Knowledge and Learning*, 0123456789. Advance online publication. DOI: 10.1007/s10758-020-09487-x

Salles, A., Evers, K., & Farisco, M. (2020). Anthropomorphism in AI. *AJOB Neuroscience*, 11(2), 88–95. DOI: 10.1080/21507740.2020.1740350 PMID: 32228388

Samarasinghe, R., Hettiarachchi, T., & Adihetti, I. (2023). Examining Teacher Perspectives on the Use of Gamification Within Classrooms to Enhance Student Engagement. *Journal of Physical Education and Sport*, 121(2), 482–491. DOI: 10.7752/jpes.2023.02060

Sampasa-Kanyinga, H., & Lewis, R. F. (2015). Frequent use of social networking sites is associated with poor psychological functioning among children and adolescents. *Cyberpsychology, Behavior, and Social Networking*, 18(7), 380–385. DOI: 10.1089/cyber.2015.0055 PMID: 26167836

Sandí Delgado, J. C., & Bazán, P. A. (2021). Diseño de juegos serios: Análisis de metodologías. *E-Ciencias de la Información*, 11(2), 80–106. DOI: 10.15517/eci.v11i2.45505

Sanmugam, M. (2021). Sustainability and Aptness of Game Elements in A Gamified Learning Environment. *2021 9th International Conference on Information and Communication Technology, ICoICT 2021*, 500–505. DOI: 10.1109/ICoICT52021.2021.9527499

Sanmugam, M., Abdullah, Z., & Zaid, N M. (2014, December 1). Gamification: Cognitive impact and creating a meaningful experience in learning. DOI: 10.1109/ICEED.2014.7194700

Sanmugam, M., Zaid, N M., Abdullah, Z., Aris, B., Mohamed, H., & Meijden, H V D. (2016, December 1). The impacts of infusing game elements and gamification in learning. DOI: 10.1109/ICEED.2016.7856058

Sanmugam, M., Mohamed, H., Zaid, N. M., Abdullah, Z., Aris, B., & Suhadi, S. M. (2015). Implementation of Gamification as an educative tool via online and offline methods; an analyses review. *1st International Conference On Educational Studies (ICES-2015), July.*

Santos, A. C. G., Oliveira, W., Hamari, J., & Isotani, S. (2021). Do people's user types change over time? An exploratory study. *CEUR Workshop Proceedings*, 2883, 90–99.

Santos, P. A. (2015). Deep Gamification of a University Course. *Conference Proceedings SciTecIN'15 Sciences and Technologies of Interaction 12-13 November 2015 Coimbra, Portugal*, 1–5.

Sarkar, S. K., Podder, A., & Roy, P. (2023). An Analysis of the Privacy and Security Related Problem with Social Networks.

Sarkar, S. K., Roy, P., Ghosh, S., Podder, A., & Paul, S. (2024). Impact of Frequency and Consistency in Preparing Students for Career Paths. In *Preparing Students From the Academic World to Career Paths: A Comprehensive Guide* (pp. 267–292). IGI Global. DOI: 10.4018/978-1-7998-7999-2.ch012

Sarma, G. P., & Hay, N. J. (2017). Robust Computer Algebra, Theorem Proving, and Oracle AI. SSRN *Electronic Journal*. DOI: 10.2139/ssrn.3038545

Sarthou, N. F. (2016). Key Points of Discussion in Scientific Research Evaluation: Peer Review, Bibliometrics and Relevance. *Revista de Estudios Sociales*, 58(58), 76–86. DOI: 10.7440/res58.2016.06

Schimanke, F., Mertens, R., & Huck, B. S. (2019). Player types in mobile learning games – Playing patterns and motivation. *Proceedings - 2018 IEEE International Symposium on Multimedia, ISM 2018, June 2019*, 247–252. DOI: 10.1109/ISM.2018.00035

Schmidt, S. J. (2009). Development and Use of Visual Explanations: Harnessing the Power of the "Seeing" Brain to Enhance Student Learning. *Journal of Food Science Education*, 8(3), 68–72. DOI: 10.1111/j.1541-4329.2009.00076.x

Schneider, S., Nebel, S., Beege, M., & Rey, G. D. (2018). Anthropomorphism in decorative pictures: Benefit or harm for learning? *Journal of Educational Psychology*, 110(2), 218–232. DOI: 10.1037/edu0000207

Schneider, S., Wirzberger, M., & Rey, G. D. (2019). The moderating role of arousal on the seductive detail effect in a multimedia learning setting. *Applied Cognitive Psychology*, 33(1), 71–84. DOI: 10.1002/acp.3473

Schöbel, S., Schmidt-Kraepelin, M., Janson, A., & Sunyaev, A. (2021). Adaptive and Personalized Gamification Designs: Call for Action and Future Research. *AIS Transactions on Human-Computer Interaction*, 13(4), 479–494. DOI: 10.17705/1thci.00158

Schrader, D. E. (2015). Constructivism and Learning in the Age of Social Media: Changing Minds and Learning Communities. *New Directions for Teaching and Learning*, 144(144), 23–35. DOI: 10.1002/tl.20160

Schrock, A. R. (2015). Communicative affordances of mobile media: Portability, availability, locatability, and multimediality. *International Journal of Communication*, 9, 18. https://api.semanticscholar.org/CorpusID:31064350

Selwyn, N. (2019). Should robots replace teachers? AI and the future of education. *Polity*.

Serice, L. (2023). Prisms of Neuroscience. *Frameworks for Thinking About Educational Gamification.*, (March), 1–30.

Shah, H., Warwick, K., Vallverdú, J., & Wu, D. (2016). Can machines talk? Comparison of Eliza with modern dialogue systems. *Computers in Human Behavior*, 58, 278–295. DOI: 10.1016/j.chb.2016.01.004

Shangguan, C., Gong, S., Guo, Y., Wang, X., & Lu, J. (2020). The effects of emotional design on middle school students' multimedia learning: The role of learners' prior knowledge. *Educational Psychology*, 40(9), 1076–1093. DOI: 10.1080/01443410.2020.1714548

Sharma, B. P. (2022). Digital Tools in Art Education: From Expanding Creative Horizons and Facilitating Collaboration to Increasing Access and Resources for a Diverse Student Population. *Applied Research in Artificial Intelligence and Cloud Computing*, 5(1), 55–65.

Sharma, H. (2018). Skill development policies in india: Implications and challenges. *Journal of Social and Development Sciences*, 8(4), 43–50. DOI: 10.22610/jevr.v8i4.2159

Shepherd, H., & Lane, J. (2019). In the mix: Social integration and social media adoption. *Social Science Research*, 82, 1–17. DOI: 10.1016/j.ssresearch.2019.02.004 PMID: 31300070

Sheshadri, S., Pradeep, A., & Chandran, M. (2021). Towards gender inclusive skill development in rural India: Factors that inhibit and facilitate skill women's enrolment in vocational training. *Environment-Behaviour Proceedings Journal*, 6(SI4), 239–243. DOI: 10.21834/ebpj.v6isi4.3032

Shrotriya, S., & Dhir, S. (2018). Innovation driven ecosystem for quality skill development in India. *Benchmarking*, 25(8), 2997–3020.

Siddiqui, S. & Singh, T. (2016). Social Media Its Impact with Positive and Negative Aspects. International Journal of Computer Applications Technology and Research, 5(2), 71-75.

Siddiqui, S. T., Fakhreldin, M., & Alam, S. (2021, August). Blockchain technology for IoT based educational framework and credentials. In 2021 International Conference on Software Engineering & Computer Systems and 4th International Conference on Computational Science and Information Management (ICSECS-ICOCSIM) (pp. 194-199). IEEE. DOI: 10.1109/ICSECS52883.2021.00042

Sidi, Y., Torgovitsky, I., Soibelman, D., Miron-Spektor, E., & Ackerman, R. (2020). You may be more original than you think: Predictable biases in self-assessment of originality. *Acta Psychologica*, 203, 103002. DOI: 10.1016/j.actpsy.2019.103002 PMID: 32004640

Siko, J. P., & Barbour, M. K. (2012). Homemade PowerPoint Games: Game Design Pedagogy Aligned to the TPACK Framework. *Computers in the Schools*, 29(4), 339–354. DOI: 10.1080/07380569.2012.734430

Sillaots, M., Jesmin, T., Fiadotau, M., & Khulbe, M. (2020). Gamifying classroom presentations: Evaluating the effects on engagement across demographic factors. *Proceedings of the 14th International Conference on Game Based Learning, ECGBL 2020, September*, 537–546. https://doi.org/DOI: 10.34190/GBL.20.105

Silvola, A., Näykki, P., Kaveri, A., & Muukkonen, H. (2021). Expectations for supporting student engagement with learning analytics: An academic path perspective. *Computers & Education*, 168, 104192. DOI: 10.1016/j.compedu.2021.104192

Simões, J., Redondo, R P D., & Vilas, A F. (2013, March 1). A social gamification framework for a K-6 learning platform. Elsevier BV, 29(2), 345-353. https://doi.org/ DOI: 10.1016/j.chb.2012.06.007

Sims, J. G., & Hampson, G. (2018). AI in architecture: Tools for creative design. *Design Studies*, 54(2), 26–38.

Singh, A. (2024). Artificial intelligence adoption in extended hr ecosystems: Enablers and barriers. an abductive case research. *Frontiers in Psychology*, 14. Advance online publication. DOI: 10.3389/fpsyg.2023.1339782

Singh, S. (2020). Emergence of Skill Universities in India. In *Emerging Issues in Business Management* (pp. 133–138). National Press Associates.

Singleton, T. (2022). *China claims youth gaming addiction resolved.* BBC News. https://www.bbc.com/news/technology-63730316

Sion, L., Yskout, K., Van Landuyt, D., & Joosen, W. (2018). Solution-aware data flow diagrams for security threat modeling. In **Proceedings of the 33rd Annual ACM Symposium on Applied Computing** (pp. 1425-1432). DOI: 10.1145/3167132.3167285

Siswantoro, M. Z. F. N., & Yuhana, U. L. (2023). Software defect prediction based on optimized machine learning models: A comparative study. *Teknika*, 12(2), 166–172. DOI: 10.34148/teknika.v12i2.634

Skinner, E. A., & Belmont, M. J. (1993). Motivation in the classroom: Reciprocal effects of teacher behavior and student engagement across the school year. *Journal of Educational Psychology*, 85(3), 571–581. DOI: 10.1037/0022-0663.85.4.571

Slabbert, C., De Lange, R. W., & Mason, H. (2022). Anthropomorphisms in multimedia learning: Do they facilitate learning in primary school learners? *Cogent Education*, 9(1), 2034390. DOI: 10.1080/2331186X.2022.2034390

Smith, C. (2022). *Understanding Middle School Teachers' Use of Instructional Practices for Online Reading Comprehension* (Doctoral dissertation, Walden University).

Snethen, G., & Zook, P. (2016). Utilizing social media to support community integration. *American Journal of Psychiatric Rehabilitation*, 19(2), 160–174. DOI: 10.1080/15487768.2016.1171176

Söbke, H. (2019). A case study of deep gamification in higher engineering education. *Lecture Notes in Computer Science (Including Subseries Lecture Notes in Artificial Intelligence and Lecture Notes in Bioinformatics), 11385 LNCS*(December 2018), 375–386. DOI: 10.1007/978-3-030-11548-7_35

Song, L., Shi, J., Luo, P., Wei, W., Fang, Y., & Wang, Y. (2020). More Time Spent, More Job Search Success?: The Moderating Roles of Metacognitive Activities and Perceived Job Search Progress. *Journal of Career Assessment*, 28(1), 147–164. DOI: 10.1177/1069072719841575

Song, P., & Wang, X. (2020). A bibliometric analysis of worldwide educational artificial intelligence research development in recent twenty years. *Asia Pacific Education Review*, 21(3), 473–486. DOI: 10.1007/s12564-020-09640-2

Song, T. W. (2019). This paper discusses the innovation of digital media art teaching mode. *Da Guan*, 12, 113–114.

Song, W., Gan, L., & Bao, T. (2024). Software defect prediction via generative adversarial networks and pre-trained model. *International Journal of Advanced Computer Science and Applications*, 15(3). Advance online publication. DOI: 10.14569/IJACSA.2024.01503119

Soslau, E., & Bell, N. (2018). The Challenges of Supporting Equity Literacy Skill Development in White Teacher Candidates: A Self-Study of Two White Field Instructors, Studying Teacher Education. *Studying Teacher Education*, •••, 156–173.

Stapleton, A. J. (2004, December). Serious games: Serious opportunities. In *Australian Game Developers" Conference*. Academic Summit.

Stárková, T., Lukavský, J., Javora, O., & Brom, C. (2019). Anthropomorphisms in multimedia learning: Attract attention but do not enhance learning? *Journal of Computer Assisted Learning*, 35(4), 555–568. DOI: 10.1111/jcal.12359

Stott, A., & Neustaedter, C. (2013). Analysis of gamification in education. *Surrey, BC, Canada, 8*(1), 36.

Streets, M. (2023). The history and evolution of social media explained. techtarget.com

Strickland, J. How Virtual Reality Military Applications Work. Available online: howstuffworks.com/virtual-military (accessed on 15 April 2021).

Su, J., & Yang, W. (2023). Unlocking the power of ChatGPT: A framework for applying generative AI in education. *ECNU Review of Education*, 209653112311684. Advance online publication. DOI: 10.1177/20965311231168423

Sun, C., Yao, Y., Wang, R., & Ye, X. (2020, June). A study on the influence of scene reality of VR environment on English learners' learning engagement and learning effectiveness. In *2020 IEEE 2nd International Conference on Computer Science and Educational Informatization (CSEI)* (pp. 181-185). IEEE. https://doi.org/DOI: 10.1109/CSEI49390.2020.00044

Sun, Y. J. (2021). *Research on immersive scene design of digital media art* (Doctoral dissertation, Chinese National Academy of Arts). DOI: 10.27653/d.cnki.gzysy.2021.000013

Sundar, S. S., & Marathe, S. S. (2010). Personalization versus customization: The importance of agency, privacy, and power usage. *Human Communication Research*, 36(3), 298–322. DOI: 10.1111/j.1468-2958.2010.01377.x

Sun, F. R., Pan, L. F., Wan, R. G., Li, H., & Wu, S. J. (2021). Detecting the effect of student engagement in an SVVR school-based course on higher level competence development in elementary schools by SEM. *Interactive Learning Environments*, 29(1), 3–16. DOI: 10.1080/10494820.2018.1558258

Sun, X., Yue, L., & Li, S. (2020). Digital Literacy in the Era of Globalization: Connotation and evaluation. *World Education Information*, (08), 13–17.

Surameery, N. M. S., & Shakor, M. Y. (2023). Use Chat GPT to Solve Programming Bugs. [IJITC]. *International Journal of Information Technology & Computer Engineering*, 3(01), 17–22. DOI: 10.55529/ijitc.31.17.22

Sweeny, R. W., & Mason, C. L. (2019). Digital media in art education: Prospects and challenges. *Journal of Art & Design Education*, 38(2), 148–159.

Tabachnick, B. G., Fidell, L. S., & Ullman, J. B. (2013). Using multivariate statistics (Vol. 6, pp. 497-516). Boston, MA: pearson.

Taipe, M. S. A., Pesántez, D. Á., Rivera, L., & Vizueta, D. O. (2017). Juegos serios en el proceso de aprendizaje. *UTCiencia*, 4(2), 111–122.

Tang, K., Zhang, Y., & Xia, S. (2024). Software defect prediction and automatic repair based on machine learning. *Highlights in Science. Engineering and Technology*, 98, 439–443. DOI: 10.54097/cwfckw19

Tang, T., Li, P., & Tang, Q. (2022). New Strategies and Practices of Design Education Under the Background of Artificial Intelligence Technology: Online Animation Design Studio. *Frontiers in Psychology*, 13, 767295. DOI: 10.3389/fpsyg.2022.767295 PMID: 35651576

Tan, Z. P. (2023). Discussion on the reform and optimization strategy of art design teaching methods in higher vocational colleges. *Journal of Harbin Vocational Technical College*, 02, 37–39. DOI: 10.16145/j.cnki.cn23-1531/z.2023.02.012

Tariq, W., Mehboob, M., Khan, M. A., & Ullah, F. (2012)... *International Journal of Computational Science*, 9(4), 407–411.

Taylor, K. (2024). The Digital Divide: What It Is, and What's Being Done to Close It. The Digital Divide: What It Is, and What's Being Done to Close It. investopedia.com

Tess, P. A. (2013). The role of social media in higher education classes (real and virtual)–A literature review. *Computers in Human Behavior*, 29(5), A60–A68. DOI: 10.1016/j.chb.2012.12.032

Thanavath, C. (2020). Digital tools with inclusive education. *Inclusive Education*, International Research Foundations, Konchnadu Publications, 320-326.

Thomas, A., & Gupta, V. (2022). The role of motivation theories in knowledge sharing: An integrative theoretical reviews and future research agenda. *Kybernetes*, 51(1), 116–140. DOI: 10.1108/K-07-2020-0465

Tibaldi, A., Bonali, F. L., Vitello, F., Delage, E., Nomikou, P., Antoniou, V., Becciani, U., de Vries, B. V. W., Krokos, M., & Whitworth, M. (2020). Real world–based immersive Virtual Reality for research, teaching and communication in volcanology. *Bulletin of Volcanology*, 82(5), 1–12. DOI: 10.1007/s00445-020-01376-6

Ting, T. (2021). Master's Degree in the Construction and Application of Digital Literacy Evaluation Model for Higher Vocational Students (Dissertation, Guangdong Technical Normal University). Master of https://link.cnki.net/doi/10.27729/d.cnki.ggdjs.2021.000067doi:10.27729/d.cnki.ggdjs.2021.000067

Tinmaz, H., Lee, Y. T., Fanea-Ivanovici, M., & Baber, H. (2022). A systematic review on digital literacy. *Smart Learning Environments*, 9(1), 21. DOI: 10.1186/s40561-022-00204-y

Tıraşın, K. D. (2023). *Games Teachers Play: An investigation of upper secondary EFL teachers' practices, beliefs, and attitudes regarding digital game-based language learning in Norway* (Master's thesis, University of Stavanger, Norway).

Toda, A. M., Klock, A. C. T., Oliveira, W., Palomino, P. T., Rodrigues, L., Shi, L., Bittencourt, I., Gasparini, I., Isotani, S., & Cristea, A. I. (2019). Analysing gamification elements in educational environments using an existing Gamification taxonomy. In *Smart Learning Environments* (Vol. 6, Issue 1). DOI: 10.1186/s40561-019-0106-1

Toda, A. M., do Carmo, R. M. C., da Silva, A. P., Bittencourt, I. I., & Isotani, S. (2019). An approach for planning and deploying gamification concepts with social networks within educational contexts. *International Journal of Information Management*, 46(May), 294–303. DOI: 10.1016/j.ijinfomgt.2018.10.001

Torrance, E. P. (1974). Differences Are Not Deficits. *Teachers College Record*, 75(4), 1–14. DOI: 10.1177/016146817407500403 transformation in project management education? Lessons learned from 10 Years of

Trowler, V. (2010). Student engagement literature review. *Higher Education Academy*. https://www.heacademy.ac.uk/system/files/student_engagement_literature_review.pdf

Tseng, H. (2022). Patterns of basic knowledge. *iScience*, 25(2), 103803. DOI: 10.1016/j.isci.2022.103803 PMID: 35198869

Tuamsuk, K., & Subramaniam, M. (2017). The current state and influential factors in the development of digital literacy in Thailand's higher education. *Information and Learning Science*, 118(5/6), 235251. DOI: 10.1108/ILS-11-2016-0076

Tuomi, I. (2018). *The Impact of Artificial Intelligence on Learning, Teaching, and Education. Policies for the future*. EUR - Scientific and Technical Research Reports.

Turnbull, D., Chugh, R., & Luck, J. (2020). Learning management systems, an overview. Encyclopedia of education and information technologies, 1052-1058. DOI: 10.1007/978-3-030-10576-1_248

UcedaVelez. T., & Morana, M. M. (2015). Risk Centric Threat Modeling: process for attack simulation and threat analysis. John Wiley & Sons.

Uddiniyah, N. D., & Silfia, E. (2020). An analysis of students' motivation in learning English at SMAN 8 Kota Jambi academic year 2018/2019. JELT. *Journal of English Language Teaching*, 3(2), 139–149.

Ullah, M., Amin, S. U., Munsif, M., Yamin, M. M., Safaev, U., Khan, H., Khan, S., & Ullah, H. (2022). Serious games in science education: A systematic literature. *Virtual Reality & Intelligent Hardware*, 4(3), 189–209. DOI: 10.1016/j.vrih.2022.02.001

Uludağ, A. K., & Satir, U. K. (2023). Seeking alternatives in music education: The effects of mobile technologies on students' achievement in basic music theory. *International Journal of Music Education*, 02557614231196972. Advance online publication. DOI: 10.1177/02557614231196972

Um, E., Plass, J. L., Hayward, E. O., & Homer, B. D. (2012). Emotional design in multimedia learning. *Journal of Educational Psychology*, 104(2), 485–498. DOI: 10.1037/a0026609

United Nations Educational, Scientific and Cultural Organisation (UNESCO). (2011). *ICT competency standards for teachers (version 2)*. UNESCO.

Urban, K., & Urban, M. (2024). "I know my idea is original!" Creative metacognitive monitoring and regulation in kindergarten children. *Thinking Skills and Creativity*, 52, 101541. DOI: 10.1016/j.tsc.2024.101541

Urban, M., & Urban, K. (2021). Unskilled But Aware of It? Cluster Analysis of Creative Metacognition from Preschool Age to Early Adulthood. *The Journal of Creative Behavior*, 55(4), 937–945. DOI: 10.1002/jocb.499

Urban, M., & Urban, K. (2023). Orientation Toward Intrinsic Motivation Mediates the Relationship Between Metacognition and Creativity. *The Journal of Creative Behavior*, 57(1), 6–16. DOI: 10.1002/jocb.558

Vaddepalli, D. (2023). The future of work: implications of artificial intelligence on hr practices. tjjpt, 44(3), 1711-1724. https://doi.org/DOI: 10.52783/tjjpt.v44.i3.562

van der Meer, N., van der Werf, V., Brinkman, W. P., & Specht, M. (2023). Virtual reality and collaborative learning: A systematic literature review. *Frontiers in Virtual Reality*, 4, 1159905. DOI: 10.3389/frvir.2023.1159905

Van Geel, M., & Vedder, P. (2020). Does cyberbullying predict internalizing problems and conduct problems when controlled for traditional bullying? *Scandinavian Journal of Psychology*, 61(2), 307–311. DOI: 10.1111/sjop.12601 PMID: 31802517

Varas, D., Santana, M., Nussbaum, M., Claro, S., & Imbarack, P. (2023). Teachers' strategies and challenges in teaching 21st century skills: Little common understanding. *Thinking Skills and Creativity*, 48, 101289. DOI: 10.1016/j.tsc.2023.101289

Varkey, B. (2020). AI and student data: Protecting privacy in the age of big data. *Journal of Education Policy*, 35(3), 407–426.

Vasconcelos, G., Oliveira, W., Santos, A. C. G., & Hamari, J. (2022). ReGammend: A method for personalized recommendation of gamification designs. *CEUR Workshop Proceedings*, 3147(June), 85–94.

Velaora, C., Dimos, I., Tsagiopoulou, S., & Kakarountas, A. (2022). A game-based learning approach in digital design course to enhance students' competency. *Information (Basel)*, 13(4), 177. DOI: 10.3390/info13040177

Viswanathan, G. (2021). *A hybrid threat model for system-centric and attack-centric for effective security design in SDLC. *Web Intelligence, 19*(1-2), 1-11.* IOS Press.

Vlachopoulos, D., & Makri, A. (2017). The effect of games and simulations on higher education: A systematic literature review. *International Journal of Educational Technology in Higher Education*, 14(1), 1–33. DOI: 10.1186/s41239-017-0062-1

Voronkova, V., Vasyl'chuk, G., Nikitenko, V., Kaganov, Y., & Metelenko, N. (2023). Transformation of digital education in the era of the fourth industrial revolution and globalization.

Vygotsky, L. (1978). *Mind in society: The development of higher psychological processes*. Harvard University Press.

Waang, G. P. (2023). Maximizing the Potential of Multimedia in Indonesia: Enhancing Engagement, Accessibility, and Learning Outcomes. *Academic Society for Appropriate Technology*, 9(3), 235–245. DOI: 10.37675/jat.2023.00409

Wang Y M, Yang X L, Hu W & Wang J. (2013). From Digital Literacy to digital competence: conceptual evolution, constitutive elements and integration model. Remote education magazine (03), 24-29.

Wang, H., Wang, M. & Li, G. (2022). The use of social media inside and outside the classroom to enhance students' engagement in EFL contexts – PMC. nih.gov

Wang, T. (2020). Research on project teaching methods for digital media art specialties. *SP, 11*, 281.

Wang, X., Li, A., Li, T., Zhao, X., Liu, S., Gai, J., & Zhang, R. (2023). Research on Strategies and Methods of Improving Teachers' Digital Literacy in Classroom Teaching in Higher Vocational Colleges. In SHS Web of Conferences (Vol. 179, p. 02016). EDP Sciences.

Wang, A. I., & Tahir, R. (2020). The effect of using Kahoot! For learning – a literature review. *Computers & Education*, 149, 103818. DOI: 10.1016/j.compedu.2020.103818

Wang, D., & Zhang, Q. M. (2022). Research on the reform and innovation of digital media art education in colleges and universities. *Grand View (Forum)*, 02, 147–149.

Wang, F. (2023). Software defect fault intelligent location and identification method based on data mining. *Journal of Applied Data Sciences*, 4(2), 84–92. DOI: 10.47738/jads.v4i2.92

Wang, F., Liu, M., & Dun, L. (2021). Augmented and virtual reality in art education: Exploring new frontiers with AI. *Computers & Graphics*, 92, 26–35. DOI: 10.1016/j.cag.2020.12.005

Wang, L. (2023). The application of project-based approach to English teaching in secondary vocational schools. *Examination Questions and Research*, 32, 106–108.

Wang, L., & He, Y. (2020). Online learning engagement assessment based on multimodal behavioral data. In *Transactions on Edutainment XVI* (pp. 256–265). Springer., DOI: 10.1007/978-3-662-61510-2_25

Wang, M. T., Fredricks, J. A., Ye, F., Hofkens, T. L., & Linn, J. S. (2016). The math and science engagement scales: Scale development, validation, and psychometric properties. *Learning and Instruction*, 43, 16–26. DOI: 10.1016/j.learninstruc.2016.01.008

Wang, T. (2021). Research on the teaching of professional English courses in higher vocational colleges based on a project-based approach. *Journal of Chongqing Vocational College of Electronic Engineering*, 02, 98–101. DOI: 10.13887/j.cnki.jccee.2021(2).23

Wang, X., Mayer, R. E., Han, M., & Zhang, L. (2023). Two Emotional Design Features Are More Effective Than One in Multimedia Learning. *Journal of Educational Computing Research*, 60(8), 1991–2014. DOI: 10.1177/07356331221090845

Wang, Y. (2020). An improved machine learning and artificial intelligence algorithm for classroom management of English distance education. *Journal of Intelligent & Fuzzy Systems*, •••, 1–12. DOI: 10.3233/JIFS-179615

Wang, Y., & An, H. (2019). The application research of project teaching methods in the course of information technology teaching theory. *Knowledge Library*, 21, 174–178.

Wang, Y., & Zheng, L. (2022). A Novel Deep Framework for English Communication Based on Educational Psychology Perspective. *Frontiers in Public Health*, 10, 916101. DOI: 10.3389/fpubh.2022.916101 PMID: 35801240

Wartman, S. A., & Combs, C. D. (2018, August). Medical education must move from the information age to the age of artificial intelligence. *Academic Medicine*, 93(8), 1107–1109. DOI: 10.1097/ACM.0000000000002044 PMID: 29095704

Webster, J., & Watson, R. T. (2002). Analyzing the past to prepare for the future: Writing a literature review. *Management Information Systems Quarterly*, 26(2), xiii–xxiii. https://www.jstor.org/stable/4132319

Webster, P. R. (2011). Construction of music learning. In *MENC handbook of research on music learning* (pp. 35–83). Oxford University Press. DOI: 10.1093/acprof:osobl/9780195386677.003.0002

Wei, T. X. (2024). Exploring the application of project teaching methods in mathematics teaching in secondary vocational schools. *Guangdong Vocational Technical Education and Research*, 01, 10–13. DOI: 10.19494/j.cnki.issn1674-859x.2024.01.034

Wenger-Trayner, E., Wenger, E., & Wenger-Trayner, B. (2020). *Learning to make a difference: Value creation in social learning spaces*. Cambridge university press. DOI: 10.1017/9781108677431

Wermelinger, M. (2023). Using GitHub Copilot to solve simple programming problems. *SIGCSE 2023: Proceedings of the 54th ACM Technical Symposium on Computer Science Education*, V.1, 172–178. https://doi.org/DOI: 10.1145/3545945.3569830

Whitby, B. (2008). *Artificial Intelligence: A Beginner's Guide*. Oneworld.

Whitton, N. (2011). Games-based learning. In Seel, N. M. (Ed.), *Encyclopedia of the Sciences of learning (pp. 1337e1340)*. Springer.

Wilder, S. (2023). Effects of parental involvement on academic achievement: a meta-synthesis. In *Mapping the field* (pp. 137–157). Routledge. DOI: 10.4324/9781003403722-12

Williams, D. A. (2014). Another perspective. *Music Educators Journal*, 101(1), 93–98. DOI: 10.1177/0027432114540476

Williamson, B. (2018). The hidden architecture of higher education: Building a big data infrastructure for the 'smarter university.'. *International Journal of Educational Technology in Higher Education*, 15(1), 12. DOI: 10.1186/s41239-018-0094-1

Williamson, B., & Eynon, R. (2020). Automation in education: Rethinking the roles of teachers and technology. *Learning, Media and Technology*, 45(2), 115–128.

Winner, E., Goldstein, T. R., & Vincent-Lancrin, S. (2018). *Art for art's sake? The impact of arts education*. OECD Publishing.

Wong, E. Y. C., Hui, R. T. Y., & Kong, H. (2023). Perceived usefulness of, engagement with, and effectiveness of virtual reality environments in learning industrial operations: The moderating role of openness to experience. *Virtual Reality (Waltham Cross)*, 27(3), 2149–2165. DOI: 10.1007/s10055-023-00793-0 PMID: 37360804

Woo, J., & Lee, S.-Y. (2024). The moderating effect of creative metacognition on adolescents' risk-taking in creative performance. *Asia Pacific Education Review*, 25(1), 99–115. DOI: 10.1007/s12564-024-09927-8

Wooldridge, J. (2022). Teaching Pragmatic Suprasegmentals in the Adult ESL Classroom. *School of Education and Leadership Student Capstone Projects,* 776. https://digitalcommons.hamline.edu/hse_cp/776

Wouters, P., Van Nimwegen, C., Van Oostendorp, H., & Van Der Spek, E. D. (2013). A meta-analysis of the cognitive and motivational effects of serious games. *Journal of Educational Psychology*, 105(2), 249–265. DOI: 10.1037/a0031311

Wu, C. F. (2023). *The project teaching method in secondary vocational "Interior design": The optimization practice research* (Master's thesis, Guangxi Normal University). https://doi.org/DOI: 10.27036/d.cnki.ggxsu.2023.001052

Wu, D. (2023). Exploring digital literacy in the era of digital civilization: A framework for college students in China. Information Services & Use, (Preprint), 1-23.

Xian, Y., & Liu, N. (2023). Research on the core curriculum construction standard of digital media art majors for vocational undergraduates. *Western Radio & Television*, 04, 85–88.

Xiao, J., Jiang, Z., Wang, L., & Yu, T. (2023). What Can Multimodal Data Tell Us About Online Synchronous Training: Learning Outcomes and Engagement of in-Service Teachers. *Frontiers in Psychology*, 13, 1092848. Advance online publication. DOI: 10.3389/fpsyg.2022.1092848 PMID: 36687926

Xiaoling, H., Lingxia, Z., & Dan, L. (2021). Effectiveness of game-based teaching: A systematic review and meta-analysis. *Open Educ. Res*, 27(02), 69–79.

Xing, W. L. (2023). Research on teaching innovation in electrical and electronic specialties in secondary vocational schools. *New Wisdom*, 36, 7–9.

Xin, Y. (2022). Influence of learning engagement on learning effect under a virtual reality (VR) environment. [iJET]. *International Journal of Emerging Technologies in Learning*, 17(5), 226–237. DOI: 10.3991/ijet.v17i05.29451

Xiong, H. F., Ning, C., & Huang, H. (2021). Project-based teaching: Reform and practice of the packaging design course in higher vocational education under the integration of industry and education. *Theoretical Research and Practice of Innovation and Entrepreneurship, 05*, 22–23+26.

Xiong, W. (2021). *Enhancing IT systems cyber resilience through threat modeling: Cyber security analysis of enterprise systems and connected vehicles* (Doctoral dissertation, KTH Royal Institute of Technology). Retrieved from https://urn.kb.se/resolve?urn=urn:nbn:se:kth:diva-300046

Xu, M. (2022). *Applied research of project teaching methods in the course of "Foundation of Fashion Design" in secondary vocational schools* (Master's thesis, Nanning Normal University). DOI: 10.27037/d.cnki.ggxsc.2022.000278

Xu, B., Chen, N. S., & Chen, G. (2020). Effects of teacher role on student engagement in WeChat-based online discussion learning. *Computers & Education*, 157, 103956. DOI: 10.1016/j.compedu.2020.103956

Xue, D. S., & Li, C. H. (2019). An analysis of the economic dynamics of personnel training in digital media art. *Times of Fortune*, 12, 168.

Xu, J. (2023). Optimizing English Education in the Information Era: A Multimodal Approach Based on BOPPPS Teaching Model. *Journal of Combinatorial Mathematics and Combinatorial Computing*, 118, 33–48. DOI: 10.61091/jcmcc118-03

Yaccob, N. S., Rahman, S. F. A., Mohamad, S. N. A., Rahim, A. A. A., Rashid, K. K. A., Aldaba, A. M. A., Yunus, M. M., & Hashim, H. (2022). Gamifying ESL Classrooms through Gamified Teaching and Learning. *Arab World English Journal (AWEJ). Special Issue on CALL*, 8, 177–191. DOI: 10.24093/awej/call8.12

Yaccob, N. S., & Yunus, M. M. (2019). Language Games in Teaching and Learning English Grammar: A Literature Review. *Arab World English Journal*, 10(1), 209–217. DOI: 10.24093/awej/vol10no1.18

Yan, L., Lu, Z., & Yu, Y. (2023). Exploration and Practice of BOPPPS Model in Enhancing Effective Teaching--Taking Business Communication as an Example. SHS Web of Conferences, Zaman, M. (2023). ChatGPT for healthcare sector: SWOT analysis. *International journal of research in industrial engineering, 12*(3), 221-233.

Yang, Y. J. (2020). The application and research of project teaching methods in the teaching of graphic design. *Journal of Science and Education (Mid-Magazine), 32*, 146–147. DOI: 10.16400/j.cnki.kjdkz.2020.11.068

Yang, J. C., Quadir, B., & Chen, N. S. (2016). Effects of the badge mechanism on self-efficacy and learning performance in a game-based English learning environment. *Journal of Educational Computing Research*, 54(3), 371–394. DOI: 10.1177/0735633115620433

Yang, J.-C., Lin, M., & Chen, S. (2018). Effects of anxiety levels on learning performance and gaming performance in digital game-based learning. *Journal of Computer Assisted Learning*, 34(3), 324–334. DOI: 10.1111/jcal.12245

Yang, M. Y. (2021). *The application research of project teaching methods in junior Chinese reading teaching*. Liaoning Normal University., DOI: 10.27212/d.cnki.glnsu.2021.001379

Yang, S., & Bai, H. (2020). The integration design of artificial intelligence and normal students' Education. *Journal of Physics: Conference Series*, 1453(1), 012090. DOI: 10.1088/1742-6596/1453/1/012090

Yan, S. (2023). The application of virtual reality technology in higher education and its impact on student learning performance. *The Educational Review, USA*, 7(11), 1808–1812. DOI: 10.26855/er.2023.11.032

Yao, S. (2022) A Study on Case Teaching of High School Geography Courses from the Perspective of. SWOT Analysis (Doctoral dissertation, Henan University).

Ye, S. Y. (2010). The application and exploration of project teaching methods in the course of art design specialty. *Vocational and Technical Education in China, 14*, 70–71+82.

Yeager, D. S., & Walton, G. M. (2011). Social-Psychological Interventions in Education: They're Not Magic. *Review of Educational Research*, 81(2), 267–301. DOI: 10.3102/0034654311405999

Yeh, E., & Swinehart, N. (2018). A model for mobile social media integration in constructivist ESL classrooms. In *Social Media in Education: Breakthroughs in Research and Practice* (pp. 258–278). IGI Global. DOI: 10.4018/978-1-5225-5652-7.ch014

Ye, L., Li, J., Yang, S., & Hang, Y. (2024). The effect of augmented reality-based serious game on traditional pattern learning. *Interactive Learning Environments*, •••, 1–29. DOI: 10.1080/10494820.2024.2327042

Ye, L., Wang, R., & Zhao, J. (2021). Enhancing learning performance and motivation of cultural heritage using serious games. *Journal of Educational Computing Research*, 59(2), 287–317. DOI: 10.1177/0735633120963828

Yeng, P. K., D., S., & Yang, B. (2020). Comparative analysis of threat modeling methods for cloud computing towards healthcare security practice. *International Journal of Advanced Computer Science and Applications, 11*(11).

Yetişensoy, O. and Rapoport, A. (2023). Artificial intelligence literacy teaching in social studies education. Journal of Pedagogical Research. https://doi.org/DOI: 10.33902/jpr.202320866

Yie, D. L., Sanmugam, M. A., Yahaya, W. A. J. W., & Abdullah, N. B. (2022, May). The dilemma of online gamified learning in Malaysian educational context: A qualitative study on Malaysian university students' perspective. In 2022 IEEE 12th Symposium on Computer Applications & Industrial Electronics (ISCAIE) (pp. 61-65). IEEE.

Yıldırım, İ., & Şen, S. (2019, July 3). The effects of gamification on students' academic achievement: a meta-analysis study. Taylor & Francis, 29(8), 1301-1318. https://doi.org/DOI: 10.1080/10494820.2019.1636089

Yimer, B. L. (2021). Social media usage, psychosocial well-being and academic performance. *Community Health Equity Research & Policy*, 43(4), 399–404. DOI: 10.1177/0272684X211033482 PMID: 34275379

Yin, K., He, Z., Xiong, J., Zou, J., Li, K., & Wu, S. T. (2021). Virtual reality and augmented reality displays: Advances and future perspectives. *JPhys Photonics*, 3(2), 022010. DOI: 10.1088/2515-7647/abf02e

Yohanna, A. (2020). The influence of social media on social interactions among students. *Indonesian Journal of Social Sciences*, 12(2), 34–48. DOI: 10.20473/ijss.v12i2.22907

Yuan, J., Liu, Y., Han, X., Li, A., & Zhao, L. (2023). Educational metaverse: An exploration and practice of VR wisdom teaching model in Chinese open university English course. *Interactive Technology and Smart Education*, 20(3), 403–421. DOI: 10.1108/ITSE-10-2022-0140

Yudha, H. T., & Mandasari, B. (2021). The analysis of game usage for senior high school students to improve their vocabulary mastery. *Journal of English Language Teaching and Learning*, 2(2), 74–79. http://jim.teknokrat.ac.id/index.php/english-language-teaching/article/view/1329. DOI: 10.33365/jeltl.v2i2.1329

Yufei, L., Saleh, S., Jiahui, H., & Abdullah, S. M. S. (2020). Review of the application of artificial intelligence in education. *International Journal of Innovation. Creativity and Change*, 12(8), 548–562.

Yu, Z., Gao, M., & Wang, L. (2021). The effect of educational games on learning outcomes, student motivation, engagement and satisfaction. *Journal of Educational Computing Research*, 59(3), 522–546. DOI: 10.1177/0735633120969214

Yuzulia, I. (2021). A study on students' motivation towards learning English language. *Eltin Journal: Journal of English Language Teaching in Indonesia*, 9(1), 10–17.

Zaidieh, A. J. Y. (2012). The use of social networking in education: Challenges and opportunities. *World of Computer Science and Information Technology Journal*, 2(1), 18–21.

Zakaria, N. Y. K., Yunus, M., Hashim, H., Nordin, M. N., Norman, H., & Adnan, N. H. (2021b). Pre-Service Teachers' Views on the Implementation of Game-Based Learning for Academic Writing Skills. *Sains Insani*, 6(1), 11–16. DOI: 10.33102/sainsinsani.vol6no1.226

Zarghami, S. A. (2022). Forecasting project duration in the face of disruptive events: A resource-based approach. *Journal of Construction Engineering and Management*, 148(5), 04022016. DOI: 10.1061/(ASCE)CO.1943-7862.0002257

Zawacki-Richter, O., Marín, V. I., Bond, M., & Gouverneur, F. (2019). Systematic review of research on artificial intelligence applications in higher education–Where are the educators? *International Journal of Educational Technology in Higher Education*, 16(1), 39. DOI: 10.1186/s41239-019-0171-0

Zeybek, N., & Saygı, E. (2024). Gamification in Education: Why, Where, When, and How?—A Systematic Review. *Games and Culture*, 19(2), 237–264. DOI: 10.1177/15554120231158625

Zhang, Y., Li, W., Luo, Y., Nie, X., Tan, G., Qin, Y., & Sin, Y. K. (2021, November). Serious game design of cultural heritage education based on the experiential learning cycle model. In 2021 2nd International Conference on Information Science and Education (ICISE-IE) (pp. 1193-1200). IEEE. DOI: 10.1109/ICISE-IE53922.2021.00269

Zhang, C. (2024). The application of project teaching methods in graphic design teaching. *PACK*, 04, 226–228. DOI: 10.19446/j.cnki.1005-9423.2024.04.073

Zhang, C. Y. (2022). Reflection and innovation research on digital media art design teaching. *Guangdong Vocational Technical Education and Research*, 05, 137–140. DOI: 10.19494/j.cnki.issn1674-859x.2022.05.036

Zhang, C., & Lu, Y. (2021). Study on artificial intelligence: The state of the art and future prospects. *Journal of Industrial Information Integration*, 23, 100224. DOI: 10.1016/j.jii.2021.100224

Zhang, H. M., Zhang, C. Y., & Liu, Q. (2020). Research on the international professional talents training of digital media majors from the perspective of creativity. *Modern Computers*, 07, 95–99.

Zhang, H., Yu, L., Ji, M., Cui, Y., Liu, D., Li, Y., & Wang, Y. (2023). Investigating high school students' perceptions and presences under VR learning environment. In *Cross Reality (XR) and Immersive Learning Environments (ILEs) in Education* (pp. 97–117). Routledge. DOI: 10.4324/9781003457121-8

Zhang, J., Ding, Y., Yang, X., Zhong, J., Qiu, X., Zou, Z., Xu, Y., Jin, X., Wu, X., Huang, J., & Zheng, Y. (2022). COVID-19's impacts on the scope, effectiveness, and interaction characteristics of online learning: A social network analysis. *PLoS One*, 17(8), e0273016. DOI: 10.1371/journal.pone.0273016 PMID: 35998175

Zhang, K. (2021). Determining the influencing factors affecting the digital competencies of colleges students in blended teaching. *Contemporary Educational Research Journal*, 11(4), 210–224. DOI: 10.18844/cerj.v11i4.5974

Zhang, K., & Aslan, A. B. (2021). AI technologies for education: Recent research & future directions. *Computers and Education Artificial Intelligence*, 2, 100025. DOI: 10.1016/j.caeai.2021.100025

Zhang, L., & Dong, F. (2024). Development Strategies of Chinese Geriatric Hospitals Based on the SWOT-CLPV Model. *Social Medicine and Health Management*, 5(1), 106–118.

Zhang, S., & Liu, Q. (2019). Investigating the relationships among teachers' motivational beliefs, motivational regulation, and their learning engagement in online professional learning communities. *Computers & Education*, 134, 145–155. DOI: 10.1016/j.compedu.2019.02.013

Zhang, S., Zhao, L., Lu, Y., & Yang, J. (2016). Do you get tired of socializing? An empirical explanation of discontinuous usage behavior in social network services. *Information & Management*, 53(7), 904–914. DOI: 10.1016/j.im.2016.03.006

Zhang, X., Lyu, F., & Cheng, S. (2018). Interaction paradigm in intelligent systems. *SCIENTIA SINICA Informationis*, 48(4), 406–418. DOI: 10.1360/N112017-00217

Zhang, Y. T., Cheng, Y. L., Wu, H. X., & Liao, Y. P. (2022). Intelligent music accompaniment system based on discrete wavelet transform. *Journal of Physics: Conference Series*, 2345(1), 012021–012021. DOI: 10.1088/1742-6596/2345/1/012021

Zhang, Y. Y. (2022). Market-oriented exploration of higher vocational art design teaching reform: Digital media art design as an example. *DAGUAN*, 10, 124–126.

Zhonggen, Y. (2019). A meta-analysis of use of serious games in education over a decade. *International Journal of Computer Games Technology*, 2019(1), 4797032. DOI: 10.1155/2019/4797032

Zhou, A. Q. (2020). Research on the application of project teaching methods in design courses: Taking the design of animation scenes as an example. *Grand Spectacle*, 06, 138–139.

Zhou, R. (2023). Digital Literacy of vocational college Students: Connotation change, theoretical logic, Framework Construction and Practical Direction. *Vocational and Technical Education in China*, (21), 5–13.

Zhou, W. T., & He, H. Y. (2023). Research and practice on the teaching reform of landscape architecture design courses in the context of rural revitalization: Taking the preliminary course of landscape architecture design as an example. *Anhui Agricultural Science Bulletin*, 19, 129–133. DOI: 10.16377/j.cnki.issn1007-7731.2023.19.031

Zhu, X. L. (2024). Research on the talent training path of the digital culture industry in our country. *Chinese Personnel Science*, 02, 45–52.

Zichermann, G., & Cunningham, C. (2011). *Gamification by Design*. "O'Reilly Media, Inc." http://books.google.ie/books?id=Hw9X1miVMMwC&printsec=frontcover&dq=gabe+zichermann&hl=&cd=1&source=gbs_api

Zielińska, A., Forthmann, B., Lebuda, I., & Karwowski, M. (2023). Self-Regulation for Creative Activity: The Same or Different Across Domains? *Psychology of Aesthetics, Creativity, and the Arts*. Advance online publication. DOI: 10.1037/aca0000540

Zou, J., & Schiebinger, L. (2018). AI can be sexist and racist—It's time to make it fair. *Nature*, 559(7714), 324–326. DOI: 10.1038/d41586-018-05707-8 PMID: 30018439

About the Contributors

Zhang Jingru is a member of the China Europe International Design Association and the Chinese Art Anthropology Society. Design works have won numerous awards, both in China and abroad, and participated in international design weeks. Completed master's degree at China University of Mining and Technology (CUMT), specializing in Visual Communication Design. Currently pursuing Ph.D. studies at Universiti Sains Malaysia (USM). Delving into the intersection of Augmented Reality and Visual Design.

Wan Ahmad Jaafar Wan Yahaya has been Director at the Centre for Instructional Technology and Multimedia (PTPM), Universiti Sains Malaysia (USM), Penang, since 2016. He is the Chairman of the Technical Committee on Audio, Video, Information Technology, and Communication Equipment at the Department of Standard Malaysia, Ministry of International Trade and Industry Malaysia. He holds a PhD in Multimedia Education from the University of Leeds and a Master of Education (Computer in Education) from the University of Manchester, United Kingdom. He has published more than 170 articles/papers in indexed journals like Scopus, Web of Science (ISI), SCSI, SSCI, conference proceedings, and book chapters, primarily in the field of multimedia education. He is the recipient of the Thailand Association International Honor Award for Outstanding Contributions to the field of Educational Communications and Technology for the year 2023.

Mageswaran Sanmugam acquired his B.Sc. (Hons) in Electrical Engineering from Universiti Teknologi Tun Hussein Onn in 2005 and Master's degree in Educational Management in 2012 from Universiti Utara Malaysia and Ph. D in Educational Technology in 2017 from Universiti Teknologi Malaysia. He worked as an Educator in both Primary and Secondary schools from 2008-2018, before being appointed as a Senior Lecturer in the Centre for Instructional Technology and Multimedia, Universiti Sains Malaysia, Pulau Pinang, Malaysia (from 2018- till 2021). Currently he is the Deputy Director of Research, Innovation and Networking in the Centre for Instructional Technology and Multimedia, Universiti Sains Malaysia, Pulau Pinang, Malaysia (from 2022- till now). His research interests encompass educational technology, ludology, game-based learning, gamification and game theory. He also serves as an exco-member in the Malaysian Educational Technology Association (META), and as a Senior Member under the Institute of Electrical and Electronics Engineers (IEEE).

Darren Lim Yie acquired his Bachelor of Education (Hons) in Teaching English to Speakers of Other Languages (TESOL) in 2021 and his master's degree in educational technology in 2023 from Universiti Sains Malaysia. He worked as a research assistant (2021 to 2023) previously and as a university tutor for now (2023 till now). Currently he is a PhD candidate in the Centre for Instructional Technology and Multimedia, Universiti Sains Malaysia, Pulau Pinang, Malaysia (from 2023- till now). His research interests mainly encompass educational technology, game theory, game-based learning, gamification, persuasive and immersive technology.

* * *

Yahya Al-Shameri is currently pursuing a master's degree in Software Engineering at Kocaeli University. With a strong foundation in mechatronics from Marmara University, they've delved deeply into artificial intelligence and deep learning, applying these cutting-edge technologies to various real-world software projects. Their experience includes hands-on development of AI-powered systems, particularly in computer vision, natural language processing (NLP), and automation. Over the course of their academic journey, they've contributed to numerous projects, such as AI-based software testing, predictive analytics, and automated code generation. Their research interests lie at the intersection of AI, software engineering, and ethical AI practices, with a strong focus on how AI can enhance and streamline development processes.

Kien Tsong Chau is Senior Lecturer in Centre for Instructional Technology and Multimedia. He hold PhD in Instructional Multimedia from USM.

Lin Chuxuan received her Master's degree in Visual Information and Publication Design from Xiamen University in 2023. In 2024, she was admitted as a doctoral candidate at the Centre for Instructional Technology and Multimedia, Universiti Sains Malaysia, where she specializes in Visual Arts Design and Educational Technology Design.

Hannatul Akila Esahak is an undergraduate student in TESL at the Faculty of Languages and Communication, Sultan Idris Education University, Malaysia.

Haddi Junaidi Kussin is a lecturer at Sultan Idris Education University. He is currently pursuing a doctorate degree and has 18 years of experience teaching at the university level. His research interests include language acquisition, language policies, and educational psychology. According to him, education is not preparation for life; rather, it is life itself.

Liu Jinya's design works have won numerous Chinese and international design awards and participated in international design exhibitions. Completed undergraduate studies at the Design School of Jiangnan University and master's degree at Beijing Institute of Fashion Technology. Currently pursuing Ph.D studies at Universiti Sains Malaysia (USM), focusing on the impact of anthropomorphic design.

Puteri Zarina Megat Khalid (Ph.D. in English Language, University of Glasgow; M. Ed. TESL, UPSI) is a senior lecturer in the Department of English Language and Literature, Faculty of Languages and Communication, Universiti Pendidikan Sultan Idris (Sultan Idris Education University, Malaysia – UPSI). She joined UPSI in 2020 before she served Universiti Kuala Lumpur for 16 years as a Senior Lecturer. She is currently the Coordinator for Offshore M. Ed. TESL Programme (School Holiday Mode) at the Faculty of Languages and Communication, UPSI. Her research interests are Discourse (Genre) Analysis and Corpus Linguistics. She has published several chapters-in-books and numerous other studies in reputable journals which span across transdisciplinary domains.

Nurihan Nasir who has over twenty-five years as an educator is an expert in mathematics education. Nurihan has a vast teaching and supervising experience of nurturing both pre-service and in-service teachers of Mathematics in several schools and at one of the education district departments in Perak, one of the biggest states in Malaysia.

Sudip Kumar Naskar is currently working as an Associate Professor at Computer Science & Engineering department at Jadavpur University, India.

Rajat Pandit is working as an Associate Professor at Computer Science Department at West Bengal State University, West Bengal, India.

Piyal Roy is an accomplished academician in the field of Computer Science & Engineering. He has completed his BSc in Computer Science, MSc in Computer Science and MTech in Computer Science & Engineering. Currently, he is working as an Assistant Professor at Computer Science & Engineering department at Brainware University, India.

Sonia Singh, PhD., is an Associate Professor of OB & HRM at JAIN (Deemed-to-be University), Bengaluru, India. She completed her doctoral degree in Management and holds double Masters in Science & Management Program. She is a University rank holder and is UGC NET qualified. She has an overall experience of seventeen years in Academics as well as Industry and has worked with some of the world's leading organizations. Her key competent areas are HR Business Partnering, Talent Acquisition & Retention and Learning & Development function. She has to her credit two Patents and authored several research papers and book chapter in Journals of repute. She is contributing her knowledge and experience as a member of Research Advisory Committee in reputed Universities and Editorial board member of International peer-reviewed Journals. Her research interests include Organizational Psychology, Agile HR, Diversity & Inclusion, Sustainable HRM and Leadership Studies.

Yun YiTan is currently a senior lecturer at the Centre for Instructional Technology and Multimedia, Universiti Sains Malaysia. She obtained her Bachelor's degree in Digital Media (Hons) in 2009 and accomplished her Ph.D. in Educational Technology at The University of Hong Kong in 2018. Her research interest stems from a deep curiosity with creative media and technology, as well as their potential to enrich learners' educational journeys.

Index

A

B

C

D

E

F

G

H

www.ingramcontent.com/pod-product-compliance
Lightning Source LLC
La Vergne TN
LVHW080352011026
849161LV00009B/2277